Korea under Siege, 1876–1945

KOREA UNDER SIEGE, 1876–1945

Capital Formation and Economic Transformation

Young-Iob Chung

OXFORD
UNIVERSITY PRESS

2006

OXFORD
UNIVERSITY PRESS

Oxford University Press, Inc., publishes works that further
Oxford University's objective of excellence
in research, scholarship, and education.

Oxford New York
Auckland Cape Town Dar es Salaam Hong Kong Karachi
Kuala Lumpur Madrid Melbourne Mexico City Nairobi
New Delhi Shanghai Taipei Toronto

With offices in
Argentina Austria Brazil Chile Czech Republic France Greece
Guatemala Hungary Italy Japan Poland Portugal Singapore
South Korea Switzerland Thailand Turkey Ukraine Vietnam

Published by Oxford University Press, Inc.
198 Madison Avenue, New York, New York 10016

www.oup.com

Library of Congress Cataloging-in-Publication Data
Chung, Young-Iob.
Korea under siege, 1876–1945 : capital formation and economic transformation /
Young-Iob Chung.
p. cm.
Includes bibliographical references and index.
ISBN-13 978-0-19-517830-2
ISBN 0-19-517830-0
1. Saving and investment—Korea—History. 2. Korea—Economic policy. 3. Korea—Economic
conditions—1864–1910. 4. Korea—Economic conditions—1910–1945. I. Title.
HC467.S3C58 2005
330.9519'09'041—dc22 2004019149

1 3 5 7 9 8 6 4 2

Printed in the United States of America
on acid-free paper

To my parents,
who have lived behind the 38th parallel

PREFACE

Korea is a small, peninsular country with rugged terrain, few natural resources, and dense population.[1] Until modern times, it attracted little interest in the outside world, since it traditionally languished in the shadow of the major powers of Asia, namely, China and Japan. In many people's minds, it was no more than an appendage to Sino-Japanese civilizations. In recent decades, however, Korea has become a household word. South Korea has gained a reputation as an underdeveloped country that has successfully undergone spectacular economic growth since the Korean War, while North Korea remains as only one of two or three surviving communist countries that are isolated from the outside world.

The so-called miraculous economic growth in the southern half of the peninsula has transformed South Korea from basically an agrarian economy to that of a major industrial power in a very short time period, and it is now considered one of the dozen or so industrialized countries in the world. During the three decades before the economic crisis of 1997, its real gross national product expanded more than 8 percent a year on average, while export earnings increased, often by more than 30 percent annually. Also, by 1988 South Korea took its place on the world stage when it hosted the summer Olympics, followed by the World Cup Soccer finals in 2001. In short, South Koreans have achieved what many people, including most Koreans, once thought impossible,[2] and this has attracted much interest in the country's achievements.

Witnessing such accomplishments, an increasing number of scholars and journalists have begun studying, writing, and reporting about South Korea's phenomenal accomplishments in economic development in the last four decades. Notwithstanding such efforts, there has been little careful analysis, especially by Western scholars, of the heritage of the Korean economy in the traditional and transitional periods, from which the southern half of the country launched into a phenomenal modern economic success. This was the period when the hermit kingdom of Korea came under siege by the world powers in the last half of the nineteenth and the first half of the twentieth centuries, before South Korea had climbed out of its economic doldrums. No study had been undertaken to examine how the traditional and closed Korean economy and a people under siege responded to the onslaught of foreign powers and the Industrial Revolution and were able to enter the market-oriented era with a bang.

The time has come to assess and reassess Korea's economic heritage of transformation and economic development fairly, objectively, and with an open mind. One of the major weaknesses of a few studies, by both Korean and Japanese scholars, evaluating the Korean economy in the seventy-year period between 1876 and 1945 often has been their one-sidedness, their lack of objectivity. They frequently have preconceived notions and are dogmatic and doctrinaire. Korean scholars frequently have taken traditional and politically correct positions, condemning the aggression and harshness of Japanese rule,[3] while their Japanese counterparts have tended to blindly justify Japan's handling and colonial rule of Korea, pointing out only the achievements in the former colony under Japanese rule.

These difficulties hopefully may be overcome by someone who was reared in Korea under Japanese colonial rule but who was trained and has conducted his entire professional career abroad. An impartial examination of the development of Korea during this early modern period, considered from a global perspective and based on empirical data, is long overdue. This perhaps "politically incorrect" and more detached approach toward Korea's development, which might have been a liability in the past, eandeavors to illuminate the truth through analysis, comparison, metaphor, and perspectives that reflect on the objective of human welfare in the long run.

This book has been in the making for many years. In spite of deliberate effort, my teaching and academic administrative responsibilities did not leave much time for research and writing, making speedy progress difficult. There still remain areas in which more time could have been spent to make this study more definitive, but I am happy that this volume is seeing the light before the follow-up volume on capital formation and economic development of South Korea is in print and available for public scrutiny.

Over the years, I have benefited a great deal from pioneers in the field, and I am indebted to many people and organizations in the completion of this book. I would like to express my appreciation to Eastern Michigan University, which assisted me through sabbatical leaves and faculty research fellowships as I carried out this work, the Korea Foundation for their financial support under its Faculty Research Fellowship program, and the Academy of Korean Studies for allowing me the use of its facilities, as I undertook research in Korea under its Research Residency program. I would also like to take this opportunity to express my gratitude to my colleagues in the economics department at Eastern Michigan University for their understanding and for allowing me to conduct this study when a greater dedication to accommodating their needs would have been welcomed by them during my long tenure as an administrator.

I am also thankful to many office staff, who assisted me in typing numerous drafts of the manuscript over the years. In particular, I would like to express my special thanks to Beverly Neville, whose encouragement and assistance in lightening my administrative load so that I could devote more time on this study were so helpful. Also, numerous research assistants have helped me by gathering and compiling statistical data, doing computer analysis, and serving as bibliographers over the years. Among them, my special gratitude goes to Bruce Gockerman, who has kept close in contact with me and continued to show interest in my project, in addition to having given much support to various projects in the Economics Department for so many years. Likewise, among many who have given me encouragement and support for this project over the years, I would like to thank in particular my longtime friend Key Sun Ryang.

The manuscript owes a great deal to the assistance of many others. James Reynold read the entire manuscript, and his judicious comments about omissions, unnecessary inclusions, and the logic of the presentation have been very helpful. An immense labor was undertaken by Janet Opdyke and Lara Stelmaszyk, who edited the entire manuscript meticulously with patience and care and whose assistance I gratefully acknowledge. Of course, I bear full responsibility for errors and misapprehension in the text. I would also like to express my appreciation to Terry Vaughn and Steven McGroarthy of Oxford University Press for their support of and assistance with this publication.

Last but not least, I would like to mention my appreciation for the sacrifices my family have made for so long to make this publication possible. While this manuscript was being prepared, my wife, Oke, and daughters, Jeewon and Jeanie, paid a heavy price in the form of my silences and absences and their foregone travels. I cannot begin to speak of what I owe to their affection. My wife, especially, endured with more forbearance and affection than I deserved.

CONTENTS

ABBREVIATIONS

GDP	gross domestic product
GNP	gross national product
NBFI	nonbank financial institution
GNBFI	public nonbank financial institution
PNBFI	private nonbank financial institution
SOC	social-overhead capital

WEIGHTS AND MEASURES

dan = 991.7 square meters
jeong or *jeongbo* = 2.45 acres
pyeong = 3.3 square meters
sen = equivalent to cent
seok = 5.1 US bushels

Korea under Siege, 1876–1945

1

INTRODUCTION

Economic development is a complicated and multifaceted process that involves the entire spectrum of human life and its environments: economic, political, social, cultural, and technological. To achieve rapid and sustained economic growth, a country emerging from a tradition-embedded cocoon of an underdeveloped economy must break out of the shell and overcome many obstacles. The transformations that enable a society to achieve a new and developed economy comprise complex internal and external forces that include changes in human attitudes, values, skills, and institutions as well as economic structure.

One of the primary requirements for economic development is the expansion of a country's capital formation,[1] or investment and saving.[2] An abrupt acceleration of investment or a sharp rise in the rate of capital formation requires a sudden increase in new or existing opportunities—through either fresh inventions or institutional changes—to utilize economic resources more efficiently. Investment demands are associated in turn with a long wave of technological innovation that can be set in motion by the opening of a country to outside contact.[3] Recent research suggests that high levels of investment may explain many so-called growth miracles, although capital is not the only or even a sufficient requirement for development.[4] All the ingredients of economic development are required: the will to develop, institutions that provide incentives to effort, attitudes that value economic efficiency, growing technical knowledge, and appropriate and high-quality human resources.

As far as the requirement for capital formation is concerned, the essential feature of converting from a low to a high economic growth rate is to set aside annually a minimum percentage of savings out of the nation's income for investment; for example, from 5 percent or less of its annual net saving to 12 percent or more.[5] In the United States, up until the Great Depression net saving averaged about 13 percent and replacement about 7 percent, for a gross savings of about 20 percent of

Gross Domestic Product (GDP).[6] The requirement that a country have adequate capital seems especially pertinent in most Asian countries, the point of which has been well demonstrated, in retrospect, by the recent development experiences of what are referred to as the Asian tigers—South Korea, Singapore, and Taiwan, as well as more recently China, in addition to Japan.

This study investigates the process, extent, and character of capital formation and its contribution to Korea's economic transformation from a traditional, independent economy in the mid-1870s to a colonial economy under Japan until 1945, the seventy-year period of its early "modern" capitalist economy. Capital formation and economic transformation in Korea in this study are examined in three distinct stages. The first is the traditional economy, which prevailed prior to the foreign incursion in the mid-1870s. This examination will enable us to assess Korea's closed economy in the period immediately preceding the modernization that followed. The second stage is the thirty-year period of an open, transitional economy, which lasted from the initial "lawful" (under the Korean law) foreign incursion of the country from 1876 to 1904. This was the period when Korea maintained its sovereignty and attempted to reconcile its traditional heritage with the Western Industrial Revolution. The third stage is the colonial period, beginning in 1905, when a Korea under siege not only failed to repel the foreign "imperialists" but actually succumbed to the forty years of harsh Japanese rule. Unlike in most studies, this study sets the beginning of the third stage before the Annexation in 1910, because for all practical purposes, especially in terms of economic policy, Japan dictated the workings of Korean government after 1905.[7]

In order to assess the contribution to capital formation and the transformation of the economy, the roles of the three groups of different nationalities then in Korea—namely, the Japanese, "foreigners" (i.e., those other than Japanese nationals), and Koreans—are examined separately whenever needed and possible. For each of these groups, the following aspects are investigated in detail: the extent of their investment, the sources and uses of capital, the main factors and motivations influencing their investments and saving, and the impact of their investments on Korea's economic transformation. Whenever possible and useful, the analysis focuses on the activities and welfare of Koreans.

There are a number of reasons why the examination of capital formation in and economic transformation of Korea during this seventy-year period is valuable and useful. First, in Korea, as in many developing countries today—particularly in Asian countries where an abundance of inexpensive and quality labor is readily available—the lack of capital is one of the main obstacles to economic progress. Unless this impediment is overcome, the prospect for economic progress is virtually doomed.

Second, to understand the modern economic development of a country, or the lack thereof, one must trace back its economic heritage and resource endowment, for there may have been powerful forces at work that affected later economic growth.[8] The Korea of today is built on the Korea of yesterday. It is hoped that this study will not only explicate the level of development prior to modernization—a factor viewed by many economists as having much significance for economic development[9]—but also reveal other, more subtle factors crucial to Korea's economic transformation.

The third reason is to examine the contribution of Koreans and foreigners, especially that of Japanese, to capital formation in and economic development of Korea during this seventy-year period. There is considerable controversy and debate relative to what prompted the beginnings and the primer of Korea's economic transformation into the early modern economy.

Fourth, hopefully, this study reveals a number of significant, if not all entirely new, patterns and characteristics of capital formation in and economic transformation of Korea. The combination of circumstances, approaches, and experiences in the country was in many respects unique among developing and developed countries, particularly many Asian countries. Korea is often compared with two northeastern Asian countries, Japan and China, which differ from Korea in some respects (e.g., their size and histories in the eighteenth and nineteenth centuries) but are similar in regard to cultural heritage, including their Confucian and Buddhist influences, their isolationist tendencies, and their neglect of the natural and economic sciences in the premodern period. Yet the timing, approaches, and patterns of their acceptance of Western ways and economic development differed. It is useful to identify Korea's unique path and compare it with the experiences of its more powerful neighbors. In light of the interest shown lately by Western scholars in the economic successes of many Asian economies, particularly the Confucian-oriented countries, the examination of the economic heritage of one of them can be helpful in understanding and appreciating the process of capital formation in and economic transformation of these developed and developing countries.

The approach in this study is more behavioral and analytical (without being mathematical, statistical, or technical, but with supporting quantitative data), rather than historical. Although narratives of Korean economic history are scarce in English, an effort has been made in this study to devote as much space as possible to the analysis of the economy based on the available data, with minimal historical description. When necessary, the techniques of extrapolation and/or interpolation are applied in order to make the analysis as comprehensive, cohesive, and meaningful as possible. It is hoped that the findings in this study will be found to provide objective and unbiased analyses, contribute to the field, and become the basis for further exploration of this crucial but understudied topic.

At the outset, some mention should be made regarding the source materials. This study relies on works by all major contributors on the subject and, for the most part, on sources available in English, Korean, and/or Japanese. The Korean and Japanese scholars who have studied the Korean economy tend to rely exclusively on Asian-language sources, and Western scholars have been inclined to limit themselves to Western-language publications. Although the sources in Korean and Japanese are helpful in understanding the country's historical development, English sources written by Asian-studies scholars, Christian missionaries, diplomats, government officials, and travelers, as well as economists, evaluate the country's economic system and its people's behavior—such as work, consumption, and saving habits—more objectively and in a detached manner and are often more useful in gaining comparative insights about the early years of the modern economy that followed the model of Western industrialized economies.[10] The data used in this book are derived from a variety of sources, but statistical data are primarily obtained from the publications of the Japanese government as well as from public banks. The studies by the Bank of Korea and the Industrial Bank of Korea provide data on business firms within specific sectors of the economy. A more detailed picture of individual firms was gleaned from statistics and from the brief company histories published periodically or in various yearbooks. Notwithstanding some researchers' allegations that the majority of Japanese statistics are either invented or based on speculation and contained numerous errors and omissions,[11] probably they are as reliable as any that may be found. Of course, they are supplemented with books and studies written by individuals and various organizations.

Notwithstanding the merits of the Japanese government's statistics and publications, they are often incomplete or inconsistent. Few data are available after 1938, for instance.[12] Even during the period for which data are tabulated, if certain facts were embarrassing to the Japanese government, they were not disclosed or revealed and the publication of certain series of statistics (e.g., on the production and trade of gold) was interrupted or discontinued. The publication of some economic statistics was even prohibited after 1938.[13] The data are particularly deficient for the period 1941–1945. The best estimates of Japanese assets at the end of the occupation of Korea were compiled by the American military government in Tokyo in a classified survey of Japanese assets abroad.

Lastly, a brief mention is in order to minimize confusion regarding the romanization of Korean words and personal names in this book. Excepting proper pronouns—in particular, personal names—Korean words are alphabetized following the newly revised official romanization developed by the National Academy of the Korean Language of the Ministry of Culture and Tourism in the year 2000. Also, because of the various ways in which Asian names, including those of Koreans, can be and are written by different authors, the names of all persons, including Koreans, have systematically been written in the English rather than the Korean tradition, that is, the given name first, followed by the surname. For example, the name of the last prime minister of the Joseon dynasty is written as Wan Yong Yi, instead of Yi Wan Yong, in order to be consistent with a name such as Syngman Rhee, the first president of the Republic of Korea, so that newcomers (and sometimes even specialists) to Korean sources will avoid identifying Yong as the family name. Also as a means of avoiding unnecessary confusion, this study has, wherever useful, employed today's most common terms for concepts, even when the new term is not technically synonymous with the old. In the case of national income data, for instance, the published data in Gross National Product (GNP) in the earlier times are treated as equal to Gross Domestic Product (GDP) throughout the text. As to figures in currency values shown in this book, they are all in current value unless specified otherwise.

2

THE TRADITIONAL ECONOMY

Some of the most important forces that affect capital formation and economic development in any economy are the people's propensities to work, produce, invest, and engage in entrepreneurship, along with the positive role of the government. The purpose of this chapter, therefore, is to examine Korea's economic heritage in terms of the state of its economy and of the important forces that affected capital formation and economic development in the traditional period before the foreign "economic incursion." Specifically examined are production and income, economic structure, people's propensity to work and produce, investment and entrepreneurship, saving, and consumption, as well as the economic role of the government in the traditional Korea. In this way, we may be able to trace and discern the new forces that brought about capital formation and economic development in Korea after the opening of the country to the outside world. Before these aspects are examined, a brief sketch of the political and social structures that prevailed in Korea at the time of the opening of the country to outsiders seems in order.

TRADITIONAL POLITICAL, SOCIAL, AND ECONOMIC STRUCTURES

The Joseon dynasty, established in 1392, remained in power until Japan annexed Korea and assumed control of the country in 1910. Compared to medieval or feudal government, the government in Korea in the mid-nineteenth century was highly centralized in its organizational structure and administration, more like some of the East European countries immediately after World War II. Political rule was centered in the capital, Seoul, which exerted a profound influence on local as well as central governments. The Joseon dynasty's political power was backed by an entourage of civil servants and soldiers headquartered in Seoul. In later years, Korean kings were hemmed in by a powerful bureaucracy that vigorously defended its own prerogatives and perquisites. The country, including the government, was rooted in the Confucian tradition, and it was guided by the principle that it was the business of the government to "govern" and the duty of citizens to be obedient and loyal to the state. Most Korean people at that time expected everything to come from the central government.[1]

Traditional Korean society was ruled by an aristocracy, the *yangban,* according to Confucian principles of given wisdom and noblesse oblige. The *yangban* were a semiaristocratic, bureaucratic elite who represented the class interests of land and slave owners in what was a slave society until the nineteenth century. The *yangban* class possessed virtually the sole privilege of receiving an education; and as an educated class at the top of the social hierarchy, it not only monopolized political power and wealth, it also enjoyed many other special privileges, including the exclusive right to hold government positions. Those who attained the status of government officials and scholars were all but worshipped by the masses. Toward the end of the Joseon dynasty, the number of *yangban* increased to approximately 2 million as ordinary citizens began to move into this class.[2]

All other citizens were members of the ruled classes. Immediately below the *yangban* was the middle class (*jungin*), consisting of a small group of professionals, mostly middle- and low-ranking government officials, accountants, geographers, interpreters, copyists, and law-enforcement officials. This group differed greatly from the middle classes of the Western countries, and their functions were not the same as those of merchants, businesspeople, and skilled laborers in the industrialized West.

The overwhelming majority of people were commoners (*sangin*), a group that included peasants, fishermen, and merchants. Among the members of this class who were not farmers or connected with farming were low level government workers, messenger boys (*yamun* runners), boatmen, miners, innkeepers, and men who lived by their wits, such as gamblers and fortune-tellers. But these people accounted for no more than one-tenth of the population—most of the commoners were closely connected with farming. Merchants, for example, who made the rounds of the markets, were often former cultivators who dealt almost exclusively with farmers.

The lowest social class in traditional Korea was composed of those who filled the ranks of the outcast professions. Known as "low-born people" (*chonmin*), these included butchers, Buddhist monks, and certain merchants. Although they were held in low regard, their services were essential to the functioning of the society as a whole and, as a result, some of these individuals were actually quite prosperous.

To maintain the rigid social and class structure of the traditional period, a government Board of Works was set up to assign members of each family to work in certain trades, which were passed from father to son. In this way, the number of workmen in each occupation could be rigidly maintained. Because the whole population, except for the noble and middle classes, was under the control of the government, it was hoped that the traditional social structure would not be disrupted. Recent studies of family lineage during the Joseon period, however, suggest that there were some deviations.[3] Over time, the exclusiveness of the *yangban* gradually gave way, and the line of demarcation between the upper and lower classes blurred somewhat.

Politically, the late Joseon dynasty was unstable. Factionalism, which developed in the early sixteenth century, became more vicious toward the end of the dynasty and prevented an effective response when the country was threatened from without. The Korean system of governance contrasted with Western notions of government and individual rights. Law, to the extent that it played any meaningful role in the country, focused on preserving social order rather than protecting the rights of the individual. Moreover, there was no separation of powers; laws were promulgated by officials who combined legislative, executive, and judicial powers. These practices, attitudes, and value systems prompted one Western observer to note that Koreans were the easiest people on earth to govern.[4]

The Korean government toward the end of the nineteenth century was ineffective and inefficient.[5] For instance, at one time currency was issued not only by the Treasury Department but also by many ministries, provincial governments, and even private businesses. Korean currency was debased as much as 500 to 700 times. Corruption raged throughout the government, and nepotism was the general means of appointment to administrative positions. Civil-service positions were often sold to the highest bidders. Due to this state of affairs, the nation was not strong enough to resist foreign invasion or protect its interests during major outbreaks of violence.

Before 1876, contact with the outside world was minimal, and the country prided itself on having been a "hermit kingdom" for 300 years. Korean citizens were prohibited from making contact with foreigners or traveling abroad. Communication with foreigners, except when sanctioned by law, was a crime punishable by death. The closed-door policy was applied to all countries, and Korea strove to keep even its Asian neighbors out, except for limited contact with China and Japan. Chinese and Japanese boats were allowed to fish along the Korean coast on the condition that they did not set foot on land or confer on the open sea with members of the indigenous population. Violators were subject to imprisonment and confiscation of their boats.[6]

Even contact with China, whose suzerainty Korea recognized, was more or less confined to the dispatch of a Korean emissary to Peking once a year, to pay tribute to the Chinese emperor, and a very limited trade. There was no known Chinese resident on Korean soil other than those diplomats who regularly made official visits. Relations with Japan, which were conducted mainly through diplomats, were also restricted. Nevertheless, Korea was forced to grant Japan a special privilege as a result of Japan's conquest of Korea in the late sixteenth century. It was allowed to maintain a 300-man garrison in the southern port city of Busan; otherwise, official relations consisted of the dispatch of congratulatory missions each time a new Japanese *shogun* (military governor of Japan) was appointed in that country.

Contact with Western countries during Korea's long isolationist period was virtually nonexistent. Only a few Westerners entered Korea before the country was open to the outside world in 1876, and even fewer left any imprint on Korean economic life. The first European is thought to have set foot in Korea in 1594, when a Portuguese/Spanish Jesuit priest arrived with the invading Japanese army. Before the country was opened to foreigners, probably fewer than 100 Westerners visited Korea.[7] These were either seamen, Christian missionaries, or government representatives. Almost all of the seamen, estimated at no more than thirty-five, had been bound for countries such as Japan and China and washed ashore from shipwrecks. Representatives of European and American governments began to arrive in Korea after about 1830. On numerous occasions they were sent by their governments to persuade, and sometimes intimidate, the country to open itself to trade. In many cases, these missions were accompanied by military forces, and negotiations sometimes ended in hostilities. The Christian missionaries, numbering no more than a dozen altogether, were nearly all Roman Catholics who entered the country in a clandestine way and lived disguised as natives. Most were discovered, and some were put to death.

A few Western visitors brought books, on such subjects as geography and mathematics, and new products, such as rifles, medicine, cloth, glassware, and clocks. Many of these items were presented to kings and local magistrates but never reached the common people, although some visitors taught farmers how to raise potatoes and introduced notions of Western thought, including Christianity, and ways of life. No businessmen were among these Westerners, and no trade between Korea and the Western countries took place before the country was opened to the outside world.

Some Korean citizens, nonetheless, had limited contact with the outside world before 1876. Diplomats, a few scholars, and artisans went mostly to China and Japan. They brought back, among other things, maps, cannons, spectacles, telescopes, calendars, texts on astronomy, and Christian books. In this way, the seeds of an intellectual awakening were sown among a very small number of scholars. Some Korean intellectuals slowly changed their views, and no longer did all Koreans believe that China was the center of the universe and the most advanced nation in the world. A very small circle of intellectuals even made some attempts to introduce Western thought, ways of life, and products to Korea, though initially with little success.[8] Catholic missionaries, in particular, challenged traditional value systems and customs in Korea, and after much difficulty the first Korean Catholic was baptized in 1784. Catholics refused to sanction local rituals, burned the inhabitants' ancestral tablets, and worshipped a "foreign god" in a Confucian society in which rituals were performed only for ancestors and earth spirits.

The lack of understanding of the outside world together with growing Western pressure drove Korea even deeper into isolation. The Korean people, especially the *yangban* elite, just wanted to be spared the incursions of foreign "barbarians." The ruling elite were firm in their resolve to fend off Western advances, and the group, though precarious, was successful in holding on to power. In addition, most Koreans saw the "barbarian" Westerners as aggressors and their religion as dangerous and destructive. The majority of Koreans, especially members of the country's elite, thought that the preaching of the Christian religion in Korea was criminal and that foreign expeditions and invasions mounted in the guise of trade and religious freedom constituted aggression and interference.

PRODUCTION AND INCOME

The Korean economy before the opening of its borders in 1876 was "traditional" in that it operated within limited production functions based on pre-Newtonian technology and attitudes toward the physical world. It was essentially stagnant, and a ceiling clearly existed on the level of attainable output per capita. It was by no means completely stagnant, however. There had been occasional marvelous advances, especially during the first half of the fifteenth century, characterized by the casting of metal printing type and the construction of an iron-clad ship in the shape of a tortoise. The quality of its pottery and lacquerware were once so exceptional that Koreans taught these arts to the Japanese. In the traditional economy there also, apparently, were some improvements in irrigation, an expansion in cultivated acreage, and an increase in production, though moderate.

Aggregate Production

Accurate figures are lacking, but the country's population growth is one indication of the increase in production. While the standard of living of most Koreans did not change much during the century or two preceding the encroachment of foreigners, the nation's population did expand modestly.[9] According to one estimate, during the last 300 years of the Joseon dynasty, the population, on average, increased at least 0.03 percent a year.[10] It also appears that the average income of the people was adequate to maintain a standard of living somewhat above the level of bare subsistence. Most early Western travelers and residents observed that the people of Korea were not poor, if poverty was to be understood as scarcity of the necessities of life. The people ordinarily had enough for themselves and for sharing with others.[11] The ratio of population to arable land in Korea was smaller than in Japan or China, but as long as Korea was closed to outsiders, the average level of comfort was higher than in either of those countries. Mendicancy was almost unknown, and rice was frequently so plentiful that travelers were provided with free meals. Farmers required far less work to secure a comfortable living than elsewhere in the Orient.[12]

It is, however, difficult to translate these qualitative observations into quantitative measures of income and production. Nonetheless, we can make some crude estimates based on a few scattered bits of data. On the whole, Koreans appear to have met at least their minimum living expenses, and it is suggested that in the 1870s per capita income in traditional Korea was at least $30 a year (or $600 in year-2000 U.S. prices).[13] While Korean farmers struggled to make a living under difficult conditions, their income and the wages of common laborers were at least at the subsistence level. The wages of workers are estimated to have averaged between 45 and 120 yen a year in the late nineteenth century,[14] which would be equivalent to $362 and $964, respectively, in year-2000 U.S. prices.[15]

To maintain a standard of living at the culturally minimum level, probably the sum equivalent to $600 was needed. Since well-to-do *yangban,* wealthy merchants, and a small percentage of the population lived above the subsistence level, and considering the contribution of the public sector while allowing some margin for error, an additional income for this class of about 20 percent may be allowed. The yearly wages of a primary-school teacher, for instance, were 216 yen and for a normal-school teacher 600 yen in the late nineteenth century,[16] the equivalent of $1,735 and $4,821, respectively, in year-2000 U.S. prices. Such observations lead one to suspect that per capita income in the mid-1870s was higher than the minimum and may have been as much as $720 (in year-2000 U.S. prices).[17] The 1997 per capita GDP of South Korea was about $11,000 (in year-2000 U.S. prices), and the per capita GDP of Korea in 1876 was about 6.5 percent of that.

On the assumption that the above calculation of per capita income is essentially sound, reasonable, and consistent with the economic conditions of the country at the time, Korea's GDP may be calculated. Several sources show that the total population in Korea at the time of the opening of the country in 1876 was approximately 12.3 million.[18] This would put the country's GDP in the mid-nineteenth century at about $8.86 billion (in year-2000 U.S. prices). In 2000 the GDP of South Korea (only half of the former country) was $511.8 billion, which is about 58 times that of the mid-nineteenth century.

Sectoral Production

Production in each sector of the nation's economy—namely, agriculture, commerce, industry, mining, communications, and transportation—was small and largely depended on manual labor. As is the case in all traditional states, the dominant segment of the traditional economy in Korea was agriculture, with nearly 90 percent of the total labor force being devoted to it. The foundation of agriculture and the chief source of income for the entire economy was the cultivation of rice, supplemented with sundry crops such as barley, wheat, beans, and common vegetables.

Land was cultivated using primitive methods that changed little over the centuries. These were labor intensive, utilizing virtually no machinery, the method passed on from father to son. Farmers depended on their own labor and sometimes that of bulls. Typically, three men would use a spade, while oxen sometimes dragged a wooden plow. Rice and barley were threshed on a board, winnowed by the simple process of tossing the grains in the wind, and milled with pestles in a wooden mortar. The work was often conducted cooperatively within one's community. Agricultural implements, such as wooden plowshares, hoes, hooks, knives, harrows, bamboo rakes, and wooden spades, were crudely designed and constructed and were not widely available.

Although its agricultural technology was primitive, compared with other underdeveloped countries in the nineteenth century, Korea utilized some complex and relatively advanced farming practices. With an irrigation network and land tenure system that had a number of what might be considered modern characteristics, the rural labor force had gradually been freed from slavery and serfdom. Unfortunately, the irrigation systems were neglected, and most fell into disrepair during the last century of the Joseon dynasty. Fragmentation of landholdings and disguised unemployment also hindered productivity. In the absence of reliable data, it is impossible to state the level of labor productivity quantitatively, but one outcome is certain. With a high labor-to-land ratio, high labor-to-capital-goods ratio, and virtually no advancements in technology, farmers were doomed to a relatively low and stagnant productivity level. And low productivity in agriculture meant meager rewards for the farmers.

There were five fairly distinct groups within the farming population: landlords, part landowner-cultivators, part landowner-tenants, tenant farmers, and farmhands.

The first group, the landlords, did not cultivate land themselves but leased it to tenants and relied for their livelihoods on land rents. The landlords, who were typically *yangban,* made up 2 to 3 percent of the population and fared well in terms of wealth, income, power, and privileges. They owned about 60 percent of the country's farmland. The richest member of this class, whose landholdings probably amounted to about 4 million *won* (the equivalent of more than $32 million in year-2000 U.S. prices), had an annual income of 250,000 *won* in the late 1890s, the equivalent of more than $2 million in year-2000 U.S. prices.[19]

Landownership at the time of the foreign incursions was the result of practices handed down over the centuries. In theory, all land belonged to the ruler, but Korean kings, like those in many feudal countries, rewarded supporters and high officials with grants of land. Some were permanent gifts that could be inherited, while others went with a position and had to be surrendered when the recipient left office. By the time the country was opened to foreigners, landownership fell into four major categories: (1) private land owned by individuals, (2) royal land owned by the king and his court but leased in perpetuity to private individuals who had the right of inheritance or sale, (3) land owned by municipalities and similarly leased to individuals who were the owners in a practical sense, and (4) land belonging to Buddhist temples and operated, typically, by monks. Private land could be purchased from landowners. By the latter part of the Joseon dynasty, most land was privately owned, in the senses just listed, freely bought and sold, and concentrated in the hands of a few well-to-do landlords.

Most of the farmers who actually tilled the land and made their livings from it were tenants. Approximately 40 percent of all farm families in the traditional period leased the land they cultivated. Although Korean tenants corresponded to the tenant class in Western countries, the former paid no stipulated rent. The arrangement was on a purely cooperative basis: the landlord furnished the land and seed, while the tenant supplied himself with a house and implements and provided the labor. The returns were divided more or less equally, and taxes were paid according to agreement. The total value of the holdings of a farmer in this group, including animals and implements, probably amounted to about 3 percent of all the possessions of the farm population.

The largest group in agriculture, tenant farmers, were typically born into tenant-farmer families and themselves remained in that position for their entire lives. During the traditional period, it was impossible for a tenant farmer to earn sufficient income by working hard to become a landowner. One author has estimated that for a tenant farmer to buy 2.45 acres (one *jeong,* or *jeongbo*) of land, an average-sized farm in Korea at that time, he would have had to save half of his yearly income for a period of 24 years.[20] Under the circumstances, saving to purchase land was virtually impossible and not expected. One author speculated that the only means available to acquire sufficient money to purchase land then were either to engage in usurious money lending or to be in a position to receive bribery.[21] Consequently, there were only a few new landowners during the traditional period.

The third group of farmers comprised those who owned and cultivated their own land. About 20 percent of all farmers in the traditional period tilled the land they owned. The fourth group included part owner-tenants, who owned and cultivated their own land as well as someone else's. About 35 percent of all farmers in the traditional period belonged to this group. The last group was the farmhands, who worked by the day, labored by contract, or were held as serfs.

On the whole, the typical Korean farmer had a small plot or plots averaging about one *jeong*, an amount sufficient to produce enough food to meet the simple needs of himself and his family in ordinary times. It has been estimated that the average annual cash income per family farm was about $30,[22] or approximately $772 at the year-2000 price level, averaging $128 a person.[23] At this scanty level of production, the agricultural sector had to sustain itself and support the aristocracy, manufacturing, and commercial networks.

In manufacturing, a number of goods—such as cloth, hand fans, paper, boxes, pottery, hemp (*mosi*) grass cloth, textiles, ceramics, ironware, coal, grass mats, and split bamboo blinds—were produced. Korean paper products were considered superior to those of the Japanese and Chinese,[24] but silk and cotton goods, though inexpensive, were typically of low quality, far inferior to those of the Japanese. In the traditional economy, a major effort in manufacturing was undertaken by the government, which organized and employed artisans and skilled workers to produce the goods it needed. These included cabinets, metalware, tile, porcelain, lacquerware, leather, paper, textiles, books, shoes, hats, vehicles, boats, and weapons (including bows, arrows, knives, and swords). There were also numerous regional government pottery factories and semipublic glass factories. At one time in the early Joseon period there were 129 artisan trades with 2,841 artisans employed by the central government, while 37 trades in local governments employed 3,511 artisans who worked in government handicraft factories such as those in Seoul (*gyeong gong chang*) and the provinces (*wae gong chang*).

Manufacturing was carried out mostly by the artisans (*gongin*), who played a crucial role in developing the handicraft industries of towns. These workers occupied a somewhat lower social stratum than the farmers and often worked in small communities. Industrial workers completely separated from agriculture and living in cities were, however, very few. In contrast to the number of farmers, there was no large manufacturing class as such. The artisans who produced the articles (coffin makers, roofers, masons, porters, and the like) were limited in number and belonged to trade guilds, constituted either by written right or prescription, which held a monopoly in their trade. They were controlled and regulated by the government Board of Works, which, among other functions, was entrusted with ensuring that the trades and industries did not fall behind in meeting the country's needs.

The efforts of these artisans notwithstanding, manufacturing was not an important economic sector. For many decades the useful arts made little progress in the country. Only a few artisans and entrepreneurs worked in private handicraft industries during the traditional period. Furthermore, the amount of these goods supplied to a larger market was insignificant; there was practically no industry supplying more than limited and local demands. Moreover, there were no manufacturers in the post–Industrial Revolution sense. At the time of the opening of the country to foreigners, excepting the government factories, most of the nation's output was produced in cottage industries by individual households. Division of labor and specialization in large scale were rare in the country at that time.

Mining in the traditional period also was elementary and inconsequential. It was under the control of the king, and exploration and exploitation of precious metals without the approval of the government was punishable by death.[25] Even if one were to mine minerals, it would have been next to impossible to sell them. Consequently, few dared to excavate them, and the development of the mining industry was severely curtailed.

Commerce in traditional Korea was limited as well, lagging far behind its development in China and Japan. Commercial activities were limited to certain transactions of goods needed to supply the government, Seoul, other cities, and villages. Much grain came from government estates, and many of the handicraft products came from government-sponsored craftsmen. A special group of guild merchants acted as tributary and purchasing agents for the taxpayers and the government. Under what was called the common tax (*daedong*) law, they collected "tribute" or taxes on behalf of the king and purchased and delivered the necessities of the government and the royal household. In this way they acted as government agents, sold the surpluses, and purchased the goods needed. They supplied nearly 60 percent of the taxes that filled government coffers. In return, they received commissions for their services in the form of rice, at a rate double that of the market price.

In Seoul, the capital, where about 200,000 people lived in the mid-nineteenth century, there were shops known as *yuguijeon* that specialized in six lines of commodities, namely, thread, cotton piece goods, silk cloth, fish, paper, and hemp. These were franchised, granted monopoly rights by the government, and housed in public galleries (*gongrang*), which were leased to the retail merchants, known as "city market merchants" (*sijang sangin*) in Seoul. These city shops (*yuguijeon*) controlled the local market.

Nearly all other commercial transactions in small cities or towns took place at the fairs or open markets that were typically held in a weekly rotation among five towns in each district market (*sijang*). The locations were geographically distributed so that the distance between them could be traversed on foot within a day. No other city in Korea had 100,000 people or was considered a commercial center, perhaps with the exception of Gaeseong (or Song-do, an old capital), which was said to have been a bustling town and a great center of the grain trade. Even in fairly large cities there were few establishments devoted exclusively to business. There were not even permanent shops in villages. In the few small shops that existed in large county or provincial capitals, visitors found little to purchase.[26]

Most of the nation's commercial activities were carried out by itinerant merchants (*pobusang*), who went around the villages (*hyangsi*) and sold and bought goods. They traveled on regular circuits to the village centers, carrying what they could in bundles or on their backs while the heavy packs were loaded on bulls or carried by porters. The itinerant peddlers, probably numbering about 200,000 persons in the country, formed influential guilds (*pusanghoe*)[27] but were under the supervision of high officers of the government. Commercial practices did not rise above the level of huckstering, and business was conducted mostly by means of barter. When and where money was used, especially in the later Joseon dynasty, it was thought to have been inconvenient due to the extensive debasement of coins by the government. Also, there were no banks.

Beyond officially sanctioned trading, commercial activities were limited, because each village was nearly self-sufficient and more or less constituted a small universe. Many necessary products were made by the farmers themselves in their leisure moments, during the winter months. The carpenter, blacksmith, geomancer, and stone mason of the average hamlet were also farmers. Fishermen generally had small holdings where they raised some of their own food, and most of their paraphernalia was made for them by farmers. Villagers engaged in producing mats, sandals, screens, and thatch, and built their own houses and furniture. Wood from the forest was free and available to everyone, and people typically gathered wood and brush for their own use or for sale in the nearest town. Some of them were also produced by the wives of farmers who raised or gathered the raw materials. Clothes were made from cotton raised on each farm.

The markets for trade of nearly self-sufficient villages and households, therefore, were small. The self-sufficient economy was supplemented with a few items that ordinary households could not produce for themselves, for example, dress shoes, medicine, salt, earthenware, wooden and wrought-iron utensils, silk, linen, grass cloth, and some luxuries, and goods traded were more or less confined to these types of products. The handicraft industries that produced them were not mechanized, and thus the supply of goods was limited. Villagers traded among themselves and took their produce to nearby market towns to trade it for the goods of their neighbors. In most parts of the country, there was no trade in the ordinary sense: no exchange of commodities between one place and another.

Prior to the opening of the country to the outside world, Korea engaged in very little international commerce, even with its neighboring countries, China and Japan. International commerce was rigidly regulated: rules limited the number of merchants who could enter into trade, the number of days during which foreign merchants could stay in the country, and the number of transactions permitted during each trading session. Official trade outside the country took place only when Korean emissaries were sent to China or Busan, where Japanese were stationed. In the north, very limited trade by land was allowed in the border towns between Korea and China for a few days a year. In the south, forty Japanese junks a year were permitted to visit Busan for purposes of trade.[28]

Commodities that could be imported or exported were strictly regulated in both kind and quantity. Typical imported items were high-quality silk, dyes, medicine, copper, books, and animal hides. Exports included ginseng, cotton cloth, handicrafts, metal products, rice, leather, salt, cows, pots, and hoes. All that gave hope of profitable trade were dried fish, seaweed, and hides. The officially sanctioned "tribute" trade, which took place when a Korean emissary was sent to China to present tribute to its emperor, and the covert private trade that accompanied it were of comparatively minor importance to the economy as a whole. Otherwise, there were almost no exports or imports by resident merchants. It is believed that some illicit trade was conducted between Korean barks and Chinese junks in the shelter of the innumerable rocks and inlets of the Korean peninsula. No comprehensive data showing the extent of Korea's trade during this period exist, but trade between China and Korea before 1876 was reported to have been at levels of about 3 million yen per year. Trade with Japan between 1873 and 1876 similarly was very small, with a total volume (imports plus exports) ranging between 110,000 and 165,000 yen a year.[29] The trade balance for 1873–1876 shows a slight deficit for Korea of about 17,000 yen. The items traded were mainly copper to Korea in exchange for such items as raw cotton, pepper, ginseng, and tiger skins.

As a result of limited internal and international trade, communications and transportation were primitive and slow in developing. There was only a system of post roads and stations for the transport of tax grain and for the use of travelers on official business. Most roads were little more than footpaths. Even the so-called grand highway from Seoul to the Chinese border was barely grand enough to admit a cart. The roads, such as they were, were usually in a state of disrepair. On the grand highway or on roads between Seoul and a few of the more important provincial centers only occasional repairs were made. In one year, "a few hundred dollars" was allocated for repairs, but three-quarters of this sum was reported to have gone into someone's pocket.[30] Men and goods traveled mainly on horseback, in ox-drawn carts, in palanquins, or by coastal shipping. There was virtually no means of country-wide communications other than those relying upon personal messenger services. It was partly because of the prevailing sad state of the nation's transportation and communications systems that Korea was not able to make much economic progress during the traditional period.

THE PROPENSITY TO WORK AND PRODUCE

There were many reasons for the underdevelopment of the traditional economy of Korea. One common explanation is the economic behavior of Korean people. Many scholars and travelers have described the uniqueness of the so-called traditional Korean.[31] Korean was said to have had low propensity to work and produce. Some observed that the energies of the people lay dormant. Foreign travelers, especially the Japanese, repeatedly described Koreans as "a lazy lot."[32] Many others, however, had opposite views of their propensity to work. One Western observer who was knowledgeable and closely associated with Koreans emphasized many times over that the reputation for laziness was unfounded and that Koreans possessed vigorous energy and mentality and worked diligently. Entrepreneurs such as producers of iron and metal goods, for instance, worked hard and were wealthy. Many Westerners in Korea in the 1880s were convinced that the Korean people were superior to the Japanese and might surpass the islanders in the learning of Western sciences. Another observer in the 1890s added that "Koreans were extremely intelligent and quick at acquiring knowledge."[33]

It is difficult to generalize about the entire Korean population in the traditional period with such sweeping characterizations. Since there were many groups and classes of people, a more meaningful and useful approach may be to divide the Korean people into two broad groups, the *yangban* and the commoners, and examine their propensities to work. As noted, most *yangban* were landlords. Many lived in comfort in Seoul and hired superintendents (*saum*) to supervise tenants and determine and collect rents. Some hired more than 100 superintendents and retained 1,400 to 1,500 tenant farmers.[34] A *yangban* theoretically was not supposed to earn a living by working.[35] Labor, especially manual labor, had long been undervalued in traditional Korea and even despised by the men of this Confucian-oriented society.

When a *yangban* failed to obtain a government position, he frequently descended into poverty, overburdened with debts, while waiting for even a minor post to turn up, and many were said to have stooped to all sorts of baseness to obtain one. Typically, the only other employment open to him was teaching. The Western observer also felt that the *yangban* had a false pride, which would lead him to starve rather than do a stroke of honest manual labor. It was perfectly acceptable and honorable to classify oneself as "not employed" or "a person with no occupation" (*mujik*) rather than soiling one's hands in gainful employment. Sometimes, a *yangban* was so poor that he had to depend on others for his daily rice, and it was no disgrace for him to go hungry or to be supported by his relatives.[36] When not employed, much of his time was often spent in traveling.

In contrast to the elite class, the majority of Korean farmers were hardworking people. Many contemporary observers described the commoners as industrious.[37] Even a cursory review would explain their high propensity to work and produce. With an average farm size of approximately 2.5 acres and typically no labor-saving devices, a farmer depended solely on his own strength and sometimes that of his patient partner, the bull. In spring and summer he left his house by daybreak and worked until twilight drove him home, spending the day barefooted and bare legged in water up to his knees in the back-breaking process of planting little tufts of grain. During the day he and his sons were probably joined in this work by his wife and daughters-in-law. Small merchants, fishermen, artisans, and other commoners worked just as hard for their subsistence.

But it would be equally justifiable to say that their greatest efforts at industry were somewhat listless and perfunctory. Foreigners, including Westerners, saw that in spite of the fact that the commoners worked harder than any other members of the community, Korean agriculture was "wasteful and untidy" and conducted in a careless and haphazard fashion. There were few crops for which the climate and soil were well suited. Farm implements were few and crude. Farmers used less manure and took less care in the culture and gathering of crops than did the Japanese. Weeds on Korean farms were not kept down, and stones were often left on the ground, in contrast to the exquisite neatness of Japanese and Chinese husbandry. In Korea there was a raggedness about the margins of fields and dikes and a dilapidation about the stone walls in Korea.[38]

These seemingly contradictory observations lead us to infer that Koreans did not have the need and/or desire to try harder to make a better living, regardless of whether they yielded poor or bumper crops. Because of the futility of trying to improve their well-being, ordinary citizens worked no harder than was absolutely necessary. It was generally observed that the commoners were content to produce only what would feed and clothe their families and were afraid to build better houses or dress respectably. According to some reports, innumerable peasant farmers reduced their acreage under cultivation year after year, raising only what would enable them to procure three meals a day. Korean fishermen, too, remained "content with such fish as would run into crudely and easily constructed traps set out along the shore, which only required attention for an hour or so each day."[39]

There appear to be two principal reasons for this low propensity to work and produce. One was the fact that commoners were subject to what might be called a long-run fatalism. Events were thought to be determined by fate, and there was contentment with the traditional patterns within the society. The opportunities open to one's grandchildren would be no better than they had been for one's grandparents.[40] This belief is well represented in Confucius's teachings and in such popular proverbs as "Wealth and social status are up to Heaven," "Wife, wealth, children, and income are all predestined," "Great possessions depend on fate," "Death and life are predestined and riches and honors depend upon Heaven," and "Embrace every chance of laying up merit, and your daily wants will be regularly supplied." Even members of the middle class had no prospect of career advancement. There were no skilled occupations to which they could turn their energies. Prominence was given to nature, and man's doings were minimized or ignored. As one Korean author explained it, "Human power is so slight compared with the great power of nature" that human manipulation of nature is out of the question.[41]

The other, and perhaps more important cause of traditional Koreans' lack of motivation for economic betterment was official suppression,[42] which is examined later in this chapter.

INVESTMENT AND ENTREPRENEURSHIP

Another reason for the stagnation of the traditional economy was low investment and a lack of entrepreneurship. The assessment of investment activities during the traditional period is difficult to undertake because few pertinent or comprehensive data on investment exist. The available statistics are fragmentary and deficient in more than one respect. Under these circumstances, estimates of the value of investment/capital stock must be tentative and mostly confined to physical capital.

Investment

All indications are that capital formation was very limited during the traditional period. Net investment was perhaps just sufficient to support very small increases in population without discernibly changing average per capita income and consumption. If the incremental capital output ratio during the traditional period was approximately three to one, then net investment must have been less than one-tenth of a percent of the country's national income, since population increase on the average is estimated to have been about three one-hundredths of a percent a year. It seems reasonable, therefore, to suggest that annual net capital formation during the 1870s was close to zero.[43] It is not possible to accurately translate this assessment into concrete net investment figures, but assuming (generously) that the average annual growth rate of GDP was one-hundredth of a percent and the capital-output ratio was three, the average annual net investment would have been no more than $2.7 million, and the average per capita investment 22¢ (all in year-2000 U.S. prices).

Productive investment in traditional Korea was mostly in farming, taking the form of the production of simple tools; the construction of roads, bridges, dikes, and irrigation and drainage systems; and the claiming of virgin land. The few investments undertaken by merchants were limited.[44] Occasionally, merchants and artisans invested in small-scale commercial activities and handicraft industries such as boat building,[45] constructing carts, and building tools for mining. Industrial investment and the accumulation of private capital were slight, and public investment in the 1870s was virtually nil.

As far as the ability to invest was concerned, the *yangban* had ample potential. Their incomes were high, and wealth had been accumulated in their hands, but few invested in productive facilities. A great deal of their income was spent on ancestor worship, weddings, entertainment, charity, and concubines. When they did save, the funds were used to finance nonproductive or low-productivity investments such as the purchase of land, the construction of mansions and monuments, charity work, and lending to finance poor peasants' consumption.[46]

The paucity of investment in traditional Korea also appears to have been due to the insecurity of income and wealth, especially among the "ruled" population. Potential investors were at the mercy of the political aristocracy. Earnings were not safe from predation, and property rights were not well protected (as examined later in this chapter). Some observers and economists also believe that high rates of interest held agricultural and industrial investment to a minimum.[47] If a man's credit was very good, he might be able to borrow at an interest rate of 20 percent for a ten-month loan from a mutual-aid association (*gae,* a voluntary organization that assisted members in their needs related to work, finance, and/or social activities). More often the rate charged was 30, 40, or 50 percent a year. It was said that a person who lent money at 30 percent a year interest would earn a reputation for giving it away for nothing. Sometimes a rate of 60 or even 100 percent was demanded.[48] At these rates, no sensible man would venture into business.[49]

Investment in human capital was also small. Some savings were used to finance a Confucian education, which was intended to maintain the social order rather than to promote innovation and economic development. On paper, all government offices, from those of the highest minister in the capital to the humblest prefectural clerk in the provinces, were open to candidates who passed the annual competitive literary examinations (*gwageo*), which were modeled after the Chinese system. To meet such needs, almost every village had a private elementary school (*seodang,* or *seowon*), but the *seodang* typically was a one-room house where a group of usually around ten pupils were taught Confucian classics. It was sponsored by local elders who were learned in the teachings of Confucius. Although no reliable data are available for the period before the arrival of Westerners in the country, the earliest count of such schools, in 1912, listed about 18,200, with fewer than 200,000 Korean children attending. There was one institution of higher learning in Seoul. The small annual net investment in human capital in order just to uphold Confucian mores hardly met the country's need for economic growth.

Entrepreneurship

Entrepreneurship was also lacking in the traditional Korean society. Entrepreneurship requires the ingredients of proper motivation, the bearing of risk and uncertainty, innovation, and the organization and management of business enterprises. In Korea's traditional economy no individuals or groups possessed all four of these attributes. In fact, the requisite qualifications constituted an affront to the existing order.

Entrepreneurship is generally associated with a personality in which the motivation to achieve is strong. There certainly was a high degree of motivation among the *yangban,* but the chief goal among that group was to become a man of morality modeled after great men in the Confucian history of China and Korea—a goal not necessarily appropriate for being an entrepreneur. In Confucian terms, "only the virtuous are able to rule all under Heaven," and the virtuous man must follow "Heaven's will." Also, the Confucian principles of filial piety and loyalty to the king were regarded as the two most important human values. The "cardinal virtues" of patriotism, filial piety, loyalty, and valor, however, did not necessarily lead to a materialist life. As a matter of fact, material wealth was thought to foul the purity of one's character. The *yangban*'s trust was thus in virtue and benevolence rather than in material things, and economic aspirations were secondary.[50]

Commoners emulated the behavior of the *yangban* class—that is, "the demonstration effect," and the nonpecuniary value system was clearly evident in daily life. One foreign observer noted that no amount of money could tempt a laborer to break faith with custom, for he regarded money as a convenience, not a necessity.[51] In other words, he never descended to the level of a business relationship on pecuniary considerations alone. Reischauer and Fairbanks went so far as to write: "In fact, Korea during this period seemed at times even more Confucian and traditionally Chinese than China itself."[52]

Traditional Korean society also encouraged maintenance of the status quo rather than activities bearing risk and uncertainty, one of the requirements of a successful entrepreneur. Maintaining the existing order in society was based on the Confucian code. The five moral codes (*oryeon*) of Confucianism that governed traditional Korean society were founded upon the central principles of obedience and loyalty. They perpetuated the subordination of son to father, wife to husband, subjects to rulers, and young to elders, as well as the trust between friends.[53] In these relationships, absolute obedience to authoritative figures was the foundation of the vertical social order.[54]

As one Korean anthropologist has avowed, traditional Korean culture cannot be fully comprehended without understanding the familism in which father, scholar, and ruler played a decisive role in guiding the perceptions and behaviors of their followers.[55] A well-respected political scientist put it more pointedly in stating that the soul of Korean culture is *euli,* a deeply held system of morality, integrity, and loyalty, and a sense of obligation developed in the context of interpersonal relations.[56] This idea of *euli* supersedes the idea of self and even national interest in dealing with friends and nation alike. According to his view, no indigenous Korean ideology is better able to explain their approach. On the basis of these principles, traditional Korea was dominated by a patriarchal, family-centered way of life,[57] creating a social pattern in which family solidarity, tradition, and social status were more important than individual rights, interests, and creativity. As one foreign observer noted, if the son of a *yangban* developed this trait of obedience to his father, he would grow up to be quite useless but a model son.[58]

Under the guiding principle of maintaining the existing social order, another essential requirement of entrepreneurship, innovation, was discouraged. Confucian traditions inhibited originality but strengthened the subordination of the self to official doctrine. A Westerner observed in 1897 that the educated Korean "often becomes so self-conceited that Socrates himself could not convince him of his ignorance. He is color-blind to everything modern. His eyes are set on the past, especially the Chinese past. He is slave to the traditions and customs transmitted from antiquity."[59]

Confucianism also instilled the idea that all actions should follow the "middle of the road" principle (*jungyeong*), which confined behavior to that which upheld the status quo.[60] In this way, traditional Korea discouraged innovation and scientific research, and social deviance meant ostracization. Thus, the *yangban* were not interested in innovation, setting up businesses, or accepting risk and uncertainty. Nor did they have the ability to innovate or an incentive to train in scientific knowledge and theory. The *yangban* were most interested in maintaining their secure position in the establishment. Appointments were dependent on one's performance on the civil-service examinations, which tested the candidate's knowledge of the Chinese classics. Education in the humanities was considered to be the key to power and wealth, since this was the only way to secure an appointment to public office, the highest goal in life. Confucianism had to do with governing people but nothing to do with business.[61] Therefore, a typical Confucian *yangban* used his own and his family's savings to acquire a literary education and have himself coached in preparation for the examinations. This was virtually the only means by which he could elevate his and his family's social, political, and economic status.

Another prerequisite for successful entrepreneurship, the organization and management of business enterprises, was antithetical to Confucianism and the existing order. Under Confucianism, the specialized expert could not be raised to a position of dignity no matter what his social usefulness might be. The dignified and "cultured" man was perceived as being "not a tool." That is, in his adjustment to the world and in his efforts to achieve perfection he was an end unto himself, not a means to any functional end. Although there were some notable exceptions, such as "practical learning" (*silhak*) in Korea, on the whole the core of Confucian ethics rejected professional specialization, a modern technocratic bureaucracy, and training. Especially abhorred was training in business or economics for the pursuit of profit.[62] Gentlemen did not meddle with such mundane matters as manufacturing and merchandising.

The fact that tradesmen and businesspeople were held in low esteem encouraged the Korean gentleman to neglect training in this area. The ruling classes were not interested in exploiting natural resources, promoting people's welfare, or increasing national wealth. They were veritable children in terms of business. Thus, as one would expect, most Confucian advisers to the government argued against investment in new technology, which to them only meant added expenses and a further burden on the people.[63] They extended to commerce and industry essentially the same static, regulatory policy that characterized their control of land and agriculture.

While the middle class (largely consisting of merchants and businessmen) in Western countries took on the role of entrepreneurs, the functions of the middle class (*jungin*) in traditional Korea were quite different. Its members were a small group of professional people who carried out menial tasks (e.g., as accountants, geographers, or copyists). Merchants and businesspeople were not even included in this class because of their low social status. Even if merchants had held some social prestige, it is unlikely that they could have served an entrepreneurial function in the traditional period. According to one foreign observer, "Korean businessmen had a weak entrepreneurial spirit, [and were] mentally lazy, wedded to old customs."[64] The major function of the merchant class was trading rather than production. Commerce was largely restricted to itinerant peddlers and open markets, where the necessities of life were exchanged through barter. Commercial activities were regulated by the government, and competition was generally absent. The special privileges of the "official" merchants and guild monopolies also stifled innovation and competition.[65]

The commoners were the least likely group to develop entrepreneurial skills, since they were poor, oppressed, and uneducated. They were heavily taxed, and poverty was pervasive. Thus, no group within traditional Korean society had the incentives, power, wealth, or ability to step into the entrepreneurial role. Commercial expansion, industrial investment, maritime enterprise, and the accumulation of private capital were greatly inhibited, and the economic dynamism that emerged from Western feudal society did not develop in Korea in the traditional economy.

In the meantime, there were no external or internal forces to promote entrepreneurship and encourage investment and innovation. As noted above, the Korean people were barred from almost all intercourse with the outside world, including neighboring countries, and to show an interest in modern technology was considered heresy and severely repressed. A well-known historian found that the receptivity of the earliest Koreans to new ways gave way to a conservative posture in later periods and that they became more resistant to external influences, both physical and intangible, as their country was repeatedly invaded by foreign forces.[66] Thus, the spirit of industrial enterprise became virtually extinct.[67]

SAVING AND CONSUMPTION

One underlying factor that contributed to low investment in the traditional period was inadequate saving for investment, which could be attributed to an excessive emphasis on consumption as well as to low income. Without adequate statistical data, it is difficult to determine the precise level of saving and consumption, but the behaviors of traditional Korean people enable us to determine the level of their savings. All signs point to the fact that aggregate savings in the traditional Korean economy was minimal and likely equal to the level of investment (i.e., probably three one-hundredths of a percent of GDP).

Saving

There is no evidence indicating that Korean people as a whole in the traditional period saved a meaningful amount out of their income; indeed, nearly all observers, foreign as well as natives, agreed that their propensity to do so was low. It was generally believed that saving was beyond the ability of the ordinary Korean people largely because of their low income. For most commoners, saving was never thought or even heard of.[68] In fact, most Koreans in the traditional period fell into debt, which contributed to dissaving. It was rare to find a person who was not indebted to others.

In contrast to ordinary citizens, *yangban* obviously had the income and ability to save large sums. However, most people in this group did not save much either.[69] Although some of them did save, a few a considerable amount, most of their personal savings apparently was used for financing the purchase of land, the construction of mansions and monuments, for charity, and/or loans to poor peasants, who spent most of their loans on consumption. In this way, much of the personal savings of the well-to-do was consumed by others and did not contribute to the nation's aggregate saving for investment.

Some government officials did save, but their savings were not significant. Undoubtedly, the well-to-do merchants and entrepreneurs had some saving, but their savings were not adequate to finance significant amount of productive investment. Iron and metal-goods producers, for instance, were relatively well-to-do, and their average annual profits from handicraft industries in the 1870s were reported to have been substantial, for example, an annual profit of 923 yen.[70] But their accumulated savings in the form of wealth did not remain with them for long. As a popular saying goes, it was "difficult to remain wealthy beyond three generations."

Consumption

In addition to the low per capita income, the small aggregate savings rate was attributable to the high propensity to consume, one of the dominant characteristics of traditional Korea. It was widely noted that Koreans in the traditional period were "spendthrifts" and that "when flush they, especially the *yangban,* cared only to live in style to satisfy their caprices."[71] Some of these habits were unique and peculiar to Koreans. Let us examine consumption by the commoners and by the well-to-do *yangbans* in two groups of expenditures: daily living expenses and extraordinary expenditures for major occasions.

In daily living, most *yangban* were affluent, led comfortable lives, and enjoyed luxuries.[72] Their houses typically had tiled roofs and were surrounded by walls pierced with a double gateway, outer and inner. Most observers, including Griffis, noted that *yangban* were prodigal: "Money glided by them and went easily the way of all the earth." The Chinese were considered miserly in comparison. Korea "is full of Micawbers, men who are as prodigal as avaricious, who when they have plenty of money, scatter it quickly."[73] Many *yangban* were also "very" married men. In the estimation of his countrymen, a fortunate *yangban* could support two, three, or more wives.[74]

In contrast, the daily expenditures of commoners were not far above the subsistence level, and they often consumed more than they earned. Their houses were humble structures, only a few feet high, constructed of mud, and roofed with straw thatch. Few had ceilings or plaster, and the floors were made of hardened earth covered with oiled paper, straw, or bamboo mats.[75] Most were furnished only with what was absolutely required, comforters and pillows. In normal years the farmers' supply of food, both vegetable and animal, was abundant and cheap. Nonetheless, the very poor often took only two meals a day, while those who could afford it took three or four. Among commoners, the merit of a meal was based on the quantity rather than the quality of the food. It was observed that the average Korean did not eat that he might live, but lived that he might eat. Typical Korean farmers, especially tenants, endured a spring hunger season (*chunggunggi*) during which they had to eat weeds and roots, especially when there had been some calamity such as a flood or drought.

The commoners were taught to maintain a humble lifestyle, as expressed in the proverb "In ordinary life, you must be economical." The government prohibited people from indulging in any luxury and even forbade the state of "being wealthy" (*buyu*). The possession of silver, gold, and even gold-trimmed dishes was prohibited. The wearing of silk and foreign-made textiles was banned. By both law and social custom, commoners had to wear inexpensive clothing made of coarse cloth.[76]

In addition to daily expenses, there were major costs associated with special occasions, such as weddings, funerals, and ancestor rituals for both *yangban* landlords and commoners, which usually required sizable sums. These extraordinary expenditures may be grouped in several categories. Established customs (*pungsok*) included four major rites (*sarae*)—namely, investiture, weddings, funerals, and ancestor worship, which were based on Confucian teachings and were very important to traditional Koreans. People went to great pains to perform these rituals faithfully without sparing resources, which placed major burdens on a family budget.[77]

Some of these traditions—for example, weddings, funerals, sacrificial ceremonies, and exorcisms, were thought to have been practiced even more faithfully, elaborately, and lavishly by Koreans than by the people of other Asian countries, including China and Japan, and many observers considered these activities to be "the outstanding features" of Korea. According to one foreign observer, "Korea was the country of decorum in the East." Because the rituals indicated the wealth, social position, and/or power of those performing them, Koreans conducted their rituals pompously.[78]

In traditional Korea, the responsibility of an individual extended far beyond himself. The place of the individual in society was considered negligible; there was more emphasis on the group as a corporate body, particularly in family relations. Thus, the moment a man attained distinction and wealth he became the social head of his clan, and his relatives were at liberty to visit, stay indefinitely, and expect his assistance, including financial support. According to one foreign observer, "every hand was in his rice bag and every dollar spent paid toll to their hungry purses." This amounted to a sort of feudal socialism in which every successful man had to divide his income with his relatives. The proverb "When a man finds the way, his chickens and dogs ascend to heaven" means that when a man attains a position of authority all his relatives and friends benefit. Not only was an individual a member of a family, the family was a unit of a clan. The clan was regarded as a larger family and a major component of society. Corporate responsibility also extended well beyond the limits of kinship to villagers, friends, and, to some extent, strangers.[79]

The social obligations of a *yangban* were much greater than those of a commoner. In addition to supporting his relatives, he could acquire dignity and prestige in the eyes of his countrymen through the constant presence in his home of a number of guests (*mungaek*). There was an enormous amount of visiting and entertaining, especially among men in the cities. The number of guests could be large or small depending on the *yangban*'s standing in official circles and his ability to support them. In the case of the very high nobility, there could be as many as 300 of these hangers-on (some called them leeches) "both fattening upon and adding to the revenues of their patron."[80] Some public men kept an open house, reportedly giving their servants as much as $60 a day (in 1890 U.S. dollars), which was about 1.5 times the average annual per capita income at the time, for the entertainment of guests. Guests performed no direct services for the host beyond the occasional writing of a letter on his behalf, reading aloud to him when he was in the mood, or transacting some piece of business. There was no stigma attached to this behavior of indulging on host by either the guests or the public.[81]

The sense of corporate responsibility applied to travelers as well. Koreans were said to have been great travelers within the confines of the country. The custom of extensive travel and the consequently unending stream of visitors in traditional times, is well documented. Buddhism also inspired Koreans to visit the place of origin of that religion. One Western traveler doubted whether there were many lands where a higher value was placed on the pleasures of travel. In years of plenty, it was the custom to feed travelers along "the great roads," and it was Korean law/custom that if a village could not entertain travelers it had the responsibility to transport them to the next stopping point.[82] According to most foreign observers, hospitality was regarded as one of the Koreans' most sacred duties.

At these special occasions, many expenditures were incurred. Numerous foreign observers noted that the Korean was lavish with his money when he had any, and when he had none he was quite willing to be lavish with someone else's money. In receiving guests, hosts had to accord generous hospitality. According to one popular saying, "One will get more money only when he spends what he already has." Hosts believed that money was made to be spent and circulated, and the Korean was mortally afraid of being labeled as stingy. Especially for *yangban,* in order to be treated as a gentleman one had to maintain the reputation of being affluent and generous, but not stingy, because that was a fatal curse for any respected *yangban*.

The consequences of these practices were numerous. For one, many were impoverished by such heavy demands on their limited resources. For another, there were no beggars on the streets, but a "crowd of lazy fellows" was allowed to take advantage of public hospitality by doing virtually nothing. Many foreign observers noted that a great and universal curse in Korea was the habit, which thousands of able-bodied men indulged in, of hanging [on], or "scorching," relatives or friends who were better off than themselves. A Korean would allow indolent friends and relatives to eat him "out of house and home." According to foreign observers, such a system bred "lechers, tramps, blackmailers, and lazy louts," who "sponged" off the benevolently disposed.[83]

Not only did such traditions place a large burden upon family finances,[84] but the waste caused by blindly continuing ancient customs was also a deterrent to domestic saving and the nation's capital formation. In spite of the fact that there was scant saving in traditional Korea, the potential was there, as shown in much superfluous consumption among almost all Koreans. This potential was attested to in a report related to the converts to Christianity. The observer noted that with proper motivation and incentives a large amount of saving was possible in Korea. It was reported in 1909 that one Christian church in Seoul, with an income not one-tenth that of an ordinary city church in the United States received over $10 in gold from each member, or $3,850 for 350 members, which was nearly one-quarter of the average per capita income in the country at that time.[85] According to the Western observer, the Christian converts gave up "tobacco and other useless expenditures" to save for the Gospel's sake. Some gave a tenth or more of their income, while others gave all they had beyond a bare subsistence living. Another indication of potential saving in traditional Korea was that there were as many savings as there were debts.

These observations seem to confirm what Lewis has observed in many underdeveloped countries. According to him, it is possible and reasonable for any people to devote 25 percent of the nation's income to capital formation and providing public services if they so desire it.[86]

THE ECONOMIC ROLE OF THE GOVERNMENT

The last, but not least, important factor contributing to the low levels of investment, saving, and production in the traditional Korean economy was the oppressive and ineffective government. On paper, the government had policies to develop the resources of the country and promote its prosperity. It had plans to organize and employ artisans and skilled workers to produce the goods it needed. These included almost all the items produced at that time: tile, porcelain, lacquerware, leather, textiles, books, shoes, hats, metal products, vehicles, boats, and arms. The government was empowered also to increase the production of silk by rewarding communities that planted mulberry trees, to foster the planting of lacquer and fruit trees, and to encourage the planting of forests.[87]

In reality, however, the government had lost much of its vigor toward the end of the Joseon dynasty. By the end of the Joseon dynasty, it was neglecting such basic services as adequate protection of life and property, street cleaning, sanitation, and measures to prevent or check epidemics. It provided practically no services to aid the people or their endeavors, including businesses. It built no roads. Nor did it improve its harbors or light its coast. Responsibility for the repair of roads and bridges was almost entirely in the hands of the citizens. Consequently, in the 1870s the roads were in a constant state of disrepair.[88]

Not only did the government neglect what should have been its basic functions, it also ignored the crucial role of improving public enterprises.[89] The technology employed in government-sponsored enterprises deteriorated over time. It was said that the government's policy was "making no improvement on anything,"[90] and at best it was oriented toward maintaining no more than the status quo. Despite the fact that public services were grossly neglected, there were large expenditures on no- or low-productivity projects. Huge amounts of the nation's resources were devoted to palace construction. Practically for each new king, a new palace was built.[91] With such large-scale, low-productivity expenditures as the construction of a palace, the nation's productive capacity barely increased over time.

In addition, the taxation policy of traditional Korea had retardant effects on investment, saving, and economic growth. The most important levy was the tax on land (*jo*). Farmland was divided into six classes and nine categories based on its quality. The tax was determined annually according to the condition of the crops and the quality of the fields. Initially, it was collected in kind. The tax burden on land became increasingly heavy during the traditional era, especially in the late Joseon period, mainly because of a decline in the amount of taxable land and the corruption of officials. According to one report, nearly 130 years after the first Japanese attack in 1592 the amount of taxable land under effective state control was reported to have been less than half that of the preinvasion level and down by two-thirds at the end of the Joseon dynasty.[92] It was estimated that only 20 to 30 percent of the revenue from the land tax reached the national treasury in the early 1800s, partly owing to rampant corruption among the officials through whose hands tax revenues passed.[93] Often local government officials did not send the full amount that was due to the central government.[94]

Taxes were also imposed on commerce and industry (*gongse*). Mechanics, artisans, and peddlers were taxed according to the scale of their businesses (e.g., for a certain number of sheets of paper or pieces of cloth).[95] The owner of a junk or fishing boat had to pay a tax in kind according to the size of the craft. When it granted a monopoly license to a few businesses, the government imposed a levy.[96] One of the most unexpected taxes on tradespeople was a levy on sorceresses arriving at the capital. Upon arrival, these ladies had to pay the government a certain number of logs or sticks of wood. There also were numerous peripheral taxes in the late Joseon period. These included levies on houses, salt, tobacco, textiles, fish, fur, lumber, minerals, and ginseng—in fact, on every product—as well as on land, water, roads, and commercial transit.

Taxes were also levied on traders at barriers on both overland and river routes. With the exception of the Seoul region, every house in Korea was subject to a tax of 1,500 yen irrespective of the size or quality of the structure, while another house tax was levied on the basis of the number of rooms regardless of their size—both regressive taxes. The government imposed so-called soldiers' taxes on farmers to help meet its military expenses. Sometimes, taxes were levied on groups, such as villages as a whole, and often relatives had to pay the taxes of their kin.[97]

In addition to regular taxes, farmers owed the government personal service or corvée labor (*buyeok*), which was calculated at the rate of six days a year for every eight acres owned or under cultivation. All commoners were taxed in this way up to the age of 65. Those who owed corvée were recruited to build and repair castles, palaces, royal tombs, roads, and dikes and to work on other public projects. When an official of rank traveled, every family in the district had to provide one male member or a substitute to put the road in order. The repairs of roads and bridges devolved entirely to the country people.[98] The provinces also paid into the national treasury a fixed amount of tribute in the form of horses, rice, hempen cloth, paper, ginseng, dried fish, and the like or their value in copper cash. Another form of taxation on a nationwide scale was the debasement of the coinage. This resulted in inflation, thereby reducing the purchasing power of currency and placing a great burden on the masses.

On top of lawful taxes, there was a universal practice of burdening the people with extralegal taxes or confiscation of property. The tax-collection system was allowed to decay, and new methods of extralegal taxation, or "squeezing," were improvised over time.[99] The most common was the collection of a tax larger than what the central government had prescribed—in many cases double or triple the legitimate sum. It was the custom to add 10 percent to the amount of a levy for the benefit of the tax collectors (*yamun* runners). Commoners were also often burdened with accommodating *yangban* officials, who were given free access to every city in the kingdom and were entitled to the best accommodations free of charge. According to one observer, "The official classes never paid for what they got when traveling."[100] Another abuse was that the property of commoners was often confiscated under various pretexts. It was alleged that anything a commoner possessed beyond what would provide him and his family with simple food and clothing was certain to be taken from him.[101]

Yangban officials levied these "taxes" and confiscated commoners' property for several reasons. One was to maintain a large staff of retainers (in most cases functionless). Some magistrates had as many as a thousand; and in a single province there were 44 district mandarins at one time, each with an average staff of 400 men, whose sole duties were policing the district and tax collection. Their food alone (at the rate of $2 a month) would cost $392,400 a year in the 1880s.[102] The magistrate replenished his meager purse as often as needed to reward those who were his servants. Although it has been argued that the needs of these officials and the amount of illegal taxation were not great, the "squeezing" was major. All kinds of taxes were levied to add to the revenue that steadily filtered into and out of the great money chest of the establishment.

Extralegal levies also helped officials to maintain elegant residences in Seoul and the countryside. Most officials of any standing lived in Seoul, leaving subordinates in charge in the province. Toward the end of the nineteenth century, 3,000 official dignitaries were said to have resided in the capital and 800 in all the other cities and provinces.[103] Officials levied taxes not only to supplement their regular incomes but also to recoup their "investment" in their official positions.[104] Some provincial governors were reported to have paid from 10,000 to 40,000 Korean currency (*won*) for their positions.[105] When the king reduced the length of the term for county governors in the late Joseon dynasty, they had to "rob" even faster to be assured of a good return on their investment. Also, squeezing enabled some to amass personal fortunes.[106] Seeing these practices, a foreign observer noted that the *yangban* was reactionary and a major stumbling block to Korea' progress. He concluded that with the ruling class only caring about personal interest, it was foolish to expect official honesty, patriotism, and public spirit to take root in Korean society. "Once in office their [the *yangban*'s] principal thought is that of the boa-constrictor—the desire to squeeze the people."[107]

The inevitable result of the relentless taxation of the populace is not difficult to predict. One obvious consequence was poverty. According to the first American minister to Korea, Horace Allen, the Koreans were "so suppressed officially that . . . their condition could be no worse" and they protested or resisted only when "the robbery" passed the limits of endurance. Having experienced these practices for decades, the Korean people were accustomed to the squeezing, illegal exactions, and rapacity of the nobles.[108] Perhaps more important, heavy taxation, together with high rents and the insecurity of property, resulted in demoralization and indifference among the Korean masses. Among Koreans, a general lack of the incentive to work, save, invest, change their occupations, or raise their standard of living much beyond the subsistence level prevailed. Some foreigners believed that Koreans were the most hopeless, helpless, apathetic, and broken-spirited people on earth. Others described their demoralization as laziness, indifference, inertia, despondency, and "mental hopelessness." They predicted that the Korean peasants would never be inclined toward industry when the products of their labor were ruthlessly appropriated by the nobles and officials and the barest pittances left to the producers.[109]

It is clear that many of the reproaches made about the attitudes of the Korean people and their propensity to work, produce, and save during the traditional period were primarily the result of the exploitation of landlords, heavy taxes, and corrupt government officials. People were convinced that their only lot in life was to act as "hewers of wood and drawers of water to their masters." They tended to view life in short and hedonistic terms. Commoners worked no harder than was necessary to keep "the wolf from the door." Many farmers reduced their acreage under cultivation year after year in order to avoid exactions or forced loans, and they raised only what would supply their families with three meals a day.[110]

Lack of motivation also prevented advances in cultivation techniques and skilled workmanship in producing important goods. Even as late as 1910, the average productivity of land in Korea was 0.769 *seok* (equivalent to 5.1 U.S. bushels) per *dan* (991.7 square meters) in comparison with 1.688 *seok* per *dan* by the Japanese in 1907. The fishing industry, like others, was said to have been paralyzed by the insecurity of earnings and the exactions of officials. Farmers generally were afraid to build better houses or dress respectably. Along with the other members of society, they sought the protection of poverty.[111] Those who purchased land and valuable objects never displayed their wealth.

Yet, at the same time many foreigners detected evidence that Korean peasants possessed great powers of endurance and moral and intellectual qualities on a par with those of the industrious Chinese.[112] They also saw physical courage that rivaled that of the bravest Japanese. In the view of these observers, such as a renowned world traveler at the time, Elizabeth Bishop, Koreans would have worked harder had they been given a reason to do so. Bishop had formed a low opinion of Koreans while visiting the country for the first time. To her, Koreans appeared to be "the dregs of a race." She saw the ragged, filthy villages, cringing servility or indolent conceit, and the suspiciousness characteristic of the Korean at home. Later, however, she noted a change and difference in Koreans who had migrated to

Manchuria and Siberia. They had settled on land, mostly as squatters there. These immigrants were not exceptionally industrious or thrifty but simple, starving folk who had fled from famine and exploitation at home. In Manchuria, there were neither mandarins nor *yangbans*. They were given the chance to make money. She saw houses well built in the Korean style, whitewashed and thatched.[113] She saw Koreans who had transformed themselves into a prosperous farming class.

She further noted that the Koreans in Russia had personalities well suited to industry and good conduct. The suspiciousness, indolence, and servility that seemed to have characterized Koreans at home had given way to independence and a "manliness of manner rather British than Asiatic." Furthermore, she detected in them alacrity of movement that was far from "the conceited swing" of the *yangban* and "the heartless lounging" of the peasant at home. Bishop attributed the transformation of Koreans in Russia to the different type of government and the officials who ruled them. In Russia, she found that there were many incentives to enterprise and no one to exploit or confiscate what had been earned. A modest amount of wealth did not attract the attention of officials. Affluence was viewed as a credit to a man rather than a source of insecurity. Many of these farmers became rich and engaged in trade, making and keeping extensive contracts.[114]

Another disincentive for investment and economic development in traditional Korea was the government's control of commerce and industry, as noted earlier. It tightly regulated business by retaining the right to grant monopolies and by restricting the number of entrepreneurial establishments. These "monopolistic" enterprises were unable to produce enough to meet the requirements of the government and, as a result, their importance toward the end of the Joseon dynasty waned.

SUMMARY AND CONCLUSIONS

This chapter has examined and evaluated economic conditions and various forces that affected capital formation and economic development in traditional Korea in the 1870s, before the opening of the country to outsiders. It has shown that, like most other traditional economies, Korea in the mid-nineteenth century was underdeveloped and essentially static. Per capita income at the time may be estimated at approximately $720, while the country's aggregate GDP was about $8.86 billion (in year-2000 prices). Other than what was necessary to support a slight rise in population, the country's per capita income remained basically static for decades, and perhaps even decreased. The underdevelopment of the economy permeated all fields of endeavor. Agriculture, which employed nearly nine-tenths of the labor force, was made up mainly of near-subsistence farms operating with capital-deficient and labor-intensive technology. Commerce consisted of infrequent transactions of essential goods conducted by itinerant merchants on regularly scheduled market days. Industry and mining were only rudimentarily developed.

The reasons for Korea's underdeveloped economy included the low propensity to work and produce, the lack of capital, and the ineffective and oppressive Korean government. The lack of capital was due to a low level of income, a high propensity to consume, little savings and investment, and the discouragement of entrepreneurial activities. These interdependent and inhibitive forces did not allow for meaningful capital formation and development of the economy in the traditional Korean economy.[115]

APPENDIX 2.1: NEGATIVE FOREIGN OPINIONS OF TRADITIONAL KOREAN PROPENSITY TO WORK

The followings are some of the other negative comments written by foreigners about the propensity to work of Koreans in the traditional period. One observer wrote that Koreans were "generally averse from labor" (Borton 1944: 73). Another writer reported that work itself was foreign to Koreans (*Korea Repository* 1895: 372). They were "sunk down to a dead level of indifference, inertia, apathy and listlessness." According to another, all economic activities were ad hoc with an exploitative method of production satisfying the minimum needs: "the average town Korean spends more than half his time in idleness. He sits contentedly on his threshold and smokes, or lies on the ground and sleeps" (Kennan 1905b: 409). According to Professor Gale, the indolence and indifference of the Koreans was "an effort on the part of the natives to fulfill their high ideal of the teachings of the sage of China." Another alleged that Korean servants had "neither initiative nor the capacity for work . . ." (Hamilton 1910: 274).

The Japanese were most critical. Some Japanese noted that the defects of Korean workers included "no desire to work, laziness, no desire to use intellect in work, very weak sense of responsibility" (Takahashi 1935: 402). They chastised that Korean heads were "very slow and dull . . . [and] . . . inept for very complicated and variable labor" (Hatobe 1931: 42). Others described that Koreans were "the rotten product of a decayed Oriental civilization . . . [with] . . . lack of inventiveness, indifference to technical improvement, and dislike of rules (Seikaku Ito 1937: 216). To the Japanese conquerors, the Koreans above all needed "the whip and the spur" (cited by S. McCune 1956: 75). Also, see Government General 1910–1911: 59; Suenaga 1895: 124–125; H. Shikata 1976: 427–428; Gale 1893: 58; Bishop 1897: 78, 336, 446; Moose 1911: 135; Seikaku Ito 1937: 216.

APPENDIX 2.2: FOREIGN VIEWS OF THE *YANGBAN*'S PROPENSITY TO WORK

To some foreigners, the cursory glance revealed the following observations of *yangban*. A *yangban* was a gentleman who did no work of a manual nature (Hulbert 1911: 39). He was not supposed to "work" (manual labor) for a living (Longford 1911: 34–35, 38), and no privation could induce him to stain his rank with labor. In their view, *yangban* were about as indolent as circumstances allowed, having the largest percentage of "gentlemen of leisure" in any body politics. According to Bishop, the upper class, paralyzed by the most absurd of social obligations, spent their lives in inactivity (1897: 101–102, 305, 446). Others described them as belonging to the so-called do-nothing-class; they neither toiled nor spun. Hosts of *yangban* passed their lives as idle, unproductive drones, jealously clinging to the ancient privileges of their rank but content to extort their livelihood and the wherewithal for their pleasure from the peasantry.

Some foreign observers noted that, down to the simplest details of life, *yangban* did nothing. Many a well-to-do *yangban*'s living consisted of a supreme command of coolie service. Even the rubbing of ink on the ink-stone or the lighting of his pipe had to be done for him. (It may be noted that the bamboo pipes were too long for the smokers to light themselves). According to other foreign observers, the use of the long bamboo pipe had contributed more than a little to making the Koreans what they were, for these "inveterate procrastinators and happy-go-lucky loafers" work was impossible with the long, unwieldy instrument functioning. In addition, some observed that many *yangban* thought that unless the pipe was in their mouths their lifestyle was not dignified (Rockhill 1905: 54; Bishop 1897: 101–102, 127).

Some noted that *yangban* also traveled enormously. "Thousands" traveled for reasons that included gathering at ancestral tablets, visiting tombs, position hunting, place keeping, attempting to deprive others of place, litigation, taking literary examinations, sightseeing, and restlessness. Their studies gave them an interest in things of the world, and this was stimulated in the antebellum days by the civil-service examination, which compelled the attendance of candidates at the prefectural cities. When a member of this class traveled, custom dictated that he take with him as many attendants as he could muster. According to a foreign observer, supreme helplessness was the conventional requirement; the *yangban* even had to be supported on his lead horse (W. K. Han 1971: 240). Also, see Moose 1911: 54, 63, 99, 101–103, 123; *Korea Repository* 1896: 167, 439; ibid.1898: 2, 230–231; Dallet 1954: 104–105. Hulbert 1911: 39; Longford 1911: 34–35, 38.

APPENDIX 2.3: EXPENDITURES AT MAJOR OCCASIONS

Of their rites, those relating to ancestor worship based on filial piety were held most dear by traditional Koreans. In this regard, the Koreans were said to have been "more set in their ancestor worship than the Chinese." Faithful children made sure that their parents had decent burials. Burial ceremonies were generally elaborate and involved large expenditures (Whigham 1904: 185; Griffis 1907: 297; Moose 1911: 178; Bishop 1897: 286–287). They were conducted in such a way that they gave "an impression of gaiety rather than grief." Many in the processions were neither relatives nor friends but those "bent on having a good time and drinking all the free wine they wanted." In all probability, funeral expenses in the traditional period exceeded 1 percent of GDP. (This inference is based partly on a survey of funeral expenditures in the more traditionally oriented area of Gyongsang Bukdo, a southern province) conducted by a government agency in 1971. The expenditures incurred for funerals in that year were as much as 1 percent of GDP (*Hanguk Ilbo,* June 26, 1971). In all probability, such expenditures in the traditional period of Korea must have been far greater (W. K. Han 1971: 254–255).

On the anniversary of the death of an ancestor, a sacrificial feast had to be hosted. The custom was to enshrine the tablets of the dead in people's homes for four generations and to conduct memorial services for those of more remote generations at the family burial ground. On these occasions, all of the sons, daughters, and other relatives were invited, and a commemorative rite was performed. This called for much drinking and merrymaking. According to foreign observers, the "loafers" of the village looked forward to such ceremonies with much pleasure at times when they could have their fill of feasting and drinking. (It was often said that the habit of imbibing alcohol was widespread among Koreans.) Christian missionaries tended to think that Koreans were fond of drinking to excess, that drunkenness was a social problem, and that it was viewed as honorable throughout the land (Bishop 1897: 91; Dallet 1954: 157; Rockhill 1905: 52; *Korea Repository* 1897: 229, 447). It is, however, doubtful whether inebriation in Korea was more extensive than in Japan and China. The grieving host who could furnish the biggest spread at these annual feasts was held in the highest esteem by his neighbors. Thus, it was very costly to have numerous close relations and ancestors, especially for the eldest son and his heirs, as the expenses fell primarily on them. Often a person in this position spent more on these rites than on ordinary household expenses, and frequently many families were cast into debt by them (Moose 1911: 197–198; Bishop 1897: 290).

Huge sums of money were also spent on religious and superstitious practices, which the people followed faithfully. A popular dictum was that one ought to "light your stick of incense at the break of every day and evening." Thousands of geomancers, sorcerers (*pansu*), and sorceresses (*mudang*) performed various acts and ceremonies, including exorcism of "devils and wicked spirits." Because their fees were high, the geomancers and sorcerers were said to have made plenty of money and lived well. According to a 1897 report, one sorceress earned an average of $15 a month, or $180 a year, which was about four times the average per capita income of the time (Rockhill 1905: 55; Moose 1911: 192; Bishop 1897: 443–444). It is believed that in the late nineteenth century the money spent on these offerings and fees annually was $2.5 million in the city of Seoul alone, and the national bill for them was estimated at $12 million a year, or three times the national government's revenue at the time (Bishop 1897: 403; *Korea Repository* 1898: 232). This custom continued thereafter. According to a survey conducted in 1972, a well-recognized geomancer could earn 40,000 to 50,000 *won* ($100 to $125) a month, about ten times the average per capita income in Korea at that time (*Hanguk Ilbo,* January 30, 1972). Also, see *Korea Repository* 1898: 192, 197–198.

One important expression of filial piety for a living ancestor was the celebration of his sixtieth birthday (*hwangap*). A man who attained this age was seen as having fulfilled his task on this planet. Nothing remained for the elderly to do but rest and reminisce. For the sixtieth birthday feast, children and friends had to "strain every nerve" and spend all their cash on the occasion (Dallet 1954: 162–163; Griffis 1907: 296). In more recent times, according to a newspaper survey conducted in 1971, a typical middle-class, middle-aged man spent an entire four months' salary on his mother's sixtieth-birthday festivities (*Hanguk Ilbo,* July 8, 1971). It was commonly observed that the wealthy freely spent much of their fortunes ordering everything possible to adorn the festival, even from distant provinces, and that the poor used their wits to collect a few savings. Wine and meat in great abundance were provided for relatives, friends, neighbors, acquaintances, and strangers. When the host's resources allowed it, abundantly provisioned tables were sent to all the neighbors as a gesture of goodwill and a symbol of affluence (Dallet 1954: 150).

Children had to marry well, and good parents would see to it that each child had an elaborate and expensive wedding (Moose 1911: 168). In general, the wedding feast, at which there was much drinking and merriment, was hosted by the parents of the bride for all their relatives and friends. A very inexpensive wedding in 1897 cost 75 yen, roughly 2.5 times the average annual per capita income at the time

(Bishop 1897: 117). According to a newspaper article published in 1976, even after the promulgation of the Family Ritual Code of 1968, which required citizens to simplify rituals and ceremonies and curb extravagant expenditures for such activities, the costs of getting married continued to remain high. An average man with a salary of $260 a month could end up spending $4,100 to set up a household ("Group Wedding Economics," *Korea Herald,* March 4, 1976). Needless to say, the birth of several daughters was considered a misfortune.

Important festivities were also held on certain birthdays. The hundredth day and first-year birthday of male children also called for celebrations. Later, when the father and family had decided that a boy should be "invested," which in nearly all cases was on the verge of his marriage, ornate clothing, a hat (*mangun*), and the other accessories were provided. The New Year's celebration was the greatest of all Korean festivals and usually lasted for fifteen days.

APPENDIX 2.4: EXTRALEGAL TAXATION AND CONFISCATION OF PROPERTY

One writer asserted that any man rumored to be "making money" or having attained the luxury of a brass dinner service would be laying himself open to the "rapacious attention" of the nearest "mandarin and myrmidons." Another attested that "Every possession they [ordinary citizens] had in the world was taken by the soldiers, runners, and magistrates" (Dallet 1954: 103; Bishop 1898: 102; *Korea Repository* 1892: 242; ibid. 1898: 306).

It was also noted that both old and new deeds to land could be taken away and that farmers were forced to surrender their fields. Confiscation of property took varied forms. One foreigner wrote that it was very common for an official, when he bought a house or field, to dispense with paying for it, for a mandarin did not usually enforce payment. If an official had no money, he might send his valets to seize a merchant or farmer. Typically, after making certain that a particular resident of the district was prosperous, these servants would launch a sudden attack by day or night at the individual's house or some unfrequented place. If the man did as he was bid, he was released. Otherwise he was led to the official's house, imprisoned, deprived of nourishment, and beaten until he paid the sum asked of him. Sometimes he was dragged to a convenient locality and flogged until he agreed to pay a sizable ransom for himself. The servants of an official might also browbeat the people and take their fowl and eggs (Dallet 1954: 103: *Korea Repository* 1895: 369; Bishop 1897: 102).

Another means of confiscation was extortion. In this scheme, under the guise of "loans," officials made exactions. For example, rich *yangban* who would not contribute to an official's cause were induced to make such loans (*Korea Repository* 1898: 246; Hulbert 1911: 513; Kennan 1905a: 310; Bishop 1897: 78–79). One observer noted that the best of the officials disguised their exactions under the name of loans. As soon as it was rumored that a merchant or peasant had laid up a certain amount of cash, an official would seek a loan. If it was refused, the man was either whipped or thrown into prison on a false charge until the sum was "loaned" by him or his relatives. Otherwise, he might be seized, held in the official's house, and starved until the money was forthcoming. Although pride and exclusiveness never hampered a *yangban* magistrate when it came to borrowing, they did prevent him from contemplating the indignity of repayment. The privilege of ignoring debts was customary, though not legal (Longford 1911: 35). It was said that there were cases of "barefaced extortion on pretexts that were so fantastic and preposterous as to be almost incredible." In essence, this made them a levy. Targeted individuals included merchants, farmers, gentleman, priests in charge of well-patronized temples or monasteries, and persons to whom good fortune had come. There is no way of knowing the extent of these illegal practices, but it was generally believed that in addition to regular levies, the imposition of extralegal taxes and the confiscation of private property were common. This added to the wealth of government officials. Although many *yangban* officials were accused, generally by Western observers as well as Koreans, of being "the vampire which sucked the life-blood of the (defenseless) people" to whom they were sent to govern, many magistrates probably were decent government officials and some even patrons of almost superhuman virtue. Nonetheless, corruption among *yangban* officials was rampant. Commenting on the relationship between the governors and the governed, Bishop characterized them as "the Robbers and the Robbed." The *yangban* were "licensed vampires of the country" and the other four-fifths of the nation "supply the blood for the vampires to suck" (Bishop 1897: 22, 27, 40, 102, 303).

On some occasions, extralegal "taxes" were collected from a group of individuals. According to one Westerner's writing, whole villages of prosperous farmers who had been taught industry, frugality, and honesty were arrested on the false charge of holding secret and seditious meetings and thrown into prison. He noted that several such men had died of starvation. In some cases, outlaws surrounded and ran magistracies. One report cited a case involving the five underlings of a magistrate. During a five-year period they collected 14,000 yen in illegal taxes. Later, the taxes were collected again (*Korea Repository* 1898: 306).

3

THE TRANSITIONAL ECONOMY, 1876–1904

The transformation of an economy entails the meshing of two conflicting forces: the entrenched indigenous economic traditions and the forceful intruding outside influences. The continuance of an economic (or any) institution in a particular form depends on convenience, belief in its rectitude, and force. When an economy begins to develop, the old institution becomes no longer convenient, because it stands in the way of opportunities for economic advancement, and people cease to believe in it. As a result, most of the traditional sanctions will erode and new institutions more compatible with economic progress are likely to emerge. It is generally believed that openness is a forceful determinant of economic progress. According to a recent study, twelve developing countries that have pursued appropriate open-door policies grew at a rate of more than 2 percent per year following the changes.[1]

The purpose of this chapter is to examine the foreign influences that affected capital formation in and economic transformation of Korea during the nearly thirty-year period between 1876 and 1904, which turned out to be a transitional period. The year 1876 signaled the opening of the country to the outside world after a long period of isolation, and the year 1904 marked the ending of Korea as a sovereign state as it succumbed to Japanese occupation of the country as a protectorate. Thus, the opening of the nation's door for trade and cultural contact with the world beyond its borders during the thirty-year transitional period provided a great opportunity to Korea for economic as well as societal transformations under its own government. In that sense, this transitional period, the first stage of its modernization, was a distinct and challenging phase of the Korean economy.

Examined in this chapter are the extent of foreign trade and investment, the Korean response to the encroaching new foreign forces in terms of institutional reforms, public and private investments in various sectors of the economy, and investment in human capital. The last part of this chapter assesses Korea's progress in national income, consumption, and saving in the transitional period. This evaluation is important, especially in light of a widely held view at the time that Korea was "incapable of reforming herself from within."[2] There are considerable controversies over the extent of Korea's readiness for economic development when Japan took over the country in 1905 and over Japan's contribution to Korea's economic development under colonial rule.

THE OPENING OF KOREA

In 1876, after having been a "hermit kingdom" for a long time and under the siege and threat of foreign countries trying to open the country by force for decades, the official renunciation of the isolationist state and the initial opening of Korea's borders to the outside world came in the form of the Korea-Japan Treaty of Amity (the so-called Gangwha Treaty). With the conclusion of the treaty, the ports of Busan, Inchon, and Wonsan were immediately opened to Japanese ships, followed by the scheduled opening of others later, which provided a limited but more amenable environment for foreign intercourse. The government assured other countries that there would be no interference by officials or others and that import and export taxes would be lifted. Only a port tax would be levied on non-Japanese ships. A more general opening of the country came in 1882 with the signing of the Korea-America Treaty of Amity and Commerce, which was soon followed by similar treaties with other countries. Normal relations commenced in 1888 when a U.S. resident minister took up his post in Korea.

From the start, the largest contingent of foreigners in Korea was the Japanese. The influx of Japanese gained momentum with the conclusion of the Sino-Japanese War of 1894. Several reports indicate that on average about 1,000 Japanese a month arrived that year and by 1895 about 7,000 Japanese were reported to reside in the country. The number reached 10,000 in 1896 and 40,000 just prior to the outbreak of the Russo-Japanese War in 1904. Japanese made up about 95 percent of the foreigners in the country in 1897, and they came to exert a significant influence on Korea's economic life, though at the same time they also stirred up much criticism against them.[3]

The Japanese resided mostly in large cities: the capital city, Seoul, and three main open-port cities. By 1895, there were nearly 1,500 in Seoul, more than 4,000 in Inchon, and over 1,300 in Busan. In Seoul they established a legation—the first foreign building in the city—teahouses, a theater, post offices, banks, and shops. The city of Busan, where only 100 Japanese lived in 1875, the year preceding the Gangwha Treaty, became a flourishing Japanese community. This quiet fishing village had turned into a bustling place of trade, with a Japanese population of 1,800 in 1882 and 5,500 in 1897. By 1897 the Japanese constituted 99 percent of all foreign residents and 14.4 percent of the total population (including Korean) of the city. A Japanese consulate, a chamber of commerce, a bank, a steamship company, and a hospital were established. The Japanese organized their own police force, fire station, post office, and telegraph system, in addition to retaining the rights to the port. Japanese teahouses and theaters were built. City services such as street cleaning and sanitation were maintained by the Japanese government. They brought in their own clerical workers and technicians, and even some city streets were renamed in the Japanese style. By 1887 one Westerner observed that Busan was "purely a Japanese town." By 1903, it was described as "thoroughly Japanese, prosperous, active, and enduring," with wide streets of Japanese shops and various Anglo-Japanese buildings. There was an appearance of industry and trade on all sides, as in any Japanese community.[4]

A similar scenario was played out in Inchon (Jemulpo) city. Before 1883 Inchon had been a small village with a dozen or so houses. By 1887 it had become a port city to Seoul and had a large congregation of foreigners (almost 40 percent of the population of the city). There were three Western-style hotels, a European club, several billiard parlors and restaurants, and excellent shops. Of the 4,357 foreigners living in the city in 1897, about nine-tenths of all foreign residents were Japanese, while about 9 percent were Chinese and the remainder were Westerners. The Japanese enclave was by far the most populous, extensive, and pretentious. Business was brisk, and there was an air of great prosperity. There were several streets of shops, where "the utmost activity prevailed," and the wharves were stacked with incoming and outgoing cargo. The Japanese section of the city even had two banks in 1890.

The port city of Wonsan, which had been a local market town for centuries, selling rice, tobacco, cotton and hempen cloth, and a few precious items from China, was opened as a treaty port in 1880. Japanese settlement began immediately. They developed the town in a fashion similar to Busan and Inchon, and established a chamber of commerce, a community hospital, and a school. Wonsan hosted the home offices of Mitsubishi and Sumitomo *zaibatsu* (Japanese business conglomerate), and the Daiichi Bank of Japan. The Japanese soon made up 96 percent of all foreign residents and 8 percent of the total population of the city.

Given the overwhelming presence of the Japanese, their influence in Korea was extensive. Most of the large and medium-sized cities at this time were founded principally by them. The Japanese dominance in Korea was such that Elizabeth Bishop, a prominent world traveler, proclaimed in 1897 that "all foreigners are Japanese." The U.S. consul general, Horace N. Allen, noted in 1900 that there was an "amazing increase of Japanese influence."[5] The Japanese played the crucial role of conduit for the modernization (or Westernization) of Korea. They introduced all kinds of Western goods, including rifles produced in Europe and the United States as well as in Japan. A Japanese exposition held in Wonsan in 1880 even before Americans set foot on the land was visited by 25,000 Koreans. Its objective was said to have been "to open the eyes and pockets of the natives." The exhibit contained mostly cotton goods and notions made in the United States and Europe, while only about 4 percent of the goods displayed were of Japanese manufacture.[6] Many Western-style buildings were constructed by the Japanese as well. The Japanese legation building, constructed in early 1885, was considered to be the first Western-style structure in Seoul. Also, it was the Japanese who introduced a modern postal service with the establishment of a post office in Busan in 1876.

No accurate data are available on the number of Chinese in Korea at the time, but a few available figures indicate that a sizable number arrived following the opening of the country. In 1897 some 2,500 Chinese were stationed in Seoul and the open ports. It was reported that the Chinese colony in Seoul was fairly large and that there was a new Chinese enclave in Busan and a solid settlement in Inchon. Although the number increased somewhat thereafter, even as late as 1904 there were no more than a few thousand Chinese, who engaged primarily in trade.

There was a small but steady influx of Westerners. While only eleven were reported to have lived in Seoul in the mid-1880s, by 1892 there were 56 U.S. citizens and 34 British subjects. The number increased to 190 to 200 Americans, including women and children, and 65 British subjects in 1897. The number of Westerners seems to have more than doubled by 1903, when there were 241 Americans, 141 English, 80 French, and few Germans and Russians. Most of them lived in foreign enclaves; with the exception of missionaries, they earned fairly high incomes and maintained standards of living comparable to those in their own countries. In Seoul, Inchon, and other cities there were European hotels, clubs, billiard rooms, saloons, restaurants, and stores.[7]

Westerners in Korea included government officials, businessmen, technicians, educators, diplomats, and missionaries. Only about a half dozen countries maintained resident diplomats in the country. Seven Westerners served as advisers to the Korean government between 1882 and 1908, providing advice on the law, the post office, customs, railroad construction, the hiring of teachers, medical care, agriculture, and the military.[8] Twenty-seven Westerners were employed in the Korean customs office. The largest number of Westerners who worked in Korea was engaged in mining. Of the 190 to 200 Americans in the country in 1897, 30 were involved with gold mines and railroads, and 3 were in trade. The Wunsan Mining Company was reported to have employed as many as 65 Westerners in 1903. The railroads employed at least 13. Others worked as mint engineers, streetcar motormen, glassmakers, textile engineers and technicians, iron workers, surveyors, and silk cloth production engineers.[9]

The most representative Westerners in Korea, however, were Christian missionaries. Of the 190 to 200 Americans in 1897, approximately four-fifths of all Westerners (mostly Americans) were missionaries by the early 1900s. The number of missionaries, including family members, increased to 141 in 1900 and 248 in 1908.[10] Their work was not confined to the spreading of the Gospel. They preached against customs that were an integral part of Korean culture such as ancestor worship and the deeply rooted belief in spirits. They introduced notions of democracy and equality and exerted a strong influence on the establishment of humane values through numerous channels. Protestant churches translated bibles into the Korean alphabet rather than difficult Chinese characters, allowing them to reach many more natives and planting seeds of thrift and egalitarianism among the middle and lower classes. They even operated a printing press.

The most significant undertaking of the missionaries, other than the preaching of their religion, was education. From 1885 to 1910 practically the entire modern (or Western) educational system was organized, directed, and maintained by them. By 1900 they were managing 39 schools in Korea, and between 1885 and 1909 over

950 Christian schools were educating about 25,000 students. The missionaries' contributions to medical science, health care, and women's education were particularly notable. The first modern hospital (Gwanghaewon) was established by missionaries in 1885. In addition to caring for the sick, it admitted 16 young Koreans to an affiliated school,[11] which was formally transformed into a medical college in 1904.[12]

The Christian missionaries thus played an important role in the modernization of the country. Probably the most important channel through which introduction to Western thought and science took place was the Christian schools. In addition to being inculcated with the new religion, natives were being infused with "modern" knowledge, the concept of equality, and puritanical mores.[13] These new values contributed greatly to the acceptance of Western styles of business and life. Koreans were also taught the means of acquiring technical knowledge and received vocational training. The schools were hotbeds of revolution and Westernization, and they produced many Korean leaders, who were later found in every liberal reform movement. Some missionaries, however, apparently set certain limitations upon the education of Koreans: one declared that Koreans should be allowed to acquire no more Western education than what the missionaries taught them.[14]

FOREIGN TRADE AND THE IMPORTATION OF RESOURCES

Volume of Trade and Net Imports

With the opening of the country, machine-made Western products slowly diffused into the traditional market in Korea. The small number of imports before the opening of the country, worth about 70,000 yen in 1875, gradually climbed up to annual imports worth 20 million yen by 1904, reflecting an average increase of about 20 percent a year. The aggregate imports between 1876 and 1904 were valued at about 163 million yen.[15] This was a much higher rate of growth than that recorded for Korea's national income.

These imports enabled the country to introduce many foreign goods and open natives' eyes to see and imagine for the first time in their lives what the world beyond their borders was like. Korea's appetite for imports was enormous and grew rapidly over time. Although imports during the early years were limited primarily to such necessities as copper, they expanded after the Gangwha Treaty to include consumer and capital goods; and nine out of ten were manufactured products.[16] Consumer goods included iron and inexpensive manufactured goods that some ordinary people could afford. The principal articles of import were cotton textile goods. The import of cotton goods increased from almost none in 1876 to 1.6 million yen in 1889, 5 million in 1897, and 12 million in 1907. Imports of textiles accounted for more than 50 percent of total imports during 1886–1898, although the import share of textiles declined to a little more than 10 percent in 1900.[17] Kerosene was another significant product imported, increasing dramatically from virtually none in 1876 to amounts worth 112,900 yen in 1896 and 323,700 in 1901. Increasing amounts of commodities, such as rifles, bullets, cannons, tin plates, glass, clocks, watches, woolens, dye, flour, and soap, were also imported.

The country was soon in need of industrial goods (metal, metal products, and machinery) to meet the needs of the country's new industries. Bags and rope for packing, machinery, and equipment for agriculture and mining were in great demand. According to one source, the total value of "machinery" imported between 1889 and 1897 was $98,000.[18] From the mid-1890s to about 1905, the value of imported capital goods expanded to reach as much as $200,000 to $500,000. In 1898, an exceptional year, imports of investment goods for mining and railroad construction alone reached as much as $677,000 ($81,000 for mining and $596,000 for railroads). The average annual worth of capital-goods imports for the period following 1898 was about $200,000.

Imports were mostly financed with exports. Exports increased from about 100,000 yen in 1877 to a little more than 17 million yen in 1904, an average increase of slightly less than 20 percent a year. Between 1876 and 1904, the cumulative total value of Korean exports was about 135 million yen. In contrast to the insatiable demand for imports under the prevailing economic conditions, there were few goods produced in Korea to export at the time. Most exports were of primarily extractive agricultural products and, to a lesser extent, minerals such as gold and silver.

Of these, agricultural products made up over 90 percent, ranging between 88 and 95 percent between 1893 and 1902. Rice and beans represented 60 to 80 percent of total exports during most of the period. The amount of rice was nearly double that of beans. Nonfood agricultural exports included hides, cattle, and raw cotton. Next to agricultural products came gold and silver exports, which made up 68 percent of all goods exported between 1886 and 1889 and 38 percent during 1901–1903.[19] Other export products included bronze, ox bones, fish, seaweed, raw silk, comforters, fur, shells for inlaying, timber, herbs, and oils. Processed goods exported included paper, cotton sheets, China grass (*mapo*), and straw mats.[20]

Korea's foreign trade during the transitional period reveals two principal features. First, notwithstanding its expansion, the total volume of Korea's trade (imports plus exports) was very small. It could not have represented more than 10 percent of the country's income (probably about 8 percent) even as late as 1904. There were still many obstacles to trade: underdeveloped industries, low income, a poor transportation network,[21] barter as the chief means of transaction, and small markets. Many businessmen believed that the import trade was not profitable.[22] Second, based on official trade statistics, Korea incurred a balance-of-payments deficit of approximately 26 million yen (163 million yen in imports minus 137 million in exports) during the transitional period. In other words, Korea imported a net amount of 26 million yen of foreign savings and resources.[23]

Some questions were being raised with regard to the comprehensiveness of the official trade statistics for the period, however. There apparently was more trade with other countries, especially exports, than what was shown in the official statistics, which affected the trade balance. These factors, such as out-smuggling and unreported exports, tended to increase exports, thus reducing the balance-of-payments deficits.[24] When proper adjustments are made, the actual deficit balance for Korea might be 15 to 20 percent smaller than the official statistics indicate and set at about 23 million yen during 1876–1904. This amount was equivalent to approximately 1.6 percent of Korea's GDP in 1904. This small balance-of-payments deficit (or import surplus) suggests that there was a net inflow of foreign resources, thus enabling foreigners to invest in Korea. In this way, the opening of the country brought not only Western goods and advanced technology, it also allowed foreign resources to enter the country for investment, the establishment of industries, and the promotion of economic growth.

Trading Countries

The bulk of Korea's trade during 1876–1904 was with Japan. Imports from Japan during this period were valued at approximately 130 million yen, which represented about eight-tenths of Korea's total imports, while its exports to Japan during the same period were about 120 million yen, representing around nine-tenths of the total.[25] In other words, about 130 million yen's worth of Korea's imports from Japan were financed with approximately 120 million yen's worth of its exports to Japan. Thus, there was a net inflow of roughly 10 million yen's worth of Japanese resources to Korea. Korean imports from Japan evolved in several stages. Immediately after the opening of the country to foreigners, goods from Japan rushed into the Korean market in massive tides. Japan held an almost exclusive position in the Korean market from 1876 to 1882, when it was the only country that had a treaty allowing it to engage in trade with that country. Imports from Japan slowed a little immediately prior to the Sino-Japanese War of 1894–1895, but they regained dominance, returning to 65 percent of the total, in 1900. On average, imports from Japan during the transitional period came in at about 70 percent of the total.

Korea's imports from Japan in the early years comprised mainly European and American manufactured products, chiefly cotton goods. Nearly 90 percent (88.3 percent) of imports from Japan between 1877 and 1882 were Western-made, machine-made goods, and over 77 percent of all imported goods were cotton products. The most prominent Western country that produced such goods was England, followed by the United States. Products from England constituted 54 to 57 percent of imports during 1890–1891. Unlike Western goods, most of the imported goods produced in Japan during the early period were the products of handicraft industries that utilized traditional methods. Cotton goods manufactured by machine in Japan first appeared in 1890, and by 1896 about 35 percent of Korea's imports from Japan were made there.[26]

The country origin of production of imported goods changed over time, however. Japan soon began to challenge the position of English manufactures, and goods exported by Japanese merchants into Korea included more and more products of their own making: 50 percent in 1885, and 90 percent by 1902. The most conspicuous example was Japan's export of textile goods to Korea. Japanese yarn arrived in Korea in ever larger quantities and gradually drove English and Indian yarn out of the market. Yarn imports from Japan in 1897 were valued at $350,000, compared with $36,000 from England. Korea's imports of Japanese-made goods represented as much as 80 to 90 percent of Japan's total exports of textiles in 1890–1902. Japanese firms sold over 4 million pounds of yarn and nearly 700,000 pounds of piece goods in 1902, compared with 111,000 sold by Britain and less than 40,000 by colonial firms in India.[27]

The Japanese success in Korea could largely be attributed to "shameless imitations," according to competitors from other countries, and to the attention they paid to the tastes and requirements of the Korean market. Also, the prices of Japanese products was considerably lower than those of Western goods, although the quality was inferior. Cotton goods that brought 15 cents a yard in the United States were sold for 50 cents in Korea in 1884, while Japanese cotton goods in 1898 cost 6 to 22 percent less than the English equivalent. A similar situation existed with regard to Japanese canned foods. These inferior but less expensive products drove the wholesale houses of England and the United States from the market. Japanese dominance in Korea was such that Bishop wrote in 1897 that even in country markets the goods displayed were nearly all Japanese. Similarly, Japanese shipping came to monopolize Korean trade. At the outbreak of the Russo-Japanese War in 1904, the Japanese controlled about four-fifths of all the tonnage engaged in shipping on the Korean coast. Later, Japan increased its hold to nine-tenths of all merchant-marine shipping.[28]

Korea's exports to Japan, which constituted, on average, over nine-tenths of Korea's total exports were composed predominantly of rice, beans, gold, and silver. Japanese tradesmen scoured the country for rice, even when the export of grain was prohibited by the Korean government. Gold exports to Japan peaked in 1887, when they represented about 85 percent of total Korean exports. The figure fell to 46.3 percent in 1893 and to about 40 percent before the Sino-Japanese War in 1894, but it regained its footing afterward, rising to about 65 percent between 1894 and 1900. Such exports were worth 3.7 million yen just before the Russo-Japanese War in 1904. Annual exports of gold to Japan represented between 50 and more than 90 percent of total gold exports during most of the transitional period.[29] Japan apparently was seeking gold in order to place its currency on a gold-standard system.

Most of Korea's remaining trade was with China and was carried out by Chinese merchants. It was largely confined to barter trade in a few articles, such as Korean tiger-skins, sables, paper, ginseng, and gold dust in return for European cotton goods and Chinese silks.[30] Significant trade with China came later. China briefly challenged Japan's dominance from 1881 to the early 1890s. The share of Korea's imports from China between 1885 and 1894 increased from 19 to 49 percent of the total, while the Japanese share decreased from 81 to 50 percent.[31] There were a number of contributing factors to China's expansion of trade with Korea. China's treaty agreement with Korea, reached in 1882, accorded its merchants certain privileges that were not available to other countries, for instance, allowing Chinese merchants to travel outside of the open ports.[32] The Chinese merchants were superior competitors to the Japanese and their customs more closely resembled those of Koreans. In addition, Japan's export taxes apparently hampered its ability to compete in the Korean export market before 1894. Finally, the Chinese achieved a dominant presence in the Korean customs office by placing in it many personnel from its own Imperial Customs Service.[33]

More important perhaps, because the Chinese brought British cotton cloth directly from Hong Kong or Shanghai to Korea, they could undersell the Japanese, who had to relay it through middlemen. Over 60 percent of total imports and practically the whole of Korea's imports of piece goods in the early years hailed from Great Britain, mostly by way of Chinese merchants. Even in the later period, goods imported through Chinese merchants contained a large quantity of Western-made products. As late as 1890–1891, of all goods imported into Inchon, a port close to China, only 13 percent were Chinese made and 24 percent Japanese made,[34] while the rest (63 percent) came from the West, primarily England.[35] Korea's imports from China were, on the whole, about 20 percent of Korea's total imports. Korea's exports to China consisted mostly of gold and some ginseng. Between 1885 and 1894, gold constituted more than 80 percent of Korea's exports from the port of Inchon. Korea exported 53.7 percent of its gold and most of its ginseng to China in 1893, for instance.[36]

Korea's early trade with the West was scant and sluggish. Merchants from the United States, who were the most numerous Westerners in Korea, did not occupy a significant position in the import trade for most of the period. The only exceptional year was 1881, when the United States was ranked the number-one country in imports to Korea even before it established diplomatic relations, while Japan was number five. The trade of British, German, Russian, and Belgian nationals was even more limited. A trading post on the Russian border was established in 1898,[37] but activity there was insignificant.

Goods imported from Western countries consisted of both consumer and capital goods. In addition to textiles, trade with the United States was mainly in kerosene, machinery, flour, cigarettes, fruit, wine, milk, canned foods, flour, cotton, clothing, provisions, household goods, and personal articles. The value of kerosene imported from the United States in 1897 amounted to $232,385, while capital goods, comprising mostly tools and machinery and valued at about $100,000, were imported for railroad construction and mining in the same year. All capital goods were imported by foreigners, primarily the Japanese. Since few articles that Korea produced suited Western tastes,[38] there were virtually no exports to non-Asian countries.

As can be seen from the preceding survey, during the transitional period, including the time when China had a favorable trade agreement with Korea, Japan maintained its dominant trade position with Korea. Yet, Korea's balance-of-payments deficit was relatively small, 10 million yen out of 23 million between 1876 and 1904, less than half of the total. The rest of the country's trade deficit, amounting to 13 million yen (out of 23 million yen), was with trading partners other than Japan, as noted earlier. Could this larger deficit in the balance of trade with countries other than Japan mean that countries other than Japan financed the rest (13 million yen) of Korea's import surplus?

Indications are that no countries other than Japan financed major portions of Korea's importation of foreign resources. The reason for the larger deficit with other countries was that most financing of Korea's imports from Western countries was primarily by Japanese investors who were headquartered in Japan and invested in Korea. As noted, 88.3 percent of the goods imported into Korea by the Japanese between 1877 and 1882, for instance, were Western made.[39] Since Japan was unable to produce goods of a high enough quality to export, it apparently financed the purchase of these goods from Western countries with its funds, which were then shipped directly to Korea.

FOREIGN DIRECT INVESTMENT AND LOANS

The net inflow of foreign resources that financed Korea's imports before 1905 was used to finance foreign investment in and loans to Korea. The next sections examine foreign direct investment, loans, and motives for foreign investment and loans in Korea.

Foreign Direct Investment

Almost all foreign investment in Korea during the transitional period was direct, and most was devoted to the development of commerce; mining; public utilities such as railroads, electric power, and communications; and the purchase of land. In the early years it was commerce that attracted most foreign investment, especially that of the Japanese and to some extent the Chinese. The Japanese were by far the most active businessmen in Korea, and eventually they came to dominate all fields of commerce. Most Japanese who lived in Korea after 1876 undertook some form of commercial activity. Those who listed "merchant" or "miscellaneous business" as their occupation made up over half of all Japanese in Korea. In the early years, more than 200 Japanese businesses operated in the country, compared with about 50 enterprises run by citizens of all other countries. The number of Japanese merchants in Korea increased to nearly 2,000 in 1899, and most of them were in retail trade (77 percent of retailers in the country were Japanese), while one-fifth of them were brokers and foreign traders, and 3 percent were wholesalers.[40]

Initially, it was small-scale businesses, not the large Japanese firms, that came to Korea. These were chiefly adventurers hoping for quick enrichment. They engaged in importing and exporting goods in open ports at first; later they expanded to retailing in local markets. There were about eighty Japanese wholesale or retail stores in Seoul in the 1890s, on which many Japanese and foreigners depended. They obtained most of the eligible business sites, and their well-stocked stores occupied prominent places in the cities. Most of them were single proprietors, and in the early years there were only a few businesses that could be called companies. According to one source, four Japanese commercial companies operated in Korea in 1904 with paid-in capital of about 1 million yen (most of which probably was invested in companies headquartered in Japan).[41]

Chinese and Westerners also pursued commercial activities such as trading. No sooner were the ports of Korea open to commerce than the Chinese established businesses there. There were about eighty Chinese business establishments in Seoul in the early 1890s, many of which, however, ceased operations after the Sino-Japan War in 1894–1895. Americans, too, engaged in foreign trade and operated a trading post. The Standard Oil Company erected substantial warehouses in Inchon harbor to supply the growing demand for kerosene, over which it had a virtual monopoly.

Americans also obtained coastwise navigation privileges, won the right to cut timber, and built a movie theater. Four major foreign countries—namely, Russia, England, the United States, and Japan—maintained coaling stations. There were a few Russian shops, a British foreign-trade agency, and a station hotel. Even some Christian missionaries engaged in commercial activities, such as apple orchards, which drew criticism from some quarters, including Koreans, American diplomats, and foreign journalists. American investors were mostly entrepreneurs operating on shoestring budgets.[42]

Banking attracted a limited amount of foreign direct investment in the early stages. It was introduced to Korea by the Japanese, who initially established three branch banks in Korea, including the Daiichi Bank. In 1883 the Daiichi was virtually the central bank of Korea, handling tariffs, issuing bank notes, and managing the Korean treasury, as well as purchasing gold and silver bullion for Japan. It also loaned money to the Korean government in the early 1900s. The bank eventually had branches all around the country. Briefly, a British bank opened a branch office for foreign customers in Inchon, and the Russians attempted to establish their own institution, the Russo-Korea Bank, which was registered in 1898 but never opened for business. A charter was also issued to Americans to form a bank, but it was never incorporated. Finally, there were many private Japanese moneylenders and pawn shop proprietors in Korea,[43] many of whom engaged in usury.

Another field that attracted Japanese investment in Korea, exclusively among foreigners, was land. Many Japanese bought farmland for speculative purposes, intending to reap profits by reselling it or leasing it to Korean tenants. Some even bought land outside the open ports before it was legal to do so.[44] They acquired large tracts, usually at bargain or "nominal" prices.[45] Often, they acquired land by unusual means: some, for instance, lent money to Koreans with land as collateral at usurious rates (sometimes as high as 10 percent for 10 days)[46] and then foreclosed when the borrowers defaulted.[47] Even after land prices skyrocketed, largely as a result of the Japanese purchases,[48] the return on investment was reported to have been high.

Another sector of the economy that attracted foreign investment was mining. Before the coming of Westerners for mining, "several thousand" Koreans were reported to have worked in mining, thus enabling the country to export gold amounting to more than $300,000 a year in the 1880s.[49] Many foreigners considered Korea a haven for the exploitation of minerals. The highly profitable investments in mining came about in a few cases in which rich, mineral-bearing lands were leased for small royalties before 1904. Foreigners were given exclusive mining rights on the best land and deposits. Starting out with the Japanese, who eventually owned and operated about 85 percent of the mines in the country before 1904, a few Westerners, including Americans, English, Germans, Russians, Italians, and French,[50] also invested in mining. There were four major foreign mining companies in Korea reportedly with about 5 million yen of capital in 1904.

Among foreign mines, the Wunsan gold mine, for which the concession was given to an American mining syndicate in 1896, was the largest and perhaps the most profitable one.[51] The company sank "huge sums" into equipment and employed a large staff. It was reported that the mining company had capital stock of 10 million yen in 1908 and at one time employed 75 Westerners, 2,300 Koreans, 600 Chinese, and 60 Japanese. As an American diplomat predicted, the mine made an operating profit of $750,000, which resulted in an initial dividend of 12.5 percent on the investment.[52] The syndicate owned and operated the mines until 1939, when it sold its rights to a Japanese concern for $8 million.[53] In four decades, these mines yielded 9 million tons of ore that had a gross assay value of $56 million, bringing in a net profit of about $15 million. Notwithstanding the success story of the Wunsan mine, most other foreign investments in mining were small, not significantly more profitable than their domestic investment, and their impact on Korea's economy was limited. The investment in other mines was relatively small, and the syndicate's franchise mines were not such moneymakers.[54] The only other foreign investment of note was a Russian timber concession.

Compared with foreign direct investment in commerce, land, and mining, investment in the manufacturing sector was relatively small and concentrated in rice hauling, tobacco, paper, glass, bricks, canning factories, and metal fabrication. Although there was no great amount of investment in manufacturing, the most dominant investors in Korea were Japanese, who probably had less than 1 million yen of paid-in capital in three companies and other plants before 1905. Although these investments were small by modern standards, they were meaningful in the Korean vacuum and played a significant role in pioneering the future development of industry and the economy. In comparison with the Japanese, other foreigners' investment in manufacturing was minuscule, probably no more than about 100,000 yen in 1904.[55] It appears that Korea was no exception to the general rule that foreign investment tended to shy away from manufacturing for native consumption in underdeveloped economies, as the lack of purchasing power among the masses offered no inducement to investment in it.

The scale of investment in factories was relatively small by modern standards, and large or medium-sized factories were rare. Industrial investment was 26,000 yen per factory and 37,000 yen per company. Two fairly large rice-cleaning plants were established at Inchon, one under Japanese auspices with steam-powered stamping machines and the other maintained by the American Townsend Company, which was fitted with the most advanced machinery. The only large-scale foreign firm was an American and British cigarette factory.[56]

Another field that attracted foreign direct investment was public utilities, including the electric power industry and railroads. Westerners introduced electricity into the palace in 1884 and 1887 and brought electric power to the capital in cooperation with Korean investors in 1898, which involved the operation of electric power lines and the main power plant.[57] Capitalized at $1 million, the plant, which was located in Seoul, employed about 270 workers.

Probably the single most important foreign direct investment during the transitional period in terms of volume and significance was in railroads. The first railroad in the country connecting the port city of Inchon and the capital, Seoul, was constructed in 1899. The route for the railroad was short, only 38.7 kilometers (24 miles). The construction was started by an American syndicate, but just before its completion it was sold to a Japanese syndicate for the reported sum of 1.8 million yen.[58] The construction of other railroads, such as the Seoul–Busan Railway and the Seoul–Wuiju Line—was started but not completed before 1905. Other railways, such as the Seoul–Wonsan and Busan–Masan Lines, had been planned but not yet built.

Similarly, there was important foreign direct investment in the field of communications. A sea cable between Japan and Korea was laid by a Danish company for the Japanese in 1884, while a Seoul–Inchon telegraph line and a telegraph line from the Chinese border with Wuiju to Seoul were installed in 1885 with the assistance of China. The Seoul–Busan telegraph line was completed by the Japanese after the Sino-Japanese War. Only a small investment was made in telephone services in Korea in the transitional period.

Korean shipping was shared between Americans and Japanese, but the latter eventually came to dominate it.[59] At the outbreak of the Russo-Japanese War, the Japanese controlled 78 percent of the tonnage engaged in shipping off the coast of Korea. There also were some foreign direct investments in other areas (construction, hotels, timber, fishing, ginseng, coal, cattle ranching, and whaling), but they were not large, nor did they have a major impact on the Korean economy.

Financial Incentives for Foreign Direct Investment

Foreign investment, like domestic investment, is typically motivated by profit, and the financial incentives for it come from the market or the intervention of external forces such as the government. Foreign direct investment in Korea was no exception. Foreign investments in commerce, land, and manufacturing appear to have been driven mostly by the profit motive in the competitive markets without the intervention of external forces. However, much foreign investment in transitional Korea, especially the large projects such as mining and public utilities, apparently were made mostly in response to financial incentives provided by either the host (Korea) or the foreign government. Most of these investments would not have taken place without those financial incentives. Foreign investors, including the Japanese, found that investment in Korea without such financial incentives was far from lucrative. The few Europeans who established enterprises in Korea complained of many difficulties and the high cost of doing business in the country.[60]

The financial incentives of the host or sponsoring foreign government took various forms. Those provided by the Korean government took the form of favorable concession rights, tax relief, and financial support given to foreign investors. In the case of mining, Korea's financial incentives included generous concession rights, low or no taxes, and legal protection from labor strife. The first mining lease was given to a Japanese firm for ten years to exploit a gold-and-copper mine. In the case of Wunsan gold mines, an American syndicate received broad and favorable franchise terms. The concession was to lease the mining land for twenty-five years with no tax on the mine, materials imported for the mine, or minerals extracted and exported from it. The Korean government assured the mining company that it would provide rights of way (to interior land), "handle natives," protect the company's foreign employees, and keep local officials from demanding bribes. Liquor was barred from the mining district, and the management was "certainly in favor of the judicious whipping of Koreans" who misbehaved.[61]

The American syndicate was relieved from compensating native miners and residents for taking over the mining land. Before the grant of the Wunsan mines to the American syndicate, the district was "honeycombed by native miners," rumored to have numbered 3,000. They were ordered to stop work to make way for the foreign company. As expected, the native miners raised a protest and wrote to the U.S. minister in Korea complaining that their livelihood had been taken away, that they had lost their trees and their ancestors' tombs within the mining district, and that their homes had been looted by foreign mine workers. They requested compensation for their losses,[62] but no payment was ever made. Most other mining concessions granted similar concession rights.

Prices for concessions to the grantees were a bargain. The price to the Japanese for a mine concession was a 30,000 yen "donation" to the Korean government in 1890,[63] and for its concession the American syndicate paid 25 percent of the stock shares (worth $25,000) to the king. Three years later, in 1899, the syndicate bought the king's share for $100,000 and a yearly stipend of $12,000.

In the case of railroads, the Korean government also provided generous concession rights to successful bidders. The Japanese government first demanded a franchise for all railroads in Korea for a period of fifty years,[64] to which the Korean government apparently assented in 1894 for construction of the Seoul–Inchon and Seoul–Busan Lines.[65] But because of vigorous lobbying by U.S. interests, the concession to construct the first railroad, the Seoul–Inchon Line, was given to an American syndicate in 1896.[66] The Korean government ceded to the syndicate for free the land that formed the route between the two cities. The company was to have complete control for fifteen years, at which time the Korean government had the option of purchasing the line at an agreed price. It had three years in which to complete the work and a full year in which to start operations. In addition, a strike-breaking clause was inserted in the concession, giving the syndicate the right to import Chinese workers. Diplomats from other countries assisted the syndicate in acquiring the concession with broad powers so that precedents for grants to other countries would be set.[67] The syndicate believed that the concession grant gave it all that a concessionaire could wish and that the enterprise would prove very lucrative.[68] It further believed that the rails could be laid inexpensively, because labor costs were low, and it was expected that all costs would be met out of freight and passenger receipts.

Following the first concession to the American syndicate, the railroads attracted foreign investors from several countries, which hotly competed to obtain concession rights on other routes. The concession for the second railway, the Seoul–Wuiju Line, was given to a French company in 1896. The Japanese received their concession for the Seoul–Busan Railway in 1898 after exerting strong diplomatic pressure on the Korean royal court. The general terms of the concession were the same as those specified for the Seoul–Inchon Line. The concession rights to construct other railways—for instance, the Seoul–Wonsan and Busan–Masan lines—were also ceded to Japan.

One immediate result of granting such a favor to one foreign country was to incite competition and jealousy among all the others. Each had to wrest a similarly profitable privilege from the Korean government or the prestige of the nation would be diminished. Thus, whenever a legation succeeded in wresting a concession from the king, the others demanded similar ones on the basis of favored-nation clauses in their commercial treaties with Korea. The acquisition of favorable concession rights thus became an official business of the foreign legation, and from start to finish it was behind the concession seeking, except in rare cases. In effect, the system functioned as a business favor granted by the conceding country (Korea) to the government of the diplomat who asked for it. Korea was the "happy hunting ground of the concessionists," and concession hunters were "getting as thick as fleas in a Korean blanket," quipped an American diplomat.[69] Everything turned on concessions—that is, the obtaining by intimidation, cajolery, or bribery a license to exploit for foreign interests some source of revenue.

First place among the holders of concessions was evenly divided between the United States and Japan. More than half of these concessions were granted to Americans, and they included the first railway, trolley, timber, electric power, waterworks, mining, and telephone concessions. The United States was successful in obtaining concession rights, because the king always viewed it as a disinterested friend on which he could rely in times of emergency. Horace Allen, the American missionary-turned-diplomat who was known to be allied with U.S. financiers, was successful in acquiring many concessions as well as tax relief. He boasted that "all the considerable financial undertakings in Korea are our own. . . . American influence predominates. . . . [It] is as great as it could be. . . . It is probably as great as we have any desire it should be."[70] He knew how to manipulate the court, sometimes by "questionable means." His work on behalf of American entrepreneurs went on in spite of scoldings and instructions from the U.S. Department of State not to seek monopolies or advantages over other nations.[71]

In addition to acquiring a much-needed supply of grain (especially rice), the Japanese also succeeded in obtaining numerous railway, telegraph, mining, timber, fishing, and whaling concessions. Before the Russo-Japanese War, the Japanese concessions also included a coal mine and four gold mines.

Eventually, the Korean government came to oppose concessions to foreigners. It declared in 1898, "Hereafter the Korean government shall not grant concessions to foreigners in building railways or working mines in the empire." As a dollar diplomat, Allen could see no justice in the declaration. According to him, "The Koreans can never see what is for their own best good."[72]

Another source of financial incentives accorded to foreign investors in Korea was from their own governments. A major portion of Japanese investment in Korea, chiefly in railroads and communications, resulted from the financial support of the Japanese government, which claimed that these investments were in the long-term interest of Japan. Many Japanese believed that Korea was essential as a source of food and industrial raw materials and a market for Japanese products, as well as a critical military base on the Asian continent.[73] In the case of railroads, the ultimate investor, a Japanese syndicate, completed the railway with the financial support of its government, which assisted in the purchase of the Seoul–Inchon Railway by providing funds.[74] The railway would not have been built or purchased without the strong financial support of the Japanese government, because the line could not generate enough profits to support itself. Likewise, the Japanese built the Seoul–Busan Railway with their government's guarantee of interest on the debentures issued by the Japanese railway company, a subsidy of 2.2 million yen, and a no-interest loan of 1.58 million yen.[75]

Communications networks—namely, telegraph and cable—were built by the Japanese government. It is significant that these investments coincided with the Japanese propensity for military expansion, which first showed itself as early as the 1870s, a few years after the Meiji Restoration.[76] This was long before industrialization had created any serious need for Asian markets or raw materials for Japan. The profit margins of these investments were either minimal or negative, and the Japanese government heavily subsidized them as an inducement to other investments in Korea. It is reasonable, therefore, to infer that these investments were not for financial gain but were politically motivated: readiness for the conquest of Korea.

No Western governments had political ambitions in the form of annexing Korea or provided any financial support to their citizens' investments in Korea. Foreign direct investment by Westerners was based solely on market forces and was exclusively for profit. In the case of the Seoul–Inchon Line, it was reported that just before its completion in 1899 the Americans sold it to a Japanese syndicate for a healthy profit of 800,000 yen.[77] When the sale was made, the American syndicate also made the Japanese buyers promise that they would purchase "things manufactured in the United States" for the railroad and "promote American interests." Most of the construction equipment was imported.[78] Even when concession rights were granted, if such investment projects were later determined not to be financially rewarding, the Western concessionaires peddled the concessions until they were disposed of or they lapsed.[79] For instance, before the construction of the Seoul–Wuiju Line began, the French company found that it would be a money loser and in 1899 offered to sell the concession to the Russian and Japanese governments. The negotiations were not successful, and eventually the concession lapsed. Other foreign direct investment by Westerners was mostly in extractive industries whose output was destined for export, which had minimal impact on the domestic economy, such as linking foreign direct investment to natives' economic activity, namely, the forward or backward linkage effects, as shown in Appendix 3.

Foreign Loans

In addition to direct investment, foreigners made loans to finance Korea's deficit balance-of-payments and investment. From the early years of foreign contact, the Korean government had relied on such foreign loans. At times, it seems the government was financially reckless, such as when the king, queen, and government officials borrowed from foreign sources, apparently without even consulting one another.[80] Official loans before 1904 totaled approximately 8.5 million yen,[81] although outstanding loans at any one time were much smaller. Future customs revenues often served as collateral.

Most official loans between 1882 and 1901, totaling approximately 4.2 million yen, came from Japanese sources; other lenders were from China, Germany, France, and England.[82] The bulk of the funds was used to meet budgetary needs, including pay for military officers, and for infrastructure improvements, such as the installation of electric lines, attempted railroad-construction projects, the installation of telegraph lines, and the purchase of steamships.[83] In addition to formal loans, there were numerous unpaid bills and sums owed to foreign merchants. The American firm of Collbran and Bostwick often acted as a kind of confidential banker, lending money to the Korean king. Interest rates on these loans ranged from 7 to 10 percent a year.[84]

In sum, it is estimated that foreign direct investment in and loans to Korea during the thirty-year transitional period amounted to approximately 23 million yen, equal to about 2.5 percent of the country's estimated GDP in 1904. These amounts were by no means large by current standards, but it was significant that foreign investment and loans did take place at all in such a poor and politically and economically unstable country. It was the Japanese who contributed a majority of foreign investment and loan in Korea during the transitional period between 1876 and 1904.[85]

THE KOREAN RESPONSE TO THE FOREIGN "INVASION"

Having examined the foreign pressures, including foreigners' investment at work in Korea, the remainder of this chapter investigates how the Korean government and how a people under siege of foreign pressure responded to the powerful outside forces in the transitional period. A fundamental process in any industrial revolution, or in any abrupt acceleration of the rate of capital formation, is a sudden increase in opportunities for making profits by producing goods and services efficiently. This can be accomplished through either institutional changes or innovations that enable the economical exploitation of available resources.

For Korea in the latter half of the nineteenth century, as for Japan in the early part of the nineteenth century, the opening of the country to the outside world affected many facets of economic life, for both the government and the Korean people. Foreign imports and foreign investment could have proved to be the key that unlocked the door of economic opportunity, providing a highway over which new impulses and technologies arrive to introduce Western economic life. Foreign arrivals brought a different outlook on life, technology, infrastructure, production, business, and consumption, and forced the country to draw increasingly on the world's industrial resources to compensate for its own deficiencies. It certainly should have had a powerful demonstration effect on the Korean people. In the following sections the responses between 1876 and 1904 are evaluated in terms of institutional reforms and modernization, physical investment (in commerce, banks, industry, mining, transportation, electric power, agriculture, and miscellaneous sectors), and human capital formation.

Institutional Reforms and Modernization

One critical function of a government is to establish and maintain the political order and legal security essential to capital formation and economic development. The task sometimes requires sweeping changes in the organization of national life. Although it is not easy to trace the responses to such challenges, because there were no consistent government policies during the transitional period, it is clear that eventually the Korean government and most of its people accepted, perhaps grudgingly, Western ideas and a new economic system and order. Even Daewongun—who was the father of the king, once served as regent, and was in the vanguard of arch-conservative political leaders in Korea at that time—was interested in science and technology and recognized the need for gradual, but not speedy, reform.[86]

The government did undertake an intermittent modernization campaign and instituted a number of reform measures. At times, it showed considerable enthusiasm over its modernization policy. The zeal with which the work of reform was initially pursued resembled the first years of the Meiji Restoration in Japan. An important and clear-cut example may be seen in the direction of new policies during the 1882 and the 1894 reforms. The 1894 Gap-O Reforms, for example, enacted 208 separate laws[87] that abolished well-guarded mores of the traditional society, such as slavery and the designation of the lower class (*chonmin*); allowed widows to remarry; and discontinued the civil-service examination system (*gwageo*) that was based on the Confucian classics.[88] Further legal reforms granted *yangban* women the right to work outdoors and even regulated such matters as the length of tobacco pipes and the styles of hairdressing.

Following the example of "modernized" countries like Japan, the Korean government also undertook a series of institutional reforms, remodeling the court, the army, and local governments and developing a "modern" budget. With the reform of 1882, a new Foreign Office and a revamped Customs Bureau were established. A postmaster was appointed in 1883, and a postal service was launched in 1895. In 1896 the first budget under the reformed system was made and published for the first time in history.[89] The reforms not only attempted to discard traditional ways of life and modify the sociopolitical structure, but also laid the foundation for establishing a modern, more market-oriented economy.

There were attempts in 1891, 1894, 1901, 1903, and 1904 to reform the chaotic monetary system, which had allowed 3,000 varieties of Korean and numerous foreign currencies to circulate at one time.[90] The nation's tax system was similarly reformed in 1894 to emulate those of supposedly modern nations. The land tax was no longer to be levied in kind but in money. As a result, grain that formerly had been diverted from ordinary channels of trade to Seoul was now released for export abroad. To survey and modernize the land system, the government set up the Land Management Office. It also began building a new national market for goods and capital linked to the outside world through expanding trade.

A similar situation prevailed in the private sector. The combination of new impulses and modes of thought introduced through Western education, a greater number of Koreans traveling abroad, increased contact with foreigners, and the influence of free discussion and the press slowly affected the nation and its people. A gradual intellectual awakening began among some impressionable members of the *yangban,* particularly those few who had traveled abroad. Koreans who traveled to Japan were startled, amused, and enlightened about modernized Japan. To its Korean guests, Japan stood for "all the outward signs of civilization that is coming in."[91] The number of Korean visitors to the United States was small, but they, too, were impressed with the country and its economic advances.

A few reformers became convinced that the adoption of Western technology and production methods was the only alternative available if Korea was to maintain its independence and advance its well-being. Some began to emulate life in these countries by "modernizing their clothing and minds,"[92] while others began to adopt and invent new tools and machinery, as well as a stronger work ethic.[93] The progressive and reform-minded young intellectuals who formed the core of the modernization movement came from well-established Seoul *yangban* families. Most had passed the highly prized royal civil-service examination, and they were regarded as young men with promising futures.

When the progressive youths returned home, several became the leaders of the movement for modernization. Following the general trend in the country as a whole, these youths spearheaded the introduction of Western institutions, science, and industrial technology. They published new magazines and newspapers that introduced Western notions and goods. Women organized numerous clubs and societies to disseminate new ideas and introduce the lifestyles and business practices of Japan and the West. The progressives pointed out the need for industrial development, agricultural improvement, and the expansion of roads and port facilities. While urging the government to reorganize its administrative structure and reform its fiscal system, they also pressed for the introduction of a modern system of factory management. The Western influences that filtered through these progressive intellectuals were felt in urban areas first and, then, the notion of modernization slowly spread to the lower classes and peasant farmers as well.

Also, as the country began to recognize the importance of business, the social status of businessmen improved, and their role in society expanded.[94] When a popular vote was taken after a debate at a high school in Seoul in the mid-1890s, for instance, the response carried overwhelmingly on the reform side.[95] Gradually, contemporary Korean life, beliefs, and customs were altered. The capital city had substantial business districts made up of brick buildings; apartments in these blocks were rented, and dry-goods and notion stores sprang up. To most foreign observers, the Korean people were by nature better disposed toward foreigners and more open to change than, for instance, the Chinese.[96]

Notwithstanding the redressing of some abuses and the realization of some people that Westernization was inevitable, the overall effectiveness of the reforms and the progress of modernization in the country, unfortunately, were not overwhelming. The attitudes and structure of the administration as a whole changed little. In contrast to the official strategy of the Meiji period in Japan, which was to learn all the "tricks" of the Westerners[97] and resulted in an astonishing speed of modernization in Japan, Korean government officials lacked the strategy, the political will, and the skills the job required. The king reverted to many of the worst abuses of the throne. Every new limit placed on his arbitrary powers was viewed with disfavor and opposed with the whole strength of the court. The old queen's place was taken over by "an equally abusive lady." The government was also inefficient. The Korean government was reckless, frequently borrowing money from the Japanese Daiichi Bank to meet budgetary needs. Even as late as the period between 1895 and 1898, government expenditures were about 10 percent above its revenues. As the monetary reforms fell into chaos, the debased currency became worthless overnight.

In addition, the Korean reforms lacked support from various segments of the society.[98] Irrespective of the discernible changes among some Korean people, traditional ideas and the old economic way of life were strongly rooted. Western ideas were too radical for most people to accept at that time, and the majority still viewed foreign cultures, innovations, and material advances as "barbarian." They did not understand much about the outside world and did not want it, wishing only to be left alone in their "hermit kingdom." Every reform attempt was met with indignation. Moreover, the reforms did not encourage the internal mobility of people that is essential to economic growth and structural change.

Political and social leadership throughout most of this period continued to be exercised by dominant groups that were not technologically progressive. These groups pursued their aims through a variety of social institutions and controls. Ultra-Confucianists continued to reject the open-door policy and insisted that all innovations cease. To them, Christianity, for instance, posed a direct challenge to the patriarchal system, which was based on ancestor worship, faith in household deities, and family rituals marking coming of age, marriages, funerals, and sacrificial rites. The usual dislocation attendant on throwing open a closed economy to concession seekers and mercantile interests with superior financial and technological powers also contributed to their unhappiness.

Powerful traditionalist forces within and outside the government, including commoners, farmers, officials, and the *yangban,* objected to the many drastic changes. They opposed the adoption of Western clothing and protested a ban against the wearing of the topknot in their hair, which to most Koreans at that time was close to sacred. The popular dread of foreigners was demonstrated by delegations of country people who came to Seoul with petitions and protestations prophesying woe. A serious drought in 1882 was attributed to the foreigners and caused a riot during which the Japanese legation in Seoul was attacked. Similarly, many Koreans blamed a drought that occurred in 1899 on the new electric wires and rioted against the "evil spirit" of the foreign electric trolley cars in Seoul. They protested the construction of telegraph systems at their expense. Some denounced American businessmen as typical representatives of countries that "eat the flesh of the weak."[99]

In 1893 an anti-Western group called Dong-hak (Eastern Learning) rioted against the adoption of Western ideas and methods by the government. Understandably, Koreans reacted especially strongly against the Japanese, who were thought to be in the vanguard of modernization, "uncivilized," and "aggressive."[100] Some agonized foreigners even believed that internal reform was impossible and that change would have to be imposed from without. It is clear that Korea in 1904 was in a state of transition. The past was in ruins, most things were undefined and indeterminate, and the present and future were unclear.

Public Investment

When Korea was still feebly functioning as a sovereign state, its response to investment was similar in both the public and private sectors. In the public sector, after the opening of the country and its somewhat limited exposure to Western technology, the Korean government initiated a variety of public investment projects to build new facilities. Municipal reforms transformed the very appearance of the capital. The new thoroughfares were lined with public buildings, the homes of various government departments, and a large Western-style structure was built for the Central Bank of Korea in 1884. In 1896 the narrow, cluttered, and unsanitary streets of Seoul were drained, widened, cleaned, and freed from the obstruction of peddler's booths. Public health measures such as smallpox vaccinations were initiated. A Western-style forty-bed hospital, founded in 1885 under royal patronage, eventually evolved into a missionary hospital and medical school. It was reported that within the first year 255 were in the hospital as in-patients and more than 10,000 out-patients were treated in the hospital and its dispensary.[101] Later, three more hospitals and dispensaries were established.

The Korean government likewise played a positive role in establishing a number of enterprises that produced goods and services and that introduced the new technologies and fields of endeavor. It established the Bureau of Machinery in 1883 to introduce Western machinery and to manufacture weapons and other war materials.[102] In the same year, the Bureau of Printing was set up to meet the government's needs, which included the printing of official forms, certificates, stamps, and reports, as well as the publication of an official gazette, Korea's first newspaper, which carried both domestic and foreign news and useful literature on the subjects of agriculture, stock raising, and forestry. In addition to printing, the bureau undertook the engraving of copper plates, designing and printing, and the manufacturing of ink, ink rollers, and paper for official certificates. The government believed that private enterprise was still in its infancy and could not supply adequate amounts of these products or services. The printing and papermilling machines were imported from Germany. Similarly, a new government Bureau of Currency, set up in 1883, began to mint Western-style coins in 1885. Minting equipment and three engineers had been brought from Germany for this purpose. Another new mint was established in 1885, for which the printing equipment was imported from Japan, and three Japanese engineers were employed to help operate it.

Also in 1885 the Bureau of Mining was set up to exploit the country's mineral resources and encourage entrepreneurs to form mining companies utilizing Western technology. The bureau imported prospecting equipment from the United States and engaged foreign miners to work in gold mines. It made frequent attempts to open mines and locate new sources of the precious metal. With the objective of founding a model coal mine and deriving revenue from it, the Korean government also assumed control of the Pyongyang mines in 1904 and operated them with modern tools, equipment, and techniques.[103]

Similarly, in 1885, the Bureau of Textiles was formed to operate a model textile mill, which was equipped with machines imported from Europe. It was designed to train Korean technicians at the mill and acquaint the business community with modern textile-manufacturing methods. In 1897, following the Sino-Japanese War, it also built a model textile mill with the aim of replacing the large quantities of Japanese cotton goods imported into the country. It was to be a half-government and half-private corporation, operated with equipment imported from Japan. The government, likewise, operated a pottery factory, set up lumber yards, and built a motor-powered flour mill, a glass works, and a match factory. It established bureaus to manufacture cigarettes and liquor in Inchon. It even had the foresight to organize a Whale Catching Commission in 1883.[104]

In like manner, the government ventured into modernizing the country's transportation network with railroads. When a French concessionaire and Korean private companies failed to construct a Seoul–Wuiju Line, as noted earlier, the government attempted to build a railway system of its own. It set up the Korea Railroad Company and drew up plans with the help of French technicians and materials.[105] In the case of the trolley railway system and electric power in Seoul, a joint American and Korean investment project was founded in 1899. The government engaged an American company to construct a tramway with nine cars (1898) and a plant that generated electric power (1902) in Seoul. The cars were run by Korean motormen and conductors under the supervision of a few Americans.

The government also formed a corporation jointly with an American syndicate to supply electric power to the capital. It installed electric power in the palace in 1884 and 1887 and in the capital city in 1900. The government (actually the king) paid \$375,000 for a half share in the trolley and lighting enterprise. Likewise, it entered into a joint venture with an American firm for the construction of a system of waterworks for Seoul at the cost of some 7 million yen.[106] Thus, Seoul was the first city in East Asia to have electricity, trolley cars, a water system, telephones, and telegraph service all at the same time.

To accommodate its navigational needs, the government purchased three steamships and assigned them to its Transportation Bureau, which was established in 1884. The ships were jointly operated by merchants and they transported government grains. The bureau was later transformed into a public corporation managed by the Japanese. It began to engage in marine transport with a German ship in 1892, and by 1895 it owned and operated 144 steamships and boats with a total capacity of 38,403 tons. It also purchased a battleship from Japan in 1903. To facilitate marine shipping, the government planned to build some thirty lighthouses on the Korean coast to facilitate ocean and coastal navigation.[107]

In the communications field, the first telegraph system, installed in 1885, extended from Seoul to Inchon, Pyongyang, and finally Wuiju. Telegraph service between Seoul and Busan, Seoul and Wonsan, and Seoul and the southwestern city of Mokpo was established in 1889 with loans from China and Germany. When the line between Seoul and Wuiju was destroyed during the Sino-Japanese War of 1894–1895, the Korean government rebuilt it. Telephones, which were introduced in the palace in 1898, were made available to the public in 1902.

In addition to building its own productive facilities and factories, the government became a medium for the introduction of advanced technology. As a means of encouraging farmers and business interests to adopt Western technology, the government established model farms and factories. In 1883 the king established an American model farm, stocked it with foreign seeds and cattle, and began to distribute seeds donated by the U.S. Department of Agriculture. The model farms were also established to demonstrate the breeding and raising of cattle and sheep, the making butter and cheese, and the grafting of fruit trees.

In like fashion, the government attempted to introduce "modern" sericulture and filatry improvement projects. Sometimes foreign firms were engaged to install modern facilities. In the late 1890s a German national under the auspices of the Korean government undertook a project to "regenerate the country" by introducing a modern silk industry. In some instances the government gave financial support to selected enterprises such as railroad construction, electric-power generation, shipping, and banking to promote private investment. Likewise, entrepreneurs were encouraged to form mining companies that would utilize Western technology. In 1903 the king sanctioned a grant of 1 million yen from the customs service to aid the navigation industry.[108]

In sum, the government directly invested in or indirectly assisted private investment in numerous modern undertakings, such as machine shops and facilities that employed advanced technology, which would enable Korean investors and entrepreneurs to acquire knowledge of advanced science and machinery and experiment with new ways of producing goods and services. Many such government investments were in fields typically left to private businesses in developed Western countries, since few Korean private companies built modern factories in the early years. Before the 1890s, it was the government that built them.

Notwithstanding these efforts, the success of public investment was rather limited on the whole. The nation's productive capacity barely increased over time. Nor were the efforts of the Korean government sufficient to have much positive impact on private investment. No records of the manufacturing of weapons or other war materials at the Bureau of Machinery have been found. The project to introduce a silk industry did not succeed. The gold-mining operation with foreign machinery and miners was abandoned before it had a fair trial. Other attempts to open mines and prospect for gold failed.[109] The model farm ceased operations, although its Korean director was still drawing a salary twenty-five years later. The government-operated shipping company was also a failure. After two years the whole operation was placed under the management of the Japan Mail-Shipping Company (the Nihon Yusen Kaisha), and three years later it was absorbed into the Japanese company, which assumed control of the Korean government's steamers and held a monopoly over coastal shipping.

Neither was the impact of public investment on ordinary citizens and businesses significant. For instance, only 490 households, most of which were probably composed of foreigners, out of 50,000 families in Seoul, had electric lights in their houses as late as 1909. Likewise, the users of the telegraph and telephone systems were mostly government employees: there were a mere thirteen private telephone subscribers in the beginning, and only 1,903 parties, probably largely foreigners, had telephones by 1902. The government plan to build lighthouses was never carried out, and the Korea Railroad Company, set up by the government, failed because of a lack of funds. Nor was the climate favorable to new investment and technological change.

There are a number of reasons why so many public-investment projects were inadequate, failed, or were inconsequential. Although the zeal with which government investment was undertaken in some years resembled some of the progressive moves found in other developing countries (e.g., in Meiji Japan), Korean reconstruction lacked cohesion and the support of the various strata of society. Powerful conservative forces in the country, including both *yangban* and commoners, opposed the sudden and drastic changes. More immediately, the financial difficulties of the government, in addition to social upheaval and political instability, were tumultuous. This was well demonstrated in a controversy involving the question of attracting foreign loans for government-investment projects. It was argued that the government needed foreign loans because it did not have sufficient financial resources to invest in development projects. Nonetheless, the issue of public bonds never got off the ground.[110]

The amount of government investment in the public sector was minuscule, probably far less than 1 percent of the country's GDP. This level of public investment was not substantially different from that which existed in the traditional economy, when capital formation in the public sector was virtually nil. In most advanced industrial economies, 2 to 3 percent of national income is usually dedicated to public works, strictly defined (roads, harbors, schools, hospitals, public buildings, irrigation and drainage systems, and port facilities). The Korean government spent on the average only two-tenths of a percent (15,000 yen) out of its national budget of 6.3 million for public works in 1896, and barely two-tenths of a percent of the total (124,268 yen) for education, mostly for the nation's elite. Moreover, when small sums were allocated to various districts for road repairs, most were reported to have gone into the pockets of local magistrates.[111] The Korean government regularly spent more money than it took in and incurred budget deficits during most years.

Furthermore, the government's incompetence and inefficiency made its investments ineffective. The government seems to have had little idea about the nation's economic goals or plans for using Western technology to build a new economy. There was no well-planned economic policy.[112] Officials often purchased obsolete equipment that they were unable to use or sell in other markets. For instance, the government was reported to have bought a number of "useless ships" in need of extensive repairs. An American who sold the Korean government a ship for $9,000 later repurchased it for one-eighth that amount and then complained about the deal.[113] The Japanese cheated Korea, too. Horace Allen, the American consul-general, observed that Japan had palmed off bad ships, worse machinery, and all sorts of worthless goods, including a one-ship navy at "a fancy figure," on the oblivious Korean government. A Japanese representative then used "bull-dozing tactics" to collect one of his country's claims.[114]

Likewise, the government sank some $500,000 into its new mint. When it was persuaded to move the mint to another location to save freight charges on copper, discarded paper-making machinery was purchased at the mint in Japan. The new facility operated for only a short time. It never placed a coin on the market or even produced a sample. The mint project thus resulted in great and useless government expenditures. Some foreign firms received government contracts to provide such items as rifles and nickel coins, both of which ended up being supplied by American firms.[115]

Another impediment to successful public investment was the lack of technical know-how. Because of the lack of capital and technology, the government mining venture did not succeed, and the gold-mining enterprise with foreign machinery and technicians was abandoned. The progress of the government's efforts to introduce foreign technology and production methods was also minimal. Many technical advisers were not employed effectively, contrary to the experiences of Japan and

Thailand. Foreign glassmakers, ironworkers, and weavers, for instance, were employed by the Korean government in 1901 "without the slightest probability of their ever doing anything in any of these lines."[116] One silk expert drew a salary from Korea while living in China, and a match factory produced matches without heads. As noted by Curzon, "too much credit cannot be given to the members of . . . [the] Customs Service" in the nurturing of Korean commerce.[117]

PRIVATE INVESTMENT

With the exposure to foreigners, their new lifestyles, commodities, businesses, and Western technology, the traditional business community in the private sector, consisting of both small businessmen and workers, needed to face the major challenge of adjusting to the new environment. The Korean response to the onslaught of modernization in the private sector is examined in this section in terms of private investment and structural changes in commerce, banking, industry, mining, transportation, electric power, agriculture, and other miscellaneous industries. Also investigated are the assessment of aggregate private investment and investors in the private sector.

Commerce and Banking

The segment of the private sector that was immediately and primarily affected by the opening of the country was commerce. One obvious consequence of modernization in commerce was the shift in its centers. Traditional centers of business, such as the city of Gaeseong, an inland city, declined, while the new open ports, such as Inchon, Busan, and Wonsan, flourished. Another consequence was the change in traders who engaged in commerce. Traditional official merchants, who previously had held franchised monopolies, suddenly faced foreign industrial competition. The intrusion of foreign merchants and goods into the trading centers of the country, particularly in Seoul, was not long ignored by the native franchised merchants. The immediate response of the official town shops (*sijeon*) and six commodities shops (*yuguijeon*) was to reject foreign merchants and their inexpensive new merchandise. Official market and tributary merchants (*jangin* and *gongin*) held protest rallies, demanding the expulsion of foreign traders from the capital. Especially vociferous were the wholesale merchants who dealt in cotton goods and general merchandise. While the guilds could cope successfully with Korean competitors, they were powerless in the competition with Chinese and Japanese merchants.

Despite the protests, international trade slowly brought about the collapse of the official merchants' monopoly, and new groups of merchants emerged in the country, especially at the wholesale level, toward the end of the Joseon dynasty. These new businesses clashed with the official guilds over commercial rights and territorial jurisdictions. The clashes between the new and the old merchants took the form of frequent petitions submitted by urban merchants to the government authorities accusing the new wholesale traders of "unreasonable practices." The discontent of the Koreans reached a climax when most places of business were closed by order of the eight guilds that ruled the trade.

Thereafter, stores that carried a small stock of merchandise gradually emerged in major, and even some small, cities. White cotton sheeting of various grades found its way to the people through city merchants. Bags, rope, farming and mining machinery, and sewing machines were in great demand. Foreigners observed that the aspirations of the few extended but slowly to the nation, progress was gradual, and the pace of change was tedious. Foreigners were helpful to Korean entrepreneurs through their advice and assistance. Some also noted that typically the businessmen who possessed capital were men from Pyongyang city (not necessarily Seoul), a large city north of the capital, where the work of Christian missionaries was most successful.[118]

The new merchants who entered into commercial activities at the wholesale level were known as innkeeper merchants (*gaekju*) and inn merchants (*yogaek*). Although the distinction between the two was blurred, in general an inn merchant was a wholesaler who sold mostly textile goods, while an innkeeper merchant was a wholesaler who sold grain. These were "free" traders with neither franchise nor monopoly rights, but they paid fixed amounts of business taxes to the government. They were also more progressive, quick to perceive new opportunities, and willing to work with Western goods and businesses. Business opportunities opened up for them first in the open ports of Inchon and Busan.[119]

Because of geographical restrictions placed on foreign merchants[120] and the language barrier, foreign merchants had to rely on local commercial networks. Korean businessmen served as the intermediaries or agents of Japanese and Chinese businessmen rather than directly engaging in foreign trade themselves. The private merchants (*yogaek* and *gaekju*) had under their aegis a large number of brokers, dealers, and itinerant merchants (*pobusang*) who were mobilized to sell imported goods. Local merchants also gathered products for export. The new merchants, in alliance with the rural producers, purchased local handicrafts at prices higher than official guild merchants and sold them in the cities. They bought fish directly from fishermen and sold them through nonguild merchants. They also stored goods, handled consignment sales, forwarded merchandise in transit, and acted as wholesalers in nearby cities. In this way, they came to occupy an important position in commerce in the early modern open economy and inflicted great damage on the official six goods merchants.

The distinction between "official" and "private" or "free" merchants gradually blurred toward the end of the nineteenth century and thus cannot easily be made now, but it is clear that the importance of the official merchant and monopoly guilds diminished precipitously while the power of free merchants increased inversely as foreign trade expanded, especially with the government adoption of the "coexistence of monopoly guild and free merchants" (*dong-gong*) policy. Also, starting in the late nineteenth century the government policy toward commerce became more laissez-faire.[121]

Private merchants apparently realized considerable profits during the late nineteenth century. Some bought goods when prices were low and sold them after prices rose. Those who accumulated considerable wealth and capital became known as "giant merchants" (*keosang*) or "wealthy merchants" (*busang*) in the late transitional era, and some of their enterprises later formed the core of modern-day businesses. K. J. Cho estimated their accumulated capital during this period at about 20 million yen.[122] The rise of the new traders not only increased the commercial activities of the servants of powerful officials, rich private merchants, and military officers, it also attracted a considerable number of *yangban* to business.[123] These developments resulted in a further decline in the vested rights of the privileged official merchants.

The private merchants (*gaekju* and *yogaek*) were interested in more than just making profits. They formed voluntary organizations, unlike the old itinerant merchant guild (*pobusangdan*), in order to improve their business practices[124] and protect themselves from foreign competition. The associations gathered information about business practices from foreign merchants for dissemination to their members. They also urged their members to pool their small amount of capital to organize modern new business firms, the so-called companies (*whaesa*). When they found that "irregular acts" (more accurately, illegal acts) had been committed by Japanese merchants operating in the open ports, the associations reported them to the authorities and petitioned for remedial action. When Japanese merchants refused to sell Japanese imports wholesale to Korean merchants and peddled their wares directly to consumers, the associations made recommendations to the government for changes in the laws and regulations pertaining to the commercial activities of foreign merchants. These organizations were also patriotic in that they fought foreign, especially Japanese, penetration. They denounced Japanese violations of the Korean government's ban on the export of rice, for instance. Similarly, they denounced alleged racketeering by Japanese organizations such as the Keirin Shogyo Dan. They protested the issuance of banknotes in Korea by the Daiichi Bank of Japan.

Organizationally, new forms of business modeled on Western-style corporations slowly emerged sometime before the 1894 (Gap-O) Reform. "Modern" firms or "companies" (*whaesa, sangsa,* and *kongsa*) began to appear after about 1880. Koreans who had studied abroad published books explaining the principles and practices of Western businesses. Modeled after the modern businesses, Daidong Sangsa was organized in 1880 and a steamship company was established in 1883, modeled after Western business corporations. The Gwanginsa Company was formed in 1884 as a modern printer of books. In 1889 a fishing company was organized to operate on the coast with equipment imported from Japan. By 1894 about four such companies had been established by Koreans.[125]

The businesses established before 1894, however, were not truly "modern" in the Western sense. Some were family owned, had a monopoly granted by the government, or received government financial assistance for the purchase of modern foreign machinery and equipment. After the reforms of 1894, a few wholesalers, many retail stores, and a few small Western-style shops emerged in Seoul, other large cities, and even many small towns. A number of companies trading in agricultural and fish products also entered the market. It was reported that there were about twenty or so rice merchants in the Mapo district of Seoul alone. A few Pyongyang merchants also figured prominently. Many itinerant peddlers opened shops. One enterprising Korean businessman bought two wooden launches in Japan to engage in fishing. According to one foreign observer, the new commercial vitality was partly attributable to the assistance of foreigners.[126]

One of the more visible early attempts to engage in large Western-style business in Korea was in banking. There was no bank owned and operated by Koreans before 1894; only the money changers, whose common practice was usury, were present. The first bank established by Koreans was the Hanil Bank (Dongil), founded in 1894 with a paid-in capital of 126,000 yen. The second was the Joseon Bank, founded in 1896 with 200,000 yen of capital. The third was the Hanheung Bank, established in 1897 with 75,000 yen of capital. The Hanseong Bank was organized in the same year, with paid-in capital of 35,000 yen and subscribed capital of 100,000 yen. These banks were followed by the Daihan Cheon-il Bank (later renamed the Commercial Bank), founded in 1899 with paid-in capital of 28,000 yen, subscribed capital of 50,000 yen. In addition to ordinary commercial banking, it had the privilege of issuing convertible currency.

These banks loaned money to businesses, typically at 12 to 24 percent interest for a short term, with commodities as collateral.[127] None of them conducted much business, however, owing to lack of loanable funds. The Korean government supported all these banks by lending money at 6 percent interest. By 1898, the Joseon Bank owed the government 12,791 yen, the Hanseong Bank owed 10,000 yen, and the Daihan Cheon-il Bank was in default of a loan of 60,000 yen from the Korean government. In spite of the government assistance, the first three banks collapsed within a year because of inadequate financial resources and poor management.

Industry and Mining

Before the 1894 Gap-O Reform, the instances of private Korean businessmen interested in industry and establishing new modern factories were rare, but a few early forms of factories that produced handicrafts slowly emerged. Small shops made wooden shoes, coarse pottery, and fine matting. Using imported paper, factories produced oiled paper, which in turn was made into cloaks, umbrellas, tobacco pouches, and sheeting for walls and floors, while some shrines and temples produced noodles, paper, fans, shoes, cloth, metal and wood products, and masonry goods. Also, small shops produced paper, pottery, and metal crafts, while farm families produced cloth and silk. Even some government factory artisans gradually turned to producing goods for the private sector that were sold directly to consumers or merchant guilds, in addition to producing goods for government use.[128]

After the 1894 Gap-O Reform and following the pattern set by the Japanese, the Koreans made increasing amounts of investment in factories. Some showed interest in Western technology, and investment in "modern" manufacturing slowly sprang up from about the late 1890s.[129] Private investment extended to such fields as rice milling, soy sauce manufacturing, ceramic (porcelain) production, printing, distilling, and confectionery manufacturing. A mechanized rice mill and a glass factory that employed Japanese technicians were established. Also set up were private refineries and wrought iron and pottery factories. A few companies also produced books, paper, textiles, cigarettes, and bricks. Many of these products were produced in small communities in cities by the people who were compelled to work for their living.

Among them, the most notable industry was mechanized rice milling. Machine-powered mills replaced the work traditionally done by hand. According to one estimate, rice mills could easily have "eliminated a million or more jobs in the fields."[130] Another "modern" field that attracted the immediate attention of Korean entrepreneurs was textiles, probably the most advanced industry in the country at that time. Since the goods imported in the greatest quantities at the time were cotton yarn and fabric intended for mass consumption, more than a few businessmen focused on manufacturing these goods. The move was also prompted by the Japanese refusal to sell textile goods wholesale to Korean merchants for retailing. Because Japanese merchants had a monopolistic hold on imported cotton textiles and peddled their wares themselves directly to consumers, it was difficult for Korean merchants to procure the merchandise for retail sale. This motivated Korean merchants to pool their resources and build their own textile mills after 1897, equipped with imported machines and utilizing technology from the West.[131] They adopted Western methods of production in their "modern" mechanized factories.

Some Koreans even introduced or "invented" new equipment and methods of production in certain areas (e.g., weaving machines, rice-milling machines, measuring instruments, and new silkworm practices). Tobacco manufacture was undertaken in 1903 by a Korean-Japanese company. A Korean engineer who had been educated in the United States returned and established a gold mining company with foreign machinery.[132]

Most industrial firms, however, invested in, owned, and run by Koreans were small handicraft operations with some motor-powered machinery that produced goods not very different from crude and simply constructed cottage-industry manufactures.[133] But unlike the businesses established before the 1894 reform, these post-1984 reform companies seldom received monopoly rights, special privileges, or financial support from the government. Thus, the Korean economy was showing some signs of vitality just before the Japanese takeover in 1905. As expected, these semimechanized handicraft industries often clashed with the monopolistic official guilds over territory.

The establishment of these enterprises clearly added to the nation's capital stock. Private investment in industrial firms by Koreans on the whole, however, was neither extensive nor very potent. The earliest Japanese government statistics for 1907 place the total private capital in Korean-owned "factories" at 71,000 yen. Although the actual figure probably was somewhat larger, it is clear that Korean private investment in industry was much smaller than that of the Japanese. As U.S. Consul-General Jordan's report indicated, "The absence of manufactures is one of the great drawbacks to the development of Korean trade."[134]

In the case of mining, Koreans were quick to take up the opportunity for the business, encouraged by foreign investments in it. They established three mining companies in 1900 and another in 1903. These companies, however, never commenced operations, because of inadequate capital and a lack of technical expertise.

In addition, it was said that there were as many as 3,000 individual Korean gold miners at work in placer mining, which was the easiest and most common method for extracting the precious metal, as was the case in the earlier years.[135]

Along with paucity in the volume of private investment in industry and mining, not many private entrepreneurs were interested in or capable of utilizing much "modern technology" to produce goods in factories. These new Korean industrial firms adopted the "bare-bones" forms of Western methods of production in their "modern" mechanized factories, which was not much more advanced than that found in manual workshops. They did not form a center for the extensive adaptation of foreign technology, and there was not much serious effort among private investors to develop innovative ways to produce goods. For instance, there was a plan to set up a ramie fiber plant using Western technology, to produce and export yarn. Support for the project came from the American firm Townsend and Co. and a few other Westerners living in Seoul, and a corporation was founded, but it was abandoned before construction of the plant began. Another example is the cultivation of ginseng. It had been in the hands of a few farmers licensed by the king for generations. In spite of new available technology, they adopted a minimal amount of modern technology while essentially maintaining the traditional style of management and operation.

Transportation and Electric Power

Transportation attracted the interest of many Koreans. A number of entrepreneurs felt that rather than letting foreigners build the railways, the Koreans themselves should build them. There were three attempts to do so by private companies, in 1898, 1899, and 1902, but none of them ever commenced construction, as noted earlier.[136] Having failed at railroad construction, Korean entrepreneurs turned their efforts to developing other means of land transportation, such as wagon and railway forwarding companies, which required a relatively small amount of capital and no modern technology at the time.

Similarly, believing that the Japanese hold on shipping was having an adverse effect on the economy, a group of Korean entrepreneurs started a shipping business. A few coastal shipping and forwarding companies were founded in 1899, 1901, and 1903.[137] They strove to secure the financial resources needed to purchase foreign vessels, with the aim of regaining control over domestic maritime transportation. The Korean steamers from which so much was expected in the coastal trade, however, experienced "an unprofitable year" and folded soon after the incorporation.[138]

One of a number of other "modern" companies the Koreans established and invested in was the Seoul Electric Light Company, as noted earlier. Prominent Koreans, jointly with the royal household and foreign investors, formed a company that lit the streets of the capital. Likewise, an electric streetcar company was formed by prominent former government officials and *yangban* with an advance of 100,000 yen from the royal household, and a trolley car service, owned and operated by the Korean-American Electric Company, was provided in Seoul.[139]

Agriculture and Miscellaneous Industries

There were a few "financial investments" in agricultural land by Koreans during this period. "Giant merchants," former government officials, and wealthy *yangban* seem to have acquired land from small farmers.[140] On balance, however, very little real investment (e.g., in the form of expansion of cultivated land, construction of irrigation systems, and land improvements that would have increased the productivity) in land had taken place through purchase. Since the individual "financial investments" of one group of Koreans—the buyers—were offset by the "disinvestment" of another group—the sellers—they canceled each other out, without any increase in real investment. There appears to have been no discernible real investment in agriculture by Koreans other than modest attempts to maintain the productivity of land, such as the introduction of small-scale irrigation systems for rice paddies.

There was some investment in miscellaneous fields, including the construction of residential houses and hospitals, in the 1890s and pharmacies in later years.[141] However, the amount of real investment in them appears to have been rather minimal.

Aggregate Private Investment

Notwithstanding all the investment activities just described, aggregate real private Korean investment was relatively small, probably no more than 5 million yen or less than one-quarter that of foreign (mostly Japanese) investment during the transitional period. During the transitional period, it was not common for many Koreans to take the bold step of starting a new business. Individuals who had money scarcely dreamed of investing it in business or in agriculture.[142] Before 1905, even in such technologically backward enterprises as rice mills and leather-processing establishments, where the introduction of simple mechanization would have had an immediate effect, investment was small and only a minimum amount of modern technology was adopted, while the traditional character of management and operations remained essentially unchanged.

Not only did few Koreans venture into new businesses, but when they did only a few succeeded. Of the individuals who did try to tempt fortune with a few hundred yen or large investment, half went bankrupt in a matter of months. For example, three of the four banks that were established in the late 1890s and the early twentieth century collapsed within a year or so after opening. Even as late as 1908, only five out of ninety-two of the rudimentary factories that had motor-powered machinery were owned and operated by Koreans.[143] Specialization of functions, new forms of cooperation, and, above all, the spirit of enterprise were lacking. The result was chaos in the private sector. One foreigner observed that without foreign capital little could be done and "under native management nothing." He also noted that whatever investment of an industrial character was to be made in Korea, close technological supervision was needed.[144]

There appear to have been several reasons for the small investment in physical capital in Korea during the transitional period. Recurring social upheavals, a state of political instability, inadequate protection of property rights, and insecurity of income and wealth certainly hindered greater investment. In addition, domestic economic conditions at that time were not favorable to potential entrepreneurs for investment. Also, Korean private businesses were ill prepared for the new environment and did not have the technical know-how to build and operate modern industries, railways, merchant marines, or mines efficiently.[145] Many technicians and managers in modern businesses in Korea were not Koreans but foreigners. Korea at that time simply was not ready to exploit the full potential of its economy.

Some economists also believe that government red tape and the prevailing disincentives to investment (e.g., needing "permission" from the government, and the low social status of businessman) discouraged potential entrepreneurs from starting new businesses.[146] Other scholars blame the high rate of interest on investment loans. Ordinary market rates of interest ranged from 36 to 48 percent and could be as high as 60 percent a year. Even the mutual-aid societies (*gae*[147]), which charged the lowest interest in the free market, imposed on their members a minimum rate of 24 percent a year. Others charged as much as 120 percent interest. Anything less than 20 percent was considered so low as to be out of the question.[148]

In addition to these factors, it also appears that other crucial elements that could have propelled large-scale Korean investment, which in turn would have promoted economic development in the country, were not present. Economic growth requires not that all should be adventurous but that there should be an adequate supply of innovators. This in turn is partly a matter of the rewards and prestige to be gained by successful innovation. Economic growth, thus, depends largely on the extent to which the social atmosphere nourishes such people and gives them scope. During the transitional period in Korea, however, there were not many men whose natural tendencies were to experiment with new techniques, new products, or new economic forms, in defiance of established opinion or of vested interests. On the whole, the Korean society in the transitional period did not admire and encourage such people; rather, they were regarded as buccaneers to be suppressed. Nor were there powerful catalytic effects, linkage effects, and external economies of foreign investment.[149] In contrast, these elements were clearly present under Japanese colonial rule after 1905. As one foreign observer noted that "without foreign capital little could be done."[150]

Investors

There appear to have been three main groups of Korean investors: landlords, large merchants, and small merchants and farmers. A number of landlords, who were former government officials and the most well-to-do group in traditional Korea, were involved in commerce, banking, public utilities, and industrial activities in the late transitional period. In the case of a plan to set up a ramie fiber plant using Western technology to produce and export yarn, *yangban* and former government officials played an important role in launching the project.[151] Other prime movers in the textile industry were "white cotton merchants" (*baekmokjeon*) and other private merchants. Chong-han Kim, for example, who came from a wealthy family, passed the prestigious civil-service exams, became a civil servant, and later founded the Hanseong Bank, the first bank in Korea. Similarly, the Hanseong

[Seoul] Electric Co., a coal company, and a shipping company were financed with capital supplied by the royal household and former government officials, many of whom later cooperated with Japan after the Annexation and continued to engage in business under the Japanese administration.[152] Some small landowners/landlords sold their land and entered into new businesses.

Most new investment during the transitional period was by the second group, the large merchants. They had capital and some knowledge of new technologies and were willing to take the risks of starting a new business. After the Gap-O Reform of 1894, a number of merchants set up new trading companies and modern factories without the support of the government. Ki-jong Pak, for example, was born in Busan in 1839 and lacked a formal education, but he learned Japanese, became an interpreter, prospered as external trade grew, and eventually helped found one of the Korean railway companies. Others built factories that produced imitation foreign goods.

In addition, the private merchants provided venture capital (*seondae jabon*) to craftsmen at high interest rates to facilitate the new line of manufacturing. Venture capitalists (*mulju*) often supplied advances to itinerant merchants and financed businesses by lending money at local city centers; some financed iron mining and refining operations, large and small. In this way the private merchants after the mid-1890s played a leading role in giving birth to a few commercial and industrial firms. A small number of new companies (*sangsa*) also were organized by merchants and former low-ranking government officials, with some of their venture capital furnished by mutual-aid societies (*gae*).[153]

In establishing these new businesses, entrepreneurs from the lower classes and the aristocracy or bureaucracy commonly undertook ventures jointly. Private companies were usually established with the cooperation of *yangban*/landlords and former government officials; it was rare for ordinary merchants to start new businesses by themselves. Typically, influential former officials were recruited to top managerial positions. Through such appointments, companies attempted to forge close ties with the government so that they might receive preferential treatment from the government. In this way the business activities of the servants of powerful officials, rich private merchants, and military officers expanded, while *yangban* and the wealthy merchants played an important role in founding new businesses and banks in Korea.

The third group—small merchants, artisans, and farmers—slowly ventured into business as they became familiar with the new environment. Starting out in handicraft production, they accumulated some savings, which were reinvested in new ventures, while small landowners sold their land to finance the new business pursuits.[154] Although their numbers increased over time, the volume of their investment was relatively small.

INVESTMENT IN HUMAN CAPITAL

The prospects for economic development also depend on the stock of human capital, which in turn is founded on the initial stock of people, progress in acquiring physical and additional human capital, and the level of technological sophistication.

Many developing economies face double jeopardy in acquiring human capital because the initial stock may be so small that it takes many years or generations for it to appreciably increase. Fortunately, in Korea the initial stock of human capital was larger than in most underdeveloped economies at that time, and the propensity to acquire education was very high, largely because of the traditional Confucian heritage. With the inflow of Western ideas, what Korea faced was the new challenge of setting different educational goals, reorienting the nature of its educational mission, and restructuring its institutions, which would be different from those of the traditional society. It was, thus, necessary to transform educational institutions so that they moved away from traditional and humanistic instruction based on Confucius teachings and toward a more material and science-oriented focus in order to meet the needs of technological and economic advancement.

After the opening of the country, there were attempts in both the public and the private sectors to invest in new human (as well as physical) capital, because trained leaders and workers were needed to cope with the changing economic and technological environment. Such investment in human capital took various forms in the transitional Korea.

First, the government employed a number of foreign advisers who were hired to modernize the country, including the government itself, and educate Korean workers. They were employed as foreign office advisers, customs advisers, military instructors, farm superintendents, mining engineers, teachers, trolley-car motormen, and industrial technicians and workers.[155] Other foreigners worked in Korea's post office, legal department, and arsenal and in mining and manufacturing enterprises. Foreign teachers were hired to provide "modern" scientific education, as well as English-language instruction. These teachers, scientists, and technicians, who were employed at great expense, included Americans, French, Germans, Japanese, and Chinese.

Second, after the opening of the country to the outside world, countless government missions and individuals, many of whom were young, went abroad to acquire Western knowledge and technology. Although the host countries included China, the United States, France, Germany, England, and other European countries, the country they most frequented was Japan.[156] The first observation and study mission, which was sent there in 1876, had seventy-five members. This was followed by missions in 1880, 1881, 1882, and 1883. Members of such missions stayed mostly in large cities, typically for a few weeks or months. There they observed the workings of the Japanese government, customs services, the mint, modern arsenals, and shipyards. They examined Western-style structures, including schools and office buildings equipped with steam heat and electricity, and observed the construction and operation of publicly owned facilities, such as the telegraph system, railroads, and electrical plants. They also studied management techniques and were briefed on the development of modern agriculture, including sericulture. The visitors were impressed with Japan's modernization. They brought back a number of useful books and maps.

The first delegation to the United States, in 1883, ostensibly was a courtesy mission to reciprocate the establishment of a U.S. diplomatic presence in Korea.[157] In about ten months its members visited New York, Boston, Philadelphia, and Washington, D.C.; toured exhibitions, hospitals, and major government offices; and studied the customs and postal services, the public school system, and military fortifications. They examined business and industrial facilities and visited farms and livestock managements. Subsequent missions, including a group of thirty-five students, were sent to the World's Fair in Chicago, European countries, and the Great Paris Exposition of 1900.[158] The first Korean to attend an American college graduated in 1891. Yet the total number of Koreans who went to Western countries before 1904, excluding emigrants, could not have been many more than 100.

Third, as noted above, an increasing number of Korean students went abroad to acquire new knowledge, especially after the change in government policy in 1881. About 180 students and junior government officials were sent to Japan during 1881–1883 to study the language, the Japanese government structure, the military establishment and its techniques, and Western technologies. Interestingly, despite the fact that Korea had officially been a vassal state of China, travel by Koreans to that country to study science and industrial technology was infrequent. Only one, possibly two, Korean missions to China were dispatched. Some eighty young men, including thirty eight students and nineteen technicians, of the average age of twenty, were sent.[159] Some were reported to have studied arms manufacturing, while others learned English.

After 1895, when the king declared that "young men of intelligence in the country shall be sent abroad in order to study foreign science and industries," many students traveled at government expense. It has been estimated that a total of 246 students were sent to Japan between 1895 and 1897, which included 117 in 1895 and 77 in 1897.[160] The purpose of dispatching these students was not only to train prospective civil servants but also to introduce Western knowledge and technology to the home country. Many studied in Japanese military schools, while a number of artisans were sent to learn modern crafts and technology, with the idea of introducing the new knowledge and technology to Korea. They learned the techniques of making copper and leather and visited printing offices and silkworm breeding establishments.

These government students had varied backgrounds, different family names, and diverse places of birth, indicating that they were recruited from a wide swath of the population and from different regions. Although the main criterion for the selection of students was supposed to have been their innate ability,[161] many were sons of nobles, artisans, and middle and junior government officials. Some Korean notables were also included in the groups. Their ages ranged from seventeen to fifty-five, but the average age was under thirty years.

In addition, many Korean students went to Japan to study at their own expense, about 210 between 1869 and 1908. There were 16 private students among the 77 Koreans studying there in 1882,[162] mostly sons of nobles and junior government officials. The background and numbers of these students varied, from those having no occupation—typically well-to-do *yangban* youth—(101) to students (30) and civil servants (77). Of these, 33 students studied at colleges, 36 at high schools, 28 at military academies, and 59 at miscellaneous institutions such as business and pharmacy schools.

Upon their return, many students were employed in government offices and businesses and became the leaders of a movement for modernization and reform.

According to one study, more than half of the students who studied in Japan were employed by the government after their return. Of these, 33 became middle-ranking civil servants, 30 became teachers, 31 were commissioned as army officers (*chamii*), and 20 were appointed to other civil-service positions.[163] In 1902 more than three-quarters of the 2,800 civil servants were reported to have either studied abroad or visited other countries. Many returning students acted as catalysts of modernization by becoming mechanics in government factories.

A few government-sponsored students also became businessmen, technicians, and engineers in the private sector. According to one report, "young technicians filled the principal role in constructing the munitions factory." One Korean engineer who was educated in the United States returned to Korea, founded a mining company, and put foreign machinery into operation in a gold mine.[164] Many of those who studied modern technology, however, were not necessarily utilized in their specializations when they returned home. According to one survey, only ten out of fifty students who studied science before 1900 later held positions in their fields of study, and the remaining forty students, who studied engineering, did not work in that field.[165] Neither were those who developed a critical attitude toward the ruling regime placed on the government payroll.

Fourth, many young people were educated in "modern" educational institutions newly established within Korea. During the transitional period, while the private sector continuing to operate the traditional Confucian schools, Korea introduced so-called modern education. The government established new primary, intermediate, English, and normal schools. As early as 1885, with the assistance of foreign advisers, it established a school for interpreters (the Royal English School). Along with the Christian missionaries, it founded schools patterned after the Western model, starting in 1886. In that year, the Yugyeong Public Institute was founded for the instruction of young Koreans in Western languages and sciences, although it closed in 1894 after training only 112 students, mostly the sons of official dignitaries. In the ensuing years, forty-six primary schools enrolled 1,176 students. Other new schools and training centers included a military academy (founded in 1896), a business and industrial school (1896), a medical school (1899), a mining school (1900), a law school (1899), a surveying school (1903), a technical school (1900), and a girls school (1900).[166] The government-sponsored schools enjoyed varying degrees of success, but they were not important enough to alleviate the intellectual stagnation that prevailed in the country at the time.[167]

Likewise, a great fever for modern education took hold of the people, and many Koreans were aroused to advance themselves by the call for education. Thus, schools patterned after the Western model sprang up in the private sector like mushrooms popping out of soil after a rain in spring. It was claimed that the first modern school in Korea was established as early as in 1878 by a Korean, not a foreigner, and reported that Koreans had opened and operated eighty-six Christian schools by 1910. Notwithstanding these advances, these schools were aimed at enrolling only the favored few whose parents could afford it. There was no intent to establish a modern school in every village to enroll all the boys or every young person in the village. Individuals and businessmen also founded schools and training programs to promote Western technology. In 1890 an industrial-technology program was established to teach manufacturing arts.

Fifth, Koreans also acquired new knowledge through informal educational institutions such as extension services and training centers. In 1902, through its network of extension services, the government trained about 200 people at a model silk filatry. In the same year, it trained technicians in weaving, paper making, metal- and woodworking, and dye making at an industrial training center in every province. These and a number of other extension services employed foreign teachers and Koreans who had been abroad. Likewise, newspapers made an important contribution to the formation of human capital by inculcating in Koreans the value of Western technology. Through the *Han-Seong Jubo* (Seoul Weekly), a government publication founded in 1888, the new intellectuals attempted to introduce Western ways and educate ordinary citizens. There were also a Korean-language weekly, the *Doknip Sinmun* (Independent News), published by a group of Western-educated young intellectuals, and a Chinese-language daily, the *Jeguk Sinmun* (Imperial News). The periodic open markets, too, besides providing rural people with a venue for social and recreational activities, offered them the opportunity to trade goods and expose themselves to urban and foreign goods and cultures.

NATIONAL INCOME, CONSUMPTION, AND SAVINGS

There are no national income data available for the period, but all indications are that there was not much progress on that front during the transitional period. It is estimated that Korea's GDP increased to approximately $9.76 billion in 1904 from about $8.86 billion (all in year-2000 prices) in 1876. The growth in GDP represents about a 10.2 percent rise during the thirty-year period and an average annual increase of about three-tenths of a percent. This figure indicates that Korea's GDP per capita in 1904 was roughly $745 in year-2000 prices—that is, a rise of about 3.5 percent in about thirty years. Thus, there was virtually no perceptible annual growth in per capita income. The growth in GDP mostly reflects the growth in the population, which is estimated to have been about 13.1 million in 1904. Even as late as 1904, there was no tangible sign of growth in the Korean economy and it, as well as the country's politics, was in shambles.

Likewise, the nation's economic structure did not change much during the transitional period. Although there were signs of technological advances, even as late as the early twentieth century almost the entire industrial sector in Korea consisted of traditional cottage and household industries and only a few foreign, government-run, and private "modern" enterprises. The production of goods and services in cottage and handicraft industries was mostly carried out in the home of the "entrepreneur" by members of his family (usually in their spare time) and/or with one or two employees. These enterprises relied heavily on labor-intensive pre-industrial-age technology and operated with little capital and low-level skills. Even businesses with a modern facade did not escape technological underdevelopment. Even the more progressive private merchants and wholesale businesses were traditional, or medieval, in the opinion of some foreign observers. Even the rudimentary factories were very few in number in Korea at the time of the Japanese takeover, with only a few operated by Japanese, other foreigners, and the government. In other words, the Korean economy during the transitional period changed little.

The habit of saving did not change much either. There were some forces in the country that functioned to expand saving. For instance, Christian Protestantism had some positive effect on Korean converts in fostering austerity and the saving habit.[168] However, net domestic saving in the country during the transitional period probably was no more than one-tenth of a percent of GDP, which represented little improvement over the estimated net saving before 1876. Certainly it was not enough to meet the investment needs of a growing economy.

There appear to have been a number of reasons for the low level of saving. For one thing, the average Korean income was still so low that increased saving was difficult, though not impossible. The average income of the majority of ordinary Koreans, mostly tenant farmers, barely improved after the opening of the country, and the wage earner's lot was not much better. No comprehensive statistics are available, but wages were very low, especially compared with those of workers abroad.[169] Korean workers' daily wages at the Wunsan mines ranged from 0.32 to 0.88 *won* in 1890s,[170] which barely met their daily needs. The small merchants, peddlers, and "manufacturers" fared little better. According to one report, the small-scale handicraftsmen and petty merchants in the Wangsim-ni and Itaewon districts in Seoul were "destitute."[171]

Second, although higher income groups did save some of their income, only a small portion of their savings was devoted to productive investment. Most saving in Korea during this period was contributed by two groups, namely, the merchants and the *yangban* (including former government officials and landlords). Many *yangban* landlords prospered, especially after 1896, when their incomes increased as a result of the rise in rent in the form of their share of harvests, the growing export trade, and new markets in Japan for Korea's rice, beans, and other agricultural products. They seem to have saved a larger portion of their income than in the traditional period, some of which was invested in businesses. Most of them, however, lacked the entrepreneurial drive and ability to expand the productive facilities of the nation, showing not much improvement over those of the traditional period.[172] Most of their savings were used to make loans and finance the consumption of the less fortunate, typically at high interest rates.[173] They also purchased more land, as was the case in the traditional period.

The "giant merchants" seem to have saved most of their profits, but these savings made up a very small portion of the nation's GDP. The available resources saved for investment were such that even the giant merchants did not have the wherewithal to start many new businesses requiring fairly large investment, such as railroad and ramie-fiber plants.[174]

Third, Koreans' high propensity, in the traditional period, to consume, described in chapter 2, not only continued but actually increased during the transitional period. Demand for consumer goods, especially the new foreign commodities, expanded after the opening of the country in 1876. As the novelties of the Western world poured in, lifestyles gradually changed and "officials in higher positions led a luxurious life."[175] Although Koreans claimed that they were "very poor," had "no money," and thus could not "afford to buy foreign things," the new goods affected "the lives of men of humble circumstances as well as those of the well-to-do."[176] Foreign products were most attractive. It was observed that a general foreign tawdriness was spreading rapidly among the young "swells" who had money to spend, "vulgarizing Korean simplicity" and setting an example to those below them of extravagant and "purely selfish expenditure."[177]

The prevalence of new consumer goods in all provinces and villages was clearly observable. The most popular imported products were textiles, wool, kerosene, matches, spectacles, needles, mirrors, dyes, and even luxury items such as cigars, chairs, liquor, and guns. Large amounts of white cotton sheeting of various grades found its way to the villages. Most popular were foreign piece cottons for a man's best clothes. About 3,000 bundles of foreign piece goods, for instance, were reported to have been imported into the city of Pyongyang in 1887. Another example was the use of kerosene. One foreign observer wrote that she never saw a Korean hamlet that kerosene had not penetrated. It displaced the fish-oil or vegetable-oil lamp and the dismal rush light in the paper lantern. It was said to have revolutionized evening life in Korea. The country's importation of it increased by twenty times in about a decade, from a little more than 100,000 gallons of kerosene in 1886 and over 2 million gallons in 1897.[178]

Increases in the importation and use of these foreign commodities led not only to changes in the nation's economic and social life but to increases in consumption, which in some cases forced Koreans to borrow money. Increased consumption resulted in less saving and thus not much investment. The savings rate in Korea also lagged as a result of the lack of a secure institution in which to keep them. Although the Postal Savings System was introduced to Korea in 1880 by the Japanese, it was confined to the Japanese and not made available to Koreans until after the Annexation. There were no other institutions (including banks) where personal savings could be safely kept.

The preceding examination reveals that Korea, during the thirty-year transitional period, did not make much progress in accumulating both physical and human capital. The additions to the existing capital stock and financing of them by Koreans were insignificant and therefore did little to expand the nation's output. In comparison with Japanese investment in Korea, the native contribution was small. Without the complement of Japanese investment, this level of investment was not even sufficient to enable the country to maintain its standard of living and support the increase in population, let alone to sustain a major economic push. Even with foreign investment (mostly Japanese), the economy continued to be sluggish and in a state of transition at best. As late as the latter half of the 1890s, it was still experiencing the dislocation attendant on throwing an economically backward realm open to foreign concession seekers and the mercantile interests of more advanced financial and technological powers.

SUMMARY AND CONCLUSIONS

This chapter has examined how the outside world thrust itself on the traditional economy of the hermit kingdom in the second half of the nineteenth century,

Korea's response to these incursions, and these changes' impact on Korean investment and economic transformation during the thirty-year period between 1876 and 1904. When Korean borders and ports were opened to the outside world upon foreign threat, foreign goods and new technologies, as well as Western ideas, penetrated the country as if fresh flood water rushed in through a broken dam. It was an eye-opening, even shocking experience to most Koreans, who had been isolated nearly completely from the outside world and who had thought that the center of the universe was China, which they had been trying to emulate for centuries.

No sooner was the country opened than new foreign goods began to pour into the local market and foreign entrepreneurs embarked on establishing new businesses to engage in selling and some producing their wares. In fact, the Koreans bought more goods from abroad than they sold to other countries. The aggregate net volume of foreign resources imported into the country during the transitional period was about 23 million yen by 1904, which was equivalent to approximately 3.5 percent of Korea's GDP in that year, thus enabling foreigners to make some direct investment in and loans to Korea. The volume of foreign direct investment was small and contributed little to Korea's capital formation and economic development, but it represented almost all of the investment in the country during the period.

Most of the foreign investment was made by the Japanese. Their investments in Korea were relatively large in number but generally small in scale, and typically were made in commerce, land, and some manufacturing by those seeking quick profits. The major portion of Japanese investment in Korea was in public utilities. While private investments by individual proprietors were relatively small in scale and were made for profit, Japanese investments in public utilities were fairly sizable, perhaps making up more than half of the total; and were in fairly large-scale undertakings. They were also composed entirely of new kinds of businesses, such as railroads and communications networks, and were made for political and expansionist reasons, not necessarily for financial gain. This strategic investment in these fields eventually enabled Japan to conquer and annex Korea. For Koreans, these Japanese investments, even in the construction of railroads, were not particularly useful and did not have a significant impact on the Korean economy at the time.

In the process of playing, with great energy, the role of pioneer in new industries, Japan became the principal investor and a purveyor of Western technology, and it best represented the forces of change and innovation in Korea. It is interesting to note that all of these changes occurred at a time when Japan itself was the most backward of the world powers, suffering under unequal treaties and inviting foreign investment at home in order to establish a dynamic capitalist economy. The bearers of Japan's advance into Korea were people with only small amounts of capital, for the advent of big businesses did not take place until after the World War I. Thus, what we see in this period is capitalism without much capital and, as its main purveyors in Korea, entrepreneurs who lacked capital. Korea's capital formation and economic development were limited as much by the capacity of Japanese investment and markets as by the wants of the Koreans. Nonetheless, Japanese investment was significant in determining Korea's unfortunate political future and also had a major impact on Korea's future economic development as both a dependent and independent economy.

While Japan was for change and looked mostly to its political future in Korea, other foreign powers played a relatively weak role in investment and transformation of the Korean economy. Chinese influence was on the side of maintaining the status quo, while Westerners were busily engaged in proselytizing, inculcating Western values, and making profits from business investments. The small investments of Westerners were mostly in foreign trade and the extractive mining industries, the products of which were intended for foreign use and had limited forward or backward linkage effects to the Korean economy. Outside of mining, where Westerners dominated, most Western countries saw no reason to invest in or make loans to Korea other than to make profit. Nonetheless, the Christian missionary's contribution to modern education in the country was integral to Korea's future development.

Korea's initial response to the foreign "invasion" was overwhelmingly negative, especially toward the Japanese, but the country eventually came to reluctantly accept the tenets of the new economic system and beliefs. The Korean government introduced limited reforms to meet the new needs of the economy and undertook modest amounts of investment in such areas as electric lighting, telegraph and telephone systems, tramways, some manufacturing, printing, and mining. Although the nature of investment in the public sector during the transitional period was substantially different from that in traditional times, the magnitude of government investment in physical and human capital was rather limited and modest. It was somewhat greater than, but not substantially different from that which had prevailed in earlier times. In general, the Korean government was ineffective as a force in economic transformation.

In the private sector the changes among Koreans were discernible. They followed the pattern set by the Japanese and made some investments in commerce and industry, especially after the 1894 reforms. A small group of merchants, a few *yangban,* and former government officials began to venture into business in such new fields as banking and textile manufacturing, mining, shipping, and the electric-power industry, utilizing imported technologies and producing and trading new products.

These physical investments in the public and private sectors were complemented by some investment in human capital, especially in Western-style education. The Korean government hired a small number of foreign advisers to train government workers, and numerous government officials, students, and citizens went abroad to study and learn about new and modern institutions and technology. Moreover, a substantial number of young men, and a few women, were educated in new, modern, educational institutions within the country. Other Koreans acquired new knowledge through informal educational channels, extension services, and training centers. Notwithstanding some progress in modernization before the Japanese takeover, neither the Korean government nor its citizens invested enough to accumulate much capital to meet the needs of a growing economy.

As a consequence, for the most part the Korean economy during the transitional period remained undeveloped. Its growth was minimal. It can be estimated that

Korea's GDP expanded by no more than 10 percent in the thirty-year period, increasing the per capita GDP only about one-hundredth of a percent a year, from $720 in 1876 to $745 (all in year-2000 prices) in 1904, if at all. The basic economic structure was still agriculture, and the industrial sector remained infantile. The disposition to overconsume relative to income continued, while the propensities to save and invest were low, as Korea's traditional consumption habits changed little, and savings continued to be negligible during the transitional period. Savings were too meager to finance large investments in such modern sectors of the economy as railroads, shipping, mining, banking, and manufacturing. Had Korea not been taken over by Japan, probably it eventually would have reformed, accumulated capital, and brought about economic development in due course. Unfortunately, such opportunity was not accorded to the country for the next forty years.

APPENDIX 3.1: TRADE STATISTICS

A number of questions have been raised with regard to the comprehensiveness of the official trade statistics for the period before 1905. Apparently, there actually were larger volumes of trade with other countries than what was shown in official statistics, which affected the trade balance. This alleged unrecorded trade are examined and some adjustments are made to the official estimates of the balance of payments. On Korea's export accounts, numerous reports indicated extensive out-smuggling of goods from Korea, especially precious metals (mostly gold), rice, and ginseng, during the transitional period. With regard to gold, there is sufficient reason to believe such reports and to make adjustments to the numbers for gold export. The main reason is that although traders were required to declare all gold, as well as all other goods, exported from Korea, some shipments apparently were not recorded.

Many observers noted that few foreigners left the country "without smuggling out a little of the precious dust upon their person." According to Denny, an American adviser to the Korean Foreign and International Affairs Department, even the Chinese High Commissioner in Korea Shi Kai Yen himself was a smuggler and a protector of other smugglers. Also, since there was no export tax on gold dust, customs officials might not have meticulously checked and recorded all the gold that was exported to China, Russia, and Japan. Likewise, in the late 1880s, one-tenth of the nation's ginseng (*hongsam*) production—that is, about 100,000 pounds—was also smuggled out while cosmetics and other Western products were imported. Extensive smuggling was carried on by Chinese and Japanese, especially by the former (*Korea Repository* 1892: 138; ibid. 1897: 293, 333; ibid. 1898: 384; Hamilton 1910: 217; Curzon 1896: 182; Longford 1911: 374; B. M. Lee 1948: 273, 316; B. Y. Kim 1983: 240).

Various amounts of unrecorded exports were reported: they were "enormous," about "two-thirds of the real value," "half of all the gold exported," and "at least as large as that declared at the customs," while "only a small portion of the actual total" was recorded for 1882–1891 (Longford 1911: 17; B. M. Lee 1948: 273; Curzon 1896: 176–177; *Korea Repository* 1892: 138; ibid. 1898: 305). Still other accounts suggested that the amount of gold that passed through the hands of customs officials did not "represent more than 20 percent of the real export" (Curzon 1896: 182; *Korea Repository* 1896: 168; ibid. 1897: 291, 293, 333, 444; ibid. 1898: 305, 383–4. Longford 1911: 17, 374).

If all of these observations are taken seriously, the value of smuggled gold during 1876–1904 could have been as much as 50 million yen. Smuggled gold no doubt found its way to both China and Japan, and certainly there were unrecorded gold exports, but it is inconceivable, that 50 million yen's worth of gold dust could have been smuggled out of the country. There is, however, no sure way of knowing the exact amount of it. Nonetheless, the amount of smuggled gold could not have been very large at least for several reasons. To begin with, according to the customs returns, the value of the gold exported to foreign countries exceeded $4.8 million or 500,000 pounds. Exports of gold dust rose in value from $1.39 million (150,628 pounds) in 1896 to $2.03 million (205,507 pounds) in 1897. It seems highly unlikely that in addition to what was exported on record there was that much gold dust being produced in Korea in those years: there was no stockpile of gold available for large-scale out-smuggling.

In addition, there was no reason to smuggle out gold since it could be openly and freely exported like any other goods. Moreover, it seems improbable that smuggling of large amounts would have been possible under the surveillance of customs officials, both Westerners and natives. Since the value of gold exports between 1887 and 1896 was a little less than $11 million, when gold exports were at their peak volume, the alleged smuggling could not have been worth more than 5 million yen. A more likely range would have been about 2 to 3 million yen (*Korea Repository* 1897: 293; ibid. 1898: 383).

Second, on the import side, corresponding to underreported gold exports, there must have been underreported imports into Korea as well. In order for the supposed gold smugglers to buy gold in Korea to export, there must have been at least as many imports as exports unless capital flight from Korea to other countries took place. Since the "smuggling" of gold was in the hands of foreigners, not Koreans, this implies that the smugglers must first have brought either foreign exchanges, goods, or services into Korea in order to purchase gold. Therefore, the import figures in the official statistics would also have been understated.

Third, on the export side, others have alleged that the official statistics did not include the "illicit" or "unofficial" export trade carried on by Koreans. There was some unsanctioned and unrecorded trade on the border between China and northern Korea and in numerous coastal inlets (K. J. Cho 1977: 127, 131; *Korea Repository* 1897: 333; ibid. 1898: 305; Hamilton 1910: 217; Bishop 1897: 396; Oppert 1880: 172–173; Carles 1888: 202). Since this unsanctioned and unrecorded trade involved equal sums of exports and imports, they did not have favorable or adverse consequences on trade balances. In addition, since many Japanese settled in Korea during this period, it is likely that the possessions they brought were not recorded at the customs office. This underreported sum, which would have adversely affected the balance of payments, was not added officially to imports.

These factors tended to reduce the impact of the gold smuggling on the balance-of-payments accounts. When proper adjustments are made, the actual deficit balance for Korea would have been 15 to 20 percent smaller than the official statistics indicate. Based on this study's evaluation of the balance-of-payments accounts, it can be estimated that during 1876–1904, the net import of foreign resources or savings to Korea, which financed Korea's imports, was about 23 million yen. This amount is equivalent to approximately 3.5 percent of Korea's GDP in 1904. K. J. Cho estimates that Japanese investment between 1873 and 1910 was 25 million yen (1977: 247).

APPENDIX 3.2: EARLY FOREIGN LOANS

The early foreign loans from Japan consisted of the following: 170,000 yen from Yokohama Specie Bank in 1882; 300,000 yen in 1884, 130,0000 yen in 1893, and 500,000 yen in 1901 from the Daiichi Bank; 3 million yen in 1895 and 1 million yen in 1897 from the Bank of Japan; and 120,000 yen from the Specie Bank (Harrington 1944: 170; Jindan Hakhwae 1961a : 531, 951; K. J. Cho 1977: 167–172, 178–184; *Korea Repository* 1895: 26, 156, 233; Nahm 1988: 95–96, 98). From China, the Korean government borrowed 510,000 *ryang* (*tael*), at current commercial rates of interest of 8 to 10 percent in 1893, comprising a Business Bureau loan 210,000, telegram cable loan 100,000, and China Merchant Steamship Navigation Co. loan 200,000. There also were loans of silver dollars amounting to 100,000 *ryang* from a Chinese merchant. This was reported to have been negotiated by a private company with the official backing of the Chinese government.

Similarly, an English bank in Hong Kong provided a loan of 500,000 *taels* in 1893. The government secured a loan of $100,000 (in Mexican pesos) from a German company at 10 percent interest for the construction of a telegraph system between Seoul and Busan. Two loans were contracted with French and Russian syndicates for 5 and 3 million yen, respectively, with customs duty as collateral, but they were never consummated (Harrington 1944: 127, 193; McCune and Harrison 1951: 88; *Korea Repository* 1895: 233; Hamilton 1910: 54, 83, 164; Kim and Kim 1967: 92–93).

APPENDIX 3.3: CATALYTIC AND LINKAGE EFFECTS AND EXTERNAL ECONOMIES

The forces of catalytic and linkage effects and external economies that could have propelled large Korean investment in the country were not present. Most Koreans did not immediately pursue the example set by foreign businesses and engage in the same activities that foreigners pursued. The catalytic effect of foreign investment, particularly that of Japanese investment that was clearly visible to many Koreans in port cities, was not overwhelming enough to catapult many Koreans to make a tradition-shattering move to start new enterprises. Apparently, to most Koreans, their contact was limited to learning a great deal about new technologies, embracing new opportunities, and/or setting in motion a long wave of investment and technological innovation. Much catalytic effect was yet to spread to most landowners, intellectuals, small landowners, and merchants. Nor did it radiate widely from open ports to urban areas and then to the provinces. In the early years, most businesses were located in Seoul, Busan, Inchon, and other open ports, and only a few small-scale businesses such as repair shops and the production of kitchen utensils, tiles, bricks, ginseng, foodstuffs and the like were established.

Another factor that did not contribute much to the expansion of Korean investment at this stage was the paucity in linkage effects from foreign investment. The cumulative nature of development resulting from linkage effects, both backward and forward, could have a positive impact on investment in Korean-owned enterprises. However, there was not much backward linkage effect from trade, Korea's most important economic contact with foreign countries. By increasing the volume of trade and investment, foreign investment in Korea could have created profit opportunities for local businesses that conducted trade at the inter- and intraprovincial levels. Nor did the substantial foreign investment in mining have a great linkage effect on Korean investment. These induced, or linkage, effects could well have been more important to Korean investment than profits (for instance, in railroads and the textile industry).

In addition to the relative absence of catalytic and linkage effects, there were little of external economies with the establishment of Japanese enterprises from which Korean-owned enterprises could benefit. They could have helped to establish an environment in which Korean investors could have made a profit from new undertakings. The presence of foreign and Japanese firms and nationals could also have created more demand for the goods and services that Koreans supplied, such as handicraft goods and food. Perhaps for these reasons, industrialization in Korea during the transitional period was not extensive and did not take off. See *Korea Repository* 1895: 231–232, 242, 243, 307–374; ibid. 1896: 364; ibid. 1898: 198; Jindan Hakwhae 1961a: 438–440, 538–539, 544, 918, 942; McCune and Harrison 1951: 55; Harrington 1944: 127–128, 141, 191, 304; Brown 1921: 78; Sands 1930: 50; Palmer 1963: 142, 167, 179–180.

APPENDIX 3.4: FOREIGN GOVERNMENT EMPLOYEES

A small number of foreign advisers and workers were employed by the Korean government for various tasks to "modernize" the country. During 1882–1883, there were twenty foreign customs officials working in Korea (McCune and Harrison 1951: 55). A farm superintendent who was hired to be in charge of the government farm was expected to breed and care for cattle and sheep, make butter and cheese, and graft fruit trees (Harrington 1944: 127–128, 141, 191, 304; Brown 1921: 78; Sands 1930: 50). Also, in building a factory to manufacture rifles, the government invited engineers from China to train the Korean workers in the model factory. The Bureau of Mining, which was established to exploit the country's mineral resources, employed three American mining experts to prospect for minerals, while Thomas Edison was secured in 1884 and 1897 to install electric lights in the royal household. In 1886 one of the first teachers, Homer Hulbert, was hired to teach English, and six French engineers and technicians were hired in 1902 to construct railroads.

Their compensations were fairly high, which placed financial burdens on the government. French engineers and technicians cost 6,000 *won* each in salary and 4,000 *won* for transportation expenses. The salaries of military instructors were especially high. Chief instructors were paid $400 a year in Mexican dollars. Subordinates were paid $190 and $500 for transportation expenses. Lodging was free (Palmer 1963: 142). Diplomat Denny's pay was 12,000 *tael* (*ryang*) a year, while teacher Homer Hulbert was hired at $1,500 a year in 1886, which was more than eleven times the pay of a Korean teacher. A Korean instructor's salary at the Baejae Hakdang boys school, for example, was $132 a year (*Korea Repository* 1896: 364). Often, the salaries of American employees of the Korean government, however, were not paid for a period of twelve to twenty months (Palmer 1963: 167, 179–180).

4

ECONOMIC REFORMS AND INVESTMENT UNDER JAPAN

Korea during the transitional period could have warded off foreign subjugation; assured the nation's political unity and order; cleared away the whole complex of political obstacles to freedom of ownership, occupation, and movement; and carried out a series of reforms that would have created a setting favorable to the emergence of new forms of productive enterprise. Instead, in spite of having struggled against foreign incursions for more than thirty years, the country succumbed to the iron grip of imperial Japan. With its defeat of China and Russia in two wars fought in Korea, triumphant Japan was free to rule Korea, which was forcibly submerged into a protectorate in 1905. The Japanese Resident General (Tokan) Hirobumi Ito was appointed to the Residency General (Tokanfu) of Korea, which placed him in total control of the country. After Korea became a protectorate, the Japanese "invaded" the country in droves. By 1906, nearly 32,000 Japanese had arrived,[1] and others poured in at the rate of about 200 a day.

Finally, with the Treaty of Annexation, which Korea signed under duress in 1910, Japan vanquished Korea and turned it into a colony, and the Government General of Korea (Chosen Sotokufu) replaced the Japanese Residency General in the same year. It remained so until the end of World War II. The number of Japanese in Korea grew to 171,500 by 1910 and reached a the peak of 752,823 in 1942. Korea's total population in 1942 was 26,361,400, and other foreigners, mostly Chinese, numbered only 83,169, revealing that the Japanese, who represented less than 3 percent of the population, ruled the country with an iron hand.

Principally examined in this chapter are reforms of the economic institutions for investment that followed the Japanese takeover, aggregate investment in Korea in the public and private sectors, investment by different nationalities, and the impact of foreign investment on Korean investment under the conqueror's rule.

ECONOMIC REFORMS FOR INVESTMENT

After it took control of Korea, the Japanese government made serious attempts to reform not only the country's political structure but also its economic institutions and infrastructure as well. Beginning in 1905, the Residency General and its powerful Japanese advisers instituted numerous national and local reforms under the puppet Korean government. National reforms included the imposition of new financial, monetary, and administrative structures modeled after those of the Japanese. The Residency General also separated the functions of court and government and lessened the number of persons paid from the public treasury, reportedly by 50 percent.[2]

Following the Annexation in 1910, the old administration was cleared away, and many traditions that had been inimical to change were suppressed. The Japanese established modern financial institutions and built necessary infrastructures, reformed the currency, conducted land surveys, and introduced new incorporation laws. The tax system, including the method of collection, was overhauled. No gratuities, personal favors (*injeong*), or "miscellaneous dues" over and above the legally sanctioned amount were allowed. Departures of government officials from the regulations resulted in dismissal or other appropriate penalties. The reforms were imposed by force, sometimes with the assistance of the police.

Once it came to rule Korea, Japan was primarily interested in developing it as a supplier of agricultural goods and raw materials to Japan, although in the early years it apparently toyed with the idea of making Korea's agricultural subsistence economy into a somewhat more diversified modern economy with some industrial development. Before 1910, however, the Japanese government more or less left the Korean economy alone, partly to avoid conflict with business interests in Japan and partly because it was believed that Koreans, especially the *yangban,* lacked entrepreneurial leadership.[3] The laws regulating incorporation were not altered by the Japanese except to make them more explicit and orderly on the Western model, so that potential businessmen would have a better understanding of their rights and responsibilities.

Under the so-called Industrial Development Policy (Siksan Gwangeob), all new incorporations required government approval. Even after incorporation, the government continued to monitor the management of companies. Apparently, the purpose of the policy was to suppress Korea's development of modern industries.[4] The consequences of the policy were obvious. In spite of the fact that the law specified the rights and responsibilities of incorporators, the continuing supervision tended to limit the establishment of new businesses. As a Japanese Residency General report explained, "After the authorities concerned commenced to reform or readjust the chronic state that existed in the realm of corporations, the Koreans, understanding better the true nature of this system, ceased to apply to the government irresponsibly for approval of the establishment of business corporations."[5]

The law discouraged the establishment of and investment in companies and, thus, on the whole resulted in only sporadic incorporation during the protectorate. Before 1906, fewer than ninety firms with less than 1.2 million yen of paid-in capital were incorporated in the entire country. In 1908 a mere eight permits for incorporation (three ordinary partnerships, two limited partnerships, and three joint stock companies) were issued. In the following year, of the eleven applications for incorporation submitted, only two were approved, while at least one company was ordered to dissolve.[6]

Following the Annexation and the establishment of the Government General in 1910, the increased Japanese immigration led to a need for more commerce and better transportation networks. New business regulations were adopted that partially relaxed the government regulation by allowing businesses to obtain only a "license" to form a company. These regulations were said to have been intended to prevent the establishment of "illegal or bubble corporations"; to provide guidance to the Koreans who "still lacked knowledge and experience concerning laws and economy" and guard against schemers; to protect Japanese businessmen who were "not familiar with real conditions" in Korea so that they would not "be misled by cunning men"; and to prevent investors from duplicating "similar businesses too frequently, with the result of incurring loss." The government believed that these regulations would result in a healthy business environment and "the advancement of industry."[7]

Under the ordinance, government regulation of business formation was scaled down somewhat, and the Government General seems to have permitted the establishment of businesses more liberally. Notwithstanding the relaxation of the requirements, the government continued to exercise control, apparently not wanting to promote the rapid development of modern industries in Korea,[8] for fear that they would compete against industries in Japan. At the same time, the colonial government cautioned leading Japanese businessmen in Korea that "in carrying on their business [they should] not . . . confine their aims to the promotion of their own individual interests but bear in mind the promotion of the interests of the state."[9] As a consequence, the new regulations resulted in only a moderate expansion of investment in businesses in the country. Eighty-three companies were established between 1911 and 1913. In the meantime, restrictive measures were taken against foreign incorporation, and after 1916, foreigners (other than Japanese) were banned from owning or operating new mines in Korea. Notwithstanding the restrictive environment for investment, imports of capital goods after Korea came under Japanese domination exceeded 1 million yen a year.

The new incorporation law drew heavy criticism from many quarters, including some in Japan. Businessmen in Japan, as well as in Korea, denounced the regulations on the grounds that they discouraged the establishment of new businesses and retarded investment, even by the Japanese.[10] Some alleged that the law imposed much stricter controls and supervision over business conducted by corporations in Korea than in Japan. Because of these criticisms, plus a 1919 Korean independence-movement uprising, the authorities concluded that their interests would be better served by reforming the incorporation regulations to encourage more private investment. This would be accomplished, they reasoned, by creating a climate within which preferred businesses (those that best met the needs of Japan) could pursue entrepreneurial goals unencumbered by government regulations. The colonial government also wanted to provide opportunities for "Japanese capital" in Japan to be invested in Korea.[11] The booming economy of Japan after World War I required Korean raw materials and food as well as strengthening the links to the Japanese economy in the areas of commerce and finance.

In 1920 a new corporation law replaced the old one. The only requirement for incorporation under the new law was "to register" with the government. The new law encouraged investment in businesses. In the meantime, the customs duty between Japan and Korea was abolished to allow free trade. The change in policy, coupled with the favorable economic conditions that prevailed in Asia and the world during and after World War I, sparked new investment, especially after 1923. Even small-scale businesses utilizing local materials to produce firecrackers, mats, lacquerware, bambooware, willow ware, straw products, textiles, rubber shoes, and the like mushroomed.

Another turn in industrial policy in Korea came as Japan tested its military might in Manchuria, a prelude to further aggression on the Asian mainland. When Japan decided to move ahead with its continental conquests, Korea was seen as the beachhead and a crucial pathway to China. After the establishment of a puppet government under the name of Manchukuo in northeastern China in 1931, Korea's proximity to the Manchurian market prompted a Japanese effort to industrialize the Korean economy. This would also provide an outlet for Japanese capital, which was seeking an aperture abroad because of huge amounts of so-called idle or saturated (*howa*) capital in Japan and the lack of investment opportunities there. When the worldwide depression of the 1930s lowered the profit margins of businesses in Japan, the government in Japan followed an industrial policy that tended to discourage new investment at home.[12] The Government General in Korea took this opportunity to develop a policy of "parallel growth of agriculture and industry" (*noko heishi*), a departure from the earlier policy, with its emphasis on rice production in Korea for Japan. From 1931 to 1936 the Japanese authorities in Korea strongly supported the expansion of heavy and chemical industries while promoting agriculture and increased gold mining.

The new move was consistent with Japan's colonial policy. The colonization of Korea was intended not only to dominate the Korean market and acquire the sources of raw materials but also to support modern industry in Japan by building the infrastructure in the colony so that it could fulfill Japan's political ambitions. This policy also meshed well with Japan's need to increase its investment in foreign countries, especially in its colonial territories, in order to expand its sphere of influence on the Asian continent. Furthermore, the low wages and long working hours of Koreans, in comparison with those of Japanese workers, and the country's inexpensive raw materials obviously were an added attraction to investment in Korea.

Even more arduous and focused industrialization came with the deployment of Japan's expansionist "Great Asia Co-Prosperity" (Dai-To-A-Kyoeiken) policy, adopted in 1937. Korea became more critical as a military base beginning with the advent of the 1937 Sino-Japanese War and thereafter until the end of World War II. As that conflict, and later the Pacific War, progressed, Japanese industry was attracted not only by Korea's strategic location, but also abundant electric power and other resources, in addition to cheap labor in the colony. The Government General took a more active stance than ever before in planning, financing, and developing private business in Japan's interest. The colonial government believed that private enterprise in Korea was falling far short of the ambitious programs blueprinted for it. With the passage of the Emergency Funds Adjustment Law in 1937, free entry into business became a thing of the past and heavy industrialization was promoted. Generous assistance was provided at one of the chief bottlenecks to national expansion, the need to import more military and industrial equipment and materials from overseas. Owing to these policies (examined later), private investment rose sharply and technologically sophisticated industry began to emerge in Korea.

In 1938 came the General Mobilization Law, which conferred virtually unlimited powers of regulation upon the government. Under the aegis of the militarists, Japan moved rapidly toward the "New Economic Structure," which was to give the government sweeping powers over economic enterprise in almost all facets. This led the authorities to direct the country's investment toward its war effort and impose far-reaching restrictions on the whole economy. Government approval was required for any capital investment in excess of 50,000 yen and the establishment of all new firms capitalized at over 200,000 yen.

AGGREGATE VOLUME OF INVESTMENT

Economists have made a number of estimates of the volume of investment in Korea under Japanese rule,[13] but these have failed to give a comprehensive and accurate picture of gross or net investment in the country. Since there are no extensive statistical data in print that include investment in human capital, most calculations have relied on incomplete and uncertain information confined to physical capital. In addition, there are numerous omissions and duplications in calculating investment. Investment and capital reported in official statistics and calculated by economists principally represented private domestic investment in increasing producers' plants and inventories. Investments in service industries such as finance, transportation, communications, and professional services were not included in most of them. Likewise missing is that portion of government outlays that went into social overhead capital.

Moreover, most estimates leave out such components of real investment as dwellings used partly for business purposes, small proprietors' acquisition of real property net of depreciation, and the capital outlays of companies charged to depreciation and current expenses. Where the financial data are fairly complete, there still remains the problem of allowing for qualitative improvements or damages. In addition, capital formation in rural areas tends to be underestimated. Even such basic changes as the increase in arable land were not recorded as investment, and they failed to include the farmer's improvements on his own land. They also failed to reflect accidental damage to capital assets, as in floods.

This latter omission is particularly relevant to small farmers. In good part, the increase in production resulting from a combination of small-scale accumulation and modest technical innovation spread more or less through the traditional occupations, in which the bulk of the population was engaged, was not accounted for. We do not know how much capital was accumulated by subsistence farmers through the opening up of new land, drainage, soil conservation, and improvements in structures. Even if they were included, the value of investment in them could not have been accurately ascertained. Also missing are investments by many small, unincorporated businesses, because accounting practices did not meet the requirement for such estimates in the world of corporate industry and trade.

Thus, the review of available measurements of investment and capital in this study yielded meager results. Under these circumstances, we need to estimate investment and capital stock in colonial Korea as well and comprehensively as possible based on accessible data, so as to draw some meaningful conclusions. The calculation of the value of capital stock and investment is focused mostly on physical capital and investment. The volume of investment is estimated in terms of funds mobilized to form and operate new businesses. Unfortunately, information on them is not always available. It should be noted, however, that the valuations of capital stock and investment in this study should be treated as tentative estimates awaiting further refinement. The estimation of investment outlined next is made for four different economic entities: companies, unincorporated businesses, individuals, and the government.

Companies

Many new business ventures in Korea were incorporated and operated as companies (*kaisha*). These companies included all profit-seeking incorporated business firms: share-issuing corporations, partnerships, limited liability companies, and public business enterprises. Because data on them are frequently available and fairly reliable, though fragmentary and not comprehensive, the growth of companies may serve as a fairly dependable index of the expansion of new investment in Korea. Nonetheless, one must be cognizant of the fact that investment in a "new" company might not always be new, since in some cases an existing enterprise merely assumed corporate form. Statistics were published separately for companies headquartered in Korea and those headquartered abroad, mainly in Japan, and they are thus examined separately here.

Let us first estimate the number of and investment in companies headquartered in Korea. The number of companies headquartered in Korea increased from 88 in 1906 to 6,719 in 1943, which represented a more than seventy-six-fold increase in thirty-seven years. Likewise, investment in companies headquartered in Korea in the form of paid-in capital multiplied many times. Reported statistics on share capital are measured in "subscribed" or "official" (*kosho*) and/or "paid-in" or "paid-up" (*furi-ire*) capital. Although they do not necessarily represent the true or market value of the capital stock in many cases, they are the best available data to indicate the volume of investment in companies. As was noted in chapter 3, there was some investment in the form of paid-in capital in new businesses in Korea prior to the subjugation of the country as a Japanese protectorate in 1905, but it was very small. After 1905 investment in the form of paid-in capital in companies expanded quickly. In 1906 companies in Korea had total paid-in capital of 1.2 million yen. This figure increased to 14.9 million in 1910, 1.09 billion in 1938, and about 2.66 billion yen in 1943, as shown in Table 4.1.[14] These figures include joint-venture

TABLE 4.1 Number and Paid-in Capital of Companies Headquartered in Korea between 1906 and 1943

	Number				*Paid-in Capital (in million yen)*			
Year	Japanese	Korean	Joint Venture	Total	Japanese	Korean	Joint Venture	Total
1906	85	3	—	88	1.0	0.2	—	1.2
1910	109	10	17	136	10.0	2.0	2.9	14.9
1911	109	27	16	152	10.5	2.7	8.1	21.3
1920	414	99	31	544	330.8	19.2	27.1	377.1
1925	938	163	88	1,189	275.9	49.8	107.2	432.9
1929	1,237	169	165	1,571	193.7	19.5	95.8	309.0
1938	3,136	2,278	—	5,414	968.6	122.7	—	1,091.3
1943	—	—	—	6,719	—	—	—	2,661.0
	Number (percent)				*Paid-in Capital (percent)*			
Year	Japanese	Korean	Joint Venture	Total	Japanese	Korean	Joint Venture	Total
1906	96.6	3.4		100.0	83.3	16.7	—	100.0
1910	80.1	7.4	12.5	100.0	67.1	13.4	19.5	100.0
1911	71.7	17.8	10.5	100.0	49.3	12.7	38.0	100.0
1920	76.1	18.2	5.7	100.0	87.7	5.1	7.2	100.0
1925	78.9	13.7	7.4	100.0	63.7	11.5	24.8	100.0
1929	78.7	10.8	10.5	100.0	62.7	6.3	31.0	100.0
1938	57.9	42.1	—	100.0	88.8	11.2	—	100.0
1943	—	—	—	100.0	—	—	—	100.0

Sources: The table is constructed on the basis of data found in the following sources: Bank of Korea 1939: Index 16; Shokusan Ginko 35–37; *Kokusei Gurafu* April 1940; Toyo Keizai Shinposha 1942: 83; Takesizu Suzuki 1942:83; Mizuda and Tsuchiya 1962: 108; S. S. Kim 1985: 259. Bank of Korea 1939: Index 16; Grajdanzev 1944: 514; Shokusan Ginko 1940b: 35–37; Nihon Takumusho 1938; *Chosen Keizainenpo* 1940.

companies headquartered in Korea.[15] According to one calculation, owners' equity contributed about 56 percent of the total capital in 1938 and 42 percent in 1943,[16] as elaborated in chapter 6.

When the full measure of investment in different forms of financing companies, such as share capital, retained earnings or undistributed profits, and borrowings from external sources by businesses are taken into account and calculated, as covered in chapter 6 in the topic of financing investment in companies, the total capital of companies headquartered in Korea increased from a few million yen in 1910 to 3.2 billion in 1938 and 5.6 billion in 1943, which represented 72 percent of the total capital in the private sector, as shown in Table 4.2. Assuming that these assumptions and estimations are appropriate and reasonable, investment in companies headquartered in Korea increased nearly 3,000-fold in the thirty two-year period, as shown in Table 4.1. If an appropriate inflation adjustment (discounted) is made, the real increase (in constant yen) in capital in companies would show considerably less than these figures indicate; nevertheless, the increase is impressive.

TABLE 4.2 Investment Capital in the Private Sector in Korea as of 1943

Sectors	Million Yen			Percent					
				Ratio of		Ratio within		Ratio between	
	Japanese	Korean	Total	Total	Private	Japanese	Korean	Japanese	Korean
Investment:									
Private:	6,570	1,210	7,780	78.2	100.0	100.0	100.0	84.4	15.6
Companies:	5,900	600	6,500	65.3	83.5	89.8	49.6	90.8	9.2
In Korea	5,000	600	5,600	56.3	72.0	76.1	49.6	89.3	10.7
In Japan	900	—	900	9.0	11.5	13.7	—	100.0	—
Unincorporated	270	290	560	5.6	7.2	4.1	24.0	48.2	51.8
Housing and misc.	400	320	720	7.2	9.3	6.1	26.4	55.6	44.4
Public	—	—	2,170	21.8	—	—	—	—	—
Total			9,950	100.0					

Sources: The table is constructed on the basis of data in the following sources: Bank of Korea 1939: Index 16; Shokusan Ginko 1940b: 35–37; Government General 1937–1938: 168; Sotokufu 1932: 356; Ibid. 1933: 336; ibid. 1937–1938: 169; ibid. 1942: 171; *Chosen Keizainenpo* 1940: 513; Kawal and Yoon 1991: 134–35; Joseon Yonguwhae 1935: 292; Toyo Keizai Shimposha 1942: 83; Takesizu Suzuki 1942: 83; Mizuda and Tsuchiya 1962: 34, 108, 141; S. S. Kim 1985:259; *Kokusei Gurafu* 1942: 26–27.

There were also a considerable number of companies headquartered in foreign countries (almost all in Japan) that had branches with sizable amounts of capital in Korea. The number of these companies expanded from probably a few to 35 in 1911 and 198 in 1941, an increase of about 5.7 times in 30 years. Their paid-in capital similarly expanded over time. The total paid-in capital of companies headquartered in Japan with branches in Korea increased from 44 million yen in 1906 to 2.68 billion in 1941.[17] These amounts, however, represent all the capital of companies that had branches in Korea but not necessarily those confined to branches in Korea alone.

It is difficult to discern exactly how much was invested by them in Korea, but paid-in capital dedicated to Korea was certainly far smaller than the sum just listed. It was reported that total paid-in capital in Korean branches of companies headquartered abroad in 1931 was 95.4 million yen,[18] which represented about 28 to 30 percent of the total paid-in capital of commercial and industrial companies headquartered in Korea and 5 percent of the total paid-in capital of foreign companies headquartered abroad (including the Japanese) that invested in Korea. If the sums invested in Korean branches on the average were about 29 percent of the total paid-in capital of commercial and industrial companies headquartered in Korea between 1906 and 1931, then their investment in Korea would have been about 1.9 million yen in 1906 and 106.4 million in 1929. As already noted, foreign (including Japanese) investment in Korea accelerated after 1929. Assuming that the increases in the paid-in capital of foreign companies with headquarters abroad that invested in Korea were somewhat slower than the pace for that of companies headquartered in Korea (29 percent), the former would be equivalent to about 300 million yen in 1938, 490 million in 1941, and 900 million in 1943 (Tables 4.1 and 4.2).[19] These amounts represent about 16.1 percent of capital investment in companies headquartered in Korea and 11.6 percent of investment in the private sector as a whole.

Based on these estimations, total capital invested in companies in Korea under colonial rule, headquartered both in Korea and abroad (Japan), may be estimated at approximately 3.5 billion yen in 1938 and 6.5 billion in 1943, as shown in Table 4.2. The foregoing analysis reveals that the most capital in the private sector was invested (83.5 percent of the total) in companies, 72 percent of which were headquartered in Korea and 11.5 percent of which were headquartered in Japan, at the end of colonial rule.

Unincorporated Businesses

Obviously, there were investments in unincorporated businesses in Korea. In contrast with large and medium-sized companies, most unincorporated businesses were small and operated mostly by single proprietors, possibly with the help of a few employees. Reliable information on investment in unincorporated businesses is scarcer than company statistics. But despite the lack of accurate records and considering the relative decline of handicraft industries and the progressive adoption of the juristic form of companies and partnerships, the increase in unincorporated enterprises is also unmistakable.

In large part, the increase in investment came from a combination of small-scale accumulations and modest technical innovations that spread through the more or less traditional occupations that engaged the bulk of the nonfarm working population. A good deal of it took place with family labor and little more than their own slender funds, without resorting to the resources of financial institutions except perhaps those supplemented by a nearby moneylender, a mutual-aid association, or possibly a local bank. Small traders and industrialists invested their meager savings in equipment and working capital. In good times, tools and machinery were purchased, buildings were constructed and expanded, and materials were accumulated. In hard times, the entrepreneur drew heavily on his capital by curtailing his stock or allowing his land, buildings, or tools to deteriorate.

One former high-ranking Government General finance administrator suggested that the stock of capital in unincorporated businesses and other individual property represented about one-fifth of that in companies.[20] Estimating that the stock of capital in unincorporated businesses was a little less than the value of other individual properties, the capital stock in unincorporated businesses in 1938 would have been about 228.5 million yen (i.e., 1,081.4 million × 0.2) and about 560 million yen in 1943, which represented about 7.2 percent of investment in the private sector (see Table 4.2).

Housing and Miscellaneous Businesses

There were also investments not represented in the "companies" and "unincorporated businesses" categories. They include the construction of housing, mostly new, and other miscellaneous projects such as the construction of irrigation works and dams. There are no reliable data to compute investment in them under Japanese rule. Based on the review of available data, investment in housing and miscellaneous items may be set at about 500 million and 720 million yen in 1938 and 1943, respectively. The latter figure, 720 million yen in 1943, represented about 9.3 percent of all private investment in the country (see Table 4.2). When all components of capital goods in the private sector under Japanese rule (incorporated, unincorporated, and housing) are combined, it is estimated that total private investment in Korea under Japanese rule increased from less than 10 million yen in 1905 to 4 billion in 1938 and about 7.78 billion in 1943 (see Table 4.2). This sum of private investment (7.78 billion) made up a little more than three-quarters (78.2 percent) of all investment, both private and public, in Korea under Japanese rule.

Public Investment

The sum given here for total private investment in Korea under Japanese rule does not include investments undertaken in the public sector. One calculation shows that government-owned property in 1938 was worth 829.8 million yen; it comprised public-use property (78.6 percent of the total), forestry land and construction structures consisting mostly of buildings (17.3 percent), and miscellaneous (4.1 percent). Public-use property included land, buildings, structures, tools, and machinery, while miscellaneous property included land, structures, and stock shares.[21] The value of the government-owned enterprises and property, such as buildings, tools, machinery, railroads, ports, and communications networks (examined in detail in chapter 5), is estimated to have been about 1.4 billion yen as of 1938 and 2.17 billion in 1943 (Table 4.2), which constituted about 22 percent of total capital stock accumulated during the forty-year period that the country was under Japanese control.[22] Most public enterprises (55 percent) took the form of joint-stock companies as of 1945.

Total Capital Stock

Total capital stock accumulated under Japanese rule, including investments in both the private and the public sectors, totaled about 6.4 billion yen in 1938 and 9.95 billion in 1943 (see Table 4.2). This level of capital accumulation under the Japanese administration in Korea is translated into an average annual net investment of approximately 9 to 10 percent of GDP, on the assumption that the average capital-output ratio was about three to one.[23] If these estimates prove to be reasonable and realistic, then annual net investment out of national income in Korea under Japanese rule increased from a little more than one-tenth of a percent of GDP in 1904 to about 10 percent in 1943, a rise of 100 times in the forty-year period.

This calculation is supported by the level of upward curves of production and technological change under colonial rule (see chapter 8). Some of the accumulated capital goods had deteriorated by the end of colonial rule because of the heavy and sustained use of industrial facilities, machinery, and equipment without needed replacement, much new addition, or adequate maintenance during World War II. Nonetheless, the colonial period left a considerable amount of capital, including industrial structures, in Korea at the end of the Japanese occupation.

PRIVATE INVESTMENT BY NATIONALITY

Who were the private investors in Korea under Japanese rule and what was the extent of their contributions to capital formation? No comprehensive and accurate data relative to investment by different nationalities in Korea during colonial rule are readily available. Moreover, some statistics, especially those dealing with investment in companies by nationality, were not regularly published in detail after 1930. Nonetheless, it is possible to take account indirectly of the extent of investment by different nationalities in Korea with a fair degree of reliability and consistency. Included in the examination of capital formation below is the volume of investment by three major nationality groups in Korea, namely, the Japanese, other foreigners, and Koreans.

Companies

To no one's surprise, all available evidence clearly points to the fact that the primary investors in Korea under colonial rule were Japanese, as shown in Appendix 4.1 and Tables 4.1 and 4.2. The Japanese dominance in investment in a variety of businesses was undisputed and overwhelming and increased rapidly over time. To begin with, paid-in capital of Japanese companies headquartered in Korea increased from about 1 million yen in 1906 to approximately 10 million at the time of the Annexation. With complete control over Korea after 1910, their investment multiplied swiftly, increasing to 16.1 million yen in 1914 and 330.8 million in 1920. With the new industrial policy and the general slowdown of the economy after World War I, Japanese investment slowed down somewhat, resulting in a drop of their paid-in capital to 193.7 million in 1929. It, however, regained its strength and accelerated quickly after 1931. The 1937 war with China made Korea even more critical as a military and industrial base, and paid-in capital of Japanese companies headquartered in Korea soared to 955.8 million yen in 1938 and 1.52 billion in 1941. As a result, their share of paid-in capital increased from 26.4 percent of the total in 1911 to about 67 percent in 1929, more than 88 percent in 1938 and 1939.

In addition to equity capital and retained earnings, many Japanese corporations financed their businesses with debenture issues and borrowing mostly from financial institutions (examined in detail in chapter 6). For example, the Korea Nitrogen Fertilizer Corporation (owned by Japanese), which had 62.5 million yen of paid-in capital in 1937, issued 70 million yen's worth of debentures, more than its paid-in capital.[24] This was not an isolated case: many Japanese corporations, especially the large ones, resorted to this means of corporate financing. When these amounts are included, the reported sum of Japanese investment relative to that of the Koreans was probably understated by a considerable margin. In this respect, the Japanese investment in business in Korea vis-à-vis the Koreans was considerably larger than what was reflected in the paid-in capital of Japanese companies headquartered in Korea alone.

In addition, Japanese invested in companies jointly owned with Koreans. The amount of investment in Japanese-Korean joint companies fluctuated widely from period to period under colonial rule,[25] which appears to have reflected the changing roles of Koreans relative to the Japanese government's economic and political needs. On the whole, their paid-in capital increased from 8.1 million yen in 1911 to 95.8 million in 1929, increasing 11.8 times during that eighteen-year period. It is not possible to estimate the amount of investment of Japanese-Korean joint business ventures after 1929 (because they were not published regularly), but the amounts seemed to have increased somewhat over time.[26] However, their proportion relative to total investment in the country seemed to have declined. The number of joint Japanese-Korean companies in relation to all companies in Korea decreased from about 11 percent of the total in 1910 to 9 percent in 1929 and 1.6 percent in 1938. Similarly, the paid-in capital of Japanese-Korean companies in the case of commercial and industrial companies decreased from 51 percent of the total paid-in capital of all companies in Korea in 1910 to about 31 percent in 1929 and 9 percent in 1938.[27]

It is virtually impossible to calculate the shares of investment in joint-venture companies between Japanese and Koreans, but it appears that the major portion was contributed by the Japanese, although the Japanese invested mostly in their own corporations (approximately 60 to 80 percent), while about 10 to 30 percent of their investment was in joint ventures during the 1910–1929 period. The 10 to 30 percent accounted for practically all the paid-in capital in the joint Japanese-Korean companies. After 1929, not only did the percentage of investment in joint ventures slip, but the Japanese investment in them appear to have declined.

The Japanese likewise invested in joint-venture companies with other foreigners. The number of companies owned jointly with foreigners changed (between one and three) over time in the early years.[28] There was only one company jointly owned by Japanese and Americans; it had subscribed capital of 2 million yen in 1912 and 6 million in 1926. After 1928 it declined sharply and ceased to exist.

When all investments in companies headquartered in Korea, including those of joint ventures, are added, the stock of capital in companies headquartered in Korea owned and operated by Japanese may be estimated to have been as much as 5 billion yen, which represented 76.1 percent of Japanese private investment in Korea in 1943 (Table 4.2).

In addition to Japanese investment in companies headquartered in Korea, a considerable number of Japanese companies headquartered in the home country had branches with sizable amounts of investment in Korea. Nearly all companies headquartered outside of Korea were Japanese. Japanese companies incorporated and headquartered in Japan, especially the large *zaibatsu*, invested heavily in Korea. On the basis of the calculation shown for companies incorporated and headquartered in Japan, capital invested in Korea could be set at approximately 600 to 900 million yen in 1941–1943, as already noted. Thus, Japanese investment in all companies, headquartered both in Korea and Japan, amounted to approximately 5.9 billion yen in 1943, which was nearly 90 percent of their private investment in Korea and exceeded nine-tenths of the capital in all companies in Korea (see Table 4.2). They made up 76.1 percent of those headquartered in Korea and 13.7 percent of those headquartered in Japan.

Investment by foreign companies other than Japanese in Korea was minimal. Only one non-Japanese foreign company was headquartered in Korea in 1912, and it was partly owned by a Japanese national,[29] and there were only two foreign companies with branches in Korea that had even a small amount of capital—430,000 yen in 1911. Some signs of increases in foreign investment were noted after the Annexation. The number of companies owned by foreigners increased to eleven in 1912. Nearly half of them were mining companies and six were American firms. No information regarding foreign businesses was published after 1931, but considering the circumstances before and after that year (for example, the economic depression and Japanese suppression of foreign business in Korea) the number could not have been larger than that of 1928.

The paid-in capital of companies headquartered in Korea owned and operated by foreigners remained about the same (about 2 million yen) until 1928. In open ports in 1906 they numbered forty-two Chinese, two American, two English, and one French. In the following years the number of foreign businesses expanded. At the time of the Annexation, there were about fifteen businesses owned and operated by Westerners. No information regarding foreign businesses was published after 1931, but it is reasonable to presume that their investment declined precipitously after 1930. There were eight branches of foreign firms in Korea in 1930, probably with a combined total of no more than 1 million yen in Korea. There was no foreign company headquartered in Korea in 1939 and, thus, no paid-in capital. In sum, foreign business investment was so small in volume that its contribution to Korea's capital formation and economy was miniscule toward the end of Japanese rule.

In comparison with overwhelming Japanese investment, the paid-in capital in Korean companies was small, though it increased over time. It expanded from less than 200,000 yen (a fraction of the 1.2 million yen total for all companies in Korea) in 1906 to 2.7million yen in 1911 after the Annexation and 19.2 million in 1920, rising nearly 100 times in fourteen years. Although the increase in investment in Korean companies was sizable, overall it was not as voluminous or vigorous as that of the Japanese. Also, the relative increase in the volume of their investment lagged far behind in the number of companies established and the investment in them, relative to Japanese investment.[30] As a result, the share of paid-in capital of Korean companies decreased from 16.7 percent of the total in 1906 to 5.1 percent in 1920 (see Table 4.1), indicating a relative lag in investment by Koreans.

Most Korean investors during the early years were wealthy individuals, merchants, craftsmen, and a few small or middle-level landowners. These were a few "enlightened," prominent landlords[31] and former government officials who had been pensioned off by the Japanese government. Some soap manufacturing companies were founded by Korean landlords. The merchants and craftsmen—especially the large merchants—were typically newly established, and some had accumulated their capital in rice trade and during the mining boom.

More intensive and popular business investment in companies by Koreans began after World War I. Paid-in capital increased from 19.2 million yen in 1920 to 122.7 million in 1938, an increase of 6.4 times in an eighteen-year period (see Table 4.1).[32] During this period, the increasing numbers of investors in Korean companies were small merchants, former middle-level civil servants, and small landlords—in addition to the well-to-do landlords, former government officials, and businessmen.[33] Most of them established small or medium-sized businesses. As a result, the average amount of paid-in capital in Korean corporations declined sharply from

168,000 yen in 1923 to 54,000 after 1929.[34] Korean investment in companies in 1939 is estimated at 11.3 percent of the total.[35] Investment in Korean companies with debenture capital and borrowing was relatively small, certainly much smaller than that of the Japanese.

In the case of joint-venture companies headquartered in Korea, as noted earlier, it is virtually impossible to calculate the share of Korean investment. Nonetheless, their investment in them may be estimated. It started out as fairly sizable relative to the aggregate investment—as much as half of the total, in the early years. Their share on the whole for the entire colonial period, however, appears to have been relatively small, probably no more than two-tenths of the total, as noted earlier in connection with Japanese investment in them. The Korean partners seem to have been confined to a small number of family-owned Korean enterprises, and they were a second tier of joint-stock ventures. Some of the most successful Korean businessmen entered into joint enterprises with Japanese investors in the later years of colonial rule.[36]

When all investments in Korean companies, including those jointly owned, are combined, the capital stock in them may be estimated to have been about 600 million yen as of 1943, which represented only 9.2 percent of investment in all companies and was just about half of their private investment (49.6 percent), a far smaller share than the nearly nine-tenths for the Japanese (see Table 4.2).

Unincorporated Businesses

The Japanese invested a considerable amount in unincorporated businesses, probably a little less than half of the total capital in the sector, or about 270 million yen, in 1943, representing about 4.1 percent of their investment in the private sector. In contrast, foreign investment in unincorporated businesses in Korea was very small. Compared with the reasonable amount of data available on Japanese and foreign investment in Korea, comprehensive data on Korean investment in unincorporated businesses are more difficult to ascertain.

Notwithstanding the paucity in data, it seems sensible to infer that Koreans established a greater number of new unincorporated businesses and invested in them relatively more extensively than in companies, considering the sheer number of enterprises, in comparison with the Japanese. Many farmers who took up trade raised the funds to start small businesses by selling or mortgaging their land.[37] The volume of investment of Koreans in unincorporated businesses may be estimated to have been as much as 290 million yen (that was a little more than that of the Japanese) in 1943 (see Table 4.2), and their relative share in this sector probably constituted as much as 24 percent of the Korean investment in the private sector. The Koreans, thus, dedicated a much larger share of their savings for investment in unincorporated businesses than did the Japanese, who devoted a small portion of their savings for investment in that sector.

Housing and and Miscellaneous Businesses

Japanese investment in housing and miscellaneous businesses likewise was dominant. The Japanese had always constructed their own housing, mostly in urban areas, and a substantial amount of investment was dedicated to it. Considering the extent of housing construction needed for as many as 750,000 Japanese residents in Korea, the Japanese contribution to it in 1943 may be estimated at approximately 400 million yen (about 6.1 percent of their total investment in the private sector). Korean investments in this category are tabulated at about 320 million yen (about 26.4 percent of their total investment in the private sector) in 1943 (see Table 4.2). As with unincorporated businesses, Japanese allocated a smaller portion of their savings for investment in housing and miscellaneous sectors than did Koreans, who directed a much larger share of their savings for the same purpose, because their investment in other sectors was relatively small.

Total

When all investments in various sectors of the economy are added, it becomes clear that Japanese contribution to investment in Korea under colonial rule was overwhelming. As shown in Table 4.2, when all investments—including those in Japanese companies and Japanese joint-venture companies headquartered in Korea and Japan, debenture capital and borrowing, unincorporated businesses, and housing—are totaled, Japanese contribution to investment in the private sector adds up to 6.57 billion yen as of 1943. This volume of capital stock accumulated by the Japanese represented about 84.4 percent of the total in the private sector in Korea in 1943 (see Table 4.2).

This estimate of Japanese investment is somewhat larger than the figures typically calculated and reported in other studies. The Industrial Bank of Korea estimated that Japanese private investment in 1938 was approximately 2.9 billion yen.[38] An estimate published by the Japanese in a statistical annual reported that it was about 5–6 billion yen in 1940.[39] Considering the fact that Korea had about a 2 billion yen balance-of-payments deficit between 1940 and 1945, and taking into account the rise in prices since 1940, the aggregate sum of Japanese capital in 1943 would have been about 6–7 billion yen.[40] In a somewhat different context, Naomasa Mizuda stated in a Japanese publication in 1962 that the property value of Japanese corporations (*hojin*) in Korea was between 50 and 55 billion yen and that of individuals about 15 billion yen in September 1945 prices. Thus, the aggregate sum of Japanese property in Korea as of August 1945 in September 1945 prices was between 65 and 70 billion yen.[41] U.S. Army investigators after World War II calculated individuals' share at 9 billion yen; otherwise, they considered the Japanese estimate to be reasonable. According to Mizuda, prices during World War II increased by 6 to 7 times.

The magnitude of Japanese net investment in Korea under Japanese rule probably required as much as 7.6–8.4 percent of Korea's GDP. Not only did Japanese investment dominate, its share increased over time. In this regard, the volume and pattern of Japanese investment in Korea appears to have been unique relative to the experiences of other countries. First, Japanese investment, at approximately 85 percent of total investment in the private sector, dominated capital formation in the colony. It should be noted, however, that this estimate is somewhat smaller than the 90 percent typically alleged by many Japanese economists and historians and accepted by some Korean economists.

Following the same rationale, when all Korean investments in companies, unincorporated businesses, debenture capital and borrowing, and housing are added, their capital stock was much smaller than that of the Japanese—about 1.21 billion yen, or approximately 15.6 percent of total private capital in the country, in 1943. The amount of private Korean net investment under Japanese rule probably represented about 1.4–1.6 percent of Korea's GDP, compared with the Japanese contribution of about 7.6–8.4 percent of the country's income for private investment. However, the figure for Korean contribution to private investment is considerably larger than many Japanese and some Korean scholars have given credit to the Koreans, which is typically around 10 percent. This assessment reveals that Korean investment was not only much larger than that number but that it prevailed during the transitional period and increased considerably over time.

THE IMPACT OF FOREIGN INVESTMENT ON KOREAN INVESTMENT

As noted in chapter 3, foreign trade and foreign investment in the transitional period opened natives' eyes but did not have the powerful demonstration effect on the Korean people needed to spur them to undertake the requisite investment to bring about robust economic growth during the same period. Unfortunately, the foreign imports and investment were not keys to unlock the door of economic opportunity, nor did they stimulate the country's economic activity. What, then, motivated Koreans to expand their investment horizon, though not as vigorously as the Japanese, beyond that of the transitional period under Japanese rule? How did this change come about? These enticing questions are explored here.

A number of factors contributed to the expansion of Korean investment under Japanese rule: relative political and social stability, the security of personal income and wealth (unlike during the traditional and transitional periods), the booming Japanese and Japanese colonial economy, the forceful catalytic and linkage effects of foreign (and chiefly Japanese) investment, and the external economies of Japanese investment. Examined in the next section are catalytic and linkage effects, together with external economies—the principal mediums through which foreign investment affected Korean investment. Also examined are what are referred to as oppression effects.

Catalytic Effects

Foreign investment—again, mostly Japanese—had a powerful catalytic effect on potential Korean investors and entrepreneurs. Their business contact with Japanese and other foreigners enabled them to learn new technologies, embrace new opportunities, and set in motion a slow but long wave of investment and technological innovation. The catalytic effect spread gradually from a small group of intellectuals, "giant merchants" (who came from the ranks of new merchants), enlightened landowners, small landlords, and, especially in the 1920s, merchants who had had shops in the open ports and sold and/or exported rice to Japan and/or imported goods. Following the example of foreign businesses, the foreign mania raged everywhere, and many goods and services were manufactured in imitation of foreign articles. Koreans under Japanese rule began to engage in the same activities, including textile manufacturing, rice milling, printing, and the making of cigarettes, that the foreigners did.

The making of Korean entrepreneurs and their investment took some time. The catalytic effect radiated gradually from open ports to urban areas and then to the provinces. In the early years most businesses were located in Seoul, Busan, Inchon, and other open ports. In 1910, for example, 102 out of 167 business firms, or 61 percent, organized their businesses in Seoul or Busan.[42] After the Annexation, modern businesses began to spring up in the provinces as well. A number of small-scale businesses such as repair shops were established by Koreans: small industries sprang up to produce such "foreign" goods as soap, matches, and shoes. Many entrepreneurs even from the commoner class began engaging in such enterprises as manufacturing socks and linen-cloth, using new technologies. By 1920 provincial Koreans had established local banks in many locations.

Initially, many of these new businesses used low-technology methods that required few skills to produce locally needed consumer goods and materials, such as kitchen utensils, tiles, bricks, and foodstuffs. Eventually, businesses established mechanized facilities to manufacture products such as textiles, ceramics, tobacco, liquor, and confectioneries. Some small and medium-sized merchants and landlords even incorporated the techniques of the more advanced foreign businesses into such traditional endeavors as flour milling and printing, thereby becoming captains of modern enterprise themselves. As they acquired experience, some of these entrepreneurs employed modern technology to produce new products such as knitted/jersey underwear and rubber shoes, and they successfully competed against Japanese businesses. It has been estimated that about 200 Koreans played a significant role in the colony's Korean business community. Three-quarters of these executives worked for Korean companies.[43]

The catalytic effect could be detected even in traditional cottage industries. As Korea drew steady infusions from the world's reservoir of new technology that kept the country from having to advance the frontier of knowledge in surges of fresh invention, continuous growth of productive capacity occurred. An infusion of the superior technology of large manufacturing companies brought about the establishment of some large Korean companies as well. Even in agriculture, although virtually constant labor and "traditional" inputs were maintained, commercial fertilizers and improved seeds contributed to increasing yields more than elevenfold and more than doubling output between 1915 and 1940.[44]

The catalytic effect also can be detected in the use of savings. Entrepreneurs, former bureaucrats, and landlords, who had used their savings to either purchase more land, make usury loans, or continue the "Confucian traditions" of the late Joseon era, increased the use of their savings for investment purposes (see chapter 8).

The foreign investors and entrepreneurs who were the precursors of many new industries and who performed an important entrepreneurial function in Korea were mainly Japanese. They were the principal transmitters of new ideas and technologies, and they inculcated in Koreans the attitudes and value systems more conducive to modern business, although many resented Japanese rule of the country. In this respect, the Japanese—who had emancipated themselves from their own feudal system not long before—brought to Korea the missionary zeal of converts to Westernization and modernization. Economic growth requires an adequate supply of innovators. To Koreans, Japanese firms were Schumpeterian innovators (following Joseph Schumpeter, who advanced a thesis that innovation is a primer of economic development) whose natural bent was to experiment with new techniques, new products, or new economic forms, in defiance of established opinion or of vested interests among Koreans.

Koreans worked in and learned from Japanese businesses. Many were later employed in Korean-owned factories or started their own businesses, while others traveled to Japan to learn new technologies. A number of Korean corporations, especially in textile industry in the 1920s, were staffed with people who had attended Western educational institutions, mainly in Japan.[45] Some provincial business leaders were exposed to Western ideas by the Japanese in Korea. The Japanese also raised the aspirations of the Koreans and provided a model for Koreans to emulate. Although a few adopted such ideas grudgingly, and some with contempt for Japanese businesses, a cluster of Korean imitators followed. Because many Koreans traditionally had a low opinion of Japanese,[46] they also gained the confidence that they could achieve what the "inferior" Japanese had accomplished only a few decades earlier.

Linkage Effects

Another factor that contributed to the rise in Korean investment was linkage effects. The cumulative nature of development resulting from linkage effects, both backward and forward, also had a positive impact on investment in Korean-owned enterprises. A huge chemical plant built by the Japanese, for instance, stimulated development in those industries that supplied materials to it. Mines were worked to supply the coal for heat and energy. The linkage effect was especially keen in the case of textiles, the most important modern manufacture in Korea before 1933.

There also was a backward linkage effect from trade, Korea's most important economic contact with the outside world, especially Japan. In the case of a chemical plant built by the Japanese, it stimulated development in those businesses that used its outputs. Likewise, by increasing the volume of trade, foreign investment in Korea created profit opportunities for local businesses that conducted trade at the inter- and intra-provincial levels. It was not long before banks were opened to finance such trade, to develop export and import processing, and to finance the founding of public utilities. These induced or linkage effects may well have been more important to investment than profits were (for instance, in railroads and the textile industry), especially for Korean investors.

External Economies

In addition to bringing in most Western goods and technology, the investment in and establishment of Japanese enterprises, public as well as private, produced external economies from which Korean-owned enterprises benefited. These external economies helped to establish an environment in which Korean investors could make a profit from new undertakings. Through the factory, the railway, the ship, the machine, and modern chemistry, the Japanese opened up revolutionary opportunities for Koreans, as well as the Japanese themselves, to reap rewards from the acquisition of capital goods and new technology. For example, the construction of railroads, in which Japanese capital figured so prominently, undoubtedly created profitable opportunities for Korean-owned firms, as well as Japanese, by reducing transportation costs and providing access to larger markets. This in turn increased the markets for both imported and domestic products, which were soon produced in Korea in order to take advantage of inexpensive labor and raw materials. Ultimately, these products became available for export and increased the nation's income. The presence of Japanese firms and nationals also created more demand for the goods and services that Koreans supplied, such as textile goods and food. Perhaps for these reasons, industrialization was more extensive in Korea than in most other colonies, Japanese or otherwise.

Economic-Oppression Effects

Notwithstanding the positive impacts of large Japanese investment in Korea, some scholars, especially Koreans, often blamed the sluggish Korean investment under Japanese rule on the presence of Japanese businesses in Korea, or what they called the oppression effect.[47] According to this view, the presence of Japanese business depressed the incentives for Korean investment and retarded the development of Korean-owned enterprises. A well-known economic historian argues that "the most important factor preventing Korea's progress was Japan, because it intervened in Korea's sovereignty and governance, infringed on Korea's economic rights (*gyeongjekwon*), and hindered Korea's economic progress through military aggression. In his view, because of the presence of Japanese businesses that had strong financial support, Korean businesses lost the business activity area (*hwaltong yeongik*), or market, which made it impossible for the latter to make a profit and accumulate capital. He further alleged that the "Japanese took away [expropriated] Korean capital" to such an extent that "no underdeveloped country experienced the cruel confiscation of native capital like Korea, e.g., through the 1905 monetary reform."[48] Also, in the view of another economist, the rapid industrialization of Korea by Japanese "monopoly capital" and government oppression prevented Korean businesses from expanding.[49]

Many Koreans also assert that the Japanese usurpation of its sovereignty, oppression, and second-class treatment of Koreans created anti-Japanese sentiments, which dissuaded the Koreans from investing. In their view, Korean industrialization under Japanese rule supported the oppressive and expansionist policies of the Japanese empire and, thus, Koreans were against investment in those industries that Japan attempted to develop, especially military-related industries.[50] Patriotism was highly revered by most Koreans, and favoring Japanese interests was, rightly or wrongly, condemned. Some Korean scholars go so far as to claim that had the country remained a sovereign state and had it not been for perceived Japanese business oppression, Koreans would have realized greater investment and economic growth.

According to one historian, the Japanese confiscation or purchase of Korean land and the capital it represented somehow "prevented the formation of Korean capital": the "Japanese stole land, agricultural products, labor, and other resources, . . . and therefore prevented the development of Korea's agriculture, capital, and industry."[51] He further argues that "high rents and land taxes constituted the foundation of Japanese industrial capital under Japanese rule." An American missionary, too, observed that Japanese oppression of Koreans was so bad that the Resident General had to "deport hundreds of unsavory imperial subjects" to curb the rapacity and brutality of his own countrymen.[52]

It has also often been asserted that Japanese economic intrusions and investment in the economy stifled the growth of the traditional or indigenous sector of the economy (e.g., that producing handicrafts and operating small mines). Some Korean people believe that Korean handicraft industries suffered an "irreparable setback"[53] because of the presence and economic oppression of Japanese businesses. Also, according to many Koreans, all profits made by foreign traders and investors were at the expense of the Koreans and drained the wealth of their country.

Before evaluating these assertions and the alleged adverse impacts of Japanese economic oppression, this form of oppression needs to be distinguished from political" oppression, although such a distinction is not easy to draw clearly. Unquestionably, political oppression did prevail, which dampened the entrepreneurial spirit of Koreans and had an adverse impact on native investment. However, the prevalence of Japanese economic (as differentiated from political) oppression and its impact are less clear. No doubt, Korean businesses on the whole were not as successful as those of the Japanese. Returns on investment in Korean businesses on the whole were lower, and their business life expectancy in general was shorter.[54] However, it did not constitute "oppression" of foreign or Japanese investment.

If the term *economic oppression* is interpreted to mean that Korean enterprises could not grow or expand as fast as the Japanese firms did because of the oppression of the former, then the argument lacks factual support. Granted, some of these claims have some merit but, as Gragert's recent study of Japanese expropriation of land from Koreans found, the assertions of Japanese economic (not political) oppression are overstated.[55] In fact, some Korean firms depended heavily on Japanese capital to expand their businesses.[56] Whether the absence of Japanese businesses would have resulted in a greater rate of investment is a matter for speculation. Even if there were no Japanese businesses in Korea and no such "oppression," it is doubtful whether the Korean people would have saved enough to finance the requisite investment, or whether their savings would have been used for investment in productive facilities.

If, on the other hand, *economic oppression* is taken to mean that Japanese firms had certain advantages—economic as well as political—over their Korean counterparts in areas such as capital accessibility and intensity, technical know-how, and favorable government policy, then the argument has a great deal of merit and force. The Japanese on the whole did have greater financial resources, government support, superior technology, better management, and therefore a greater ability to earn profits than did the Koreans. They enjoyed more economies of scale, while Korean businesses typically operated under a mix of business and household management and did not have specialists to manage the business, buy raw materials, or exploit new markets. Some Japanese viewed Korean products as crude, sloppy, of poor quality, and unreliable.[57]

The only economic-oppression arguments that have much merit are those based on the ideas that government policies favored Japanese businesses over those of the Koreans and that large Japanese *zaibatsu* had the monopolistic and monopsonistic powers as sellers and buyers (see chapter 7). Other than those that cooperated closely with the Japanese government, most Korean businesses did not receive government favors in the form of subsidies, tax advantages, or low-interest investment loans from the public banks or GNBFIs (see chapter 6).

It is difficult to discern in quantitative terms the overall net impact of catalytic, linkage, and economic-oppression effects and external economies on Korean investment. Were such an assessment possible, the impact would probably be found to be of a mixed nature, perhaps with one effect reinforcing or canceling another. Nonetheless, the net effect appears on the whole to have been positive and probably significant for Korean investment. For these reasons industrialization was more rapid and pervasive and economic dislocations less severe in Korea under Japanese rule than in most other colonies, Japanese or otherwise. The lag in Korean investment was not solely or mainly a result of the Japanese economic oppression.

INVESTMENT IN HUMAN CAPITAL

The stock of human capital, in addition to physical capital, is critical to economic development, and the task of investment in human capital in Korea at that time involved two principal undertakings: the development of appropriate educational institutions structured to meet the needs of a market-oriented economy and increasing the level of technological sophistication of the country's labor force. These tasks are examined below in aggregate and by nationality.

Aggregate Investment

As noted in chapter 3, after the opening of the country to foreigners, there was a movement to adopt as a model new and modern Western educational institutions and their orientations. A number of Western-style schools began to emerge under sovereign Korea, before Japan came to control the country. However, the extent and scope of Western education available in the entire country were limited, while the traditional institution of education—the private village school (*seowon* or *seodang,* a one-room elementary school that propagated Confucian teachings)—was left in place and continued to predominate, especially outside of the capital city, in provinces. The earliest count of village schools numbered about 18,200 in 1912 following the Japanese takeover.

After taking over Korea as a protectorate, the Japanese government slowly expanded the modern, Western-style schools as Western influences gradually took hold of the country. Under the firm control and guidance of the Residency General, the Korean government established a number of vocational and industrial training schools (the first one was established in 1906), a medical school, a commercial school, and a normal school. There were sixty-five such schools in 1906, and by 1910 the number increased to 146 public schools.[58] Before the Annexation, there were nine national (*kanritsu*) schools established by the central government and fifty-one public so-called modern Korean schools. In addition, new private schools, including secondary schools, emerged in the country.

After the Annexation, the Japanese government expanded the number of public educational institutions modeled after the Western educational system at all levels and to the rural regions. It began with the elementary schools. By 1939 a total of 2,727 public schools and 1,327 two-year primary schools were established. The government also launched industrial, vocational, and professional schools and colleges to cultivate the habits of industry and economy. Between 1919 and 1935 the number of vocational and technical schools grew from twenty-one to seventy-two. In 1939, there were eleven national schools, which included one university and seven or eight post-secondary public professional schools.

Along with the increased number of schools, enrollment in them grew at all levels. The number of students, including Japanese and those in "nonstandard schools," increased from 110,800 in 1910 to 1,407,100 in 1939, a nearly thirteen-fold increase in about thirty years, as shown in Table 4.3. Primary-school enrollment increased from 35,600 to 1,311,200 (a nearly thirty-seven-fold expansion) during the same period, while the number of students registered in high schools grew from 1,100 to 69,200 (a nearly sixty-three-fold increase).

Likewise, the number of students enrolled in industrial and professional schools rose thirty-one-fold (from 1,100 to 34,100) during the 1910–1939 period, while the number of students attending colleges showed a twenty-nine-fold expansion (from 400 to 11,560). Vocational and technical school enrollment increased almost fivefold (from 1,872 to 9,233) between 1919 and 1935. Similarly, the number of students graduating from all levels of educational institutions multiplied. Graduates of elementary schools increased by nearly nine times (from 14,556 in 1915 to 128,254 in 1935) in a twenty-year period. Graduates of high schools showed a more than eightfold rise in twenty years (from 1,348 in 1915 to 10,831 in 1935).

Notwithstanding the overall expansion of the school system and student enrollments that provided the opportunities for modern education, the colonial government's effort to raise human capital via formal education was limited. Only about 0.3 percent of the government budget was dedicated to education, while as much as 5 percent was reserved for agricultural experiments, extension stations, and other, related programs. The increases in the number of schools and student enrollment were too small to meet the educational needs of all citizens. As a result, the educational level of people living in Korea on the whole was low. As of May 1944, about 91 percent of people living in the southern half of the country (for which statistics are available), for instance, had less than an elementary education, while only about 2.4 percent had more.[59]

Beyond formal education, human capital in Korea was formed through more practical training. A number of institutions that served workers and farmers were established under both the Korean and colonial governments. Under the tutelage of Japanese advisers, a technical-training extension service was added in 1907, and a

TABLE 4.3 Number of Registered Students in Educational Institutions between 1910 and 1939 (in thousands)

Educational Institutions	1910	1919	1930	1937	1939
Primary					
Japanese	15.5	42.8	67.4	89.8	92.8
Korean	20.1	89.3	450.5	901.2	1,218.4
Nonstandard	71.8	39.2	47.5	142.6	—
Secondary, boys					
Japanese	0.2	2.0	5.8	7.8	21.3
Korean	0.8	3.2	11.1	15.6	28.9
Secondary, girls					
Japanese	0.5	1.9	8.3	11.9	—
Korean	0.4	0.7	4.4	7.1	—
Vocational	1.1	4.5	15.3	26.6	—
Professional					
Japanese	—	—	—	—	7.9
Korean	—	—	—	—	26.2
Colleges	0.4	0.9	2.8	4.4	—
Japanese	—	—	—	—	4.7
Korean	—	—	—	—	6.3
University	—	—	0.6	0.5	—
Japanese	—	—	—	—	0.4
Korean	—	—	—	—	0.2
Total	110.8	184.5	613.7	1,207.5	1,407.1

Sources: Based on G. McCune 1950: 261–263; Sotokufu Tokei Nenpo 1915, 1920, 1925, 1930, 1935; and Grajdanzev 1944: 261–263.

textile institute and technical-training center in 1909. After the Annexation, the Japanese provided opportunities for Korean workers to acquire knowledge and skills through on-the-job training. The colonial government also maintained model forests and farms, seed nurseries, sericulture training institutes, and cattle-breeding stations that demonstrated modern methods of sericulture, the raising of rice, sugar beets, cotton, and livestock, and forest management. In this way, the colonial government facilitated the education of farmers by providing them with practical and theoretical lessons.

In the private sector, when Japanese factories were established, many Koreans were employed as operatives. They were provided with the necessary training on the job. Some of these men were later employed in factories owned by Koreans or became employers themselves. In this way, human capital formation through the learning-by-doing approach and the demonstration effect of development under Japanese rule provided important lessons for the development of the Korean economy.

Investment by Nationality

As just examined, investment in education under Japanese rule expanded rapidly, thereby enhancing human capital. But the opportunities for education differed vastly by nationality, endowing uneven human capital between Japanese and Koreans as well as between genders. The educational disparity between Japanese and Koreans (the dominance of the Japanese) was present at two levels: in the availability of educational opportunities and in the attainments of Koreans, with the latter being a consequence of the former. The percentage of Koreans receiving a formal education was much smaller than that for the Japanese. While 91.2 percent of school-age Japanese children in Korea attended public primary schools in 1919, only about 3.7 percent of Korean children did so. While the percentage of Japanese children attending school was near 100 percent, the number of Korean children attending school was only about one-third of that, even as recently as 1942.[60]

The disparity in enrollments of Japanese and Korean students was even greater at the secondary-school level. While nearly all school-age Japanese children attended secondary schools in 1935, only one out of 2,200 school-age Koreans did so, and as late as 1939 the percentage of Korean children attending high school was a mere 4 percent. In addition, both elementary and secondary schools were segregated along the Japanese and Korean lines.[61] Even in towns where there were only small numbers of Japanese children—perhaps fewer than thirty—a separate public school was built for them rather than putting them in the existing school for Korean students. Also, the Japanese schools always had better facilities and equipment than those for Korean students.

The schools beyond the elementary-school level where both Japanese and Korean students attended, quotas were set for Korean students, while there was no such limitation for Japanese students. In a normal school, for instance, nearly all Japanese applicants (which usually numbered about 80 percent of the total in the early 1940s) were admitted, while only about 20 percent was set aside for Korean students, for whom the school application to admission ratio was typically ten to one. Such a situation existed even in the less formal vocational and "industrial education" programs. For example, the public Railroad School, with programs lasting from one month to three years, graduated 1,509 students, of which 89.3 percent (1,348) were Japanese while the rest (10.7 percent, or 161 students) were Koreans.[62] The entire railroad training program over a fourteen-year period under colonial rule graduated a total of 4,379 students, of which 76.4 percent (3,345) were Japanese and 23.6 percent (1,034) were Koreans.

Interestingly, in spite of limitations placed on Korean students, the number of Korean students registered in all schools expanded much faster over time than the number of Japanese students. The number of Korean students registered in schools during the colonial period increased by 13.8 times, while that of Japanese students multiplied 8.27 times. Especially notable was the number of Korean students enrolled in primary schools, which increased by 60.61 times during the thirty-year period, compared with 6 times for Japanese students.

As a result of the discrepancy in educational opportunities, there was a wide gap in the level of education obtained by the two nationalities. While 73.1 percent of Japanese in Korea in 1944 had at least an elementary-school education, only 7.6 percent of Koreans did. In the same year, while 51.5 percent of Japanese in Korea had attended at least through junior high school, only 1.15 percent of Koreans had. Likewise in 1944, whereas 4.6 percent of Japanese in Korea had attended junior college or beyond, only about one-tenth of a percent of Koreans had.[63] There were only 206 Korean college students in 1939, while 350 Japanese students, or 63 percent of all university students in Korea, attended institutions of higher learning. At the time, Japanese constituted less than 3 percent of the population in Korea.

In addition, the Japanese government discouraged or banned Korean students from going abroad to study anywhere other than Japan. The number of Korean students studying in the United States, for instance, decreased from 542 during a ten-year period between 1910 and 1920 to 289 during a twenty-four-year period between 1921 and 1945.[64]

The educational institutions that played a pivotal role in narrowing the educational gap between the Japanese and the native population in Korea were the private schools. Although the traditional private village schools were not the appropriate educational institutions to meet the needs of modern society, nonetheless they were important in the effort to teach Koreans how to read and write. The number of Koreans who attended traditional village schools during their heyday under Japanese rule was up to 25,500 by 1920; in total, they educated some 245,000 Korean children. But the modern private, Western-style educational institutions played a much more critical role in educating Koreans. It was reported that there were sixty-five private schools in 1906 (of which forty were reported to have been so-called modern schools), which increased to as many as 950 by 1909 and to 2,131, of which as many as 823 had a religious (Christian) affiliation, by 1910.[65] Altogether, private schools enrolled 2.5 percent of all students in primary schools, 26.2 percent in high schools, 15.5 percent in professional schools, and 56.5 percent in colleges in 1939, all of whom were Koreans.[66]

Especially notable was the establishment of Christian schools. All Christian missionaries and many private individuals (including a queen) established these private schools. Devoted exclusively to educating Korean students, private schools sprang up rapidly on the heels of the Christian missionaries. One prominent member of the royalty, a queen, who was close to the king and the mother of the last crown prince, for instance, established three "modern" church affiliated schools (one for boys and two for girls) in 1905 and 1906. As a result of the efforts of the Christian missionaries and private individuals, the number of so-called unaccredited primary and secondary schools (private and mostly Christian schools) increased from 450 in 1915 to 778 in 1918. Although the number decreased to 279 in 1920 under the pressure of the colonial government, it surged to 406 in 1935.

These private schools beyond the elementary-school level played a particularly crucial role in educating Korean leaders and in narrowing the educational gap between the Japanese and the native population. The Japanese government approved 7 private high schools for Korean boys and 4 for Korean girls before 1919. The number (including not-government-approved) increased from 18 in 1919 to 45 in 1935 and 117 in 1939, while the number of students attending these institutions increased from 2,781 in 1919 to 3,841 in 1935. The number of students who attended the so-called unaccredited primary and secondary schools in 1935 was nearly 80,000 (79,998). Likewise, four private colleges were established for Koreans, of which some were affiliated with Christian missionaries and churches. Most of the Korean college graduates were educated in private colleges, and only a few graduated from the colleges and universities established by the Japanese government.

SUMMARY AND CONCLUSIONS

In this chapter, we have examined economic reforms and investment under forty years of Japanese rule (1905–1945). When Japan took control of Korea in 1905, it instituted numerous reforms to transform the autonomous, traditional, and transitional economy into one that served the needs of the colonial power. It removed numerous obstacles and established infrastructure to accommodate the workings of a government-controlled but market-oriented economy. The reform measures not only involved changes in the physical environment and technology they altered public attitudes and beliefs toward business investment and saving.

Under the Japanese administration, a substantial amount of investment—one of the crucial ingredients of economic development—took place, with the accumulation of physical capital valued at about 10 billion yen by 1943. The endowment of capital assets left at the end of World War II was substantially greater than that before the Japanese takeover, which laid the foundation for future economic expansion. In terms of annual averages, net investment under Japanese rule probably constituted 9 to 10 percent of Korea's GDP. The rapid rise in investment certainly represented a radical departure from the past. This volume of investment was at a level sufficiently high to expand the national income at an average of 3 percent per year (see chapter 7), in contrast with a near-zero level of net investment, and a resulting virtually stagnant economy, in the traditional and transitional periods.

Investment was undertaken by both the public and private sectors. After taking over the country, the Japanese government's levels of investment in Korea greatly exceeded that which occurred during the traditional and transitional periods and that typically found in many developed countries. Its investment was nearly 22 percent of the total in the country, while the private sector invested more than three-quarters (78.2 percent) of the total under Japanese rule. The major portion, i.e., 84.4 percent of investment in the private sector, was made by the Japanese residing in both Japan and Korea. The magnitude of the Japanese capital contribution is striking in the sense that even under the most favorable circumstances investment from nonnative citizens is apt to be small, even if investment is made for strategic purposes. In this respect the Japanese investment in Korea was different from that found under the British colonial system, for instance. For this reason, Japanese colonialism did leave a richer and more permanent legacy of institutional forms and capital formation than was typically found in Western colonialism.

Following the example set by the Japanese, Koreans likewise invested in new businesses under colonial rule. Their investment gained momentum after World War I and clearly exceeded the levels that had prevailed in the traditional and transitional periods. Korean investment was undertaken mostly by well-to-do Korean aristocrats and merchants and to some extent by small and mid-sized landowners. Korean investment in comparison with that of the Japanese, however, was relatively small, probably about 15.6 percent of the total private investment in the country. Their investment in new enterprises was significantly influenced by Japanese investment in Korea, stemming from the catalytic and linkage effects and combined with the Japanese-generated external economies. To Koreans, Japanese firms were Schumpeterian innovators, and a cluster of Korean imitators followed them. The cumulative nature of development resulting from both backward and forward linkage effects positively affected Korean-owned enterprises. The Japanese also raised the aspirations of the Korean people for success in new investments.

Contrary to the allegations made by some Korean scholars and laymen, the relatively small amount of Korean investment in comparison with that of the Japanese was not a result of the presence of the latter's investment in Korea. The hypothesis of "economic-oppression effects" (distinguished from political oppression, which unquestionably pervaded the country) of Japanese investment on Korean investment are not well founded. Whether the absence of Japanese business would have resulted in greater investment and the growth of Korean enterprises is a moot question. The only bases upon which such a claim can be supported are the privileges accorded to Japanese businesses by the colonial government and the monopoly power of the Japanese *zaibatsu*, as shown in chapter 5. Otherwise, compared with their indigenous counterparts, the Japanese on the whole had greater financial resources, better management skills, superior technology and, thus, a greater ability to earn profits. No doubt, these forces adversely affected Korean businesses, but their presence itself did not constitute oppression.

In addition to physical capital, a substantial amount of investment in human capital did take place under Japanese rule. While the importance of the traditional form of education declined, modern, Western-style schools that started modestly during the protectorate period expanded at all levels after the Annexation and raised the general level of modern education, including elementary science, of the country's labor force. Also, in addition to formal education, human capital was formed through more practical training. After the Annexation, the Japanese provided opportunities for Korean workers to acquire knowledge and skills through on-the-job training. The colonial government also facilitated the education of farmers by providing them with practical and theoretical lessons in the form of model farms, seed nurseries, sericulture training institutes, and cattle-breeding stations. In the private sector, when Japanese factories were established, many Koreans were employed as operatives, and they were provided with the necessary training on the job.

Notwithstanding the overall expansion of the school system, Korean student enrollment and opportunities for informal education, and, thus, the enhancement of Korean human capital under colonial rule were much limited. The colonial government's investment in formal education was too small to meet the educational needs of all citizens, particularly of Koreans. The level of educational attainment of Koreans through the public school system was grossly inadequate, although private schools, notably beyond the elementary school level, often run by the Christian missionaries, played a pivotal role in educating Koreans and narrowing the educational gap between the Japanese and the native population.

APPENDIX 4.1: JAPANESE INVESTMENT IN EARLY YEARS

The estimates of Japanese capital in Korea before 1910 range from about 10 million to 163 million yen. One report estimated that there were 210 Japanese businesses in open ports in 1906, with the assets valued at 15.7 million yen. Others placed the total value of Japanese assets in Korea in 1910 at 162.8 million yen, comprising 147.1 million in land and buildings (for further discussion, see Appendix 8.4), 12.9 million in company capital assets, and 2.8 million in individual and single proprietorship assets. The latter estimate appears to have inflated the value, possibly reflecting the padded claim of the Japanese government on the eve of the Annexation. Many of these estimates either inflated the amount of Japanese investment in Korea, by including all the capital of companies headquartered in Japan rather than that amount invested in Korea, or they counted the value of land confiscated by Japanese or simply added extra digits (Joseon Yeonguwhae 1935: 292). The most reasonable amount of investment at the time of the Annexation appears to have been about 10 million yen. Prior to the Annexation, Japanese investment in Korea was reported to have increased from 5.1 million to 7.4 million (with declared or official capital of 20.8 million) in 1910 (D. Chung 1987: 140). Also see B. M. Lee 1948: 294–295, 325; *Chosen Keizainenpo* 1940: 514; Y. Chung 1977: 140; K. J. Cho 1965: 375, 382; ibid. 1973b: 431–432; ibid. 1977: 244; *Kokusei Gurafu* April 1940; Shokusan Ginko 1940b: 35–37; Tokanfu 1910: 260–261; Sotokufu 1910: 160, 260; ibid. 1931: 190–193; ibid. 1932: 194–197; Shokusan Ginko 1940b: 35–37; Takesizu Suzuki (1942: 83); Far Eastern Survey 1939; Mizuda and Tsuchiya 1962: 108.

5

SECTORAL INVESTMENT

Having examined the investment in the economy as a whole in chapter 4, this chapter investigates the important and unique features and attributes of physical investment in various sectors of the Korean economy under Japanese rule. The features and attributes of sectoral investment are investigated in two broad groups, namely, the public and private sectors, which are further broken down into the subsectors of public works, social-overhead capital, industry, manufacturing, mining, commerce, financial institutions, agriculture, and miscellaneous. Examined within those subsectors are the volume, investors, and nature of sectoral investment.

The volume of investment in different economic sectors should reveal the underlying forces for the structural changes in the economy over time, while the scrutiny of investors may identify the contribution to capital formation made by different economic entities, such as government and different nationalities—in this case, the Japanese, non-Japanese foreigners, and Koreans. The examination of the nature of sectoral investment should disclose the reason for which certain types of industry and business firms expanded rapidly under Japanese rule while others grew at slower pace. The types of industry and firms examined are large versus small-scale business firms, capital- and technologically-intensive industries and firms versus labor-intensive and low-tech industries and firms, and heavy versus light industries. In this way we may be able to discern the cause for and the nature of structural change of the economy.

SECTORAL INVESTMENT BY VOLUME

There are a number of ways to group different sectors of an economy, but in Korea under Japanese rule the most common divisions used and the categories statistics were published for were agriculture, manufacturing, commerce, public works and utilities, and miscellaneous. The areas of investment examined in this chapter, therefore, fall into broad categories along the lines of the groupings listed above: social-overhead capital, industry, mining, commerce, finance, the traditional sector (including agriculture, forestry, and fishing), and miscellaneous industries.

Social-Overhead Capital

A system of adequate public works and the presence of social-overhead capital (SOC), which comprised public goods including public utilities, such as, railroad, communications, and electric power, as well as road, are prerequisites for economic development and the critical foundation for capital formation. As all physical investment depends on adequate public works and SOC, no country enjoys economic progress without them. The foundation of public works and the establishment of a framework of SOC set in motion a series of technical innovations that create opportunities for profitable investment in fields such as manufacturing and commerce. Notwithstanding these critical needs, long-term investments in them, such as the construction of national systems of transport and communications, make heavy demands on a country's resources. They are highly capital intensive and almost always represent the biggest portion of investment in developing economies. Typically, their capital-output ratios are five to six times as high as the ratios in manufacturing and agriculture. In most advanced industrial economies as much as 35 percent of gross fixed investment is in SOC—about 7 percent of GDP—and in very few does it fall below 2 percent.[1]

Considering the fact that less-developed countries need to make heavy expenditures in the areas of public works and utilities, a large investment in them is particularly important but difficult in the first decades of development. The government typically plays an important role in investment in public works and SOC, although the government's share of gross investment depends partly on the extent to which it leaves public utilities to private enterprise. Of the 7 percent of GDP needed for SOC, 2 to 3 percent is usually dedicated to public works, strictly defined (roads, harbors, schools, hospitals, public buildings, etc.), and 4 to 5 percent is generally allocated to public utilities, which may or may not be publicly administered. Let us examine the investment in them in Korea under Japanese rule.

Public Works

After taking over Korea, the Japanese government carried out extensive public works projects to provide better public services and preventive hygiene in the colony. It constructed and upgraded roads, port facilities, public structures, river navigation, waterworks, hospitals, and sanitation systems in the principal cities and towns. It is not possible to calculate the total amount of investment in public works, but according to one source the government spent about one-third of its investment, or 161 million yen, for the construction and improvement of roads, port facilities, and river navigation as of 1935, and additional outlays were planned.[2] Of these, about 40 percent was spent on ports, 33 percent on river projects, and 27 percent on roads. In general, new roads were built to meet Japanese needs, especially those of the military, which often far exceeded the demands of the Korean economy at the time.[3]

Transportation

In the traditional and transitional periods the various regions of Korea, being more or less self-sufficient, did not require extensive transportation and communications networks. Rivers and coasts carried the bulk of what trade there was. But under colonial rule two of the first and most rapidly expanding sectors of the Korean economy were transportation and communications. Some new transportation facilities were added during the transitional period (e.g., the Seoul-Inchon Railroad and new shipping services), but the improvement in transportation in the country had been woefully limited before Japan came to rule Korea.

After subjugating Korea under control, the Japanese devoted a substantial amount of resources to constructing railroads in the country. Among all forms of public-overhead capital, the construction of railroads was the most important and challenging project undertaken by the Japanese. It began in 1904, immediately after the outbreak of the Russo-Japanese War. The Japanese army completed two lines, the Seoul-Busan Line, 451 kilometers (280 miles) and the Masanpo Line, 40 kilometers (25 miles) in length, in May 1905, and the Seoul-Wuiju Line, 521 kilometers (323 miles), in March 1906. The cost of these two lines was reported to have been 25.4 million yen, which were the most important and costly investment projects at the time.

When the Japanese government nationalized the principal railroads in Japan in 1906, the policy was extended to Korea. By the time of Annexation in 1910, the aggregate sum that the Japanese government invested in railroads climbed up to nearly 96 million yen, which covered 1,088 kilometers of roadbeds. After the Annexation, the Government General continued to build railroads, and by 1929, total Japanese investment in public railroads was estimated at more than 300 million yen. It spent more than three-quarters of its investment funds for transportation on railroads prior to 1935.[4] Altogether, by 1942, eight trunk lines had been constructed, and the total capital stock in public railroads was reported to have been more than 1.3 billion yen at cost, averaging about 30 million yen per year. The investment in public railroads probably was more than one-half of total public investment. The public railroad system increased from 1,620 kilometers in 1910 to 4,537 kilometers in 1942, an average of about 100 kilometers a year. In 1945 there were 1,130 train engines, 2,016 passenger cars, and 15,247 cargo trains.[5] Most of the lines in Korea were constructed, owned, and operated by the Japanese government until its withdrawal from Korea in 1945.

In contrast with government efforts, private investment in railroads was not widespread. In 1906, when the Japanese government nationalized the major lines, private businesses had invested far less than 5 million yen in building railroads. However, when private corporations were again allowed and encouraged to build nontrunk spur and freight lines in 1910, they renewed construction and spent 4 million yen in that year. Private railroads included trolley lines, which had increased substantially after they were introduced around the turn of the century. By

1942 their total paid-in capital was about 412 million yen: 279.2 million for private railroads and 132.6 million for private tracks, which included mining railways.[6]

In sum, total capital invested in railroads, both public and private, as of 1942 was 1.71 billion yen, of which 76 percent went into public railroads, 16.3 percent in private railroads, and 7.7 percent in private tracks. More than 200 engines, 752 passenger cars, and 3,990 boxcars were imported from Japan during 1941–1945, while Korea produced more than 20 engines, 99 passenger cars, and 7,000 boxcars during 1930–1944. The total sum invested in railroads was slightly more than the total paid-in capital and reserves of all industrial companies in Korea, nearly one-fifth of all capital stock accumulated under Japanese rule.

Investment in these railroads does not appear to have been particularly profitable, however. Relative to the volume of investment in railways, the net income from them was rather small. It registered less than a 5 percent return as late as in 1938. Reportedly, not only was the net profit minute but even gross revenues were small. Private railroads received annual subsidies of 7.23 million yen as late as 1944, for instance, while public railroads probably also were heavily subsidized.[7] One report indicated that the demand for passenger service and freight transport was insufficient, especially in the early years, and so the railroads were not built for profit. Apparently, military rather than economic considerations governed the construction of Korean railways by the Japanese government.[8]

In addition to railroads, a number of other transportation companies, such as those involved in coastal and inland navigation, trucking, busing, and warehousing, were established in the private sector. The number of such companies increased and made up 10 to 11 percent of all companies in Korea during 1923–1938, while the amount of paid-in capital similarly increased more than 100-fold in twenty-eight years and threefold in fifteen (between 1923 and 1938).[9] However, the paid-in capital of the other transportation and warehouse companies (excluding railroads) increased rather moderately. Consequently, their share of paid-in capital declined from 16.2 percent of the total to 9.1 percent during 1923–1938.

Communications

Following the takeover of Korea, the Japanese government secured control of the country's two main communications networks, telegraph and telephone, under an agreement between the two governments concluded in April 1905. From that time onward, the communications network was a monopoly enterprise in the hands of the Japanese government. After the Annexation, the colonial government invested a large portion of its financial resources in the construction and maintenance of communications networks. It extended the telegraph lines from 5,500 kilometers in 1910 to 9,000 in 1938, while expanding telephone lines from 500 kilometers in 1910 to 13,400 in 1942.[10] It also had a well-established network of post offices and founded a public radio station in 1926. It is difficult to estimate the exact amount of investment in these enterprises, but based on data related to public expenditures, investments in communications appeared to have been substantial, perhaps more than 50 million yen, as their operations were quite capital intensive. This represented about a half percent of all capital accumulated under Japanese rule.

Industry

When Japan took control of the country in 1905, industry (which included manufacturing, gas, and electric power)[11] in Korea was underdeveloped, as shown in chapter 3, comparable to the state of industrial development at the end of the medieval period in Europe. Typical enterprises were of the traditional handicraft and cottage-industry type, which produced mostly the necessities of the traditional economy. Korea's industries included carpentry, blacksmithing, dyeing, brewing, pickling, and canning, all of which were cottage industries found in rural communities. The goods these small operations produced, namely, candles, cotton goods, and soy paste and sauce, were sold mostly in cities.

With the continuing influx of foreigners, adventurers, and speculators hungry for quick profits, small-scale industrial firms sprang up in the early years of Japanese domination. Immigrants and domestic entrepreneurs who duplicated foreign goods renewed existing industries and established new enterprises, manufacturing such items as bricks, tile, coal, metal goods, canned food, tobacco, wood products, bean oil, confections, and leather goods. Only a few "new" industrial establishments could be found among the cottage and handicraft industries in the early years. There were 11 and 27 of these industrial companies in 1906 and 1907 and 123 factories (*kojo*) in 1907. Factories with more than ten employees and motor-powered machinery numbered eighty-nine in 1907.[12] After the Annexation in 1910, the number of industrial companies mushroomed, from 25 in 1910 to 1,541 in 1940, while their paid-in capital (including that of mining) increased from less than 1 million yen to 430.1 million in 1938.[13] Similarly, the number of industrial factories expanded from 151 in 1910 to 14,856 in 1943, while their paid-in capital increased from an insignificant sum in 1907 to 469 million in 1938 and eventually 1.7 billion in 1943.[14] Capital invested in industry made up about 43 percent of all private capital accumulated in 1938.

Manufacturing

The expansion of investment in the industrial sector was notable in manufacturing. The number of manufacturing companies rose from fewer than 5 in 1905 to 1,964 in 1941, while their paid-in capital expanded from 26,000 yen in 1908 to 1.1 million in 1910 and 4.9 million in 1913.[15] After World War I, paid-in capital in manufacturing companies ascended to 19.8 million yen in 1921, 245 million in 1938, and 536.7 million in 1941. The paid-in capital of manufacturing companies thus expanded more than 500-fold between 1910 and 1941, which outpaced the expansion of investment in companies in the country as a whole. As a result of such rapid expansion, the share of paid-in capital of manufacturing companies expanded from less than 10 percent of all companies in 1921 to 22.6 percent in 1939 and probably more than 30 percent after 1941. When investment in unincorporated businesses is added, investment in manufacturing in 1941 probably was more than a fifth (about 22 percent) of the total capital accumulated under Japanese rule.

HEAVY AND CHEMICAL INDUSTRIES Within manufacturing, the sector in which investment expanded the most rapidly under Japanese rule was producer-oriented

TABLE 5.1 Paid-in Capital of Manufacturing Companies Headquartered in Korea in 1938

	In Million Yen			*Percent*					
							Share of Paid-in Capital		
Industries	Japanese	Korean	Total	Japanese	Korean	Total	Japanese	Korean	Share*
*HCI***									
Metal, equipment	23.7	1.9	25.6	92.6	7.4	100.0	11.0	6.3	10.4
Chemical	100.7	3.0	103.7	97.1	2.9	100.0	46.9	9.9	42.3
Subtotal	124.4	4.9	129.3	96.2	3.8	100.0	57.9	16.2	52.8
Light Industries									
Textiles	23.1	6.1	29.2	79.1	20.9	100.0	10.8	20.1	11.9
Food processing	9.6	0.2	9.8	98.0	2.0	100.0	4.5	0.7	4.0
Distillery/Brewing	13.8	12.1	25.9	53.3	46.7	100.0	6.4	39.9	10.6
Milling	9.9	2.5	12.4	79.8	20.2	100.0	4.6	8.3	5.1
Pharmaceutics	0.9	1.7	2.6	34.6	65.4	100.0	0.4	5.6	1.1
Pottery	15.8	0.4	16.2	97.5	2.5	100.0	7.4	1.3	6.6
Wood	10.6	0.6	11.2	94.6	5.4	100.0	4.9	2.0	4.6
Printing	1.5	0.6	2.1	71.4	28.6	100.0	0.7	2.0	0.9
Others	5.2	1.2	6.4	81.3	18.8	100.0	2.4	4.0	2.6
Subtotal	90.4	25.4	115.8	78.1	21.9	100.0	42.1	83.8	47.2
Total	214.8	30.3	245.1	87.6	12.4	100.0	100.0	100.0	100.0

*Each category's share of the total.
**Heavy and chemical industry.

Sources: Based on Himeno 1940: 330 and Kawai and Yoon 1991: 130.

heavy and chemical industries, such as metal, machinery, and fertilizer manufacturing. Investment in this subsector multiplied briskly from a negligible amount in the early years to 16.5 percent of investment in the entire industry in 1930, 28 percent in 1936, and 40 percent in 1939, followed by a slight decrease to 36 percent in 1941.[16] The sector made up 53 percent of paid-in capital of all manufacturing in 1938, as shown in Table 5.1. In all probability, far more than half of capital in manufacturing was in the heavy and chemical industries at the end of Japanese colonial rule.

Unequivocally, the most dramatic expansion of investment in manufacturing was the chemical industry. The number of chemical manufacturers increased from 393 in 1929 to 997 in 1931 and 1,588 in 1938.[17] By 1938 these plants constituted about 23 percent of all manufacturing facilities, and by 1943 there were more than 2,000 chemical plants. The number of chemical companies also increased, from a minuscule number in 1905 to 144 in 1941, while their paid-in capital increased correspondingly. By 1938 paid-in capital was 103.7 million yen, making up 42.3 percent of all capital in manufacturing (see Table 5.1). Companies in the chemical industry thus had the largest amount of paid-in capital of all manufacturing companies in Korea.

As the country became more industrialized, investment in the metal and machinery industries also followed the suit.[18] The number of such companies rose from virtually none in 1923 to 154 in 1938 (10 percent of all manufacturing companies and 3 percent of all companies in Korea). In 1941 there were 234, representing 12 percent of all manufacturing companies. The number of machine and tool manufacturing plants increased from 224 in 1930 to 613 in 1939 and 1,354 in 1943. The metal and machinery industries alone expanded more than tenfold during the 1923–1938 period. The number of plants in the metal industry, which was next in importance to chemical plants, remained fairly constant at about 200 to 300.

Paid-in capital in metal and machinery companies likewise rose from virtually none in 1923 to 25.6 million yen in 1938 and 150.8 million in 1941, representing 10.4 percent of investment in all manufacturing companies in 1938 (see Table 5.1) and 28 percent in 1941. As a result of such rapid expansion, factories in the metal and machinery industries made up 8.8 and 5 percent, respectively, of all companies in Korea in 1938, and they were just behind the chemical industry in terms of their shares of paid-in capital. The machinery and tool industry was the third largest in the manufacturing sector, while the metal industry was fourth.[19]

LIGHT INDUSTRIES Investment in light industry (producing processed food, textiles, earthenwares, wood products, printed materials, and other similar goods) also increased but rather modestly in comparison with the heavy and chemical industries. A small number of companies with meager capital expanded slowly after the Annexation. By 1938 paid-in capital in light industries was 115.8 million yen, and by 1941 the number and paid-in capital of such companies had increased to 1,586 and 192.7 million yen, respectively. Paid-in capital in light industries in 1938 made up less than half (47.2 percent) of the total in manufacturing (see Table 5.1). Among the light industries, the food industry, which comprised food processing, milling, and brewing/distillery, accounted for the largest number—that is, nearly half of all the industrial "establishments"—in Korea in 1929, and increased from 1,958 in 1929 to 2,399 in 1938, an increase of 22.5 percent in 10 years. Likewise, the number of companies in the food industry increased from 122 in 1931—to as many as 273 companies in 1938.[20] Similarly, investment in the food industry rose rapidly under Japanese rule (more rapidly than the increase in overall investment in Korea) and came to represent a significant part of the industrial sector. By 1938 the paid-in capital of food companies had expanded to 48.1 million yen, which constituted nearly an eighth of the total invested in manufacturing companies in that year.

Within the food industry, the most common business was rice milling.[21] The number of rice mills increased from 33 in 1907 to 2,137 in 1923 and about 6,000 in the 1930s, more than all other factories put together. The number increased to 7,142 rice mills and related establishments in 1941. Rice-milling companies had 12.4 million yen in paid-in capital in 1938 and 14.4 million in 1941, each averaging a little over 2,000 yen. The largest amount of corporate investment within the food industry was in brewing and distillery. The amount of paid-in capital in distillery companies was 25.9 million yen in 1938 (see Table 5.1) and 34.1 million in 1941. In 1938 about three-tenths of, or 449, companies in manufacturing (1,544), were distilleries/brewers.

The second largest investment in consumer-oriented light industry was textiles. Even in the early years of Japanese rule, there were a fair number of mechanized factories producing textile goods in Korea.[22] The number of textile companies increased from twenty-four in 1923 to seventy-six in 1938 and ninety-one in 1941. However, the number of textile companies did not increase as much as other manufacturing concerns, and its relative share actually decreased from about 11 percent of the total to 8 percent during the same period. Paid-in capital in textile factories increased from 7.1 million yen in 1917 to 29.2 million in 1938 (Table 5.1) and 47.7 million in 1941. The rapid expansion of the textile industry in Korea in the early years slowed after 1938. It was not only the war that compelled the Japanese administration to increase taxation on businesses but the shortage of cotton and other raw materials, the obligatory addition of other staple fibers to cotton goods, and difficulties in exporting that contributed to the decline of the industry. As a result, paid-in capital in textile companies relative to paid-in capital in manufacturing as a whole decreased from 31.3 percent in 1923 to 20 percent in 1938 and from about 23 percent of the paid-in capital of all companies in 1923 to about 12 percent in 1938 and 8.9 percent in 1941.

Electric Power and Gas

Ever since the gas and electric-power industries were introduced to Korea in the 1890s, they played a major role in the country's industrialization. There were two electric power companies in 1906 and seven gas and electric companies in 1911. To accommodate expanding Japanese needs, especially in manufacturing, the number of electric and gas companies expanded to fifty-nine by 1931. Thereafter, however, many were forced to merge, and the number steadily declined to sixteen in 1938, followed by a slight rise in number to twenty in 1940. As far as paid-in capital in electric and gas companies is concerned, there was a more dramatic rise in them from 5.9 million yen in 1923 to 213.1 million in 1938, a thirty-six-fold jump during the fifteen-year period. The nominal capital of these companies was 553 million yen in 1940.[23] As a result of such rapid expansion in investment, the industry's share of paid-in capital in companies in Korea increased from 3 percent of total capital in companies in 1923 to 19.7 percent in 1938. The entire industry was owned and operated by private interests under government patronage.

Investment in the electric-power industry expanded particularly rapidly. The number of companies generating electricity increased from two in 1906 to sixty-two in 1932, and then consolidated into twenty-one in 1937, while paid-in capital increased from 225,000 yen in 1906 to 34.5 million in 1928. Thereafter, an even more dramatic rise in investment in electric-power facilities ensued. With the support of the Japanese authorities, the Bujeon River Dam and electric-power stations were constructed in 1929, with paid-in capital of 63.1 million and subscribed capital of 85.7 million yen. This expansion was prompted by the increasing energy requirements of chemical factories, textile mills, and food-processing plants. Another large-scale expansion came in 1931, ostensibly for the production of nitrogen fertilizer, which was important in the manufacture of gunpowder as well as fertilizer for agriculture. Paid-in capital jumped up to 100.4 million yen in 1934.[24]

Further expansions commenced when the Japanese government adopted a new policy to meet its war needs. With the support of the colonial government, a private company constructed huge hydroelectric-power plants on the Yalu River and its tributaries in northern Korea. The Supung Dam and its generating stations were constructed in 1937. The total paid-in capital of electric companies jumped to 267.6 million yen in that year and to 337.5 million yen in 1940. This represented a 847-fold increase in a twenty-seven-year period and made up more than one-fifth of the paid-in capital of all companies in Korea, which was nearly equivalent to the paid-in capital of all manufacturing companies combined.[25]

Investment in the gas industry, which operated with coal, was rather modest. Although the first company was established in 1908, in 1938 it reported total paid-in capital of only 3 million yen.[26]

Mining

As noted in chapter 3, one industry that attracted a great deal of investment among Japanese and foreign nationals was mining. Korea was reputed to have rich deposits of minerals, such as gold, silver, iron, aluminum, magnesium, copper, graphite, lead, mercury, tungsten, zinc, coal, and nickel.[27] The number of mines increased 263-fold in a thirty-nine-year period,[28] while the number of mining companies increased to represent 3.5 percent of all companies in Korea in 1931 and 17 percent in 1938. Similarly, paid-in capital in mining corporations multiplied twenty-six-fold under Japanese rule.[29] Gold and silver mining were among the most popular investments. A total of 2,455 out of 2,785 mines in Korea in 1935 were of these precious metals. The number of gold and silver mines increased to 3,664 in 1943.

Agriculture, Forestry, and Fishing

Reliable and comprehensive investment figures in agriculture, which constituted the largest sector of the economy, are scarce, but limited data show that there was some real investment (i.e., investment in resources that increased the ability to produce more output) under Japanese rule. The rise in real investment in agriculture was reflected in such varied forms as increases in the amount of cultivated land, land improvements, the introduction of machinery and modern equipment, and advances in agricultural technology and management, some of which are examined in the following section. As a result of the increase in real investment, substantial gains in agricultural productivity did take place (see chapter 7).

First of all, there were serious efforts to expand the acreage of arable land. Following the takeover of Korea, much virgin land, wetland, and "waste" or uncultivated land was turned into arable land by reclaiming and investing in it, often with the support of the Japanese government. Permits granted for the cultivation of virgin land started out early; for example, in 1909 113 permits were issued and involved 3,995 *jeong* of land valued at 1,980 yen, and permits granted in 1910 numbered 136 and involved 4,732 *jeong* valued at 2,366 yen. Typically, it was Japanese who obtained permits to convert uncultivated into arable land. As of January 1910 a total of 1,800 Japanese had applied for 118,751 *jeong* of land, though only 155 permits were granted for 8,261 *jeong*.

After the Annexation, virgin land was cleared at a faster rate by land-development companies such as the Oriental Development Company and other private firms, such as the Shibuzawa, Ohhashi, and Otaka firms. Gisaku Fujita, for instance, obtained 350 *jeong* of land by filling wetlands with excavated dirt and rocks from mines. As a result of such efforts, the acreage under cultivation expanded. Altogether, the amount of cultivated land in Korea increased probably a little more than 10 percent under Japanese rule, from about 4.35 million *jeong* in 1905 to 4.85 million in 1945.[30] Arable land constituted approximately 20 to 21 percent of the total land area of Korea in 1940.

Second, the maintenance and improvement of land was a major form of agricultural investment in Korea, as it was in all Asian countries. Such investment took several forms, including the construction of dams and irrigation systems and the afforestation of hills and mountains. Most rice farming in Korea required irrigated land, and its expansion was necessary in order to increase rice production. Because Korea was looked upon as a colony that could supply Japan's need for rice, the Japanese government undertook ambitious projects to expand the acreage of irrigated rice paddy.[31] Thus, when a plan to increase rice exports to Japan was being contemplated, local authorities were "advised," or, more accurately, forced, to irrigate land for rice production.[32]

It was reported that acreage in irrigated paddy increased 13.2 percent between 1919 and 1938. By 1938 approximately 1,751,000 *jeong* were being irrigated, an increase of 204,000 *jeong* over 1919 figures. This represents an average annual increase of 10,700 *jeong* of irrigated paddy fields, or an average annual rise of three-fifths of a percent, a considerable achievement. A total of 428 irrigation associations formed after 1908 serviced 305,500 *jeong* of farmland in 1942. Total land under irrigation associations' jurisdiction in 1938 was 1,216,000 *jeong*,[33] nearly 70 percent of all irrigated land in the country (see chapter 6).

In rural Korea productive assets were also created simply by employing one's labor to improve agricultural land and forest and fishery resources. Farmers used their spare time to convert hillsides to irrigated paddy fields, villages reclaimed coastal strips by building dikes. Although no official records are available, these investments were visible.

Third, there were also investments in capital goods such as farm machinery, equipment, new buildings, simple agricultural or industrial tools, and vehicles purchased and/or constructed by a myriad of homeowners using their own labor and earnings. Professor Ban has calculated the fixed capital of Korean farms in terms of horsepower (on the basis of the number of cows). The number of cows increased by 244 percent between 1910 and 1943, an average yearly rise of 2.75 percent. The use of foot and mechanical pumps, improved plows, and winnows increased at rates of 53, 357, 600, and 59 percent, respectively, between 1929 and 1938, while the use of oil increased by 100 percent during the same period.[34] According to Ban's calculations, the working capital increased almost 3 times from 1910 to 1918, 12.3 times by 1925, 42.9 times by 1930, and 134.1 times by 1936. After 1936 it decreased to 51.7 times the 1910 level.

In spite of these advances, farm mechanization in Korea remained slight, and it contributed not much to the increase in agricultural productivity. For instance, only one out of eleven farm households had improved plows and one out of 863 farm families was using mechanical pumps in 1940. The average expenditure on equipment per farmer in Korea was only 1.4 yen (less than US$1) in contrast to $329 spent by American farmers in 1940.[35] Apparently, mechanization was not a significant factor in Korean agriculture. A Japanese historian wrote in 1940 that the agricultural implements used by the Koreans were very primitive.[36] Compared with farmers in Japan in 1931, the amount of capital goods used in Korea was one third of the Japanese per farm, one-fifth per acre, one-half per farm expenditures, and one-half per farm worker.

Fourth, additional real investment was made in agriculture by improving inputs such as seeds, farming methods, and management systems. Between 1905 and 1909, the Korean government and the Residency General invested in and operated model farms to improve the cultivation of rice, sugar beets, sericulture, livestock, cotton, and forest products. The government after the Annexation developed a network of agricultural experiment stations and other technical agencies, which tackled problems of land management, insect control, seeds, and fertilizer. Impressive achievements were recorded in such areas as silkworm breeding. No other public expenditure was more productive than this technical aid to agriculture, as far as it went. Under colonial rule, small-scale but pervasive improvements in agriculture served to raise the physical productivity of labor on farms by 100 percent, despite the lack of mechanization, the persistent shortage of capital, and inefficient forms of land tenure.[37]

The most notable contributing factor to the improvement in agricultural productivity was the use of commercial fertilizers, Their use increased from none in the early 1910s to 8,513 tons in 1915, 48,000 in 1919, 285,800 in 1928, 367,600 in 1938, and 868,025 in 1939.[38] Also increased was the use of improved varieties of seeds, from 22 percent of all seeds sown in 1915 to 84.4 percent in 1932. This more than doubled agricultural production between 1915 and 1940. Other contributing factors were new methods of cultivation, modern techniques, and the improved quality of cocoons and raw silk.

These investments were made by the majority of the farmers (individual proprietors or unincorporated enterprises) with little more than family labor and their own slender resources, possibly supplemented by moneylenders or a bank. In one government official's view, these achievements were made possible by "government leadership, encouragement, and support."[39] Nonetheless, these investments—even such basic changes as the increase in arable land—were typically not included in official statistics and, when they were their value was not accurately ascertained. Unfortunately, no one has estimated the amount of investment in these areas involved in increasing agricultural productivity.

In forestry, three major developments under Japanese rule affected investment. First, the Japanese government "nationalized" large portions of Korean forest land. Before the coming of the Japanese, there were very few state forests, and those that did exist were either in private hands or the hands of the king. After the Annexation, most of the king's lands became the colonial government's property. Also, some private woodland was nationalized because their owners failed to register them under the land law of 1908. It was reported that in this way the Japanese government acquired more than four-fifths of the forests of Korea.[40]

A second development that affected investment in forestry was a 1906 agreement between the Korean and Japanese governments to exploit the northern forests.

The fund to be invested for the harvesting of the forests was fixed at 1.2 million yen, to be shared equally by Japanese and Korean governments. For the purpose of raising revenue, the Korean government agreed to harvest timber along the Yalu and Tumen rivers to meet the lumber demands of Japan. When work began in 1907, with half of the paid-in capital of 600,000 yen, the Forestry Undertakings Station was established.[41] The Japanese government later transferred forest land to Japanese owners not only for the purpose of afforestation but with the aim of harvesting timber for Japan's use.

A third development in forestry occurred in 1937 when the Korea Forestry Development Company (Chosen Ringyo Kaihatsu Kabushiki Kaisha) was organized with subscribed capital of 20 million yen and paid-in capital of 2 million yen. The purpose of the corporation was to manage (mainly harvest) state forests and "help" the owners of private forests. This corporation received 500,000 *jeong* of the best timber land in Korea (about one-fourth of the remaining prime-quality forest) from the Government General for free. Moreover, the company was to receive a subsidy of 7.4 million yen in annual government installments until 1946.[42] These arrangements led to both deforestation and disinvestment, as most harvested lumber was used to meet the war needs of Japan.

There was only one initiative worth noting that might have enhanced investment in forestry, the "reforestation" policy/campaign of the Japanese government during the colonial period. This program restored some of the denuded timberland before 1905, which helped to contain soil erosion. Thus, on the whole, colonial Korea experienced a decline of wealth in forests, as the Japanese seem to have cut more timber than they restocked.

Investment in fishing under Japanese rule started out small, but it expanded steadily. The number of companies engaged in fishing increased from one in 1911 to ninety-six in 1938,[43] while paid-in capital climbed from almost nothing in 1911 to 2.8 million yen in 1931, 14.6 million in 1938, and 19.4 million in 1940. Paid-in capital increased sevenfold between 1931 and 1940.[44] The number of boats and ships engaged in fishing increased from 14,300 in 1911 to 69,300 in 1942. Although investment in the fisheries expanded under Japanese rule, it occupied a relatively small niche and decreased over time relative to the increasing volume of aggregate investment in the country. Paid-in capital in fishing companies constituted only about 5 percent of investment in all companies in Korea in 1923, which decreased to about 1.4 percent by 1938.

Commerce

Commercial activity and investment in Korea under Japanese rule expanded on two fronts. One was the popularization of traditional markets. It was estimated that in 1940 more than 1,400 itinerant markets had traded 400 to 1,000 million yen's worth of goods.[45] On another front, a number of new commercial enterprises emerged. The number of commercial companies increased from 28 in 1906 to 1,896 in 1938, a more than sixty-seven-fold increase, which was a faster rate of growth than that of companies in all other fields. They made up 37 percent of all companies in 1923 and 42.5 percent in 1938. Paid-in capital in commercial companies likewise increased, from 1.3 million yen in 1906 to 89.1 million yen in 1938, after a slowdown in 1931 during the worldwide Great Depression. On the whole, investment in commercial companies showed a less spectacular growth than the rises in sectors such as mining and industry. As a result, the relative value of paid-in capital in commercial companies decreased from 74 percent of the total for all companies in 1911 to 14.5 percent in 1921 and 8.2 percent in 1938.

The extent of investment in commerce by unincorporated businesses is difficult to gauge, but it probably was sizable and increased relatively more than it did in commercial companies, since many new enterprising individuals were attracted to them. Although the number of these establishments increased substantially, their investments were small to modest.

In sum, investment in commerce as a whole, including both incorporated and unincorporated businesses, probably expanded by three to four times under the Japanese colonial administration. It seems reasonable, therefore, to note that aggregate investment in all forms of commerce, including corporations, single proprietorships, and partnerships, probably did not exceed 110 million yen in 1938, representing about 8 percent of total capital accumulated under Japanese rule.

Financial Institutions

Like commerce, the financial institutions expanded under colonial rule, the number increasing from a few in 1904 to 178 in 1938, accompanied by a rapid rise in investment in them. There are no consistent statistics on the paid-in capital of financial institutions, especially those of banks headquartered in Japan and nonbank financial institutions (NBFIs), such as savings-and-loan associations (*mujin kaisha*), insurance companies, and mutual-aid societies. Notwithstanding the lack of reliable data of certain financial institutions, the paid-in capital of banks and NBFIs headquartered in Korea was reported to have increased from approximately 7.2 million yen in 1911 to about 125 million in 1942, a rise of 17.4 times in a thirty-one-year period. The retained earnings of banks and NBFIs were about three-quarters of the amount of their paid-in capital, or approximately 95 million yen, in 1942.[46] Thus, the total paid-in capital and retained earnings of all financial institutions may be estimated at about 220 million yen.

The investment in financial institutions constituted the largest investment in companies in the early years of Japanese rule. However, because of more rapidly expanding investment in other sectors of the economy in Korea, such as public utilities and manufacturing, the share of paid-in capital of financial institutions in relation to total paid-in capital of all companies in Korea declined markedly over time. While paid-in capital of financial institutions was about 43 percent of that invested in all companies in 1921, the percentage decreased more than half to about 20 percent in 1931 and a mere 7 percent in 1939.

Banks

Among the financial institutions of the country, banks that played the dominant role in all financial transactions expanded most rapidly. The number of banks established in Korea increased from two in 1904 to twenty-three in 1920, although it slowly decreased thereafter to five in 1944. Likewise, their paid-in capital increased from 88,000 yen in 1904 to 84.7 million in 1921, constituting 42.4 percent of the paid-in capital of all companies and representing the largest investment in all companies in Korea. Since then, the amount of paid-in capital in banks gradually decreased to 56.4 million yen in 1925, thereafter regaining slowly back to 127.2 million in 1940, but then declined to 107.2 million in 1942. In relation to all companies in Korea, their share of paid-in capital decreased to 19.6 percent in 1931 and 8 percent in 1938.

There were two types of banks established under colonial rule, public and private, and each played a rather unique role, as shown in chapter 6. The public banks were founded under the auspices of the colonial government, while private banks were established by individual shareholders. Public banks included the Bank of Korea, the Industrial Bank of Korea, the Savings Bank, and the Postal Savings System.

The Bank of Korea (Hanguk Eunhaeng) was organized in 1908 under the tutelage of the Japanese financial adviser to the Residency General of Korea, Tanetaro Mekata, and replaced the Daiichi Bank of Japan, which had acted as the central bank of Korea until then. After the Annexation, it was reorganized as the Bank of Korea (Chosen Ginko) in 1911 and acted not only as a central bank that issued currency but also as a commercial bank that made loans and received deposits from the general public. When the Bank of Korea was reorganized in 1909, it had paid-in capital of 2.5 million yen, which gradually inched up to 50 million in 1944, constituting 19 percent of the paid-in capital of all financial institutions in 1942. The bank's retained earnings also increased from 1 million yen in 1927 to 27.1 million in 1944.[47]

The Industrial Bank (Shokusan Ginko) was established in 1918 as one of the two "policy banks" in Korea under the aegis of the colonial government.[48] This was the successor bank of the Agricultural and Industrial Bank System (Nonggong Eunhaeng), which had been launched in 1906 by the Korean government under Japanese adviser Mekata's supervision. The Agricultural and Industrial Bank System, organized as "Korean banks," initially had eleven Agricultural and Industrial Banks assigned to each province. It started out with paid-in capital of 774,110 yen, of which the Korean government subscribed 40 percent (313,540), while the rest of the shares were subscribed by Korean citizens. Later, paid-in capital was increased to 1.46 million yen with nominal capital of 2.6 million. However, as capital shares were limited only to Koreans, who had few savings and lacked knowledge of investing in stock shares and bonds, there apparently was not enough investment in the banks. Consequently, the banks had to obtain a government loan of 756,100 yen, of which 60 percent (450,000 yen) was advanced by the Industrial Bank (Kogyo Ginko) of Japan at no interest.

In 1918, the Agricultural-Industrial Bank System was reorganized as the Industrial Bank, with paid-in capital of 10 million yen and nominal capital of 20 million.[49] Unlike its predecessor, the Agricultural and Industrial Bank System, it was established as a "Japanese bank managed by Japanese." Although there were 300 times more share subscribers in Japan than anticipated, no such enthusiasm was found among Koreans. Paid-in capital was increased to 30 million yen in 1937 (that was 20 percent more than the paid-in capital of the Bank of Korea in the same year) and 52.5 million in 1942. The bank had 24 percent of the paid-in capital of all financial institutions in 1942, while its retained earnings increased from 4 million yen in 1926 to 34.8 million in 1944. The bank was to make long-term loans to individuals, businesses, and public organizations, in addition to conducting ordinary commercial banking business.

The two public banks had the most financial resources among the financial intermediaries.[50] Together they held 43 percent of the paid-in capital of all financial institutions in 1942: 19 percent (40 million yen) for the Bank of Korea and 24 percent (52.5 million yen) for the Industrial Bank; and also about four-fifths of the paid-in capital of all banks headquartered in Korea. Like paid-in capital, the retained earnings of the two public banks accounted for the largest share of the retained earnings of all financial institutions.

The Japanese government also launched the Savings Bank (Tyotiku Ginko) of Korea and the Postal Savings System to collect the savings of ordinary citizens. The Savings Bank was established in 1928, at the urging of the president of the Industrial Bank, Tanetaro Mekata, with paid-in capital of 1.25 million yen, principally to mobilize the savings of middle-class people and nonprofit organizations. The amount of paid-in capital was increased to 3.75 million in 1937.[51] The bank's retained earnings increased from less than half a million yen in 1935 to 4.4 million in 1944. The Postal Savings System (established in Korea in 1880 to serve the Japanese and made available to Koreans after 1910) typically collected the small savings of ordinary and low-income earners.

Like the public banks, private commercial banks expanded from insignificant institutions in the early years of colonial rule to complementary partners providing financial services in the private sector.[52] The number of private commercial banks headquartered in Korea increased from two in 1905 to eleven in 1913. During the World War I economic boom, many small banks (some with capital of as little as 50,000 yen) were established, the number of which then expanded to twenty-one in 1920. After the government policy of consolidating banks was implemented in 1923, the number plunged precipitously, to fourteen in 1928, four in 1941, and two in 1943. The growth of paid-in capital of commercial banks headquartered in Korea followed a rather modest swing. Paid-in capital increased from 7.2 million yen in 1911 to 16.5 million in 1926, a rise of 230 percent in fifteen years. It then declined to 14.7 million yen in 1930 and less than 11 million in 1944, a decline of one-third in eighteen years. The paid-in capital of private banks was much smaller than that of public banks and represented about one-tenth of the paid-in capital of all banks in Korea in 1944. Their retained earnings increased from 3.2 million to 8.7 million yen between 1926 and 1944.

Nonbank Financial Institutions

To serve special financial needs of the country, a number of NBFIs came into being. As was the case with banks, there were two types of NBFIs, semipublic and private. The semipublic NBFIs (GNBFIs) were established principally at the instigation of the government, while private NBFIs (PNBFIs) were established by individual shareholders. The GNBFIs were composed mainly of the Oriental Development Company and the Agricultural Credit Cooperative Societies (Kinyu Kumiai, or credit unions), while PNBFIs included trust companies, savings-and-loan associations, insurance companies, and the like. Their limited banking functions included receiving deposits and/or supplying credit to designated segments of the population, such as farmers, small businesses, and individuals, subject to prescribed regulations.

The Oriental Development Company (Toyo Takushoku Kaisha) was founded by the Japanese parliament as a national policy company in 1906 with the strong support of the Japanese military and opened for business in Korea in 1908.[53] It started with 10 million yen of subscribed capital, of which the Japanese government was to contribute 5 million yen and the Korean government 50,000 *joeng* of land.[54] The paid-in capital of the company gradually increased from 2.5 million yen in 1910 to 62.5 million in 1942. By then the company had retained earnings of 22 million yen. Initially, its main purpose was to settle Japanese immigrants as well as to improve land and agriculture in colonial Korea in order to meet Japan's needs for agricultural products, particularly grain. It recruited and settled Japanese immigrants in Korea; dealt with the purchase, sale, leasing, management, and reclamation of land for agricultural use; and made loans and provided mortgages to settlers. In addition, it invested in fishing and lumbering and financed other projects.

The Agricultural Credit Cooperative Societies were another form of GNBFI established under the auspices of the Japanese government. The credit unions were cooperative credit societies aimed at promoting the welfare of members by using deposits to make loans to them. They also engaged in buying farm machinery, selling farm products, and providing leadership in the agricultural sector. Staff members of the credit unions even taught farmers how to build rice beds, transplant, fertilize, weed, harvest, and store grain. They were organized at the national, provincial, city, and village levels. The number of credit unions increased from 120 in 1910 to 723 in 1939 and then declined to 613 in 1943. So did their paid-in capital, which increased from less than 100,000 yen in 1910 to 15.1 million in 1939 (7.8 yen per member), and 36.2 million in 1944 (18.7 per member). The largest bloc of retained earnings held by the financial institutions was in the credit unions, which had 60.4 million yen in 1944,[55] more than their paid-in capital.

Similar to GNBFIs, PNBFIs expanded from insignificant institutions in the early years to useful providers of financial services in the private sector.[56] A small number of PNBFIs in the early years sharply expanded since the 1920s, when many private commercial banks were forced to merge or close under the onus of the banking laws of 1923 and 1928. They mushroomed from twenty-one in 1923 to ninety-five in 1938. Reportedly, there were forty-nine insurance companies in 1932. There are no consistent or comprehensive statistics on the paid-in capital of PNBFIs, but it seems to have increased moderately from about 4 million yen in 1923 to 15 million in 1938, which represented about 5 percent of the paid-in capital of all financial institutions. One PNBFI, the Korea Trust Company, was organized in 1932 with a subscribed capital of 2 million yen, which had increased to 2.5 million by 1937. The paid-in capital of a large number of savings-and-loan associations, the mutual-aid credit companies, increased from 2.6 million yen in 1926 to 12.7 million in 1939. It then decreased to 10.9 million in 1940, equal to that of the private commercial banks. The retained earnings of NBFIs are not known, but it is likely that they were small.

It is clear from the above examination that the bulk of investment in financial institutions was in public banks and GNBFIs. Their paid-in capital in 1939 was nearly 90 percent of the total in all financial institutions headquartered in Korea, while the paid-in capital of private banks had less than 10 percent of the paid-in capital of all financial institutions[57] and the PNBFIs had even an insignificant amount. All of these public financial institutions (the public banks and GNBFIs), which played a very important role in capital formation (examined in chapter 6) were established and largely directed by the Japanese government. In most developed countries, financial institutions typically emerged when attitudes conducive to lending other than face-to-face developed and when technical progress and "modern" economic institutions became well established in the country.[58] In Korea however, financial institutions did not "automatically" emerge when they were needed; they were "planted" by the government to meet what the colonialists thought were the needs of the economy at that time.

Miscellaneous Sectors

No comprehensive statistical data are available on investment in the so-called miscellaneous sectors, which comprised mostly service industries. They included construction, services, traditional medicine and drugs, printing, entertainment facilities, restaurants, hotels, and hospitals in the private sector. Nonetheless, they exhibited a similar pattern of increasing investment under Japanese rule. The number of companies in this category in 1938 was 740, representing about 14 percent of all companies in Korea, and their paid-in capital was 85.9 million yen, which constituted 7.9 percent of the paid-in capital of all companies in Korea.

SECTORAL INVESTMENT BY NATIONALITY

Investment in Korea under Japanese rule varied among different sectors of the economy, as examined in the previous section, but also among diverse economic entities. For example, investment activity differed among the various nationalities (namely, Japanese, non-Japanese foreigners, and Koreans) and between the public and private sectors. The variations are detected not only with regard to the volume of investment in different economic sectors but also with the nature of investment, such as scale, capital, and technological intensity, and the types of goods produced in manufacturing. They are examined here.

The volume of investment by different economic entities varied clearly in all sectors of the economy without any exception. As shown in the sections that follow, Japanese investment, unquestionably, dominated all sectors of the economy, especially those closely related to Japan's needs. The only difference among sectors is the matter of degree of Japanese dominance, and in some sectors it was greater than others. The greatest effort in Japanese investment was found in transportation, electric power, heavy industrial goods and chemical manufacturing, and mining.

Transportation

In addition to public investment, such as railroads, Japanese private investment dominated the private transport industry from the beginning of its colonial rule. The number of Japanese companies in transportation increased from 14 in 1913 to 274 in 1938. It is impossible to estimate the exact amount in the later years, but according to one estimate, Japanese private companies headquartered in Korea alone in the nonrailroad and warehouse industries invested 90.9 million yen in 1938, or 92.4 percent of total investment in companies in the industry.[59] Allowing for investment in unincorporated businesses, the aggregate capital accumulation in all forms of transportation other than public railroads by Japanese nationals was about 93 percent of the industry and 9 percent of all capital accumulated in the private sector under Japanese rule. As noted earlier in this chapter, all investment in private railroads was of Japanese, and none was Korean.

The Japanese were especially active in investing in coastal and inland navigation and monopolized the industry. Under an agreement between the Korean and Japanese governments, reached in August 1905, Japanese vessels were at liberty to navigate the coasts and inland waters of Korea for the purpose of trade. Japanese shipowners were also free to lease land for the purpose of building warehouses at the ports where their vessels called. In 1906 there were four Japanese transportation companies, including those headquartered in Japan, with 34.4 million yen of subscribed capital.[60] Paid-in capital in shipping companies, including those headquartered in Japan, was 40.3 million yen in 1908. Japanese eventually came to monopolize the shipping industry in Korea.

Koreans showed some interest in transportation. The number of Korean transport companies increased from 2 in 1913 to 18 in 1923 and 258 in 1938. Likewise, paid-in capital of Korean companies in motor vehicles, water transport, and warehouses increased from 400,000 yen in 1923 to 6.7 million in 1938, constituting 11 and 20 percent of the paid-in capital of all Korean companies, respectively.[61] Although this field became increasingly attractive to Koreans, their investment in the transportation industry as a whole was relatively minor. Korean investment in transportation and warehouse businesses was only about 8 percent of paid-in capital in transportation companies headquartered in Korea, 7.4 percent of the Japanese investment in the sector, and about 6 percent of paid-in capital of all Korean companies in 1938.

Industry

Japanese investment in the industry was launched very modestly in the early years, but it gradually came to dominate the sector. In 1906 there were only 3 Japanese industrial companies and 223 Japanese "industrial establishments" (*kogyo kigyo*) in Korea. The number of industrial companies increased to 25 in 1913. Many new medium-sized and large industrial companies joined their ranks after World War I, thus increasing the number to 480 in 1929 and approximately 1,300 in 1939,[62] which represented 52.1 percent of all companies in industry and commerce. While the number of Japanese industrial companies represented more than half of all those in industry and commerce, Japanese paid-in capital came to dominate even more prominently, representing a staggering 87.6 percent of such capital in industrial companies headquartered in Korea in 1938 and 88.5 percent in 1940. Similar increases have been noted for industrial factories.

Japanese also invested in joint-venture companies, most of which were owned and operated with Koreans (one or two ventures were between Japanese and Westerners). Likewise, there was investment in single proprietorships. These small-scale Japanese enterprises were quite common in the manufacturing of confectioneries, tile, and food. The amount of capital in Japanese hands in the entire industrial sector was reported to have been about 93 percent of the total in 1938 (Table 4.1).[63]

In comparison with the Japanese, the investment of "foreigners" (non-Japanese) in the industrial sector was minuscule. There were only two foreign-owned factories in 1907, eight in 1913, and thirteen in 1917. After World War I, the "foreign" industrial sector seems to have expanded somewhat—the number of factories have increased to fifty by 1931. However, after 1931 it showed a rapid decline, and by 1939 it had vanished altogether. The volume of foreign investment in the industrial sector was also small and inconsequential. One estimate indicated that a negligible amount of investment, 200,000 yen, was made by other foreigners in industrial companies in the early 1900s. According to the Residency General's statistics, foreign-owned factories in 1907 possessed about 2 million yen (jointly with Japanese investors) in subscribed capital. Although no reliable figure is available, the total capital of foreign companies could not have been much more than 2 million yen in 1913. Foreign paid-in capital then increased to 3.1 million yen in 1917 and somewhat more after World War I, reaching a peak of 10 million yen in 1931. Thereafter, it showed a steady decline, and by 1939 it was down to 200,000 yen.[64]

Following in the footsteps of the Japanese, the Koreans established their own industrial firms, in which their investment multiplied over time. There were only 8 Korean industrial companies in 1913, but when the incorporation movement gained momentum after the World War I economic boom, the number shot up to 202 in 1923 and 445 in 1931. When the number reached 740 in 1938, there were almost as many Korean industrial companies (48 percent of the total) as Japanese.[65] This was almost a 100-fold expansion in twenty years. Although Korean factories experienced similar growth, in comparison with that of the Japanese their expansion was even more rapid.[66]

The amount of paid-in capital in Korean-held industrial companies also increased, from 71,000 yen in 1907 to 722,632 in 1911, 7.8 million in 1921, and 30.2 million in 1938. Korean investment in the industrial sector expanded relatively more than in other fields. Consequently, the share of Korean investment in industrial companies increased from near zero in 1905 to 10.7 percent of Korean investment in all companies in 1923, 20.5 percent in 1931, and 30.2 percent in 1939.[67] These increases represented a considerable accomplishment. Nonetheless,

Korean investment in the industrial sector remained relatively small. It constituted only about 6.8 percent of all investment in industry in the country and about 7.3 percent of that of the Japanese in 1938.[68]

In a similar manner, Koreans also started single proprietorships and cottage industries with small investment. Likewise, they also invested in joint-venture companies owned and operated with Japanese. In sum, total investment by Koreans in all industrial firms accounted for roughly 7.2 percent of that of Japanese in 1938.

The Koreans who were most responsible for investing in the industrial sector in the early years were a few former government officials (who confined their role to financing rather than running businesses in the early years) and wealthy merchants. Later, some traditional landlords, merchants, and artisans began to invest in industry as well; and some former government officials and/or *yangban* actually began managing such enterprises themselves in later years. However, most wealthy Korean landlords who possessed the means were not interested in investing in businesses or in "stooping so low as to become businessmen."[69]

Electric and Gas

Investment in the electric and gas industry was monopolized by the Japanese. Although four electric power plants were owned and operated by Koreans (as compared with fourteen Japanese owned) in the early years of the colony, they were relatively insignificant. Koreans continued to own three electric and gas companies in 1913, but only one remained in 1937, at which time the last Korean electric company closed down. The gas industry, too, was dominated by the Japanese. Foreign investment in the industry, which began in 1898,[70] ceased to exist after the Annexation in 1910. Koreans did invest some funds in gas in the early years of the colony, but it is clear that the gas and electric industries in Korea were developed, owned, and operated primarily by the Japanese.

Manufacturing

Manufacturing, too, Japanese investment came to dominate from the beginning. The number of Japanese factories expanded from 79 in 1908 to 1,150 in 1941, while Japanese-owned and -operated manufacturing businesses, including household industries, numbered 2,144 in 1938. In addition, there were 19 Japanese manufacturing companies in Korea headquartered in Japan in 1939. Even faster expansion was seen in their paid-in and subscribed capitals in manufacturing companies in Korea. There were only 1.3 million and 1.78 million yen, respectively, in 1906. After the Annexation, Japanese investment in manufacturing companies soared to 9.2 million yen in 1911 and 33.7 million in 1917. Especially after World War I, paid-in capital in Japanese manufacturing companies quickly expanded to 68.3 million yen in 1930, 214.8 million in 1938 (that came to represent 87.6 percent of the total; see Table 5.1), and 487.8 million in 1941. In addition, Japanese manufacturing companies headquartered in Japan had 117.8 million yen of paid-in capital in Korea in 1939.[71]

Having seen the Japanese invest in modern industry and produce new commodities, Korean entrepreneurs slowly began to invest in manufacturing as well.

Korean-owned and -operated manufacturing businesses (including some household industries) increased from a negligible number in 1905 to 2,652 in 1938, exceeding that of the Japanese (2,144). Mills that cleaned and hulled grain with machinery attracted the most interest among Korean investors. However, the amount of their investment in manufacturing was relatively small, only about 14.3 percent of that of the Japanese in 1938 and 8 percent in 1941.[72] Before 1938, only about a third of all "plants" owned by Koreans (employing 18 percent of all manufacturing workers) produced 16.3 percent of manufacturing output.

In addition to the private investment by Japanese and Koreans examined above, the government also invested in and operated a number of manufacturing plants.[73] It established enterprises primarily for the purpose of controlling output and deriving revenue, although some were established during the protectorate to augment the inadequate supply of goods and services in the private sector. One investment undertaken by the Korean government before the Annexation but under Japanese control was earthenware manufacturing. When the government decided to construct substantial brick buildings, the supply of domestic bricks was found to be inadequate. Because imported bricks were too expensive, it decided to manufacture them itself by investing 234,000 yen in a brick factory, which began operating in 1907 and produced 30,000 bricks a day. The cost of the bricks produced at this plant was reported to have been much less than that of imported bricks. As a branch of this enterprise, a factory making earthen drain pipes and tiles, as well as bricks, was added in the same year. After the Annexation, these factories were transferred to the Justice Department to be operated by the prison system. Similarly, the Printing Bureau was established to meet the printing needs of the government.

After 1910 the colonial government was a major entrepreneur in the peninsula. Their investment included some large undertakings—for instance, a number of public-monopoly enterprises as a means of deriving revenue and controlling production and distribution of products such as salt, cigarettes, tobacco, ginseng, and opium.[74] After the takeover of the country, the colonial government expanded these enterprises and also continued to operate a printing company to publish textbooks. The revenues and expenditures of public enterprises increased from 11.9 million yen in 1911 to 235 million in 1937. No data on government investment in these manufacturing enterprises are available, but based on their scale, their relative importance, the nature of their manufacturing technology, and the value of their output, the total value of the investment in government manufacturing enterprises in 1938 was not insignificant.

In spite of its active involvement, the government share of investment in manufacturing on the whole was relatively small and declined over time. Statistical data are scanty for the early years of Japanese rule, but as the Korean economy expanded and more firms with larger volume of investment came to be owned and operated by private entrepreneurs, the importance of public investment in manufacturing clearly declined over time. In 1936, when about 82 percent of the factories in the heavy and chemical industries were operated by private businesses and 17 percent by household industries, the government operated only 1.5 percent of them. When business ownership expanded to 92.3 percent (and 7.1 percent by the household operations) in 1939, the share of government enterprises declined to

0.6 percent. In light industries, while private ownership increased from 51.3 percent in 1936 to 92.3 percent in 1939, government operations decreased from 10 to 8.4 percent. Household operations also decreased during that period, from 38.7 percent in 1936 to 35 percent.

It seems reasonable, therefore, to note that, except for investments for revenue and control purposes, the Government General did not invest in new fields of manufacturing that private businesses ordinarily dominated. The phase of government entrepreneurship thus passed rather quickly, and government investment itself was a small part of the total, and the main goal of government did not lie in taking over the manufacturing sector. This was in contrast to the experience in Japan in the early years of the Meiji Restoration, when the Japanese government vigorously engaged in modernization of the manufacturing industry.

Mining

From the beginning the most aggressive investors in mining in Korea were the Japanese, and their investment reigned this sector.[75] The number of Japanese-operated mines was an overwhelming 77.2 percent of the total in 1907 and about 85 percent (of 368 mines) in 1909. Their preponderance magnified after the Japanese Annexation of Korea, and mining became increasingly more important and profitable during and after World War I. The number of mine permits granted to and operated by Japanese was about two-thirds to twice that of the Koreans. The Japanese owned and operated about four-fifths of all mining companies in Korea in 1920 and a little more than half in 1937.[76]

By 1938, mining companies owned and operated by the Japanese had paid-in capital of 171.1 million yen, which represented about 93 percent of the total paid-in capital in mining companies and about 17 percent of paid-in capital in all corporations in Korea. Japanese companies headquartered in Korea alone invested a total of 168.4 million yen in mining in 1939, which represented 87.5 percent of all paid-in capital in mining companies headquartered in Korea. Also active in mining were companies headquartered in Japan. According to the Bank of Korea, about one-quarter of all capital invested by companies headquartered in Japan was in mining. These firms, mostly *zaibatsu*, invested huge sums, especially in gold mines.

Altogether, Japanese capital invested in mining, including external financing, was 765.7 million yen in 1945, which represented about 95 percent of the total capital in all mining companies in that year.[77] Japanese domination was also shown in terms of its increasing share of mineral output. Following the Annexation, the value of Japanese mining output was about one-quarter of the total until 1917 and about two-fifths after 1918. Thereafter, Japanese mines accounted for about three-quarters of total mineral output between 1918 and 1932, 82 percent in 1933, about 90 percent in 1936, and more than 90 percent in the early 1940s. During the entire colonial period, Japanese mines produced about three-quarters of the total mining output of the country.

Other non-Japanese foreigners invested the largest amount of their capital in mining and occupied an important position in the years prior to 1917. Some of the most productive mineral resources were exploited by them under concessions granted by the Korean king, as noted in chapter 3. The mines owned and operated by foreign companies other than Japanese increased from eight in 1906 to twenty in 1907, thirty-one in 1909, and forty-one in 1910.[78] Four such companies were reputed to have had total capital of $6.1 million in 1913. The production of minerals by Western operators accounted for between 50 and 75 percent of total mining output until 1917.[79]

After 1917, the prominence of foreign mining in Korea gradually waned. A law passed by the Japanese government in 1916 forbade the granting of additional mining permits to "foreigners." By means of this and other measures intended to obstruct foreign investment, foreign mining enterprises were gradually forced out of Korea. Their numbers dwindled to eleven in 1921 and two in 1931. Paid-in capital of Western companies decreased to 8.7 million yen in two mines in 1931 and to 2.7 million yen in 1939. Likewise, their share of minerals excavated gradually decreased to 20 to 25 percent of the total between 1918 and 1924 and about 14 percent by 1928, when total mineral production in Korea was valued at about 25 million yen. Foreign mine operators extracted 3.7 million yen's worth of minerals in 1932, a little less than 10 percent of total mining production. By 1941 all foreign mining enterprises had been either bought out by the Japanese or forced out of Korea. The major foreign investors were Westerners, namely, American, English, German, Italian, and French.

Encouraged by foreign and Japanese investments, Koreans were also drawn into mining. Prior to the Annexation, with the object of establishing a model coal mine and increasing the nation's revenues, the Korean government assumed complete control of the Pyongyang coal mines and operated them.[80] In the ensuing years, the number of private Korean mines and their paid-in capital expanded quickly. Only four mining permits were granted to Koreans in 1906, which represented about 13 percent of all mining companies in Korea, but it was increased to about 20 percent in 1927 and 47.5 percent in 1937 and then fell to 31 percent in 1945. The number of Korean-owned mines increased to 3,512 in 1937,[81] which was almost equal in number to that of the Japanese. Due to native landownership, Korean participation in mining was greater than that in the industrial sector.

Paid-in capital of Korean-owned mining companies likewise increased, but slowly, from about 10,000 yen in 1905 to 12.45 million (in 29 companies) in 1938.[82] In spite of the fact that Korean mining activity expanded, its importance in the industry, however, was relatively minor. The paid-in capital of Korean-owned mining companies in 1938 was only 7.3 percent of that of the Japanese and less than 5.2 percent of the paid-in capital of all mining companies in 1945. Also, the production of minerals by Korean-owned companies contributed relatively little, although it increased over time. The Korean share of mining taxes ranged between 6.1 and 6.8 percent during 1907 and 1920, but the extraction of minerals by Korean-owned companies contributed less than 10 percent prior to 1920. However, the Koreans' share gradually increased from less than 10 percent in 1932 to 10.5 percent in 1936.[83]

There seem to have been at least two reasons for the relatively small amount of investment in mining by Koreans. First, the Japanese government appears to have erected barriers to Korean investment in mining: some of their applications for mining permits did not receive approval. The government also organized a special corporation to activate dormant mines in 1939, and it took over many Korean-owned enterprises. In addition, among those who began mining, many had to either shut down or sell out to big Japanese corporations. In this way, powerful firms, such as the Mitsubishi and Sumitomo *zaibatsu,* were able to secure control of nearly the entire mining industry in Korea toward the end of colonial rule.[84] Second, of the few who obtained permits, a significant number lacked sufficient capital to launch mineral exploration.

Agriculture and Fishing

As examined in chapter 3, from the time of their arrival in Korea, the Japanese were continually attracted to acquire land,[85] and their landholding increased over time. The Japanese financial investment in land may be estimated as much as 200 million yen in 1938. However, it is interesting and perhaps significant to note that their share of such investment relative to both their investment in agriculture and total investment in Korea decreased over time. Japanese financial investment in agriculture relative to their total investment in Korea declined over time and occupied a relatively small portion. Paid-in capital of Japanese-owned agricultural companies in Korea decreased from about 67 percent of the total Japanese investment before 1905 to 6.4 percent in 1943. Also, paid-in capital in Japanese agricultural and forestry corporations was reported to have been 94.5 percent of total capital stock invested in land (by both Japanese and Korean) in 1931 (the rest, 5.5 percent, being Korean), but the percentage dropped to 81.9 percent in 1939. There was virtually no other foreign (non-Japanese) investment in agriculture during the colonial period.

In contrast to the relative decline in the share of Japanese investment in land over time, the number and amount of investment in Korean companies in the agricultural sector actually increased relative to the private and total investments in Korea. Traditionally, Koreans considered land more valuable than other forms of assets, as is the case in traditional society in most Asian countries. Holding a large tract of land not only gave a family a handsome income, it also provided security and prestige. Most, however, did not invest in land in order to improve its productivity. Some wealthy and middle-income Koreans followed suit and formed agricultural companies. As early as 1913 one Korean company and one jointly owned with Japanese were established, and the number of Korean companies in the agricultural sector increased thereafter.[86] Between 1921 and 1927 the number of Korean agricultural companies increased by 12 percent, and by 1938 there were eighty-six Korean companies in agriculture. Also, the size of Korean landholdings between 1921 and 1927 grew by 7 percent.

Similarly, paid-in capital in Korean agricultural companies increased from 2 million yen in 1923 to 13.5 million in 1938, which represented about 11 percent of Korean investment in all companies.[87] In contrast to the relative decline in the share of Japanese investment in land over time, paid-in capital in Korean agricultural companies increased from about 5.5 percent of all investment in agriculture in 1931 to 18.1 percent in 1939 and 20.7 percent in 1942. Although the paid-in capital of Korean agricultural companies was small relative to the nation's aggregate investment and decreased over time, as investment of companies in other sectors increased faster, the paid-in capital of the Korean-owned companies in agriculture was as much as 54 percent of that of the Japanese investment in 1942.

These findings lead us to observe two meaningful developments in investment in agriculture. On the one hand, while the sum of Japanese investment in land increased substantially, their share relative to total Japanese investment in Korea in land shrank over time. On the other hand, both the amount and share of Korean investment in land relative to total Korean investment increased over time.[88] These developments indicate that while the Japanese investment in land did not increase as much as their investment in other sectors, Korean investment in land did increase more than in other sectors. Therefore, it can be inferred that while the Japanese were more interested in investing in industry, the Koreans were less interested in investing in sectors other than land.

Just as they dominated all other industries, Japanese also dominated fishing.[89] Reportedly, there were two Japanese corporations with subscribed capital of 200,000 yen and paid-in capital of 85,000 yen as early as 1906. By 1938, the number had increased to 69 Japanese companies with paid-in capital of 13.7 million yen, which represented 93.7 percent of total paid-in capital in the fishing industry in Korea. In other words, Japanese fishing companies represented 72 percent of all fishing companies in Korea and had 94 percent of the paid-in capital in the industry. Twenty-seven Korean companies, representing 28 percent of all fishing companies in Korea, had 900,000 yen in paid-in capital in 1938, which represented 6.3 percent of paid-in capital in the industry as a whole. The number of Korean fishing companies declined toward the end of Japanese rule.

Commerce/Trade

Outside of traditional commerce, that is, the itinerant market, the Japanese dominated Korean commerce from the very beginning. Upon gaining a secure foothold in the country, they "invaded" the future colony in droves, as noted earlier. With their coming, Japanese investment in trade in Korea also expanded rapidly. Twenty-eight Japanese commercial "companies" constituted two-thirds of all Japanese companies in Korea in 1906, with 1.3 million yen in paid-in capital.[90] The number increased to 61 (79 percent of total companies in commerce) in 1909. After the Annexation, the Japanese continued to invest in this line of business, gaining even greater momentum after 1920. The number of Japanese commercial businesses expanded to 75 in 1923 and about 1,050 in 1938, making up 55.4 percent of the total in the country. In 1940 more than 28 percent of the Japanese in Korea were engaged in commerce, more than the Koreans.

Paid-in capital in Japanese commercial companies increased likewise. It grew from 1.3 million yen in 1906 to 58.6 million in 1931, representing 87.6 percent of total paid-in capital in commerce.[91] After 1931, however, Japanese investment in commercial companies slowed down considerably. In subsequent years, their paid-in capital increased only modestly, to 66.8 million yen in 1938, after which time their investment in commerce actually decreased to 65.7 million yen in 1939. As a consequence, their share of paid-in capital declined to 73.7 percent of the total for companies in commerce in 1938 and 64.4 percent in 1939. There are no statistics on the paid-in capital of commercial companies headquartered in Japan, but it appears to have been rather small in volume.

Japanese investment in commerce by unincorporated businesses, mostly in retail trade catering chiefly to Japanese customers, probably was modest. No data are available on the nationality of merchants, but retail trade attracted a sizable interest among Japanese, especially in urban areas. The Japanese dominated the field in terms of the volume of business conducted throughout the entire colonial period. Based on these data, it seems reasonable to estimate that aggregate investment in commerce by the Japanese (including single proprietorships, partnerships, and companies) was roughly about 100 million yen in 1938.

Foreign investment in commerce, though larger than most other fields, was negligible, especially toward the end of colonial rule. One foreign business was involved in the wholesaling and retailing of kerosene, and two operated foreign trade companies in the early years of Japanese rule. Foreign commerce gradually declined and totally withdrew by the end of colonial rule.

Unlike in the industrial sector, Korean investment in commerce under Japanese administration was more substantial in relation to Korean investments in other fields and also relative to Japanese investments in commerce. Other than traditional businesses, such as itinerant peddling and wholesaling, which supplied handicraft goods and grain for local needs, there was virtually no new Korean investment in commerce in the traditional economy. However, Korean investors had accepted new means of conducting daily business during the transitional period, and commerce, especially the retail trade, gained much popularity among Korean investors under Japanese rule. There appear to have been more Korean than Japanese retail outlets. The trade was easy to enter into in terms of knowledge and the required amount of capital funds, and it demanded no new technology. Commercial undertakings also offered minimal legal and political constraints on investors, for business was not an activity closely identified, in their view, with the aggressor Japan. Therefore, the Korean presence in commerce was more pervasive than in any other occupation outside of farming from the moment the country was opened to the outside world. Even commoners were able to make a profit and accumulate considerable amounts of capital in their new commercial ventures.

Korean investment in commerce expanded markedly after 1905. By 1913 17 Korean companies were in commerce, 21 percent of the total.[92] The number of companies rose to 75 in 1923 and 846 in 1938, representing higher rate of growth than that of Korean companies in other fields. The percentage of Korean companies in commerce compared with all Korean companies rose from 37 percent in 1923 to 42.5 percent in 1938, making commerce the most popular of all Korean business activities under Japanese rule outside of farming. The percentage of Korean commercial companies increased to 64.4 percent in 1939, a greater increase than for Japanese companies. Similarly, the paid-in capital of Korean commercial companies increased from 7 million yen in 1923 to 8.3 million in 1931 and 23.4 million in 1938–1939. This represents a threefold increase in paid-in capital during the sixteen-year period and about 26 percent of the paid-in capital of all commercial companies headquartered in Korea. The paid-in capital of commercial companies in

Korean hands expanded at approximately the same pace as the growth of companies in all fields during the colonial period.

No figures are available, but Korean investments in unincorporated commercial businesses probably were substantial and increased more than in other areas of business, as was the case with the growth in the number of Korean commercial companies. The aggregate amount of Korean investment in commerce in 1939 may be estimated to have been as much as 40 million yen or nearly one-third of the total investment in commerce by both Japanese and Koreans.[93]

Financial Institutions

The banking business attracted equally the interest of Japanese and Koreans in the early years, and their contributions to investment in commercial banks and NBFIs were skewed surprisingly away from Japanese during most of the period under colonial rule. When Japan took control of Korea in 1905, Japanese already had two private branch banks in the country with about 100,000 yen of paid-in capital. The number of Japanese banks increased to three in 1906 and six in 1907, with paid-in capital of about 600,000 yen. Although the number of Japanese commercial banks decreased to three in 1933 and one in 1938, their paid-in capital increased to about 9 million yen in 1923 and then declined to 5 million yen in 1943.[94]

Koreans, who had been attracted to banking since their earliest contact with foreigners, followed an investment pattern similar to that of the Japanese but with greater enthusiasm. Before 1906 six commercial banks were organized by Koreans.[95] Although three failed, the remaining three operated with the reported total paid-in capital of 325,000 yen in 1909, averaging a little more than 100,000 yen per bank. The number of Korean banks increased to nine in 1921, of which three had more than 5 million yen in capital. By 1923 the number of Korean-owned commercial banks reached twelve, double that of the Japanese, with 11.9 million yen in paid-in capital, a third larger than the Japanese. Then the number plummeted to one after 1923, with a paid-in capital of 6 million yen, as was the case with Japanese banks, in 1943. Most of these Korean banks were organized and established by *yangban* (including pensioned-off government officials), landlords, wealthy or "giant" merchants, and other well-to-do Koreans. Four Korean-Japanese joint banks were also operated in 1912–1913.

A similar, but somewhat different, situation seems to have developed in the PNBFIs. A few large trust companies and insurance companies in the hands of Japanese emerged, while Koreans organized countless small savings-and-loan associations, and mutual-aid societies sprang up. Likewise, Japanese PNBFIs had sizable paid-in capital and retained earnings in their organizations and expanded over time, while Korean PNBFIs were numerous but had relatively small amounts of funds and decreased over time. The paid-in capital of Japanese companies (76.7 million yen) made up 88.4 percent of the total in 1938, while Korean investment in financial institutions was less than 13 percent of that of the Japanese in the same year.[96] In 1939 the paid-in capital of Korean-owned banks and PNBFIs was 10.2 million and represented 11.7 percent of the total paid-in capital of all financial institutions headquartered in Korea.

When all these financial institutions, namely, banks and NBFIs, are included, Japanese clearly dominated practically all the financial institutions and controlled nearly 90 percent of financial resources in the country. Clearly, all public banks and GNBFIs were in the hands of Japanese. In the realm of commercial banks, Koreans were able to enjoy their financial power during the interwar period, but their financial weight was reduced substantially when only one bank remained and when it came under government control in the later years. As far as NBFIs were concerned, the number of financial companies owned and operated by Koreans expanded during the interwar years but eventually decreased from 16 percent of all companies in 1923 to less than 5 percent in 1938. Their share of paid-in capital decreased even more drastically, from 40 percent of total paid-in capital in companies to about 8 percent during the period between 1910 and 1943. Thus, it is clear that the control of financial institutions was mostly in the hands of the Japanese.

Miscellaneous Sectors

Japanese investment was also prominent, but less so, in the miscellaneous-businesses sector. In 1938 Japanese companies headquartered in Korea invested 61.2 million yen in the miscellaneous sector,[97] which made up about 71.4 percent of the total funds invested in the sector. The number of Korean companies in the miscellaneous sector in both 1923 and 1938 constituted approximately 5 to 6 percent of all companies, while paid-in capital in it was 28.6 percent (24.6 million yen) of the total and 2.3 percent of that of all companies in 1938. Korean share of investment in this sector, thus, was relatively larger than in all others and it continued to play a significant role in this sector of the economy. Korean investment in this category made up as much as a fifth of their paid-in capital in all companies and was only 60 percent less than Japanese capital in the field.

There were a number of areas in miscellaneous light industries that Koreans made substantial investments in, compared with investments in those areas by the Japanese, although their investment was small in volume and decreased absolutely and relatively over time. Five areas in the miscellaneous sector are worth noting: real estate, printing, traditional papermaking, traditional/oriental pharmaceuticals, and construction. Particularly significant in this sector was real estate, which involved the transaction of Korean-owned property. The number of Korean-owned companies constituted 34.7 percent of the total, while their paid-in capital was 40.6 percent of the total.[98] The Koreans also occupied a prominent position in the traditional paper industry. There were already three mechanized printing factories in 1907, representing 43 percent of all factories in the industry. They attracted about 2 percent of all company investments in 1938. Similarly, there were fifteen paper manufacturing plants in 1907, and investment in them increased to about 1 percent of all company investments in 1938.

Another exception to the general pattern of Korean investment being small compared to that of the Japanese was the pharmaceutical industry, which primarily produced traditional products such as herbal medicines. Koreans dominated the production of traditional medicines and drugs. The number of Korean pharmaceutical companies was 178, and 116 percent of that of the Japanese in 1939 and

1941, respectively. Korean investment in pharmaceutical companies in 1938 was nearly two-thirds more (1.7 million yen) than the Japanese (0.9 million) and accounted for nearly 50 percent of all paid-in capital of companies in the industry in 1941. Similarly, the paid-in capital of Korean-owned pharmaceutical businesses on the whole was 113.4 percent that of the Japanese. Also, Korean-owned businesses were about 138 percent larger in scale than those of Japanese in 1938. However, the share of paid-in capital in all miscellaneous industries decreased from 23.5 percent of Korean-owned manufacturing companies in 1923 to 2.1 percent in 1938.[99]

NATURE OF SECTORAL INVESTMENT BY NATIONALITY

Another difference in investment between Japanese and Koreans was the nature of investment, namely, the scale, capital and technology intensities, and the types of goods produced in manufacturing in which investment was made.

Scale of Investment

The scale of investment in businesses varied in all sectors of the economy, but the difference in the scale of investment between the Japanese and Koreans was clearly evident in almost all sectors. Japanese investment in all sectors was in fairly large corporations for the most part, while Korean investment was typically small and in small businesses. This characteristic could be seen in transportation (e.g., railroads and shipping) electric power and gas, manufacturing (e.g., textiles and chemicals) mining, banking, and even agriculture. In the case of rice milling, the scale of the Japanese companies on the average was 5.3 times larger than that of the Koreans. Koreans typically invested in single proprietorships and cottage industries. The small-scale enterprises dominated the manufacture of brassware, tile, and eating utensils. There were some exceptions, such as the textile and brewing industries. Another exception to the general pattern of Korean enterprises being small compared to those of the Japanese was the pharmaceutical industry.

Capital and Technical Intensity

Similarly, tendencies in investment between Japanese and Koreans differed with regard to capital and technological intensities of industrial firms. As noted in the preceding analyses, Japanese investment in industry was in more capital- and technologically intensive enterprises. As with the scale of investment, this characteristic could easily be found in almost all sectors, such as transportation—(e.g., railroad and shipping) electric power and gas, manufacturing (e.g., textile and chemical) mining, banking, and even agriculture. Most enterprises in light industries in which Korean investment typically took place were labor intensive but not highly capital intensive or mechanized.

Types of Goods Produced in Manufacturing

Another difference in the nature of investment between the Japanese and Koreans was the type of goods produced by manufacturing industries that they heavily invested in. Although the Japanese dominated investment in all manufacturing, the Japanese investment was more focused on industrial users and on chemical and heavy industry-related manufacturing, while the Koreans devoted investment to the consumer-goods-oriented light manufacturing industries that were mainly intended to cater to Koreans, as elaborated on in the sections that follow.

Heavy and Chemical Industries

The majority of investment in the heavy and chemical industries was by the Japanese, who dominated the industries. Along with metal and machinery manufacturing, the Japanese companies were prominent in the iron and steel industry. The Japanese owned ninety-five companies in the heavy and chemical industries in 1938, while fifty-eight were Korean owned.[100] The Japanese owned 62 percent of the companies in the industry and contributed nearly 95 percent of the paid-in capital, which amounted to 24 million yen in 1938 and 142.12 million in 1941. Korean businessmen were active in the manufacturing of metal consumer goods, such products as brassware and cooking utensils, to meet domestic demand in the early years of Japanese rule. There were ten brassware and eighteen utensil factories in 1907. By 1938 the number of Korean companies in the machinery and tool industry had increased to about half that of the Japanese. The number of Korean companies was sixty-five in 1941, representing 27.8 percent of the total for the industry, but their investment in 1941 was 8.6 million yen, representing a mere 6.3 and 5.7 percent of the paid-in capital of companies in manufacturing and the entire industrial sector respectively.

In the chemical industry, there were seventy-five Japanese-owned companies with more than 100 million yen in paid-in capital in 1938 (Table 5.1).[101] The number of Japanese companies made up 67 percent of the total, while their investment occupied 97 percent of the total in the chemical industry. In 1938 the amount of their investment in chemical companies represented about 47 percent of their investment in all of their manufacturing companies headquartered in Korea and about 23 percent of investment in all companies in Korea. By 1939 92 percent of all production in the chemical industry took place in factories owned and operated by the Japanese. No foreign investment was found in producer-oriented heavy industry.

The Koreans likewise slowly began to invest in the chemical industry. However, there was only one chemical company owned and operated by a Korean, with 125,000 yen in paid-in capital, in 1923. These figures increased to thirty-seven companies and 3 million yen in 1938 and forty-three companies and 3.8 million yen in 1941.[102] The Korean-owned chemical companies made up as much as 30 percent of the total and had as much as 10 percent of Korean investment in manufacturing, but they constituted less than 3 percent of total paid-in capital in the chemical industry and less than 4 percent of investment in manufacturing in 1938 (see

Table 5.1).[103] Less than 8 percent of output of the chemical industry took place in Korean cottage industries in 1939. It is clear that in spite of the expanding numbers of Korean investment in the chemical industry, it produced a small amount of output.

One commodity within the chemical industry that attracted considerable investment by Koreans was the manufacturing of rubber shoes for Koreans, which was introduced in the late 1910s and which most Koreans wore, especially in rural areas.[104] Although the Japanese invested heavily in the production of other rubber products, it was the Koreans who dominated rubber-shoe manufacturing and played a major role in its development and expansion. By 1920–25, twenty companies producing rubber shoes were set up by Koreans, compared with eleven by the Japanese. Koreans had 1.6 million yen in paid-in capital in rubber-shoe factories that had more than five employees and power-driven machinery. In 1926 there was only one Japanese rubber-shoe manufacturing company, and Japanese factories employed, in aggregate, fewer than 100 workers. By 1930, the Korean-invested and/or owned rubber-shoe manufacturers numbered thirty out of forty-seven, which increased to sixty-one in 1942.[105] Korean factories produced 53.1 percent of total output in rubber-shoe manufacturing and 63.6 percent of the total output in the chemical businesses owned by Koreans in 1928, and they contributed 3.5 percent of chemical-industry output in 1940.[106] Some Korean companies even supplied the Manchurian market, having developed rubber shoes suitable for the Chinese. The Koreans continued to dominate the rubber-shoe industry until World War II, when the shortage of raw materials forced many factories to close. The-rubber shoe producers in the Pyongyang region were mostly Christians.

Light Industry

Japanese dominance was clearly evident in light industry, too, but less prominent in it than in the chemical and metal-related heavy industries. They contributed about 78 percent of total paid-in capital in the industry, devoting 42 percent of their total paid-in capital in manufacturing in 1938 (see Table 5.1). In 1941 Japanese companies represented 55 percent of the total number and had about 81 percent of paid-in capital in the light industry.[107]

Other foreign (non-Japanese) investment in manufacturing was minimal and mostly clustered around light industries such as rice cleaning and the manufacturing of cigarettes and bricks. Notable examples were 30,000 yen invested in a rice-cleaning mill by an American named Townsend (established in 1892 and employing about forty workers in 1907) and 5,700 yen invested in a Chinese brick-manufacturing firm that employed fifty-four workers.[108] There also were two foreign firms manufacturing cigarettes. No foreign investment was found in nonfood light industries such as textiles. Most foreign investors were Americans, whose six firms were medium-sized enterprises with average per factory capital of 13,680 yen in 1921 and 18,609 yen in 1927.[109] Foreign manufacturers produced about 5 million yen's worth of commodities in 1931.

In contrast to the paucity of their presence in the heavy and chemical industries, a substantial number of Korean companies that made a relatively large investment in light industry was established and increased over time.[110] The number increased from a few before the Annexation to thirty-five companies in 1923 and 706 in 1941, while paid-in capital increased from less than 3 million to 36.53 million yen during 1923 and 1941. The number of Korean-owned companies in light industry was about 45 percent of the total, while their paid-in capital was nearly 22 percent of manufacturing in 1938 and 19 percent of the industry in 1941. Korean manufacturers, employing 18 percent of all manufacturing workers, produced 16.3 percent of manufacturing output in light industries, mostly for native consumption. In comparison with other industrial sectors—for instance, the heavy and chemical industries—these ratios are more than double.

One of the major components of the light industry, food-related industries, too, the Japanese investment was larger than that of the Koreans, but not as much as that found in the chemical industry. The paid-in capital of Japanese companies in the food industry occupied 60 percent of the total in 1938 and nearly two-thirds in 1941, although the number of Japanese companies was fewer than 41 percent of the total. The Japanese devoted about 15.5 percent of their total paid-in capital to the food industry.

In comparison with the limited amount of Japanese investment in the food industry, Koreans devoted a major portion and an increasing amount of their resources to the industry and played a more important role in it than in other fields.[111] The number of Korean companies increased from about 27.7 percent of all manufacturing companies in 1923 to more than 31.7 percent (338) in 1938 and from about 5 percent of all companies to more than 7 percent during the same period. They composed 15.6 percent of the total in the industrial sector in 1941. Similarly, the paid-in capital of Korean companies in the food industry increased from 9.1 percent of all manufacturing companies under Korean management in 1923 to 49 percent (14.8 million yen) in 1938. The Koreans invested 43 percent as much capital in the food industry as the Japanese (34.2 million yen), and the share of Korean investment in it was 12 percent of total Korean investment in 1938. Consequently, Korean firms contributed a large share of output in the food industry as well. However, the importance of their investment in it cannot be overstated. Their investment in 1941 was only 3 percent of the paid-in capital of all companies in industry.

The segments of the food industry that attracted many Korean investors were rice milling and brewing/distillery. There was only one motorized Korean-owned rice mill in 1907, but by 1911 more than 60 percent (fourteen in number) of all motor-powered plants owned and operated by Koreans were rice-hulling mills. As many as 1,544, constituting one-third of all Korean factories, were rice mills in 1938. In the same year, Korean-owned rice-milling companies numbered ninety-four, compared with seventy owned and operated by the Japanese. The number of Korean rice mills continued to exceed that of the Japanese in 1941, with 51 versus 49 percent of the total. However, as in other fields, Korean investment in this sector was relatively small. While the Japanese invested 9.8 million yen in 1938, the Korean investment in flour and rice-milling companies was only 2.5 million yen, or about one-fifth of the total.

Another field in food industry that Koreans invested heavily and played a major role in was the brewing/distillery industry. The number of Korean-owned distilling companies employing more than five workers, using power-driven machinery, and producing more than 5,000 yen's worth of output was 321 in 1938, nearly triple the number the Japanese owned (128), while the paid-in capital in Korean-owned distilling companies attracted the largest investment in industry by Koreans: 12.1 million yen in 1938 (see Table 5.1). The total paid-in capital of Korean-owned distilling companies in 1938 was equivalent to 46.7 percent of the industry, nearly equaling that of the Japanese (13.8 million yen). Korean investment in distilleries represented more than 70 percent of the total investment of all Korean companies in 1941, more than 40 percent of total paid-in capital in Korean industrial companies, and nearly 11 percent of total paid-in capital in the industry. Japanese investment in distilling companies devoted only 6.4 percent of their total paid-in capital in manufacturing companies. By 1941, the paid-in capital of Korean companies had increased to 15.8 million yen. The output of Korean-invested and -owned distillery companies accounted for nearly half of all food products and produced almost 92 percent of the "Korean liquor" output in 1928.

The dominance of Korean investment in rice-wine distilling is even more conspicuous. They invested 4.4 million yen in the form of paid-in capital in their factories in 1928, which represented about 64.1 percent of total paid-in capital in the industry (for plants with more than five employees, power-driven machinery, and more than 5,000 yen's worth of output), and produced about 70 percent of the total rice-wine output of factories in the country. Their dominance expanded in later years. Korean-owned factories of this type attracted 84 percent of all paid-in capital in the country's liquor industry and produced 92 percent of its total output in 1938.[112]

Another industry that attracted much Korean investment was textile manufacturing. Following the general pattern, investment in the textile industry was dominated by the Japanese, but not as much as in the chemical and heavy-machinery industries.[113] Paid-in capital in Japanese textile companies made up nearly 80 percent of the total in the industry in 1938 (see Table 5.1). It was four times that of Korean companies, although the Japanese invested in it less than 11 percent of their paid-in capital devoted to manufacturing and 5.4 percent of their investment in all of their companies in Korea in 1938. The number of Japanese businesses in the textile industry was 61.5 percent of the total in 1941, but their investment was more than 85 percent of the paid-in capital of all companies in the industry.[114]

Korean investment in textiles was substantial, the second largest amount of investment in manufacturing by Koreans and next in importance only to the food industry. Beginning with the World War I economic boom, many traditional Korean merchants and weavers were transformed into entrepreneurs in the modern textile industry. Having enjoyed a measure of success, the number of Korean textile companies increased from 4 in 1923 to 37 in 1938, which was nearly equal in number to Japanese-owned enterprises and ranked fourth in number among all firms owned and operated by Koreans. The Koreans not only established as many textile companies as (and in some years even more than) did the Japanese, but their investment was relatively large. Paid-in capital in the industry made up more than one-quarter that of Japanese-owned companies, slightly more than one-fifth of

Korean investment in all manufacturing companies, and 14.6 percent of the total investment in industry in 1941.[115]

Within the textile industry, knitwear, which included such products as heavy underwear (*naebok,* jersey, or thermal underwear), and socks, attracted considerable investment by Koreans. Paid-in capital in Korean-owned factories with more than five employees, power-driven machinery, and more than 5,000 yen's worth of output in 1928 represented 62.3 percent of total paid-in capital in all factories producing knitted goods. In 1938 Koreans had paid-in capital of about 6.4 million yen, which represented 20 percent of all investment in textile companies. It attracted a considerable amount of investment from small Korean merchants and craftsmen,[116] who proved to be both competitive and successful. In this industry, Korean investment exceeded that of the Japanese, and most of their enterprises were successful. There was no significant Japanese competition in knitwear. As a result, knitted goods manufactured in Korean-owned factories represented more than 62 percent of the total output in 1928.

The manufacturing of socks by Koreans, which began in 1900, also firmly established their prominence by about 1917, when their firms accounted for 60 to 70 percent of production in the industry.[117] The business typically required a small amount of capital, and many manufacturers of socks had worked as assistants or apprentices to other producers or merchants, working hard, saving, and later starting their own companies. Apparently, almost all of these entrepreneurs were Westernized and/or Christians. However, after 1937 and during World War II, when the Japanese government suppressed the operation of Korean textile factories, the rapid expansion of the industry came to an abrupt halt. Under the pretext of wartime control, the supply of raw materials was curtailed, and about a third of the Korean factories came into Japanese possession, mostly through acquisitions that left little choice for the former owners.

SUMMARY AND CONCLUSIONS

This chapter has revealed several unique features and patterns of investment for different segments of the economy, for example, the nature of products between public and private sectors, between nationalities, between Japanese and Koreans, and motivation for investment under Japanese rule. They are summarized in five main groups. First, one of the outstanding features of sectoral investment under colonial rule was the large investment in SOC. The originally almost nonexistent, small, and insignificant investment in it in the early years expanded rapidly and came to represent one of the major portions of capital formation in Korea under Japanese rule. It is difficult to discern whether investment in Korea followed the "typical" investment pattern of other developed and developing countries, but it appears that it followed a somewhat different pattern from what was being suggested as typical, average gross fixed investment in advanced industrial countries,[118] that is, 35 percent of total fixed investment. The cumulative value of capital stock in SOC may be set at more than 35 percent, or probably as much as half of the net value of physical capital accumulated under Japanese rule, representing more than 3.5 percent of GDP.

Investment in SOC included the construction and extension of modern railroads, communications networks, and electric power, in addition to public works. The single most important investment in the country was the construction of railroads, which was equal to slightly more than the total paid-in capital and reserves (about a third) of all industrial companies in Korea. Next in importance was the electric-power industry, which eventually attracted about 15 percent of all investment under colonial rule. The third most important industry within the SOC sector was communications networks. Investment in these facilities was crucial in stimulating private investment and economic development that occurred at the time and that followed later, in addition to meeting Japanese military needs. The large investment in them facilitated the exploitation of resources and industries developed to meet Japanese needs.

A second outstanding feature of sectoral investment under colonial rule was the increased investment in the industrial sector and mining, which expanded more rapidly than investment in other sectors. Particularly notable is the large investment in modern manufacturing industries. Within the manufacturing sector, the chemical and metal industries attracted the most investment, while consumer-oriented industries such as textiles and food processing showed relatively modest gains.

The least amount of private investment was in agriculture, relative to its dominance in the economy. Investment in agriculture was more or less limited to the modest expansion of cultivated land, the improved quality of selected land, especially of rice paddy, and the introduction of technological innovations to expand rice production. There were no serious efforts to mechanize Korean agriculture. Investment in commerce, banking, and miscellaneous industries showed increases, but not as much as that in SOC, manufacturing, and mining. Compared with the 10 and 30 percent rates of investment for commerce and combined agriculture and manufacturing, respectably, as was the typical situation in other countries, there was more investment in manufacturing and less in agriculture in Korea under Japanese rule. Fixed investment in housing in Korea under Japanese rule was far less than 25 percent, which was considered typical and appropriate.[119]

A third outstanding characteristic of sectoral investment in Korea under Japanese rule was the fact that private businesses have carried the burden, but the colonial government also played a crucial and unique role in investment in Korea. While private investment was focused mostly on businesses in the manufacturing field that provided "modern products"—such as heavy and chemical industries, rice cleaning, brewing, ore smelting, mining, and electric power—the government played a dominant role in infrastructure development through the construction of railways and communications networks, as well as a number of other public-works projects. More than three-quarters of the total investment in railroads was by the government. The expansion of these facilities for SOC greatly enhanced the development potential of the Korean economy in the long as well as the short run. It also established and operated manufacturing facilities to produce revenue for itself. In this connection, the colonial government, in some cases in partnership with large private investors, played the crucial role in building public overhead capital and economic development. Nonetheless, the government did not intrude and engage in manufacturing in the private domain extensively: the share of government investment in manufacturing was relatively small and declined over time.

Fourth, the scope, amount, and areas of Japanese and Korean investment in the private sector varied widely from one sector to another. Japanese investment dominated in almost all sectors of the economy, but it was more focused on "modern" industries such as electric power, the chemical and metal industries, textile industry, and mining. Their investment typically was in large firms as well as in capital- and technologically intensive industries. In spite of the fact that the Japanese contributed the most investment in sectors crucial for meeting Japan's needs, such as the military, it is questionable whether some of it really contributed significantly to the economic development of Korea and the welfare of its people in either the short or the long run. The benefits of Japanese investment in aircraft, arsenals, and certain chemical industries (such as high explosives) at that time were dubious at best.[120] The excellent harbors of Korea, with their modern facilities constructed by the Japanese government, had little to do with Korean shipping. Even some railroads did not have much impact on the Korean economy at that time, although in the long run they did. Some of the infrastructure and material assets (e.g., the transportation system, factories, and mines) had also deteriorated by the end of World War II.

While Japanese investment dominated in all fields, Korean investment was confined to certain areas, but not all pervasive. Most was in commerce. Korean investment in public utilities was virtually nil and certainly less than 10 percent of the total in manufacturing. In manufacturing, it was essentially in the first-stage processing of raw materials, and agricultural goods; more focused on light and consumer-oriented industries; and concentrated in enterprises that produced traditional products and items to meet daily Korean consumer needs. Korean investment in the modern industrial sector as a pioneer in the field was limited.

Fifth and last, Japanese investment in Korea was not solely for profit but also to obtain primary products and for political and military reasons.[121] Most other colonial powers did not become capital exporters when they needed to import raw materials and food or use the colony as a base for its conquest of neighboring countries. Great Britain and the United States, for instance, invested wherever they thought there was money to be made, irrespective of their level of imports. Great Britain used its earnings on foreign investments and repayments of principal not to pay for imports but to add to its overseas capital. It merely reinvested what it was owed overseas.[122] In this respect, the Japanese investment in Korea was different from that of the British colonial system. For this reason, in a broad sense Japanese colonialism did leave a richer and more permanent legacy of institutional forms and capital formation than was typical of Western colonialism.

APPENDIX 5.1: FARMLAND STATISTICS

According to official records, land under cultivation in Korea increased from 2.16 million *jeong* in 1905 to 2.3 million in 1909, 2.46 million *jeong* in 1910, 4.96 million in 1939, and 4.85 million in 1942 (Tokanfu 1909: 387; Sotokufu 1912: 720; ibid. 1942: 4–5; *Chosen Keizainenpo* 1939; Nihon Takumusho 1938; and Bank of Korea 1948: III, 14). Had these increases been accomplished under Japanese rule, the farmland would have expanded 225 percent in forty years, at an annual average of 2.2 percent. Such an expansion of farmland in Korea was impossible for a number of reasons. In all probability, the increase in the cultivated acreage was not as spectacular as these statistics indicate, because of extensive underreporting of land under cultivation before the completion of the land survey in 1918.

Close examination reveals that the increases reported between 1910 and 1918, when the cadastral land survey was carried out, were illusory. According to the official statistics, cultivated land increased from 2.32 in 1910 million to 4.5 million *jeong* in 1918, at the stunning rate of 94 percent in an eight-year period, averaging nearly 10 percent a year, while number of farm households increased from about 2.2 million in 1909 to 2.6 million in 1918, an 18 percent rise in nine years. The government statistics also show that in one year alone, between 1917 and 1918, the arable land increased by an implausible 16 percent. Such large increases in arable land were not possible.

In contrast, the increase in cultivated land between 1919 and 1939 was only 10 percent, averaging far less than 1 percent a year. In addition, the amount of cultivated land actually decreased by 2.2 percent between 1939 and 1942. It seems reasonable to determine that the extraordinary increases in arable land in official statistics in the first nine years of the Japanese administration (1910–1918) could not have been feasible when the country was being transformed radically from an independent country to a colony. In fact, neither the Japanese government nor the private sector between did much to increase the amount of cultivated land between 1910 and 1918.

Realistically, the increases in farmland must have been much smaller in the early years, when no vigorous arable land expansion program was undertaken. These inflated government statistics seem to reflect the incomplete and poor quality of the data before the completion of the land survey and improvements in record keeping after 1918. The amount of arable land at the time of the Japanese takeover was probably much larger, approximately 4.35 million *jeong,* than that recorded in the official statistics. In that case, the percentage increase in the amount of arable land during the 1910–1918 period would be smaller. Ban calculates that cultivated land increased from 4.510 million *jeong* (11 million acres) in 1910 to 4.938 million *jeong* (12.1 million acres) in 1939, when the acreage cultivated was the largest, a rise of 9.5 percent, or less than one-third of a percent, each year (1983: 18). A more likely increase in cultivated land was about 5 to 8 percent (1983: 4). Also see Tokanfu 1909: 387; Sotokufu 1912: 720; ibid. 1942: 4–5; Nihon Takumusho 1938; Bank of Korea 1948: III, 14; *Chosen Keizainenpo* 1939; Ban 1983: 18, 2; K. J. Cho 1977: 164–165; ibid. 1994: 434; S. J. Ko 1988: 232.

6

SOURCES AND POLICIES FOR INVESTMENT

This chapter examines two aspects of capital formation: the sources and mobilization of resources and the policies for investment. The government has a crucial role in providing the institutions and economic environment conducive to capital formation. Government supports are essential to initiating and nurturing so-called underdeveloped economies to bring about economic progress. Past experience clearly demonstrates that public policy is one of the most important sources of cross-country growth differentials. A standard explanation for the extraordinary rates of economic growth achieved in Hong Kong, Singapore, and Taiwan, as well as South Korea in recent decades, is that these countries had strong government support and sound public policies that directed public and private investment into promising sectors of the economy. The government support ranged from legal security, freedom of enterprise, technical research, and education to routine services such as agricultural extension programs and financial and technical assistance that amounted to virtual partnerships with private interests in certain key industries.

In contrast, policies that reduce the rewards of private investment slow the rate of economic expansion. There are abundant examples of the effects of such policies: high and inequitable taxes, unsuitable and inefficient educational systems, lax patent protection, poor protection of general property rights, and political instability (as shown in Korea during the traditional/transitional periods). In the case of Korea, the role of the government under Japanese rule was unique in a number of areas. The volume, character, and pattern of investment and its financing were by no means coincidental. Prevailing conditions and powerful forces, especially those of the government, led economic resources to be directed toward investment and development of certain sectors of economy and away from consumption and uses for nonstrategic fields.

In governing Korea, the Japanese colonial government played a decisive role in shaping economic as well as political policy. It was convinced that the Korean economy had to be guided.[1] The colonial government not only expanded its budget over time the Government General also increased its share of revenues (e.g., from 71 percent of its revenues in 1932 to 85 percent in 1939). There were a number of government policies, such as those dealing with labor and tariffs that could have affected capital formation and development of certain economic sectors. However, the policies under Japanese rule examined in this study are limited to those that directly affected capital formation, that is, investment and saving. These are fiscal policies involving taxation and subsidies, directing financial resources for investment, and promoting saving.

The second part of this chapter examines the mobilization of resources for investment. Having examined earlier the extent and nature of investment in various sectors, the ensuing requisite question is how Korea has mobilized economic resources needed for its investment, a crucial challenge that faces all developing economies and, that faced all developed countries in the past. It has been argued that in less-developed countries, such as Korea prior to World War II, it is nearly impossible to secure resources for even the minimum investment needed to support the native population at the prevailing standard of living, let alone to enable the country to mobilize sufficient resources for large investments for rapid economic growth.

Examined in this chapter, therefore, are the means through which resources were mobilized for investment both from abroad and domestic sources, such as financial resources, direct investment, and forced saving. They are investigated in two broad policy means, namely, fiscal and financial policies.

FISCAL POLICIES FOR INVESTMENT

Fiscal policies under Japanese rule were clearly based on the principle of promoting investment in certain economic sectors. Taxes and subsidies, which were typically used as a primary fiscal means of increasing investment and attracting it into desired sectors of the economy, are examined in the sections that follow.

Taxation

Japanese tax policy in Korea after the Annexation evolved gradually from the traditional and transitional policies administered under the Korean government before 1904. Once the Japanese government took hold of the administration, a number of tax reforms were undertaken. The arbitrary levies exacted at the whim of a political aristocracy in the traditional and transitional periods became a thing of the past, and the Government General assumed increasing power in taxation, at the expense of local governments. Tax revenues increased from a few million yen in 1904 to 68.7 million in 1937, 163 million in 1941, and 309.4 million in 1943 and became a reliable and major source of government revenue.[2]

One aspect of tax policy under Japanese administration that stands out clearly is the incidence of taxation. In spite of the reforms and increases, the incidence of taxation under Japanese rule did not change much from what had prevailed prior to 1905. The major tax burden was still squarely placed on the masses who depended on agriculture for their livelihood and rested lightly on high-income earners and businesses. The land tax, which had been the principal tax before 1905, continued to serve as the primary source of revenue after the Annexation. Before 1915, the land tax furnished more than 50 percent of all government revenues, and it continued to supply more than 40 percent until 1926. Until about 1930, both the national and local governments were financed largely through real estate taxes paid by the rural population. In fact, under colonial rule more of the incidence of land taxation shifted from landlords to tenants. In the traditional period, the land tax had been paid by landowners. Although there was a tendency for the land tax to be shifted from landlords to tenants in the transitional period, such a shift seems to have accelerated and become more prevalent under Japanese rule. In addition, there was a considerable shift of water taxes (or irrigation fees) from landlords to tenants.[3]

After about 1930, the land tax as a source of revenue in relation to total tax revenues fell progressively—to about 20 percent of all tax revenues in 1937 and 7 percent in 1943—far short of providing the necessary government revenue.[4] In its place, levies on consumption goods gained increasing importance. High taxes were levied on consumer goods, for which demand increased rapidly with modernization of the country's economy during the colonial period, and import duties with high marginal tax rates were implemented. These new levies took three forms: (1) direct excise taxes on such consumer goods as liquor, sugar, soy products, textiles, and a few other items; (2) indirect taxes, basically lucrative fiscal monopolies imposed in 1910 on the sale of widely used products and necessities such as tobacco, salt, and ginseng; and (3) import tariffs.

Direct taxes on consumption goods increased over time and were an important source of government revenue in the later years. In 1937 the revenues derived from taxes on liquor alone represented 28.8 percent of all tax revenues and constituted the largest single tax in Korea.[5] Although revenue from the liquor tax gradually declined to 15 percent in 1943, it continued to far exceed land-tax revenues. Another source of government revenue from consumption was the tax on sugar (nearly 70 percent of the retail price), which accounted for 6.7 percent of total tax revenues in 1929. In 1939 the government collected 4.1 million yen in taxes on the sale of 6 million yen's worth of sugar.[6]

After 1930, indirect taxes on consumer goods financed the growing requirements of the national budget. The government monopoly on tobacco, cigarettes, salt, and ginseng also brought in considerable amounts of monopoly profit or tax revenues. It is not possible to calculate accurately the profits of these monopoly businesses, but according to government statistics on public enterprises, "monopoly profits" were lucrative, ranging from 35.7 million yen in 1929 to 286 million in 1943.[7] The opium and morphine monopolies were particularly profitable, yielding 6.7 million yen in 1940. The government monopolies generated 15 to 17 percent of all tax revenues. In addition, some portion of the tariff revenue must be attributed to consumers. If we were to assume that one-half of customs duties was collected on imports of consumer goods, the revenues from consumption taxes would be even larger than the sum given here.

In addition, a number of taxes in kind were levied on the Korean people. This took the form of a corvée labor "tax." Although the Japanese government after the takeover of Korea virtually eliminated the sorts of informal taxes of the traditional period, they survived in certain forms. When road repairs were undertaken, corvée labor was required of persons unable to pay their assessments. On many occasions, Koreans were "conscripted" to construct roads without wages.[8] They also had to work at the convenience of the officials, however inconvenient this might have been for workers, such as for spring sowing or the fall harvest season. Railroad construction also utilized some free Korean labor.[9] It is not possible to estimate the value of these informal, in-kind taxes.

While heavy taxes were levied on land and consumer goods, income and business taxes were nonexistent, low, or light under the Japanese administration. Apparently, to encourage saving and investment, no personal income tax was levied in Korea until 1934; even then, the tax rates were lower in Korea than in Japan. According to one official explanation, "special circumstances" in Korea dictated that the tax rate be only a quarter and a half that of Japan proper in 1934 and 1935, respectively.

The income tax was based on a low marginal rate. As a result, it contributed relatively little to the government coffers, only 14.85 percent of all tax revenues in 1937 and 25 percent in 1943.[10] Moreover, it was less progressive and imposed a heavier burden on the middle- and lower-income brackets than that in Japan. While an annual income above 1,200 yen was taxable in Japan, the minimum taxable income in Korea was as low as 800 yen. Persons earning between 1,500 and 3,000 yen were allowed to deduct 100 yen in Japan, but the deduction allowed in Korea was only 30 yen. Those with family incomes under 3,000 yen, which included three quarters of the population, were overwhelmingly farmers and wage earners; those earning more than 3,000 yen were predominantly property owners. Large personal incomes were subject to only mildly progressive levies until 1938. Even the income-tax schedule of 1940 showed a levy of only 27 percent for the income bracket of 100,000 to 200,000 yen.

In addition, virtually all interest income and 40 percent of corporate dividends and bonuses were immune to the progressive rates. Interest income (except the yield on national and savings bonds, which was entirely exempt) was separately taxed at rates of only 4 to 5 percent. The inheritance tax was low as well; the tax on a sum as large as 1 or 2 million yen was only 22 percent. By modern standards, the Korean tax system was very lenient in its treatment of large income earners and property owners.

Taxes on business were also low. Until the corporate income tax was inaugurated in 1920, based on the Japanese model, they were almost nonexistent. None of the early taxes on business income and property, except those on real estate, was heavy enough to yield much government revenue. Taxes on non-Japanese foreign enterprises were either nonexistent or low before 1916, because of the provisions written into their mine concessions by the Korean king before the Japanese Annexation. For instance, according to tax returns from 1907, when foreign mining firms mined 70 percent of the minerals in Korea, they paid only 16.3 percent of total mining taxes. In the following year, the share was even lower, 9.9 percent. Large corporate incomes continued to be subject to only mildly progressive levies until after 1937. Applied to corporate profits, the basic rate was only 5 percent. Surtaxes on excess profits raised it by no higher than 10 percent, even when a firm was making 30 percent on its invested capital.

General business and interest taxes were introduced in 1927. While Korea maintained a common tariff system with Japan, taxes on business were lower in Korea. The tax on mining was small, for instance, and its terms were favorable to the mine operators. Mining taxes consisted of 1 percent of the value of minerals mined and 50 *sen* per *pyeong* (3.3 square meters) of mining land on concession. Only a small fixed levy on imported machinery and equipment was imposed.[11]

In addition, businesses were given numerous tax exemptions, especially in industries founded in Korea or designated as "nationally strategic." Although non-Japanese foreigners had been barred from mining, the 1915 mining regulations eliminated the tax on gold, silver, and copper to encourage the mining of the precious metals.[12] Similarly, companies engaged in the iron industry or working certain chartered mines were exempted from business taxes altogether. On the other hand, the colonial government imposed several miscellaneous business taxes that drew heavily on those with small and medium incomes.

Only after 1935 did the Government General increasingly rely on progressive taxes applied to personal and corporate incomes, but the burden of business and income taxes under Japanese rule was lighter than what the laws prescribed. Both the laws and those who administered them dealt leniently with business and large property incomes, which were the sources of a large share of the country's savings. Where political influence could be exerted on the collector, evasion of business and personal income taxes was commonplace in Korea, as it was in Japan.[13] Evasion was widespread as a result of lax enforcement and fictitious bookkeeping. Whatever the legal rates, the taxes paid by corporations and well-to-do individuals depended in no small degree on a process of individual negotiation in which political influence and financial bargaining power carried a good deal of weight in Korea as well as Japan. As a result, business taxes made up only a small portion of tax revenues. They accounted for little more than 3 percent of all tax revenues even as late as in 1937 and 1943.[14] They provided less than half of what was collected from excise taxes and the tax on monopoly revenue. As one scholar who has carefully examined the modernization of Korea under Japanese rule observed, Korea "was a capitalist's paradise [and] taxes on business were almost non-existent."[15]

This analysis demonstrates that the major portion of tax revenue came from the masses. It has been calculated that real estate and consumption levies furnished as much as 80 percent of all tax revenues prior to 1923. Thereafter, it still accounted for more than 50 percent until the end of colonial rule. As late as 1935, the combined national taxes on personal income, business profits, and interest income yielded little more than the liquor tax. Around 70 percent in 1936–1940 came from the entire population in the form of consumption taxes, while land, income, wartime profit, interest income, corporate, and inheritance taxes constituted the other 30 percent.[16] This heavily regressive tax structure had a significant impact on peasants, workers, small industrialists, tradesmen, and professionals. It placed the heaviest burden on the largest segment of the Korean population, especially the small farmers.

Subsidies

Continuing a tradition, the Korean government after 1905, under the direction of Japanese advisers, provided a limited amount of financial assistance to businesses. No comprehensive statistical data on direct subsidies to private businesses under Japanese rule are available, but the amount seemed to have been rather small. Before the Annexation, the Korean government could not have provided much financial support to businesses because of the lack of financial means and the Japanese military threat.[17] After the Annexation, attempts to encourage private investment in Korea through subsidies slowly accelerated and then were vigorously and systematically pursued. In the Japanese view, Korea needed government support and entrepreneurial leadership.[18] Between 1910 and 1919, the Government General provided modest (an annual average of about 2.5 million yen) subsidies, while the provincial governments allocated on average about 1 million yen per year.[19]

With a new policy of encouraging local industries, promulgated in 1920, the amount of these subsidies increased sixfold. Between 1920 and 1931, the Government General increased its subsidies to an average of 13 million yen a year, while the provincial governments raised theirs to about 7 to 8 million yen. The new official policy was to encourage "desirable" small-scale industries that utilized local raw materials. Among these were businesses manufacturing firecrackers, mats, and lacquerware.[20]

When Japan adopted an expansionary policy on the Asian continent, the subsidy to businesses in Korea leaped up dramatically. According to one Japanese scholar, "millions [of yen] of government subsidies were given after 1937."[21] Another observer has noted that the Government General provided liberal accommodations to such an extent that it was criticized for breaking its own regulations. The subsidy of the Government General rose to 17 million yen in 1931, 37 million in 1939, 73 million in 1941, and 105.1 million in 1943, a more than eightfold increase in a twelve-year period. The total subsidy granted by the Residency General and the Government General was approximately 710 million yen between 1908 and 1943.

The subsidy provided by the provincial governments during the same period was approximately double that of the period before 1930, averaging about 15 million yen per year. The total amount of the provincial subsidies was roughly 280 million yen between 1908 and 1943.[22] Local governments also granted subsidies to business, although no accurate data are available. It is known that in 1939 the county and township governments (*bu* and *myon*) allocated "more than 2 million yen of subsidies to business," while the municipal governments allotted "several million yen."[23]

It is difficult to calculate the aggregate sum for direct subsidies, but the available figures lead us to estimate that national and provincial subsidies amounted to approximately 1 billion yen during 1908–1943. In annual terms, this would be approximately 30 million yen (22 million from the Government General and 8 million from the provincial governments), which is equivalent to 5 to 10 percent of regular government budgets on average. If we were to add the subsidies of local governments, the aggregate subsidy would certainly exceed a billion yen.

Direct subsidies were granted to certain sectors of the economy, which included mining, railroads, manufacturing (especially the chemical and heavy industries), and rice production, to meet Japanese economic needs and further its expansionary policy in Asia. The largest and most generous subsidies were given to mining, especially of gold. The gold mines received an annual government subsidy in the amount of 650,000 yen in 1918 and 4.3 million in 1936.[24] After 1937, when Korea was designated to supply large amounts of gold to meet Japan's needs, the government provided the necessary financial incentives to mining. These subsidies were reported to have reached 57.5 million yen in 1940–1941—two-thirds of all subsidies allotted by the Government General in that year.

The production of other minerals (silver, iron ore, mineral oil, aluminum, and magnesium) was also supported.[25] Generous subsidies were given to producers of aluminum and magnesium. Large sums were spent on exploration, development of substitutes for scarce materials (e.g., liquid fuels), repair and improvement of roads to mines, purchase of machinery and equipment, freight charges for the transport of ore, development of refining and cooperative facilities, and electrical transmission. In 1944 a major portion of the government expenditure of 2.3 billion yen—15.6 percent of the total, or 360 million yen—was allocated to gold production, other mining, and various industries, in contrast to only 0.3 percent spent on education and 5 percent on agricultural experimental stations and other programs.[26]

Subsidies were granted also to strategic industries such as railways, shipping, aviation, and timber.[27] In step with the construction of public railroads, provisions were made in 1914 and 1921 to grant special subsidies to important private lines. Since the railroads were not yet profitable, subsidies augmented deficiencies in profits below a certain percentage, usually 6 percent, on paid-in capital, enabling them to construct and operate private lines. They received a subsidy of 7.23 million yen, for instance, in 1944. Subsidies were likewise granted to the shipping industry in the early years and the aviation industry after 1929. Similarly, when the Korea Lumber Corporation was organized in 1908, the government granted a subsidy of 300,000 yen annually for eight years. The Korea Trust Company was given an annual subsidy of 100,000 yen for five years, and the Industrial Bank also received a subsidy of 300,000 yen annually.

Another sector that received government subsidies was agriculture. Improvements in agriculture took two main forms: upgrading facilities, including experiment stations and extension services; and encouraging land improvement. Subsidies in agriculture were specifically targeted at increasing Korea's rice production for Japan. Initially, in 1919 the government awarded 10,000 yen in subsidies to irrigation associations. In 1926, by halving the initial thirty-year rice production plan (Appendix 6.1), a fifteen-year plan to improve 420,000 *jeong* of rice land was developed at a cost of 168 million yen in order to increase rice production by 4.6 million *seok*. The government subsidy in the initial plan was 35.18 million yen, but in 1931 an additional subsidy of as much as 3.83 million yen was allotted, thus making the total subsidy 26.1 percent of total projected costs.

The drainage project to convert so-called wasteland into arable land was carried out with 60 percent of the costs being paid by a government subsidy, while bank loans and owners' equity covered the rest. The Government General also allocated 40 million yen to agriculture, mainly to assist in the purchase of fertilizers and improved seeds and to develop modern farming methods. The Japanese government likewise provided financial help to the credit unions during most of the period and awarded an annual subsidy of 300,000 yen to the Oriental Development Company beginning in 1909.[28]

Indirect subsidies were also provided to businesses in various forms after 1910. First, the government provided financial assistance to the shareholders of certain businesses through dividend guarantees. The Government General, for example, guaranteed shareholders of the Industrial Bank an annual dividend of 7 percent for a five-year period while exempting itself from dividends on its holdings of capital shares for fifteen years. The average dividend was 7 percent in the first half of the year and 14 percent in the second. When the Korea Lumber Corporation was organized in 1908, the government guaranteed its shareholders an annual dividend of 8 percent.[29]

Second, the governments made interest-free loans to public banks and some private institutions at low subsidized or no-interest rates. The most conspicuous examples of Korean businesses receiving loans were the early Korean commercial banks during the protectorate period. When these banks faced financial difficulties soon after their establishment, the Korean government under the direction of Japanese advisers provided financial support. The Hanseong and Cheonil Banks were given interest-free loans and other assistance to support their operations, as elaborated in Appendix 6.1. Similarly, the government loaned the Agricultural and Industrial Banks 692,100 yen, which was more than the paid-in capital of the banks, without interest, between 1906 and 1918. Before 1930, there also were government loans totaling 1.2 million yen to the Bank of Korea and 1.5 million to the Industrial Bank.[30] The loan to the former was increased to 70.2 million yen in 1930.

Third, the government supplied venture capital to new businesses. There are numerous examples of this type of government support. When the Agricultural and Industrial Bank system was established in 1906, the government subscribed more than 50 percent of its stock shares, a subsidy amounting to 277,740 yen. By the end of 1907 the authorized capital had increased to 12 million yen and the paid-in capital to 559,610, of which the government had contributed sixty percent or 335,960. When the Oriental Development Company was organized in 1908, the Korean government, under Japanese advisement, supplied 30 percent of the company's capital. The government also subscribed capital shares of the Bank of Korea and the Industrial Bank. The share subscription of the Bank of Korea ranged from 800,000 yen in 1910 to 3 million in 1915, while the subscription of the Industrial Bank was 6,600 shares of capital stock for 300,000 yen.[31]

Fourth, the government sold or transferred land for free or below market prices to land-development firms such as the Oriental Development Company. Fifth, the government provided an indirect form of subsidy to industries by charging them low prices for public utilities. While the average price of electricity charged to residential consumers was 15 to 16 *sen* per kilowatt hour in 1937, industrial users paid 2 *sen,* only 12.5 to 13.3 percent of the price paid by residential users.[32] In addition, only a small portion of the available electricity was allocated to residential users and an even smaller share to Korean residential customers. Electric service, which was initially household oriented until about 1920, was increasingly diverted to industry thereafter. In 1925 the share of electrical service to households decreased to 14.8 percent of total electricity consumed, and in 1930, to 6.6 percent. By 1930 business was utilizing as much as 93 percent of the supply, although industrial use declined slightly to 92 percent in 1940.

The price of electricity also differed according to industry. The electric and chemical industries enjoyed the lowest rates in 1938, between 0.3 and 1.5 *sen* per kilowatt hour, while other industries paid between 1.43 and 4.1 *sen*. Financial assistance also included low freight charges for transporting ore from the mines to the nearest railroad or waterway. A total of 25 million yen was assigned for this purpose (including the improvement of mining roads and electrical transmission) in the 1939 budget.[33]

Subsidies were also targeted at certain businesses. The favored groups were large firms. The government lavished grants and subsidies on the large producers. In the case of gold mining, subsidies were given to companies that (1) had been in business for at least three years, (2) had a value of production of more than 10,000 yen per year and growing, and (3) used power-driven drilling machines. Discriminatory pricing policies also were biased toward large, monopolistic firms. The average price of electricity charged to large industrial users was only 1.4 to 2.2 *sen* per kilowatt hour, less than half the amount charged to small firms, which paid 4 to 5 *sen* in 1937. Likewise, when the supply of labor and raw materials was rationed during World War II, the Japanese government allocated scarce production inputs at favorable controlled prices and wages to large *zaibatsu* firms while denying the same privileges to small and medium-sized consumer-oriented businesses.[34]

Second, the chief beneficiaries of government subsidies were Japanese business firms and landowners, while discriminatory pricing policies consistently favored Japanese firms.[35] The large companies were almost exclusively Japanese owned, the core of which constituted the military-industrial complex. They were controlled by *zaibatsu* such as Mitsui, Mitsubishi, Sumitomo, and Noguchi. For instance, until 1930 the Government General granted a 200,000-yen annual subsidy to Mitsui to produce textiles in Korea, and a subsidy of 300,000 yen was given to Noguchi to build a gold refinery. In the case of mining, the Japanese officials licensed good mines to Japanese and poor mines to Koreans.[36] As a result, the Japanese prospered while many Korean mines struggled to be profitable and some went bankrupt. Nor were Korean businesses successful in obtaining labor and raw materials at controlled prices and wages during World War II.

In agriculture, most irrigation projects (which were typically subsidized) were targeted at Japanese-owned land. Japanese farmers received land-improvement support 2.7 to 4.2 times more frequently than Korean farmers did in 1920, for instance.[37] As a result, by the end of colonial rule roughly 20 percent (5,749 in 1944) of Japanese farmers (owning 51,499 *jeong* of land) had irrigated rice paddies. Japanese farmers, who made up only one-tenth of a percent of the farm population, had more than one-third of the irrigation systems and, on a per capita basis, were 100 times more likely than the Koreans to own irrigated land; conversely, 97 percent of farmers were Korean (81,220, owning 100,386 *jeong* of land) but had only two-thirds of the irrigated paddy land,[38] and the probability of their land being irrigated was equal to 1 percent of that of Japanese farmers. The Koreans who received handsome subsidies for selected land reclamation projects, mining, and industrial ventures were mostly confined to a core of business leaders and landlords who worked closely with the Japanese.[39]

FINANCING OF INVESTMENT BY FINANCIAL INSTITUTIONS

In addition to equity capital, investment may be expanded with debenture capital, including loans financed by financial institutions and sometimes with government grants and loans. In this regard, financial institutions play a key role in augmenting investment for economic development when industry depends heavily on external financial resources. When banks and other financial institutions pool risk, they tend to be more willing to invest in the development of new technologies by allocating financial resources to investment. However, they do not retard development by their absence or facilitate it by their early presence. When the necessary institutions have become a part of the culture, the financial institutions play an important role in accumulating and transferring resources for investment.

The role of financial institutions is particularly important during the early years in a country that does not have a large public securities market, where corporations are prone to pay out most of their earnings in dividends, and/or where most individual savings are in the form of bank deposits. In Korea under Japanese rule, there was no large public market for securities, and bank funds and business savings were the chief sources of supplanting investment to share capital. As noted in chapter 4, the share capital, especially from domestic sources, was relatively scarce. Consequently, financial institutions played a more strategic role in funding investment in Korea than in most developed countries.

Examined in the next sections are the means by which savings—both domestic and foreign—were mobilized for supplementing the share capital for investment in Korea. They comprise the amount of loans granted by financial institutions, the purposes for which the loans were made, and the borrowers. The financial institutions examined below are grouped in two categories, namely, banks and NBFIs, and in two sectors, public and private.

VOLUME AND USE OF LOANS

Before the Annexation, loans extended by financial institutions in Korea were very small.[40] The total volume of loans in 1906 was less than 8 million yen. Following the Annexation, this figure grew nearly fivefold to 38.7 million yen in 1910, 147.3 million in 1918, 1.61 billion in 1938, and 3.73 billion in 1943, as shown in Table 6.1. The amount of loans expanded by more than 467 times in a thirty-seven-year period at an average annual compound rate of nearly 20 percent. Most of these loans were made by banks. As much as 86.6 and 94.5 percent of the loans of all financial institutions that funded investment projects in 1938 and 1939, respectively, were made by banks,[41] whereas three-quarters to four-fifths of all long-term loans were made by banks in 1939 and 1940, while the NBFIs contributed the rest.

TABLE 6.1 Loans of All Financial Institutions and Banks between 1905 and 1944

	Million Yen				Percent			
		Banks				Banks		
Year	Financial Institutions	Public	Private	Total	Banks/Financial Institutions	Public	Private	Total
1905	—	3.0	8.0	11.0	—	27.3	72.7	100.0
1906	8.0	—	—	—	—	—	—	—
1909	—	7.0	—	—	—	—	—	—
1910	38.7	—	—	—	—	—	—	—
1918	147.3	—	—	—	—	—	—	—
1921	—	—	57.0	—	—	—	—	—
1926	—	267.2	105.0	372.2	—	71.8	28.2	100.0
1928	631.9	292.8	107.2	400.0	63.3	73.2	26.8	100.0
1932	—	420.1	117.0	537.1	—	78.2	21.8	100.0
1938	1,610.0	843.3	210.2	1,053.5	65.4	80.0	20.0	100.0
1940	2,560.0	1,571.6	391.6	1,963.2	76.7	80.1	19.9	100.0
1943	3,730.0	2,383.8	677.8	3,061.6	82.1	77.9	22.1	100.0
1944	—	2,730.8	864.4	3,595.2	—	76.0	24.0	100.0

Sources: The table is constructed on the basis of data from Bank of Korea 1948: III, 74–87; Tokanfu 1906: 117–118, 140; ibid. 1908: 383–385; ibid. 1909: 383–388; Sotokufu 1932: 275–277; ibid. 1933: 98; ibid. 1942: 125–127; K. Takahashi 1935: 500–501, 532–533; Mizuda and Tsuchiya 1962: 56, 101; S. Suzuki 1939: 321, 346–347; Himeno 1940: 374, Takeo Suzuki 1941: 268–269; Hosokawa 1941: 324–325.

The purposes for which loans were extended covered a wide range of economic activities, but they were aimed primarily at promoting Japanese interests and followed a pattern that supported the Japanese government's economic policies in Korea. In the early years of Japanese domination (1905–1920), most loans were directed toward commerce. At that time, when the Japanese were mainly interested in undertaking business ventures to exploit the new market by buying Korean goods for export and selling Japanese wares within the country, most financial resources were directed toward supporting these activities. Nearly four-fifths of all bank loans were extended for "commercial" use in the 1910s, as shown in Table 6.2. The practice of allocating the largest share of loans to commerce continued until about 1920. As Japan got a foothold in Korea and its population continued to increase in Japan, it began to view the country as a primary source of food.[42] Loans for commercial activities gradually shifted away from it (from about 80 percent in 1910 to 51.2 percent in 1928,[43] and 23 percent in 1937, except for a slight increase to 29 percent in 1942) to agriculture. Bank loans to the agricultural sector (as a percentage of total loans as well as an absolute amount) increased dramatically from about 3 percent in 1910 to about 43 percent in 1930. The purpose of the majority of agricultural loans was to increase rice production for export to Japan. As an influential Japanese financial newspaper editorialized, Korea's "contribution to the Empire's demand for rice . . . is very important."[44] It entailed the financing of irrigation and land-improvement projects that focused on the construction of drainage systems, dams, and dikes for rice paddy.

TABLE 6.2 Loan Allocation of Banks between 1910 and 1942

Year	Total (in million yen)	Annual Changes (Percent)	Allocation Ratio (Percent): Agriculture	Industry	Commerce	Miscellaneous	Total
1910	23.0	—	3.0	8.0	79.0	10.0	100.0
1914	47.5	20.0	6.5	12.5	67.2	13.8	100.0
1919	201.1	33.5	6.3	6.2	81.0	6.5	100.0
1922	248.4	7.5	17.7	5.8	60.3	16.2	100.0
1924	308.6	11.0	20.3	3.2	55.3	21.2	100.0
1926	309.6	0.1	30.6	3.0	50.4	16.0	100.0
1928	372.9	10.0	35.1	2.7	51.2	11.0	100.0
1930	425.2	7.0	42.8	4.2	38.2	14.8	100.0
1932	480.3	9.8	39.7	5.5	39.9	14.9	100.0
1933	490.6	2.1	38.7	8.4	36.2	16.7	100.0
1934	542.3	10.5	35.0	9.3	42.3	13.4	100.0
1935	642.7	18.5	33.9	10.5	41.8	13.8	100.0
1936	775.7	20.7	31.3	12.9	40.3	15.5	100.0
1937	1,377.3	77.6	32.5	17.2	22.9	27.4	100.0
1938	1,466.4	6.5	30.9	22.2	26.3	20.6	100.0
1939	2,019.5	37.7	27.0	25.6	29.4	18.0	100.0
1940	2,487.1	23.2	25.9	27.8	26.8	19.5	100.0
1941	2,791.7	12.2	25.7	30.4	27.5	16.4	100.0
1942	3,237.3	16.0	24.5	30.2	29.1	16.2	100.0
Average	—	18.0	26.7	12.9	44.5	15.9	100.0

Sources: The table is constructed on the basis of data from Hanguk Eunhaeng 1952: 105; Takahashi 1935: 521; S. Suzuki 1939: 323, 344, 347; *Chosen Nenkan* 1939: 351; Ibid., 1941; J. B. Kim 1977: 367. Toyo Takushoku Kaisha 1928: 26–28; *Chosen Keizainenpo* 1939: Appendix, p. 36: Shokusan Ginko 1938b: 71; Shokusan Ginko 1940: 30–32; F. Fujita 1993: 236; K.J. Cho 1977: 164–165. Chosen Kinyu Kumiai Kyokai 1935; Sotokufu 1932: 294–295; ibid. 1942: 130–131; Bank of Korea 1948: III, 84–85; H. J. Kim 1990: 360; Himeno 1940: 371–374.

When Japan decided to move ahead with its continental conquests and Korea was seen as a crucial pathway to the mainland, Japan adopted a policy of expanding its industrial facilities in Korea. Loans to the industrial sector, which had ranged from about 3 to 5 percent of total loans between 1910 and 1932, increased to 8.4 percent in 1933, 20 percent in 1937, and more than 30 percent after 1940, while loans to agriculture slowly declined to 24.5 percent in 1942. Loans to the industrial sector constituted the largest share after 1940.

Loans extended by the financial institutions in the later years were channeled to new undertakings, such as the iron, steel, and chemical industries; mining (gold, iron, and coal), electric power; and transportation (automobiles). A policy focused on diverting financial resources to the industrial sector was closely associated with the development of the military-industrial complex in Korea. After the 1930s, when Japan needed industrial development, especially military related, their financial needs were met with more bank loans. The major proportion of loans (60 to 70 percent) to industry went to those that were closely related to military needs. About 65 and 57 percent of the total loan funds of all financial institutions extended to industry were directed to heavy and military industries in 1938 and 1939, respectively, while limited support was provided to other industries, such as consumer-goods manufacturing in textiles.[45]

THE ROLE OF FINANCIAL INSTITUTIONS

Each financial institution, whether it was a bank, an NBFI, or public or private, played a different and unique role in financing loans to businesses.

Public Banks

The Bank of Korea was one of the two major policy-oriented public banks. The amount of its loans increased from a very small amount in 1905 to 7 million yen in 1909, 53.5 million in 1926, 207.8 million in 1937, 837.6 million in 1943, and 1 billion in 1944.[46] The bank accounted for about 15 percent of the loans of financial institutions in 1937 (as shown in Table 6.3) and 22 percent in 1943, which was more than all the loans made by private commercial banks in the same year. The Bank of Korea's credit policy was expansive. Its loans often outstripped its financial resources (paid-in capital, retained earnings, and deposits), typically by more than 50 percent of that amount. For instance, in 1936 it loaned 156.6 million yen, which was 1.5 times the 104.6 million yen of its paid-in capital, "reserve funds," and deposits combined (the total volume of loans was equal to 2.18 times deposits in 1943).[47]

The Bank of Korea served as the central bank in fulfilling the demands of the government and also in meeting the financial needs of the private sector as a

TABLE 6.3 Loans of Financial Institutions in 1937

	Million Yen			*Percent*		
Institutions	Loans	Commercial Paper Discounts	Total	Loans	Commercial Paper Discounts	Total
Bank of Korea	207.8	218.0	425.8	15.0	54.3	23.8
Industrial Bank	547.8	43.1	590.9	39.4	10.7	33.0
Savings Bank	26.6	31.0	57.6	1.9	7.7	3.2
Commercial banks	195.7	21.0	216.7	14.1	5.2	12.1
Local banks	159.8	9.0	168.8	11.5	2.2	9.4
Branch banks	35.9	12.0	47.9	2.6	3.0	2.7
Credit unions	237.4	—	237.4	17.1	—	13.3
Trust Company	44.7	9.2	53.9	3.2	2.3	3.0
Oriental Development Company	101.9	78.3	180.2	7.3	19.5	10.1
Insurance companies	27.9	1.0	28.9	2.0	0.2	1.6
Total	1,389.8	401.6	1,791.4	100.0	100.0	100.0

Sources: The table is constructed on the basis of data from Bank of Korea 1948: I, 278 and III, 74–75, 82–87; Takahashi 1935: 500–501; Takeo Suzuki 1941: 268–269; S. Suzuki 1939: 321, 347; Himeno 1940: 369, 371, 374; Hosokawa 1941: 335–336; K. J. Cho 1977: 477.

commercial bank. As a principal financial agent of the government, it channeled financial resources into supporting government programs. In the early years of the Japanese administration, as much as three-quarters of the Bank of Korea's lending was made to the government. This figure declined to 22 percent in 1921 but regained to 51.3 percent in 1925. It decreased once more later, but even as late as 1929 loans to the government made up 26.5 percent of the total. No statistics were published after 1929, but it seems reasonable to assume that loans to the government continued to account for more than a quarter of the bank's loans for the remainder of Japanese rule. As the Japanese empire extended its hegemony into the Asian continent in later years, the Bank of Korea also served as a fiscal agent for the Japanese army in Manchuria. It financed a series of needs of the puppet regime in Manchuria and companies on the Asian continent. It was rumored that the bank was even engaged in the smuggling of silver, opium, and textiles into China.[48]

As a commercial bank, the Bank of Korea supplied financial resources to the private sector as well, mainly large-scale financing aimed at industrial and commercial enterprises that produced strategic goods and services. Many of these loans were made more on political rather than financial considerations and the Bank of Korea concentrated its loans on Japanese companies. As early as 1910 a Japanese bank in Busan received a "relief loan" from the Bank of Korea.[49] The bank also played a large part in the introduction of modern technologies in industry. For instance, it made a 40 million yen loan, or one-third of its total loan amount in 1930 to Noguchi Jun's Korea Chemical Nitrogen Company (Chosen Jitsuso Kaisha). In 1938, under the direction of the Government General, the Bank of Korea financed four-fifths of a Yalu River Hydroelectric Company project, while additional capital needs were supplied by other *zaibatsu*. The practice of making loans on bases other than financial considerations often resulted in default, however. In 1920, for example, about half of the bank's loans were either in default (worth 10 million yen) or classified as "troubled" (worth 50 million yen). In contrast to its heavy loans to industry, Bank of Korea loans to agriculture were minimal, making up no more than 1 to 2 percent of the bank's total loans.

The Industrial Bank, which started out as the Agricultural and Industrial Bank System in 1906, was supposed to have extended loans to agriculture and industry,[50] but about 70 percent of them were short-term loans, mostly to commerce. Its predecessor's banking business was sluggish in the early years and was not able to meet the challenges of a successful banking system until 1918, largely because of its lack of financial resources, managerial inexperience, and reckless credit policy. In 1918, it had outstanding loans equal to 18.6 million yen,[51] which included large numbers of bad loans on which it was difficult or impossible to collect. Huge losses ensued. Bad loans represented 26 percent of all loans, and some of its provincial banks incurred losses of as much as 50 percent of their loans. The two largest Agricultural and Industrial Banks—one in Seoul and another in Pyongyang—alone incurred 1.7 million yen in losses.[52] As a result, the number of provincial banks was reduced from eleven to six.

When its predecessor was reorganized into the Industrial Bank in 1918, it became the main source of long-term loans and debenture capital provided by banks to entrepreneurs, civil and business organizations, and companies headquartered in

Korea.[53] Its loans quickly multiplied, amounting to about 25 million yen in 1919, 73.7 million in 1921, 213.7 million in 1926, 547.8 million in 1937 (see Table 6.3), 1.45 billion in 1943, and 1.65 billion in 1944, a sixty-six-fold increase in a twenty-five-year period and an average annual increase of about 11 percent.

Industrial Bank loans represented approximately 37 percent of loans made by all financial institutions in 1938, 50 percent between 1931 and 1937, 57 percent in 1938, and 60 percent in 1943. They were typically more than double of its financial resources. In 1936, for example, it loaned 488.2 million yen, three times its financial resources. In 1942 it loaned 1.25 billion yen when it had only about 600 million in paid-in-capital and deposits. Its loans typically were about three times its deposits. After 1918, the Industrial Bank made the largest amount of loans of all banks in Korea and became the most important bank for financing investment for the development of agriculture and industry under Japanese rule.[54] In 1937 the loans accounted for nearly 40 percent of the loans of all organized financial institutions (see Table 6.3) and were as much as 4.31 times deposits. Between 1919 and 1945 the bank made, on average, about 56 percent of its loans in the country for long-term investment purposes. In some years (e.g., in 1931), it made as many as 83 percent of its loans for investment purposes.

In fulfilling its mission, the principal concern of the Industrial Bank's loan policy was to implement the established government policies and promote Japan's interests.[55] It acted as a partner of the government and was in step with it, as one former bank official put it, like "a well-oiled cogwheel." According to one economic historian, the colonial government used it like "a private bank" to direct financial resources to meet Japan's needs. Likewise, the bank played the role of a coordinating agency for the government in financing investment in Korea. For instance, it was at the center of a network of agricultural credit agencies sponsored by the government, including the credit unions and the Oriental Development Company.[56]

In the early years, when Japan's interests were centered on commerce, the bank financed that sector heavily, making as many as 51.8 percent of its loans to it in 1922. The focus shifted abruptly thereafter, reflecting a change in Japanese government policy. When Japan faced an acute shortage of rice, loans were redirected from commerce to agriculture, and the largest amount of the Industrial Bank's loans were directed to the agricultural sector. One of the major investment projects in agriculture was a thirty-year plan, originally developed in 1921, to increase rice production in Korea for export to Japan, in which the Industrial Bank was instrumental and a principal agency in financing the project, as explained more fully in Appendix 6.2.

The Industrial Bank's loans to the agricultural sector increased from 4.8 million yen in 1919 to 24.4 million in 1922, 71.5 million in 1928, 165.9 million in 1931, and 212.52 million in 1937, an average annual increase of 11.6 percent. The percentage of loans to agriculture increased from only 5.5 percent of the bank's total loans in 1922 to 47.5 percent in 1921, 37 percent in 1927, and 51.2 percent in 1939. In 1930 as many as 62 percent of its loans were allocated for the agricultural sector. The majority of agricultural loans were for irrigation and land-improvement projects, which included land reclamation and the construction of drainage systems, dams, and dikes. Between 1919 and 1937 the Industrial Bank directed an average of

47.7 percent of its total loans to agriculture, with the aim of improving and irrigating land for rice production.[57] Of all the loans of the bank to agriculture, about 40 percent were for irrigation projects, 12.5 percent for land-improvement projects, and 47.7 percent for general farming needs such as the purchase of fertilizers. While loans to the agricultural sector ranged from 37 to 51.2 percent between 1921 and 1939, loans of the Industrial Bank to "public organizations" (such as government) came in second, accounting for between 5 and 34 percent of the bank's total loans. Loans to commerce came in third, followed by "others." Industry, mining, and fishing received relatively small amounts during 1921–1939, although the share of the industrial sector increased toward the end of Japanese rule.[58]

Finally, when Japan undertook its military course in Asia, the Industrial Bank's credit policy was redirected again. With the aid of government guarantees, the Industrial Bank, with other lending institutions, gained increasing importance in financing investment in industrial enterprises, as all sorts of "national policy companies" were launched to support the war effort. In the early years, the bank's loans to industry were rather modest (3.6 percent in 1921, 3 percent in 1927, and 2.3 percent in 1932). As Japan launched its military expansion into China, the Industrial Bank financed an increasing amount and share of loans to the military-industrial complex after 1935,[59] while the share of its loans to agriculture declined to less than half by 1933. Its loans to industry, which were 3 percent of its total in 1937, increased to 8.2 percent in 1939. Especially with Governor General Minami's policy of developing Korea as a military base (*heitan kichi*), the Korean economy was tailored to establish military-oriented industries to supply food and ammunition to the Japanese armed forces. Although no comprehensive data are available, an even more drastic shift in the Industrial Bank's loans to industry probably took place after 1941.[60] Under this policy, the Industrial Bank gave active financial support to companies producing what were identified as the fifteen national strategic goods. The bank also financed small to medium-sized machinery companies to help meet military needs, and it even financed fish-oil firms in order to increase the production of fish oil to supplement food.

Similarly, the bank also made increasing amounts of loans in "other" areas (national-defense-related organizations). These loans increased from 4.8 percent of its total in 1921 to 6.4 percent in 1932, 8.1 percent in 1937, and 13.6 percent in 1939.[61] It was instrumental in financing the "nonprofit public organizations" (*koko-dantai*) and special corporations (e.g., *eidan, kodan*) that were supported by the Japanese government. The share of its loans to these public nonprofit organizations was large but fluctuated widely; for example, from 13.2 percent of the total in 1921, to 29.6 percent in 1927, 33.9 percent in 1932, 25 percent in 1937, and a mere 5.9 percent in 1939.

The Industrial Bank also focused its loans to serve the financial needs of the businesses and public institutions that it nurtured and controlled. It extended a larger share of loans to them than to businesses that were not closely affiliated with the bank. Approximately 7.5 percent of all companies (mostly major and large) in Korea had close ties with the bank in 1942. In 1933, for instance, 69 percent of the bank's loans went to businesses that were closely affiliated with it, while 27.3 percent went to the firms connected to the Bank of Korea. These included more than twenty major companies in Korea, which possessed nearly 100 million yen of paid-in capital, and which engaged in mining, mineral refining, electric-power generation, railroads, automobile, airplane, and electric-wire manufacturing, shipping, printing, banking, savings and loans, trusts, fire insurance, rice storage, iron-ore production, heavy industry, animal husbandry, and agribusiness (*nojo*). Some scholars believe that the Industrial Bank was in fact a holding company of these business enterprises. It directly invested 26.4 million yen in companies in which it had major shares. For example, it owned a 27 percent interest, or 54,100 shares out of a total of 200,000, in a gold refinery that it kept under its wing.[62]

The Industrial Bank also actively engaged in setting up new companies.[63] It established many corporations as a "venture capitalist" (*hakkijin*) in close consultation with the Government General. Many were in electric-power generation, railroads, and smelting, all of which were closely tied to the military. The Japan High Voltage Heavy Industry (Nihon Koshuha Chukogyo) Company was one of those that received the active support of the Industrial Bank, with a strong military endorsement, as a "policy company" (*kokusaku kaisha*) for military needs. The Industrial Bank financed most of the capital for the establishment of the iron refinery. The bank's involvement with the company was such that some people expressed concern about the bank's excessive involvement in and financing of the company.

Likewise, the bank not only contributed 10 million yen but also was actively involved as a venture capitalist in the construction of the Seoul-Chuncheon Railroad. It helped to establish the Korea Fire and Marine Insurance Company and the Korea Savings Bank. The insurance company and the bank deposited their insurance premiums and deposits in the Industrial Bank, and these, in turn, were used to finance the Industrial Bank's loans.[64] Frequently, loans were extended also to those who had close personal or political ties to the bank and government officials. In making long-term investment loans without collateral, the bank apparently relied more on the borrowers' credibility or "trustworthiness" (*shinyo*) than on the financial soundness of their projects. Likewise, the bank catered more to organizations than to individuals.[65]

The success of the bank's lending policies was mixed. In the case of loans for the rice-production plan, for instance, the positive impact of its financing may be seen in the increased number of irrigation associations formed, more irrigated land, and increased food production. In 1918 there were only fourteen irrigation associations, which were organized largely for Japanese entrepreneurs and immigrants, and covered a total of 26,000 *jeong* of land. The number of irrigation associations increased to 190, servicing 227,900 *jeong*, in 1936. Of these, about 70 percent had dams, 15 percent had water pumps, and 15 percent used natural flows. These projects irrigated 149,161 *jeong* of land and increased rice production by about 1.3 million bushels (254,900 *seok*).[66] Irrigated land was then producing 2.03 million bushels of rice annually.

In spite of these accomplishments, compared with the bank's supply of vast amounts of financial resources, the outcome was less than satisfactory. Many people who were affected by bank-financed projects expressed dissatisfaction with them. No irrigation association was immune from complaint. Newspapers frequently reported disputes involving irrigation projects. Some landlords complained that irrigation fees were too high to warrant the increases in production, while tenants complained that the fees were often being passed on to them.[67] Also, irrigation association fees or water taxes became a major component of the increased production costs of rice. There were cases in which irrigated land was seized for nonpayment of fees. When the price of rice fell, fees became an especially heavy burden, often resulting in the sale of the irrigated land. Moreover, many small landowners fell victim to the projects when their land was targeted for the construction of dams, dikes, or canals. Some complaints and disputes required intervention of the police.[68] Overall, in spite of the fact that 80 percent of the planned amount was spent on the project, only 43 percent of the designated acreage was irrigated and a mere 27.5 percent of the anticipated increase in output was realized.[69]

The efficacy of some bank loans was also questioned. As of 1933 the Industrial Bank's loans to public institutions, such as irrigation associations, without collateral and at low interest rates totaled more than 77 million yen.[70] Some irrigation associations failed to pay interest or repay the principal. As of 1935 70 (out of 190) were described as needing "assistance," of which 5 eventually ceased to operate, 35 needed additional support, and 30 had difficulty remaining solvent. They were given further assistance in the form of lower interest charges, extension of the repayment period, and/or outright government subsidies. The Industrial Bank also lowered interest charges to agricultural plantation companies (Fujin) when it had difficulty in producing planned output. According to the bank, they were given the break because they were supporting a "national policy."

The Savings Bank made some loans, but their volume was small.[71] Their value ranged from 6 million yen in 1929 to 27 million in 1938 and 80.2 million in 1943, which represented only about 3.2 percent of total bank loans in 1937 and 2.5 percent in 1943. The loans were far smaller than the bank's financial resources, representing a little less than 20 to 28 percent of deposits. It, thus, played a very limited role in directly financing investment.

Private Banks

Like those of the public banks, loans extended by private commercial banks also increased. They expanded from less than 8 million yen in 1905 to 57 million in 1921, 195.7 million in 1937 (see Table 6.3), and 677.8 million in 1943 (see Table 6.1). However, unlike in many other countries, the volume of loans extended by the commercial banks in Korea under Japanese rule was relatively small. On average, the commercial banks made up less than one-quarter of the loans of all banks during most of the years of Japanese rule.[72] Such loans constituted about 14.1 percent of the total loans of the financial institutions in 1937 and 17.4 percent in 1943.

The principal reasons for the limited amount of loans by commercial banks were the bounded financial resources and the constraints placed on them by the government, in contrast with the relative lack of restrictions on public banks. As will be examined in the next section, financial resources of commercial banks, such as the volume of deposits, were relatively small, as is shown later in this chapter. In addition, the activities of commercial banks were subject to considerable government restrictive control, and decision making by bank management was bound, especially with regard to loans. The ability of the commercial banks to make loans was limited to an amount equal to or less than their financial resources. Commercial banks did not even loan as much as the amount received in deposits for most of the period, especially after 1938, and the ratio of loans to deposits decreased over time. The commercial banks loaned less than 90 percent of deposits received (391.6 million out of 446.8 million yen) in 1940, for instance. The ratio decreased to 77 percent in 1942 (572.4 million in contrast to 746.6 million yen) and 62 percent in 1944 (1.38 billion in deposits as opposed to 864.4 million yen in loans). Moreover, the relative volume of the loans of all commercial banks compared with that of public banks decreased over time, from about twice the amount loaned by the Bank of Korea before 1934 to about a third more in 1935, a third less in 1940, and about 85 percent in 1944. It is clear that commercial banks in Korea played a more important role in mobilizing savings and a less demanding and diminishing role in making loans for investment.

The volume of loans was even more limited among the commercial banks headquartered in Korea, because they had even more limited loanable funds. Local private banks headquartered in Korea had only 8.6 percent of all loanable funds in 1937, and the Japanese branch banks in Korea had 3.4 percent.[73] The share of loanable funds possessed by Korean-controlled banks was even smaller. In 1943 they made only 8.3 percent of all bank loans.

Moreover, the commercial banks made primarily short-term loans, mostly to businesses engaged in trade. Private bank loans made up more than half of such loans, although loans to commerce gradually declined from 85.8 percent of all loans in 1910 to 61.2 percent in 1932, while loans to other sectors increased. Their lending to the industrial and agricultural sectors, which were typically long-term loans, was very small in the early years, hovering around 3 to 5 percent between 1910 and 1932. Loans to the industrial and "miscellaneous" sectors increased slowly from about 1 to 20 percent during the 1910–1932 period.[74] This trend appears to have continued after 1932.

Public Nonbank Financial Institutions

In addition to banks, a number of NBFIs, both public and private, played a unique role in lending. Public nonbank financial institutions (GNBFIs) included the Oriental Development Company and the credit unions. The Oriental Development Company engaged in substantial loan activities in Korea, increasing from about 600,000 yen in 1910 to 7.4 million in 1912, 30.4 million in 1918, 172.5 million in 1938, and 205.4 million in 1942.[75] Its loanable funds represented 7.3 percent of those of all financial institutions in Korea in 1937 (as shown in Table 6.3) and 5.7 percent in 1943, about 2.6 times the company's paid-in capital and deposits.

The Oriental Development Company extended loans mainly to serve the needs of the agricultural, forestry, and fishing sectors. It allocated 79.3 percent of its loans to agriculture (and some to forestry and fishing) in 1912, 83 percent in 1917, 37.8 percent in 1937, and 51.2 percent in 1939, primarily to increase production and exports of grain (mainly rice) to Japan. In other words, the company allotted as many as four-fifths of its loans to the agricultural sector. Other loan recipients were public organizations such as irrigation associations (about a quarter), commercial enterprises (about one-tenth), and mining, manufacturing, transportation, and gas and electric power companies (the rest).

The major agricultural projects financed by the Oriental Development Company were in irrigation, land improvement, and agriculture in general.[76] In 1931, for instance, the company, along with the Industrial Bank, allotted more than 42 percent of its loans to irrigation projects and about 10 percent to land improvement. The remaining loans were to support of sericulture, animal husbandry, and agriculture in general. Similarly, the company's loans in 1938 amounted to 29.3 percent (33.2 million yen) for irrigation projects, 34.2 percent (38.7 million) for farming, and 5.6 percent (6.4 million) for fertilizer purchases, as well as 30.9 percent (35 million) for urban land reclamation.

The company made loans to some "modern" nonagricultural sectors as well, especially toward the end of colonial rule. Loans to these sectors increased from none in 1912 to 17 percent of total loans in 1917 and 32.8 percent in 1927. Its loans included mining (10.5 million yen), textiles (9 million), gas and electric companies (6.8 million), and others (172.5 million). Also included were railroad, distilling, heavy and chemical industries, oil, paper, and grain-storage projects. The company even financed the Agricultural and Industrial Banks by purchasing its bonds, totaling 3 million yen (1 million in 1913 and 2 million in 1918).

Credit unions likewise made loans, which increased from about 16,000 yen in 1907 to 2.2 million in 1915, 123.4 million in 1930, 237.4 million in 1937 (see Table 6.3), and 549.5 million in 1943. This accounted for 17.1 percent of total loans made by all financial institutions in 1937 and 14.2 percent in 1943. Thus, the volume of loans by the credit unions was substantial and increased over time but lagged far behind their financial resources (examined in the following section). Their loans represented about 1.4 times their deposits in the early years, but the ratio declined sharply to about three-quarters in the 1930s, one-third in the later years, and less than one-quarter by 1944. Their loans did not even keep pace with deposits. This low loan-to-deposit ratio contrasts strikingly with the high ratio of the public banks and the Oriental Development Company.

Credit unions made loans, mainly to the agricultural sector which constituted more than 70 percent of the total.[77] Nearly a third of the loans in 1936 were used by borrowers to repay their debts, and one-fifth were to finance their purchase of land, and only about 8.5 percent of the total was used for real investment in farm instruments or inudstrial tools, tool houses, cows, horses, or establishing shops and factories. They also financed some small urban businesses, including manufacturing, which began to expand toward the end of the colonial period, but loans for these purposes still were rather modest.

For investment purpose, credit union loans tended to finance land-improvement projects for large landholders, as was examined above in connection with Industrial Bank loans. Since many large projects that the credit unions financed were undertaken by Japanese entrepreneurs, Japanese companies (especially those in agriculture) also tended to receive more loans.[78] In contrast to wealthy landlords, ordinary farmers—especially the small Korean farmers—received little assistance in the form of loans. Because of their stringent terms, such as land as collateral, most small farmers did not qualify for loans. Most of them were tenants and lacked land, the only collateral available in villages. Several investigations conducted among farmers in 1933 revealed that loans from credit unions played only a small part in the financing of small producers.[79] According to Hoon Ku Lee, the credit unions supplied fewer loans to small farmers than those financed by individual lenders in 1930, which was estimated at about 30 percent of the total debt.[80] Another estimate of farmers' indebtedness made in 1932 shows that only 17.4 percent of loans to farmers were supplied by the credit unions, while 26 percent were supplied by private persons, mostly usurers who charged high interest, typically 30 to 40 percent a year. Likewise, in 1938 the credit unions financed only 31 percent of farmers' debt and the banks 34 percent, while the rest was financed by individuals.[81] It is difficult to calculate the precise amount of farmers' debt not financed by these institutions, but it was large.

Private Nonbank Financial Institutions

There also were private nonbank financial institutions (PNBFIs)—which included trust companies, savings-and-loan associations, mutual-aid societies, and insurance companies—that performed limited but useful financial services by supplying credit to farmers and small businesses in cities while receiving deposits of people's savings.[82] Among them, trust companies provided small but increasing amounts of loans to businesses. The value of their loans was minuscule before 1937, but in that year it increased to 45.1 million yen and rose to 69.4 million in 1944. Trust company loans were usually secured with real estate and securities as collateral.

Similarly, a large number of savings-and-loan associations and mutual-aid credit unions (*mujin whoesa*) provided small but increasing numbers of loans. Their loans expanded slowly, from 3.2 million yen in 1930 to 34.7 million in 1944, but their relative share of loans was small and decreased over time: 3.1 percent of total loans of the financial institutions in 1938 and 1.5 percent in 1943. Insurance companies also contributed financial resources to businesses, including government-directed investment projects.

Private individuals also engaged in lending. There were as many Japanese as Koreans in the private lending business, particularly in the early years. Many Japanese who began as merchants providing for people's daily needs turned to dry goods and then to moneylending businesses.[83] As early as 1905 there were 114 Japanese lenders in three cities.[84] The fund of these individuals was reported to have increased modestly from 1.5 million yen in 1923 to 1.84 million in 1931 and 4.6 million in 1938. Several investigations conducted among farmers in 1933 indicated that loans extended by individuals to individuals made up more than 60 percent of all personal loans. Private individuals financed loans to small farmers and others. Typically, landlords extended credit to their tenant farmers for major family events and the purchase of food, fertilizer, seeds, and equipment. Most Japanese landlords in Korea and their Korean counterparts were reported to have engaged in such lending to their tenant farmers.[85] Their loan activities appear to have had little impact on the nation's real investment.

The preceding analysis reveals three features of loan activities of financial institutions under Japanese rule. First, as expected, the major portion of institutional loans was extended by banks. For example, as much as 86.6 and 94.5 percent of the loans of all financial institutions in 1938 and 1939, respectively, were made by banks. Likewise, three-quarters to four-fifths of all long-term loans were made by banks in 1939 and 1940, while the NBFIs contributed the rest.

Second, unlike the situation in most developed countries, the dominant proportion of loans was made by two public banks and two GNBFIs. The special or public banks (the Bank of Korea and the Industrial Bank) dominated lending. The loans supplied by these two banks made up more than half (50.2 percent in 1938 and 59.2 percent in 1943) of the loans of all financial intermediaries in Korea. When short-term lending is included, their loans represented more than 60 percent in 1943. Thus, the loans of the public banks were far larger (3.9 times in 1938 and 3.4 times in 1943, or 80 and 77.3 percent of all bank loans) than those made by private commercial banks. The GNBFIs accounted for nearly a third of the loans of all financial institutions in 1938 and 20 percent in 1943. In contrast, the share of loans of private banks and PNBFIs was relatively small (16 percent of the loanable funds of all financial intermediaries in 1938 and 19 percent in 1943) and played a limited role in financing long-term loans for investment, especially in the early colonial years.

Third, the financial institutions as a whole supplied more loans than was warranted by their financial resources, in fact nearly twice as much.[86] In 1939 the total value of loans extended by all banks was 1.38 billion yen, compared with about 975 million in official capital and deposits. In 1942 total loans extended by all banks were valued at 2.45 billion yen, compared with about 1.9 billion in official capital and deposits. The lending of three public financial institutions, namely, the Bank of Korea, the Industrial Bank, and the Oriental Development Company, typically exceeded their financial resources, while other financial institutions, including private commercial banks, did not loan out as much as their available financial resources. Through these loans, the public financial intermediaries exercised power over the nation's business, which relied on them. Major economic expansion would not have been possible in colonial Korea without the state-controlled credit channeled through them.

The credit policies of these public banks and GNBFIs were coordinated with the economic policy of the colonial government, because the prime mover in them was the government. The public banks and GNBFIs were closely tied to, supervised, and guided by the government. The appointment or approval of the principal officers and directors of these financial intermediaries was made by the Government General, and all major administrative decisions, such as the making of major loans for "certain purposes," required the explicit or tacit approval of the government. Obviously, these financial intermediaries supported the goals of the government and were in partnership with it,[87] and the government did not hesitate to use them as instruments of national policy. The colonial government dictated their loan policies, including the allocation of their financial resources to targeted users.

Private banks and PNBFIs were not under the direct control of the Japanese government, but some of their loans were also directed toward government-sponsored investment projects, since their activity was regulated and monitored through the imposition of certain conditions. One of the conditions of the Government General for setting up an insurance company, for instance, was that all insurance premiums had to be deposited in the Industrial Bank or invested in its bonds.

TERMS OF LOANS AND BORROWERS

The terms of loans of financial institutions varied widely, depending on the type of financial institution that made the loan and the kind of collateral offered (in most cases, loans with collateral carried lower interest rates than those without it),[88] but they clearly reflected the economic policy objectives of the government in the purposes of the loans and the types of borrowers to whom loans were extended. Loans of the public banks and GNBFIs typically were made at lower rates of interest than the market rates (usually by 25 percent) and those charged by private banks and PNBFIs. They were also made for a longer duration, since many were for development projects that usually had long gestation period. Loans for the purposes approved and supported by the government bore even lower rates of interest than ordinary loans.[89] Also, interest rates on large loans typically were lower than those on small ones. Likewise, interest rates charged by banks depended on the nationality of the borrower. They were lower for Japanese (and some selected Korean borrowers) than for most Koreans. Korean enterprises as a rule paid 25 percent higher interest than did the Japanese.[90]

It is difficult to determine exactly who the borrowers were, but the bulk of loans were made to large businesses and landlords. This outcome can clearly be seen in the case of loans extended by public banks and GNBFIs. In the case of industry, since most projects for which the public banks extended loans were large, loans were mostly for large enterprises, as shown in the financing of chemical, heavy industries, and hydroelectric-power plants. In agriculture, since irrigation projects were carried out mostly by and for large landlords to increase the production of rice, they were the major recipients of loans financed by the public financial institutions.

In contrast, small farmers and businesses were underserved by banks and NBFIs, particularly public banks and GNBFIs. Little was done to stop the growth of tenancy by means of inexpensive credit or other financially beneficial measures to assist tenant farmers in becoming independent farmers with their own land. Even the credit unions and the Oriental Development Company, whose main missions were in agriculture, were of little help to them. They together furnished only about a quarter of the funds borrowed by farmers. The continuing inability of peasants to finance debt through financial institutions remained a conspicuous feature of the Korean scene under Japanese rule. As a result, usury continued to flourish and tenant farming expanded.

It has often been argued, mostly by Korean scholars, that in making loans, financial institutions discriminated against the Koreans and favored the Japanese.[91] This assertion was made on the bases of the following four main reasons: (1) Japanese borrowers received larger loans than Koreans borrowers did; (2) Japanese companies had a higher ratio of debt to equity; (3) almost all large firms, which derived the most benefit from loans of financial institutions, were Japanese owned; and (4) loans to Japanese businesses were made with more lenient requirements. According to scholars' rationale, the financial advantage enabled the Japanese investors to expand their businesses and landholdings.

First of all, there is evidence that Japanese companies relied more heavily on borrowed money from the financial institutions, which is closely associated with the growing financial resources of the public banks, than did the Korean firms. According to available data, the Japanese, during 1920–1939, typically received between 50 and 65 percent of total volume of loans, and the Korean share was limited to between 35 percent and 50 percent.

Second, many Japanese corporations did finance their businesses with debenture issues and borrowing more than the Koreans did. In the case of manufacturing, the Japanese companies relied on more borrowed money, while Korean companies financed their businesses with more owners' equity. As of 1943 29.9 percent of Japanese companies' business financing was in the form of owners' equity, on average, while 53.6 percent of Korean companies' investment was financed with owners' equity. In other words, borrowed money financed more than 70 percent of the Japanese investment in their companies, in comparison with only 46.4 percent in the case of Korean businesses.[92] Of agricultural loans, more than half of the irrigated acreage under the jurisdiction of irrigation associations that received large loans from the Industrial Bank and GNBFIs, which were closely associated with the growing financial resources of the public banks, were owned by the Japanese.[93] More than four-fifths of the irrigated land was owned by large Japanese landowners (those with more than 50 *jeong*), and more than half (52.5 percent) of Japanese owners of irrigated land held more than 100 *jeong*.[94] Therefore, they benefited the most from the loans of the financial institutions.

Third, that large businesses, including agribusinesses, received more loans than small and medium-sized businesses implies that the Japanese were favored to receive, since large businesses, including agribusinesses, typically were Japanese. As noted earlier, most large businesses were Japanese owned. Fourth, Korean borrowers had to meet more stringent requirements for loans, such as the possession of collateral and their motive for taking loans. Apparently, the discriminatory lending policy was intended to choke off funds for Korean independence movements.

Contrary to these views and data, other bank loan data show that Koreans were not necessarily being discriminated against in the business of receiving bank loans. In fact, they seemed to have received more than their fair share. Compared with their deposits in these financial institutions, the amount of loans extended to Koreans relative to those granted to Japanese was not unfairly small. While the Koreans did receive smaller amounts of loans than did the Japanese during 1920–1939, their deposits in banks were merely 15 to 24 percent of the total during the same period. Therefore, the amount of loans to Koreans was more than twice their deposits.[95] On the other hand, while the Japanese typically received between 50 to 65 percent of total loans during 1920–1939, their deposits in banks were 76 to 85 percent of the total during the same period. The ratios of loan advances to Japanese, thus, were only 67 and 76 percent of their bank deposits, respectively.[96] In other words, relative to the amount of deposits Koreans made in financial institutions, they received bank loans in amounts more than twice their share of deposits, while the Japanese received bank loans at less than their share of deposits.

Let us examine this development in more detail, using the loan activities of 1939. Loans to Japanese nationals in that year equaled 55 percent of total loans, while Koreans received 45 percent.[97] In relation to deposits, the Japanese share of loans was not out of the ordinary, nor was the Korean share unfavorably small. While the banking system in Korea as a whole loaned out twice the amount of deposits it received in 1939, the Japanese received loans equal to only about 150 percent of their deposits, while the Koreans received 375 percent; thus, the ratio of loans to deposits for the Koreans was 2.5 times that for the Japanese, which means that, in relation to deposits, Koreans borrowed more than the Japanese did. In this respect, it could be said that Koreans received more than their fair share of such loans.

Moreover, the ratio of loans to deposits to Koreans versus the Japanese increased over time. Loans to Koreans multiplied 34.7 times during the 1910–1934 period, while loans to Japanese increased only 14.1 times.[98] Also, the Korean share increased from 41.8 percent of that of the Japanese in 1910 (6.6 million yen to Koreans and 15.8 million to Japanese) to 97 percent in 1928 (151.1 million yen to Koreans and 155.7 million to Japanese) and 103 percent in 1934 (229.2 million yen to Koreans and 223.4 million to Japanese). By 1932 Koreans were receiving nearly half of all bank loans, or about an equal amount as the Japanese. The Korean loan-deposit ratio increased from about 3.2 (12.5 million yen in loans to 3.9 million in deposits) in 1919 to 4.1 (154.1 million yen in loans to 37.4 million in deposits) in 1934. Thus, while the share of deposits of Koreans fluctuated between 21 percent of the total to 24 percent during the same period, their loans were four times the deposits, and the gap in the amount of loans between the two nationalities narrowed considerably over time.

There are no comprehensive records available regarding which Koreans received loans, but they appear to have been largely limited to businessmen who had won the backing of the colonial administration.[99] Korean-owned companies such as the Tongil Bank, Whashin Trade, and Gyeongseong Spinning and Weaving received financial assistance from state-affiliated financial institutions. In order to address and gain more insight into the allegation of discriminatory loan policies, it may be helpful to separate the loan activities of public banks and GNBFIs on the one hand and the private banks and PNBFIs on the other. There are few published records showing the amount of loans of the public banks and GNBFIs to Japanese and Koreans, but in all likelihood the public banks and GNBFIs did extend far greater amounts of funds, especially long-term loans for investment, to the Japanese than to the Koreans. Financial resources were tightly controlled by the Japanese government, especially during World War II, and it did favor large firms owned and operated by the Japanese.

As noted above, many public financial institutions were set up by and for the benefit of not only the Japanese government but also Japanese businesses including agri-businesses. The preferred customers of the Oriental Development Company and the Industrial Bank were Japanese.[100] The company automatically made loans to Japanese immigrants on very favorable terms (e.g., at 7 percent annual interest for twenty-five years for the purchase of land) but not to Korean farmers. Although the company's loans to Japanese immigrants were relatively small, they increased from 238,000 yen in 1918 to about half a million in the early 1930s. The Industrial Bank, too, was described by a former Japanese bank official as "a Japanese bank managed by Japanese."[101] It directed, for example, most of its efforts to a particular region, e.g., Jeolla provinces, where many large Japanese agribusinesses were concentrated.

Many Japanese took advantage of banks' loan programs and of government subsidies and undertook projects requiring huge amounts of investment and advanced technology, for instance, under the rice-production expansion plans.[102] According to government and bank officials, one reason for the limited amount of loans to Koreans was that they did not take advantage of bank loans to undertake "sound and profitable projects" for increasing rice production. A case in point is the irrigation projects of the 1920s and the early 1930s. In the view of Japanese government and bank officials, government and financial-institution support for land-improvement programs was such that the potential benefit to entrepreneurs was great.[103] However, few Korean landlords were willing to participate or borrow money for the projects.

Japanese government and bank officials blamed Koreans for not investing in projects for which government subsidies and financial institutions' loans were forthcoming. To them, Koreans were not interested in land improvement and lacked the desire and technical skills to take advantage of these opportunities. Government officials also suggested that even the most modern Korean agricultural companies had little interest in making a real investment in agriculture to increase rice production. According to the Japanese officials, Korean landlords figured that the returns on investment in farmland were too small compared with the potential earnings from other businesses and moneylending. They cited a survey showing that most of the twenty-two Korean agricultural companies in 1930 diverted profits from farming to moneylending and retail businesses. In addition, they pointed out that many of the Korean landlords were absentee owners who were not interested in farming but enjoyed the luxuries of city life and relied on their superintendents to oversee farming operations.[104] In 1930 absentee landlords in Korea represented, on average, about 31 percent of the total, ranging from 11 to 46 percent in 13 provinces.

In response to these accusations, Korean landlords pointed out that many irrigation projects were not sound investments and were not financially profitable.[105] Notwithstanding this controversy, three facts are clearly notable. One is that the returns on investment of these projects in farmland were typically small compared with the earnings to be made from other businesses and moneylending.[106] The second is that many irrigation associations were in financial difficulties due to inefficacy of their irrigation projects. In these ways, the assessment of Korean landlords proved to be correct. The third fact is that, after 1910, the most owners of irrigated land were Japanese. The land-improvement projects financed by public banks and GNBFIs were undertaken mostly in areas where a large number of Japanese owners were concentrated. There was as much Japanese-owned land (51.3 percent of all irrigated land) being served by irrigation projects as there was irrigated land owned by Koreans in the late 1930s, in spite of the fact that Japanese were a very small minority, while an overwhelming majority of farmers were Koreans.

Contrary to the allegation of Koreans being discriminated against, private banks and PNBFIs did extend more loans to Koreans than to Japanese. It is interesting and perhaps significant to note that the commercial banks and probably PNBFIs were more inclined to make loans to Koreans than to Japanese. There seem to have been at least two reasons for the relatively large amounts of loans extended to Koreans by commercial banks and PNBFIs. One is that most large Japanese firms but few Koreans had access to financial markets in Japan, where interest rates were lower than in Korea. The large companies headquartered in Japan, as well as some large Japanese companies headquartered in Korea, relied on financial markets in Japan. Another reason was that banks were able to charge about 25 percent higher interest rates to Koreans than to Japanese borrowers in Korea.

RESOURCES OF FINANCIAL INSTITUTIONS

One crucial challenge facing underdeveloped countries today, as was the case in all developed countries in the past, is the mobilization and expansion of savings for investment. Typically, it is the inability of financial institutions to assemble savings that prevents investment and development, not the lack of a market for loans. People are always willing to borrow the savings of others,[107] and Koreans under Japanese rule were no exception. The financial resources with which the banks and NBFIs financed their loans to businesses were derived from four main sources: owners' equity, deposits, currency issues, and borrowed funds. These are examined next.

Owners' Equity

There are no comprehensive and consistent statistics on the owners' equity of many financial institutions, including banks headquartered in Japan and PNBFIs, but the amount was not very large. The owners' equity in the form of paid-in capital of those institutions headquartered in Korea in 1938 represented about 6.2 percent of the financial resources of all financial institutions. The paid-in capital of those headquartered in Korea in later years was even slimmer. Total paid-in capital in 1943, for instance, represented only about 2.7 percent of the financial resources of all financial institutions in Korea, as shown in Table 6.4. The owners' equity in the form of retained earnings of all the financial institutions in Korea was also relatively small, representing less than 3.5 percent of their financial resources in 1938, while those in later years were even smaller; for example, about 1.9 percent in 1943. The largest bloc of retained earnings held by the financial institutions was in the credit unions, while those of the commercial banks showed only about 1 percent of their financial resources in the same year. The combined total of owners' equity in paid-in capital and retained earnings of all financial institutions declined from 9.7 percent of their financial resources in 1938 to 4.6 percent in 1943.[108]

TABLE 6.4 Paid-in Capital and Retained Earnings of Financial Institutions (percent)

	Paid-in Capital		*Retained Earnings*	
Financial Institutions	1938	1943	1938	1943
Bank of Korea	3.5	1.8	1.3	1.1
Industrial Bank	4.8	3.0	2.7	1.8
Savings Bank	5.2	1.0	1.8	1.2
Oriental Development Company	29.2	11.7	12.9	4.1
Credit unions	6.2	2.6	—	4.4
Private banks	4.5	1.3	2.0	1.0
PNBFIs	5.9	3.6	—	—
Average	5.5	2.5	2.3	2.3

Sources: Based on Bank of Korea 1948: I, 277 and III, 74–77, 80–81, 84–85, 86–87, 173; Takahashi 1935: 508; S. Suzuki 1939: 332; *Kokusei Gurafu* April 1940; Hosokawa 1941: 335–336. Also see Sotokufu 1916: 110–113; ibid. 1926: 108; ibid. 1932: 294–295; ibid. 1935.

Deposits

Because financial intermediaries are in business not with the owner's equity but with someone else's savings, the primary financial resource of the financial intermediaries is the public's deposits in them.[109] They contributed 46.3 percent of the resources of all financial institutions in Korea in 1938 and 61.5 percent in 1943. Of these, deposits in banks represented the bulk (62.2 percent) of the total deposits in all financial institutions.[110] Deposits of Japanese were much larger than those of Koreans, with the ratios between the two nationalities from 1910 to 1932 ranging between about three to one and four to one.

The major portion of bank deposits was in the two principal public banks, namely, the Bank of Korea and the Industrial Bank, which held more than half of all bank deposits.[111] The Bank of Korea typically received 10 to 15 percent of all deposits in financial institutions, and its deposits constituted more than one-fifth of its financial resources.[112] The largest deposits were in the Industrial Bank.[113] It received 15 to 20 percent of all deposits in financial institutions between 1932 and 1943, which were 10 to 50 percent more than those received by the Bank of Korea, and the bank's deposits supplied about 30 percent of its financial resources in 1938 and more than 46 percent in 1943. The depositors in the Industrial Bank were mostly by financial and industrial institutions closely affiliated with it: the Savings Bank, the Postal Savings System, the Trust Company, the credit unions, the Oriental Development Company, commercial banks, and insurance companies.[114] Between them, they accounted for 55.7 percent of all deposits in 1933, compared with the 32.3 percent deposited by institutions that were more closely affiliated with the Bank of Korea. These depositors were predominantly nonborrowers who were attracted by the government guarantee of deposits and high interest payments.

The Savings Bank, established primarily to collect savings of individuals and nonprofit organizations, relied on deposits for its financial resources. It was successful in collecting the savings of landlords, middle-income farmers, some businesses, professional workers, and semipublic institutions such as irrigation associations. Deposits in the bank represented 8.7 percent of those of all banks in 1941, 10.3 percent in 1939, and 12.5 percent in 1943. Deposits constituted 98 percent of its financial resources.[115]

A number of GNBFIs also collected savings.[116] The credit unions, whose primary function was the mobilization of members' savings, played an important role in mobilizing savings, mostly from the rural areas and small towns. They paid higher interest rates on deposits than the public banks (4.3 percent, which was 0.7 percent higher than the banks). The deposits of the credit unions, which had the most deposits of any NBFIs in Korea, represented nearly one-quarter (23.6 percent) of deposits in all financial institutions between 1918 and 1943.[117] Deposits made up more than three-quarters (84 percent in 1943) of credit unions' financial resources, and the second largest bloc of deposits among financial institutions. Deposits in the credit unions that were not loaned out were deposited in the Industrial Bank or invested in public and bank bonds.

The Postal Savings System likewise collected the savings of small-income earners, workers, mostly in urban areas, via the postal service, in excess of those received by the Savings Bank.[118] By 1944, the deposits in the system amounted to nearly one-fifth of total deposits in all financial institutions in the country. The Postal Savings System, which was under the direct control of the government, thus played an important role of mobilizing the savings of small income earners and supplying the public banks (via deposits in the Industrial Bank and the purchase of bonds) and the government with funds they could use for investment. Their deposits in the Industrial and other public banks increased from a small sum in 1910 to 38.5 million yen in 1929, 234.3 million in 1940, and 1.41 billion in 1944.

The commercial banks similarly attracted large deposits, which increased over time.[119] Their deposits constituted approximately 35 to 38 percent of deposits in all financial institutions during 1932 and 1934, respectively, and then decreased to 20 percent in 1943. On average, they comprised approximately 30 percent of the deposits of all banks from 1926 to 1944. Deposits received by the commercial banks represented 96 percent of their total financial resources in 1943. The PNBFIs also performed a limited but useful service by mobilizing savings. Their deposits, however, were relatively small, most of which were deposited with the Industrial Bank.

Currency Issue

Another major source of funds for financial institutions was the issuance of bank notes by the Bank of Korea. Other than during the last two years of colonial rule (1944–1945), this source represented about 13.5 percent of the total resources of all financial institutions in 1938 and 17.8 percent in 1943.[120] Currency issues supplied approximately 45.8 percent of the financial resources of the Bank of Korea before World War II and 66.7 percent in 1943. The bank's reserve against currency issues was based almost entirely on the Japanese yen, government bonds, and commercial papers. Between 1939 and 1945, for instance, it had only 4 to 10 million yen in gold and silver reserves against the total currency issue of about 1 billion yen.

The creation of money by means of the printing press allowed the Bank of Korea to finance some of the investment projects that helped to meet Japan's industrial needs.

Borrowing

The fourth source of financial resources that financial institutions obtained was external borrowing. Large amounts were raised by floating bonds, which represented 30.4 percent of total financial resources of all financial institutions in 1938 and 15.6 percent in 1943.[121] The institutions that borrowed most heavily from external sources were the public banks and GNBFIs.[122] There are no statistical data showing the borrowing of the Bank of Korea, but its outstanding sums represented 21.3 percent of its financial resources in 1938 and 7 percent in 1943.[123]

Unquestionably, the bank that borrowed the most money through bond issues was the Industrial Bank.[124] The bank was given the authority and had the ability to raise funds. It was authorized in 1918 to float government-secured bank bonds bearing 8 percent interest up to ten times its paid-in capital, or 100 million yen.[125] In 1925 it was permitted to issue greater sums, in amounts up to fifteen times its paid-in capital.[126] This limit was lifted altogether after 1930, when the bank was given virtually unlimited borrowing power. By 1939 the value of bonds outstanding was 156 percent of deposits, which was equal to more than twenty times its paid-in capital.[127] Interest paid on these bonds ranged from 4.3 percent to 8.5 percent.

The Industrial Bank thus became the institution that floated the largest number of bonds and brought in the most external financial resources, which represented the most significant source of its financial resources and allowed it to make loans in an amount far greater than its own financial resources. The borrowed funds represented between 65 and 78 percent of its loanable funds between 1924 and 1937 and between 50 to 60 percent after 1937. Since deposits were not suitable for long-term loans, external borrowing became one of the main sources of financing investment in businesses and agriculture in Korea.[128]

Because the Industrial Bank had the ability to raise funds in Japan at low interest rates, most of its bonds were sold there. The principal buyers were the Deposit Bureau of the Japanese government and the Industrial Bank of Japan (Nihon Kogyo Ginko). Of the funds raised through bank bond issues between 1921 and 1937, the Deposit Bureau bought about one-fifth.[129] Other financial institutions, corporations, and the Government General purchased about one-tenth, while the bond market absorbed the rest, or a little less than two-thirds, mostly in Japan. The Deposit Bureau came to assist many fund-raising efforts of the Industrial Bank, including loans to pay off an Agricultural and Industrial Bank loan in 1920 (at 5.5 percent interest for 10 years) and to finance the rice-production projects. In 1934 loans from the Deposit Bureau of Japan and bond issues represented about 36 percent of the loanable funds of all banks in Korea.[130]

After 1938, the subscribers to Industrial Bank bonds shifted considerably from Japanese to Korean sources. Of the government-guaranteed Industrial Bank bonds issued after 1938, Japanese sources purchased 58.5 percent, while Korean markets took in as much as 41.5 percent.[131] The Deposit Bureau of the Japanese government continued to supply about 27 percent of the total. In Korea a large number of shares were taken up by the credit unions and the Korea Savings Bank, which were supported by small- and medium-income earners through depositing their savings. They absorbed more than a third of the total funds raised by the Industrial Bank, 19.3 percent and 17.3 percent, respectively. Of the Industrial Bank's ordinary (nongovernment guaranteed) bonds, Korean sources supplied about one-half of the total, while about a third was bought by bond markets in Japan.[132] To suit small savers in Korea, the bank issued small-denomination bonds, the so-called patriot bonds. It was reported that all of the funds raised through the issuance of bonds were devoted to such investments as land-improvement programs, irrigation and dam projects, and chemical and heavy industries.[133]

The Oriental Development Company also issued large numbers of bonds, mainly in Japan.[134] It had the authority to issue corporate bonds and did so with the assistance of the Industrial Bank of Japan.[135] The borrowed sums were equal to 21 percent of the financial resources of the company in 1938 and 49 percent in 1943. The credit unions also raised funds by selling bonds and borrowing in Japan.[136] The borrowing of the credit unions represented 26.5 percent of their financial resources in 1938 and 10.5 percent in 1943. The Credit Union Federation issued somewhat smaller amounts of bonds in 1939 and 1940.[137] Likewise, the Irrigation Association raised small amounts through bonds between 1913 and 1932.[138]

Unlike most public banks and GNBFIs, the commercial banks and PNBFIs did not finance their loans with borrowed funds, as they were restricted to borrowing money in the capital market. The commercial banks had borrowed small amounts of funds between 1926 and 1942, representing only about 16.2 percent of their financial resources in 1938 and a mere 1.9 percent in 1943.[139]

The foregoing analysis clearly shows that the amount of financial resources raised through bond issues by the public banks and GNBFIs was large, equal to 93.4 percent of the debenture capital raised by all financial institutions in 1938 and 98.7 percent in 1943. It made up 33 percent of their financial resources in 1938 and 20.7 percent in 1943.[140] Borrowing thus enabled them to finance nearly one-third of the value of all loans made by financial institutions in Korea, and with these financial resources they were able to make long-term loans beyond their own financial resources.

This examination also reveals the nature of the financial resources of the financial institutions, the types of financial institutions that possessed sufficient resources to make loans, and the extent of the loans they made. First, the largest share of financial resources came from deposits, which represented approximately 52 percent of the total (e.g., 46.3 percent in 1938 and 59.5 percent in 1943). This was followed by external borrowings, which contributed about 25 percent (30.4 percent in 1938 and 18.1 percent in 1943), mostly from Japan. The third major financial resource was currency issued by the Bank of Korea, which constituted about 15 percent of the total financial resources of the financial institutions. Paid-in capital and retained earnings of financial institutions made up the remaining portions, which were very small. The government provided little support in the form of share capital, yet it did secure sufficient financial resources to carry out its economic policies through the banks and GNBFIs.

Second, public banks and GNBFIs possessed the most financial resources, typically about 86 percent of the total, and played the dominant role in credit market.[141] Third, the value of the loans extended was far greater than the financial resources of the financial institutions. Through such expansionary financial practices, mainly by the public banks and GNBFIs, a great deal of new investment in Korea was made possible.

There was, however, a price to be paid for the recklessness with which the public banks extended credit. One adverse consequence of Japan's expansionary and lax credit standards was a chronic waste of capital resources, which were easily diverted into speculation and ill-conceived projects, often resulting in default. Banks, especially the two public banks and the Oriental Development Company, often gambled on risky loans. In 1937, for instance, nearly 15 percent of the loans of all financial institutions and approximately 11 to 31 percent of all loans made by banks in Korea from 1926 to 1944 were either in default (10 million yen) or classified as "troubled loans."[142]

Lax credit policies, guarantees instigated by government officials (which made possible low-interest bank credits to risky projects), and failure to repay this credit indicated distorted resource allocation, which probably dampened the incentives otherwise present for technological improvement. Low-interest bank loans extended to unproved projects also imposed a heavy burden on the most innovative and potentially productive segments of the economy, including small and medium-sized enterprises, and they inhibited investment and economic growth, thus lowering the living standard of people in the country.

Another consequence of the expansionary bank credit policy was its contribution to the inflationary spiral, especially toward the end of colonial rule.[143] The inflationary spiral, in turn, aggravated income inequities and poverty (some benefited from it, but not the poor). The inflationary spiral likewise tended to shift government spending away from socially beneficial investments (such as health, education, good roads, and communications) toward military-industrial projects, the rice-production program, and low-quality infrastructure.

SUMMARY AND CONCLUSIONS

This chapter has examined how the colonial government promoted capital formation and transformed the Korean economy from the transitional economy to a modern one. It was found that this was not effected through a greater disposition by the government to invest, nor were there more profit opportunities in Korea. Instead, it was the result of more effective inducements for high rates of investment in the economic sectors and enterprises that Japan needed and promoted. The colonial government provided incentives to private investors to invest in newly produced capital assets by three principal means—low taxes, generous subsidies, and financial loans to strategic industries—in addition to encouraging investment through guarantees against loss, dividend warranties, and technical assistance.

One of the more effective inducements was tax incentives. No income or business taxes were levied in Korea until 1936, and even thereafter the tax burden was light on business and high incomes. These taxes in Korea were lower and less progressive than those that prevailed in Japan, and low tax rates and exemptions were accorded to what the colonial government then considered strategic to Japanese interests. Government tax revenues were mostly derived from taxes that fell directly or indirectly upon the low-saving masses, especially peasants, who made up more than two-thirds of the population. These taxes were mostly derived from land in the early period and consumption in later years. The land tax made up more than 60 percent of government revenues in the early years, while consumption taxes (including government monopoly profits and tariffs) were most important in later times.

The second government inducement for investment was the provision of generous subsidies, which represented more than 5 to 10 percent of government expenditures, to targeted sectors, namely, rice producers, gold miners, and strategic industries. The chief beneficiaries of government subsidies were Japanese business firms and landowners. Upon alleged grounds of economies of scale, they were also bestowed primarily upon large firms. Exceptional privileges were accorded to groups capable of commanding capital and skills, namely, the *zaibatsu,* which were virtual partners of the government (see chapter 8). Discriminatory pricing policies for input goods and services also consistently favored Japanese firms. The Japanese government allocated scarce production inputs at favorable controlled prices and wages to large *zaibatsu* firms.

The third and the most important instrument for promoting private investment was the extension of loans to finance investment in agriculture and industry with subsidized interest by the public banks and GNBFIs, which enabled new and/or expanding businesses to employ idle resources to produce goods and services. The largest portion of these loans was directed toward meeting the changing needs of Japan: initially in commerce, followed by agriculture, and in modern industries in the later years. Loans in agriculture were mostly for rice production and involved the construction of irrigation systems for paddy fields, dams, and the conversion of wasteland into farming land, while loans in industry went mostly to manufacturers using modern technology and often producing military-related goods. Loans were channeled mostly into investments that Japan prescribed to large agricultural operations and industrial firms, which were owned and operated mostly by the Japanese.

More than four-fifths of these loans were extended by the government-established public banks and GNBFIs and were typically made for the long term at rates of interest lower than market prices. Resources that enabled the financial institutions to extend such loans came mainly from bank deposits and external borrowings. One-half to three-fifths of their total financial resources came from deposits, which were institutionalized mostly (over four-fifths of the total) in the hands of public banks and GNBFIs. It is, thus, clear that the government-established public banks and GNBFIs played a strategic role in mobilizing savings in Korea and borrowing from Japan. In this sense, they were borrowing from renters and lending to entrepreneurs. Their role in capital formation is particularly notable in the absence of a public securities market in the country, where businesses were increasingly dependent on big public banks.

In contrast to the public banks and GNBFIs, the private banks and PNBFIs were able to attract relatively small amounts of deposits in the early years, and their ability to loan was constrained by the government. Only in the later period did they garner considerable amounts of private savings (still less than one-fifth of the total) into their deposit accounts, but they were not able to make many long-term investment loans, because private banks and PNBFIs were limited from lending much money out of deposits or borrowing from external markets. Their loans were typically less than one-fifth of those of all financial institutions and, in addition, most of them were for short-term commercial rather than long-term loans for industrial and agricultural investment. This pattern, whatever its shortcomings, served to divert a considerable amount of savings into investment for the expansion of rice production and industrialization prescribed by Japan.

The remaining financial resource of the financial institutions was external borrowing by means of their bond issues and printing machines. The public banks and GNBFIs obtained almost all the credit by floating government-guaranteed as well as regular bank bonds, mostly in Japan until 1937, after which time they obtained a little more than half of their funds from Japan. Such debenture capital and borrowings ranged between one-fifth and one-third of their financial resources. Some of these funds were made available to the financial institutions from the increased savings in Korea toward the end of colonial rule.

Notwithstanding the positive role of the government, the excessive intervention, through the adoption of preferential schemes such as directed credits, subsidies, and tax exemptions, carried with it a considerable economic burden. It led to excessive speculation and a high incidence of bad loans, making the allocation of resources less than optimal and often shifting government spending away from socially beneficial investments toward the building of a wasteful military-industrial infrastructure. It thereby caused inflation, inhibited economic growth, and ultimately constrained the improvement of living standards of the people. It also tended to aggravate income inequalities and poverty and reduce domestic savings while discriminating against Korean and foreign businesses.

APPENDIX 6.1: GOVERNMENT LOANS TO BANKS BEFORE 1910

In the early years the poor management of Korean businesses, including private commercial banks, was often noted. In the cases of the Hanseong and Cheonil Banks, their capital was inadequate, their organizations were deficient, and their management was so far from commanding confidence that their business could not be conducted without government aid. Cheonil Bank shareholders were reported to have squandered the greater part of the share capital and even of the deposits, so that the bank was compelled to suspend payments in August 1905. In order for these banks to maintain financial health, the government, in 1906, had to create a rescue fund (*seili shikin* or *jeongli jageum*), which loaned the bank 240,000 yen without interest. Similarly, the government had to accommodate the Hanseong Bank with a loan of 100,000 yen, without interest, in the same year (K. J. Cho 1973: 369). The First Bank (Dai-Ichi Ginko) of Japan also rendered assistance to them (Residency General 1907: 54–55). Subsequently, many Korean banks received numerous forms of assistance, including interest-free loans and share subscriptions by the Korean government, which enabled them to survive.

By the end of 1907, government loans amounted to 1,058,680 yen. The Hanseong Bank also received a 3 million yen loan from the Oriental Development Company and came under heavy Industrial Bank supervision (S. J. Ko 1988: 338–340). The banks had a total of 274,714 yen on deposit and 1,571,409 in loans and balanced their accounts for the first time at the end of June 1907. At the end of the second half of 1907, the deposits and loans were 520,973 and 2,253,525 yen, respectively. In 1909 the government provided financial support of 180,000 yen each to the Cheonil and Hanseong Banks. At that time, each had 500,000 to 850,000 yen of deposits and loans (Tokanfu 1910b: 168; K. J. Cho 1994: 402). Under the protection and supervision of the government, the Hanseong Bank was able to pay a dividend of 15 percent, the Cheonil Bank a dividend of 10 percent, and the Hanil Bank dividends of 11 and 10 percent. Nonetheless, even in later years, because of reported inefficient management, a number of banks were closed or merged with other banks (K. J. Cho 1973: 368; Residency General 1907: 54–57).

APPENDIX 6.2: A THIRTY-YEAR FINANCIAL PLAN TO INCREASE RICE PRODUCTION

The Government General developed, in 1921, a thirty-year plan to increase rice production in Korea in order to export it to Japan. The plan called for an increase in rice production of 895,000 *seok* (an increase of more than 60 percent of total rice production), of which 458,300 would be designated for export to Japan, while leaving less than half of the increased output in Korea. This plan was developed on the basis of the Japanese consuming 1.2 *seok* of rice per year per person versus 0.89 for Koreans.

The challenges of the rice-production plan were two: the implementation of irrigation projects and their financing. The plan was to be founded on private entrepreneurship in the hands of local irrigation associations. The government "advised" (more accurately, forced) the landowners to form irrigation associations as a legal entity responsible for the administration and repayment of the financial obligation for the projects (Takeo Suzuki 1941: 112). Also see Hamanuma 1982: 141; Grajdanzev 1944: 97, 99.

The original thirty-year rice-production plan would have cost 280.73 million yen, which would have been financed with a government subsidy of 65.15 million yen, 193.5 million yen of low-interest bank loans of the Treasury Deposit Bureau in Japan and the Industrial Bank and the Oriental Development Company (each covering one-half the amount), and 22 million yen paid by a number of agribusiness entrepreneurs. Another source stated that the initiatives were supposed to have been financed with 115.3 million yen furnished by the Government General and 94.7 million contributed by the provincial governments.

When the rice-production plan was abandoned in 1936, only 48 percent of the planned amount, or a total amount of 134.51 million yen, had actually been spent on the project. Of this, 83.21 million yen was in government-secured bank loans, 35.18 million in government subsidies, and 16.11 million in private investment.

These investments represented 43, 54, and 73 percent, respectively, of the originally planned amounts. In other words, the largest contribution in terms of loans, representing 62 percent of the total, was made by the banks and GNBFIs, while the owners contributed only 12 percent of total costs. The Industrial Bank was a close collaborator.

As the sponsors of the projects, members of the irrigation associations were responsible for the debts. The debts and interest charges (actually, taxes) for the loans were supposed to have been paid off through charges for the use of water. Some members, however, complained about the high construction costs, high interest rates, excessive cost of management, and high charge for water. In addition, many Koreans expressed their displeasure at having no voice in the management of the associations, since the associations were in Japanese hands. Most of the Korean members were recruited against their will (Sotokufu 1932: 749, 841; ibid. 1942: 351–352; Shokusan Ginko 1938b: 70–71; ibid. 1940b: 30–32; S. J. Ko 1988: 245; T. Suzuki 1941: 132; F. Fujita 1993: 290–291, 346, 366, 366–367, 381, 391, 406; S. Suzuki 1939: 477; S. J. Ko 1988: 335).

7

MOBILIZATION OF SAVINGS FOR INVESTMENT

Having examined the government fiscal and financial policies for investment in chapter 6, the ensuing question is, how has Korea mobilized economic resources needed for its investment, which is and was the crucial challenge facing all developing economies as well as entire developed countries in the past. It has been argued that in less-developed countries, such as Korea prior to 1905, it is nearly impossible to secure adequate resources for even the minimum investment needed to support the native population at the prevailing standard of living, let alone to mobilize sufficient resources for large investments for solid economic growth. The ability of a country to make investment is dependent upon the ability to set aside a certain portion of income or available resources for investment either from domestic and/or foreign sources.

The task in this chapter, therefore, is to examine the mobilization of resources for investment from abroad as well as domestic sources. Obviously, resources for investment that enabled the economy to expand had to come from foreign countries as well as from domestic sources. Analyses in this chapter evolved through investigation of the magnitude of savings available for investment, the means of mobilizing savings or resources available for investment in Korea, the venues for obtaining foreign resources/savings, and the policy applied to promoting domestic savings under Japanese administration.

IMPORTATION OF FOREIGN RESOURCES/SAVINGS

In order to gain insight into the importation of foreign resources or savings overall, examined first is the net imports of foreign resources, followed by analysis of

Japanese financing of imports and its contribution to the importation of foreign resources into Korea for purposes of investment.

Net Imports

Resources available to Korea for investment that came from foreign savings may be ascertained by calculating the net inflow of resources into the country from abroad. The trade statistics should indicate whether there was an overall net importing or exporting under Japanese rule. If an import surplus is indicated, then there were net imports of foreign savings or resources that were available for investment in Korea. According to the official trade statistics, Korea imported 18 billion yen's worth of goods and services between 1905 and 1944.[1] During the same period, about 14.33 billion yen's worth, or approximately four-fifths of imports, were financed with Korea's exports. Thus, there was an import surplus of 3.67 billion yen or about one-fifth of imports. This sum represents the net foreign savings or resources imported into Korea.

The official data, however, are reputed to be inconsistent and incomplete, and some assert that the official trade statistics should be adjusted to reflect more accurate and representative figures. One possible adjustment involves Korea's gold exports to Japan. Apparently, there was a sizable amount of unrecorded gold smuggled out of Korea and into Japan. Korea was a base for Japanese smuggling or unregistered exporting of gold for many years. Officially, the value of net exports of specie and bullion from Korea to Japan recorded between 1910 and 1936 amounted to 434.2 million yen, or about 98 percent of all recorded gold exports from Korea.[2]

After the outbreak of the Japanese invasion of China in 1937, there was no accounting of Korea's gold exports to Japan. Considering the fact that gold mining in Korea was much energized with very generous subsidies during this period, as noted in the preceding chapter, and that Japan was much in need of foreign resources to prepare for its planned military campaigns in China followed with the ensuing war in the Pacific, it seems reasonable to assume that there were sizable exports of gold to Japan after 1936. In fact, the Japanese official who headed the Finance Department in Korea during this period admitted after World War II that Korea had "sent a large quantity of gold to Japan during World War II," presumably in secret. One estimate shows that the value of gold production between 1937 and 1939 alone could hardly have been less than 300 million yen. On the conservative assumption that exports between 1937 and 1944 were the same as those in previous years,[3] when the adjustments were made for gold exports, Korea's balance-of-payments deficit would be reduced to about 3.37 billion yen during the colonial period.

Some scholars also proposed that remittances to the mother country sent by Koreans living abroad should be incorporated into the official trade statistics. Grajdanzev has estimated that the annual remittances of Koreans in Japan, Manchuria, and China were as much as 180 million yen.[4] No doubt, Koreans abroad sent a substantial amount of money home, which could have been used to pay for imports. But a similar situation probably existed for Japanese residing in Korea, and they were financially far better off than most Koreans living abroad. It is highly likely that they sent more money from Korea to Japan than the sum Koreans living abroad remitted to their homeland. Moreover, there also were sizable inflows of possessions brought in by Japanese immigrants to Korea. Thus, even if allowances are made for Korean remittances, the allotment for Japanese remittances and imports of their possessions would probably have been more than offset those sent by Koreans.

The data can be made more useful, however, by making one adjustment to reflect more realistically the weight of each year's trade balance. Because of rapidly changing prices, the official statistics tended to inflate the deficit value of the balance of payments during inflationary periods, especially in the later years, while understating it during depressed times, particularly in the early years. This means that, in general, there were upward biases in the later figures and downward biases in the early ones. It is therefore necessary to correct these biases with an appropriate price index.

Unfortunately, the only available price indexes are those for cost of living and wholesale prices.[5] Between the two, the latter seems more suitable for adjusting foreign trade figures, since the prices of goods in foreign trade in general would likely have reflected primarily wholesale prices. It must be noted, however, that the wholesale price index does not accurately reflect price changes in foreign trade, since domestic wholesale prices generally do not necessarily fluctuate in proportion to changes in the prices of foreign trade goods and services. Once these shortcomings are recognized, on the basis of adjusted 1936 prices, the deficit balance-of-payments figure is reduced to approximately 2.34 billion yen. Thus, Korea received that net amount of foreign resources and savings for its use. This represents an annual average sum of about 60 million yen.

Japanese Financing of Imports

Most of the imports under colonial rule came from Japan. Korea's imports from Japan were valued at about 14.62 billion yen, four-fifths of the country's total imports. They formed as much as 88.6 percent of the total in 1939. Most of its imports (84 percent of the total, or 12.35 billion yen) were financed through Korea's exports to Japan. This trade relationship shows an adjusted balance-of-payments deficit for the period 1905–1945 of 2.21 billion yen at the current prices (the prices prevailing then) and 1.09 billion yen at the adjusted value in 1936 prices. Korea's balance-of-payments deficit with Japan thus represented 47 percent of the total during the period. This net inflow of foreign resources was obviously financed by Japanese savings in Japan.

A closer examination of the data also reveals that its deficits varied substantially from period to period, which seems to reflect the changing political and military needs of Japan. During the first ten years of Japanese domination, 1905–1914, Korea incurred an import surplus of nearly 100 million yen, which represented the initial Japanese investment in its colony. This was the period when Japan was solidifying its hold on Korea, by investing substantial amounts of its resources in the country. The most sizable capital imports, however, occurred during 1936–1944, when Japan invaded China and started the war in the Pacific. As Japan pursued its expansionist policy in Asia and made Korea an integral part of its military-industrial complex, it invested heavily to expand the colony's industrial capacity. During this period, Korea's total deficit with Japan was 2.84 billion yen, or about four-fifths of the entire deficit for the 1904–1945 period. The deficit during the period averaged about 315 million yen annually.

Other import balances occurred following the 1919 Korean independence movement uprising and the Manchurian War. The colony incurred a deficit of about 150 million yen during the four-year period following the 1919 uprising, while the other surge in capital imports from Japan occurred during the prosperity of 1927–1930 and after the Manchurian War, which amounted to about 220 million yen. During the forty-year period under Japanese rule, Korea had small export surpluses in trade only during the eight-year period between 1914 and 1935.

A large portion of Korea's balance-of-payments deficit during most of the twenty-one-year period between 1914 and 1935 was with countries other than Japan. Although Korea's trade relations with foreign countries, primarily the non-yen bloc countries, were far less substantial than those with Japan, Korea's imports exceeded its exports to them fairly consistently during the 1915–1934 period. Korea's balance-of-payments deficit with foreign countries (excluding Japan) for the entire period was 1.13 billion yen in current prices (1.24 billion in 1936 prices), about 53 percent of its total during the period.

This deficit with foreign countries other than Japan, however, does not represent Korea's net imports from foreign countries or foreign countries' net exports of resources or savings to Korea. Korea's deficits with foreign countries were financed by the Japanese in Japan, which in effect meant that Japanese capital was being exported to Korea via other foreign countries. As was noted in chapter 4, no substantial foreign (non-Japanese) investment took place in Korea. Most goods imported from foreign countries (other than Japan) were either luxury items intended for the well-to-do Japanese and a small group of wealthy Koreans (but not intended for wide distribution among the Korean population) or, more important, materials designated for the expansion and support of industry in Korea. Japanese investors in Japan had to purchase such goods as machinery, railway equipment, other capital goods, and industrial raw materials from abroad to use for investment and production in Korea.

The value of imported machinery from foreign countries exceeded 1 million yen even during the early years (1905–1910). The proportion of imports for production purposes (such as machinery, chemicals, metals, minerals, and ores) rose from 25.2 percent of total imports in 1929 to 43.6 percent in 1939, or in absolute figures from 106.6 million to 604.2 million yen during the same period. Most of these goods were imported from the United States, China, the Japanese colony Taiwan, Canada, Germany, and the United Kingdom. While imports from the United States accounted for only 1.7 percent of the total imports in 1939, they could be attributed almost entirely to the purchase of much-needed American machinery.[6] In this way most investment in Korea during the bulk of the years under Japanese rule was financed directly or indirectly from funds derived from Japanese savings in Japan.

How were these net imports from Japan financed? They may be grouped in five categories: (1) Japanese government grants, (2) colonial government borrowing and public debt, (3) the borrowing of financial institutions and businesses, and (4) business borrowing.

Japanese Government Grants

The first lump-sum Japanese government grant was made to Korea when Korea was annexed. As discussed in chapter 3, when Korea was a protectorate between 1905 and 1910 the Korean government borrowed about 46.6 million yen from Japan, including the Japanese government.[7] When Korea was annexed in 1910, the Japanese government relieved a major portion of these loan obligations with a lump-sum grant of 30 million yen. In addition, after the Annexation, the Japanese government annually made outright grants-in-aid to the Government General of Korea. The grant fluctuated somewhat from year to year, but it averaged about 12 million yen a year until the colony was liberated after the defeat of Japan in World War II. The annual grants made up a substantial portion of the Government General's budget, especially in the early years. In 1910, for instance, the annual 12 million yen grant constituted as much as 20 to 30 percent of the Government General's budget.[8] However, because the amount of the grant was relatively fixed, while the government budget increased over time, its relative importance gradually waned, and by 1940 it represented only about 2.3 percent of the budget.[9]

Total Japanese government grants to Korea under its rule amounted to about 450 million yen, which was equivalent to approximately 14 percent of Korea's total balance-of-payments deficit.[10] This amount enabled Korea to import resources from abroad beyond the level of its exports. These grants did not include the Japanese government's outlay for military expenditures in Korea.

Government Borrowing and Public Debt

The second venue for financing Korea's imports was borrowing of the Government General in the form of public bonds.[11] As noted above, before the Annexation, the Korean government had borrowed a total of 46.6 million yen at 5 to 7 percent interest.[12] Between 1910 and 1945 the Government General incurred a total of nearly 3 billion yen in public debt. When Japan began its aggressive military campaigns in Asia in 1937 and the Pacific, the public debt was increased to 2.6 billion yen. In relation to the Government General's revenues, the national debt increased from about 87 percent of the budget in 1911 to 120 percent in 1939. Since a little less than half of the bonds were redeemed during this period, the net debt figure outstanding was 1.58 billion yen at the end of colonial rule. In 1936 prices, this represented approximately 1.22 billion yen. Based on the figures available for the period between 1910 and 1932, it may be estimated that nearly one-fifth of the inflow of foreign savings into Korea under Japanese rule came via public bonds.

Most of the funds raised through public bonds came from Japan. Before 1941, about 98 percent of these public bonds were sold in the market in Japan and only 1 to 2 percent in Korea. After 1941, the Government General continued to rely on the Japanese financial market; for example, the Deposit Bureau of the Japanese government continued to supply about 27 percent of the total. However, its reliance diminished and came to depend more heavily on Korea after 1941.[13] The exact figure is not available, but the amount of bonds sold in Korea after 1941 must have been significant, because there was much pressure on the residents of Korea to purchase them during World War II, as noted in next section. Also, according to a former high-ranking Japanese official in the Government General, "some portion" (certainly more than 1 or 2 percent of the total) of it was subscribed in Korea after 1941. Considering the facts that of the government-guaranteed Industrial Bank bonds issued after 1938 Korean markets took in as much as 41.5 percent while Japanese sources purchased 58.5 percent[14] and a large number of shares were taken up in Korea by the credit unions and the Korea Savings Bank, it is reasonable to presume that as much as four-tenths of funds were raised in Korea.

The total net amount of loans actually financed by Japan, therefore, was certainly less than 98 percent but was perhaps as much as two-thirds of the total during World War II. On the basis of this observation, Japan's absorption of Korea's public debt during the entire period may have represented a sum somewhat smaller than 1.5 billion yen. The financiers of these bonds and loans in Japan were reported to have been the Daiichi Bank, the Bank of Japan, the Japan Industrial Bank, the Deposit Bureau of the Japanese Government, and wealthy individuals, including Japan's royalty. Japan's savings imported through public bond financed about one-fifth of the balance-of-payments deficits. According to a study covering the period between 1910 and 1932, public bonds supplied 19.1 percent of the total balance-of-payments deficits,[15] but for the entire period under Japanese rule public debt averaged about 43 million yen a year and financed about one-fifth of Korea's deficits.

The extent of financing of the Government General's budget through bond issues varied considerably from year to year, reflecting Japan's political conditions and economic needs. Prior to the Annexation, the sum of 44.7 million yen that the Residency General raised funded about one-third of its budget. Between 1911 and 1919, borrowing valued at 670 million yen covered between 15 and 20 percent of its annual budget.[16] After 1919, the Government General raised the public debt limit to 3.1 billion yen and relied on it even more heavily. Government borrowing financed 15.5 percent of its budget in 1936, 20 percent in 1937, 33.9 percent in 1938, and 36.4 percent in 1940. On average, an annual sum of about 45 million yen raised from public bonds, which was almost equal to tax revenues, financed a little more than 20 percent of the Government General's budget. When this is combined with the grants from the Japanese government, the financing of the Government General's revenues increased from 21.8 percent of the total budget in 1936 to 38 percent in 1938 and 38.7 percent in 1940.[17]

Public debt in Korean provincial governments was insignificant—less than 1 million yen a year on average—until 1930. From 1931 to 1937, provincial debt increased from about 12 million to 34 million yen. The provincial debts mostly financed construction and relief projects, local development, subsidies, and education.[18] No detailed information is available with regard to their sources, but probably most of these funds were raised within Korea.

Borrowing by Financial Institutions and Businesses

The third means by which Japan supplied its savings to Korea and financed the latter's imports was through lending to the country's financial institutions and businesses. Several of the public banks and GNFIs that the colonial government established and supported borrowed heavily in the Japanese capital market. As examined earlier, these included the Bank of Korea, the Industrial Bank, the Oriental Development Company, and the Credit Cooperative Associations (or credit unions),[19] which regularly issued bonds in Japan to augment their financial resources for lending in Korea.

In 1940, the year before Japan entered the war against the Allied Forces in the Pacific, the sum of outstanding bonds that had been issued by the financial institutions totaled 1.3 to 1.65 billion yen, with approximately 98 percent having been raised in Japan. Of the government-guaranteed Industrial Bank bonds issued after 1938, Japanese sources purchased 58.5 percent, while Korean markets took in as much as 41.5 percent. The Deposit Bureau of the Japanese government continued to supply about 27 percent of the total. In Korea, a large number of shares were taken up by the credit unions and the Korea Savings Bank, which were supported by small- and medium-income earners through depositing of their savings. Since some institutions (mainly the Bank of Korea) apparently made sizable loans to Manchuria and China on Japan's behalf, not all of these loans represented Japan's net lending to Korea's financial institutions. When the loans applied to neighboring countries are subtracted from the total, Japan's net supply of loans to the financial institutions of Korea for use in Korea must have been at least 1 billion yen, and possibly as much as 1.1 to 1.3 billion, which was equivalent to about 30 percent of Korea's balance-of-payments deficit. Another means of importing Japanese savings/resources was by private businesses. Noguchi's hydroelectric and chemical companies, for instance, borrowed directly from the capital market in Japan either by floating corporate bonds or obtaining direct loans from banks and other financial institutions in Japan. When all business borrowings from Japan are added, they probably contributed about 13 percent of the Japanese financing of Korea's trade deficit during the colonial period.[20] According to studies covering the period between 1910 and 1932, bank and corporate loans from Japan met 22.8 percent of Korea's balance-of-payments deficits, and 29.7 percent during the entire colonial period.[21]

Foreign Direct Investment

The principal means of financing foreign investment in the private sector typically is direct business investment. According to a former Japanese official of the Government General, about 30 percent of the savings and resources imported from Japan was supplied by Japanese investors in the form of paid-in capital, direct company investment, and retained earnings of companies headquartered in Korea. When this is combined with direct investment in Japanese companies headquartered in Japan, approximately 23 percent of Korea's balance-of-payments deficits were financed in the form of direct investment with Japanese savings in Japan.[22]

The preceding analysis reveals that Korea's balance-of-payments deficits were largely financed with Japanese savings in Japan in the form of loans, mostly by the two public banks and two GNBFIs, which made up approximately 30 percent of the total. The next source of financing the deficits was Japanese direct investment in private businesses in Korea, which was equivalent to approximately 23 percent of the total, while colonial government loans financed approximately one-fifth of the total. The Japanese government's grants to Korea and business borrowing each mobilized about 14 and 13 percent of the total, respectively, from Japanese financial markets.

DOMESTIC SOURCES OF FINANCING INVESTMENT

Obviously, not all of the net savings/resources imported from Japan were dedicated to investment in Korea, nor was this the only source of savings that financed investment in the country. The next question to examine is who the domestic savers were and the magnitude of their savings that financed investment in Korea, both private and public. There are no suitable and comprehensive data to trace and estimate the financial sources of investment in Korea, other than fragmentary information, such as limited amount of information on savings for private railroad investment.[23] No doubt, the resources were available for investment—through either foreign or domestic savings—in the country.

There are a few studies examining the domestic sources of financing investment in Korea. Hosokawa examined the relative contribution of different sources of financing investment during 1910–1932. According to his study, nearly nine-tenths of all investment in Korea was financed by Japanese: 28.8 percent in corporate bonds, nearly 23 percent in bank and corporate loans, 19.6 percent in public bonds, and 16.6 percent in direct investment by corporations headquartered in Japan. According to his estimate, direct investment by corporations headquartered in Korea financed a little less than 12 percent of the total.[24] The Bank of Korea's study of Japanese financing of investment in Korea in 1931 estimated it at 2.13 billion yen, or 93.2 percent of total investment in Korea: 42.2 percent from the Japanese government's budget, 20.4 percent from company investment, 30.6 percent from Japan, and 6.8 percent from Japanese in Korea.[25] Unfortunately, these studies do not adequately reflect Korea's contribution to investment after 1932. Japan continued to supply most funds for investment, but the share of investment financing in Korea changed, and the colony financed more investment out of its savings after 1932.

The Industrial Bank of Korea calculated Japanese financing of investment in Korea in 1938, which was estimated at about 3.6 billion yen[26]: 700 million in loans to national and provincial governments (19.4 percent of the total); 400 million in corporate bonds and loans (11.1 percent); 650 million in loans to public financial institutions, namely, public banks and other financial institutions (18.1 percent); 820 million in paid-in capital of companies (22.8 percent); and 1,030 million in other sources (28.6 percent). Specifically, in manufacturing, according to a Japanese economic newspaper, investment in Korea in 1938 was financed by direct Japanese investment of 74 percent, domestic major investment of 18 percent, and investment by other companies in Korea of 8 percent.[27] Also, according to its estimate, the major industrial capital was made up of special-purpose companies (17 percent), the companies under the umbrella of the Industrial Bank of (29 percent), other Japanese capital (48 percent), and Korean capital (6 percent). Still another study estimated that the wealth (*furyoku*) of Korea as of 1938 was 7 billion yen: 1.7 billion in public wealth (24.3 percent) and 5.3 billion in private wealth (75.7 percent). The Japanese in Korea owned about 60 percent of all private wealth of about 3.2 billion yen.

According to an estimate made by the chamber of commerce in Seoul (Japanese) in 1944, Japanese capital accumulation in Korea during 1910–1941 was 7.33 billion yen. In a somewhat different grouping, it identified five different sources, grouped under the headings of government funds, loans of banking systems, corporate investments, private funds, and other "investments," during 1910–1941.[28] It calculated that the largest Japanese "investment" was made by corporations, representing 53.8 percent of the total, followed by government funds (28.2 percent), individuals (13.3 percent), and others (less than 1 percent). The study is a useful guide to ascertaining sources and estimating the extent of their financing of investment, but unfortunately it is confined mostly to the financing of investment in tangible facility expansion of companies.

As one may detect from this survey, these studies are fragmentary. They cover different time periods and durations and do not reveal the identity of those who saved their incomes for investment. Therefore, a somewhat different approach for estimating all sources of financing investment in Korea, both private and public, may be attempted below. Since investment, both in private and public sectors, in Korea during the forty-year period between 1905 and 1945 was financed with both foreign and domestic resources or savings, the amount of resources or savings available for investment from foreign and domestic sources are examined to determine the extent of their savings that financed investment in the country by Japanese and Koreans. The sources of financing investment in the private sector are examined in companies, headquartered in both Japan and Korea, unincorporated businesses, and housing and miscellaneous categories.

Companies

As was shown earlier in chapter 4, the most significant investment in Korea under Japanese rule was in companies. Capital stock in companies, headquartered in both Korea and Japan, is estimated to have been about 6.5 billion yen as of 1943, or about 83.5 percent of the total capital stock in the private sector (see Table 4.2). This section examines the sources of saving and their extent of financing companies in Korea. Investment in private companies obviously was financed by the Japanese in Japan and Korea, and by Koreans.

Savings in Japan

No comprehensive and detailed data are available to calculate savings accurately, but limited data allow us to estimate the volume of savings/resources imported

TABLE 7.1 Financial Sources of Investment of Japanese Companies Headquartered in Korea in 1943

	In Korea		*In Japan*		*Total*	
Sources	In Million Yen	Percent	In Million Yen	Percent	In Million Yen	Percent
Direct company investment	117.0	14.0	8.0	1.1	125.0	8.0
Retained earnings	180.6	21.7	(38.6)	(5.3)	142.0	9.1
Paid-in capital	148.7	17.8	250.0	34.1	398.7	25.4
Corporate bonds	10.0	1.2	60.0	8.2	70.0	4.5
Bank borrowings	333.3	40.0	366.3	49.9	699.6	44.6
Other borrowings	43.7	5.2	88.0	12.0	131.7	8.4
Total	833.3	100.0	733.7	100.0	1,567.0	100.0
Sources of financing investment (percent)	53.2		46.8		100.0	

Source: This table is constructed based on Mizuda and Tsuchiya 1962: 108.

from Japan that was used for investment in private companies in Korea. It is obvious from the preceding analysis that Japanese exported large amounts of their savings to Korea in various forms during the period of colonial rule, and it is clear that much of this was dedicated to financing investment in Korea. One estimate for 1942 shows that investment from Japan, mainly by the *zaibatsu,* was set at 2.15 billion yen, or 74 percent of total capital accumulated in Korea shown in that year.[29] The estimate in Table 7.1 shows that nearly half (46.8 percent) of the capital stock invested in Japanese companies headquartered in Korea as of 1943 was supplied with savings and resources imported from Japan, while more than half (53.2 percent) of the total was supplied by Japanese in Korea.

Of the two groups of Japanese companies, namely, those headquartered in Japan with branches in Korea and those companies headquartered in Korea, the savings or resources dedicated for investment to the former are estimated at about 900 million yen as of 1943, while Japanese residents in Japan also contributed as much as 2.62 billion yen toward capital stock in Japanese companies headquartered in Korea (Table 7.2). The combined total investments in Japanese companies, headquartered both in Japan and Korea, by residents in Japan thus represented about 54 percent of capital stock in all companies and contributed 45.2 percent of the entire capital formation in the private sector in Korea.[30]

Savings in Korea

In addition to Japanese savings imported from Japan as a source, savings in Korea also financed investment in companies headquartered in Korea. Obviously, a portion of savings in Korea was directly invested in the forms of share capital and business savings, such as retained earnings and capital depreciation allowances. As noted in chapter 4, owners' equity contributed about 56 percent of the total capital

TABLE 7.2 Savings That Financed Investment in Korea as of 1943

	Million Yen			*Percent*					
				Ratio of		*Ratio within*		*Ratio between*	
Sources	Japanese	Korean	Total	Total	Private	Japanese	Korean	Japanese	Korean
Total savings:	8,582	1,369	9,950	100.0	100.0	23.9	59.8	86.3	13.8
Private:	6,520	1,260	7,780	78.2	100.0	100.0	100.0	83.8	16.2
Companies	5,850	650	6,500	65.3	83.5	89.7	51.6	90.0	10.0
Headquartered:									
In Korea:	2,330	650	2,980	29.9	38.3	35.7	51.6	78.2	21.8
Korean	—	650	650	6.5	8.4	—	51.6	—	100.0
Japanese	2,330	—	2,330	23.4	29.9	35.7	—	100.0	—
In Japan	3,520	—	3,520	35.4	45.2	54.0	—	100.0	—
Branch	900	—	900	9.0	11.6	13.8	—	100.0	—
Japanese*	2,620	—	2,620	26.3	33.7	40.2	—	100.0	—
Unincorporated	270	290	560	5.6	7.2	4.1	23.0	48.2	51.8
Housing**	400	320	720	7.2	9.3	6.1	25.4	55.6	44.4
Public:	2,062	109	2,170	21.8	—	23.9	8.2	95.0	5.0
Private savings:	6,520	1,260	7,780	100.0	—	100.0	100.0	83.8	16.2
In Japan	3,520	—	3,520	45.2	—	54.0	—	100.0	—
In Korea	3,000	1,260	4,260	54.8	—	46.0	100.0	70.4	29.6
Public savings:	2,061	109	2,170	100.0	—	100.0	99.5	95.0	5.0
In Japan	1,953	—	1,953	90.0	—	94.8	—	100.0	—
In Korea	109	109	217	10.0	—	5.3	99.5	50.0	50.0
Total savings:	8,581	1,369	9,950	100.0	—	100.0	100.0	86.2	13.8
In Japan	5,473	—	5,473	55.0	—	63.8	—	100.0	—
In Korea	3,109	1,369	4,477	45.0	—	36.2	100.0	50.0	50.0

*Japanese companies headquartered in Korea.
**Housing and miscellaneous.

Sources: The table is constructed on the basis of data based on the following sources: Bank of Korea 1939: Index 16; ibid. 1948: III-82; Shokusan Ginko 1940b: 35–37; *Kokusei Gurafu* April 1940; Toyo Keizai Shinposha 1942: 83; Takesizu Suzuki 1942: 83; Mizuda and Tsuchiya 1962: 108; S.S. Kim 1985: 259.

in 1938 and 42 percent in 1943. They consisted of paid-in capital of 25 percent, retained earnings of 9 percent, and working capital of 8 percent in 1943. No comprehensive data regarding retained earnings are available, but an estimate may be made based on the average retained earnings of companies in Korea cited by Mizuda. According to him, the average retained earnings and capital depreciation allowance represented about 9 and 8 percent of total company capital, respectively, in 1943.[31] If this ratio is applied to the financing of all companies, then the aggregate retained earnings, which had been close to zero in the early years, would have climbed up to about 500 million yen by 1943.

In addition to paid-in capital and retained earnings, the other part of investment in companies was financed typically through external borrowing. Most corporations relied heavily on loans from financial institutions, especially banks, as examined earlier. According to the same high-ranking official in the Government General, while debenture capital and borrowing financed about 44 percent in 1938, they made up 58 percent of the total financing of companies—comprising borrowing from the financial institutions of 53 percent and debenture capital of 5 percent—in 1943.[32] These loans came mostly from banks but also from other financial and nonfinancial institutions. Bank loans to companies alone represented 44.6 percent of the total financial sources of investment in companies in 1943. The outstanding loans of the financial institutions in 1938 and 1943 were 1.58 billion and 3.86 billion yen, respectively. The major portion of these funds was loaned to companies.

It is difficult to obtain accurate data showing savings in Korea under Japanese administration, but it is clear that they increased over time. Savings deposits in banks, for instance, increased by 250 percent in the fourteen years between 1925 and 1939. Total deposits in banks, financial associations, and post offices multiplied 3.5 times, while commodity production increased by about 50 percent in current prices during the same period. Thus, relative to commodity production, monetary savings in Korea increased by 2.3 times, from 9 percent in 1925 to 21 percent in 1939.[33] Postal savings increased from 3 to 90 million yen, showing a thirtyfold increase in about thirty years during the 1910–1938 period, at an average of about 12 percent a year.[34]

The rise in savings was particularly remarkable after 1938. Korea, which had contributed nothing before 1937, supplied 180 million yen to Japan's war chest between 1940 and 1941. Also, savings absorbed through public bond sales, including public bank bonds, rapidly increased to 20 percent of national income in 1941, 30 percent in 1943, and 50 percent in 1945, while business savings and investment remained fairly constant at 17 to 18 percent of national income. As a result, the savings ratio increased to 33.7 percent of national income in 1941, 45 percent in 1943, and a staggering 67.3 percent in 1945.[35] Savings in 1944 were more than double the sum reported in 1940–1941.

Most of these savings were deposited directly or indirectly in various banking institutions, chiefly in the Industrial Bank, credit unions, the Savings Bank, the Postal Savings System, commercial banks, and in various government-sponsored bonds. They increased from a few million yen in 1905 to 193.1 million in 1926, 258.8 million in 1931, 624.8 million in 1938, 1.39 billion in 1941, and 2.56 billion in 1943 (see Table 7.3). The deposits in financial institutions as a whole multiplied to 3.7 billion yen in 1943. There was not much savings being invested directly in capital shares. Part of the reason for the paucity of equity financing was the lack of institutions to channel people's savings into equity share capital: no large public market for securities in Korea, such as a stock market, existed where equity investment in shares could be made. Even if there had been one, not many savers were accustomed to utilizing the institutions for investment purpose.

JAPANESE SAVINGS IN KOREA All available data indicate that Japanese savings in Korea increased very rapidly and that it financed investment in Japanese companies headquartered in Korea. At the minimum, their savings in banks increased thirtyfold times in about 30 years during the 1910–1938 period, averaging about 12 percent a year.[36] Other than investing directly in their own businesses, most of their savings were deposited in financial institutions. Since there was no well-developed stock market, investments in stock shares were small, and most savings

TABLE 7.3 Deposits and Loans of Financial Institutions* and Banks (in million yen)

	Deposits		*Loans*	
Year	Financial Institutions	Banks	Financial Institutions	Banks
1910	18.4	—	38.7	—
1914	35.8	—	63.7	—
1917	54.5	—	99.9	—
1918	86.7	—	147.3	—
1919	131.9	—	293.7	—
1921	188.4	—	346.4	—
1923	246.3	—	448.4	—
1926	256.8	193.1	511.3	372.2
1928	315.4	232.7	631.9	399.9
1934	437.1	376.3	757.1	613.7
1937	642.0	462.5	1,220.0	957.8
1939	1,176.5	867.9	1,933.9	1,506.5
1941	1,982.0	1,395.8	2,177.5	2,177.5
1943	3,708.3	2,562.3	3,732.8	3,061.5

*Financial institutions include the Bank of Korea, the Industrial Bank, commercial banks, Savings Bank, and credit unions.

Sources: This table is based on K. Takahashi 1935: 500–501; Bank of Korea 1948: III, 74–87.

were kept in deposit accounts in banks. These deposits made up between 76 and 85 percent, averaging about 83 percent, of the total deposits in all financial institutions in Korea.

Japanese savings in Korea that financed investment in Japanese companies headquartered in Korea comprised two components: capital share and external loans. One estimate indicates that for the entire country, including Japanese and Korean companies, 53.6 percent of savings that financed investment in Korea was in the form of paid-in capital and retained earnings, while 46.4 percent came from debenture capital and loans, mostly from financial institutions.[37] In the case of Japanese companies headquartered in Korea, it seems appropriate to apply a somewhat lower average rate of share capital—50 percent of the total investment in companies, rather than the national average of 53.6 percent—because the Japanese companies had proportionately less owners' equity and more loans, especially from the public banks, than the national average and than the Korean companies. When this ratio is applied, the total owners' equity supplied by Japanese residents in Korea would be equal to 1,190 million yen.[38]

Another source of financing investment in Japanese companies headquartered in Korea, namely, loans and debenture capital, supplied mostly by financial institutions, filled the remaining requisite capital. The loan share of Japanese companies is set conservatively at 50 percent of their capital stock, which is somewhat higher than the national average ratio estimated above (46.4 percent), because the Japanese companies headquartered in Korea acquired relatively more loans from banks, especially from the public banks, than the national average and than Korean companies, as already noted. Since, on average, the share of loans of Japanese companies was equal to 83 percent of the total loan pool, the volume of investment acquired with loans and debenture capital would have been equal to 1,140 million yen.[39]

When the two sources of investment financing in Japanese companies headquartered in Korea—the share capital and loans—are combined, the sum that contributed to capital accumulation in Japanese companies headquartered in Korea by Japanese residents in Korea would be equal to 2,330 million yen as of 1943 (see Table 7.2).[40] This amount contributed by Japanese residents in Korea represented 47 percent of capital in Japanese companies headquartered in Korea, 39.8 percent of all Japanese companies headquartered both in Korea and Japan, 35.7 percent of all companies headquartered both in Korea and Japan, and 29.9 percent of all capital in the private sector in Korea in 1943.

If the financing of Korean branches of Japanese companies headquartered in Japan is included (900 million yen noted above), then nine-tenths of capital stock accumulated in companies in Korea,[41] headquartered both in Korea and Japan, were financed by savings of Japanese residents in Korea and Japan. It may be noted that the sum of Japanese investment in Japanese companies headquartered in Korea—2.38 billion yen (2.33 billion yen plus 50 million yen)—is 50 million yen (or 2.1 percent of the total) larger than what the Japanese saved for investment in their companies headquartered in Korea (2.33 billion yen), as shown in Table 7.2.

KOREAN SAVINGS Like the Japanese, Korean savings on the whole also increased over time, as evident in the increases in their deposits in the Postal Savings System and banks, and the purchase of war bonds (see the last section in this chapter). More Koreans placed their savings in the Postal Savings System than in any other financial institutions. The number of depositors increased from 4,200 in 1908 to 1.9 million in 1932 (the latest data available), while the amount of their deposits rose from less than 30,000 to 6.4 million yen during the same period,[42] increases of 452.4 and 21.3 times, respectively. Likewise, deposits in banks, where the more affluent Koreans and businesses deposited some of their savings, also multiplied. Korean bank deposits increased from 3.9 million yen in 1910 to 104.9 million in 1938.[43] Similar to the Japanese, a rapid increase in savings was notable after 1938. Korean savings on the whole came to represent as much as 3 to 4 percent of disposable income. They were partly responsible for the sharp rise in the ratio of saving to income in the country.

The rise in savings seems to have been partly due to a decline in people's resistance to keeping their savings in financial institutions as they gained more confidence in them and the availability of a whole range of savings institutions developed under Japanese rule—post office accounts, cooperative credit societies, insurance companies, banks, and the like—for the people to deposit their savings in. Even if they had had such institutions in the traditional and transitional periods, most Koreans would have had little confidence in them.[44] In addition to the increases in income, a sharp rise in savings toward the end of the 1930s and World War II was largely a result of policies of forced saving imposed on them by the colonial government, as shown in last section of this chapter.

Yet, for the size of the population the amount of savings remained small. Notwithstanding the fact that the increases shown in yen appear impressive, they are partly illusory. A closer examination of the data shows that the savings of Koreans under Japanese rule were rather limited on the whole. Published data show that the number of Korean depositors in the Postal Savings System as late as 1933 represented less than one-tenth of the native population. Only about a third of Korean households had deposits in post offices, the most widely used financial institution by Koreans. In other words, the Koreans, who constituted more than 97 percent of the country's population, made up only about two-thirds of the savers in the postal system during the 1910–1933 period, when such data were published by nationality.

Also, the volume of Korean savings continued to be small during most of the period of Japanese rule. The overall amount of Korean savings in the Postal Savings System accounted for less than one-fifth of the total. In 1933 Koreans deposited only 7.4 million yen. These records may be compared with those of the Japanese. The number of Japanese deposit accounts in the Postal Savings System in 1933 was 667,400, which was more than the Japanese population in Korea at that time, and they deposited 37.4 million yen, more than five times the deposits of the Koreans.[45] Moreover, compared with the average deposit of the Japanese, the average Korean savings deposit in the system, 3.4 yen, was very small, about 6 percent that of the Japanese (56 yen). In addition, Korean deposit per capita not only ceased to increase but actually decreased over time, in contrast with Japanese deposits, which were large and showed sizable growth. The average deposit by Koreans decreased from 5.4 yen in 1910 to 2.2 in 1920, although it bounced back slightly to 3.4 yen in 1933. When adjusted for price increases using the official price index, the real value of Korean savings deposits remained virtually constant during the 1920–1932 period. In contrast, the average savings deposit per account for Japanese increased from 29 yen in 1910 to 56 in 1933, which reveals increasing differences between the average deposits per account between Japanese and Koreans (or the ratios of average Japanese deposits to average Korean deposits) between 1910 and 1933 from 5.37 and 16.47 to 1, respectively.

There are no published statistics, but based on limited and fragmentary information available, some estimation of Korean savings that financed investment in Korea may be made. Similar to the method used to calculate the financing of investment in Japanese companies, Korean savings that financed investment in Korean companies took the form of direct investment in their own businesses, such as share capital, and loans from financial institutions. As noted earlier, although the national average of investment financed with owners' equity (paid-in capital and retained earnings) in companies headquartered in Korea was 53.6 percent, the owners' equity of Korean companies is calculated on the basis of it being 70 percent of total investment in companies, since Korean companies relied far more on share capital than did the Japanese. Following the similar rationale and methods applied in estimating the Japanese contribution, Korean investment in share capital is estimated at 420 million.[46]

The second component of savings that financed Korean companies, as was the case with the Japanese companies examined, was loans, mostly from financial institutions. Since 70 percent of financing investment in Korean companies consisted of paid-in capital and retained earnings and they were not particularly successful with bank loans, only three-tenths of their investment were assumed to have come from borrowing, rather than the 50 percent assigned to the Japanese companies.[47] Based on similar reasoning as that described in the case of the Japanese, loans that financed investment in Korean companies were equal to 17 percent (as compared with 83 percent to Japanese companies) of the total loans extended to companies in Korea on average. The sum total that indirectly contributed to capital accumulation in companies by Korean savers via banks was equal to 230 million yen as of 1943.[48] When the two sources of financing investment in companies are combined, the sum total that contributed to capital accumulation in companies was 650 million yen as of 1943.[49] This amount constituted 51.6 percent of Korean investment in their private sector investment and 16.2 percent of the total investment in companies.

On the basis of these calculations, the financing of investment in companies headquartered in Korea as a whole by residents of Korea, both Japanese and Koreans, may be set at 2.98 billion yen, while Japanese in Japan supplied 2.62 billion yen, as of 1943 (see Table 7.2).[50] These figures indicate that Korea supplied a little more (53.2 percent of the total) than Japan (46.8 percent) did. But of the combined total investments in Japanese companies, headquartered both in Korea and Japan, Japan supplied more funding (60.2 percent of the total, or 3.52 billion yen) for investment in them than did Korea (39.8 percent, or 2.33 billion yen).[51] It is also clear from this analysis that the Japanese citizens dedicated more resources to financing investment in companies in Korea than did the Koreans. The Japanese residents in Korea dedicated 78.2 percent of investment in companies headquartered in Korea, including those that were Korean owned, in contrast with 21.8 percent for the Koreans. Also, the Japanese living in Japan as well as in Korea financed 88.4 percent of investment in all companies headquartered in Korea, in contrast with 11.6 percent for the Koreans. Japanese in Korea as well as in Japan financed 90 percent of investment in all companies headquartered both in Korea and in Japan, while the Koreans devoted 10 percent.

It is interesting to note that the sum of Korean savings (650 million yen) that financed companies in Korea was more than the capital stock of Korean companies (600 million yen) in 1943, while capital stock of Japanese companies headquartered in Korea (2.38 billion yen, calculated in chapter 4) was more than what the Japanese saved for investment in their companies headquartered in Korea (2.33 billion yen). It thus appears that Korean savers actually financed 50 million yen or 2.1 percent of investment in Japanese companies headquartered in Korea,[52] indirectly through their bank deposits, which were loaned out to the Japanese companies (see Table 7.2).

Other Investments

In addition to financing companies headquartered in Korea and Japan, other Korean investments were financed by both Japanese and Korean residents of Korea (see Table 7.2). As examined earlier, among these were investments in unincorporated businesses as well as housing and other remaining sectors. Total capital stock in them as of 1943 was 7.2 percent of the total capital stock in the private sector for unincorporated businesses and 9.3 percent for housing and others. Japanese devoted 4.1 percent of their savings to investment in unincorporated businesses, while Koreans dedicated 23 percent of their savings to investment in unincorporated businesses. Likewise, Japanese used 6.1 percent of their savings for investment in housing and miscellaneous sectors, while Koreans directed 25.4 percent of their savings to investment in housing and miscellaneous sectors.

This analyses reveal that the magnitude and pattern of financing private investment differed widely between Japanese and Koreans. Japanese, both in Japan and Korea, financed 83.8 percent of investment in the private sector with their savings, while the Koreans dedicated 16.2 percent (see Table 7.2). Within Korea, more than 70 percent of investment in the private sector was financed with Japanese savings, while Korean savings financed less than 30 percent. The Japanese also dedicated more of their savings to financing investment in companies than did the Koreans. The Japanese devoted nearly nine-tenths of their private savings to investment in companies, while the Koreans allocated only about 52 percent of their private savings for the same purpose. On the other hand, the Japanese dedicated relatively small amounts of their savings to investment in unincorporated businesses, housing, and miscellaneous sectors—approximately 4 to 6 percent each—while the Koreans dedicated nearly half of their savings to the same sectors, namely, about a quarter of their savings to each group.

Public Investment

There were two sources for financing public investment: foreign savings or resources and budgetary revenues. Most of the funding for public investment came from Japanese savings or resources derived from Japanese government grants and Japanese credit extended to the colonial government. The first means of financing public investment, namely, the colonial government borrowing by issuing public bonds, raised a total of nearly 3 billion yen in public debt between 1910 and 1945, as examined earlier. Most of the borrowings were plowed into public investment projects and, reportedly, none was used for current government expenditures or to offset budget deficits.[53] As of 1938, nearly 98 percent of the public debt (580.7 million yen) had actually been used to construct public overhead facilities, 0.1 percent (0.6 million yen) for bond administration costs, and 2.1 percent (12.3 million yen) for "other purposes." The only exception was said to have been the use of bond proceeds for the operation of the penitentiary and improvements in sanitation and education immediately after the Korean uprising of 1919. In other words, nearly all of the major public investments in Korea were financed with savings imported from Japan through public bonds issued by the Government General. Some portion of grants from the Japanese government in Tokyo apparently was also used for the construction of public investment projects in Korea.

Among the public investment projects, the construction of railroads was the most important. More than three-quarters of all public bond money raised during the 1910–1918 period and four-fifths between 1919 and 1930 were allocated for railroad construction. As of 1938, over four-fifths of the funds raised from public bonds were reported to have been used for the construction of railroads, although the percentage dropped off to 64.2 percent in 1940. On the whole, two-thirds of the proceeds of the public debt, or 2.1 billion yen, was used for the construction and operation of railroads during colonial rule.[54]

The second means of financing public investment was government budgetary revenues. Although it is not too difficult to trace the source of funding public investment with borrowing, it is not easy to discern the sources of financing public investment with government budgetary revenue, because there is no reliable data on this. A relatively small amount for financing public investment projects does, however, seem to have come mostly from the profits realized by public monopoly enterprises producing and selling such products as tobacco, salt, and ginseng. It is clear that regardless of the real source, the overwhelming portion of public investment was financed by savings imported from Japan. It seems reasonable to estimate that it financed as much as nine-tenths (1,952 million yen) of the total (2,170 million yen), while only about a tenth (218 million yen) was financed with savings in Korea. It is difficult to assign any concrete figures to the Japanese and Korean shares within Korea, but it may be reasonable to set the share of Japanese in Korea and Koreans equally at 5 percent each of Korea's share (10 percent) of financing public investment, namely 109 million yen. There is some arbitrariness in the estimate, but the split seems conservative and reasonable enough. Based on these calculations, it may be stated that the Japanese (both in Japan and Korea) share of financing public investment was 95 of the total (2.1 billion yen)[55] and the share of Koreans at about 5 percent (109 million yen), as shown in Table 7.2

Aggregate Investment

Based on these estimates, the aggregate investment of 9.95 billion yen, comprising 7.78 billion of private investment and 2.17 billion of public investment, Japan supplied 55 percent of the total for investment in Korea,[56] while Korea financed the rest, or 45 percent of the total.[57] Resources available for investment in both public and private sectors in Korea under Japanese rule were largely supplied by Japanese. It is estimated that Japanese savings both in Korea and Japan supplied as much as 86.2 percent of the total in the country, constituting 83.8 percent of private investment and 95 percent of public investment, while Koreans financed approximately 13.8 percent of the total, comprising 16.2 percent of private investment and 5.5 percent of public investment. The figures attributed to Japanese and Koreans in this book are somewhat different from those assigned by many other scholars, especially the Japanese. Typically, the Japanese were credited with financing more than nine-tenths, while the typically attributed figure to Koreans was less than one-tenth. It is also notable that a small fraction (eight-tenths of a percent) of Japanese private investment was financed by the Koreans indirectly through bank loans to the former with the latter's bank deposits.

SAVINGS POLICY

When Taro Mishima became the first president of the Industrial Bank of Korea in 1918, he found the lack of savings in Korea "shocking," but, as has been illustrated, Korean saving increased substantially in the ensuing years of the Japanese administration. What accounted for the increase in savings in Korea under colonial rule? Among the many reasons, such as the rise in income and the establishment of varieties of banks and NBFIs in which savings could be deposited conveniently and safely, one of the more vital reasons for the rise in savings, especially toward the end of colonial rule, appears to have been the policy of forcefully altering Korean people's saving habits and a series of aggressive government programs for promoting saving,[58] mainly to fulfill Japan's ambitious and grand goals.

Numerous Japanese government and civilian leaders urged Koreans to live within their means and save. A campaign known as the Self-Help and Rejuvenation Movement (*Jinryoku Kyosei Undo*) exhorted Korean people to live within their means by reducing expenditures and by saving. Governor General Ugaki's Movement of Rural Revival (*Noson Fukuko Undo*) stressed the need to balance one's income and expenditures to achieve self-sufficiency in foodstuffs in each household and to repay debts. Families were urged to reduce rice consumption and wear homemade straw footwear instead of purchasing rubber shoes. The government gave prizes to those who met its goals. After 1941, the Japanese government virtually forced the people to save and buy its savings bonds. In addition, many Japanese agribusinesses instituted compulsory savings programs in their establishments.[59]

Under these slogans, movements, and policies, indebtedness was reported to have been reduced. According to one provincial governor's report, 92.06 percent of 8,056 households in 204 villages in Jeonbuk Province were in debt in 1932, and 80.6 percent were suffering an "absolute shortage" of food. Of these, in 77.2 percent of farm households (6,221) expenses exceeded revenues by an average of 5.7 yen annually. One year later, "because of the Self-Help and Rejuvenation Movement," nearly 11 percent of these households had enough food to eat, 11.2 percent had reduced their debts by half, and 20.9 percent balanced their budgets. The debts of some were reduced as much as 20 percent within a year, and 13.8 percent completely repaid their loans. According to the report, this feat was accomplished by reducing "wasteful expenses" and increasing income from supplementary employment. The reduction in debt was also due to the replacement of usurious loans with low-interest credit-union loans and the "tireless efforts of the police and county and village officials."[60]

To augment savings by reducing consumption, the government went so far as to prescribe how much could be spent on major occasions. A government decree stipulated that spending was not to exceed 50 yen for funerals, weddings, and other major celebrations. Some counties went even further, adopting schedules of expenditures for various occasions (e.g., 20 to 200 yen for a wedding and 5 to 100 yen for a funeral).[61] After 1936, the government mandated saving to support Japan's expansionist policies. Under the Korea Savings Promotion Movement (*Chosen Chojuku Zyosei Undo*) inaugurated in 1937, the government attempted to siphon off "excess income" by restraining consumption and forcing saving. Under the compulsory savings plan (*tenppiki*), which was similar to a surtax, a certain percentage (e.g., 10 percent) of sales or production was taken for saving.

These programs seem to have achieved some success in reducing expenditures and enlarging domestic savings.[62] Forced saving was especially prevalent during World War II. The targeted amounts of Korea's savings ranged from 200 million yen in 1938 to 2.3 billion in 1944. Residents of Korea were forced to save an increasing proportion of their income: 36.7 percent in 1941, 50.9 percent in 1943, and 71.4 percent in 1945. The targets for 1943 were based on average saving, tax, and consumption ratios of 30, 20, and 50 percent of income, respectively. The 1944 plan called for even more ambitious ratios of 36, 24, and 40, respectively. One of the means of achieving the target for savings was the Japanese war bond sales program during World War II.[63]

The results of these savings programs were phenomenal. It was reported that public bonds sold in Korea after 1936 always exceeded the quotas set by the Government General by 10, 20, or 30 percent. During the period between 1936–1937 and 1940–1941, the amount of income available for saving increased from 20 to 50 percent, and Korean bond sales increased from almost nothing in 1936–1937 to 180 million yen in 1940–1941. The targeted goals for bond sales were not published after 1941, but based on the prevailing circumstances and reports that are available it seems reasonable to infer that the total value of bonds sold was much larger during World War II than the sum reported for 1940–1941. A report suggested that the results often exceeded the goals by as much as 155 percent (in 1944).[64] Savings ratios in Korea increased from 33.7 percent of income in 1941 to 45 percent in 1943[65] and a staggering 67.3 percent in 1945.[66] On the basis of these data, it seems reasonable to infer that saving in 1944 was more than double the sum reported in 1940–1941. Obviously, increased income made the gain in savings possible, but the actions of the government together with the shortage of consumer goods during the war years probably contributed a great deal, especially considering that most Korean people did not even have enough to eat. These savings were from the masses[67] as well as the high income earners.

SUMMARY AND CONCLUSIONS

This chapter has examined the mobilization of savings/resources of both foreign and domestic sources for financing investment in Korea. Of the investments in the private sector in Korea, which constituted more than three-quarters of the total, slightly more than half of the total was supplied within the country, while Japan financed the rest. The resources available to Korea for investment infused from Japan were principally of those of the borrowed funds of the two public banks and two GNBFIs—which made up a little less than a third of the total balance-of-payment deficit—the direct investment equivalent to a little more than one-fifth, and the colonial government's borrowing of approximately one-fifth. Also, the Japanese government's grants to the colonial government and business borrowing supplied about one-seventh of the total.

The resources available for investment in Korea under Japanese rule were largely supplied by Japanese. Their savings in Korea and Japan supplied more than 86 percent of the total in the country, while Koreans financed the remainder. The Korean contribution thus was considerably larger than many scholars give them credit for. It is also notable that the Koreans financed a small fraction of Japanese private investment indirectly, through bank loans to the latter made with their bank deposits.

The financing of investment from Japanese and Korean sources varied widely among different areas within the private sector. While Japan contributed more than half of investment in companies, Korea's dedication to it was less than half. Investments in unincorporated businesses, housing, and miscellaneous sectors were all financed within Korea. In the case of public investment, which was a little less than a quarter of the total investment in the country, the overwhelming portion (e.g., nine-tenths) of it was financed with the money borrowed by the colonial government from Japan and supplemented with Japanese government grants and profits of public enterprises.

The magnitude and type of investment financed between the Japanese and Koreans also showed distinct differences in a number of ways. The Japanese residing in both Japan and Korea financed more than 86 percent of the total investment in the country, while Koreans devoted approximately 14 percent of the total. Of them, Japanese dedicated nearly 84 percent of private investment and 95 percent of public investment, while Koreans contributed a little more than 16 percent and 5 percent, respectively. It should be noted that the Japanese financing of investment in Korea was somewhat smaller than what typically was alleged (90 percent) by many Japanese economists and historians and accepted by some Korean economists. In contrast, the Korean contribution to financing investment in the country with increased savings was considerably higher, and, through their bank deposits, they indirectly financed a small sum of investment in Japanese companies. Paradoxically, the diversion of Korean savings to the Japanese investment promoted the expansion of Japanese businesses at the expense of Korean businesses, which were typically consumer-goods-oriented enterprises.

It may also be noted that one of the principal reasons for larger savings among Koreans toward the end of the colonial era than during the traditional and transitional periods was the government savings policy and the related programs, some of which were compulsory and aggressively enforced. These programs seem to have had some successes in enlarging Korean domestic savings. Some of the results of these savings programs were phenomenal, especially considering the habitually low level of savings during the traditional and transitional periods. Korean saving increased to exceed 50 percent of income toward the end of colonial rule. Certainly, increased income and the shortage of consumer goods during the war years made the gain in savings possible, but the actions of the government seem to have contributed a great deal. These savings were from the masses as well as from the high-income earners.

8

ECONOMIC GROWTH AND STRUCTURAL CHANGES

Under Japanese rule, vast changes took place in the Korean economy. Some were the natural consequence of the introduction of "modern ways" into traditional economic life in Korea, but many came at the instigation of the Japanese. The impact of investment and government policies on the Korean economy under colonial rule is assessed in the remainder of this study. Examined in this chapter are the consequences of colonial rule for Korea's economic growth and structural changes. Korea's economic growth is gauged in terms of the expansions of its population, commodity (goods and services) production, and, the most comprehensive measure, GDP. They are followed by the assessment of structural changes in the economy relative to all major sectors: industry, mining, transportation, communications, commerce, finance, agriculture, forestry, and fishing. Also scrutinized are the volume and patterns of foreign trade, Japanese domination of the Korean economy, and Korea's dependence on the Japanese economy.

The Korean economy also underwent other significant economic changes, namely, agricultural and industrial organization, which in turn affected both income and wealth distribution in Korea under Japanese rule and in the post–World War II Korean economy. Aspects of structural changes in industrial and agricultural organization under colonial rule scrutinized include the transformation of the traditional sector and rise of the modern sector, the scale of business, and monopolies in industry, as well as landownership, the scale of landholding, the status of working farmers, and land tenancy in agriculture.

ECONOMIC GROWTH

Perhaps the most important economic impact of colonial rule was Korea's economic growth. Unquestionably, the Korean economy at the end of Japanese rule in

1945 was considerably more developed than the economy of the nation that had fallen apart only two generations earlier. Yet it is difficult to measure it quantitatively, for there are no accurate and comprehensive data suitable to compute it with a high degree of confidence. Under the circumstances, it seems necessary to rely on certain quantitative measurements that enable us to assess the country's economic growth in as meaningful a way as possible. There are essentially three available data sets for this purpose: the growth of population, commodity production, and limited data on the GDP.

These three sets of data clearly show that the Korean economy under Japanese rule did expand. First of all, the population of Korea during the forty-year period increased from approximately 13.1 million in 1904 to 26.5 million in 1943, more than doubling during that period and increasing at an annual average rate of about 1.8 percent. The official statistics also show that the average size of the family swelled from 4.7 persons per household in 1906 to 5.5 in 1942, indicating that over time the average household was able to support a larger number of family members. During the same period, the standard of living in the country by no means deteriorated. These developments clearly indicate that the Korean economy during the period grew, at the minimum, at the rate of population growth, or 1.8 percent a year.[1]

The second data that reveals economic growth in Korea, commodity production, shows a substantial increase under Japanese rule. According to the Japanese government's estimate, which is more comprehensive than many other sources for the period, the gross value of commodity production (mining, fishing, forestry, agriculture, and manufacturing) in current prices increased 19.3 times from 246.4 million yen in 1910 to 4.75 billion in 1940.[2] When these figures are adjusted for price rises during the period using a price index to eliminate nominal increases in value,[3] the real increase in commodity production is less spectacular, more than sixfold (635 percent) between 1910 and 1940, according to one study.[4] This places the annual increase in commodity production at approximately 6.3 percent. This estimate, however, is based on underestimated values in the early years, similar to the underestimated acreage of arable land examined in a previous chapter. The official figures understated the value of commodity production during 1910–1912 by as much as 23 percent.[5] When the adjustment is made, commodity production in Korea increased about 370 percent or at an annual average rate of 4.4 percent between 1910 and 1940. According to the government, commodity production between 1940 and 1944 also increased at an annual rate of 5.5 percent.[6]

A more recent estimate places the annual rise in the value of commodity production lower. According to calculations, the net value in 1936 prices increased from 645 million to 1.66 billion yen during the 1910–1940 period, an average annual increase of 3.7 percent. The average annual increase per capita in commodity production is estimated at 1.9 percent. Similar figures can also be found in publications of the Industrial Bank and a study of the issue.[7] From these data, it seems reasonable to infer that the annual increase in the net value of commodity production during the colonial period ranged between 3.7 and 4.4 percent, or an average of approximately 4 percent. However, similar to other data examined above, these data, too, suffer from underestimation of commodity production before 1918.

When an appropriate adjustment for the underestimation is made, the average annual growth rate of per capita commodity production may be set at about 2.2 percent for the period under Japanese rule. The per capita value of commodity production in Korea in 1938 may be estimated at 126 yen, which was a little more than a third of that of Japan, which was 358 yen. Judging by the value of many commodities whose prices are known, a ratio of 3 yen to $US1 corresponded fairly closely to the level of prices in these two countries in 1938 and can be used as a basis of comparison for that year.[8] Based on an exchange rate of 3 yen to $1, the value of per capita commodity production in Korea may be set at about $67 in 1938,[9] or $802 in year-2000 prices.

Lastly, fragmentary national income data support the rise in the nation's production. There are no definitive national income data for Korea before 1945, but a few fragmentary GDP data enable us to derive some reasonable and realistic estimates. They clearly show the increases in aggregate and per capita GDP during the forty-year period. One early estimate shows an average annual increase of real national income of 7.65 percent between 1931 and 1935,[10] while another source—covering the period between 1937 and 1944—shows an increase in real national income (corrected by the wholesale price index) of about 37 percent, indicating an average annual increase of about 4 percent. More recently, Yoon Keun Lee estimated that real GDP between 1926 and 1935 increased by 48.9 percent, an average annual increase of about 4.5 percent.[11] These calculations show average annual growth rates of GDP at different periods ranging from 4 to 7.65 percent. These estimates give us some idea of the improvement in Korea's economy. However, since these estimates calculate the economic growth of different time periods and duration, and they typically focus on periods of rapid growth, they are not representative of the average annual rise in GDP for the entire period (1905–1945).

Two recent attempts have been made to estimate the growth in GDP for most of the period. Suh estimates that the nation's income increased about three times during 1910–1941, for an average annual increase of about 3.6 percent. His estimates of national income for 1905 and 1938 are approximately 770 million and 2.3 billion yen (in 1938 prices), respectively. Kahng calculates that Korea's GDP increased from about $5 billion in 1910–1914 to about 11 billion (in 1980 U.S. dollars) in 1940–1944, an increase in real GDP of approximately 2.1 times, representing an average annual rise of 2.6 percent between 1910 and 1940.[12] These two estimates place the average annual increase in GDP between 2.6 and 3.6 percent under Japanese rule.

More careful analysis may show that the annual growth rate was somewhere between the two. It appears that the higher estimate might not have fully taken into consideration the undervalued figures before 1918, as examined in chapter 5 and later in this chapter, while the latter calculation showing a low growth rate did not seem to have given full credit to increased production in later years. This study estimates that Korea's GDP more than tripled under Japanese rule, implying an average annual growth rate of about 3 percent. Since Korea's population increased at an average annual rate of 1.8 percent, the increase in per capita GDP was estimated at 1.2 percent. This figure compares favorably with Kahng's estimate of 1.1 percent.

Based on these calculations, we can set the per capita GDP in 1942 at about $1,130 in year-2000 U.S. prices,[13] which is slightly more than that of Philippines today (which was $1,040 in the year 2000). This figure shows an increase in per capita income of about 1.56 times in about forty years, from $745 in 1904 and reflects the moderate expansion and development of the Korean economy under Japanese rule. This estimate contrasts with Kahng's and Y. K. Lee's estimates. Kahng estimated that the increase was from $322 in 1910–1914 to $435 in 1940–1944 in 1980 U.S. prices (or from about $660 to approximately $892 in year-2000 U.S. prices), while Y. K. Lee estimated that per capita GDP increased by 3 percent, from 91.36 yen in 1926 to 118.8 in 1935.[14] Since the population is estimated to have been 26.36 million in 1942, the nation's GDP would have been approximately $29.8 billion in 1942, an increase of 305.3 percent in forty years. Not having grown much for the prior three decades, the rate of growth of 3 percent between 1910 and 1942 was substantial, though not spectacular.

With the growth of the economy, the nation's employment also increased. Because of the lack of accurate data, it is not easy to correctly assess the growth of employment under colonial rule, but indications are clear that the increase was positive and ample. The official statistics indicate that employment in Korea increased from about 2.3 million in 1905 to 3.2 million in 1942, an increase of nearly 40 percent over the forty-year period at an average annual increase of nine-tenths of a percent. Increased investment provided more and better opportunities to Korean workers, some of whom would have been unemployed, partially employed, or employed in less productive and rewarding fields like in the traditional and transitional economies.

One persistent and widely held hypothesis in the analysis of the Korean economy under Japanese rule is that economic development was accomplished by means of draining off Korean resources for the benefit of the Japanese. It has been pointed out that there was destruction of the standing forests and intensive exploitation of gold and other minerals by Japanese lumber and mining companies. According to one official figure, the amount of standing timber decreased from 247 million cubic meters in 1927 to 198 million in 1936, a decrease of nearly one-fifth in a nine-year period.[15] Timber felled in Korea in 1939 alone was reported to have been 2.8 million cubic meters. Similarly, huge amounts of gold, silver, and iron ore were mined to meet Japanese needs. In a similar vein, it has also been alleged that the increase in agricultural production resulted in the draining of Korean resources.[16]

These arguments are somewhat misleading, however. Increased production and economic growth almost always require the use of resources. There is no evidence that the Japanese deliberately engaged in exploitation, except during the desperate years of World War II, when it extracted resources without adequately replenishing them. Likewise, it is mistaken to imply that Korean farmers would have been better off had they disregarded new technologies and not used fertilizers to increase output. It certainly is an injustice to suggest that these resources and products were stolen from Korea, although some, such as minerals and timber, would have been available to Koreans after 1945 had Japan not extracted them extensively.

In fact, there were conscious attempts on the part of the Japanese administration to replenish natural resources whenever possible. It attempted to reforest certain denuded areas (which it had inherited) and was proud of its accomplishments in this field. It was reported that no less than half a billion young trees were planted by the Japanese forestry service.[17] Standing timber increased, for example, from 198 million cubic meters in 1936 to 202 million in 1938. It is probable that reforestation proceeded more slowly than the destruction of the standing forests, but over the years the reforestation program, which was initiated in 1911, planted billions of seedlings and reduced soil erosion.[18]

It seems fair to point out that there was no overt attempt on the part of Japanese to exploit Korean resources without due consideration of the long-term effects on the colony's economy. On the contrary, Japanese colonialists were very much interested in using resources in Korea, as well as those in Japan, optimally. After all, the Japanese conquerors were planning to hold onto Korea forever as their territory in the Japanese empire. Thus, the Japanese government even resorted to force to bring about optimal resource utilization such as the protection of forests. When the government decided to promote sericulture in Korea, it imposed its own program on farmers. It determined the number of mulberry trees necessary for the program and distributed saplings to provinces, districts, and villages, though without addressing the immediate needs of the farmers.[19] Also, since Korea typically had supplied nearly half of its rice production to Japan, the latter undertook numerous costly irrigation projects during colonial rule to insure the continual flow to Japan in the decades to come.

SECTORAL EXPANSIONS AND STRUCTURAL CHANGES

Another clearly visible impact of Japanese rule was a perceptible change in its economic structure. Structural changes in production, employment, technology, and foreign trade are discernible in all segments of the economy, intra- as well as inter-industry. Virtually all sectors grew, though not simultaneously or equally. Consequently, the relative makeup and contribution of different segments of the economy were altered considerably under colonial rule. In this section, the analysis of structural changes follows sectoral divisions—agriculture, industry, mining, commerce, transportation, communications, and miscellaneous—traditionally found in Korea's statistical data. Whenever the data allow, other types of sectoral breakdown, such as primary, secondary, and tertiary sectors, are also examined.

Industry

One of the most notable structural changes in Korea under Japanese rule was the rapid expansion and increasing importance of the industrial sector. With the increase in investment in the industrial sector, as shown in chapter 4, employment in it also expanded. The number of persons employed in industry increased, probably from a few thousand in 1904 to 8,200 in 1910 and about 280,000 in 1942, a rise of thirty-four-fold in thirty-two years.[20] Relative to the total labor force, employment in the industrial sector increased from almost none to 5 percent during that period. The growth of industrial employment was especially rapid in later years. From 1931 to 1936, for instance, as the number of industrial enterprises in Korea increased 28.5 percent, the number of employees rose more than 75 percent. Also remarkable was the rise in the average number of workers employed per enterprise, from about twenty-three persons in 1920 to thirty-seven in 1938, a rise of more than 60 percent. In later years this growth probably accelerated. Total employment in the industrial sector, however, was relatively small in comparison with more developed countries, for example, 7.2 percent that of Japan in 1938.

The industrial sector, likewise, experienced an impressive rise in labor productivity. The value of output per industrial worker in constant prices increased 366 percent between 1920 and 1940, representing an average annual rise of 7 percent, much higher than the national average, which was slightly less than 3 percent. The value of net production per worker in industry in 1938 was 3,000 yen, fourteen times the 214 yen in agriculture.

As a consequence of increases in investment, employment, and labor productivity, output in the industrial sector expanded speedily, similar to the experiences of most developed countries. The expansion of the industrial output under Japanese rule started out slowly but mustered speed very quickly thereafter. When the inflationary factor is expunged, real production multiplied about thirty times between 1910 and 1943, an average annual growth rate of about 11 percent. Thus, the industrial sector grew at a much faster rate than that of the entire economy, for instance, by as much as four times during the 1910–1943 period. The increase between 1930 and 1943 was particularly impressive. The contribution of the industrial sector to overall growth in commodity production rose from about 14 percent in the 1910s to about 80 percent in the 1930s.[21]

As a result of the speedy rise in industrial production, its share of commodity production in the country expanded from 3.8 percent in 1912 to 11.3 percent in 1915, 16.4 percent in 1925, 23.4 percent in 1930, 29.1 percent in 1935, 39.1 percent in 1940, and 37 percent in 1943.[22] Also, the share of production in industry to GDP climbed from 6.7 percent in 1910–1912 to 29 percent in 1939–1941. In comparison with Japan, however, the gross value of industrial production in Korea remained fairly small, for example, only 5.8 percent that of the former (1.14 billion compared with 19.67 billion yen) in 1938. Industrial output represented only 37.8 percent of Korea's total commodity output in 1938, in contrast with 76.4 percent in Japan.

Manufacturing

Within industry, the expansion of manufacturing was most notable. Productivity in the manufacturing sector increased more rapidly than in most other sectors. Real product per worker in manufacturing in comparison with agriculture increased from 109 percent in 1920 to 411 percent in 1940 and from 130 percent of the countrywide average in 1930 to 340 percent in 1940. The value of production in manufacturing, including a small percentage in mining, increased the most, from 29 million yen in 1920 to 498 million in 1940, a more than seventeenfold increase in twenty years.[23] Within manufacturing, one clear structural change was the shift from light to heavy industries.

LIGHT INDUSTRY In the early years of Japanese rule, the insignificant amount of manufacturing in Korea was carried out mostly in light industries, such as processed food, textiles, pottery, wood products, printing, and bookbinding. Production in light industry increased at a fast rate during the early years; for example, at an average of about 9 percent a year during the 1914–1927 period, but its output expanded at a slower rate: for example, an average of about 5.7 percent a year, in later years, thereby approximately doubling output in a thirteen-year period between 1930 and 1943. On the whole, the output of the light industrial sector expanded about 7.3 percent a year between 1914 and 1943, which was more than double the national average but rather modest in comparison with heavy industry, as examined in the next section.[24] Because of the modest rise in comparison with the heavy and chemical industries, the relative share of output of the light industry declined rather precipitously over time—for example, from 61 percent of industrial output in 1936 to 49 percent in 1943, a seven-year period—as shown in Table 8.1. Nonetheless, the number of workers employed in light industry continued to exceed those in heavy industry. About 160,000 workers, or about 72 percent of all employment in manufacturing, were on payroll in 1943.

Within the light industrial sector, food processing (rice hulling, milling, sugar refining, distilling, canning, and soy sauce and paste manufacturing) occupied the most prominent place, especially during the early years of Japanese rule. Its facilities, even as late as 1929, constituted 49 percent of all industrial plants in Korea. The food-processing industry, however, expanded only modestly in later years and gradually lost its prominence.[25] It accounted for 33.8 percent of manufacturing in 1939 and 18.8 percent in 1943 and was second to the chemical industry in later years. The number of food-processing plants during the 1914–1940 period expanded between 7 and 8 percent a year.

TABLE 8.1 Share of Industrial Production between 1936 and 1943 (percent)

Industry	1936	1939	1943
Heavy and Chemical Industry:	34.0	47.0	49.0
Chemical	27.0	34.0	29.0
Metal	5.0	9.0	14.0
Machinery and equipment	2.0	4.0	6.0
Light Industry:	61.0	51.0	49.0
Food	27.0	22.0	19.0
Textile	14.0	13.0	17.0
Ceramic	3.0	3.0	4.0
Printing	2.0	1.0	1.0
Wood	1.0	1.0	6.0
Miscellaneous	14.0	11.0	2.0
Electric Power and Gas	5.0	2.0	2.0
Total	100.0	100.0	100.0

Sources: This table is based on Bank of Korea 1948: I, 100, 106–107; Takeo Suzuki, 1941: 223, 235.

Likewise, in terms of value of output, the food industry occupied first place in output within the manufacturing sector even as late as 1929. But it lost its prominence even more quickly than the number of plants did in the later years. Although the value of output increased 232 percent between 1930 and 1939 at an average annual rate of about 8.2 percent, when the inflation factor is discounted the increase in real value was very modest.[26] Consequently, its share decreased from 67 percent of total industrial output in 1929 to 27 percent in 1936 and only 19 percent in 1943 (see Table 8.1). Similarly, employment in the food-processing industry decreased from 31.7 percent of the total industrial labor force to 21 percent during the same period.

As found in the early stages of economic growth in most developing countries, the textile industry in Korea expanded steadily under Japanese rule. The number of factories more than doubled in nine years, between 1930 and 1939, for instance. Textile plants employed 19.3 percent of the industrial work force in 1943, making textiles the third largest employer in manufacturing. Although the production of textile goods increased at an average annual rate of 4.71 percent between 1914 and 1927, the growth of output during the 1928–1940 period was at an average annual rate of about 10 percent.[27] As a result of this brisk expansion, the textile industry's share of production increased from 6.3 percent of total industrial output in 1930 to 13 percent in 1939 and almost 17 percent in 1943 (see Table 8.1).

The ceramics industry, which included the production of cement, ceramics, glass, pencils, bricks, and tile, similarly expanded as a result of increasing demand and kept pace with other industrial sectors.[28] It grew rapidly by an average of 15 percent a year between 1914 and 1927 and 11.8 percent annually after 1928. Although the number of factories remained fairly constant from 1930 to 1939, the total output increased by 377 percent at an annual average of more than 10 percent.[29] Overall, the ceramics industry sustained a share of total industrial output of about 2 to 4 percent.

HEAVY AND CHEMICAL INDUSTRY In contrast with light industries, the heavy and chemical industrial sector, which produced such items as metals, machinery, and chemicals, expanded modestly in the early years but very rapidly in later years as Japan's territorial expansionist policies were pursued on the Asian continent. Eventually it came to dominate manufacturing in Korea. While its output increased at about 6 percent a year on average during the early years between 1914 and 1927, its production surged more than elevenfold at an annual average rate of more than 20 percent between 1930 and 1943.[30] Employment in heavy industry expanded with a similar speed but remained relatively small in comparison with light industry. By 1943 heavy industry employed about 28 percent of the work force in the manufacturing sector.[31]

As a result of a rapid expansion of the heavy and chemical industries and the slow growth of light industry, the relative share between the two changed, and the importance of key heavy and chemical industries oriented toward producer uses gained over time. The percentage of plants in heavy and chemical industries increased from nearly zero in the manufacturing sector in 1910 to about 23 percent in

1930, 36.33 percent in 1939, and 49 percent in 1943, while that of light industry, conversely, decreased during the same period. Similarly, the proportion of output of heavy and chemical industries dramatically expanded, while the share of output of light industry sharply declined. The proportion of output of heavy and chemical industries increased, for instance, from 34 percent of the total industrial production in 1936 to 49 percent in 1943, an increase of more than 44 percent in seven years (see Table 8.1).

Especially rapid was the expansion of the chemical industry, which produced fertilizers, explosives, pharmaceuticals, soap, oil, and rubber products. Its annual growth rate increased from 8.87 percent a year during the 1914–1917 period to as much as 21.62 percent a year during 1928–1940. Employment in the chemical industry grew from 12 percent of the industrial work force in 1929 to 31 percent in 1937, while worker productivity was 158 percent of the industrial average. As a result, the insignificant chemical industry of 1905 grew to represent 12 percent of all manufacturing plants in 1930 and 24 percent after 1936.[32] Likewise, the value of its output increased nearly elevenfold at an average annual rate of more than 20 percent between 1930 and 1943. In relation to manufacturing output, production in the chemical industry gradually increased from an insignificant 4.6 percent of the total manufacturing output in 1928 to 27 percent in 1936 and 39.6 percent in 1940 (although it declined to 29 percent in 1943) (see Table 8.1), making it the largest and the most important segment of the manufacturing sector by the 1930s.

Within the chemical industry, the production of fertilizers was most important in the early years, but later the production of chemicals for industrial use came to occupy the dominant position, making up more than 40 percent of all chemical production, followed by 20 percent for fertilizers and 25 percent for mineral, vegetable, and animal oils.[33]

Next in importance to manufacturing was the metal industry. The number of plants remained fairly constant at about 200 to 300, but the number of employees grew rapidly, especially during the 1930–1943 period, when it increased about fourfold. [34] Consequently, employment in the industry expanded from 5.4 percent of the industrial labor force in 1930 to 6.6 percent in 1939. The percentage of output of the metal industry also increased slowly, from 7.7 percent of total industrial output in 1928 to 9 percent in 1939 and then 14 percent in 1943. In terms of output per worker, it produced at a rate of 183 percent of the industrial average. Especially rapidly growing was the iron industry: the percentage rise in production multiplied more than threefold in twenty years, from an average of 3.2 percent a year between 1914 and 1927 to 11.6 percent a year between 1928 and 1940.[35]

As the country became more industrialized with growing iron and steel production, machine and tool manufacturing likewise expanded.[36] The number of plants increased from 5.3 percent of total factories in 1930 to 8.8 percent in 1939 and 9 percent in 1943, while employment during the same period expanded fourteenfold.[37] As a result of expansion in the number of plants and workers, the value of output increased at an average annual rate of 6.5 percent during 1914–1927, while the increase between 1930 and 1943 was by 5.1 times at an average annual rate of 13 percent.[38] Because of this rapid expansion, the value of output rose from

0.6 percent of the total industrial output in 1928 to 4 percent in 1939 and 6 percent in 1943. Employment in it accounted for 11 percent of the industrial labor force in 1939. Labor productivity, however, was low. In terms of output per worker, the machinery and tool industry, together with wood products, achieved only about 50 percent of the industrial average during the 1930s and early 1940s. In spite of their expansion, the metal, machinery, and tool industries remained fairly small.

This examination reveals that the industrial sector in Korea experienced a rapid structural change in the types of goods produced. Although the production of consumer goods in light industry expanded, its share gradually declined over time, while the share as well as the absolute amount of producers' goods in the heavy and chemical industries grew very quickly. The production share of foodstuffs in the consumer goods industry decreased from 83.5 percent in 1919 to 68 percent in 1940, while the share of producers' goods in relation to total finished goods grew from about 4 percent in 1920 to 18 percent in 1940. These trends clearly show that manufacturing in Korea under Japanese rule was becoming more producer-goods oriented in relation to total finished goods.

The examination of production in the industrial sector above indicates that the industrial sector became more balanced over time. Even as recent as 1936, the production in light industry recorded as much as 61 percent of total industrial production, which was almost double of that of heavy and chemical industry (34 percent). But by 1943, they were equal (49 percent each) (see Table 8.1). The structural change of the industrial sector was even more dramatic in production between food and chemical industries. Their relationship reversed over time. The percentage distribution was much larger for food industry than chemical industry in the early years as noted earlier, but by 1936 the two industries were identical in (27 percent each), and by 1943, the production in the chemical industry surpassed (29 percent of the total) food industry (19 percent).

The degree of product processing also changed over time. Manufacturing slowly moved away from the production of semiprocessed goods toward more finished products. Semiprocessed goods represented 85 percent of total output in 1920 but fell to about 67 percent in 1940. The proportion of so-called manufactured and nonmanufactured consumer goods likewise changed over time. The percentage of manufactured goods increased from 20.5 percent in 1919 to 44 percent in 1940, while nonmanufactured goods decreased from near 80 percent to 56 percent during the same period. The production of crude foodstuffs decreased from 91.5 percent of all consumer goods to 75.3 percent, while that of manufactured foodstuffs expanded from 8.5 percent to nearly 25 percent during the same period.[39]

Electric Power and Gas

The electric power industry likewise expanded rapidly under Japanese rule. Although the number of electric power and gas plants did not change much, not only the amount but the share of output expanded quickly. Yet, the output of the electric-power and gas industries together contributed relatively small portions of industrial output and decreased over time; for example, from about 5 percent of the total output of the industrial sector in 1936 to 2 percent in 1943 (see Table 8.1). Output per worker in the power industry was the highest in the industrial sector, at 560 percent of the industrial average in the 1930s.

Particularly notable was the speedy expansion of the electric-power industry. The capacity to generate electricity in Korea, mostly with coal in the beginning and with hydroelectric power in the later years, expanded from 1.7 kilowatts in 1910 to 1.5 million in 1943.[40] Since industrial development was focused almost entirely on Japan's strategic needs, electricity was generated in Korea in vast amounts found nowhere else in the Japanese empire. The increasing size of the capacity represented an astonishing accomplishment: 342 times in twenty-five years and almost a million times in thirty-three years. The construction of hydroelectric-power stations enabled the fast development of the heavy and chemical industries. Most of the electricity was used for industrial production, particularly in the chemical industry, the major "high-tech" sector of the pre–World War II period in Korea.

The gas industry, which was launched in 1909, expanded only modestly under Japanese rule, eventually serving fewer than 30,000 households in 1942. Following the outbreak of World War II, the coal shortages caused existing gas enterprises to decline, and new construction ceased by government decree.

Mining

Another structural change noted under Japanese rule was the gaining of importance of mining for industrial expansion. The rich endowment of minerals in Korea attracted much investment and caused a rapid expansion of mining soon after the country opened its doors to outsiders, as examined in chapter 3, but the most vigorous expansion in the exploitation of mineral resources took place after the Japanese came to rule the country. Mining held a prominent place in the Japanese economic design for Korea, and the country soon became an important source and processing center of mineral raw materials. Employment in mining likewise grew, eventually drawing in more than 2 percent of the labor force in 1942. Its productivity was high. According to one calculation, commodity production per worker in mining was 400 percent of the country average in 1930 and 340 percent in 1940, which was one of the highest in Korea, higher than in manufacturing as a whole.[41]

The value of mining output expanded swiftly. The average annual growth rate of mining accelerated from 6.33 percent during the 1914–1927 period to 19.7 percent during 1928–1940. A certain portion of this expansion is illusory, because of the rise in prices, yet on the whole the dramatic increase in mineral production was real. If the expansion of value were to be discounted by a price index, the annual increase would still exceed 8 percent annually, and the value of mining production multiplied seventy-three-fold between 1910 and 1942, rising on average between 9 and 10 percent a year.[42] As a result of such rapid expansion, the share of mineral production increased from 1.3 percent of the total output of goods in 1912 to 2 percent in 1931, 4.7 percent in 1935, and 5.9 percent in 1940.

Especially important among minerals was the gold and silver mining. The Wunsan mines alone extracted 82 tons of gold in a forty-year period prior to

1939,[43] comparable to the best gold mines in Japanese history, which had produced 60 tons since the Tokugawa period. Korea was similarly blessed with rich deposits of iron, estimated at about 20 million tons of high-grade and over a billion tons of low-grade ore.[44] By 1944 about a million tons of iron was produced, largely depleting Korea's ore reserves by the end of World War II. It was also richly endowed with coal reserves, which were estimated at 1.75 billion tons in 1939.[45] The output of coal increased about eighty-eight-fold between 1910 and 1941.[46] Coal was the leading source of energy in Korea, and it was either used directly as fuel or converted to electricity. In 1937 it accounted for 84.5 percent of all the energy used in industry (oil accounted for 8.9 percent and hydroelectricity 6.5 percent). In the same year, it supplied 75 percent of the energy used in transportation.

Transportation and Communications

Two of the quickly expanding sectors of the Korean economy under colonial rule, transportation and communications, were well developed and contributed to economic expansion of the country. New and modern transportation and communications networks were introduced prior to 1905, but the principal means of transportation infrastructure, such as roads and harbors, were later improved and expanded under colonial rule, largely to meet the needs of the Japanese. Employment in transportation increased from almost zero in 1904 to about 1.4 percent of the labor force in 1942. As Korean highways were modernized, their total length extended to 9,000 miles by 1938.

The most important means of transportation developed in Korea following the opening of the country was railroads. Under Japanese rule, track mileage expanded from about 39 kilometers in 1904 to nearly 3,400 kilometers in 1944, with numerous locomotives, coaches, boxcars, and a work force.[47] Likewise, private spur lines and other private tracks with a total length of 1,726 kilometers were built.[48] These railroad lines provided the major means of land transportation in the country, especially the north–south connection. The utilization of the system expanded swiftly in the 1930s, and the railroads transported more than 100 million passengers and 28 million tons of freight in the early 1940s. The movement of freight products, especially the transport of minerals and industrial goods, increased by 217 percent between 1930 and 1938. In other areas of transportation, private businesses augmented the railroads. Transportation companies (other than railroads) in the private sector represented 10 to 11 percent of all companies in Korea between 1923 and 1938. In shipping, the tonnage of bottoms multiplied fourteenfold between 1910 and 1937, and the tonnage of ships entering Korean ports expanded to more than 15 million in the late 1930s.[49]

Likewise, the telephone and telegraph systems were enlarged to facilitate the nation's communications. Although Korea had a fairly well-established telegraph network before 1905, the colonial government expanded both communications systems more extensively. Telephone lines were increased from 500 kilometers in 1910 to 13,400 in 1942, while telegraph lines were extended from 5,500 to 8,800 kilometers during the same period.[50] The telephone and telegraph systems, as well as trunk-line railroads, were operated as government monopolies.

Commerce/Trade and Finance

Also expanded in Korea under Japanese rule were the commercial and financial sectors. Because no comprehensive data on commerce in Korea are available, it is difficult to assess its growth and structural change in quantitative terms. However, there is no question that commerce/trade and finance expanded and experienced structural change under Japanese rule. While itinerant merchants continued to tour a circuit of rural town markets, merchants gradually opened stores and conducted business along the main streets of towns and cities. Employment in commerce expanded from 4.6 percent of the country's labor force in 1926 to 7.3 percent in 1942, about 50 percent more than industrial employment.[51] By the end of Japanese rule, many commercial activities, including those small merchants, were thriving. Although domestic trade expanded, its growth lagged behind that of the industrial sector.

As the economy expanded, the virtually nonexistent financial institutions of the transitional economy came to play a critical role in mobilizing savings and extending loans for investment, as scrutinized in earlier chapters. They enlarged the value of their deposits and loans from about 20 million yen in 1905 to about 3.5 billion in 1943. This was a new experience for most Koreans. While the role of the public banks and GNBFIs expanded and catered mostly to the investment needs of large businesses and landlords sponsored by the Japanese government, the shrinking commercial banks and PNBFIs confined their business mostly to commercial interests. At the end of the Japanese administration, the two private commercial banks—one Japanese and one Korean—were extending only a small portion of bank loans, mainly short-term credit to traders, although they mobilized substantial amounts of deposit funds. No financial institutions, however, adequately met the financial needs of small-income earners, especially landless tenant farmers.

Agriculture, Forestry, and Fishing

The largest and most important sector in the traditional economy, agriculture, also expanded under Japanese rule, but rather modestly. According to official statistics, agricultural production increased about tenfold from 207.7 million yen in 1910 to 2.2 billion in 1941.[52] The published statistics, however, need to be scrutinized for accuracy, since the rapid increases in agricultural production recorded in the official statistics overstated the rate of expansion for two reasons: (1) underreported amounts of agricultural production, of workforce size, and workers' productivity before 1918; and (2) rising agricultural prices over time.

As noted in chapter 5, agricultural data before 1918 are based on extensive underreporting of crop areas and harvests as well as missing data for many crops. A critical evaluation of the data shows that the value of agricultural output in current prices increased considerably less than tenfold, from 240 million to 2.2 billion yen, but the value in constant prices probably increased by about two-thirds between 1911 and 1943, at an average annual rate of about 1.6 percent.[53] This calculation places the increase in agricultural output somewhat lower than other estimates. Japanese officials and economists placed the increase in agricultural production during 1910 and 1942 at rates between 1.7 and 3 percent a year.[54] One study calculates that agricultural output increased by 77.5 percent between 1910 and 1942, an average annual increase of 2.1 percent,[55] while another study sets the average annual growth rate of agricultural production during 1911–41 at 2.13 percent.[56]

Accompanying the expansion of agricultural production, employment in agriculture also increased. According to the official statistics, agricultural employment, including forestry and fishing, increased by nearly 40 percent, from 2.21 million households in 1909 to 3.07 million in 1941,[57] an annual increase of just under 1 percent. These increases would have allowed the value of production per worker in constant prices to rise about 40 percent during this period, at an average annual increase of approximately nine-tenths of a percent. This places the annual growth rate of production in the agricultural sector at less than one-fifth that in the industrial sector. Agricultural production in Korea was far behind that of other countries, such as Japan, and its productivity of land was about 48 percent of that of Japan during 1910 and 1920.

These increases have resulted in the value of product per worker in constant prices to rise modestly. Labor productivity in agriculture increased about 50 percent between 1910 and 1942, reflecting an average annual rise of about 1.25 percent. Some other estimate shows that real product per worker in agriculture increased 24.1 percent between 1920 and 1940, an average annual rise of about 1 percent.[58]

Within agriculture, rice continued to be the dominant crop, accounting for about 60 percent of total production until about 1935 and more than 50 percent even in later years.[59] It supplied about 60 percent of the population's total calories. The published data show that rice production increased from 10.4 million *seok* in 1910 (this figure is probably too low, because of underreporting by farmers) to 21.5 million in 1942, a more than twofold rise and an average annual rise of about 2.3 percent. Agricultural productivity of rice likewise increased. The rice productivity of land increased about 70 percent between 1910 and 1940, from about 0.77 *seok* per *dan* to 1.31 *seok*, an average annual rise of about 1.8 percent, while labor productivity also increased about 70 percent. However, the understated figures before 1918 tended to inflate the increases. Accomplishments were actually considerably less than these figures might indicate. Rice productivity in Korea was only about one-half that of Japan; for example, 1.163 *seok* per *dan*, compared with 2.160 *seok* in Japan, in 1938.

The increase in agricultural productivity may be attributed to many factors, including new management techniques, improved seeds, increased use of fertilizers, better irrigation systems, and improved methods of cultivation. Among them, the most notable contributing factor was found to be the increased use of commercial fertilizers. The application of fertilizers increased from 8,513 tons in 1915 to 285,800 in 1928 and 868,025 in 1939, an increase of 102 times in a twenty-five-year period. Experiments conducted on plots of land planted to rice, wheat, and barley showed that average yields declined by as much as 50 percent when no fertilizer was applied.[60] The same was found to be the case with cotton. A decline in productivity experienced in 1940–1945 was largely a result of the shortages of commercial fertilizers during the war years. Also important were the expanded irrigation system and improved varieties of seeds. Newly developed rice-seed strains raised output, on average, 17 percent (from 8.86 to 10.34 *seok* per *jeong*). As was shown in chapter 5, however, the increased use of capital goods played a limited role.

In spite of the rises in production, productivity of land, and employment, the increase in labor productivity in agriculture was much lower than that in the industrial sector. The annual growth rate of agricultural commodity production was about one-fifth that of industrial production (2 percent versus 9.7 percent) and two-thirds that of commodity production in Korea as a whole (3 percent) between 1910 and 1939.[61] As a result, the increases of per capita production in agriculture lagged far behind those of the other sectors. According to one calculation, commodity production per worker in agriculture was 90 percent of the national average in 1930 and 80 percent in 1940.

As a result of slow growth in agricultural productivity, the agricultural sector expanded at a much slower rate than the rest of the economy, especially the industrial sector, and the relative importance of agriculture gradually diminished. The sector, which had accounted for 93 percent of total commodity production (excluding tertiary industry) at the dawn of the twentieth century, declined to 73.9 percent in 1925, 54.8 percent in 1935, 43 percent in 1940, and 37.4 percent in 1944.[62] In relation to Korea's GDP, agricultural output probably decreased from 84.6 percent in 1910–1912 to 49.6 percent in 1939–1941. Similarly, employment in the traditional sector, primarily in agriculture, relative to other sectors of the economy declined. The percentage contracted from over 85 percent in 1905 to less than 67 percent at the end of colonial rule.[63] The incursion of modern industries led some farmers to become wage-earning laborers in industrial, mining, trade, and service sectors. Along with the relative decrease in agricultural production, the importance of rice declined as well, from over 80 percent of all agricultural output in the early 1910s to about 70 percent in 1940. Meanwhile, the share of products such as cocoons and manure slowly expanded.

In spite of agriculture's relative decline in importance in the Korean economy, Korea at the end of colonial rule remained primarily an agricultural country with low income. It continued to occupy a much more significant position in the Korean economy than it did in neighboring countries such as Japan. Agricultural output in 1940 represented 37.4 percent of total commodity output in Korea, in contrast with only 16.1 percent in Japan in 1938. Also, the majority of workers in Korea were in the agricultural sector. In comparison to farmers in some other countries, the Korean farmers' output continued to be small. Gross value of production per farm in Korea was only $153 in 1938, in comparison with $248 for the Japanese and $1,828 for the American farmers.[64]

Forestry likewise expanded, but its relative position in the economy under Japanese rule remained fairly constant. Timber production increased at about 5 percent a year,[65] but the relative position of the forestry sector remained at about 5 percent of all commodity production in Korea, although its share of GDP increased from 5.3 percent in 1910–1912 to 7.2 percent in 1939–1941.[66]

The primitive fishing industry in Korea expanded much more than forestry did and gradually gained in importance to the Korean economy under Japanese rule.[67] The value of fish production in constant prices increased 12.7 times, while the number of fishing households increased 268 percent in thirty years or 8 percent a year. These figures indicate that the productivity of households in the fishing industry increased at an average annual rate of 5.1 percent between 1911 and 1941, considerably higher than the average for the entire economy. By 1939, Korea ranked sixth in the world as a supplier of fish products (accounting for 15 percent of world production). More than half of the fish harvested were exported. As a consequence, the fishing industry's share of total commodity production expanded from about 2.6 percent in 1910 to 7.3 percent in 1940, while its share of GDP rose from 1.9 percent in 1910–1912 to 6.5 percent in 1939–1941. Employment in fishing increased from 1.2 percent of the total labor force in 1910 to 1.9 percent in 1942.

The increase in fishing was largely a result of increased investment and government efforts. It established schools and experimental stations, improved harbor and market facilities, developed fish farms, introduced processed fish, and expanded the export market. Although most government support went to large Japanese firms, local enterprises were also encouraged to pursue new cooperative-credit, purchasing, and marketing arrangements.

Foreign Trade

Structural change under Japanese rule is also clearly visible in foreign trade, even more than in the industrial sector, in several ways. First, Korea's ability to trade multiplied many times. The ratio of commodities traded to the total available products in the economy (domestic production plus imports) increased from 20 percent in 1911–1915 to 60.4 percent in 1936–1940. The export ratio (the ratio of exports to total commodity products plus imports) increased from 6.6 to 25.8 percent during the same period, while the import ratio expanded from 13.4 to 34.6 percent.[68] Since no accurate national income data is available, it is difficult to make reliable comparisons, but the ratio of foreign trade to national income must have increased precipitously, probably from less than 5 percent in 1904 to more than 30 percent in 1940. Foreign trade thus gave the Korean economy the boost that set it on a progressive road. Production for export did not have the same disadvantages as production for the domestic market. It did not depend on growing demand within the country, and it gave rise to no competitive struggles at home since world demand in the early years was large relative to the output of individual producers in a single country. Exports stimulated home industries in other ways, such as through linkage effects, while imports created new tastes.

Second, the composition of the goods and services traded changed over time. Initially, Korea's exports consisted mainly of unprocessed foodstuffs and raw materials, such as rice and gold. Most were produced by means of traditional farming, extracting resources, and handicraft methods. As Korea's economy developed under Japanese rule, the export of crude foodstuffs decreased relatively from about 66.5 percent of the total before 1910 to about 26.1 percent in 1939, as indicated in Table 8.2. In their place, exports of finished manufactured goods, processed raw materials, and processed foodstuffs became increasingly important. Exports of finished manufactured goods climbed from about 3.3 percent of total exports in 1910 to 22.6 percent in 1939, while exports of processed raw materials increased from six-tenths of a percent in the late 1910s to 25 percent in 1939. Toward the end of Japanese

TABLE 8.2 Share of Korea's Imports and Exports between 1910 and 1939 (percent)

	Imports			*Exports*		
Goods	1910	1933	1939	1910	1933	1939
Raw materials	10.4	10.8	12.9	19.2	13.7	17.4
Intermediate goods	10.2	13.5	14.0	0.6	16.6	24.7
Crude food	3.3	8.5	8.5	66.5	51.9	26.1
Processed food	11.3	6.4	4.7	0.1	3.4	3.7
Manufactured goods	56.3	55.6	55.4	3.3	8.7	22.6
Miscellaneous goods	8.5	4.7	4.2	9.3	5.5	5.2
Reimport goods		0.5	0.3	1.0	0.2	0.3
Total	100.0	100.0	100.0	100.0	100.0	100.0

Sources: This table is based on Bank of Korea 1948: I, 117, III, 50–59.

rule, fertilizers, pulp, hard oil, explosives, and other manufactured and semimanufactured goods bolstered exports. Capital equipment went largely to the protected markets of Korea and other Japanese-occupied countries, such as Manchuria.[69]

Korea's demand for foreign goods likewise changed over time, reflecting the industrialization of the Korean economy. On the one hand, imports of industrial materials, whether raw or partly processed, grew inexorably decade by decade, from 20.6 percent in 1910 to 26 percent in 1939 (see Table 8.2; these numbers reflect the combination of "Raw materials" and "Intermediate goods" categories). On the other hand, Korea's imports of finished goods (excluding foodstuffs) actually declined in volume. Its demand for manufactured goods decreased from 56.3 to 55.4 percent of the total during 1910 and 1939, while the demand for processed raw materials increased gradually, from about 10.2 percent of total imports in 1910 to 14 percent in 1939. While the imports of crude foodstuffs increased from 3.3 percent to 8.5 between 1910 and 1939, the demand for processed food declined slowly, from about 11.3 percent of total imports to 4.7 percent, during the same period.

Another dimension of the trends in trade reflected the process of industrialization of the Korean economy. While imports of consumption goods relative to the total declined over time, the portion of imported finished items in the form of capital goods such as machinery and equipment increased. The ratio of commodity imports destined mainly for consumption (such as living plants, animals, cereals, liquor, tobacco, and textiles) fell from 51.5 percent of total imports in 1929 to 36.8 percent in 1939, while the proportion of a group of imports destined mainly for production increased in the same period, from 25.2 to 43.6 percent of the total. The classification of commodities in these statistics is by no means faultless, but the contrast is convincing. Moreover, the remaining share of imports contained goods used chiefly for production, such as fertilizers, timber, and dyes.[70]

ECONOMIC DEPENDENCY

It has often been pointed out that under Japanese rule the Korean economy was molded into one that depended on Japan—the so-called dependency theory.[71]

According to this view, the Korean economy became an integral part of the Japanese economy and was incapable of standing alone. Also, it has been argued that the Japanese in Korea intended to use the colony to meet Japan's needs, not those of the Koreans. In this view, the Korean economy became not only overly dependent on Japan but also was unbalanced and unstable.

The Korean economy's dependency was certainly reflected in its trade relations with Japan. The volume of trade between Japan and Korea was unusually large, and it intensified over time. The trade ratio (the export ratio plus the import ratio) tripled in about thirty years, rising from 20 to 60 percent between 1905 and 1943.[72] Its exports to Japan increased from about 60 percent of total exports in 1910 to about 90 percent in the 1930s, averaging about 83 percent during the 1910–1941 period. On a broader scale, Korean exports to yen-bloc countries accounted for as much as 97 percent of its total exports in 1939. The Korean share of Japanese imports expanded from 3 percent of total imports in 1910 to about 16 percent in 1940, as shown in Table 8.3. Korea developed into an important Japanese supply depot, especially for military materials and foodstuffs.

Korea likewise depended heavily on the Japanese market, especially for its rice. Rice exports to Japan, the main source of Korea's export revenue, increased briskly throughout the 1920s and 1930s. Averaging 4.4 million *seok* per year in 1922–1926, rice export to Japan increased to 6.2 million in 1927–1931 and 9.6 million in 1932–1936, more than doubling in ten years.[73] Exports of rice to Japan expanded from 4.5 percent of Korea's total rice production in 1912 to 30 percent in 1922–1926, 40 percent in 1930, and 51.5 percent on average in 1932–1936. Korean rice export grew from about a quarter of Japan's imports of rice to nearly two-thirds during that period. For the entire period, rice sent to Japan constituted nearly one-third of Korea's total exports. This represented 40 percent or more of all the rice produced in Korea.

Korea's dependence on the Japanese market for rice placed it at the mercy of Japan. As was examined in chapter 6, whenever the Japanese government changed

TABLE 8.3 Share of Trade between Korea and Japan, 1910–1940 (percent)

	Japanese Share in Korea's Exports and Imports		*Korean Share in Japan's Exports and Imports*	
Year	Exports	Imports	Exports	Imports
1910	60.7	63.7	5.1	3.0
1915	81.4	69.6	5.3	6.5
1920	86.0	57.4	6.5	6.3
1925	92.9	69.0	8.8	10.2
1930	90.3	75.8	14.9	12.1
1935	88.2	85.9	17.1	14.9
1940	78.2	86.9	24.7	15.9
Average	82.5	72.6	11.8	9.8

Note: All other yen-block countries—Taiwan, Manchuria, and China—had similar increasing trends.

Sources: Based on Bank of Korea 1948: I, 117, III, 50–51.

its agricultural policy, which was frequently, Korea had to comply and accommodate it. In the very early years, the Japanese government's main concern was to settle Japanese farmers in Korea.[74] In later years, its aim was to retain the basic agricultural orientation of the Korean economy and make its agriculture more efficient so as to better cater to Japan's needs. In other words, a principal objective of Japan was to use Korea as a source of food and raw materials, by placing the emphasis on rice production, because rice was essential in the growing industrial and commercial cities of Japan. Between 1912 and 1917, Korean rice sent to Japan represented between 56 and 88 percent of the country's total rice exports. A rice riot in Japan in 1918 made Korea even more critical as a supplier of rice and in 1919 prompted the Government General to develop the thirty-year plan to increase rice production in Korea and to export more than 90 percent of it to Japan. Between 1923 and 1930, virtually all Korean rice exports went to Japan.

Then, in 1933, as a result of the overproduction of rice in Japan in 1930, low prices in Korea, and many complaints in Japan about imported Korean rice, Governor General Ugaki began to urge Koreans to eat more rice and export less. He adopted a "cotton in the South and sheep in the North" (*nanmen-hokuyo*) policy, encouraging cotton production and sheep raising as substitutes for rice farming. In 1934 the colonial government abandoned its rice-production plan and implemented the policy of "parallel development of agriculture and industry" (*noko heishin*).

Again, starting 1938, to meet growing needs emanating from the wars in China and the Pacific, the colonial government developed rice-production plans. In 1939 Governor General Minami advised the Korean people to stop eating rice and developed a series of plans to increase rice production: a five-year plan in September 1939, a seven-year plan in October 1939, and a six-year plan in January 1940. Exports of rice to Japan continued at a high level even in the face of a decline in production (largely attributable to the shortage of commercial fertilizers) and an increasing population in Korea. It is thus clear that the Japanese agrarian policy was carried out exclusive with a view toward the needs and interests of the Japanese.

Korea also depended on Japan to purchase its gold. As much as 99 percent of Korea's gold production (4 percent of total exports) went to Japan.[75] Similarly, over four-fifths of Korea's iron and steel production was exported to Japan.

Korea likewise depended on Japan for imported goods and services. Imports from Japan expanded from 62.4 percent of total imports during 1910–1912 to 88.3 percent during 1939–1941. Korean imports of Japanese goods and services increased from 5.1 percent of Japan's total exports in 1910 to 25 percent in 1940. On a broader scale, imports from the yen-bloc countries made up 95.1 percent of Korea's total. Imports from the United States in 1939 amounted to only 1.7 percent, and this was almost entirely attributable to the purchase of much-needed American machinery.[76]

The goods Korea traded with Japan were quite different from those traded with other countries. Exports to Japan between 1915 and 1939 consisted, on average, of 76.2 percent crude materials (foodstuffs and industrial goods) and 19.1 percent manufactured goods (semifinished and finished products), the rest being "miscellaneous." The share of manufactured products in Korea's imports from Japan was far greater than that of crude materials (79.1 percent versus 12.6 percent, respectively). The former was approximately 6.3 times the latter. Like other Japanese territorial acquisitions, Korea served as a market for Japanese manufactures. With nations other than Japan, Korea's imports and exports of crude materials and manufactured goods were fairly evenly divided: 51.3 percent versus 39.6 percent and 40.2 percent versus 39.6 percent, respectively.[77]

Also, Korean industries were largely dependent on complementary industries in Japan, as shown in Table 8.4. Many large or key plants in Korea were designed principally for the manufacture of parts to be used in the final assembly of completed articles in Japan. The Korean economy was not geared toward producing the goods and services needed to meet its own needs. Even for textiles, Korea relied heavily on Japan, meeting only 56 percent of its own needs, with cotton goods serving as the only exception. Heavy industry in Korea met a mere 55.7 percent of domestic needs and the metal industry only 60 percent in 1941. The machine and tool industry met about a third in the same year, while it met only about 7.8 percent of its needs for printed materials, for example, with Japan supplying the rest. The economy was also heavily dependent on Japan for capital, technology, and skilled workers.

As a consequence of Korea's dependence on the Japanese economy, its reliance on trade with Japan distorted its postliberation economy because the country was "overdeveloped" in areas inappropriate to early development stages (e.g., those that were chemical and military related), while other areas (in particular, the consumer-goods industry, producing such goods as textiles) were neglected and underdeveloped. Industries concentrated in certain regions—for example, the heavy, chemical, and electric-power industries in northern Korea—also proved to be unsuitable when

TABLE 8.4 Self-Sufficiency Ratios in Industries in 1940–1941

Industries	Percent
Food	95.1
Chemical	82.8
Wood products	76.1
Miscellaneous	74.2
Ceramics	68.1
Metal	59.5
Textiles	55.9
Machine and tools	34.7
Printing	7.8
Aggregate Average	72.1
Railway stock car, ships, and parts	29.5
Reproduction machine	19.6
Power motor	7.1
Watch, telephone, school equipment	6.2
Engine and parts	3.7
Railway engine car	—
Structural machinery	—
Average	9.4

Source: Based on Bank of Korea 1948: I-101.

Korea became became independent countries after World War II. It thus seems reasonable to suggest that Japanese investment in selected areas in Korea did not optimally promote Korea's economic growth, and thus the welfare of Korean people suffered, especially in the short run.

Many Korean scholars also believe that because of their country's dependence on Japan the latter was exploitative and brought instability to the Korean economy. Clearly there was a dependency relationship, but whether it was truly exploitative is not clear. There are some indications that Japan brought trade advantages rather than exploiting a disadvantaged Korea. Good examples are rice and iron ore exports to Japan: Japan paid higher prices to import those commodities from Korea than those prevailing in world markets at the time.[78]

In the meantime, Korea was also developing its own economic structure to suit the changing needs of the economy and paradoxically was becoming less dependent on Japan over time. The changes in Korea's trade are notable in opposite directions at least in two respects. First, with time, Korea's manufacturing became more balanced in the sense that the production of producer, as opposed to consumer, goods expanded. The share of finished producer goods increased from 3.6 percent of the total during 1919–1921 to 18.1 percent during 1939–1940, while the percentage of finished consumer goods produced decreased from 96.4 percent of total finished goods to 81.9 percent during the same period. Likewise, the share of producer goods increased from 15.4 percent during 1919–1921 to 33.4 percent during 1939–1940, while the percentage of manufactured consumer goods decreased from 84.6 percent of all finished manufactured goods to 66.6 percent during the same period. Similarly, the chemical and ceramics industries were meeting 83 and 68 percent of domestic needs on average in 1941, respectively, while the textile industry met 56 percent of domestic needs and the food industry met more than 95 percent in the same year, as shown in Table 8.4. In the case of machine and tool manufacturing, the self-sufficiency rate increased from 24.7 percent in 1939 to 51.7 percent in 1944.[79]

Second, as Korea's exports horizon widened under Japanese rule, it expanded its own network of foreign trade, and its trade with Japan and other countries grew more balanced over time. Korea's exports to countries other than Japan increased from 6 to 8 percent of total exports in the late 1920s to 21 percent in 1940.[80] Exports of crude materials, including unprocessed food, to countries other than Japan decreased from 72.6 percent of total exports in 1910 to 27.4 percent in 1939, while exports of manufactured products increased from 3.7 percent to 65.5 percent of total exports during the same period. At the same time, imports of crude materials from countries other than Japan increased (e.g., from 17.1 percent of the total imports in 1910 to 74.4 percent in 1939). It might have been that Korean exports were principally to yen-bloc nations and so were part of Japanese-controlled markets. Nonetheless, Korea was gradually establishing markets in a wider circle of nations. This development is similar to what it has experienced since the 1970s: South Korea and Japan have been close trading partners since the former gained its independence.

In the meantime, Korean exports to Japan decreased over time, from 93.2 percent of total exports in 1924 to 87.2 percent in 1936, 73.3 percent in 1939, and 72.8

percent in 1943.[81] Likewise, the percentage of Korean exports of crude materials (such as food and industrial raw materials) to Japan steadily decreased from about 89.5 percent of total exports in 1910 to less than 49.5 percent in 1939; more dramatically, exports of unprocessed food products decreased from 69.5 to 27.9 percent of the total during the same period. At the same time, exports of manufactured products increased from 4 percent to 45.8 percent of the total during the same period, a more than elevenfold increase. On the other hand, imports of crude materials rose somewhat, while imports of manufactured products remained fairly stable. Korea's trade thus was becoming more independent of Japan by the end of the colonial period.[82]

Regardless of whether a country is a sovereign nation or a colony, a certain degree of dependency, especially among neighboring countries, where there is much to gain from a close trade relationship, often prevails. In this sense, some degree of the dependency of Korea on Japan may have been natural, as is well demonstrated in the trade relationship between independent South Korea and Japan today.

There is no empirical evidence to suggest that an unbalanced or "unhealthy" export relationship developed under colonial rule and/or that economic instability was the end result of Japanese domination. On the contrary, considering the relative stability and booming economy of Japan during the colonial period, e.g., more steady economies in Japan and Korea than in the Western economies during the Great Depression of the 1930s, the relationship probably brought about more economic stability than otherwise. Furthermore, the balance of trade between agricultural and manufactured products barely changed in spite of the fact that Korea exported increasing amounts of rice to Japan. On the other hand, the share of Korea's imports of crude materials rose dramatically during the period when the proportion of its imports of manufactured products plummeted.

INDUSTRIAL ORGANIZATION

As with the sectors just examined, the industrial sector also underwent structural changes in production technology, management, and scale of firms in the process of transformation of the economy under Japanese rule. This process is clearly visible in all industrial sectors. The modus operandi of restructuring the industrial sector under Japanese rule is examined next, in terms of the country's adaptation to the Industrial Revolution, the scale of business, and domination of the market.

Traditional and Modern Sectors

One easily discernible transformation that took place in the industrial sector under colonial rule is its modernization. Except for a few run by Japanese and "foreigners,"[83] modern-style factories were not common even at the time of Japanese takeover. Only after 1919, positively influenced by the World War I economic boom, did the industrial sector make many advances. The so-called factories with employer and employees slowly came to dominate the industrial sector, and greater reliance was placed on machinery and motor power. There also sprung up new enterprises producing for the foreign as well as the domestic market: such Western-style manufactures as commercial fertilizers, metal, machine parts, rubber shoes, and toys. Many of the new businesses employed modern methods, some comparable to the best in the world at the time. Most "modern" businesses in Korea were Japanese owned.

As the modern manufacturing and factory system expanded, production increased. Commodity production in the modern sector increased, on average, more than 20 percent a year during the 1920–1939 period. As the modern sector expanded, employment in it also increased, not only absolutely but relative to the total labor force. Employment in the modern industrial and mining sectors, for instance, increased from far less than 1 percent of the labor force in 1910 to nearly 7 percent in 1942.[84] As a result, the share of the modern manufacturing sector expanded from less than 10 percent in 1904 to nearly 60 percent of total factory production in 1932–1933, 75 percent in 1938, and 80 percent in 1943.

Some scholars have argued that modern industry destroyed the traditional or indigenous sector in Korea, causing an irreparable setback.[85] In the early years, factory goods imported from overseas did cause some displacement of domestic handicrafts, especially in textiles and oil. Cheap cotton goods woven from machine-spun yarns proved superior to native hempen cloth, and modern cotton cloth and yarn made up a third of total imports during the first two decades of the twentieth century. Imported kerosene, sugar, indigo, and raw cotton likewise began to replace native products. According to this argument, since a large proportion of Korean business was in cottage industries, this development hurt the growth of native-owned businesses.

Notwithstanding these assertions, the destructive effect of imported foreign manufactures and domestically produced modern goods on traditional handicrafts seems to have been neither pronounced nor widespread under Japanese rule. Rather than replacing the traditional handicraft/cottage industries, the modern sector actually augmented them in most cases. In 1932 most households still engaged in cottage industries,[86] and probably more than half the businesses in Korea were organized around small unincorporated enterprises as late as the 1940s. In fact, these household industries expanded their output under Japanese rule. From small handicraft plants, such as blacksmith shops and motor-powered rice mills, came most of the traditional necessities and luxuries of the Korean people: textiles, soy products, dyed goods, spirits, straw mats, footwear, silks, pottery, lacquerware, and processed food.

Statistics on household industries are less reliable than those on manufacturing by companies and factories, but a tendency toward growth is clearly evident. Obviously, as the modern sector rapidly expanded the relative share of output in traditional industries in the economy decreased. The share of household industries decreased from probably more than 90 percent in 1904 to 40.5 percent of total factory production in 1932, 25 percent in 1938, and less than 20 percent in 1943. However, they did not suffer an absolute decline in most cases. The value of production in cottage industries, in fact, increased from about 20 million yen in 1910 to 130 million in 1932 and 328 million in 1939, an increase of 16.4 times in thirty years.[87] Taking into consideration the rise in prices during the period, the real increase is still clearly visible and substantial: more than fivefold during the period and with real growth of about 5.5 percent a year. Only once, during World War II, were there signs of decline in household industries, which resulted largely from the shortage of raw materials for the cottage industry during the war. Cottage industries were prevalent in almost all sectors of the economy and remained dominant in many sectors, producing light consumer goods such as woven cotton, textiles, processed food, wood, and paper, as late as in the 1930s. Coexistence persisted between the traditional and modern sectors in many fields.

The main reason for the survival, and even modest growth, of the traditional sector seems to have been the fact that traditional technology employed more labor compared with capital-intensive methods of production in the modern sector. Since the price of labor relative to that of capital goods was low, the unit cost of production using traditional technology was relatively low as well. Second, transportation costs for products of the traditional sector were also low. Third, the modern sector sometimes made an important contribution to cottage industries by supplying the necessary materials and introducing technological improvements. The most illustrative case is the hand-weaving industry, where the yarn used on the hand looms was first supplied by imports and then by textile factories established in Korea. Without a regular and reliable supply of high-quality intermediate products, the hand-weaving industry would probably never have been able to develop as much as it did. It also relied on the modern sector for materials such as dyes. Another essential factor in the growth of hand weaving is believed to have been the introduction of the iron hand loom, which replaced the age-old wooden type.

Improvements in technology could also be found, though on a limited scale, in handicraft industries such as silk reeling, oil pressing, flour milling, and cotton fluffing and ginning. "Modern" products such as matches and soap were imitated by the handicrafts. Socks and knitted or jersey underwear factories in Pyongyang and cotton sheet factories in Seoul adopted new technologies. Improvements in handicraft industries sometimes occurred as a result of the pressure of competition from the modern sector. In this sense, the modern sector helped the traditional sector survive and expand. In rare cases, a handicraft enterprise was completely transformed into a modern factory.

Fourth, the development of the modern sector led to increasing demand for a variety of traditional products that still constituted an essential part of consumption, even for urban residents. The masses showed great interest in such new products as kerosene, oil, lamps, matches, needles, and towels, to name a few, but these products accounted for only a minor part of mass consumption in the early years (although demand for them expanded in later years). Moreover, costly modern products were often beyond the means of the average Korean at the time.

The expansion notwithstanding, traditional businesses did not constitute the most important segment of the Korean economy under the colonial regime, nor did they develop as rapidly as modern enterprises. As noted previously, the share of household industries decreased from more than 90 percent of total factory production in 1904 to less than 20 percent in 1943. Neither did traditional businesses play a critical role in modernization through the development of leaders or innovators. They were typically the reluctant and conservative followers of modern industries. At the end of Japanese rule, modern and traditional businesses coexisted side by side, with traditional enterprises employing primitive techniques and a few corporations with the most modern techniques producing most of the output.

Scale of Business

Not only did the industrial sector in Korea modernize, it was also increasingly dominated by large-scale corporations during the colonial period, in terms of numbers, paid-in capital, employment, and output. In the early years of Japanese rule, most new businesses were very small. A total of twenty-four textile factories in 1910, for instance, had average capital of 8,226 yen. The average capital per company (which tended to be larger than other types of businesses) in 1910 was 13,000 yen, and only four had nominal capital of more than 300,000. Prior to 1904, only nine firms were considered medium in size (with between 30 and 99 employees), while only one was classified as large (with more than 100 employees), the latter being an iron refinery established by the Japanese.

As the Korean economy expanded, an increasing number of medium-sized and large factories and companies were established after about 1923. The number of large companies multiplied from 1 in 1905 to 100 in 1938. The percentage of large factories increased from 2.1 percent of the total number of factories in 1932 to 5 percent in 1940, an increase of 2.4 times in eight years, whereas the percentage of medium-sized factories increased from 3.4 to 14 percent during the same period, an increase of 4.1 times. In contrast, small factories (with between 1 and 29 employees), which once accounted for more than 95 percent of all factories, diminished to about 82 percent in the later years.[88]

As the number of medium-sized and large businesses increased, the average paid-in capital of all companies increased from 66,100 yen in 1910 to 209,700 in 1917, and 336,000 in 1920. Thereafter, it precipitously declined to 186,300 yen in 1925 and 160,400 in 1928. But the average bounced back to 220,100 yen in 1935, 304,000 in 1938, and 535,300 in 1941.[89] The large companies came to dominate the nation's output more conspicuously after 1933. Large factories with more than 200 workers, which employed only 1.2 percent of the country's factory workers, produced 61.8 percent of factory output in 1938. In 1940 the large factories (those employing more than 100 employees), which constituted only 4.7 percent of all companies and employed 51.6 percent of all factory workers, produced 69.5 percent of the output in industry.

Almost all new large businesses were incorporated. Most were organized in Korea or Japan after 1929, were engaged in modern industrial activities, and maintained close relationships with banks. Included among these large businesses were a few towering combines that dominated industry, mining, agriculture, and commerce. Many in Korea were organized even on a scale larger than were corresponding enterprises in Japan.

The domination of large companies was most conspicuous in public utilities. The gas and electric industries were reigned over by large companies, and their predominance grew over time. In 1933 there were sixty-three electric companies, but through mergers mandated by the colonial government, ostensibly to derive economies of scale, the number was reduced to eighteen in 1939. Each of these corporations was capitalized, on average, at 13.3 million yen. Only three had capital of less than 1 million yen, thirteen had 10 million yen or more, and three had more than 50 million yen. These corporations were even bigger than those in Japan, where only 13 to 14 percent of all electric-power corporations had capital of 10 million yen or more.[90] The scale of their operations in Korea accelerated over time. The Yalu River dam and power station at Supung, constructed in 1937, for instance, surpassed the size of Boulder Dam in the United States and was the largest installation in the world at the time. Chemical companies also figured prominently. The Korea Nitrogen Fertilizer Corporation in Heungnam, for example, built in 1930, was said to have been the second largest in the world at the time.

Although large companies dominated the Korean economy in terms of paid-in capital, employment, and output, a majority of the business firms in Korea under Japanese rule were small in scale. Typically, these small businesses operated as single proprietorships, some of which were too small to be classified officially as factories, which had to have five or more operatives. These small business establishments continued to prevail even after World War I. They constituted 81.7 percent of all factories, employed only 26.1 percent of the workers, and produced a mere 16.5 percent of total factory output in later years.[91] In 1930 one in every three or four Koreans gainfully employed outside of the farming sector probably was in some sense an entrepreneur, carrying some risk and responsibility for his business. Even as late as 1940, the typical Korean-owned rice mill, for example, had an average investment of a little more than 400 yen. Even smaller businesses produced kitchen utensils, manufactured tiles, and processed ginseng.[92]

The resulting situation at the end of Japanese rule was the coexistence of large and small businesses side by side.[93] The prevalence of small businesses in number and the dominance of large and medium-sized businesses in terms of paid-in capital, employment, and output were seen in all sectors, including the chemical, metal, machinery, and tool-making industries and mining.

Who were the large entrepreneurs and small-business owners? Almost all of the large corporations were Japanese, although they started out as small-scale businesses in Korea in the early years. In 1910 the average amount of capital invested per capita in Japanese businesses in Korea was 26.5 yen.[94] In 1908 there were seventy-nine Japanese "factories" capitalized on average at about 1,000 yen, which employed an average of forty-one workers producing 41,600 yen of output. Only a few factories had more than 100,000 yen in capital in 1910.[95] These included a soy sauce plant, a rice mill, electric-power plants, and a lumber mill. The average capital of companies was 27,850 yen in 1908. Only three so-called large companies had been established by the Japanese in Korea by 1910. Their average subscribed and paid-in capital in 1911 were 96,400 and 46,000 yen, respectively. This situation prevailed until about 1916. Venturesome Japanese speculators with small amounts of capital, and modest factories (five to fifty employees) continued to account for about 80 percent of all factories, but in time medium-sized and large Japanese businesses gradually overshadowed them.[96] The average paid-in capital of such companies increased to 288,000 yen in 1919 and 306,000 at the end of 1938, showing an expansion of eleven times in thirty years between 1908 and 1938.

The large companies were usually connected with the Japanese *zaibatsu*. Between 1931 and 1939, some thirty large *zaibatsu* established their businesses in Korea, and they had the requisite financial resources, manpower, and technical know-how to undertake major economic projects. These large companies eventually constituted the military-industrial complex, and toward the end of the colonial period they were at the core of Japanese military and economic policy.[97] By this time, according to one economic historian, 50 percent of Korea's industry was devoted to meeting military needs. Even if the needs were to be narrowly defined, the manufacturing sector, according to his calculations, allocated 36.7 percent of its resources, 40.8 percent of its employees, and 38 percent of its production to military purposes.

Similarly, non-Japanese foreign-owned companies and plants, on average, had large amounts of paid-in capital, most even larger than the Japanese (e.g., average capital of 684,000 yen in twenty plants in 1921 and 200,000 yen in ninety-three plants in 1927). Most foreign investors were the six American firms involved in medium-sized enterprises (e.g., with average per factory capital of 13,680 yen in 1921 and 18,609 in 1927). Even a few joint Japanese-Korean and Japanese-Western companies were considerably larger in early years—many even larger than the Japanese-owned firms—having average capital of 103,433 yen in 1910 and 237,391 1917.[98]

Unlike the pattern set by the Japanese, the establishment of new businesses by Koreans followed a somewhat different path. Surprisingly, new Korean businesses in the very early years were fairly large in size, though small in number. The average size of Korean-owned companies in 1908 in terms of capital was more than twice (10,000 yen) that of the Japanese and nearly six times that of Chinese companies in Korea (1,700 yen).[99] The average paid-in capital of Korean companies increased to 181,950 yen in 1919 and 252,000 in 1922.[100] It thus appears that those who established companies in the early years were not small businessmen but rather wealthy individuals and/or "giant" merchants.

After World War I, however, an increasing number of small Korean businesses joined the ranks, including brick manufacturers, food processors, and retailers, all providing goods and services essential to the masses.[101] As a result of small businesses joining the ranks, the average paid-in capital of Korean companies dropped down to 168,000 yen in 1923 and plummeted to 5,588 by 1928, which represented about 6 percent of that of Japanese-owned companies during the same period. Then the average paid-in capital of Korean companies slowly regained to 54,000 yen in 1938 and to nearly 100,000 yen in 1941. It bounced back to 17.5 and 16.7 percent of that of Japanese-owned companies, respectively, in those years. Although the relative size of Korean companies compared with the Japanese recovered somewhat, the majority of Korean businesses continued to be relatively small. The difference in the scale of businesses between Koreans and Japanese was also clearly shown in the number of employees. Of the 2,504 Korean companies registered in 1938, more than nine-tenths were small and operated with a workforce consisting of between five and forty-nine employees.

There were only a few prominent large businesses owned and operated by Koreans. These included the Seoul Textile Company (Gyeongseong Bangjik), the

TABLE 8.5 Amount of Paid-in Capital of Industrial Companies by Scale of Business and Nationality in 1933

	Million Yen			*Percent*		
Amount of Paid-in Capital	Japanese	Korean	Total	Japanese	Korean	Total
Less than 50,000 yen	6.0	3.2	9.2	65.2	34.8	100.0
50,000–100,000	5.0	1.6	6.6	75.8	24.2	100.0
100,000–300,000	7.9	2.2	10.1	78.2	21.8	100.0
300,000–500,000	4.0	0.4	4.4	90.9	9.1	100.0
500,000–1,000,000	7.6	1.8	9.4	80.9	19.1	100.0
More than 1,000,000	90.3	—	90.3	100.0	—	100.0
Total	120.8	9.2	130.0	92.9	7.1	100.0

Source: This table is constructed based on Himeno 1940: 329.

Korea Mill (Joseon Jebeon) Company, and a major department store owned and operated by an entrepreneur who was also active in airplane manufacturing.[102]

The Japanese dominance of large businesses and the preponderance of small Korean businesses prevailed in all fields, as further elaborated in Appendix 8.3 and also shown in Table 8.5.[103] Even in sectors in which the size difference in businesses owned by the two nationalities was small, such as commerce, the wood products industry, printing, and possibly textile and food, most small businesses were owned and operated by Koreans.[104] Therefore, in spite of the increase in the number of businesses owned by Koreans, they lacked ability to compete and take advantage of economies of scale, largely because of a continual decline in the scale of their businesses relative to Japanese firms.

There were a number of reasons for the dearth of large companies and the large number of small businesses owned and operated by the Koreans. For one, there were few wealthy Korean families who were willing to engage in business at that time. According to a survey conducted by the Government General in 1911, there were only 32 Koreans with more than 500,000 yen's worth of assets (while there were more than 10,000 Japanese with that volume of assets).[105] Second, most wealthy Koreans, chiefly large landowners, did not venture into new businesses. Following the Confucian tradition, many were still averse to entering into any business and taking risk, so they avoided investing in new enterprises. Third, many large Korean companies founded in the early period soon failed, examples of which were noted in earlier chapters.

Industrial Monopoly

Another development in industry under colonial rule was that many large corporations, typically Japanese-owned *zaibatsu,* gained monopoly power. According to Hosokawa's estimate, four Japanese *zaibatsu* invested a gross sum of about 1 billion yen in Korea (a net sum of about 900 million) as of 1938, which represented about 50 percent of total capital in Korea at that time, which was then estimated at 1.9 billion yen.[106] The *zaibatsu* domination in Korea included the manufacturing and power industries. Most were engaged in steel milling, the metal industry, shipbuilding, automobile and airplane assembly, machine-tool fabricating, chemicals, and textiles, which required abundant financial resources and technical know-how. Initially, the *zaibatsu* based in Japan controlled nearly three-quarters of all businesses in Korea, while only about 18 percent of all businesses were being dominated by financial groups based in Korea (e.g., the Industrial Bank and special semipublic companies) and 8 percent by other companies headquartered in Korea.[107] The prominent *zaibatsu* based in Japan were Nissan, Mitsubishi, Mitsui, and Sumitomo. The Mitsubishi *zaibatsu* alone had twenty-three branches, forty-two subsidiaries, and fifty-four affiliates in Korea in 1930.

In the later years, the *zaibatsu* based in Korea (e.g., the Noguchi, the Totaku, the Industrial Bank, and special semipublic companies) gained control of nearly 61 percent of the country's businesses, while the rest, approximately 39 percent, remained in the hands of *zaibatsu* based in Japan.[108] The Noguchi *zaibatsu,* based in Korea, alone controlled nearly 26 percent of all businesses in Korea. It dominated many heavy industries in Korea and controlled 45 percent of the electric industry, 35 percent of the chemical industry, 13 percent of mining, and 7 percent of railroads.[109] Shimizu Gumi dominated civil engineering and large construction projects, while Kanebo dominated textile manufacturing. Two construction firms, Kajima and Shimizu, virtually monopolized the construction of large industrial plants and hydroelectric facilities and dams. Most light manufacturing was in the hands of the Asano *zaibatsu.*

The Mitsui, Mitsubishi, Furukawa, and Fujita companies dominated mining in Korea, accounting for about 70 percent of mineral production between 1908 and 1916. Although there are no data available after 1916, their domination probably continued until they came to control most of the major mines in Korea. In addition, many *zaibatsu* heavily subscribed capital shares in semipublic companies such as Nitetsu, a iron refinery. Through stockholdings in subsidiaries, they also directly controlled assets in such firms.

The interests of the large corporations were closely tied to the needs of the Japanese government, which acted as partners and worked for their mutual benefit in developing and implementing the economic policies of the Japanese government, especially after 1930. On the one hand, the government looked to the *zaibatsu* for assistance in financing public budgets, building foreign trade and colonial enterprises, and creating the heavy and chemical industries required by the military. In return, the government reasoned that the best way to fulfill its objectives was to give large corporations control over their industries through legislation and regulation and by allowing them to exercise monopoly power. Japanese colonial government policies thus were geared toward the concentration of industrial and financial power in the hands of either the government or large Japanese business interests, with which the authorities had a close working relationship.

The large businesses, on the other hand, promoted their interests by working closely with the government through helping to establish the industries essential for maintaining power. Obviously, the *zaibatsus*' command over capital and their role as agents of the Japanese government gave them decisive advantages. It assisted the government in developing and promoting semiofficial institutions like public banks and the Oriental Development Company at home and abroad.[110] In return, the large businesses promoted their own interests in developing a system of laws that imposed few restrictions on monopolistic practices by working in close association with the bureaucrats.

Monopolies of large corporations were acquired in three principal ways: the domination of markets by eliminating competition, creating interlocking corporations, and colluding with competitors. All three tactics had the full endorsement and support of the Government General. The number of competitors in various markets was reduced, mainly through mergers (forced as well as voluntary) and acquisitions. The Government General promulgated a number of laws facilitating the elimination of competition. For instance, the banking laws of 1923 and 1928 promoted mergers by mandating that banks organize a joint stock company with minimum capital of 2 million yen.[111] This requirement was in contrast with that of 1 million yen in Japan. Because of this legislation, many small private banks either folded or were forced to merge with others, and the number of commercial banks gradually decreased from twenty-one in 1923 to two (while leaving three public banks) in 1943. Similarly, when electric companies were forced to merge after 1933, the number of companies was sharply reduced, from eighty-eight in 1930 to forty-five in 1935 and fifteen in 1936. Mergers were numerous even in rice milling, especially when Japanese firms took over Korean enterprises. Once numbering more than 6,000, the mostly native-run rice mills were rapidly taken over through mergers. Via mergers, shipping companies came to enjoy a virtual monopoly of intra-empire trade from early on. The government accommodated Japanese businesses to such an extent that it was accused of breaking its own laws.

The monopoly position of large firms was also strengthened by means of collusive agreements with competitors and exclusive sales agencies widely employed to build vertical trusts in their industries. The law was lax in its requirements for full and accurate disclosure of information on company activities in the steel, metal, machine-tool, coal, fertilizer, chemical, and textile industries. Apparently, these practices prevailed in both Korea and Japan. Not only did it allow them to collude, it increasingly persuaded large firms to enter into collusive agreements with competitors. Concerted efforts were made, with the support of the government, to organize cartels, associations, and agreements to reduce competition. By 1936 there were nearly fifty industrial cartels in Korea and Japan. Match producers in 1939, for example, organized associations and reached an agreement concerning quotas and prices.[112] By 1941 there were many associations engaged in "controlling [business] activity" with some degree of government authority. Thus, industries in Korea, already dominated by Japanese, were blanketed with a system of government-supported cartels in the form of controlled associations of every description. Small producers were helpless to defend themselves. Being engaged mainly in the production and sale of consumer goods, many Korean businesses suffered.

In addition, many large businesses maintained close working relationships, formally and informally, among themselves, and arranged intercorporate stockholding and interlocking directorates. The interlocking of banking and large businesses and landowners was common, especially with the Industrial Bank. Sometimes corporations secretly, but legally, entered into partnerships with the bank. Exclusive sales agencies were widely employed to build vertical trusts in major industries. The exercise of monopoly power by large corporations such as the *zaibatsu,* by mergers and other means, was also made easy by their close business relationships and lack of competition. The various *zaibatsu* vied with each other for prestige and influence in the government, but they promoted their common interests.[113]

These collusive activities were made easier by the fact that the large firms were controlled by a small band of business executives. Auditors were likely to have been appointed by insiders. In this way, whenever political domination was secured, Japanese industrialists and traders automatically won a preferential position. They also gained a good deal of their momentum from the absorptive power of the government banks. As one economist aptly described it, industrialization in Korea was undertaken with "Japanese monopoly capital."[114] Toward the end of the colonial period, however, these conglomerates lost much of their freedom to the military, and few Japanese businesses were able to make decisions in conformity with company strategies. In this sense, the *zaibatsu* became the victims of the system they helped create in Korea.

The segment of the economy most adversely affected by the domination of the *zaibatsu* was Korean businesses. Korean enterprises were small and numerous, and their market was, as a rule, a highly competitive one in which both prices and profits were low.[115] Many were unable to compete and survive. A good example may be found in banking. The number of banks in Korean hands decreased from 18 in 1922 to 1 in 1943. Many were forced to merge with other private banks. For instance, the Chosen Commercial (Shogyo) Bank, which was established by wealthy Korean merchants and former government officials, merged with a number of private banks, the last of which was the Dongil Bank in 1943. Many small Korean banks were converted into PNBFIs or had to go out of business. Moreover, Korean-owned banks were forced to open themselves to the Japanese. In 1920 the Hanseong Bank had to allow Japanese to hold its stock shares, resulting in heavy infiltration by the *zaibatsu.* Also, the existence of great aggregates of financial power in the large monopoly firms, reinforced by political influence, tended to discourage from early times the growth of a middle class with sufficient capital and opportunity to develop medium-sized, modern enterprises on their own.

AGRICULTURAL ORGANIZATION

In addition to the structural changes already examined, there were four organizational changes under colonial rule that affected the agricultural sector: landownership, the scale of landholding, the status of working farmers, and land tenancy.

Landownership

One development in agriculture that stood out vividly was the change in the ownership of much of land from Koreans to Japanese. There are many conflicting data relative to Japanese ownership of land in Korea, but the overall trends are unmistakable. Japanese purchases of land began soon after the 1876 treaty and accelerated after Japan took control of the country in 1905. The major interest of Japanese investors in Korea in the early years was Korean farmland. Of the reported 15 million yen invested by the Japanese in Korea in 1906, for instance, approximately one-third was said to have been invested in land and other permanent structures, especially in the southern provinces. Japanese purchases of land increased after that time. By 1908, they were reported to have invested about 10 million yen in about 46,000 *jeong* of land. Another report indicated that they also acquired about 62,268 *jeong* by 1909.[116] By the time of the Annexation in 1910, 2,254 Japanese owned 86,961 *jeong* of land, comprising 26,727 *jeong* of cultivated land, 42,584 *jeong* of wetland, and 17,650 *jeong* of virgin land, valued at 13.7 million yen.

After the Annexation in 1910, Japanese land acquisition accelerated.[117] The year after the Annexation, a total of 3,839 Japanese invested 22.5 million yen in agriculture, which increased to 45.6 million in 1915.[118] Their landholdings rapidly expanded to 205,538 *jeong* in 1915 and 236,586 in 1918. Following the completion of the land survey of 1918, the reported figures climbed up to 242,500 *jeong* in 1921 and 346,200 in 1927, a rise of 43 percent in six years, while the number of Japanese landowners increased by 48 percent during the period.

Actual Japanese landholdings, however, appear to have been even larger than what was officially reported. Edmund deS Brunner, who visited Korea in 1926, wrote: "Government statistics show less than 6 percent of agricultural and residential land registered as Japanese in ownership. But this fact needs careful scrutiny. Various careful estimates of fair-minded non-government Japanese and Koreans place the proportion of land owned, actually or virtually, by Japanese at a point between 12 and 20 percent."[119] A total of 65,922 Japanese paid land taxes in 1927, meaning that they were landowners. It is perhaps significant that the colonial government ceased to publish statistics on Japanese landholdings after that year.

There is little doubt that, after 1927, Japanese landholdings continued to expand.[120] According to the limited data available, the number of Japanese landholdings in Korea increased from 6,528 to 13,804 between 1921 and 1933, while 2,841 Koreans lost their land during the same period. Some have estimated that the Japanese owned as much as 3.7 million *jeong* of private forests and 1 million *jeong* of cultivated land, totaling 4.7 million *jeong,* in 1938. Others have alleged that as much as one-quarter of all cultivated land and more than half of the total land in Korea was in Japanese hands. According to this estimate, two-thirds of Korean land passed into Japanese control.[121] Another estimate places Japanese landholdings at 22.8 percent of all land in Korea (35.4 percent of private forests, 23.5 percent of all forests, and 22.6 percent of all farmlands).[122] On the other hand, Hatobe estimated in 1931 that only about 15 percent of dry land and 10 percent of paddy fields, or a total of 10 percent of all land, was in Japanese hands.[123]

In sum, it seems reasonably certain that Japanese farmland holdings increased from less than three-tenths of a percent of total farmland in 1908 to about 2 percent in 1910, 6.5 percent in 1915, 12.3 percent after the 1918 land survey, and about 16 percent in 1944.[124] Japanese landholdings, therefore, may be estimated at about 719,330 *jeong* of farmland[125] and 3,293,280 *jeong* of wooded land (a total of a little over 4 million) by 1944,[126] or approximately 21 percent of the total (about

16 percent of cultivated land and 22 percent of forest land) in the country.[127] By 1938 the Japanese investment in land may have been as much as 200 million yen.

How did the Japanese acquire so much land? There apparently were a number of ways in which Japanese acquired land in Korea. The first means was the procurement of land from Korean landowners in the course of normal market transactions. The most compelling reason for the Japanese to acquire large plots of land was that it was a good financial investment for them. As one Governor General wrote, Japanese buying rice fields in Korea was aimed to make a profit by leasing them to Korean tenants or reselling them. Many Japanese bought land from Korean farmers at bargain prices. Land prices in Korea before 1910 were reported to have been between one-tenth and one-thirtieth of those in Japan. Numerous reports indicated that hundreds of thousands of acres were acquired by the Japanese during the early years at a nominal price, often "less than one-twentieth" of "the real value." Even one of the royal families sold 600 *jeong* of land to a large Japanese landlord at about half the market price.

The rise in Korean land prices after 1929 apparently narrowed the gap somewhat, but it did not eliminate the transaction of land. The price of paddy fields between 1929 and 1939 increased by approximately 60 percent and dry land by about 56 percent. But even as late as 1931, the price of medium-quality land in Korea was almost one-quarter that in Japan: 27 yen per 100 *pyeong* (approximately 0.082 acre or 330 square meters) of paddy field in contrast with 100 yen in Japan. Another source indicated that the price of Korean land increased 3.5 times between 1931 and 1940, considerably narrowing the gap, but the discrepancy persisted, and Korean land prices in 1940 were still 55 percent of those in Japan.[128]

In either case, most Japanese, especially the large landlords, acquired land not for farming but for financial investment or speculation purposes. Most of them leased it to Korean tenants. The returns on investment in agricultural land were reported to have been high. A landlord's revenue capitalized (after taxes) against low-priced land at the market rate of interest guaranteed a higher return than most other kinds of investment. Rice fields offered the best return on investment, which was reported to have been 10 percent in 1914, 11 percent in 1917, and 20 percent in 1921, compared with 9 percent, 9 percent, and 16 percent, respectively, on dry fields in the same years. The returns on investment in land in Korea were more than 100 percent higher than those in Japan. Average rates of return on investment to landowners in Korea in 1931 ranged between 7.7 percent (paddy field) and 8.3 percent (dry land) in comparison with 3.69 percent (dry land) and 3.89 percent (paddy field) in Japan. A similar situation existed in 1937, when an Industrial Bank survey found that average rates of return on investment to landowners on dry land and paddy fields were 8.5 and 8.0 percent, respectively, in Korea in contrast with 4.89 and 5.46 percent, respectively, in Japan.[129]

Returns on land in Korea were even higher than the average earnings of major manufacturing firms. Rates of return from land in 1931 were higher than the 6.9 percent rate of return on major common stocks. In 1937 they were more favorable—between 8.0 percent on paddy field and 8.5 percent on dry land—than the rates of return on major common stocks in Korea and Japan (6.1 and 5.3 percent, respectively). It was reported that returns on investment in farmland were about 10 percent in 1931–1937, a figure higher than the returns on investment in manufacturing, which were about 6 to 7 percent at the time.[130] On average, therefore, investment in land had a 20 to 30 percent higher rate of return than that in manufacturing. Such high returns may be attributable to the low price of land, cheap labor, low taxes, and low maintenance costs.

The second means by which Japanese acquired land in Korea was converting wasteland into farmland, as examined in chapter 5.

The third means Japanese used to acquire land was through usury loans to Korean farmers. According to some Koreans, Japanese seized Korean land by resorting to all sorts of "immoral and illegal means and techniques." As one former high-ranking Japanese official admitted in 1958, many Japanese did "pretty vicious things" to Koreans in order to acquire land. Some were so "unprincipled and rapacious" that the authorities were compelled to send them back to their homeland. One of these illegitimate means resorted to by the Japanese was the seizure of land when Korean borrowers failed to repay their loans on time.[131] Some Japanese groups, such as the Ikki-gumi, charged usurious interest rates on loans to Korean farmers, rates as high as 10 percent for ten days. When Korean farmers did not repay the loans on time—a common traditional custom in Korea—the Japanese creditors would take the land forcibly.[132] Thus, much collateral land ended up in the hands of the Japanese. According to the former official, a good deal of this foreclosed land came into the possession of the Oriental Development Company.[133]

The fourth venue through which Japanese acquired land was the alleged confiscation of land in massive scale by the colonial government. Koreans often accuse the Japanese of "nationalizing" private land under the pretext of enforcing the land-registration law, with the aid of the 1918 land survey. Let us examine this allegation in more detail. In the traditional period, the legal owner of all land was the king; there was no private ownership in the modern sense. But over the years this de jure public land (*gongjun*) became de facto private land (*sajun*), which evolved in four ways. The land was (1) given by the king to war heroes and officials who served with distinction; (2) inherited; (3) purchased from previous owners who might have acquired it through inheritance, by building on it, or by cultivating it; and (4) acquired through the process of "squatting" on unoccupied crown land.

In the traditional period owners were not required to register their land with the government. Thus, when land was bought or inherited there was no government record of the new owners. In the case of "squatting," no official notice was taken until the fourth year, when an officer was deputized to survey the land under cultivation and assess yearly taxes. The size, grade (quality classification), and location of the land were entered on a yeomen's land register, and the tract was given a number. The owner's name was not even recorded, nor did he receive any document. When land was sold, the seller merely made out a deed, which he handed to the purchaser. This deed was not even registered with local officials.[134]

Then, in 1895, a new law was promulgated under which buyers of land were ordered to register with the local government. The registration of all land was required after 1906. In 1910, following the Annexation, in order to "modernize" the landownership system in the Western tradition, the colonial government enforced the law that required the registration of landownership. Many farmers apparently did not fully understand the significance and consequences of not complying with the law, and they failed to register their land within the required time. As the Japanese Resident General observed, the confusion concerning the survey of lands and their price and the distribution between public and private ownership greatly impeded the settlement of the question and caused misunderstanding on the part of certain Koreans.[135] In addition to confusion and ignorance, anti-Japanese sentiments apparently led some Koreans to defy the law and reject land registration.[136] In all cases, the burden of proof of ownership of land was on the person who claimed it.

After the Annexation of Korea, the Japanese government conducted land surveys throughout the country for eight years between 1910 and 1918 at a hefty cost of 25 million yen, employing 7,000-plus workers at the height of the survey, to establish the "legal" title to land in the Western tradition based on the 1895 law.[137] Once the land survey was completed, in addition to public land, all land that did not have clear title was nationalized without consideration of traditional ownership and compensation.[138] Reportedly, a total of 133,633 *jeong* of farmland, representing 5.7 percent of the country's total arable land,[139] was nationalized, thus making the Government General the largest landlord in the country. Included in nationalized land was much acreage belonging to the king's household (25,800 *jeong* of newly cultivated virgin land, 19,400 of wooded land, and 50 of house sites) and land allotted to maintain "road stations" (*yeokdonto*), which are comparable to today's railroad stations (134,000 *jeong*).

Nationalization aroused much anger among Koreans. There were numerous protests from the Korean "owners."[140] A total of 39,937 cases involving 99,445 units of land (5.2 percent of the total) were brought contesting ownership. There were more disputes (about 65 percent) over so-called national or public land (acreage cultivated by farmers but with registration either lacking or improperly done) than disputes over "private land" (35 percent) and borderline land (1 percent). There were a total of 3,132 legal disputes involving 14,200-plus units of land. Controversies over the ownership of royal land (*gungjangto*) were the most difficult and frequent. Although many people, including Japanese officials, recognized the difficulty of distinguishing between public and private land, the decision went against the Korean farmers. The nationalized land included family property held for generations and some virgin land on which farmers had regularly paid taxes. Similarly, large parcels owned by government units and Buddhist temples that had been leased to farmers in perpetuity for little or no rent were nationalized, without compensation.

Many farmers also lost communal land, tracts used for firewood collection and grazing that were traditionally owned and used by several families in a community but for which there was little documentary evidence (since it was not needed). Many such cases were arbitrarily determined. For instance, anyone who registered community land (village, family, or clan) in his own name got title to it. Tenants and cultivators as well as nonclan members (*munwae*) lost family plots and/or village communal land. In many cases it ended up in the hands of large landlords or the leaders of clans or communities.[141]

After 1929, Japanese "expropriation" of Korean land was also supposed to have taken place. Some historians have argued that the Japanese alienated Korean land on other pretexts as well. When the Government General was in need of land for the construction of roads or railroads, for instance, the owners were "induced," or, more accurately, forced, to surrender it at "far below the market price, and often without compensation."[142] Some of the nationalized land was later sold to Japanese companies and individuals, including immigrants. The confiscated land the Government General transferred included 20,000 *jeong* to railroad companies[143] and 6,000 *jeong* to construct "military railroads." Edwin H. Gragert, however, has questioned the validity of these allegations. His findings show that instead of confiscation of Korean property on a mass scale, the worldwide economic depression of the late 1920s and early 1930s was responsible for the loss of land by Koreans in the last two decades of the colonial period.[144] If his finding is valid, a nagging question is, Why did the economic depression adversely affect Koreans but not Japanese?

Scale of Landholding

Another change in the agricultural sector under colonial rule was the increasing concentration of land in the hands of large landowners. At the time of the land surveys (1910–1918), large landlords constituted 1.8 percent of the agricultural population and owned 51.1 percent of the land.[145] In 1929–1932 these figures increased to 3.7 and 64 percent, respectively, a more than doubling of the number of large landlords and a more than 25 percent increase in their landholding in about a twenty-year period. While the scale of landowning expanded, there also was an increasing tendency for nonfarming landlords to take over land. Between 1918 and 1932, for instance, the number of nonfarming landlords increased from six-tenths of a percent of the agricultural population to 1.2 percent, doubling in fourteen years. As the economy became more modernized and grew, more and more land fell into the hands of large landlords. One study reveals that in Chungnam Province there were only three large landowners before 1875, but during the following twenty-eight-year transitional period (1876 to 1904), twenty-eight new large landowners emerged.[146] During the next twenty-six-year period under Japanese rule (1910–1936), a total of thirty-seven new large landowners emerged in the province. The Chungnam Province example was not an exception.

No comprehensive statistics are available, but the fragmentary data strongly indicate that, in general, landholdings became larger over time under colonial rule.[147] One-quarter, or about 33,000 out of 104,000 of the landowners in Korea in 1932, were large absentee landlords. The number of landowners with more than 5 *jeong* of land increased by 47.8 percent in six years (from 43,305 in 1921 to 63,989 in 1927), while the acreage owned by them increased by 42.8 percent (from 242,469 to 346,232 *jeong*). This increased concentration of land in a few hands was more conspicuous in Korea than in the rest of the Japanese empire. While there were only 35 who owned 500 *jeong* or more of land in Japan proper and 50 in Hokkaido, there were 100 such landowners in Korea.

The increase in large landholdings was principally a result of the acquisition of large tracts of land by Japanese. Japanese landholdings in the early years were relatively small in size, though larger than those of most Koreans, but the size of their holdings increased over time. After the Annexation, the number of Japanese who owned between 5 and 10 *jeong* of land increased by 211.5 percent in a twelve-year period (from 6,528 in 1921 to 13,804 in 1933).[148] They made up about 9 percent of all landlords and owned about 5 percent of the total land. Along with the medium-sized Japanese landowners, there also were large Japanese landlords who owned larger tracts of land. One report indicated that there were 85 large landowners with more than 100 *jeong* of land in 1909, while another reported that 172 operators of large farms (or 7.6 percent of all Japanese operators) owned 58,944 *jeong* of land in 1910, averaging 343 *jeong* per farm with an average investment of 55,814 yen.[149] The number of large Japanese landowners increased rapidly and held the dominant position in agriculture, while the number of large Korean landlords decreased over time.[150]

The difference in the number of large Japanese and Korean landlords was widened relative to the size of the landholding: the larger the size of the landholding, the greater was the gap between the two nationalities. The number of Japanese who owned and operated tracts of 100 *jeong* or more farm increased more than thirty-three-fold from 1905 to 1933–1942, and they came to represent more than half of all landowners in this group. The number of Japanese landlords owning more than 200 *jeong* of land increased 7 percent between 1921 and 1936. Similarly, there were 192 Japanese owners with more than 300 *jeong* in 1927, but only 45 Koreans, the ratio being four to one. Likewise, Japanese owning more than 500 *jeong* in 1942 accounted for 85 percent of the total in this group, while Japanese owning 1,000 *jeong* or more accounted for 95 percent.

Another notable aspect of enlargement of the scale of landownership was an increase in the amount of land owned by corporations. Semipublic Japanese corporations owned large tracts of land. The most active and prominent one was the Oriental Development Company, whose landholdings increased from 2,535 *jeong* in 1908 to 11,000 in 1910, 74,700 in 1917, 166,000 in 1935, and 200,700 in 1942.[151] At the end of Japanese rule, the company owned about 4.5 percent of all cultivated land in Korea and 13.4 percent in southern Korea.

Similarly, many large landowners who were in agribusinesses and whose sole aim was to earn profits by leasing the land to tenants or engaging in agribusiness and speculation owned large tracts of land. Corporate financial investment in agriculture expanded rapidly.[152] Most of these landowning corporations were Japanese owned and operated, and almost all large Japanese companies in Korea held large pieces of land.[153] Many Japanese executives also invested in large parcels. It was reported that in 1938 7 to 10 percent of them (out of a total of 523) were large landowners and 35 percent of these were connected to companies.

Status of Korean Farmers

One obvious consequence of the concentration of agricultural land in the hands of large (typically Japanese) landowners was a decrease in the number of Korean landowners, especially the small owner/cultivators and part-owner/tenants, and their share of farming. Between 1921 and 1933, for instance, 86 percent of the landowners (2,457 out of 2,841) who owned plots up to 5 *jeong* lost their land, a decrease in their ranks of 1.8 percent.[154] According to official figures, the number

TABLE 8.6 Composition of Agricultural Population between 1914 and 1941 (percent)

Year	Landlord	Owner/ cultivator*	Owner/ tenant	Tenant	Others**	Total
1914	1.8	22.0	35.2	41.0	—	100.0
1919	3.5	19.7	37.6	39.2	—	100.0
1924	3.8	19.5	34.5	42.2	—	100.0
1929	3.7	18.0	31.5	46.8	—	100.0
1934	—	18.0	24.0	51.9	6.1	100.0
1939	—	17.8	23.8	52.4	6.0	100.0
1941	—	17.3	23.9	53.8	5.0	100.0

*According to Takeo Suzuki, the ratio of owner/tenants or proprietors/tenants decreased from 38.9 to 25.3 percent, a 35 percent decrease, during the same period (1941: 72–73; 1942: 246.

**Included are slash-and-burn farmers and farm employees.

Source: This table is constructed based on Bank of Korea 1948: I, 28–29.

of small owner/cultivators decreased from 22 percent of total farm households in the early 1910s to 19.7 percent in 1919, 18 percent in 1934, and 17.3 percent in 1941, a decline of nearly 21.4 percent, as shown in Table 8.6. Similarly, the number of part-owner/tenants, representing 41.1 percent of the farming population, who owned 10.3 percent of land at the time of the land survey (1910–1918), had decreased to 23.9 percent by 1941. When the part-owner/tenant farmers are added to the landowner group, the decrease in all owner/cultivators was from 57.7 to 41.2 percent between 1914 and 1940. The share of farming by landowners and part-owner/tenant farmers, thus, decreased by 28 percent from 1914 to 1941.

Many small Korean landowners lost their land, because they could not meet their expenses, including assessments for irrigation services. Assessments to pay for the reclamation and irrigation projects that were more or less forced on them were often so high that some Koreans mortgaged their land and then lost it.[155] After losing their lands, many of these owner/cultivators and part-owner/tenants were transformed into landless farmers (contract tenants who owned no land and were obligated to share their harvest with or pay rent to landlords), slash-and-burn farmers, or farm laborers. Others left farming for new and/or different occupations.

One obvious consequence of the concentration of agricultural land in the hands of large, nonfarming landlords was an increase in the number of tenants. At the beginning of the land survey in 1910, tenant farmers constituted 35.1 percent of the total farm population, but their ranks swelled under Japanese rule.[156] The percentage of so-called pure tenant households increased to 39.4 percent in 1917 and 55.7 percent in 1939, a 41.4 percent rise in about twenty years. In terms of the amount of land cultivated, tenant farming increased from 53 percent of all cultivated land in 1917 to 58 percent in 1944, a 9 percent rise in a twenty-five-year period. Paddy fields cultivated by tenant farmers increased from about 65 percent in 1917 to 68 percent in 1939, showing a rise of more than 7 percent, while dry land cultivated by tenant farmers remained at about 45 percent. Thus, the burden of agricultural production was placed primarily on the shoulders of the tenants.[157]

When slash-and-burn farmers and agricultural employees are added to the tenant group, their increase is from about 35 to 58.8 percent during the same period. When the part-owner/tenants are included, farm tenancy in Korea can be estimated to have increased from less than 40 percent in 1910 to 73 percent in 1945. In other words, the share of farming by landless tenant farmers, slash-and-burn farmers, and agricultural employees increased about 68 percent. Thus, the burden of agricultural production was placed primarily on the shoulders of the tenants.

Another change in agriculture under Japanese rule was a decrease in average farm size. As the number of farmers increased relative to the amount of arable land during the colonial period, farm size per farm household, especially that of tenants, obviously declined. The average acreage under cultivation per farmer decreased about 10 percent, from 0.31 *jeong* in 1914 to 0.28 in 1932. Similarly, the average amount of arable land per farm family decreased 12 percent from 1.70 *jeong* in 1919 to 1.5 in 1943. Although the typical farm family of six was reported to have cultivated more than 2.45 acres (1 *jeong*) in 1938, about half of the total agricultural population cultivated less than 0.5 *jeong*. About 83 percent of the farms consisted of less than 2.5 *jeong* of farmland, and about 38.4 percent had less than 0.5 *jeong*, as shown in Table 8.7.

Land Tenancy

Another significant structural change in the farming sector under Japanese rule was the embellishment of the rights and abridgment of the duties of landlord vis-à-vis tenancy. Under the traditional system, landlords (*jiju*, literally "land masters") had "the right to collect rent," such as in the form of a certain amount of the harvest, while the tenants (*sojakin*, literally "small cultivators") were obliged to pay rent in order to retain the right to occupy and farm the land.[158] Although the landlord had the right to collect rent from the land (*jip-cho-kweon*) that he controlled, he de jure "did not hold ownership of the land (*soyukweon*)." It was owned by neither the landlords nor the tenants in the traditional society. In other words, the tenant actually held the land and had the right to farm it. The children of tenants inherited the right to

TABLE 8.7 Scale of Farming in 1938 by Farmers' Groups (percent)

Farming Area (in *jeong*)	Landowner	Owner/ cultivator	Owner/ tenant	Tenant
Less than 0.3	13.0	14.0	20.0	17.0
0.3–0.5	17.0	21.0	23.0	21.0
0.5–1	21.0	26.0	26.0	25.0
1.0–2.0	21.0	22.0	18.0	20.0
2.0–3.0	16.0	12.0	9.0	11.0
3.0–5.0	9.0	5.0	3.0	5.0
5.0+	3.0	—	1.0	1.0
Total	100.0	100.0	100.0	100.0

Sources: Based on data in Bank of Korea 1948: I, 14, 18, 343; Daehan Geumnyung Johap 1955: 101; Takeo Suzuki 1941: 248; K. Takahashi 1935: 397; G. McCune 1950: 26; S. McCune 1956: 91.

occupy and cultivate the land, while the landlords had the duty to provide at least the minimum requirements for "livelihood." This was a legally binding contractual relationship.

The land reform could have accorded ownership either to tenants (as was the case in Japan in the 1870s) or landlords, but the decision favored the latter in Korea. Land reform in Korea, established through land-related laws, surveys, and the public policies of the colonial government, abolished the traditional contract, redefined the rights and duties of landlords and tenants, and legitimized private ownership in the modern Western tradition.[159] In this way, the reform gave landlords ownership of land in the Western sense, which included the right to freely sell and buy it. It thus brought about the abolishment of the "shared right" to land between landlords and tenants. Under the modern system, a new owner-tenant relationship was established in which the landlord gained the additional right of terminating the tenancy contract at will and the tenant became a mere contract farmer, an "employee," or simply a tenant in the Western tradition. Since the best rice fields were in southern Korea, the impact of this change was most pronounced there.

Once the initial reforms were imposed in Korea, the issues of land tenure and distributive justice in the countryside were preempted, despite their importance for technical modernization. Inefficiencies in the land-tenure system were perpetuated by continuation of the traditional arrangement but with embellished landlords' right. A particular problem was, the lack of written contracts, which would have given the tenant security and compensated him for making permanent improvements in the land. In addition, farm prices remained at the mercy of the weather and the operations of the "free" market, where the hard-pressed peasant was typically at a bargaining disadvantage. As a result, the number of landlord-tenant disputes skyrocketed in the 1920s.[160] There were 237,238 cases of disputes in 1929–1930 alone, about 93 percent of which involved tenants with less than one *jeong* of land. The colonial government typically sided with the landlords (especially the Japanese) and supported the tenant system, which enhanced the rights of the landlords, including their bargaining power and high rents.

SUMMARY AND CONCLUSIONS

This chapter has shown that substantial gains in the production of goods and services were made in Korea under Japanese rule. Its real GDP between 1905 and 1944 grew by about 215 percent, an average annual increase of 3 percent, while its population doubled at an average annual rate of 1.8 percent. This resulted in a rise in per capita GDP of 56 percent, from US$745 to $1,130 (in year-2000 prices), an average annual increase of 1.2 percent. The rate of increase was not phenomenal, but it certainly represented a solid gain. In comparison with the transitional period (1876–1904) and/or many developing economies at that time, the Korean economy under Japanese rule clearly grew and improved.

The Korean economy under Japan also underwent substantial structural transformation. Most obvious was the change from a predominantly agrarian to a semi-industrial economy oriented toward serving the needs of Japanese empire. The primary economic sector, agriculture, including forestry and fishing, which made up nearly nine-tenths of the nation's output and employment, very much resembling Japan before the Meiji Reformation, expanded at an average annual rate of about 1 percent but gradually declined, contributing less than half of its output and about two-thirds of its employment toward the end of colonial rule. The secondary industrial sector expanded much more rapidly, thus, increasing the nation's output from less than 5 to near 40 percent of the total output during the same period. Especially notable in the industrial sector was the growth of public utilities (railroads, communications, and electric-power generation), manufacturing, and mining, which utilized modern technology.

Within the manufacturing sector, the type of goods and services produced also altered prominently, particularly in the heavy and chemical industries, which expanded at an average annual rate of more than 15 percent, eventually occupying about the same importance as light industry. The chemical industry especially experienced a phenomenal growth, about 20 percent a year, and became the most important component of the manufacturing sector in Korea under colonial rule. The expansion of the metal industry, and to a lesser extent the manufacturing of machinery, was also rapid. Light industry expanded but experienced varied growth rates and structural changes. The food-processing industry, which produced the most output in the industrial sector in the early years, gradually lost its prominence in spite of its growth. In its place, the textile industry achieved an important position within light industry. Ceramics, wood products, printing, and bookbinding also sustained their shares of growth in output.

Structural change can also be detected in the extent of product processing. "Manufactured goods" increased their portion of the total industrial output over time, while the share of "nonmanufactured consumer goods" and cottage industries declined. While the proportion of processed foods rapidly expanded, the production share of crude foodstuffs decreased. The shares of other processed consumer goods, such as clothing, increased modestly to markedly. Structural changes may also be detected in the finished-goods category. The share of goods produced for consumers declined, while those manufactured for producers expanded.

Likewise, not only was Korea's ability to trade expanded remarkably under Japanese rule, the kinds of goods and services traded changed over time as well. While exports in the early years consisted mainly of unprocessed raw materials (gold and foodstuffs such as rice), the export of finished goods as well as processed raw materials and food gained in importance in later years. Korea's demand for foreign goods also changed. While imports of processed foods, semiprepared raw materials, and finished manufactured goods gradually declined over time, the demand for raw materials and capital goods such as machinery and equipment expanded. These trends clearly reflected the industrialization of the Korean economy.

Another clear indication of structural change was the dependence of the Korean economy on Japan. The more dependent the Korean economy became, the larger the market it provided for Japanese goods, and vice versa. It is significant to note that at the same time, Korea gradually established its own network of import and export markets in a wider circle of countries, making its trade more balanced and less dependent on Japan. However, there is no empirical evidence to support the claim that Korea's dependence on Japan led to an unstable economy.

This chapter has also shown that industry and agriculture underwent important organizational transformations under colonial rule. The industrial sector underwent a transformation in its organization in a number of ways. One significant structural change was the rise of modern industries and factories on the one hand and the relative decline of household enterprises on the other. The factories, with their greater reliance on machinery and motor power, came to dominate the industrial sector in capital, output, and, to a limited extent, employment, despite the fact that their number was not large. New industries sprang up to provide the foreign and domestic markets with Western-style goods. In the meanwhile, the relative share of traditional cottage industries gradually declined from over 90 percent of the sector's output to probably less than a fifth under Japanese rule. Notwithstanding these changes, cottage industries expanded their output—instead of experiencing an absolute decline—and continued to be significant in almost all sectors of the economy, although their relative contribution declined over time.

As Korean industry modernized under Japanese rule, the scale of business enterprises also expanded. Included among large businesses were a few towering combines that dominated industry and commerce in terms of capital, employment, and production. The share of capital controlled by the leading Japanese *zaibatsu* was estimated to have been as large as three-quarters of the total capital in Korea. In terms of output, by 1940 the large factories, constituting less than 5 percent of all factories, produced as much as 70 percent of total factory output. Their dominance was especially prominent in manufacturing, mining, and the gas and electric industries, in terms of production and employment, and their influence on the nation's economy was preeminent.

The large corporations, particularly the *zaibatsu,* enjoyed monopolistic/oligopolistic powers in markets—acquired through mergers, interlocking corporations, and collusion—that reduced or for all practical purposes eliminated competition. Big-business interests worked in association with government bureaucrats to create a system of law that imposed few restrictions on monopolistic market powers and practices. The situation at the end of Japanese rule was one of coexistence between large and small businesses. Typically, the large businesses were Japanese owned and operated, while most small businesses, ample in number, were dominated by the Koreans.

Agriculture, too, experienced major organizational changes, in landownership, the scale of land holding, the status of Korean farmers, and tenancy. Most conspicuous was the dramatic increase in Japanese landownership, accounting for more than one-fifth of all land in the country, which led to the increasing concentration of land in the hands of large Japanese landlords. Most new large landowners were Japanese corporations, whose objective was to derive income from leasing land to tenant farmers. The groups that lost out on land were Korean landlords, including a few large and many small part-owner/cultivators and part-owner/tenants, some of whom were reduced to being tenants.

Major agricultural or land reform, in terms of redistributing land to farmers who actually tilled the soil, was never seriously contemplated by the Japanese administration; instead, the rights and duties of landlord vis-à-vis tenants were significantly strengthened. The land-related laws, surveys, and public policies destroyed the traditional landlord-tenant contract, legalized private ownership in the Western tradition, and took away the tenants' right to farm the land their ancestors had tilled for generations.

APPENDIX 8.1: COEXISTENCE OF LARGE AND SMALL BUSINESSES

The coexistence of large and small businesses in Korea under Japanese rule was common in all sectors of the economy. In the chemical industry, the most important industry in Korea in 1940, for instance, there were numerous small enterprises making fish oil and fertilizers and pressing vegetable oil, while a few giants produced the bulk of the output. In the metal industry, the large factories, which constituted only 3.3 percent of all plants, accounted for 88.4 percent of total production, while small factories, which represented 79 percent of the total, contributed a mere 4.8 percent of production in that sector. Similarly, in the machinery and toolmaking industries, the large factories represented only 3.2 percent of all plants but produced 53 percent of the total output, while the small factories, made up 75 percent of the total, produced only 17 percent of the output. The cement and ceramics industry was made up totally of medium-sized and large factories (Bank of Korea 1948: I, 104).

In the textile industry, as late as 1939, 68 percent of all factories were small, employing fewer than thirty workers, while one-quarter were of medium size and 7 percent were large. The large factories employed 67 percent of the workers and produced 85.8 percent of the output, while the small factories constituting 67.8 percent of all factories and employing 11 percent of the workers produced a meager 5.9 percent of the output. In food processing, a similar picture emerged. In 1940 about 1 percent of the firms in this industry were classified as large and produced 6 percent of the industry's output, while the medium-sized factories, 9 percent of the industry, produced 53 percent of the output. Small factories, constituting 90 percent, produced only 41 percent of the output. Large and small businesses also coexisted in mining. A total of 200 mines that produced more than 50,000 yen's worth of ore accounted for 80 percent of the output in the sector, while the remaining 3,000 mines produced only 20 percent (Bank of Korea 1948: I, 111, 113; Suh 1978: 109; S. J. Ko 1988: 385).

APPENDIX 8.2: THE SCALE OF JAPANESE AND KOREAN BUSINESSES

The large scale of Japanese businesses in comparison with Korean-owned businesses became clearly evident after the Annexation, especially after World War I. In 1931, of twenty-three industrial companies that had paid-in capital of between 300,000 and 1 million yen, 85.2 percent were Japanese, while only four were Korean owned. All eleven industrial companies that had more than 1 million yen in paid-in capital in 1933 were Japanese owned. By 1934, 86.7 percent (111 out of 128) of large companies, including banks, with more than 1 million yen in capital were owned and operated by Japanese. The total subscribed capital of large Japanese industrial corporations with more than 1 million yen in capital in 1940 was 1.1 billion yen, the equivalent of 94 percent of the total capital stock in all industrial corporations. If the companies headquartered in Japan are included, the percentage becomes even more skewed toward the Japanese. The average paid-in capital in Japanese industrial companies was about 6.7 times that of Korean companies in 1938. The average paid-in capital of Japanese companies in 1941 was 8.67 times larger than that of Koreans, 397,200 yen in contrast to 45,800 yen.

A similar picture emerges with regard to the paid-in capital of large factories (or plants) after 1917. Paid-in capital of Japanese-owned factories between 1917 and 1927 averaged about 15.7 times that of the Koreans. While nine large Japanese factories had average capital of 4.5 million yen in 1921 and fourteen had average capital of 8.3 million in 1927, Koreans had none. In 1940 the Koreans' share of the paid-in capital of factories with more than 1 million yen in capital had expanded to only 5.3 million yen. If we were to compare only the "modern" factories, the gap between the Japanese- and Korean-owned plants was even greater. The average nominal capital in Japanese industrial plants in Korea was 14.3 times larger than in Korean-owned plants (94,100 and 5,900 yen, respectively). There were 125 Japanese factories with more than 200 employees in 1939–89.3 percent of the total—in contrast to only 15 Korean-owned factories (Bank of Korea 1948: I, 100, 318; K. J. Cho 1973: 413, 419–429, 439–440; H. J. Choi 1962: 406; B. M. Lee 1948: 352–353; Himeno 1940: 329–330; and Grajdanzev 1944: 172–173, 176).

The disparity in scales of businesses owned and operated by Japanese and Korean varied widely among different sectors. One of the most conspicuous examples of Japanese domination of large businesses was in the electric-power industry. Only four electric plants were owned and operated by Koreans in the early years of the colony in contrast to the fourteen owned by the Japanese. The Korean-owned ones were small, with each possessing less than 1 million yen in paid-in capital. The number of Korean-owned electric and gas companies fell to three in 1913 and to paid-in capital of 200,000 yen in 1923. Only one (or possibly two) remained in business in 1937, at which time the last Korean company ceased operation. Average paid-in capital per firm was 13.3 million yen in 1938, while Koreans held virtually no share in large gas or electric companies (Kajimura 1989: 325).

Among the large manufacturing firms, the dominance of Japanese companies was most prominent in the chemical industry. In 1938 Japanese-owned chemical companies had average paid-in capital of 1.34 million yen in contrast to 80,000 for Korean-owned companies, the difference between the two being about 17 to 1. The gap between the two became even greater in 1941, when the average paid-in capital of Japanese-owned companies was 1.88 million yen in contrast to 87,600 yen for Korean-owned companies, the difference between them being about twenty-two to one. Japanese ownership of chemical companies with more than 1 million yen in paid-in capital was nearly 100 percent in 1940, the largest and most important one being the Korea Nitrogen Fertilizer (Jisso Hiryo) Company. The subscribed capital of Japanese chemical factories with more than 1 million yen in paid-in capital was 276.3 million yen in 1940, in contrast to 1 million yen for Korean companies. An even greater difference emerged between the Japanese- and Korean-owned chemical plants. The average subscribed capital of Japanese-owned plants in 1940 was 99,600 yen in contrast to 400 for Korean-owned plants, the former being 249 times larger than the latter.

In the case of the metal and machinery industries, Japanese companies were 7.7 times larger than the Koreans'. Japanese-owned plants with more than 1 million yen of nominal capital in 1940 accounted for 98 percent of the industry total, while Korean businesses made up only 2 percent. Japanese-owned metalworking plants had 61.5 times more nominal capital than did Korean-owned plants. There were seventeen Japanese metalworking factories with more than 200 employees, in contrast to only one Korean-owned company. The machinery and tool-making industry had eight Japanese and only one Korean-owned company.

A similar situation emerged even in the food industry, in which Koreans played a more significant role than in most other fields. Japanese firms were almost ten times larger than Korean companies. The average paid-in capital of Japanese-owned companies in 1938 was 128,000 yen, in contrast to 13,000 yen for Korean-owned companies. Similarly, in 1942 the average was 128,500 yen, in contrast to 21,100 yen for Koreans, the Japanese firms being more than six times larger. Japanese-owned industrial plants with more than 1 million yen of nominal capital in 1940 accounted for 93 percent of the food industry.

In flour and rice milling, the average size of Japanese companies was more than five times that of the Korean companies. Even in the distillery/brewing industry, where relatively large Korean firms were present, the average size of Korean companies was 36 percent that of the Japanese-owned. The Korean-owned plants in the wood industry with more than 1 million yen of nominal capital in 1940 made up only 10 percent of the industry (*Kokusei Gurafu,* April 1940; Tokanfu *Tokeinenpo;* J. B. Kim 1977: 209; and S. J. Ko 1988: 385).

The industrial sector in which the Japanese were least dominant was the textile industry. The number of Japanese factories with more than 200 employees increased from twenty in 1930 to thirty-eight in 1939, almost doubling in ten years, in contrast to an increase in Korean factories from four to five, increasing only 25 percent, during the same period. The average paid-in capital of Japanese-owned textile companies in 1938 was 593,000 yen in contrast to 164,000 yen for Korean-owned companies. The average paid-in capital of Japanese-owned textile companies increased to 728,000 yen in 1940, in contrast to 198,500 yen for Korean-owned companies. The average size of Japanese-owned textile companies in relation to those owned by Koreans was thus nearly four to one. The Chosen Textile Company, the Japanese textile giant, had 5 million yen in capital in contrast to the largest Korean company, the Seoul Textile Company, which eventually had subscribed (not paid-in) capital of 3 million yen. Japanese-owned textile plants with more than 1 million yen of nominal capital in 1940 made up 85 percent of the textile industry (Kajimura 1989: 343; K. J. Cho 1977: 499).

In the ceramics industry, which included cement, the average size of Japanese-owned companies was 6.7 to 11.1 times larger than those owned by Koreans. The average paid-in capital of Japanese-owned companies in 1938 was 395,000 yen, in contrast to 36,000 yen for Korean-owned companies, the former being nearly eleven times more than the latter. In 1942 the average was 418,100 yen, in contrast to 61,800 yen for Koreans. Koreans had virtually no share in the large ceramics companies. The average size of Korean factories in the wood-product industry was 24 percent that of the Japanese-owned firms. Korean printing businesses, which had the largest share of paid-in capital of all industrial companies, with more than 1 million yen in paid-in capital, made up only 57 percent of paid-in capital in the industry.

The dominance of large Japanese firms also prevailed in mining. The Japanese already had one mining company in 1913, when the Koreans had none, while one joint Japanese-Korean company had been founded. Thereafter, large Japanese mining companies dominated the field. Nineteen of the twenty companies producing more than 500,000 yen's worth of minerals in 1935 were Japanese owned. Even the single Korean firm was bought out by the Japanese in 1939. The Japanese commercial banks were more than ten times larger than Korean banks in terms of paid-in-capital. Likewise, the average paid-in capital of Japanese insurance companies in 1938 was ten times larger than the average in the industry. In the transportation industry the average paid-in capital of Japanese companies in 1938 was 11.5 times that of Korean companies.

A similar situation was found even in fishing. The average amount of capital per Japanese fisherman was 265 yen in 1932, in contrast to 15.2 yen per Korean. The value of capital goods (such as tools) in Korean fishing households likewise was small. The value of capital goods per Japanese fishing household increased 8.5 times, from 130 yen in 1911 to 1,109.7 in 1930, while that of Koreans increased only 4.4 times, from 13.2 to 57.7 yen, during the same period. The value of tools and equipment used by Korean fishing households was 15.2 yen in 1932, which was only 5.7 percent of that of Japanese fishermen, which averaged 265 yen. Thus, the amount of capital goods available to Japanese fisherman was ten to twenty times more than that available to the Korean, and the gap widened over time. Moreover, on average, every two Japanese fishermen had a boat, in contrast to every thirteen Koreans. According to one foreign observer, Korean vessels were small boats of the type "used in the previous century." Their average size as late as 1938 was only 13 tons. Sailing vessels and rowboats accounted for 63 percent of the tonnage and 88 percent of all fishing craft. Although the number of boats per Korean fishing household increased more than threefold between 1912 and 1930 (from 0.22 to 0.74), while that of the Japanese increased from 2.2 to 4.45 during the same period, the number of boats available to Korean fishermen was only one-sixth to one-tenth that of Japanese-owned boats (Sotokufu 1932: 141–143, 194–201; G. McCune 1950: 130; Grajdanzev 1944: 197).

In "miscellaneous" (officially classified as "other") fields Korean companies were somewhat larger, but, on average, the size of Korean companies was about one-seventh the size of Japanese companies. Although the average relative size of Korean companies in miscellaneous industries was considerably larger than in other fields, it nonetheless was smaller than the Japanese. The average paid-in capital of Japanese companies in this category was 2.4 times the Korean capital. Paid-in capital of "miscellaneous factories" owned and operated by Japanese, which was also large (e.g., 121,000 yen in 1921 and 134,000 yen in 1927), averaged about sixteen times of that of the Korean-owned (7,000 yen) in 1921 and more than seventeen times that of the Korean-owned (9,000 yen) in 1927 (S. J. Ko 1988: 302, 323). Korean-owned industrial plants in miscellaneous industries with more than 1 million yen of nominal capital in 1940 made up only 8 percent of the total. Among the miscellaneous industries, the average paid-in capital of Korean companies in the printing industry was highest, at 40 percent of Japanese capital (K. J. Cho 1973: 383–84; ibid. 1977: 457–459, 489–501, 507; Grajdanzev 1944: 284). Also see Sotokufu 1925, 1927, ibid. 1932: 195; J. B. Kim 1970: 18; Moon 1966: 144–146.

APPENDIX 8.3: LARGE KOREAN BUSINESSES

Among the most successful and prominent Korean businessmen were Tae-sik and Kyu-sik Min (of the Dongil Bank and the Gaesong and Yonbo real estate companies), Youn-su Kim (the Samyang Agricultural Company and Seoul [Gyeongseong] Spinning and Weaving), and Heung-sik Pak (the Whashin firms). Other leading entrepreneurs were Sang-yong Han (the Hanseong Bank and Joseon Trust), Chun-ho Hyon (the Honam Bank and Opa Agricultural Company); Yong-chol Pak (the Chosen Commercial Bank), Ui-sok Pang (active in finance and transport businesses), Chang-hak Choe (active in mining), and Sa-yon Kim (Chosen Yeast). Some of the wealthiest Korean businessmen in 1942 were reported to have been Yonsu Kim (worth 18.5 million yen), the Min family (7.8 million yen), Hung-sick Park (3.9 million yen), and Ui Suk Bang (3.6 million yen) (K. J. Cho 1977: 457–459; S. J. Ko 1988: 323).

One of the largest corporations owned and operated by Koreans was the Seoul Textile Company (Gyeongseong Bangjik), which was founded by two brothers, Sung-su and Yon-su Kim, in 1911 with 100,000 yen of capital. It was reorganized and expanded to become a joint stock company in 1919, with subscribed capital of 3 million yen and paid-in capital of 250,000 yen by 182 shareholders. It opened the market in the northwestern region and successfully competed against such Japanese giants as the Chosen Textile Company. The principal owners and shareholders of the Seoul Textile Company were landowners and merchants who joined with craftsmen who were interested in developing a modern industry. The latter shareholders were traditional merchants and craftsmen who had no connection to the government. Other textile-factory owners were former high- and middle-level government officials, large merchants, and/or landlords who either sold or mortgaged their land or borrowed money to start businesses. Some of them were successful, wealthy, and well-known Koreans. Some small entrepreneurs in the textile industry in later years were commoners, almost all of them small merchants who had worked previously for cloth and dry-goods merchants. A department store, the Whashin Company, which was established in 1929 with paid-in capital of 250,000 yen, had 8 million yen in capital and competed successfully against three Japanese-owned department stores in Seoul. Other large Korean businesses included the Korea Flour Mill (Joseon Jebun) Joint Company, established in 1920 with 1 million yen in capital; the Joseon Soap Company; and the O. B. Brewing Company. The small number of Koreans with fairly large and family-owned domestic enterprises were able to maintain control of their core businesses throughout most of the colonial period (K. J. Cho 1973: 383–384, 413, 419–429; 439–440; ibid. 1977: 489–501, 507; S. J. Ko 1988: 302–303, 385; Sotokufu 1921, 1927; ibid. 1932: 141–143, 194–201; Bank of Korea 1948: I, 100, 318; Himeno 1940: 329–330; B. M. Lee 1948: 352–353; G. McCune 1950: 130; Grajdanzev 1944: 172–173, 176; H. J. Choi 1962: 406; J. B. Kim 1977: 209; Kajimura 1989: 325, 343).

APPENDIX 8.4: JAPANESE LANDHOLDING IN THE EARLY YEARS

Statistics on Japanese landholdings in the early years reported in Japanese government statistics appear to have been exaggerated and are certainly confusing, since some of them are unreasonably high and conflict with other evidence. One published source stated that 8,474 Japanese had invested 147.1 million yen in land (Regency General 1910: 5–18, 21). Conroy (1960) also cites Masao Kanbe (1910), who suggested that the total investment in land and buildings by the Japanese in 1908 was 147.1 million yen, consisting of 75,970 *jeong* (186,200 acres) of land valued at 135 million yen and 12.1 million yen in buildings. It has been said that this sum was published in the Japanese government's statistics yearbook to inflate Japanese landholdings before the Annexation (Tokanfu 1910a: 5–18, 21). But it might also have been a printing error, perhaps a misprint for 14.7 million yen. If the official figure was correct, it certainly seemed highly exaggerated.

Most statistics show that Japanese landholding was small in the early years. In terms of investment in land, the Japanese invested, on average, 1,735 yen per farm in 1908 and 3,185 yen in 1910. One source cites that 14,036 Japanese invested 44.7 million yen in real estate in 1910, comprising 31.1 million yen in 34,127 *jeong* of land and 13.6 million yen in buildings (B.M. Lee 1948: 359). Therefore, the figures published by the Japanese government for 1908 were either exaggerated or misprinted intentionally to inflate their claims in Korea before the Annexation. Other, more feasible and reasonable estimates show that the average amount of investment was 6,078 yen (J. B. Kim 1974: 96–97), which set Japanese landholding at about 12 million yen at most. Although the investment in land increased somewhat thereafter, most of the farmers were not large landowners. The year after the Annexation (1911), Japanese investment in land averaged 5,861 yen (*Chosen Keizainenpo*

1939: 38–39; J. B. Kim 1974: 96–97; Kwon 1984: 305). Their landholdings were about 38.56 *jeong* in 1910. Altogether, the majority of Japanese farmers in Korea—about 82.4 percent—owned 13,400 *jeong* of land, investing on the average 2,017 yen per farm in 1910 (Sotokufu 1910: 182). See also Bank of Korea 1948: I, 341; and H. K. Lee 1936: 145–146.

APPENDIX 8.5: LARGE JAPANESE AND KOREAN LANDLORDS

The increasing dominance of large landholdings by Japanese is clearly demonstrated in all published data, in contrast to the declining tendency for large Korean landholdings. The number of Japanese who owned and operated tracts of 100 *jeong* or more increased from 18 in 1905 to 69 in 1911–1915, 74 in 1916–1920, 490 in 1921, and 598 for the period of 1933–1942, which came to constitute more than half of all landowners in this group. In contrast, between 1918 and 1927, the number of Koreans with more than 100 *jeong* decreased and comprised fewer than half. Between 1921 and 1933, their numbers fell by 18 percent (from 426 to 351). Also, the number of Koreans who owned between 100 and 200 *jeong* of land and their acreage decreased by 19.4 percent (from 360 to 290 *jeong*) and 19 percent (from 49,700 to 40,250 *jeong*), respectively, between 1921 and 1927.

The number of Japanese landlords owning more than 200 *jeong* of land increased by 13 percent (from 169 to 192) between 1921 and 1933, although it fell to 181 by 1936, while the number and acreage of Koreans who owned more than 200 *jeong* decreased by 32 percent (from 66 to 45 and from 13,200 to 9,000 *jeong*, respectively) during the same period. The number of Japanese owners with more than 300 *jeong* increased, while the number of Korean counterparts fell by 31 percent (from 65 to 45) in the ten years between 1918 and 1927. In 1927 there were 192 Japanese owners with more than 300 *jeong,* while there were only 45 Koreans, the ratio being four to one (Nihon Noshomusho 1932: 422–423; Bank of Korea 1948: I, 340–341; J. B. Kim 1970: 101; Hosokawa 1941: 338–340; Himeno 1940: 320).

The difference in the number of large Japanese and Korean landlords was greater as the size of the landholding increased. Japanese owning more than 500 *jeong* in 1942 accounted for 85 percent of the total in this group, while Japanese owning 1,000 *jeong* or more accounted for 95 percent (Bank of Korea 1948: I, 29–30; J. B. Kim 1974: 143; H. C. Choi 1962: 345; Kobayakawa 1941: 94). In contrast, there were more small- to medium-sized Korean than Japanese landlords. There were 4,152 Korean landlords with more than 30 *jeong* of land, constituting about four-fifths who had less than 100 *jeong* and one-fifth who had more than 100 *jeong* in 1934 (H. K. Lee 1936: 145–146). There was a slight increase in the number and acreage of those Koreans who owned more than 5 *jeong*. See also Sotokufu 1910: 182; Conroy 1960; Kanbe 1910; *Chosen Keizainenpo* 1939: 38–39; J. B. Kim 1974: 96–97; Kwon 1984: 305; K. J. Cho 1979: 5.

APPENDIX 8.6: LANDHOLDINGS OF CORPORATIONS

A number of Japanese companies began agribusinesses growing rice in the early 1900s. It was reported that in 1906 there were four agricultural corporations with paid-in capital of 190,000 yen, which expanded to 370,000 in 1907 and 5 million in twenty-one companies in 1908. The paid-in capital and new landholdings of corporations were large and expanded over time. According to official statistics, paid-in capital in agricultural (combined with forestry and fishing) companies increased from 21 million yen in 1921, to 51 million in 1931 and about 65.2 million in 1939, showing about a threefold increase during the eight-year period. The number of companies in agriculture increased fourfold during the 1921–1939 period, comprising nearly four-fifths of the total paid-in capital of all agribusiness companies in Korea. In spite of the increase in the amount of paid-in capital in agribusiness corporations, its relative share decreased over time, from 10.5 percent of paid-in capital of all companies in Korea in 1921 to 7.4 percent in 1939 as more Japanese invested in sectors other than agriculture (Tokanfu 1910; Governor General 1914; Chosen Ginko 1933: 35, 39; ibid. 1940b: 35–37; Chosen Nokai 1944: 588; Shokusan Ginko 1940b: 35–37; F. Fujita 1993: 357; Grajdanzev 1944: 175; H. Shikata 1933: 202; B. M. Lee 1948: 294–295; Huh 1989: 372; J. B. Kim 1974: 64; K. J. Cho 1994: 435; *Kokusei Gurafu* 1940; S. J. Ko 1988: 224–237).

These firms included companies headquartered in Japan as well as in Korea. The *zaibatsu,* which occupied the dominant position, included Iwazaki, Hosokawa, Ohkura, Mitsubishi, and Yamazaki (Sotokufu 1932: 321; Chosen Ginko 1933: 39; Reeve 1963: 19). Their possessions were mostly in the southern provinces. It was estimated that about 52 percent of land owned by Japanese companies was controlled by firms headquartered in Japan. Likewise, the landholdings of the railroads increased from 6,270 *jeong* in 1920 to 10,800 *jeong* in 1930.

APPENDIX 8.7: LAND REFORMS OF MEIJI JAPAN AND KOREA

Cultivated land in traditional Japan before the reform was fairly evenly divided among millions of small cultivators who held a qualified title to the soil, subject to heavy seignorial dues and other, lesser obligations. When Japan entered the modern era with the Meiji Restoration in 1868, it was confronted with neither the necessity nor the opportunity for a sweeping revolution in the techniques and organization of agriculture. Japan, however, decided to distribute land to those who actually farmed it and removed landowners and nobles from the land. By buying out the feudal rights of nobility, the state swiftly deprived them of their administrative functions and transformed them into capitalists in new businesses, including industries. It also took over the debts of the feudal lords. Finding themselves with plenty of money (or rather government bonds) and no duties, some nobles took up banking in 1880 and, when the government decided that it was ready to sell some of the factories it had established for pioneering purposes, it found a ready market. This swift transformation of an old-style aristocracy into a new capitalist class was profoundly important for increasing entrepreneurship in a crucial period. At the same time, the commercial classes now had a new freedom to invest productively and were powerfully reinforced by the entry into their ranks of some of the richest and most powerful families in the country.

Land "reform" in Korea was much different from the Meiji land reform in Japan. In Korea the ownership of land and the rights and privileges of the landlord were greatly strengthened, rather than weakened as was the case in Japan, and they were encouraged to remain landlords rather than becoming entrepreneurs. Gragert (1994: 210) argues that Japanese administrators, by legitimizing the position of the Korean landlord class, were in fact adapting themselves to Korean realities. He characterizes the role of the Japanese colonial government as having been neutral in matters pertaining to land (Hosokawa 1941: 247, 250; K. J. Cho 1977: 349; Takeo Suzuki 1941: 72).

9

INCOME DISTRIBUTION, CONSUMPTION, AND SAVING

As examined in earlier chapters, forty years of Japanese rule after 1905 brought about vast changes in Korea's economic, as well as political and social, conditions. It transformed the country from an agrarian to a semi-industrial economy while increasing the economy's agricultural, industrial, and mining output, as well as expanding the railways, communications networks, and educational facilities. It also brought about structural change in industrial and agricultural organizations. The final chapter of this assessment of the impact of Japanese rule investigates the impact of Japanese rule on income distribution, consumption (standards of living), and saving in Korea, focusing on Koreans. This examination should reveal a clear picture of the ultimate beneficiaries of economic transformation and development, as well as their contribution to capital formation under colonial rule. Income distribution, consumption, and saving in Korea are examined relative to various economic sectors, income groups, and nationalities.

INCOME DISTRIBUTION

The preceding chapter showed that national income in Korea expanded more than three times and per capita GDP increased about 56 percent during the forty-year period under Japanese rule. The first question in this chapter is, How has the increase in national income affected the distribution of income among different segments of the economy? This question is examined below relative to different economic sectors, income groups, and nationality in the country.

Sectoral Incomes

For the convenience and simplicity of analysis, income distribution among economic sectors is examined broadly in two categories: agriculture and industry. Although the grouping of income in these two broad groups is less than satisfactory, their analysis nonetheless should reveal certain significant dimensions of income distribution in Korea under Japanese rule.

Agricultural Income

As shown in chapter 8, output in the agricultural sector increased by about two-thirds during 1905–1943 and, thus, agricultural income should have reflected it and increased at about the corresponding rate, since income is dependent largely on output. However, the level and increases in agricultural income were rather modest and limited, in comparison with those of other sectors of the economy. Such a modest increase in agricultural income appears to have resulted from the limited increases in cultivated land and its productivity, as evaluated in an earlier chapter, and the poor terms of trade for agricultural products.

The unfavorable terms of trade for agricultural products were attributable to low agricultural prices relative to industrial prices, brought about by a Government General's low-price policy on agricultural products during most of its administration in order to supply cheap grain, especially rice, to Japan. The price of Korean rice, the product of the sector, for instance, was a little less than nine-tenths of the price of Japanese rice.[1] The terms of trade between agricultural and manufactured products between 1911 and 1940, based on official statistics, were less than parity and remained fairly constant at about 85 percent for the period.[2]

The terms of trade of agricultural products deteriorated even more sharply after 1940. The government, toward the end of the period of colonial rule, placed price controls on agricultural goods and established "collective sale" and "compulsory delivery" requirements. As was noted in earlier chapters, the Japanese government attempted to increase rice production in Korea to export large quantities of it to Japan, and farmers were forced to sell their products at officially set low prices ("collective sale" [*kongdong panmae*]). After 1941, they had to deliver ("compulsory delivery" [*kongchul*]) more than 70 percent of over forty major agricultural products at the officially set low prices, which, according to some farmers, covered only "a small fraction of their cost." The compulsory delivery of grain affected 56.3 and 64.1 percent of grain production during 1942 and 1944, respectively. The compulsory delivery quota for rice ranged between 42.7 and 63.8 percent of production during 1940 and 1944, while the quota on barley between 1940 and 1943 rose from 18.1 to 37.6 percent of production.[3]

The impact of these policies is clearly reflected in the wholesale price indexes of 1940 and thereafter. When Korea's average price index on all goods was 180.3 (based on 1910 prices) in 1940, the prices of cereals and other foods were 159.7 and 168.7, respectively, while the price indexes of textiles and metals were 190.8 and 240, respectively. These disparate price movements between the agricultural and industrial products resulted in unfavorable terms of trade for agricultural products, in spite of the fact that the worsening of the terms of trade for agriculture was somewhat mitigated by the Japanese government policy of relying on the import of Korean rice and restricting food imports into Japan from sources other than its colonies. The terms of trade for agricultural products in 1940 deteriorated to between 70 and 81 percent.

As a result of maintaining low food prices, the increase in the prices of agricultural products was modest, thereby constraining the rise in agricultural income. The gross income per farm in Korea in U.S. dollars (3 yen = 1 dollar) increased by about 1 percent a year, from $100 in 1905 to about $153 in 1938. This income was much lower than those in Japan ($248) and the United States ($1,828).[4]

Moreover, the limited increases in agricultural income had an unequal impact on the earnings of different groups within the farming sector, the landlords and tenant farmers. No comprehensive statistical data are available on levels and changes in income for landlords, but there is no doubt that the income of landlords increased substantially under Japanese rule. Their share of income increased primarily for two reasons: rises in agricultural productivity and augmented rental income from leased land to tenants. As examined in chapter 8, productivity in the agricultural sector increased by nearly 60 percent under Japanese rule. There is no uniformly accepted figure for rent, but it is generally believed that rental income did go up under Japanese rule. It is known that before 1905 the average rent was approximately 50 percent of the crop, while the most commonly cited figures of land rent during the colonial period were between 55 to 60 percent. Variations in land rent aside, the average land rent slowly inched up above the 50 percent level, possibly reaching as high as 60 percent.[5] This increase was the natural consequence of a growing population/labor, which resulted in an unfavorable ratio of population/labor to land and capital assets in a system of private ownership at the mercy of market forces. Other factors that contributed to the high and rising incomes of landlords were the strengthened tenancy system, which favored landlords (examined in chapter 8), and the government suppression of tenant movements to improve various facets of the well-being of tenants, including their income.

As a result of rises in productivity, land rent, and enhanced bargaining position, landlords' income from tenants slowly inched up. According to one official source, while the average rent per 100 *pyeong* (approximately equal to 0.082 acre, or 330 square meters) of dry land increased by nearly 50 percent in ten years (which was more than the increases in price index), from 1.62 yen in 1930 to 2.42 yen in 1939,[6] the average rent for paddy fields climbed by more than 15 percent in ten years, from 0.39 *seok* per *tan* in 1929 to 0.45 in 1939, an average annual rise of about 1.35 percent. Another study indicates that between 1933 and 1939 rent for owner-tenants increased from 93 to 162 yen, a 74.2 percent rise, and for tenants from 117 to 210 yen, a rise of nearly 80 percent. When inflation is discounted, the increase in real terms was probably about 1.3 percent a year.[7] The higher rise in rental income of landowners than that of the income of tenants resulted in the landlords' increased share of agricultural income.

As a result of these contributing factors, returns on investment in land to landlords were high and increased. The rise in landlords' income is well demonstrated in a government report. According to an investigation launched in 1932 by the Government General to determine the amount of rice Korea could export to Japan, a total of 6,486,000 *seok* out of 17,398,000 *seok* of rice produced in that year, or 38.3 percent, went to landlords, who made up less than 2 percent of the agricultural population.[8] This meant that the average rice income per member of the landlord families was 11.43 *seok*. Taking 1.5 *seok* as the maximum per capita rice consumption for a year, the total quantity that could be consumed by the landlord class was about 850,000 *seok*. The remainder, over 5,600,000 *seok* of "landlords' surplus," would have been available for export to Japan at a handsome profit.

In contrast to those of the landlords, the incomes of the tenant farmers (part-owner/tenants and tenants) were low and increased very modestly. They constituted as much as 79 percent of the agricultural population by the end of Japanese rule but received less than 47 percent of rice production in 1938.[9] The incomes of tenant farmers and part-owner/cultivators were one-third and three-quarters of the average agricultural income, respectively. Earnings in 1938 in terms of rice were 0.41 *seok* per capita for cultivator families. After paying rent and taxes, tenant farmers were left with only a fraction of the harvest, perhaps no more than 40 percent of the rice they had produced. Obviously, an income of 40 percent of the harvest was very hard on tenants, especially when the price of rice was sharply depressed. According to one investigation, the 210 yen in rent paid by tenants in the study represented 73 percent of their total farm income of 288 yen in 1939.[10] Cash income was between 50 and 100 yen per year. Moreover, in spite of a discernible rise in agricultural productivity, the rise in cultivators' (especially tenants') incomes was very modest, probably far less than 1 percent per year on the average.

There were three principal reasons for the modest rise in the incomes of small farmers. First, harvests were modest, and they were derived from small and decreasing plots of land. Typically, an average Korean farm family cultivated only a little more than 1 *jeong* (2.45 acres) of land,[11] while a Korean tenant family of 6 persons cultivated less than 1 *jeong* in 1938. Half of the total agricultural population tilled less than half a *jeong*, 69 percent farmed less than 1 *jeong*, and 87 percent farmed less than 2. Farm size also decreased about 13 percent on average, from 1.7 *jeong* in 1919 to 1.6 in 1929 and 1.48 in 1938. These figures include not only the tenants but also the medium-sized and large owner/cultivators. Thus, in spite of the fact that agricultural production increased under Japanese rule, the improvement in the farmers' share of the harvest was not commensurate, but smaller.

The second reason for the merely modest increase in the incomes of small farmers was the high and increasing rents. Because the majority of the farming population had to hand over larger shares of their crops as rent, they were left with smaller portions of their harvests.

The third reason was the increased cost of farming. In addition to higher rent, tenants often bore the increasing tax burden, such as of paying land taxes and water bills to irrigation associations. They paid fees for the inspection of rice; arranged for animal power, seeds, and commercial fertilizers; made gifts to landlords; and provided corvée labor for the repair of roads on the landlord's behalf, in addition to delivering the landlord's share of grain to his premises (when he lived in a city, this could be expensive).

Moreover, since most of the large landlords were absentee owners, their agents exploited tenants in many ways, such as by charging interest on land improvements and demanding gifts. Tenants were obligated to entertain managers, repair landlords' and managers' houses, clean, and help out at major social occasions, such as weddings and funerals. One report indicated that when all of these expenses were deducted, the net income of owner-tenants was as low as 14.8 percent of their gross, while the net income of tenants was mere 10 percent. According to Shirushi, the tenants in Gangwon Province were left with only 18 percent of the rice crop and those in the Gimhae region with 25 percent. It is little wonder, then, that so many poverty-stricken Korean farmers lost hope.[12]

The traditional poverty of Korean farmers did not seem to have changed much under Japanese rule; they were much poorer than Korean city workers.[13] The average tax payments of Koreans living in rural areas in 1939 were about 32 percent of what the city dwellers paid (2.78 yen as compared with 8.66 yen). Although the differences in tax payments may not show exactly the differences in incomes, they nonetheless reflect the vast gap in income levels in rural areas and also, to a large extent, city residents. One of the consequences of this prevailing poverty was emigration of a large number of Koreans to other countries, especially Manchuria. As many as 1 million Koreans had emigrated to that region by 1942. If all Koreans living in other countries—including Japan, Russia, and China—are added, there were as many as 2.3 million in 1942, which was more than 10 percent of the total farm population in Korea.

It is clear from this examination that there emerged an increasing disparity in income distribution in agriculture between the landlords and the peasants and that these small farmers, who made up nearly three-quarters of the population, were relatively untouched by the economic and social transformation that took place in the towns, which was much different from the conditions that prevailed in Japan at that time. The Japanese often blamed the Korean farmers for their own poverty and contended that the government's inability to remedy conditions after the Annexation was due to the farmers' lack of self-confidence.[14] The Japanese showed little disposition to employ the power of government to redistribute land and/or to shelter the peasants from poverty and the rigors of competitive markets. Instead, the Tenant Dispute Regulations (*Gosakulei*) of 1932 and the Agricultural Land Regulations (*Nochilei*) of 1934 were designed to protect the interests of landlords and financial institutions.[15]

Profit Income and Wages

Information on industrial income is scanty, but all available data indicate that profits and the returns on investment in industry on the whole were high for most of the period under colonial rule. Average corporate profits on paid-in capital ranged between 5 and 15 percent in most of the interwar years.[16] According to one estimate, the rates of return on the common stocks of major firms even in 1931 and 1937 when the world economy experienced the Great Depression were 6.9 percent and 6.5 percent, respectively. Banks in Korea in 1932 reported net profits of 6.2 percent per share of subscribed capital and 10.2 percent for paid-in capital. In 1938 they were reported to have been 9.4 percent and 13.1 percent, respectively.

Profits in industry seem to have grown relative to national income over time, but the increases in their incomes affected disparate groups within the industrial sector differently. There are no comprehensive data to indicate the level of business income, but it is clear from the analysis of sectoral growth of production examined in chapter 8 that business profits were unmistakably high and significant, which ultimately enabled the business sector to realize business profits increasing from less than a tenth of GNP to about four-tenths.

Another indication of large business profits under Japanese rule was the fact that dividend payments by business were relatively high. Dividends were reported to have been at the level of 6 to 9 percent per share of paid-in capital, on average.[17] One report indicated that approximately 7.5 percent of all companies in Korea paid annual dividends of 7 percent on average. The average annual dividend of the Wunsan Mine Company for the period between 1903 and 1938 was more than 9 percent. Dividend payment of the mine company was as much as 12 percent a year, on average, from 1903 to 1917. Even in hard times, dividends were paid. Although dividends for the mine declined somewhat after World War I, profits went up again in the Great Depression years. The Industrial Bank paid dividends of 8 to 9 percent, although returns on paid-in capital of commercial banks were relatively low, ranging between 4 and 5 percent.[18]

The high returns on business investment in Korea seem to have been principally attributable to three main factors. The first was the low costs of production arising from the "unlimited" supply of labor at near subsistence wages and the technological progress that contributed to increased productivity. The value of output per industrial worker in constant prices increased 366 percent between 1920 and 1940, representing an average annual rise of 7 percent, which was much higher than the national average. The value of net production per worker in industry in 1938 was 3,000 yen, fourteen times the 214 yen in agriculture. The large increase in productivity, in turn, contributed to an increase in profits. Another factor that contributed to high business profits was increased prices, which seems to have helped to arbitrarily redistribute income in favor of business owners, which promoted industrial expansion.

Business profits in industry also seem to have varied directly according to the size of business investment. Returns on investment for large corporations were higher than for small businesses, especially in good years. Profits of 20, 30, and 50 percent were not uncommon among large Japanese corporations. The net profits of the largest textile corporation in Korea during 1939–1940, for example, were reported to have been 49 to 50 percent of paid-in capital, respectively.[19]

More data are available for wage income than for business-income figures, but there is no accurate, comprehensive, and representative measure of wage income in Korea during the colonial period. The official statistics show that money wages did increase, though rather modestly, under Japanese rule. According to the wage index of the city of Seoul (which is the only statistic available), the money wages on the whole rose 362 percent between 1910 and 1944,[20] showing an average annual rate of increase of 3.8 percent. The gains in money wages were eroded by inflation, however.[21] When the rise in money wages is corrected for inflation with the official price index, real wages during the 1910–1944 period show an overall decrease to about 87 percent of that of 1910. The real wage level based on the official wage index showed a higher level than the one in 1910 base year only during the periods 1921–1923 and 1932–1937. It is probable that the wage controls that prevailed toward the end of the colonial period contributed to the decline in real wages.

Apparently, based on these official data, some economists went so far as to declare that the Korean populace, at least half of them, suffered a decline in real income during most of the colonial period.[22] Had this been the case, the benefits of increases in labor productivity did not go to workers in the form of wage increases at all, but entirely to profit earners. Were the wage statistics the sole guide, workers' real wages in Korea in fact would have even been much worse than the calculations have shown, for in reality the declines in purchasing power following 1937 were far worse than the official statistics on prices indicated. Naomasa Mizuda, a former Japanese official of the Government General in charge of the Finance Department and an expert on financial affairs in colonial Korea, confessed after World War II that the official price index after 1937 represented prices that were far below the black-market level and contended that market prices in Korea during the war were much higher than what was shown in the official indexes. While the official index showed an increase of 100 percent between 1937 and 1944, market prices in 1944 were as much as six to ten times higher than that.[23] This estimate seems reasonable based on the reports of prices in newspapers and other media at that time.

Given all these developments, did most wage earners actually experience a sharp decline in real wage income under Japanese rule? That this situation prevailed for most of the period of Japanese rule is highly unlikely. We need to carefully examine the official statistics before reaching any definitive conclusion. First, since the official wage statistics were based principally on the wages of day laborers (mostly manual workers), an inference based on them leads to distorted, if not erroneous, conclusions. If a representative, weighted sample of the wages of all workers (including regular full-time and salaried employees) were included, the wage statistics would probably show a discernible rise in average real wages during the colonial period, with the exception of the World War II years. As proof, it can be seen that people, including wage earners, lived better in the 1930s than in 1910, as shown in the next section.

Second, we need to take into consideration the possible sources of employment income that are not directly reflected in the official wage index. Although more people continued to rely for their livelihood on the farming sector, an increasing portion of workers depended for their earnings on the expanding "modern" industrial sector, where the increases in labor productivity and wage earnings were higher, away from the farming sector. The expansion of modern industry provided greater employment opportunities to many Koreans, as well as to the Japanese, at higher wages. The widening of labor markets, specialization of labor, and development of the transportation infrastructure would have played a part in rising wages.

Within the industrial sector, employment in relatively high-paying jobs such as in the heavy and chemical industries increased rapidly, from probably a very low, single-digit percentage in 1910 to 25.4 percent of workers in industry in 1930 and 46.7 percent in 1940. The percentage of mostly low-paying jobs in light industry, on the other hand, decreased over time. As much as 75 percent of the industrial labor force was employed in light industry as late as 1930, but this figure decreased to 52.3 percent in 1940. The contrast can easily be seen in employment in the machine and tool industry, which increased from 3.2 percent of the industrial labor force in 1930 to 11.9 percent in 1940. The chemical industry expanded its employment from 16.8 to 28.1 percent during the same period. On the other hand, the low-paying food industry, which employed as many as 34.3 percent of all industrial workers in 1930, employed only 14.2 percent in 1940.

Also, as a result of the expanded educational system, there was increased employment in better-paying jobs. As Japan began its military campaign in Asia, the demand for industrial workers with skills and a modern education expanded, which tended to push wages up. The expansion of modern industry provided employment opportunities for many Koreans who earlier had been either unemployed or employed in less remunerative jobs. Compensation for longer and steadier employment and upward mobility in jobs also should have resulted in higher real income for the workers than what the government statistics show. When these adjustments are made, it may be seen that wage earners on the whole realized some real gains, or at least modest gains beyond the level they had achieved in the past, such as during the transitional period.

In spite of their realization of higher real income, however, the increase in workers' real wages lagged far behind the rise in their productivity. Labor productivity increased substantially under Japanese rule, especially in the modern manufacturing sector, as examined earlier (e.g., 366 percent between 1920 and 1940, representing an average annual rise of 7 percent). In this way, even where it helped to build the country's productive power, the benefits were not shared fairly among different earning groups. In common with tenant farmers and small independent workers with comparable status, the typical wage earner depended solely on his or her labor and had virtually no property income.

In addition to modest wage gains, working conditions in Korea saw limited improvement under colonial rule. Working hours were long. Factory operatives commonly worked for eleven to fourteen hours, day and night, as late as 1938, for an average (41.1 percent) of twelve-hour-plus working days in all factories, as shown in Table 9.1. In the textile and food industries, as many as 64 and 53 percent of workers, respectively, toiled more than twelve hours a day, respectively. According to a 1931 Government General survey of working conditions in factories and mines employing more than ten workers, the average number of hours worked by women and children was eleven hours. As late as 1939, workers (including women and children) even in large-scale enterprises labored, on average, more than ten hours a day and six days a week. In small and medium-sized enterprises, it was not uncommon to work as many as thirteen hours a day.[24] One coal mine in northern Korea employed two twelve-hour shifts in 1929. In the textile industry as many as 63.6 percent and in the food industry 53.2 percent of all factories had average shifts of more than twelve hours. In the machine and tool industry, 42.9 percent of factories had eleven- to twelve-hour shifts, and 39.8 percent of chemical plants employed workers for ten to eleven hours a day.

In other regards, except for general laws relating to property and contracts, there were no labor standards of any sort, and legislation to protect workers was absent.

TABLE 9.1 Distribution of Average Workhours per Day in Factories in 1938 (percent)

Industries	Less than 8 hours	8.0–9.0	9.0–10.0	10.0–11.0	11.0–12.0	12.0+	Unknown	Total
Total	0.9	4.9	8.5	24.6	19.5	41.1	0.5	100.0
Textile	0.7	0.7	4.3	16.4	14.3	63.6	—	100.0
Metal	1.6	8.2	4.9	27.9	29.5	27.9	—	100.0
Machinery and Equipment	—	1.6	7.9	28.6	42.9	19.0	—	100.0
Pottery	—	3.2	9.6	22.3	27.7	36.2	1.0	100.0
Chemical	2.3	5.7	12.5	39.8	10.2	28.4	1.1	100.0
Woodwork	—	1.4	2.4	9.6	42.8	43.8	—	100.0
Printing	1.8	11.7	31.5	50.5	3.6	0.9	—	100.0
Food	1.0	3.8	4.6	18.8	17.1	53.2	1.5	100.0
Gas and Electric	—	28.6	21.4	28.6	—	21.4	—	100.0
Others	—	6.6	9.2	30.3	21.0	32.9	—	100.0

Sources: This table is based on Himeno 1940: 294; K. Hosokawa 1941: 353.

There were few attempts on the part of the colonial government to protect or improve the workers' lot. In spite of the fact that businesses in Korea employed many women and children at low wages, no government action was taken against unfair labor practices. In the manufacturing sector, nearly one out of every ten workers was a child below the age of sixteen, while women made up 35 percent of the industrial work force in 1931 and about 30 percent in 1932. In the textile industry 22 percent of the work force was made up of children, and 80 percent of women as late as 1939.[25] Trade unions did not exist, and attempts to form them were brutally suppressed. Neither did the government shelter workers from the rigors of market competition.

Income by Nationality

There are no comprehensive statistics showing income distribution between the Japanese and Koreans. One form of available data that may shed some light on it is tax records. Based on Hosokawa's calculations of the tax burden of national, provincial, and local governments per person, it is clear that the Japanese bore much higher taxes than the Koreans did. The Japanese paid an average of 48.21 yen in taxes in 1939, while the Koreans paid only 4.84 yen,[26] the ratio being almost ten to one. The tax payments were not dependent solely on one's income, and the differences in incomes, therefore, may not be as much or as little as the above figures imply, but they nonetheless reflect the vast differences in income levels of the two nationalities. The disparity between Japanese and Koreans prevailed in all types of income, whether rental and tenant incomes, profits, or wages.

Rental and Profit Income

In the case of rental income, returns on investment in land owned and operated by the Japanese were higher than those of Korean landlords. Many Japanese-owned farms were reported to have been managed more efficiently by individuals or corporations and run by competent technicians and professional staffs than those managed by the Koreans. The Japanese used the land more skillfully by improving its quality and constructing irrigation facilities, which resulted in increased productivity. Returns on Korean investment in agriculture likewise were reported to have been high, but lower than those of the Japanese. Very few Korean landowners utilized modern management techniques or operated their farms efficiently.[27] It was said that the typical Korean landowner lived in the city, was not particularly dedicated to improving his land, and left farm management to his agents.[28] This left tenants to farm in traditional ways and led to an inefficient and antiquated operation, resulting in low productivity.

As with Japanese landowners, Japanese business entrepreneurs earned considerably higher profits than those of the Koreans. Japanese corporations in Korea brought especially high returns on investment. The average annual profits of Japanese companies headquartered in Korea were reported to have been 21.4 percent, while dividends were 6.6 percent a year.[29] In many cases these annual profits of Japanese companies in Korea were higher than those of comparable corporations in Japan. For example, while the Japan Nitrogen Corporation was making 11 to 13 percent net profits in Japan, those of the Korea Nitrogen Fertilizer (Chosen Chisso Hiryo) Company were 31 to 33 percent in 1936, more than 2.6 times the former.[30] Although this example may not be representative, higher profits in Korea than in Japan are shown in other data as well.

There appear to have been three principal reasons for the higher profits of Japanese businesses than those of the Koreans. As examined in earlier chapters, Japanese businesses received more tax breaks and subsidies from the colonial government and paid lower input costs, for example, lower interest rates.[31] Also, Japanese businesses on the whole were larger than those of the Koreans and thus enjoyed economies of scale. They also yielded monopoly profits of 20, 30, and even 50 percent in some years. Japanese *zaibatsu* often dominated the market and realized profits through monopolistic practices such as entering into agreements with competitors. On the other hand, Korean enterprises were typically small and numerous, and their market, as a rule, was a highly competitive one in which prices were low, resulting in low profits.[32] Compared with Japanese firms, many Korean businesses were also less mechanized, less efficient, poorly managed, and not specialized, resulting in lower income. Likewise, the life expectancy of Korean businesses in general, especially in the early years, was shorter than that of the Japanese.

Wages and Tenant Income

A similar pattern of unequal income distribution between Japanese and Koreans prevailed in wage and tenant incomes. Before the Annexation, Japanese wage earners in Korea typically were engaged in commerce or cottage industries such as blacksmithing, brick manufacturing, textiles, soy sauce making, rice milling, dyeing, and canning, not much different from many of their Korean counterparts. In 1906, for instance, one-third of so-called industrial workers were blacksmiths and one-fifth were in rice milling.[33] After the Annexation, however, the occupations and provision for real wages and working conditions vastly changed, and the differences between Japanese and Korean workers became more pronounced.

The occupations of Japanese workers were swiftly transformed, reflecting the changing needs of the colonial administration. An increasing number of Japanese filled managerial and professional positions in government and businesses in Korea. Civil servants and professionals in private employment accounted for about 15 percent of the Japanese workforce in Korea in 1908, but they increased to 20 percent in 1911, 30 percent in 1920, 41.4 percent in 1937, and 43.8 percent in 1942, nearly half of the Japanese labor force. Japanese held 63.4 percent of all civil-service and professional jobs in 1938 and made up 55.5 percent of all government employees, despite the fact that they represented less than 3 percent of the population of Korea. Korean workers constituted 36.6 percent of all government employees and professionals and represented 44.5 percent of all government employees in 1940.

Similarly, the number and percentages of Japanese workers employed in aspects of the business sector other than commerce—for example, industry, manufacturing, and transportation—were relatively small in the early period. But as the Korean economy expanded and industrialized, Japanese employment increased to meet the soaring demand in those fields. Almost as many Japanese were employed in manufacturing, commerce, and transportation as were civil servants and professionals. In the railroad system too, there were more Japanese than Koreans. The public railroads, for instance, employed 24.4 percent more Japanese (6,693) than Korean workers (5,381) in 1919.[34]

A rapid increase in employment in businesses took place during the period of heavy Japanese investment in Korea after 1936. Nearly 40 percent of all Japanese workers were in manufacturing, commerce, or transportation toward the end of Japanese rule. Of these, about 20 percent were employed in manufacturing, 13 percent in transportation, 3 percent in mining, and 23.5 percent in commerce. The percentage of Japanese workers in industry and mining increased from about 12 percent in 1910 to approximately 22 percent in the 1940s. On the other hand, Japanese employment in the agricultural and blue-collar occupations was insignificant, with less than 4 percent of Japanese workers in Korea engaged in agriculture in 1942. Thus, by 1942 the employment of Japanese workers was mostly in civil service, professional service, industry, mining, transportation, and commerce. The employment in these sectors increased from 64.3 percent of all Japanese workers in 1911 to 86.4 percent in 1942.[35] In contrast, more than three-quarters of Korean workers were engaged in agriculture.

Not only were the majority of the Japanese and Korean workers employed in different sectors of the economy, the natures of the positions held by the two groups were vastly different. As the primers of development in Korea, management and professional positions were the more or less exclusive domain of the Japanese, and they held nearly all of the important positions and the major portion of white-collar jobs in government and business. The post of public-school principal, for instance, was reserved exclusively for Japanese until 1919,[36] and even thereafter it was very rare for a Korean to be appointed to that position.

It has been estimated that 83 percent of all so-called skilled workers in Korea were Japanese.[37] Of 188,000 Japanese males between the ages of sixteen and sixty in Korea in 1944, about 28 percent, or 52,000, were managers or professional and technical experts who provided the leadership in government and businesses. Nearly all the engineers and technicians who operated the industrial plants, mines, and public utilities were Japanese. In the business sector, nearly all executives, more than 80 percent of the skilled technicians, 81 percent of the skilled industrial workers, 62 percent of the skilled miners, and 89 percent of the skilled transportation workers were Japanese.

In contrast, Korean employment in the professional and business sectors remained modest even as late as 1942. In 1940 a mere 11.1 percent of all Korean workers were in the civil service and professions, mining and manufacturing, and commerce (1.9 percent, 3.6 percent, and 5.6 percent, respectively).[38] Also, only a small portion (about 1,600) of Korean workers were skilled; for example, just 17.2 percent of this category in 1943.[39] They ranged from 11 percent in the metal and chemical industries to 42.9 percent in the printing industry. Even during the rapid industrialization of 1932–1945, the status of skilled Korean workers did not improve much. Only 29 percent of so-called technicians in mining and 11 percent in refining were Koreans in 1941. Similar situations existed in almost all sectors, including the metal, machine, chemical, electric, ceramics, textile, and construction industries. On average, Korean technicians made up less than one-fifth of the total number. Exceptions were found in forestry, printing, and food processing, where Koreans made up 65, 43, and 36 percent of all technicians, respectively. Also, only a very few Korean business executives were employed by Japanese companies.[40]

Among government employees in Korea, there were more ranked Japanese officials[41] at senior level than there were Koreans—in 1920, almost twice as many (21,799 Japanese versus 11,432 Koreans). Moreover, the number of ranked Japanese officials increased more rapidly than did the Koreans over time. By 1940 there were 2.1 times more ranked Japanese than Korean officials (35,553 as opposed to 16,757); the Japanese percentage of ranked officials expanded from 65 percent in 1920 to 68.5 percent in 1940. On the other hand, the percentage of unranked Japanese government employees decreased from 59.2 to 42.7 percent during the same period. In contrast, Koreans occupied more of the low-level jobs. A total of 91.5 percent of all Korean workers in the Government General's offices were probationary employees (*shokutaku*). Korean employees held only 28.4 percent of bureau appointments (*hanninkan*), 18.7 percent of minister's appointments (*soninkan*), and 9.4 percent of imperial appointments (*chokuninkan*) in Korea.[42]

In the railroads, prior to the mid-1930s Koreans held only 2 to 7 percent of middle-level positions, while most held the lowest-paying jobs.[43] Hardly any held main-office supervisory or management positions. Following the mid-1930s, when the Japanese experienced shortages of manpower, more Koreans were hired, and they came to make up about 70 percent of all employees in the railroad system. Some were promoted to management positions (they held 94 out of 868 management positions, or 11 percent, in 1940).

Moreover, in most cases Koreans held only lower-echelon and nonregular technical and office positions in Japanese companies and public enterprises. They were often employed on a temporary basis (*shokutaku*), while Japanese were hired as regular employees (*kaishanin*) on a permanent basis. In public railroads, the ratio of

Korean to total regular company employees was 1.3 percent (13 out of 1,010).[44] Only one out of nine probationary employees (11 percent), and 5.7 percent (119 out of 2,071) hourly employees (*koyonin*) were Koreans. Korean workers also dominated at the lowest level, that of so-called day laborers (*yonin*). In addition, almost all of the female and child laborers, who were used extensively, especially in the textile industry, were Koreans. In 1938 approximately 30 and 10 percent of industrial workers were women and children, respectively, while about 80 and 22 percent, respectively, of the workers in the textile industry were women and children.

The paucity of Koreans in leadership and skilled professional positions was often attributed to their lack of education and training. Although the majority of Koreans had no formal schooling (85.7 percent in 1944), nearly 70 percent of the Japanese in Korea had formal education ranging from elementary to high school. Nearly half (48.1 percent) of all Korean industrial workers had no education, in contrast with only 10 percent of the Japanese workers (see Table 9.2). In 1944 about 4.6 percent of the Japanese in Korea, but only about 1 percent of Koreans, had a college education. According to a 1943 survey of industrial and mining firms with thirty or more workers, 97.5 percent of Korean workers but fewer than 7 percent of Japanese had less than an elementary school education.[45] Only four-tenths of a percent of Korean workers in industry had a high school education, while 54 percent of Japanese workers did, in the same year.[46] As the evidence clearly shows, Korean workers were far less educated than were the Japanese workers, which contributed to their lack of employment in professional and managerial occupations.

The wide difference in occupations between Japanese and Korean workers, however, seems to have reflected more than the disparity in their educational attainments. Discriminatory Japanese employment policies can clearly be seen.[47] Well-educated Koreans, unlike their Japanese counterparts, did not get jobs commensurate with their education. The chance of being employed in the government was less than one in ten for Koreans, in contrast with much higher probabilities for Japanese workers. Few banks hired Korean employees.[48] Approximately

TABLE 9.2 Educational Level of Workers in Industry and Mining in 1943 (percent)

	Industry		*Mining*	
Educational Level	Korean	Japanese	Korean	Japanese
No Education	48.1	0.1	75.2	4.7
Some Elementary Education	17.7	1.8	7.6	2.2
Elementary School	31.8	22.7	16.0	26.8
Some Secondary School	0.1	3.1	0.1	2.2
Secondary Education	0.4	54.0	0.2	43.2
Vocational School	1.5	15.4	0.8	18.5
College	0.4	2.9	0.1	2.4
Total	100.0	100.0	100.0	100.0

Sources: This table based on Sotokufu Report on Labor Skills 1943; Ahn 1989: 417.

43.6 percent of all teachers in Korea were Japanese. There were more Korean teachers in the primary schools, but in the higher grades the Japanese outnumbered Koreans by a factor of three to one.

Partly as a consequence of such discriminatory employment policy, the unemployment rate of Korean workers was higher than that of the Japanese. A Government General survey of 1932, for instance, indicated that the average unemployment rate for Korean workers was 3.4 times higher than that of the Japanese (12.2 percent of the labor force versus 3.6 percent).[49]

In addition to Japanese workers commanding higher salaries as managers and skilled workers, almost all Japanese employers in the country, including the Government General, local governments, banks, companies, and businesses, routinely engaged in discriminatory wage practices for the same positions.[50] Although they varied somewhat by occupation and employer, the wages of Korean workers were, on average, considerably lower than those of the Japanese. The regular government surveys and reports on wages based on nationality, gender, and age revealed that Korean workers typically earned somewhat less than half of what the Japanese workers with the same qualifications received. Such wage differentials prevailed in all segments of the economy, including the civil service.

Clear differences in wages between Japanese and Korean workers prevailed for common laborers and school teachers alike. As shown in Table 9.3, the daily wages of common laborers for Japanese and Korean workers were at a ratio of about two to one, on average, during the 1930s. In the public school system, as shown in Table 9.4, monthly salaries of regular teachers for Japanese and Koreans, both male and female, varied widely, ranging from 3.17 to 1.19 to one in favor of Japanese teachers from 1913 to 1942. In 1913 Korean elementary school teachers made 18 yen per month, compared with 57 yen for the Japanese. The monthly salary of public-school teachers even as recently as 1940 was 58 yen for Korean males and 97 for their Japanese counterparts, while Korean females were paid 46 yen, compared with 79 for

TABLE 9.3 Daily Wage Rates of Japanese and Korean Workers During 1929 and 1937

	Yen				*Ratio*		*Yen*	
	Japanese		*Korean*		*Japanese/Korean*		*Juvenile Korean*	
Year	Male	Female	Male	Female	Male	Female	Male	Female
1929	2.32	1.01	1.00	0.59	2.3	1.7		
1931	1.36	0.98	0.93	0.57	1.5	1.7	0.37	0.33
1933	1.93	1.00	0.92	0.50	2.1	2.0	0.40	0.25
1933	1.94	0.96	0.92	0.50	2.1	1.9	0.46	0.28
1934	1.83	0.88	0.90	0.51	2.0	1.7	0.36	0.31
1935	1.83	1.06	0.90	0.49	2.0	2.2	0.49	0.30
1936	1.85	1.04	0.92	0.47	2.0	2.2	0.41	0.30
1937	1.88	0.98	0.95	0.48	2.0	2.0	0.42	0.32
Average	1.87	0.99	0.93	0.51	2.01	1.94	0.42	0.30

Sources: This table is based on Sotokufu surveys of factories with more than 50 employees reported in K. Takahashi 1935: 430; Himeno 1940: 301.

TABLE 9.4 Monthly Salaries of Regular Japanese and Korean Teachers During 1913 and 1942 (yen and ratio)

	Male			*Female*			*Gender Difference*	
							Male/Female	
Year	Japanese	Korean	Japanese/ Korean	Japanese	Korean	Japanese/ Korean	Japanese	Korean
1913	57.00	18.00	3.17	27.00	15.00	1.80	2.11	1.20
1915	56.00	19.00	2.95	27.00	15.00	1.80	2.07	1.27
1920	112.00	52.00	2.15	70.00	45.00	1.56	1.60	1.16
1925	114.00	51.00	2.24	77.00	47.00	1.64	1.48	1.09
1930	115.00	53.00	2.17	80.00	49.00	1.63	1.44	1.08
1935	109.00	55.00	1.98	81.00	48.00	1.69	1.35	1.15
1940	97.00	58.00	1.67	64.00	46.00	1.39	1.52	1.26
1942	107.00	90.00	1.19	76.00	71.00	1.07	1.41	1.27
Average			2.19			1.57	1.62	1.18

Sources: This table is based on Sotokufu Statistics 1932: 684–685; ibid. 1942: 206–207.

their Japanese counterparts. Often, when foreign-service bonuses were added, Japanese pay was double that of Koreans. A Japanese graduate of an agricultural school received more than double the monthly salary of 50 yen received by a Korean. Similar wage differentials prevailed in the business sector as well.[51]

It is not surprising that Japanese wages and salaries in Korea were even higher than those in Japan. Japanese executives, administrators, and other white-collar workers were paid more in Korea than they were in Japan. The wages of Japanese employed in manufacturing, construction, and most service industries in Korea were about 30 to 40 percent higher than those in Japan,[52] in spite of the fact that wages in Korea were less than one-half the general wage level in Japan and the costs of living were lower in Korea. There was one modest exception to the general employment and discriminatory compensation practices under Japanese rule, namely, the Industrial Bank, where it was said that equal wages were paid to workers of different nationalities in the same position.[53] Wage differentials existed not only between the two nationalities in factories and in public schools but also between males and females, as shown in Tables 9.3 and 9.4.[54]

The disparity in earnings between the Japanese and Koreans, in both business incomes and wages, was also reflected in tax payments. According to Hosokawa's data, Japanese living in urban areas paid on average as much as 5.6 times the amount paid by Koreans urban residents, 48.56 versus 8.66 yen.[55]

Also, the discrepancy between Korean and Japanese workers was partly reflected in the supplementary compensations Japanese workers received in addition to the base pay. Regardless of the place of employment, public or private, the Japanese workers were paid an additional 40 to 60 percent as supplemental compensation in the form of bonuses for overseas service. The average pay of Japanese government employees was 57.5 percent higher than that of the Koreans. A high government official (*kotokan,* fifth degree), for instance, received 140 percent of his regular monthly salary of 200 yen (or 280 yen), while Japanese workers of the middle rank (*hanninkan*) received, on average, 58.4 percent higher wages than those of their Korean counterparts. For the highest-ranking Japanese employees (*chokuninkan*), the premium was 46 percent.[56]

In addition to clear differences in wages, there also were disparities in fringe benefits such as free or subsidized housing, education, better rations, and bonuses, which were typically given to Japanese workers but not to the Koreans.[57] Disparities between Japanese and Koreans extended even to shoe rations during World War II. For example, an unlimited shoe ration was given to Japanese teachers, while Korean teachers were allowed only one pair every nine months. When all forms of compensation, including bonuses and supplementary compensations, were counted, Japanese workers typically received more than double a Korean worker's compensation.

It was often said, especially by some Japanese, that the main reason for the lower wage of Korean workers than that of the Japanese in Korea was low productivity of the former. This low productivity was said to have been attributable to the "many defects of Korean workers."[58] Judging from the contradictory views on the subject, it is difficult to accept the assertion that the productivity of Korean workers was less than half that of the Japanese workers. There is no study showing the productivity differences between the two nationalities, but, on average, the production level of Korean workers certainly could not have been less than half that of Japanese workers in comparable positions, if there was any difference at all. There also is ample evidence to show that the difference in wages mainly originated in discrimination based on nationality, rather than being rooted in rational economic grounds.

There appear to have been different working conditions for Japanese and Korean workers as well. The working conditions under colonial rule on the whole were poor, but poorer conditions prevailed for Korean workers than for the Japanese. As shown in Table 9.5, which exhibits a Government General survey of conditions in factories and mines employing more than ten workers in 1931, the majority of Korean workers (47 percent) toiled more than twelve hours a day, while 45.3 percent of the Japanese worked less than ten to twelve hours. Also, nearly 47 percent of Koreans worked more than twelve hours a day, but only 0.3 percent of Japanese did the same. Of these, only 28.7 percent of Koreans and 45.3 percent of

TABLE 9.5 Average Workhours of Japanese and Korean Workers in Industry in 1930 (percent)

Workhours	Korean	Japanese
Less than 8 Hours	0.8	1.4
8.00–10.00	28.7	45.3
10.00–12.00	11.9	43.6
More than 12 Hours	46.9	0.3
Unknown	0.3	—
Total	88.6	90.6

Source: This table based on K. Hosokawa 1941: 353.

Japanese worked less than ten hours. The average workday of male Korean and Japanese factory employees in 1930 was 9.48 and 8.48 hours, respectively, while for females it was 10.42 and 9.30. Korean children worked on average 10.42 hours per day, while no work hours were cited for Japanese children, indicating that they were not in the labor force. The average shift for women and children in 1938 was eleven hours long.

Provision for health care of Korean workers was also being neglected. Health-care programs for employees were seldom provided, especially in the factories where Koreans typically worked. Living quarters were poor. Live-in workers (mostly young Korean women) were lodged in factory dormitories on a three-year contract. It was said that as many as half of these workers deserted within nine months.[59] Also, night-shift work was assigned without any premium pay. The old paternalistic system, which carried with it reciprocal obligations of protection and subordination, was supposed to have extended to modern industry, but it seems to have lost most of its kindness and humanity in consideration of profits.

Notwithstanding such discriminatory practices, toward the end of colonial rule there were some notable improvements for Korean workers. While lower wages prevailed, the gap between Korean and Japanese workers eventually narrowed, because Korean workers' wages increased more rapidly at the end of colonial rule than did those of the Japanese. According to the Government General's statistics, the relative wages of Korean workers improved over time, especially between 1936 and 1942 (Table 9.4), for educated workers, while the same improvement apparently did not take place for day laborers. While Japanese wages increased by 35.8 percent during the period, those of Koreans advanced by 72.1 percent, which was about twice the level of increases realized by the Japanese, largely because of the tightening of the labor market during the war period. Labor shortages after the late 1930s forced changes in Japanese labor policies on the Korean Peninsula, further improving the opportunities for the Korean workers.[60] As a result, the wage gap between Japanese and Korean workers narrowed over time. The average salary of regular male Japanese teachers in 1912 was 3.2 times higher than that of Korean teachers, but it was only 1.2 times higher in 1942. Similarly, the average salary of female Japanese teachers in 1912 was not as large as that of males, but it was 1.8 times higher than that of the Koreans. This gap slowly narrowed to 1.1 times in 1942. In spite of the war economy, there also were signs of relative improvement in working conditions toward the end of colonial rule.

The income of small farmers, especially that of tenants, did not increase much, showing the least improvement among all Korean income earners, and it remained low under Japanese rule, as has been the case for centuries.[61] According to Hosokawa,[62] the average Korean living in a rural area paid as little as 5.9 percent (=2.78/47.36) of the taxes paid by the Japanese living in rural areas in Korea. Also, Korean rural residents were much poorer than Korean city inhabitants, as shown earlier. A Governor General noted the misery of Korean farmers by stating that nearly half were in poverty, yet the inequalities inherent in the economy were allowed to continue largely unchecked.

Notwithstanding this disregard for the welfare of Korean tenants, the Government General did assist small Japanese immigrant farmers generously. Under the government colonization policy, they were recruited from Japan by land development companies. The Oriental Development Company, for example, provided them with 2 *jeong* of land per household: twice the average acreage of the typical Korean farm household.[63] The average plot gradually increased to 2.15 *jeong* in 1920 and 2.56 after 1930, when the company leased land to 3,943 Japanese farm families.[64] Also, under the company's program small and medium-sized Japanese tenant farmers were able to purchase land on installment.[65] Notwithstanding the encouragement and assistance in the form of government grants, subsidies, low-interest loans, and help with moving costs, the number of Japanese farmers who actually settled in Korea to farm remained small. The 4,000 who settled in Korea in 1908 (on about 2,000 farms) constituted only about 4 percent of the Japanese population in Korea at the time, a figure roughly equivalent to the number of Japanese geishas and prostitutes reported to be in the colony.[66] After the Annexation, the number of Japanese farm households increased somewhat to 2,254 in 1910 and 9,573 in 1915. It peaked at 10,800 in 1931, declining thereafter to 7,300 in 1938, 5,892 in 1942, and probably fewer than 5,000 in 1944.

The majority of Japanese farmers in Korea came to own adequately large plots (in comparison with Korean farmers) and earned fairly comfortable incomes. On average, the landholdings of Japanese farmers were five to six times the average size of Korean farms. Ordinary Japanese farmers (numbering 2,094) in Korea owned 13,400 *jeong,* an average of 6.4 *jeong* per farm, in 1910.[67] Between 1910 and 1918, a total of 7,240 *jeong* was appropriated for the settlement of 1,035 Japanese families, averaging about 7 *jeong* per family, which decreased to roughly 5.43 in 1927. As noted earlier, most Japanese engaged in agriculture were not farmers but landowners who leased plots to Korean tenants.

Similarly, Japanese fisherman had much higher income than the Korean fisherman, since they operated better boats and equipment. In 1932, for instance, the value of the fish catch per Japanese fisherman was 1,910 yen in contrast to 102 for Koreans.[68]

PERSONAL CONSUMPTION

Having examined the level of income for different income groups, it is necessary to investigate their personal consumption as a whole and then among different income groups—landlords, farmers, businessmen, and wage earners, in particular—in order to determine their standard of living under colonial rule. However, satisfactory data are scarce. Except for isolated family budget studies, the limited data constrain a detailed analysis of personal-consumption patterns and the prevailing standard of living under Japanese rule. Nonetheless, there is sufficient evidence, though fragmentary, to indicate the magnitude and general patterns of personal consumption in Korea under Japanese rule in aggregate and among the four segments of people in Korea.

Aggregate

It is well known that the principal determinants of personal consumption are the level and distribution of incomes in an economy. They greatly influence the use of goods and services for consumption by all segments of the population. Most data suggest that with an overall rise of national income, personal consumption and the standard of living in Korea rose and improved over time. Most Koreans, as well as Japanese, in Korea had a greater opportunity to enjoy the fruits of their labor than they did during the traditional and transitional periods. One major exception to this general tendency was during World War II, when resources devoted to personal consumption were drastically slashed, to 63.3 percent of national income in 1941, 52.3 percent in 1943, and an astonishing 32.7 percent in 1945.[69] In other words, in the final years of Japanese rule just before Korea was liberated, less than a third of Korea's income was spent for consumption purposes.

Until World War II, increases in consumption under Japanese rule prevailed in all components of economic goods. Of public goods, railroads and roads were improved, and communications facilities were "modernized" and made more accessible to all. Gas and electricity became available to many urban dwellers, while public health conditions and the literacy rate improved. Of consumer goods, the average per capita expenditure for domestic use increased by 36 percent between 1919 and 1940. Consumption of fish, tobacco, sugar, liquor, cloth, kerosene, paper, and pottery multiplied. The amount spent on liquor, tobacco, and sugar jumped two to three times. Tobacco consumption per capita climbed up from 0.42 yen in 1915 to 5.23 in 1942.[70] Spending on clothing and in all other nonfood categories in constant yen expanded 74 and 300 percent, respectively. The percentage of income spent in these two categories rose from 10 to 13.1 percent and from 6.5 to 19 percent, respectively, between 1920 and 1940. In terms of relative consumption, the percentage of income spent on nonfood items was boosted from 16.5 percent in 1920 to 32 percent in 1940.

The quality of goods and services consumed also improved. Consumers on the whole used more refined manufactured goods. One estimate shows that the use of manufactured consumer goods expanded from about 20 percent in 1920 to 44 percent in 1940, while the use of coarse nonmanufactured goods declined proportionately. The quality of some foodstuffs appears to have improved. While consumption of crude foodstuffs declined radically, that of processed foods clearly increased. A similar picture emerged in the area of health care. The number of physicians, dentists, pharmacists, and nurses increased under colonial rule. Deaths from contagious diseases declined, and life expectancy and survival rates improved.[71]

Notwithstanding the rise and improvements of goods and services, not all embellishments contributed to the improvement of people's welfare. The construction of roads and railroads in Korea, for instance, was undertaken mainly for military purposes, especially in the initial stage. As one Western observer noted, the broad, straight, and well-constructed road system developed in Korea would never have been built for the needs of the natives, as Korea's commerce did not require it. Also, the number of vehicles per person in Korea increased but was still inadequate to meet the people's needs. There were 3.3 bicycles, horse and cow carts, pushcarts, rickshaws, motorcars, and motorcycles per 100 persons in 1938, in contrast to 14.7 in Japan.[72] Also, most modern conveniences were provided in urban areas, benefitting city and urban inhabitants, but the residents in the rural areas, where far fewer modern amenities were available, did not realize this benefit. The urban population increased from about 4 percent of the nation's total population in 1910 to 14 percent in 1938.

Consumption by Nationality

Another feature of personal consumption under Japanese rule was that the increase in consumption and improvement of standard of living affected the Japanese and Koreans quite differently. The rapid advances in modern conveniences, including public utilities and social-overhead capital, did not benefit both nationalities equally. As far as the majority of Japanese were concerned, the increased spending and an improved standard of living were clearly visible.[73] Since 71 percent of Japanese were concentrated in cities in 1938, the majority of them were obviously on the receiving end of modern public goods. Again, the majority of Koreans who lived in the rural areas, where far fewer modern amenities were available, derived little benefit.

Whether families had electricity and gas varied widely between Japanese and Koreans. As late as 1939, only 12.5 percent of Korean families had electricity in their houses, whereas more than 90 percent of Japanese families did. Gas service was available only in large cities. Even in Seoul, only 1 out of every 103 Korean families used gas in 1938, while one out of every two Japanese families did. In the second largest city, Pyongyang, the ratio was even worse for Koreans, 1 out of 905. Even as recently as 1943, the Korean families with gas service in Seoul, Daegu, and Busan made up only 6.7 percent (1,855 out of 27,700) of all households, while Japanese households made up 97.1 percent.[74] As one official source reported, the demand for gas in Korea was almost exclusively from Japanese and foreigners.

A comparable situation prevailed in the use of telephones. As the economy developed, the number of telephones increased in Korea, from 8,353 in 1912 to 43,502 in 1941 for the Japanese and from 483 to 17,620 for Koreans during the same period. Although the number of telephones used by Koreans increased more (fortyfold between 1912 and 1941) than for the Japanese (fivefold), the Japanese, who constituted less than 3 percent of the population in Korea, had 71.1 percent of all the telephones in the country. In 1942, one out of every four Japanese households had a telephone, while only one out of every 250 Korean households did. A similar situation was found in the use of the telegraph. Between 1910 and 1930, telegraph usage in Korea was only 10 percent of that in Japan. The number of post offices in Korea increased from 516 in 1905 to 1,296 in 1940, and the number of telegraph stations increased as well. The Japanese used postal and telegraph services far more frequently than did Koreans, about ten times more in 1937.[75]

Health care received by the Japanese was far superior to that available to Koreans. Japanese had seven to twenty-one times more access to hospitals, physicians, dentists, pharmacists, midwives, and nurses. Although the number of Korean medical doctors increased from 72 in 1912 to 836 in 1930 and the number of Japanese physicians rose from 353 to 779, the number of doctors available per Japanese overwhelmed the number of those available to Koreans. Since most Japanese and Koreans tended to go to their own health-care providers, the health-care services rendered to Japanese far outpaced those available to the Koreans, apparently, by as much as thirty-three times. Figures for 1938 show that almost as many Japanese, who made up less than a fraction of the population, as Koreans were cared for in government hospitals. The percentage of deaths from contagious diseases was about 20 percent of the afflicted for Koreans and 13 percent for Japanese.[76]

In contrast to most consumption goods and services, there was a progressive deterioration in the quantity and quality of food consumed over time by the majority of Koreans under Japanese administration. Although calculations of grain consumption vary from one data source to another, one common finding is an absolute decrease in food consumption by Koreans under Japanese rule, as the figures in Table 9.6 demonstrate. The supply of rice, which accounted for about 60 percent of all calories consumed by Koreans and Japanese, fluctuated from year to year, depending on the harvests. However, on the whole, Korean consumption of rice clearly declined over time (e.g., from an annual average of 33,576,000 *seok* in 1922–1926 to 33,063,000 in 1927–1931 and 32,063,000 in 1932–1936), a decrease of about 4.5 percent in about fifteen years. During the same period, the population

TABLE 9.6 Production and Domestic Consumption of Rice During 1910 and 1930 (million *seok* and percent)

	Million Seok				
		Domestic Consumption			
Year	Production	Total	Change	Marginal Propensity to Consume	Ratio of Consumption to Production in Percent
1910	1.04	—	—	—	—
1911	1.06	—	—	—	—
1912	1.09	1.04	0.05	—	95.4
1913	1.21	1.15	0.06	1.00	95.0
1914	1.41	1.26	0.15	1.73	89.4
1915	1.28	1.07	0.21	1.04	83.6
1916	1.39	1.19	0.20	0.75	85.6
1917	1.37	1.18	0.19	0.68	86.1
1918	1.53	1.29	0.24	0.83	84.3
1919	1.27	1.02	0.25	0.79	80.3
1920	1.49	1.27	0.22	0.68	85.2
1921	1.43	1.12	0.31	0.99	78.3
1922	1.50	1.15	0.35	0.88	76.7
1923	1.52	1.15	0.37	0.80	75.7
1924	1.32	0.91	0.41	1.06	68.9
1925	1.48	0.96	0.52	1.45	64.9
1926	1.53	0.97	0.56	1.16	63.4
1927	1.73	1.03	0.70	1.25	59.5
1928	1.35	0.77	0.58	1.04	57.0
1929	1.37	0.80	0.57	1.60	58.4
1930	1.92	1.16	0.76	1.44	60.4
Average	1.39	1.08	0.35	1.06	76.2

Sources: The table in constructed on the data supplied in H. Kajimura 1989.

of Korea increased from 17.6 to 22 million persons, or 25 percent. Thus, rice consumption per capita decreased nearly 30 percent during the fifteen-year period. Similarly, the Bank of Korea's data show that per capita rice consumption in Korea decreased from about 0.71 *seok* during 1915–1919 to 0.43 during 1930–1936, a 40 percent drop. A more representative estimate appears to have been a decrease of about 22 percent, from 0.7 *seok* in 1915 to 0.55 in 1944. In normal times, much of the rice sent to Japan was obtained by curtailing the rice consumption of the Koreans. For example, Koreans produced 24,138,874 *seok* in 1942 but were forced to export nearly 40 percent of it (or 9,521,000 *seok*) to Japan, keeping only about 60 percent of the harvest for their own consumption.[77]

Per capita consumption of rice in Korea was considerably lower than that in Japan. It has been calculated that when annual Korean rice consumption decreased from 0.78 *seok* in 1912 to 0.41 in 1933, that of Japan actually increased from 1.07 *seok* to 1.1 *seok*. Other data show that while per capita consumption of rice in Korea decreased 41 percent, from 0.694 to 0.412 *seok* between 1914 and 1933, the per capita consumption of rice in Japan increased by about 10 percent, from 0.981 to 1.095 *seok*. In 1934–1938, the average per capita consumption of rice in Korea was 0.396 *seok* in contrast to 1.089 in Japan.[78]

The decrease in rice consumption by Koreans was somewhat offset by an increase in the consumption of grains such as millet and barley. Consumption of millet per capita increased 15 percent, from 0.27 to 0.31 *seok*, during 1912–1938. However, according to one estimate, per capita consumption of rice, barley, and millet combined (the main staple foods in Korea) declined from 1.25 *seok* in 1912–1915 to 1.08 in 1931–1935, a decrease of 14 percent. The daily per capita calorie intake from these grains declined from 2,133 during 1912–1915 to 1,812 during 1931–1935, a decline of about 15 percent.

The decline in food consumption beyond 1935 was even greater than those figures indicate. The Japanese government introduced the rationing of cereals and other basic foodstuffs during the war years. Compared with the Japanese consumption of cereals, the average per capita consumption of Koreans in 1936 was about 71 percent (248 and 176 kilograms, respectively). The percentage of income spent on foodstuffs in Korea decreased from 83.5 percent in 1920 to 68 percent in 1940. Worst of all, food consumption from 1938 to 1944 probably decreased at least 15 percent. One calculation shows that per capita consumption of cereals and beans in Korea decreased from 2.032 *seok* in 1915–1919 to 1.32 in 1941–1944, a 35 percent drop.[79]

In addition, the quality of the grain consumed certainly deteriorated over time, although Mitsuhiko Kimura did not find that the nutritional status of Koreans suffered under Japanese rule.[80] In Korea, as well as in most other Asian countries, including Japan, rice was generally considered the superior grain.[81] Thus, the increased substitution of "inferior" grains, such as millet, for rice in Korea represented a deterioration of the country's standard of living.

Income Groups

The available data on the personal consumption levels of different income groups among Koreans, though limited and fragmentary, indicate that various income groups not only enjoyed different standards of living, but they also derived varying degrees of improvement under Japanese rule. Although the propensity to meet the requirements for "proper" Confucian ethics and those expenditures involving traditional rituals, such as ancestor worship, funerals, weddings, and anniversaries,[82] diminished somewhat under Japanese rule, the wealthy, upper strata and some middle-income Koreans continued to maintain these habits and expenditures. Surpluses were also spent to support a large number of hangers-on, to extend charity, and to entertain extensively and lavishly. Moreover, some Koreans indulged in conspicuous consumption by maintaining mansions and concubines. They improved their standard of living as their incomes increased, but they also acquired the higher standard of living by imitating Japanese and Western ways of life.

In contrast, the working farmers—the majority of the Korean people—did not fare as well as the wealthy landlords. The expenses of the average Korean farm household were much less than those of the average Japanese farm household. The Korean household spent 78.9 percent of its income on necessities, while the Japanese spent 62.6 percent. The major portion of the Korean family budget was spent on food—60.7 percent compared with the Japanese's 42.4 percent. Thus, it is not surprising that only small amounts of Western-type consumer goods were imported for mass consumption. Korean farm households spent much less on such "luxuries" as entertainment, health care, education, and hobbies than did the Japanese (e.g., 21 percent of total expenditures in Korea in contrast to 37 percent in Japan).[83] In yen, it was only one-half. Korean farm households spent, on average, only 7.4 percent of their budgets on entertainment, while the Japanese spent almost double, 14.2 percent. While Japanese farmers spent 5 percent on hobbies and 5.7 percent on health care, Korean farmers spent 1.9 percent and 1.4 percent, respectively.

The low standard of living of Korean farmers was reported in a number of surveys and studies over time. A colonial-government investigation conducted in 1929 showed that 837,000 families lacked the adequate means of subsistence. Another survey indicated that 1.25 million families (48.3 percent of all farm households) were gathering grass and bark for food in 1930, a year that had experienced an excellent harvest. Farmers who had consumed all of their grain by early spring were subsisting on a "starvation diet" until the summer crops could be harvested in June. Most in this group were tenants (68.1 percent of the total), but 37.3 percent were owner-tenants and 18.4 percent were owner-cultivators.[84] A similar situation prevailed in 1933, when 71.4 percent (1,233 out of 1,728 surveyed) of tenants and 42.3 percent (786 out of 1,859 surveyed) of owner/tenants experienced food shortages. Even as late as 1939, 39 and 26 percent of these groups, respectively, were short of food.

Shirushi, writing in 1940, reported that 1.4 million families, making up more than 40 percent of all farmers, did not have enough food.[85] Yet he described overall conditions as "a striking picture of the gradual improvement of the Korean village" and spoke of the return to a "natural economy," because the farmers had no means with which to buy much. The most difficult time for farmers continued to be "the spring hunger season" (*chungunggi*). Family budgets of three representative Korean farmers showed that 75 to 80 percent of them had a deficit budget and experienced a "shortage of foodstuffs."[86] On the whole, farming under Japanese rule changed little and experienced what today would seem to be very modest improvements: elementary sanitation, the kerosene lamp, machine-made cloth, and rubber shoes.

Among all Koreans, the tenants, who constituted the majority not only of the farmers but also the entire population in Korea, experienced the least improved standard of living. Thus, most tenant farmers lacked the resources to consume much beyond the subsistence level. Even the supply of food was scarce in some years. Rice available for consumption by the family was only 0.41 *seok* per person, which was barely adequate to meet its nutritional needs. Most tenants (80 percent of 2.9 million farm households or 2.3 million families) found themselves in this situation almost every spring.[87] It thus seems reasonable to deduce that small tenant farmers were relatively untouched by the increased agricultural productivity and production and general economic expansion in the country under Japanese rule.

Korean businessmen, similar to the *yangban* aristocracy, were ambitious, but their path to power lay in a different direction. Unlike the aristocrats of the traditional period, businessmen knew that their power rested in their businesses. The mere fact of their independent status as profit makers and employers of other people, combined with their wealth, assured them social prestige. There is little evidence to show that they engaged in conspicuous consumption, and most of them seem to have maintained a relatively frugal way of life.

There are no comprehensive data indicating the level of consumption of wage earners, but it is clear that poverty prevailed for most Korean workers (mostly laborers). The base of the pyramid that rested on the wage earners as well as peasants during the traditional and transitional periods continued after the Japanese takeover. An investigation conducted by the Government General in 1929 showed that while the daily earnings of a laborer in Korea were 70 *sen*, his daily expenses were 54 *sen,* leaving only 16 *sen* to support his family. According to another study, the monthly wage of an urban worker was about 28 yen, and a family of five, which was probably below the average at the time, needed 1 yen a day for rent, electricity, rice, firewood, soy paste, textiles, sugar, tobacco, and soap. The family budget for most Korean workers had no provision for meat, fish, alcoholic beverages, paper, shoes, or the expenses of frequent births, burials, and the like.[88]

Thus, the majority of Korean workers (mostly laborers) could not easily support their families on their earnings of a single breadwinner. For many families, more than one earner was needed to support the entire family. One American businessman observed that the workers looked pale and seedy. As far as housing was concerned, Kimura found in his study little if any improvement in housing.[89] Worse, he concluded that it generally deteriorated as people left their villages for urban shanty towns. They lived in single-room houses or apartments where their families swarmed "like rabbits."[90] Korea under colonial rule lagged far behind most industrial countries in the provision of social security. Some signs of improvement in the standard of living of the mass of the Korean people on the whole were detected in the later years of colonial administration, but the character of consumption did not change much under Japanese rule. As a result, the inequalities and insecurities inherent in the economic situation were allowed to continue largely unchecked.

While consumption among the majority of wage earners continued to be low, there was a slow rise in the level of consumption among salaried and professional workers under colonial rule. The rise in their income stimulated consumption among some of these Koreans. Many of them came to enjoy modern conveniences, such as electricity, better housing, and education. Some were able to maintain a standard of living comparable to that of the middle- and the lower-middle-income Japanese; and toward the end of colonial rule a few even maintained a high standard of living comparable to that of the well-to-do Japanese.

It is difficult to aggregate the standard of living into an overall index, but it is reasonably clear that a net improvement in the standard of living for the majority of Koreans, though limited, did prevail. However, they did not really benefit much from the amenities of economic expansion, nor did they experience much improvement in their standard of living. While the standard of living of the upper class clearly improved, the character of consumption for most, especially among tenant farmers and laborers, changed little under Japanese colonial rule.[91]

PERSONAL AND BUSINESS SAVINGS OF KOREANS

Having noted aggregate private savings in Korea under Japanese rule in chapter 7, let us now probe in detail the savings of four income groups: landlords and the wealthy classes, businessmen, farmers, and wage earners, to determine their contribution to capital formation in the country. Although the limited data do not allow a thorough assessment, a few pieces of information reveal reasonably clearly the magnitude and pattern of the personal and business savings of these groups for capital formation.

Personal Savings

It is obvious from the information assembled here that the potential of saving for landlords was high and certainly improved markedly under colonial rule over the earlier traditional and transitional periods. According to a government study, the average landlord with more than 20 *jeong* of land had a surplus of 52.1 percent out of an average income of 10,712 yen in 1925.[92] In 1932 the average landlord enjoyed a "surplus" of about 87 percent of his rice income, most of which would have been available for saving.[93] According to another government study, the landlords, who constituted less than 4 percent of the farm population, received 38.3 percent of the harvest (or on average 11.43 *seok* of rice per person) as income in 1938. This amount was more than ten times their needs, enabling them to save nine-tenths of it. A limited number of well-to-do Koreans (the wealthy, the landlords, *yangban,* former government officials, and even some small owner/cultivators) actually did increase their savings by depositing money in banks and other venues, such as investment in business. Deposits in private commercial banks increased about 30 times under Japanese rule. Some savings were dedicated directly toward investment in businesses.

However, the potential for saving was not fully realized in actual saving for investment in the country. In addition to maintaining a high standard of living, the savings of the well-to-do were used to purchase more land. To a large extent, the practice of *yangban* increasing the size of their estates to achieve power in the traditional period continued under colonial rule. There is no easy way to discern the amount of this financial "investment" in land, but it is thought to have been substantial, as shown in chapter 5. This type of financial investment probably raised the price of land and altered the distribution of landownership without increasing real investment or raising the productivity of land. Some also invested in new businesses in commerce, financial intermediaries, industry, and mining.

The personal savings of the well-to-do were also diverted toward the personal consumption of others. Many funds were used to finance loans to private individuals,[94] continuing the customs and practices common in traditional communities. It was reported that the number of known private lenders in Korea increased from 8,212 in 1927 to 12,088 in 1931, a 47 percent rise, in four years.[95] As there were no banks from which ordinary Korean citizens could readily borrow money, the rich in Korea acted as lenders. A significant portion of loans of small farmers was obtained from these individuals. The reported figures ranged from 25.6 percent of total indebtedness to more than 60 percent in 1932 and 43.1 percent in 1936.[96]

In contrast to landlords, most Korean farmers did not have much income to save, nor did they actually save. Instead, the majority appear to have had deficit family budgets. A government report of 1935 described three representative Korean farmers, each with a cash deficit, as noted earlier. Another survey of the condition of three representative Korean farmers in 1939–1940 revealed that all three had experienced family budget deficits ranging from 10.80 to 23.20 yen and average debts ranging from 40 to 130 yen. The budget deficits of small farmers were somewhat smaller. Tenant farmers registered deficit family budgets between 13.91 to 31.6 yen in 1938–1941, while a typical Korean farmer in 1942 incurred a deficit of 44.81 yen. As consumption expenditures accounted for all of or more than their incomes, the majority of farmers were left with virtually no savings. Many actually dissaved. The dissavings of Korean farmers were larger than those of the Japanese. A typical Korean farmer in 1942 incurred a deficit 4.65 times higher than the average Japanese farm household incurred (9.63 yen).

One consequence of dissaving was indebtedness, which continued into the colonial period, as was the case during the traditional and transitional periods. Indebted families accounted for 46.6 percent of all farm households in 1924,[97] approximately 77 percent of all tenant farmers in 1930, 92.6 percent of sampled households in one province in 1932, about 78 percent in 1933, and 40 percent (more than 1.4 million families) in 1940. A Rural Self-Help Movement report indicated that out of the total number of households (78,472) under its guidance in 1935–1936, about 80 percent were in debt and 55 percent showed a debit balance for those years.[98]

There are no comprehensive or accurate data on debts per capita, but they were small in amount. This type of small debt prevailed in every province, the sum ranging from 38 to 121 yen per household. The indebtedness of small farmers was somewhat smaller than the average farmers. Their indebtedness seems to have increased over time, however. The official average debt per farm household in 1930 was 58.34 yen,[99] with the highest being 420 yen. The average indebtedness increased to 103 yen in 1932, 115 in 1933, and 232 in 1936, though it decreased to about 200 in 1940. The debt per family seems small but, in relation to the farmers' income the debt burdens were sizable, incurring large interest payments. Most farmers had to hand over a large portion of their crops as interest for loans at a rate of 3 or 4 percent per month.[100] The annual interest payment of an average borrower was 46.16 yen, which was equivalent to about a quarter of farm operating costs. The debts of all tenant farmers except a small number of large tenants represented 0.8 to 5.7 percent of their income, and the debt of the typical poor farmer averaged 4 percent of his income, although the average farmer had a surplus of 9.2 percent from farming. The payments of interest on farmers' debts together with rent on tenanted land probably amounted to a third or more of total net income in farming. Aggregate indebtedness of these farm households in the country was substantial. The total debt of 1.73 million farm households in 1930, according to official reports, was estimated at 101.1 million yen, which increased to 128 million in 1932.[101] However, many studies showed that the total debt in agriculture was even much larger than the reported sum. One estimate sets the amount borrowed by farmers including that from private individuals at 491.2 million yen,[102] while Hoon Ku Lee calculated the total indebtedness of the agricultural sector in 1930 at not less than 500 million yen,[103] which far exceeded the value of capital stock owned by Koreans in modern industries at the time. Another estimate placed total agricultural indebtedness, including the debts of the irrigation associations, even higher, at 700 to 800 million yen in 1940. Private moneylenders typically charged interest rates as high as 48 percent a year,[104] based usually on the pledge of the coming fall crop as collateral.

Many of these loans were used for purposes other than productive investment. As a matter of fact, most of them were made for living expenses so that the borrowers would be able to tide themselves over. A survey of loans in a province (Hamgyeong-bukdo) showed that loans to farm families were made primarily for consumption purposes, mainly for food. Similarly, a survey in another province (Hamgyeong-namdo) indicated that the largest percentage of loans (39 percent) was contracted so that the borrowers could purchase food. This was followed by 18 percent for weddings, funerals, and other ceremonies; 9 percent for disasters; 5 percent for the repayment of previous loans; and 6 percent for other purposes. Loans for investment comprised only 23 percent of the total. Similar survey results were reported in other provinces in 1930, 1931, 1932, 1937, and 1939–1940.[105]

There are no comprehensive statistics on the savings of wage earners, but a situation similar to that of tenant farmers prevailed during most of the period under Japanese rule. Poverty among the majority of wage earners was such that savings were minimal. This is indicated in a number of ways. One good piece of evidence is the small amount of savings deposited by the masses in the postal savings system and banks. Deposit balances in the postal savings system averaged between 3.3 to 5.4 yen between 1910 and 1938. The savings of small earners in Korea under Japanese rule was no different from those in other developing countries, where typically less than 1 percent of national income was saved. In more prosperous countries, these savings were around 4 percent of national income.[106] Wage earners in Korea under Japanese rule probably contributed an insignificant amount, certainly no more than 1 percent of national income.

While saving among the majority of the wage earners continued to be low, there were, however, signs of a slow rise in the savings of salaried and professional workers and even small-wage earners toward the end of Japanese rule. No reliable or comparable statistical data are available, but fragmentary evidence shows that such savings increased over time. Middle-class families that earned 2,000 yen a year typically saved 10 to 20 percent of it in the later years of the colonial period. Some of their savings were deposited in banks or used to start small businesses. White-collar workers also saved to educate their children or provide for their old age. However, as these savings represented merely a postponement of future consumption and were largely offset by other forms of postponed consumption, they were not particularly important in the context of productive investment. Moreover, on the whole these savings were too small to contribute much to the country's aggregate need for investment. Thus, the savings of the middle classes appear to have had not much impact on the nation's productive investment. It seems reasonable, therefore, to conclude that the mass of the people—upward of 75 percent of the population—who received about 40 percent or so of total household income, were able to contribute little to the nation's capital formation.

Business Savings

For the businessman, since the road to success lay in his business, his independent status, and personal security depended mainly on family thrift and saving. In no other way could a businessman provide for the future. Unlike the *yangban,* businessmen believed that they had a duty to produce a surplus. The profit maker knew that the best investments were those that exploited new technologies and resources by dedicating their savings to it. As their incomes increased and the safety of their wealth under Japanese rule became better guaranteed, their profits were saved and invested in their enterprises. The profit motive operated among small industrialists and tradesmen as well as large-scale entrepreneurs.

A major portion of the nation's savings invested in business may be attributable to businesses, which were owned and operated by the upper-income and some middle-income groups, as well as some small businesses. No reliable or comprehensive statistical data are available, nor is it possible to calculate them. Nonetheless, a few scattered figures, such as the rise in business investment, show that saving among members of the business class was substantial. Certainly, it was greater than during the traditional and transitional periods. The mere expansion of businesses and investments in them under Japanese rule are a clear indication of increased savings for real investment. For 1930, corporate savings in the country were estimated at 204 million yen, or 24 percent of corporate profits, and they rose to 756 million yen, or 37 percent of net profits, in 1937. As a fraction of aggregate savings, they may have run to 20 to 40 percent, and their share of the total rose steadily with the spread of the corporate form of organization.

In this way, profits grew relative to national income and the share of national income that was reinvested increased over time. Assuming that the share of savings of the Korean-owned company was about 8 percent of the total, their contribution to aggregate savings in the late 1930s would have been as much as 2 percent of national income. The major benefits of the growth in production, thus, went to business owners who channeled their saving into investment in industry and industrial production.[107] Likewise, the increase in production, in turn, opened up new opportunities for trade and profits. This was a key mechanism through which savings potential was augmented for investment and economic development under Japanese rule.

SUMMARY AND CONCLUSIONS

This chapter has examined the impact of capital formation, economic development, and structural changes on income distribution, consumption, and saving for investment in Korea under Japanese rule. We have found a number of unique and significant features. As far as income distribution is concerned, while the level of income per capita increased overall, its fruits were not shared equitably, nor were they enjoyed equally by different sectors or segments of people in the country under colonial rule. Farm income on the whole did increase, but only modestly. Within the agricultural sector, the income gains of the landlords were substantial, certainly greater than during the traditional or transitional periods and significantly larger than those of the tenants, whose earnings improved the least among all groups of Korean people under Japanese rule, as has been the case for centuries. On the other hand, the majority of Japanese farmers in Korea came to own adequately large plots and earned fairly comfortable income.

Business incomes in the form of profits multiplied many times and were substantially more under Japanese rule than during the traditional or transitional period. Much of the benefits of rising productivity went to profits rather than being shared fairly with workers. Within the business sector, the rates of return on investment in large corporations in general were higher than those in small businesses. In comparison with profits, workers on the whole made only modest gains, substantially below their productivity increases, and continued to suffer under low wages and poor working conditions, although these improved somewhat toward the end of the colonial administration.

One glaring feature of income distribution under Japanese rule was the prevalence of conspicuous differences in earnings between Japanese and Korean workers. Japanese had higher incomes in all walks of life. In the farming sector, many of the large Japanese landlords had higher returns on investment than their Korean counterparts. Likewise, in the business sector, Japanese enterprises were larger and enjoyed higher profit margins than did the Koreans. Korean enterprises were almost as numerous as the Japanese, but as a rule they were small and engaged in businesses in highly competitive markets in which prices were kept low, resulting in low profits.

In the labor market, while the Japanese held most of the well-paying, white-collar, managerial, professional, and skilled positions in government and businesses, Korean workers typically made up almost all of the seemingly unlimited supply of unskilled workers, who held subordinate and low-paying positions in all sectors. Moreover, Koreans with similar qualifications in the form of education, training, and/or experience received substantially lower wages (about half), than their Japanese counterparts in the same occupations. Fringe benefits for Japanese workers were superior to those of Koreans. Moreover, the working hours of the majority of Koreans were longer and the working conditions poorer than those of the Japanese. Likewise, the unemployment rate for Korean workers was much higher than that of the Japanese. These differences between Japanese and Koreans narrowed somewhat toward the end of Japanese rule, however.

The second main question examined in this chapter, the impact of economic development and structural changes on the standard of living of people in Korea under colonial rule, is not easy to aggregate into an overall index, but it is clear that the standard of living for the majority of Koreans did improve, though in a limited way. However, there were notable differences in the level of consumption between Japanese and Koreans. The standard of living for well-to-do and some upper-strata Koreans as well as Japanese living in Korea improved markedly. Even some middle-income Koreans imitated Japanese and Western ways of life and maintained higher standard of living than during the transitional period as their incomes increased. There is little evidence to show that businessmen engaged in conspicuous consumption, but they seem to have also maintained a relatively comfortable, yet frugal, way of life.

The majority of Koreans, however, did not really benefit much from the amenities of "economic progress," nor did they experience much improvement in their standard of living. For most, the character of consumption changed little under Japanese rule. In fact, for most Koreans there was a progressive deterioration of food consumption. Among Koreans, the worst off were the small farmers, especially the tenants, who constituted more than half of the total population. The lives of these farmers under colonial rule were relatively untouched by the general economic expansion. There are no comprehensive data indicating the level of consumption of wage earners, especially manual laborers, but it is clear that poverty prevailed for most Korean workers as well. While consumption among the majority of wage earners continued to be low, there was a slow rise in the level of consumption among salaried and professional workers under Japanese administration.

As the national income expanded, the ability and willingness of Koreans to save enhanced. It is obvious from the examination in this chapter that the potential of the landlords for saving was high and certainly expanded markedly under colonial rule. The *yangban* and landlords saved more than in the transitional period, although only small amounts of savings were directed toward productive investment. In contrast to landlords, the majority of Korean farmers did not have much income to save, nor did they actually save. Instead, they continued to dissave and fall into debt. Many of their loans were used for purposes other than productive investment. There are no comprehensive statistics on the savings of wage earners, but a situation similar to that of tenant farmers seems to have prevailed during most of the period under Japanese rule. Poverty among the majority of wage earners was such that savings were minimal.

While saving among the majority of the wage earners continued to be low, there were, however, signs of a slow rise in the savings of salaried and professional workers and even small-wage earners toward the end of colonial rule. Some of their savings were deposited in banks or used to start small businesses. White-collar workers also saved to educate their children or provide for their old age. Nonetheless, as these savings represented merely a postponement of future consumption and were largely offset by other forms of postponed consumption, they were not important in the context of productive investment.

Unlike the *yangban,* businessmen believed that they had a duty to produce a surplus, and most of them did save their profits and invest them in their businesses, including profits in the form of corporate savings. As their incomes increased and the safety of their wealth under Japanese administration became better guaranteed, their profits were saved and invested in their enterprises. A major portion of Korean savings invested in business may be attributable to businesses, which were owned and operated by the upper-income and some middle-income groups. Nonetheless, the savings of Korean people on the whole were not sufficient to support the country's investment needs to accommodate the economic growth achieved under colonial rule.

10

SUMMARY AND CONCLUSIONS

Through a focus on capital formation, economic development, and structural changes, this study has examined the transformation of the isolated and independent Korea into a dependent colonial economy between 1876 and 1945. During this seventy-year period under sieges by foreign powers, Korea went through three distinct stages of economic transformation: the traditional economy, before the opening of the country to the outside world in 1876; the transitional economy, between 1876 and 1904; and the colonial economy under Japan, between 1905 and 1945. This examination has revealed a number of significant, though perhaps not all unique, patterns and characteristics of capital formation, economic development, and structural changes in Korea. The combination of circumstances, approaches, and experiences in the country was in many respects atypical, and several major conclusions may be drawn from them.

Before the Korea, a hermit kingdom, was forcibly opened to the outside world in 1876, it had the familiar underdeveloped, agrarian-based economy of the preindustrial age. Its traditional economy was isolated and essentially static, characterized by a relatively low propensity to work and produce, and under the rule of the oppressive and ineffective government of the Josean dynasty. There was a lack of capital, because of a combination of low level of income, dampened propensity to save and invest, and the discouragement of entrepreneurial activities: the vicious cycle of poverty. These interdependent forces inhibited capital formation and economic development. In this respect, Korea before 1876 was no different from many traditional economies, including those of China and Japan before the onslaught of Western influence and the Industrial Revolution. Capital formation was inadequate to warrant economic development beyond what could accommodate a slight increase in population. The aggregate GDP of Korea in 1876 probably was about $8.86 billion, and per capita income of approximately $720 (in year-2000 U.S. prices).

During the transitional period between 1876 and 1904, after the country was opened to the outside world, the Korean economy experienced some changes but, unfortunately, not much headway was made under its own sovereign government. No substantial progress in capital formation, economic development, or structural change took place. Initially, the country resisted alien beliefs, ways of life, and investments before these were imposed upon it from without, and they were accepted by most Koreans only passively in later years. Slowly, outsiders, especially the Christian missionaries, Japanese, and more progressive Korean leaders educated abroad, began to awaken the Korean people to the challenges of the external forces. However, these influences were trifling. As late as 1904 the Korean economy was in shambles, with cottage industries continuing to supply the bare essentials. Capital formation was just sufficient to support a small population growth without much improvement in the standard of living of the people. Aggregate GDP had expanded perhaps by no more than 10 percent, to about $9.76 billion in 1904, while per capita income virtually stood still ($745 in year-2000 U.S. prices, a 3.5 percent rise) during the thirty-year period, as in the traditional period.

It seems reasonable to conclude that during the traditional and transitional periods Korea was simply not transformed sufficiently to make discernible economic progress. Koreans were not as receptive to Western ways as the Japanese were in the Meiji Reformation period, although they were perhaps more ready for Western ideas and technology than were the Chinese at the time. The majority of the Korean people were staunchly conservative and wedded to the traditional isolationist Confucian beliefs. No group, neither the leadership of the government, the nation's elite, nor the masses, had gained ample knowledge, experience, or the will to inspire the country to modernize its economy. Neither did the country have the desire to save an adequate amount of resources and invest in new capital goods for economic development. There were some attempts at reform before 1905, but they were ineffectual and failed to muster sufficient forces to adequately meet the needs of the new and modern economy before the country was taken over by the Imperial Japan.

With the onset of Japanese rule, a major economic, as well as political, transformation took place in Korea. Japanese administration swiftly and mercilessly undertook institutional and economic reforms under forceful government stewardship and began its active participation in molding Korea's economic path. After it annexed Korea, Japan effectively abolished the established authority of traditional political, religious, and social leaders and swept away many traditions inimical to economic change. In their place it laid the foundation of a modern economy with opportune infrastructure and financial institutions, including the freedom of entrepreneurship, the protection of property rights, accommodating incorporation laws, currency reforms, and land surveys and improvements, all modeled on its own image.

Japanese rule was accompanied by large investment in the colony. Net investment under Japanese rule is estimated to have been about 9 to 10 percent of GDP. Investment in Korea was undertaken by both the public and private sectors. The government contributed nearly 22 percent of all investment in Korea, while the private sector contributed more than three-quarters. It is worth noting that after taking over Korea, the colonial government invested more heavily in the country than what was found before 1905 and, also, that typically was seen in many developed economies at that time. Public investment focused on the construction of social-overhead capital, such as railways, communications systems, modern ports and harbors, irrigation works for farmland, and hospitals. The largest and most important investment of the colonial government was in railroads, which came to represent nearly one-fifth of all capital in Korea under Japanese rule.

Private investment was largely concentrated in manufacturing (both heavy and light industries), mining, and electric-power generation, which used modern technology and produced the necessary light consumer and heavy military-related goods. In comparison, a relatively small amount of real investment took place in agriculture other than that devoted to rice production for export to Japan, which involved the construction of irrigation systems for paddy fields, dams, and the conversion of wasteland into farmland. Investments in commerce and banking were relatively modest.

The magnitude and the nature of private investment were largely influenced by financial incentives provided by the government through fiscal and financial policies favorable to investors. In addition to the benefits provided by generous indirect subsidies, direct government subsidies to businesses constituted more than 20 percent of the government budget, while few taxes were assessed on income and business before 1936. Even thereafter, these taxes were lenient, lower, and less progressive than those in Japan, and the government budget was financed largely with land and consumption taxes, which fell most heavily upon the shoulders of peasants and consumers, supplemented by Japanese government grants from Tokyo. The subsidies, low taxes, tax exemptions, and subsidized bank loans were provided mostly to industries and enterprises considered to be of strategic interest to Japan, such as chemical and heavy industries, mines, rice production, and were mostly to favored Japanese businesses. The greatest beneficiaries of these government policies were the big *zaibatsu*, which emerged as virtual partners of the government.

Another important, perhaps crucial, instrument for promoting private investment was the extension of loans for financing investment to designated industries and agriculture. These credits, which constituted the major portion of business and agricultural investment, enabled new and/or expanding businesses to employ idle resources and produce targeted output. Faithfully following government policies, more than four-fifths of long-term loans were extended by the government-established banks and GNBFIs at the subsidized interest rates. The largest portion of these loans was directed toward meeting the changing needs of Japan: initially in commerce, followed by agriculture, and in modern industries in later years. In contrast, the private banks and PNBFIs were more limited in their ability to finance investment, since their loanable funds were constrained by government policies. Their loans were typically less than one-fifth of those of all financial institutions, and most of them were extended for short-term commercial rather than long-term industrial and agricultural loans. Also, more loans were extended to Japanese businesses and landlords than to the Koreans. Japanese businesses relied more on loans from public banks and GNBFIs than their Korean counterparts did. In contrast, Korean investments were financed mostly with their own savings in the form of equity capital, relying less on loans from banks and NBFIs.

Resources that enabled the financial intermediaries to extend business loans for investment came mainly from deposits and external borrowing. One-half to three-fifths of financial resources of the organized financial institutions were acquired from deposits, while most of their remaining sums were derived from external borrowing by means of bond issues floated by the public banks and GNBFIs, as well as the printing machine of the Bank of Korea. The public banks and GNBFIs thus played the important and strategic role of mobilizing savings in Korea and Japan and then channeling them into investment that Japan prescribed. Their role in capital formation was especially notable in the absence of a public securities market, the lack of which left businesses increasingly dependent on big public banks for financing their investment. This setup, whatever its shortcomings, served to divert a considerable amount of savings into investment for industrialization and the expansion of agricultural production dictated by Japan.

The volume and the nature of investment made by Japanese and Koreans differed a great deal. In terms of the volume of investment, the Japanese dominated. Approximately 84 percent of private investment was made by them, and their investment was prevalent in all fields during 1905–1945. A large volume of their investment was in electric power; heavy, chemical, and defense-oriented industries, and mining, and the Japanese played a critical role as leaders and innovators in the modernization into an open but state-led economy. Not all Japanese investments in Korea were profit motivated: some major public investment projects, such as railroads and communications systems, were undertaken for political, rather than financial, reasons. This practice was rather unique among colonial powers.

Of the total investment in Korea, in both the public and private sectors, more than half of the investment was financed from Japan, while about 45 percent of the total investment was financed in Korea. Resources that financed investment in Korea were largely supplied by Japanese savings in Japan and Korea. It is estimated that more than 86 percent of the total investment (including both public and private) in the country was financed by Japanese savings in Korea and Japan, constituting more than 95 percent of the total public investment and nearly 84 percent of the private investment. Japanese resources were brought to Korea through their direct investment—mostly in companies headquartered in Japan and Korea—Japanese government grants, credit extended to the colonial government, public financial institutions, and businesses, as well as the savings of individual Japanese in Korea and some Korean savings.

The magnitude of Japanese contribution to capital formation in Korea is striking in the sense that even under the most favorable circumstances the financing of investment by a foreign country in a less developed country that is poor in natural resources is apt to be small, however strategic it might be in other respects, such as politically. The difference in Korea's capital formation under colonial rule from that of Japan in its early stages of economic development was not only the difference in timing but also the role of foreign capital in the two countries. While Japan relied more or less exclusively on its own, not foreign, savings or resources for investment in its development effort more than a half century earlier, Korea relied heavily on Japanese savings for its investment. This unique aspect of Japanese investment in Korea reveals that the motivation for foreign investment in developing countries is not always solely dependent on profit—political motives, too, weigh heavily.

Following the example set by the Japanese, Koreans likewise invested in new businesses under colonial rule, especially after World War I, clearly exceeding the level that had prevailed in the transitional period under its own government. But in comparison with those of the Japanese, investments by Koreans were relatively small, accounting for a little more than 16 percent of total private investment in the country. Notwithstanding their relatively small contribution, it should be noted that the level of investment was over 60 percent more than they were given credit for by most Japanese scholars, usually 10 percent of investment. In contrast with the Japanese, their investment was more or less limited to commerce and light industries oriented toward consumer goods, such as food processing, distilling, and textiles, which typically met the traditional and daily needs of Koreans, and many were in business ventures not far advanced from traditional native manufacturing. Korean savings were contributed mostly by well-to-do Korean aristocrats, former government officials, merchants, and, to some extent, by small and mid-sized landowners.

Substantial capital formation under Japanese rule enabled the Korean economy to realize discernible economic gains, namely, growth and becoming a semi-industrialized modern economy. Korea's GDP and population expanded approximately 120 and 62 percent, respectively, resulting in a rise of per capita GDP of about 56 percent, from about $745 to $1,130 (in year-2000 U.S. prices). Average annual aggregate and per capita GDP during the forty-year period increased about 3 and 1.2 percent, respectively. These rates of growth were not spectacular, but they did show solid gains in production and income compared with the earlier period of modernization in Korea under its own government and with many developing economies at that time.

Accompanying the economic growth, there were substantial changes in the nation's economic structure, from a predominantly agrarian to a semi-industrial economy. Agriculture continued to dominate, but the industrial sector was increasingly modernized, expanded, and important in the economy. Although small businesses were pervasive, also enlarged was the scale of businesses, a change that started slowly but became rapid after World War I. Included among the large-scale businesses were a few towering combines (the Japanese *zaibatsu*), which dominated the economy. Not only did the country's foreign trade expand, the pattern and composition of goods and services traded altered substantially as well. At the same time, and in spite of the fact that the Korean economy became more dependent on Japan, it also developed its own trade network.

Economic reforms, capital formation, and economic development under Japanese rule also had profound effects on later economic growth, public attitudes, and beliefs. Certain Japanese accomplishments eased the path of Korea's future development, because the traditional political and social hierarchy, which often was inimical to future modernization in many other countries, was largely rooted out by the colonial administration. The overthrow of traditional political and economic values and systems under Japanese rule mitigated the potential difficulties of transforming the traditional economy into a rapidly developing and market-oriented economy after World War II in South Korea. Similarly, the catalytic effect, linkage effect, and external economies of Japanese investment had positive impacts on Korean investment. Also, the Japanese contributed to motivating Koreans to do everything possible to show that they could do as well as, if not better than, the Japanese had during and after colonial rule of their own country. This competitive spirit prevails among Koreans to this day. On the other hand, many claims of the so-called drain effect, destruction effect, and economic (not political) oppression effect on the Korean economy from Japanese rule have been exaggerated.

The large Japanese investments in Korea also brought about a few other blessings in disguise for Korea. Capital stocks, human as well as physical, formed and left by the former colonialists—for which the Korean people did not have to pay financially—became the necessary and important ingredient for economic growth during the colonial period and the foundation for economic growth after the liberation from colonial rule. Likewise, the Koreans gained confidence in their ability to accomplish what the Japanese had achieved earlier in their own country, and the former colonized people used Japan's development path and techniques as a model for their own development in South Korea after liberation from Japan. Japan continues to be a country that Koreans watch closely and emulate. In these senses, there were a few silver linings for Korea in Imperial Japan's ambitious but hurtful domination and rule of the country.

Notwithstanding the Japanese contribution to capital formation, economic transformation, and development of Korea, the Japanese imperial adventure in Korea imposed enormous sacrifices on Korean people. Most of all, the Korean people paid a heavy political price. Not only did they suffer the worst political defeat and humiliation in their history when they were subjugated by a country many had considered inferior, but it was also degrading to be treated as second-class citizens in their own country: the large gaps in income distribution and standards of living between Japanese and Koreans in all walks of life and the severely limited opportunities available for education of Koreans. The Koreans who realized the fewest gains under Japanese rule were the tenant farmers, the largest single group in the population, and wage earners, while the landlords and some business owners enjoyed many economic benefits.

Meanwhile, Korea's energy was sapped and its time and creativity were wasted in the service of wanton Japanese imperial ambitions. Some of Korea's savings and resources were drained off for the purpose of financing Japan's reckless imperial and war efforts. The extent of the benefits of the Japanese investment in arsenals, chemical industries, and even railroads to the indigenous population were overstated. How much advantage did ordinary Korean citizens derive from the establishment of an industry that produced sulfate of ammonia in modern Japanese plants to be exported to Japan, even if the proceeds were invested in new Japanese enterprises in Korea for their military? Moreover, heavy industrialization and dependence on trade with Japan distorted Korea's economic growth, because it became "overdeveloped" in areas inappropriate to Korea at its early stage of development and deprived Korea of other areas that were essential to the Korean economy but not important to Japan.

What would have been the prospects for economic development and structural change for Korea had Japan not colonized and instead left it alone as an independent state? Some Korean scholars believe that had the country remained a sovereign state it would have realized greater economic success. It is futile to speculate on this moot question, but it is questionable whether Korea would have achieved greater economic growth as an independent state. The pertinent and crucial questions relative to Korea's possibility for rapid economic growth are, Would Koreans have saved enough resources to finance the necessary investment (e.g., 9–10 percent of GDP)?; Would they have invested more to make up for what Japanese invested in colonial Korea?; and if they had, would their savings have been invested productively?

Had Korea remained an independent country, its economy would probably have developed eventually, but at a later date, at a slower rate of growth, and with greater economic sacrifices to Korean people (in order to save more to make up the foregone Japanese investment) in the short run. It is clear that Korean savings were too meager to adequately support the required investment needs of the country and stimulate economic growth. Moreover, it is questionable whether savings would have all been directed toward productive investment. Considering the marginal attractiveness of investment in Korea at the time, it is doubtful that other foreign countries would have filled the gap had Japan not dedicated its resources to the colony.

Was it, then, worthwhile for Koreans to have substantial capital formation and to realize speedy transformation and economic development under Japanese colonial rule? To most Koreans, it certainly was not. If the Korean people had had a choice, they unquestionably would have chosen the path of political freedom and independence even if it demanded greater economic sacrifices and attained economic growth more slowly than was forced on them by the Japanese. Most Koreans would not have voluntarily traded their sovereignty for accelerated economic growth under colonial rule.

The findings in this study go beyond the matter of Koreans and their economy under Japanese rule; Japanese colonial rule of Korea obviously also had major economic implications on Japan and Japanese. To Japan, the annexation of Korea might have had some benefit in the form of heightened self-esteem and momentary euphoria as it exercised its domination over Korea, as well as enabling Japan to use the country as a springboard to conquer a part of the Asian continent and fulfill its longtime political dream of becoming an empire, for at least forty years. Japanese residents in Korea also were privileged to maintain a high standard of living, However, the question is whether such political solaces and economic gains to some colonialists were worth the enormous sacrifices, human as well as material, that the Japanese people as a whole had to bear. The colonization of Korea placed heavy economic burdens on the entire Japanese population.[1] To conquer and administer the colony, Japan diverted vast amounts of its resources, human as well as material. According to Lockwood, from 1895 to 1935 some 40 to 50 percent of Japan's national budget was regularly allocated for military purposes, which included furnishing grants and servicing loans to support Korea.[2]

In spite of huge amounts of its savings and resources being diverted to Korea, Japan failed to amalgamate Korea into its empire or bring about reconciliation between the two peoples. It did not transform the majority of Koreans into "imperial subjects" (*kokoku shinminka*) or meld them into a "single body" in the Japanese empire (*naisen ittai*). According to a 1940 publication of the Japanese government, as of 1937 only 664 Korean women had married Japanese men and mere 474 Korean men had wedded Japanese women.[3] In the end, Japan had nothing to show for its immense human and material sacrifices. It had no claim on its vast capital assets in Korea at the end of World War II, and the extensive capital resources it had accumulated in Korea during nearly the first half the twentieth century became the assets of the former colony. In fact, it had to pay substantial reparations to South Korea after its defeat, and North Korea is also demanding a large sum.

Had it not engaged in empire building, Japan would have profited a good deal more by gaining access to Korean markets and raw materials through trade and investment without having to shoulder the immense costs of administering and developing the colony. Taxes that supported the administration of the colony came increasingly out of private Japanese income that otherwise would have been saved and invested to improve Japanese citizens' standards of living. Moreover, conquering, administering, and investing in Korea lured capital and skills away from more productive employment at home, diluted the country's capital assets, crippled its educational system, and precluded welfare measures that only a government could have undertaken. In addition, some of the products Japan imported from Korea, such as rice and iron ore, could have been purchased more advantageously at lower prices in open world markets. Not only has the Japanese empire disappeared from the world map now, but Japanese imperialism and colonialism also incensed Koreans, as well as many other Asians, and led to their hostility toward Japan, which is still very evident more than a half century after the end of colonial rule and its empire. It thus is clear that both the Koreans and Japanese alike were the misguided or oppressed victims and suffered heavy losses from Japan's costly and willfully miscalculated adventure in Korea, as well as in China and other Asian countries.

NOTES

PREFACE

1. Of the 220,000 square kilometers that make up the peninsula, only about one-quarter of the land is arable. With a population density of 363 persons per square kilometer (in 1987), Korea is even more densely populated than Japan (294) and the Netherlands (333).

2. According to Lockwood, "The pattern of organization and entrepreneurship which produced such rapid economic growth in Japan can hardly be duplicated elsewhere in Asia" (1954: 591).

3. As Wagner observed, the Korean scholar was himself a product of the traditional culture under scrutiny (1975: 45).

CHAPTER 1

1. One of the first modern economists to examine the importance of capital formation in economic development was Professor Ragnar Nurkse (1953).

2. The term *investment* in this study, as defined by economists, refers to the creation of real goods, which are used for the production of other goods and services. Investment is often thought of as the expansion of physical assets for production purposes, but investment in human capital is also an essential ingredient of growth. Investment in human capital involves acquisition of the knowledge and skills needed to be more productive. This view includes the acquisition of knowledge and skills through informal education, as well as through formal education in the institutional framework.

3. Gould and Ruffin 1993b: 25–40.

4. De Long and Summers find evidence suggesting that investments in machinery and equipment are a strategic factor in growth and possibly carry great positive benefits in generating further technological progress (1991: 445–502).

5. Lewis 1955: 201–225.

6. The formation of new capital is of smaller proportions, because gross investment includes depreciation charges and other allowances for business consumption of durable goods.

7. Although Korea did not come under the complete domination of Japan until the Annexation in 1910, the protectorate turned out to be a transitional setup for annexation. It therefore seems more meaningful to examine the period following 1905 rather than using the time span from 1910 to 1945, which is found in most writings.

8. Many postwar government policies—including those of an independent South Korea after World War II, such as using banks as policy tools and promulgating regulations to curb consumption—are very similar to policies that prevailed under Japanese rule.

9. See especially Gerschenkron 1962.

10. It should be noted at the outset that this book cites more sources written in English than in any other language, especially in the early chapters, for at least two reasons. First, since this book is written in English, it is presumed that the readers will be mainly English-speaking students of Korea. Second, the English sources are in many cases more objective, detached, and critical, since the authors are typically foreigners looking at Korean affairs with a more discerning, dispassionate, and interpretative view. Many of the sources that contain descriptive and factual information were written in Korean and Japanese.

11. Ahn 1971: 87.

12. Mizuda and Tsuchiya 1962: 131.

13. S. J. Ko 1988: 397.

CHAPTER 2

1. *Korea Repository* 1896: 347; Carles 1888: 220.

2. At the time of the Japanese Annexation in 1910, it was estimated that about one-fifth of the entire population of Korea was *yangban* (Longford 1911: 33, 367; Hulbert 1911: 508).

3. Wagner 1975. A class breakdown of one southern county may give some idea of social class in the traditional period and its evolution. According to a 1717 survey of a county in a southern province (Danseong-gun, Gyeongsang-do), the *yangban* constituted 19.9 percent of the population, the middle class and commoners (*jungin* and *sangin*) made up 52.5 percent, and the lowest slave class (*nobi*) including *chonmin* 27.6 percent. Seventy years later, in 1786, the composition was 32.2 percent *yangban*, 59 percent middle class and commoners, and 8.8 percent lower classes. A northern county would have had a smaller percentage of *yangban*, as the Joseon dynasty discriminated against northerners and shunned their appointment to government offices, thereby, blocking the opportunities to be *yangban* (Na 1984: 45–47).

4. Hulbert (1905: 61), who was one of the first Westerners to enter the country after it was opened to outsiders, noted that persons sacrificed upon the altar of party strife numbered in "the hundreds of thousands" (Henderson 1968; *Korea Repository* 1898: 231).

5. According to *Korea Repository* (1896: 167–168), the government could have operated effectively with just a third of the extant work force, provided that each official performed his duties faithfully. Private businesses that coined currency surrendered a certain amount to the government (B. Y. Kim 1983: 349–352). A former vice consul at the U.S. Legation in Seoul in 1905 describes the king's household treasury, which held revenues from the sale of offices and from other unscrupulous activities. These funds were used for all manner of strange things, according to the whim of the ruler. L. Graves (1922) includes detailed personal accounts of this, drawn from diaries and memoranda. Also, see *Korea Repository* 1895: 114; ibid. 1896: 211, 222–253; ibid. 1898: 246; Kennan 1905a: 310 ff.; W. K. Han, 1971: 312, 339; D. Chung 1987: 105–106; Hulbert 1911: 51.

6. Dallet 1954: 180, 182–183. The isolationist tendency may be consistent with Professor De Bary's observation that Asian civilizations in general have tended to look inward (1970: 47–51).

7. This calculation is based on fragmentary data found in numerous sources, including Curzon 1896: 87, 183; H-J. Choi 1962: 291–292, 296; *Korea Repository* 1895: 183–184, 186–188, 195–196, 201–202, 205, 207, and 212; Brown 1921: 487, 500; Hatada 1951: 162–163; B. M. Lee 1948: 253; U.S. Department of State 1962: 45–46; Jindan Hakhwae 1961a: 92, 99, 748.

8. Experiments imitating Western technology were also attempted. During the isolationist period, there were some signs of the Korean government attempting to learn about and imitate the production of Western products. Western-style rifles were reproduced in the late seventeenth century with the help of shipwrecked Westerners, and the construction of steamships was also attempted in the 1860s, without success. For instance, Tae Won Gun, the regent of the royal court, ordered the duplication of a captured American merchant ship and its guns and gunpowder. After much expenditure of time, labor, money, copper, and iron, none of these attempts succeeded (K. J. Cho 1994: 361).

9. This inference is supported by Dallet's observation that the Koreans were convinced that the population was increasing and that "certain facts . . . uphold their conclusion" (1954: 8). Data on stature and weight collected for European countries support the soundness of this observation. Similar experiences are found in England and France during the eighteenth and nineteenth centuries (Fogel 1994).

10. This information is drawn from D. Chung 1987: 195.

11. Bishop 1897: 78; *Korea Repository* 1898: 118.

12. Hulbert 1911: 44.

13. According to various price indexes for the United States, the price level increased by about 20 times, from 25.8 in 1876 to 515.8 in 2000, based on the base-year price index of 1967.

14. According to Gale (1909: 196–197), the daily wage of common laborers in the late nineteenth century was between 15 and 40 cents. The rewards of mining were minimal, with the daily wage of mine workers in the 1890s ranging from 10 to 40 cents. Silver miners' wages were about 40 cents a day in silver, which was equivalent to about 20 cents in gold (*Korea Repository* 1898: 149). The average earnings of a more efficient gold miner (placer mining) were about 80 cents a day. These gold miners seldom made more than 16 shillings a month, and only about 50 shillings when working even in the best gold fields (Bishop 1897: 108. Moose 1911: 88; *Korea Repository* 1898: 149). In good diggings, miners earned from 20 cents to a dollar or two a day (Ibid. 1897: 292). Some speculators were reported to have earned as much as 80 cents a day (Bishop 1897: 103, 335). According to a report in the *Kyong Hyang Shinmun* (July 29, 1974), the hiring of a horse and driver from Inchon to Seoul cost 2.50 yen, while the cost of a four-person palanquin was 6 yen (1.50 yen per person) and rice wine, which was a common liquor among Korean people.

15. Korean people appear to have had adequate incomes to sustain the needed calorie intake. Most underdeveloped nations report a daily consumption of calories of more than 1,900 and per capita income of more than $500. While India's official report in 1950 showed 1,850 calories, many scholars believe the figures substantially understate actual consumption. According to Farnsworth's calculations, even in India, where a large proportion of the population was chronically underfed, the calorie supply per person in 1953–1954 was 2,200 a day (1958: 57, 189–212). India's per capita income in 1953–1954 was the equivalent of US$60 (or $300 in year-2000 prices).

16. *Korea Repository* (1896: 284) reported that the monthly wages of a primary-school teacher in the latter part of the eighteenth century were 14 yen, and 40 yen for a normal-school teacher, equivalent to $112 and $321 (annually, $1,344 and $3,852), respectively, in

year-2000 prices. Moose (1911: 123) reported that a teacher received his board as well as the cash equivalent of $12 to $36 a year for his services, the equivalent of $90 to $289 in year-2000 prices.

17. This estimate seems consistent with other available data. First, compared with that of the Japanese around 1860, the standard of living in Korea seems to have been somewhat lower, by about 10 percent. National income per capita in Japan in 1860 has been estimated at $40 (or about $800 in year-2000 U.S. prices), while for China in the same period it has been estimated at $44 ($880) and, for the Far East as a whole, at $50 ($1,000). In North America the average per capita national income in the same year was more than ten times those of Japan and China ($420 in 1860 prices and $9,165 in year-2000 prices) (Zimmerman 1965: 34). Second, an interpolation from 1940s Korean national income figures also supports this estimate. The calculations in chapters 3 and 7 set the per capita income in Korea in 1943 at $1,130 in year-2000 U.S. prices, its average annual per capita GNP growth rate during the colonial period at about 1.2 percent, and the growth rate of per capita GNP during the transitional period (1876–1904) at near zero. Based on these calculations, an interpolation puts Korea's per capita income for the mid-1870s at about $720.

18. Estimates of the Korean population at this time vary greatly from one source to another. Dallet cites official government statistics that place the figure at 7.5 million in 1844. His computation for the early 1870s places it at 10 million (1874: 9), which is supported by Carles (1888: 116). Bishop (1897: 391) places the population in 1897 at 12 million. The highest figure cited is 17 million in 1898 (*Korea Repository* 1898: 30–31). My computation confirms Bishop's figure for 1897 (1897: 391), which is consistent with the more accurate data for the post-1910 period.

19. *Korea Repository*1898: 234.

20. G. McCune 1950: 112. On average, one *jeong* of paddy was valued at 2,160 yen, and the same acreage of dry field at 750 yen in 1938–1939.

21. Ahn 1975: 7–8.

22. Bishop 1897: 448; Griffis 1907: 499; Hulbert 1911: 444. This figure is taken from an 1890–1900 estimate, but conditions had not changed much since 1875.

23. This seems to coincide with Zimmerman's calculation that per capita income in the primary sector was about one-third that prevailing in the other sectors in Japan between 1881 and 1890 (1965: 51).

24. *Korea Repository* 1898: 381; Longford 1911: 375.

25. Dallet 1954: 3; Oppert 1880: 171; *Korea Repository*1897: 292.

26. Curzon 1896: 136; Dallet 1954: 179; Moose 1911: 53; *Korea Repository* 1896: 440; Hatobe 1931: 43–45. When Westerners arrived in the late nineteenth century, Korea did not have a single respectable retail outlet, and very few merchants kept a store even in their own house. There were only two storied shops, or warehouses, in Seoul. They belonged to the king and were leased to the merchants of the six great trading guilds of Korea, which paid him a substantial price for the privilege of controlling the sale of Chinese and native silk or cotton goods, hemp and grass cloth, and Korean paper.

27. Moose 1911: 143. Even shamans and female entertainers (*gisaeng* or *geisha* in Japanese) were incorporated into guilds (Bishop 1897: 402; Griffis 1907: 291).

28. Dallet 1954: 182–83; Carles 1888: 3, 197–198; Hamilton 1904: 182.

29. Dallet 1954: 182–183; Longford 1911: 306; Hamilton 1910: 182; Nihon Noshomusho 1905: 192–193.

30. Hulbert 1911: 252.

31. One scholar who made such an attempt is Professor Byong Do Lee, an eminent historian who published a series of articles on the subject in a widely read popular magazine, *Sam-Toh*, from 1979 to 1981.

32. See Appendix 2.1.

33. Savage-Landor 1885: 291; Bishop, 1898: 79. 235–236; *Korea Repository* 1896: 253–254; von Richthofen 1943: 101–398; S. B. McCune 1956: 75.

34. Hosokawa 1941: 219.

35. See Appendix 2.2.

36. Western travelers noted that the *yangban* might live on the clandestine sewing and/or laundry work of his wife or wives.

37. Bishop 1897: 447–448; *Korea Repository* 1898: 230.

38. Longford 1911: 369; Bishop 1897: 160–162; *Korea Repository* 1892: 135; ibid. 1897: 445; ibid. 1898: 381; Gale 1972: 25.

39. Bishop 1897: 158, 446–448.

40. Some of these traditions prevail even today, as noted by one anthropologist who conducted a village field study. The villagers showed little confidence in their capacity to effect substantial change and no apparent interest in gradual improvement (Brandt 1972: chap. 3).

41. N. N. Lee 1963: 114–116.

42. Gifford (1898) characterized their laziness as apathy resulting from the dominance of the ruthless *yangban* gentry.

43. In contrast, India in 1955 was estimated to have invested 4 to 5 percent of its national income (Lewis 1955: 207).

44. Some of these entrepreneurs (e.g., iron and metal-goods producers) were reported to have been wealthy investors in iron mines, fuel (wood charcoal), and clay to make iron. Sometimes they invested the entire profit from the previous year (Oh 1989: 182).

45. M. G. Kang 1970; Kwon 1984: 207–208.

46. Griffis 1907: 295.

47. Bishop 1897: 305; H-J. Choi 1982: 173–253; D. Chung (1972) suggests that high interest rates brought about the downfall of the Yi dynasty.

48. *Korea Repository*1895: 47; Dallet 1954: 180. Gale (1909: 109, 196–197) wrote that "twenty years ago the interest rate was 12 percent a month. Little by little it has fallen till today when it is 4 or 3 or 2 percent monthly, the lowest on record."

49. Interest rates were prohibitively high in part because most Koreans did not consider the repayment of loans to be obligatory. Only a very small proportion of those who borrowed from foreigners ever repaid their loans. One Westerner reported that he was told by a Korean, "The Christians are very bad.... They lend the Koreans money... but they want to be repaid, and that is very bad" (Hulbert 1911: 40).

50. This type of motivation is well reflected in what might be labeled the Confucian ethos. It is illustrated in the following teachings of Confucius: "The gentleman understands what is right; the inferior or small man (*soin*) understands what is profitable"; "One should not seek gold, jade, and such valuables; rather desire that each of one's descendants be virtuous"; and "Men should warn against covetousness, for wealth thus coveted would provoke the wrath of Heaven." Similar beliefs and attitudes may be discerned in the following adages: "Gold and silver are but vain things; after death how could they remain in one's hands?" "Wealth is but dung; benevolence and righteousness are worth thousands of gold pieces"; and "It is better to understand the classics than to amass riches." Also, see *Korea Repository* 1898: 381.

51. *Korea Repository* 1896: 253–254, 479.

52. *Korea Repository* 1896: 253–254. Reischauer and Fairbanks 1960: 426. Whigham suggested that a Korean was "more Confucianist than Confucius" himself (1904: 185).

53. Some of these traditions still predominate today, as noted by Brandt. In a village study, he found that a man's prestige still largely rests on his lineage, rank, age, and moral behavior (1972: chap. 4).

54. Jin Young Choi was quoted in "Loyalty Dominates Confucian Thought," *Korea Herald*, August 26, 1983.

55. S-P. Kang 1982.

56. Koo 1982.

57. Yim 1963: 57; see also the series of articles written by Hyo-chae Lee (1978).

58. *Korea Repository* 1898: 5.

59. Gifford 1898.

60. In Korea today, great emphasis is still placed on conviviality and harmony. Personal pride and courage are not regarded as highly as harmonious adjustment to the community (Brandt 1972: chap. 7).

61. K. J. Cho 1973: 409; Y. M. Kim 1972.

62. Weber 1951: 246.

63. For a few sample observations, see Oppert 1880: 178; *Korea Repository* 1898: 4; Hulbert 1911: 515; Moose 1911: 54. Some of these traditions persist today, as noted by Brandt, who described "pure prejudice based on professional distaste for innovation" (1972). This attitude is consistent with that found in China (De Bary 1970: 48, 50).

64. Cited in B. Y. Kim 1983: 217, 220.

65. Bishop 1897: 305; H. Shikata 1929: 427–428.

66. H-J. Chun 1976.

67. Oppert 1880: 175; *Korea Repository* 1898: 381.

68. *Korea Repository* 1897: 26; Bishop 1897: 78; Hulbert 1911: 40; Shikata 1929: 427–428.

69. Dallet 1954: 156; Griffis 1907: 289; Gale 1909: 109–110.

70. Kwon 1984: 207–208; H-J. Choi 1957; M. G. Kang 1970.

71. Dallet 1954: 156; Bishop 1897: 114; Gale 1909: 109–110; Griffis 1907: 289.

72. Descriptions can be found in *Korea Repository* 1896: 167; ibid. 1898: 3; Gale 1909: 109–110; Moose 1911: 104. The *yangban* continued to be spendthrift in 1965, according to a survey conducted by Ki. Hyok. Park (1965: 57).

73. Griffis 1889: 289

74. Moose 1911: 104.

75. Hulbert 1911: 444; Longford 1911: 305–306. The costs of such a dwelling should not have been more than 9,999 *ryang* (old currency unit equivalent to yen) in Seoul and 999 *ryang* in other cities. B. Y. Kim 1983: 186–187; Bishop 1897: 154; Dallet 1954: 156; Lowell 1888: 55; Hosokawa 1941: 337.

76. Griffis 1889: 232; B. Y. Kim 1983: 186–187. According to Griffis (1907: 232), only high-ranking men (above the third rank) were allowed to wear silk. Petty officials had to wear cotton. Merchants and farmers could not imitate official robes and instead donned tighter or more economical coats and trousers.

77. See Appendix 2.3.

78. One foreign traveler saw more intoxicated people in Seoul in a week than he had in twenty years in China (*Korea Repository* 1897: 229, 447). Most Western travelers observed that Koreans loved to drink and that distilled liquor was widely used (Bishop 1897: 91, 114, 360; Dallet 1954: 156–157; Rockhill 1905: 52; Huang 1967; B. Y. Kim 1983: 142; Hulbert 1911: 36, 38). Even today, according to surveys and studies, *gyongjo,* the time-honored Korean custom of spending great sums on these special functions, is a heavy burden on people (*Newsreview*, September 20, 1997: 30–31).

79. Many foreigners observed that a great virtue among Koreans was their innate respect for and daily practice of the laws of "human brotherhood." Mutual assistance and generous hospitality were said to be distinctive national traits, "and they were hospitable to a fault among themselves." The home of one was the home of well-nigh all, and the wealth of one was practically a common fortune. The expense incurred in carrying out such social and

corporate responsibilities was sizable. Often a man with income, however small, had to support many of his and his wife's relations. When a noble obtained some post, he was often obliged to support all his relatives, even distant ones. When there was a celebration or formal dinner in a house, all the relatives were invited. The willingness with which the Korean would depend on his friends when in poor circumstances was to a large extent offset by the willingness with which he let others depend on him when he was in better circumstances. It was a grave and shameful form of misconduct to refuse a portion of one's meal to anyone, known or unknown, who presented himself at mealtime (G. McCune 1950: 74; Moose 1911: 64; Gale 1909: 111; Hulbert 1911: 37–38; Dallet 1954: 105, 131, 149–150; *Korea Repository* 1895: 346–347; Griffis 1907: 288). Some of these traditions prevail today, as noted by Brandt (1972).

80. Bishop 1897: 132.

81. Dallet 1954: 150, 156; *Korea Repository* 1895: 367–368, 347; ibid. 1897: 228; Bishop 1897: 132, 329, 356; Hulbert 1911: 263; Griffis 1907: 288–289; Gale 1909: 109–110; Longford 1911: 49.

82. Lowell 1888: 58; Bishop 1897: 127; *Korea Repository* 1895: 347; ibid. 1898: 230–231.

83. Hulbert 1911: 37.Bishop 1897: 445–446; Dallet 1954: 150; *Korea Repository* 1896: 253; ibid. 1895: 346–347; ibid. 1896: 253; Griffis 1907: 289.

84. Even as late as 1971, expenditures for such traditions were considered to be an unbearable burden on a family's finances. All the people interviewed for a newspaper article in Seoul in July 1971 expressed the desire to institute a rule to reduce such expenditures. And, in fact, a law and regulations imposing heavy penalties upon violators were instituted to reduce such expenditures (*Hanguk Ilbo,* July 8, 1971).

85. Gale 1909: 199–200.

86. Lewis 1955: 201–203.

87. Rockhill 1905: 51.

88. In the cities, the streets were indescribably filthy. There was no sanitation or drainage, and nothing was being done to remove the accumulation of household refuse and trash that was piled up all along the sides of even the best streets, rendering them equally offensive to sight and smell. Longford 1911: 305–306. The priorities of leaders were the effective use of mountain resources (*jisan*) and the control of water (*jisu*), but not the provision and maintenance of roads (*jido*). The latter policy was apparently intended to discourage foreign invasion (Kennan 1905a: 310; Bishop 1897: 301).

89. Kennan 1905a: 310.

90. Griffis 1907: 174.

91. Hulbert (1905: 61) cited the particulars behind the building of one of the many palaces erected during the Joseon dynasty: "About this time a monk gained the confidence of the superstitious king and induced him to build the In-gyeong Palace. To do this, heavy taxes were levied throughout the country."

92. One reason for the decline in tax revenue was that over the years cultivated acreage increased, but it was not reported or recorded, and tax collection was based on the old records (Hulbert 1905: 319; Reischauer and Fairbanks 1960: 445).

93. Bishop 1897: 396–397; Rockhill 1905: 46.

94. One magistrate, for instance, "appropriated $2,600 of the government revenue" and "pigeon-holed" it. *Korea Repository* 1897: 110–111. Corruption resulted partly because many provincial taxes and expenditures were left to local management (B. Y. Kim 1983: 312).

95. Members of guilds were required to pay a monthly tax to the head of their organizations. *Korea Repository* 1896: 43.

96. For example, 500,000 yen in 1884 (Carles 1888: 136).

97. Dallet 1954: 131.

98. Rockhill 1905: 51–52; Bishop 1897: 301.

99. *Korea Repository* 1898: 231; Tokanfu 1907: 36; Bishop 1897: 337; B. Y. Kim 1983: 301.

100. Rockhill 1905: 47; Carles 1888: 136; Bishop 1897: 25; Hulbert 1911: 228; B. Y. Kim 1983: 312; *Korea Repository* 1898: 2; Longford 1911: 36.

101. See Appendix 2.4.

102. *Korea Repository* 1895: 114, 369; Bishop 1897: 329.

103. Bishop 1897: 303; Griffis 1907: 233.

104. *Korea Repository* 1896: 339. The salary of postmasters of first-class post offices in 1896 was $480 a year, with clerks earning $240. Postmasters of second-class post offices received $360 a year, and clerks were paid $240.

105. Historian Chong Wha Park reported that these positions were sold for as much as 50,000 to 100,000 Korean *ryang* (1970).

106. Kennan 1905a: 310; Sands 1930: 119–120; Harrington 1944: 252; *Korea Repository* 1898: 243; Bishop 1897: 303. The ruling classes were parasites (Hatobe 1931: 234–235) and were mainly interested in the extraction of monies from the people (W. D. Yoo 1977: 493).

107. Gifford 1898.

108. Longford 1911: 35; Hamilton 1910: 97; Harrington 1944: 252; Kennan 1905a: 310.

109. Bishop 1897: 447–448; B. Y. Kim 1983: 230; Oppert 1880: 175; Longford 1911: 40–41. Hatobe (1931: 234–235) accused the ruling classes of being parasites who were interested mainly in the exaction of money from the people (W. D. Yoo 1977: 493). Also, see Government-General of Chosen 1910–1911: 59; Government-General of Chosen 1937–1938: 218.

110. Hatobe 1931: 158, 232–234; Oppert 1880: 175; Longford 1911: 41; B. D. Lee 1979–1981; Bishop 1897: 446–448.

111. Bishop 1897: 78–79, 158; Harrington 1944: 252; Hosokawa 1941: 220; Hatobe 1931: 158, 336.

112. *Korea Repository* 1896: 439.

113. Bishop 1898: 305. The same observation was made by Harrington (1944: 312–313).

114. Bishop 1898: 235–236, 336; *Korea Repository*1897: 44.

115. The effect of these impediments becomes clear when the economic climate of traditional Korea is contrasted with the dynamics that emerged from Western feudal society prior to the Industrial Revolution, the accomplishments of Korean immigrants in Manchuria, and the more recent economic development of South Korea. It is interesting to observe that the environment that prevailed in traditional Korea may be discovered in numerous ways in today's North Korea, where one group of isolationists rules the country and where a lack of incentive to produce economically, heavy taxes, a stagnant economy, and poverty among the masses persist.

CHAPTER 3

1. Sachs and Warner 1999.

2. This view was also expressed by many Japanese at the time, including Fukuda (1921: 138–146). Also, see Bishop 1897: 452; Hulbert 1911: 508.

3. Hamilton wrote that "the scum of the Japanese nation" had come to Korea. With their "puffed-up arrogance," they were sowing the seeds of future disaster. The Japanese "think might is right," he declared, and "master and man alike terrorize the Korean. . . . Any Japanese coolie thinks he's the better of them . . . .The modesty, cleanliness, and politeness, so characteristic of Japanese, are conspicuously absent in their settlements in this country"

(1904: 129–131). Their "known combativeness" and "rude ways" were rebuked (Harrington 1944: 307; Government-General of Chosen 1914: 11). The Japanese authorities, too, were critical of their citizens' behavior. Count Okuma commented that the 10,000 Japanese in Korea were acting in such a way as to injure the honor of Japan (cited in *Korea Repository* 1896: 493–494). Count Inouye was quoted in *Japan Gazette*, June 29, 1895: "Japanese residents in Korea must be reformed. . . . The Japanese are not only impolite, but often insult the Koreans. They are rude in their treatment of Korean customers and when there is some slight misunderstanding they do not hesitate to appeal to fists, and even go so far as to throw Koreans into rivers or use weapons" (*Korea Repository* 1895: 310–311).

4. Dallet 1954: 12; Hamilton 1910: 157, 171–173, 176; Carles 1888: 16, 82, 275, 277; Government-General 1914: 11; Altman 1984: 685; Griffis 1907: 425; Bishop 1897: 23–26, 31–32, 43–44, 173, 175–176, 314; Curzon 1896: 90; *Korea Repository* 1897: 380, 469; ibid. 1898: 401; Harrington 1944: 194.

5. Bishop 1897: 20, 325, 328; Harrington 1944: 194; Hamilton 1910: 176; Hatobe 1931: 57–58.

6. Griffis 1907: 426–427. The display also featured porcelain vases worth 40 yen and a "glass roof." Jindan Hakhwae 1961a: 446; *Korea Repository* 1895: 241; Government-General of Chosen 1937–1938: 165, 168.

7. Savage-Landor 1885: 17–18, 26; *Korea Repository* 1896: 301; ibid. 1897: 380; Curzon 1896: 94; Hamilton 1910: 149–150; Sands 1930: 145.

8. When the Korean customs office was first established under the direction of a foreign adviser named Mollendorf, there were twenty-seven Europeans and four Chinese on the Korean government payroll. The first Western military academy was established in 1888 with the help of the U.S. Army and those of other countries. Foreign officers not only acted as military advisers and instructors but were instrumental in purchasing rifles and other guns from the United States. Also, see Hamilton 1910: 151; *Korea Repository* 1898: 307.

9. *Korea Repository* 1898: 307; Harrington 1944: 27, 141, 151, 191, 305.

10. This estimate is based on *Korea Repository* 1895: 241, 320, 325, 339–344; ibid. 1898: 307; Bishop 1897: 20, 63–64; Hamilton 1910: 149–150. Also, see Brown 1921: 500–503; Harrington 1944: 49; Paik 1929: 99–118; Gale 1909: 227, 258–259.

11. The report for the first year, beginning in 1885, shows a record of 255 in-patients, on 150 of whom surgical operations were performed, while in that year 10,460 cases were seen in the out-patients department, with 394 operations of a minor nature having been performed (*Korea Repository* 1892: 356).

12. The medical school was founded with a donation of $150,000 by an American businessman, L. H. Severance (Harrington 1944: 120; Paik 1929: 120; *Korea Repository* 1896: 308–309).

13. It was reported that many converted Christians stopped drinking, smoking, gambling, buying expensive clothing, and indulging in spending sprees (Huang 1967: 48–50).

14. According to Horace G. Underwood (1992), the Korean missions were in many ways anti-intellectual and anti-institutional. He noted that in 1900 a gift of $10,000 to establish a medical school was almost refused. One missionary cautioned against the training of a native ministry: "Never think of sending a bright and apparently earnest Christian native off to America to be educated on foreign money unless you want to spoil him. That will be the surest way to blight his future usefulness. The Orientals who can stand such a process without ruin are few. It is dangerous to say the least" (*Korea Repository* 1897: 174). Missionary Rev. W. D. Reynolds stated: "Don't employ him as a preacher or evangelist on foreign pay. . . . Don't send him to America to be educated. . . . Don't train him in any way that tends to lift him far above the level of the people among whom he is to live and labor (*Korea Repository* 1896: 200–201).

15. Nihon Noshomusho 1905: 110, 112, 113–114; Chosen Boeki Kyokai 1943: 55–56; Bank of Chosen 1920: 166–167, 174–175.

16. Oppert 1880: 173; Griffis 1907: 426, 447; Hamilton 1910: 134, 151; Longford 1911: 379; Daiichi Ginko 1926: 72ff.

17. *Korea Repository* 1898: 109; B. M. Lee 1948: 260. Foreigners observed that trade grew in volume rather than in variety.

18. The estimated total of imports from the United States in 1897 was approximately $400,000: $232,385 in kerosene, $100,000 in machinery (mostly for mines and railroads), $25,000 in household supplies, and $42,615 in miscellaneous other products (including nearly $25,000 worth of piece goods). The English open-port trade amounted to about $2 million, three-fourths of which was in cotton products (*Korea Repository* 1898: 305–306).

19. Gold and silver exports made up 780,000 yen in 1881, increasing to 2.91 million in 1900 and 5.6 million in 1903.

20. The estimate is based on S. J. Ko 1959: 320–323, 326–327; ibid. 1975: 129, 389; Conroy 1960: 459; Toyo Keizai Shinposha 1935: 579; B. Y. Kim 1983: 242–243; Carles 1888: 169; Griffis 1907: 426; *Korea Repository* 1898: 109; Harrington 1944: 56; Chosen BoekiKyokai 1942: 58–59; B. M. Lee 1948: 267–268, 270–271; Jindan Hakhwae 1961a: 444–445.

21. It was observed that about one-third of the goods imported were carried inland on the backs of men and horses. Delays at barriers on both the overland and river routes were intolerable to traders. In 1895 the main road connecting Seoul and China was widened to twenty feet and improved with $8,000 in support from the king (B. Y. Kim 1983: 150–151). The absence of large rivers and of land transportation other than on the back of a bull or horse made it next to impossible for the little communities in the numerous mountain valleys to get their produce to market (*Korea Repository* 1897: 444).

22. Carles (1888: 101), for instance, observed that "even the Japanese, economically as they lived, found that trade in Korea was far from being a source of wealth, and many of them failed, while the few Europeans who were established in the place complained of the difficulties in the way of obtaining payment. . . ." (Curzon, 1896: 180).

23. K. J. Cho (1965: 385) estimated that Korea's balance-of-payments deficit between 1873 and 1910 was about 118 million yen, most of which accrued in 1885 and 1910 (K. J. Cho 1977: 244).

24. See Appendix 3.1.

25. Nihon Noshomusho 1905: 110, 112, 113–114; Chosen Boeki Kyokai 1892: 55–56; Bank of Chosen 1920: 166–167, 174–175.

26. B. Y. Kim 1983: 197; Chosen Boeki Kyokai 1942: 42–43; Conroy 1960: 458, 461; Palmer 1963: 195; *Korea Repository* 1897: Appendix, 465. According to others (S. J. Ko 1959: 341; Tsuchiya and Okazaki 1937: 154–158), goods produced in mechanized textile factories were imported from Japan only after about 1903.

27. Hamilton 1910: 133, 150–151; *Korea Repository* 1898: 305–306; Kitakawa 1932: 74; Miyamoto 1944: 47–77; B. M. Lee 1948: 265.

28. *Korea Repository* 1897: 446–447; ibid. 1898: 305–306; Bishop 1897: 32, 20, 325, 328, 393; Hamilton 1910: 133, 165–167; Harrington 1944: 57, 195; Nihon Noshomusho 1905: 157; Brown 1921: 151; B. Y. Kim 1983: 199–206; Curzon 1896: 178n.

29. Shinobu 1901: 12–13; Curzon 1896: 177; *Korea Repository* 1897: 374, 444; Conroy 1960: 459–460; Griffis 1889: 426; Bishop 1897: 33; J. B. Kim 1977: 71, 123; Chosen Kyokai 1892: 5; Daiichi Ginko 1926: 77; Toyo Keizai Shinposha 1935: 579; K. J. Cho 1965: 389–390; ibid. 1977: 126–132; S. J. Ko 1959: 325–326. The major portion of "official" gold exports entered Japan through the Daiichi Bank. Almost all gold export activities were carried out by the Japanese. B. M. Lee 1948: 268–271.

30. Carles 1888: 3, 197–198; Oppert 1880: 172–173; *Korea Repository* 1897: 336; Hamilton 1910: 182.

31. Carles 1888: 167–168; Bishop 1897: 328.

32. For example, the Chinese were given the privileges of traveling, residing, and trading outside the open ports (Hatada 1951: 172; McCune and Harrison 1951: 27–28).

33. Savage-Landor 1885: 26; Curzon 1896: 178–179; Bishop 1897: 31–32; Miyamoto 1944: 47–77; K. J. Cho 1977: 277–282.

34. Curzon 1896: 177; Bishop 1897: 32; *Korea Repository* 1898: 385; B. Y. Kim 1983: 247; Miyamoto 1944: 47–77; K. J. Cho 1973: 263.

35. The Chinese businessmen who were agents and distributors of British goods in Korea were increasingly compelled by market demands to provide the Japanese with piece goods (*Korea Repository* 1898: 385).

36. *Korea Repository* 1987: 444; S. J. Ko 1959: 325–326; B. M. Lee 1948: 271.

37. *Korea Repository* 1897: 946; Palmer 1963: 249–250.

38. Hamilton 1910: 134, 144–145, 151; Bishop 1897: 392; *Korea Repository* 1897: 159–160, 199–200, 398, 444; ibid. 1898: 80, 305–306; Harrington 1944: 56; McCune and Harrison 1951: 8.

39. Immediately after Korea's opening, 88 percent of Japan's exports to Korea consisted of foreign-produced goods (K. J. Cho 1983: 16). French navy commander Fournier reported in 1880 that three-quarters of Japan's exports to Korea were foreign-made products. His report, "Mission in Korea," was discovered in 1980 and was reported on in the *Korea Herald*, September 4, 1980. In 1877 62 percent of Korean imports from Japan were Western goods (Chosen Boeki Kyokai 1942: 42–43). By 1882, the proportion changed to only 6 percent Japanese and 94 percent Western goods (ibid: 112–114).

40. Government-General of Chosen 1914: 20; Conroy 1960: 462.

41. Government-General 1914: 11, 20; *Korea Repository* 1895: 278; ibid. 1896: 440–441; Grajdanzenv 1944: 75; Griffis 1889: 267; Kim and Kim 1967: 67; Bishop 1897: 44, 314; H. Shikata 1933: 202.

42. Griffis 1889: 267; Kim and Kim 1967: 67; Bishop 1897: 44; *Korea Repository* 1895: 451; ibid. 1898: 76, 308; Harrington 1944: 106–108, 118, 127–29, 137–138, 186, 194; Hamilton 1910: 261–265; Sands 1930: 94.

43. *Korea Repository* 1895: 337; Hamilton 1910: 150; Shikata 1933: 86ff.; B. M. Lee, 1948: 266, 312, 313; Conroy 1960: 467, 475.

44. Government-General of Chosen 1914: 12; Takeo Suzuki 1941: 75; Nihon Noshomusho 1905.

45. Many reports indicate that "hundreds of thousands of acres" were acquired, often at "less than one-twentieth of the real value" (Takeo Suzuki 1941: 78; *Chosen Keizainenpo* 1939: 53; McKenzie 1908: 81; Grajdanzev 1944: 41).

46. Hatobe 1931: 116; Mizuda and Tsuchiya 1962: 24; Hatada 1951: 179–180.

47. Sands 1930: 76. There were, for instance, Japanese groups, such as Ikki Gumi, which charged Korean farmers exorbitant interest rates on collateral loans on land. When the farmers could not pay back the loans promptly, the Japanese creditors took the land, a practice not common in traditional Korea. In this way the collateral land ended up in the hands of the Japanese, including the Oriental Development Company. As one former high-ranking Japanese official in the Government-General admitted in 1958, many Japanese did "pretty vicious things" to Koreans in order to acquire land (Mizuda and Tsuchiya 1962: 23–24, 51).

48. Land prices before the opening of the country to foreigners were fairly stable, but they rose quickly after the opening in 1876. For instance, the price of a piece of land rose from 950 *ryang* in 1768 to 1,500 in 1788–1805, 1,700 in 1822, and 1,800 in 1848, nearly doubling in

80 years. However, after the opening of the country, prices skyrocketed to 2,700 *ryang* in 1876 and 18,500 in 1893 (J. B. Kim 1970: 81).

49. *Korea Repository* (1897: 292) estimated it at about $3,000. See also Harrington 1944: 129 and Carles 1888: 244.

50. Residency General of Korea 1909–1910: 125; Iwaya Hosai, cited in the *Oriental Review*, December 24, 1910, as quoted in Brown 1921: 9, 142; *Korea Repository* 1895: 311–312, 328; ibid. 1898: 478–479; Harrington 1944: 165, 193–194; Hamilton 1910: 146–148, 163, 219–220, 218; S. J. Ko 1959: 335–339.

51. *Korea Repository* 1895: 284; Harrington 1944: 156–157, 161–162; Hamilton 1910: 151.

52. The American diplomat H. Allen wrote, "I feel confident that our big money will come from our mines. . . . We have a 'Cripple Creek' there all of our own" (quoted in Harrington 1944: 160–161).

53. Allen expected a large financial reward from the syndicate in exchange for his efforts to obtain the mining concession, and he did receive sizable gifts on two occasions. But he complained that the gifts were "small . . . considering what I have done." He received a few thousand dollars for launching an enterprise that was to net $12 million in his lifetime (quoted in Harrington 1944: 157–159, 167).

54. Harrington 1944: 144, 166.

55. Harrington 1944: 146; Bishop 1897: 26; B. M. Lee 1948: 263–264; Shikata 1933: 202; Shokusan Ginko 1940b: 35–37.

56. *Korea Repository* 1897: 379; Hamilton 1910: 146–148; Takeo Suzuki 1941: 78; *Chosen Keizainenpo* 1939: 53; B. M. Lee 1948: 263–264.

57. Tokanfu 1907: 286–287. About 500,000 yen in capital was invested in the power-generating station, which employed about twenty workers. Most of these systems were installed and run by Americans: the Seoul Electric Light Company, the Seoul Electric Car Company, and the Seoul "Fresh Spring" Water Company.

58. Zinsenfu 1933: 835; The rail line realized a $1 million profit, according to German consul Krien (cited in Harrington 1944: 182).

59. *Korea Repository* 1896: 486; B. Y. Kim 1983: 199–206; Brown 1921: 151; McCune and Harrison 1951: 8; Curzon 1896: 178n.

60. Carles 1888: 101; Griffis 1889: 427.

61. Harrington 1944: 162–164; S. J. Ko 1959: 324; ibid. 1988: 232.

62. Harrington 1944: 163–164.

63. S. J. Ko 1959: 324; ibid. 1988: 232.

64. Hamilton 1910: 99–100; Palmer 1963: 154–155.

65. Sotokufu 1915: 7, 10, 21–22, 25, 44–45.

66. Residency General 1907: 74; Sotokufu 1915: 7, 10, 21–22, 25, 44–45; *Korea Repository* 1895: 11, 307.

67. *Korea Repository* 1896: 169; Harrington 1944: 169, 171, 173, 179.

68. *Korea Repository* 1898: 272. In fact, it was felt that the prospect for a handsome profit was so great that the syndicate should have given the Korean officials who were instrumental in acquiring the concession stock worth $10,000–15,000 as a reward (Harrington 1944: 171–172, 175).

69. Whigham 1904: 186; Harrington 1944: 193; Sands 1930: 55–56, 197–98.

70. Harrington 1944: 142–143, 165, 190–191. Allen successfully pressured the king to rescind the tax on silver and gold in 1896 (Palmer 1963: 202). As a result, the mining tax revenue tumbled from 43,106 yen in 1896 to 2,953 yen in 1987 (S. J. Ko 1959: 337–338).

71. U.S. Department of State 1962: 52–53. See also Harrington 1944: 125, 128, 132, 147, 183, 196–197, 245–247; McCune and Harrison 1951: 39.

72. Harrington 1944: 164, 296; *Korea Repository* 1898: 38.

73. Hatada 1951: 177, 185; Conroy 1960: 463; H-J. Choi 1962: 333–334; D. Chung 1987: 465.

74. The Japanese government made itself responsible for the payment of the debenture bonds and guaranteed 6 percent upon the company's subscribed capital for a period of fifteen years. The capital of this company was 25 million yen (2.5 million British pounds). The Japanese government decided in 1903, however, to fund the capital necessary for the immediate completion of the railway. An additional million pounds sterling was allotted for this purpose (Hamilton 1910: 152; Kim and Kim 1967: 97).

75. *Korea Repository* 1896: 297; Hamilton 1910: 161; Harrington 1944: 174; Sotokufu 1937: 130–133, 137–140, 151–152; B. M. Lee 1948: 332; Residency General of Korea 1907: 74.

76. The construction of the Seoul–Inchon Railroad had strong backing from the military, which was willing to partly finance its construction and subsidize it after construction. Throughout, the Japanese government worked closely with the syndicate (Zinsenfu 1933: 823–836).

77. Zinsenfu 1933: 835.

78. Harrington 1944: 180–181; *Korea Repository* 1897: 159–160, 199–200, 398; ibid. 1898: 80; Hamilton 1910: 144–145; B. M. Lee 1948: 262.

79. Sands 1930: 198. The American Trading Company's president sold a concession worth several million for $30,000. Harrington 1944: 160.

80. Jindan Hakhwae 1961a: 951; Harrington 1944: 127.

81. This sum does not include a loan from Japan of 1 million yen in 1897 for the construction of a railroad between Seoul and Inchon that was later abrogated (Nahm 1988: 96).

82. See Appendix 3.2.

83. They were financed by the Yokohama Specie Bank, the Daiichi Bank, the Bank of Japan, and the Japanese government, generally at prevailing commercial rates of interest, which were about 8 percent (*Korea Repository* 1895: 156).

84. Townsend and Co. often provided this service (Harrington 1944: 127, 188; Hamilton 1910: 148).

85. A sum of 10.1 million yen of investment from Japan before 1910 was reported by K. J. Cho (1977: 249).

86. Daewongun believed that there should be some reform works in Korea, such as installing railways or developing mines, although he preferred gradual changes.

87. Harrington 1944: 287–288; Lew 1972.

88. The 1905 Gwageo Reform had abolished the civil-service examinations that were based on the Confucian classics, preceding China's abolition of them by 21 years.

89. *Korea Repository* 1896: 31, 167; Bishop 1897: 385.

90. K. J. Cho 1994: 370–375. In 1903 the Korean government banned the use of Japanese bank notes, which the Japanese government had attempted to force on Korea (*Korea Repository* 1895: 344–445).

91. Griffis 1889: 422.

92. Griffis 1907: 432.

93. Among the tools and machinery were textile machines, grain-cleaning equipment, record players, and photographic equipment. Moose (1911: 60–61) reported that it was to the credit of Koreans that young men had proven themselves capable of handling the trolley cars as motormen in such a short time. Also, some scholars believe that Christian Protestantism gave birth to a stronger work ethic (Huang 1967: 48–50).

94. Gil-Joon Yu was the first Korean who had studied in the United States; he argued for change and became one of the pioneers of introducing Western thought and the Western way of life to Koreans, especially for business.

95. *Korea Repository* 1896: 301; 1897: 278.

96. As one foreigner remarked, the Koreans were "less arrogant, less unfriendly towards all kinds of betterment and progress and less fanatical in their pretended superiority over the barbarians [Westerners] than other Asians" (Dallet 1954: 186). Other contemporary observers thought that the advances were solid and "rapid." In fact, by 1903 Korea was showing ample evidence of the progressive movement that had stimulated its people.

97. Buruma 2003.

98. The masses were not convinced that Western influences would eventually dominate the country or that the modernists would gain sufficient force to overcome the difficulties of capital formation and economic development. Bishop 1897: 262–263. Sands 1930: 37–38. Gale 1909: 127–128. See also Hamilton 1910: 14; F. Fujita 1993: 142–144, 150; Harrington 1944: 189; Sands 1930: 37–8.

99. Harrington 1944: 189, 287–288.

100. Koreans complained about Japanese combativeness and rude ways (Harrington 1944: 307; *Korea Repository* 1895: 310–311; Hamilton 1910: 129–130). Even Japanese officials in Korea conceded that "not a few Japanese" held themselves "very haughty towards Koreans and treated them with scant respect" (Residency General of Korea 1910: 22; Government General of Chosen 1914: 11; *Korea Repository* 1896: 493–494). Bishop 1897: 452; cited in Hulbert 1911: 508.

101. Allen 1908: 205; Brown 1921: 502; *Korea Repository* 1895: 241; Paik 1929: 429–430; Harrington 1944: 45, 64–65, 95; Jindan Hakhwae 1961a: 919.

102. It was reported that rifles were manufactured at the factory, but it is not known what other weapons were produced there (*Korea Repository* 1895: 223–224, 232; Residency General of Korea 1907: 78; Jindan Hakhwae 1961a: 402–405, 436–438, 542, 557; Griffis 1907: 422, 434).

103. *Korea Repository* 1898: 148; Curzon 1896: 182.

104. *Korea Repository* 1895: 67, 232, 335; ibid. 1896: 67; ibid. 1898: 148; Curzon 1896: 182; Hamilton 1910: 19, 39; Harrington 1940: 39, 128, 133.

105. Hamilton 1910: 158–159. The Korean government was supposed to have contributed 100,000 yen (10,000 British pounds) annually (Harrington 1944: 304–305). The railroad was eventually built by the Japanese, who completed it in 1906.

106. The Seoul Electric Company was formed by prominent Koreans (*Korea Repository* 1895: 333; ibid. 1898: 118, 315; Harrington 1910: 188; Government-General of Chosen 1937–1938: 165).

107. Bishop 1897: 459; B. M. Lee 1948: 328; Hamilton 1910: 20; *Korea Repository* 1895: 338.

108. Hamilton 1910: 14, 20; *Korea Repository* 1895: 232–233; ibid. 1898: 148; Griffis 1907: 447–448; Curzon 1896: 170, 182.

109. Sands 1930: 50; Curzon 1896: 182, 170; Harrington 1944: 141; *Korea Repository* 1898: 148.

110. Y. H. Kim 1972; *Korea Repository* 1896: 486; Bishop 1897: 459; Hamilton 1910: 159.

111. *Korea Repository* 1896: 167; Government General of Chosen 1938: 147.

112. Cumings 1997: 108; Palais 1975: 42.

113. Edward Lake, quoted in Harrington 1944: 195.

114. Harrington 1944: 195, 248–249.

115. Palmer 1963: 290; Jindan Hakhwae 1961a: 924; *Korea Repository* 1895: 232; Harrington 1944: 188; McCune and Harrison 1951: 55.

116. *Korea Repository* 1895: 335.

117. Curzon 1896: 170, 178–179. There is no record indicating the location of the factory or how the plan was implemented (Harrington 1944: 133).

118. Moose 1911: 143–148; Hamilton 1910: 14–15, 134; Carles 1888: 107.

119. *Korea Repository* 1898: 229; S. J. Ko 1988: 316–317. Busan had the most *gaekju* (about 160 in 1890), followed by Inchon and Wonsan. (K. J. Cho 1994: 346).

120. Shortly after the opening of Korea, foreign merchants were barred from extending their businesses more than forty kilometers beyond their settlements and were confined to the open port areas.

121. Oh 1989: 181–182.

122. K. J. Cho 1977: 284.

123. Oh 1989: 181.

124. These organizations became the core of the chamber of commerce at a later date.

125. U.S. Consul-General Jordan's report, reprinted in *Korea Repository* 1898: 381; K. J. Cho 1994: 378.

126. Carles 1888: 107; *Korea Repository* 1897: 377; Oh 1989: 180; Hamilton 1910: 14.

127. Residency General of Korea 1907: 55; Government General of Chosen 1935–1936 (combined edition): 64; K. J. Cho 1973: 369–370; ibid. 1983: 368–369; B. Y. Kim 1983: 167; B. M. Lee 1948: 314.

128. M. G. Kang 1966.

129. In 1890 artisans established a porcelain factory that employed Japanese technicians (K. J. Cho 1977: 345–346, 384; Hamilton 1910: 27).

130. Hamilton 1910: 27.

131. K. J. Cho 1994: 386–389.

132. Hamilton 1910: 27; Government General of Chosen 1935–1936: 57; Palmer 1963: 197.

133. *Korea Repository* 1895: 348; ibid. 1898: 381; Hamilton 1910: 14; K. J. Cho 1977: 346. Bishop 1897: 296; Moose 1911: 54.

134. *Korea Repository* 1898: 381.

135. Hamilton 1910: 219.

136. Some former high-ranking government officials, businessmen, and landlords actually set up companies to build railroads in the early years (K. J. Cho 1973: 397, 401).

137. *Korea Repository* 1897: 377, 446; K. J. Cho 1977: 378.

138. *Korea Repository* 1897: 377, 446.

139. *Korea Repository*1898: 80, 118, 308.

140. K. J. Cho 1977: 391.

141. K. J. Cho 1994: 378.

142. Dallet 1954: 178.

143. On the other hand, seventy-seven factories were owned and operated by Japanese, six by Chinese, and three by Americans (Tokanfu 1910a: 325–330).

144. Hamilton 1910: 138; Curzon 1896: 182–183.

145. K. J. Cho 1994: 382–383.

146. K. J. Cho 1994: 382–383.

147. A *gae* is a voluntary organization that assists its members with their needs related to work, finance, and/or social activities.

148. *Korea Repository* 1895: 47; B. Y. Kim 1983: 169–170.

149. See Appendix 3.3.

150. Curzon 1896: 182–183; *Korea Repository* 1896: 439.

151. K. J. Cho 1994: 381–382.

152. Eckert 1991: 18; S. J. Ko 1988: 349–353; K. J. Cho 1977: 390.

153. K. J. Cho 1977: 232–247, 378; Eckert 1991: 18; S. J. Ko 1988: 215.

154. Kwon 1984: 208.

155. See Appendix 3.4.

156. *Korea Repository* 1897: 402–406, 436–438, 440; Griffis 1907: 422, 427, 432, 434, 446; K. J. Cho 1977: 261–262; Jindan Hakhwae 1961a: 402–406, 436–438; Kim and Kim 1967: 43. This group included a trio of bright Koreans, Young-hyo Park, Ok-gyun Kim, and Kwang-bom So. They visited Japan for six months to observe the remarkable achievements in the country after the Meiji Reform. With 25,000 *won*, the proceeds from the sale of whaling rights, sixty-one additional students, including Chae-pil So, were sent to Japan (S-Y. Park 1991: 24).

157. U.S. Department of State 1962: 48–49; Griffis 1889: ix; Jindan Hakhwae 1961a: 744–745; *Korea Repository* 1897: 744–745.

158. *Korea Repository* 1895: 359; ibid. 1897: 350; Hulbert 1905: 328. Korean immigrants to the United States between 1903 and 1905 numbered 7,843. This estimate is based on the fragmentary data available in Korean, English, and Japanese publications.

159. Jindan Hakhwae 1961a: 436–438, 440; Griffis 1889: 432, 446.

160. Bishop 1897: 250, 391; *Korea Repository* 1895: 197; ibid. 1897: 320; Y. M. Kim 1972.

161. The opportunity was supposed to have been open to all men, and it was reported that one of those selected was the slave of a political leader (Jindan Hakhwae 1961b: 436–438).

162. *Korea Repository* 1897: 320; Y. M. Kim 1972.

163. Griffis 1889: 422.

164. Palmer 1963: 197.

165. The *Whang Seong Sinmun*'s report was cited in *Kyong Hyang Sinmun*, November 8, 1973.

166. Bishop 1897: 388, 390–391. The city of Seoul had five primary schools that averaged 100 students each (*Korea Repository* 1895: 328; ibid. 1896: 284; ibid. 1898: 389; Moose 1911: 121–122, 236; Brown 1921: 79; Sands 1930: 53; Hamilton 1910: 27, 59).

167. Palmer 1963: 236; Gale 1909: 144.

168. Huang 1967: 49.

169. Korean workers, for example, received less than one-fifth of foreigners' salaries in the Customs Office. The British Customs Office chief received 380 silver dollars, German executives 130 *won*, Chinese 115 *won*, Japanese 80 *won*, and British low officials 70 *won*, but a low-level Korean official received only 15 *won*.

170. It was reported that wages ranged from 8 pence to 1 shilling 2 pence (Hamilton 1910: 151). These figures were converted at exchange rates of $4.80 to 1 pound and 1 dollar to 2 *won*. In 1885 rice cost 0.6 *won* per bushel (*gama*), and a cow cost 15 *won* (reported in a column by Sunwhan Um, "Segwan Yasa," *Joong-Ahng Ilbo*, June 10, 1975).

171. K-T. Kim 1982.

172. Takeo Suzuki 1941: 111; Kwon 1984: 362.

173. D. Chung 1972.

174. K. J. Cho 1994: 382–383.

175. K-T. Kim 1982.

176. Carles 1888: 169.

177. Oppert 1880: 173; Bishop 1897: 24, 90–91; Carles 1888: 166, 176; *Korea Repository* 1896: 320; Harrington 1944: 132–133.

178. Carles 1888: 166–168; *Korea Repository* 1896: 320; ibid. 1897: 279, 446; ibid.1898: 278; Lowell 1888: 57; Harrington 1944: 132–33; Bishop 1897: 24, 78, 90–91, 293, 395; B. Y. Kim 1983: 256–257.

CHAPTER 4

1. Tokanfu 1906: 22–23.

2. Hulbert 1911: 514.

3. Takeo Suzuki 1941: 112, 220.
4. K. J. Cho 1977: 351.
5. Residency General of Korea 1909–1910: 120.
6. Residency General of Korea 1908–1909: 139; ibid. 1909–1910: 120; Takeo Suzuki 1941: 219.
7. Government General of Chosen 1914: 32–33.
8. Takahashi (1935) quoted a statement made by Hozume, the chief of the Bureau of Industrial Development (Shokusan-kyoku), who claimed that after the Annexation, the Japanese government deliberately checked Korea's industrial development.
9. Government General of Chosen 1914: 12–13, 33.
10. Professor K. J. Cho believed that the law was intended to prevent the establishment of new and modern businesses and industries in Korea (*Dong-A Ilbo,* March 4, 1979). Also, a German Foreign Office report on Korea wrote, "The Japanese officials did everything possible to prevent the Koreans from starting new businesses" (*Kyong Hyang Sinmun,* March 13, 1979). See also Grajdanzev 1944: 52, 173–174; Government General 1915–1916: 113.
11. K. J. Cho 1977: 405–406.
12. Takeo Suzuki 1941: 225.
13. The only available data are what was reported in K. J. Cho (1965: 375). He reported that the Bank of Korea estimated Japanese capital imports to Korea during the 1910–1931 period.
14. According to the Government General of Chosen (1914: 33), between 1911 and 1913, eighty-three companies possessing an aggregate capital of 14.84 million yen were established. In 1938 there were 15,000 factories with 1,090.4 million yen of paid-in capital in 1938 (Mizuda and Tsuchiya 1962: 108).
15. In addition to companies owned by one nationality, there was investment in companies jointly owned by Japanese and Koreans or foreigners. The amount of investment in joint-venture companies fluctuated widely from period to period under colonial rule, reflecting the changing roles of Koreans and foreigners, as dictated by the Government General of Chosen to meet the Japanese government's economic and political needs, but the paid-in capital in them increased from 8.1 million yen in 1911 to 95.8 million in 1929, showing an increase of about 11.8 times during the nineteen-year year period. The figures for paid-in capital are not available after that year, but on the whole it must have increased modestly to about 200 million yen in 1943. The share capital in the joint-venture companies relative to total paid-in capital in companies headquartered in Korea ranged between over 50 percent in the early years to less than 5 percent in the later years.
16. Mizuda and Tsuchiya 1962: 108.
17. Government General of Chosen 1914: 33; Sotokufu 1932: 194–201; ibid 1942: 118–119.
18. Chosen Ginko 1933: 35.
19. Another method of calculation produces somewhat smaller figures. This calculation is based on the formula that a little over one-quarter of the total foreign investment in Korea was made by foreign companies headquartered abroad that had branches in Korea. This formula is based on two assumptions. One is that one-half of all the foreign capital in Korea came from abroad, one-half of that amount was in the form of paid-in capital, and the rest was made up of retained earnings and debenture capital. The second is that approximately one-tenth of the paid-in capital of foreign companies headquartered abroad that had branches in Korea was devoted to Korean business operations. On the basis of the this formula, the total capital of foreign companies headquartered abroad that had branches in Korea is estimated at 6.9 million yen in 1911, 58.3 million in 1921, 212.8 million in 1929, 270 million in 1938, and 500 million in 1942 (see chapter 7).
20. Mizuda and Tsuchiya 1962: 141.
21. Hosokawa 1941: 335–336.

22. Some scholars suggested that public investment constituted approximately a quarter of the total investment in Korea under Japanese rule.

23. Lewis 1955: 201.

24. Miyake 1937: 75, 143–144.

25. Sotokufu 1910: 160; 1931: 190–193.

26. Sotokufu 1921; ibid. 1931: 190–193; ibid. 1932: 194–197; Takesizu Suzuki 1942: 83; *Chosen Nenkan* 1942: 83; K. J. Cho 1973: 431–432.

27. S. Miyake 1937: 75, 143–144.

28. Sotokufu 1931: 190–193; ibid. 1932: 196–201.

29. Sotokufu 1912: 261–262; ibid. 1913: 197–198.

30. K. J. Cho 1973: 431–432; *Chosen Keizainenpo* 1940; Grajdanzev 1944: 515.

31. Sotokufu 1910: 260. Many writers, including K. J. Cho, suggested that the traditional upper classes of Korea were more interested in preserving their social position under Japanese rule than in seeing their country freed from foreign rule. The old Confucian literati contributed little to the independence movement (K. J. Cho 1977: 559).

32. Sotokufu 1931: 190–193; ibid. 1932: 194–197; Takesizu Suzuki 1942: 83; Shokusan Ginko 1940b: 35–37; Grajdanzev 1944: 175.

33. D. H. Yun 1999.

34. Y. M. Kim 1972. According to a survey conducted by the Government General of Chosen in 1911, there were 10,018 capitalists with more than 500,000 yen. Of these, only thirty-two, or three-tenths of a percent, were Koreans. The rest were Japanese.

35. Mizuda and Tsuchiya 1962: 108; Shokusan Ginko 1940b: 35–37.

36. They included the Mins, Youn-su Kim, and Heung-sik Pak. Many wealthy Koreans invested and worked in a variety of enterprises largely owned by Japanese interests, among them Doka Industries (Doka Sangyo) and Korea Doa Trade (Chosen Doa Boeki). The former was led by Han Sangyong and Ha Chun-sok and had an authorized capital of 2 million yen and branches in China. These included the Daiko Trade Company, an export-import venture between Korea and Mongolia. It was registered with authorized capital of 1 million yen and paid-in capital of 500,000 yen. About 18 percent of the company's shares were held by Whashin Trade, 10 percent by Gyeongseong Spinning and Weaving, and 9 percent each by the Bank of Korea, the Korea Industrial Bank, and the Japanese imperial household. The Daiko Trade Company in turn invested in two other ventures, including Chosen Doa Trade, a large general trading company with authorized capital of 5 million yen. The Japanese investors with 5 percent of the shares of the company were Shibuya, Nakatomi, and Noguchi Jun's Japan Nitrogenous Fertilizers. Mitsui Commerce held 4 percent. The venture declared assets in 1945 of 75 million yen. There were also smaller joint-venture businesses. See Akihishi 1942; Nakamura 1941; Kobayashi 1968, 1973.

37. S. J. Ko 1988: 349–353; K. J. Cho 1977: 450.

38. Shokusan Ginko 1940b.

39. *Chosen Keizainenpo* 1940: 514.

40. Considerations have to be made with regard to the worth of capital goods at the end of World War II. For instance, the railroads were nearly worn out, and there was scant replacement of essential parts and equipment. By August 1945 Korea's entire railroad network was in precarious condition (*Korea Herald*, September 18, 1979: 5).

41. Mizuda and Tsuchiya 1962: 141.

42. Sotokufu 1910: 60.

43. Huh 1989: 374, 386–387. The Seoul Textile Company employed only Koreans (K. J. Cho 1977: 496).

44. Huh 1989: 378; Suh 1978: 77.

45. K. J. Cho 1977: 400. One example is Yonsu Kim of the Kyungsung Textile Company.

46. Cumings 1997: 91.

47. K. J. Cho 1977: 366, 555; Bank of Korea 1948: I, 101.

48. K. J. Cho 1977: 366, 555–556. No explanation was given, however, as to how such expropriation prevented capital formation.

49. Ahn 1971: 83, 92.

50. Yong Mo Kim, speaking at a colloquium sponsored by and reported in the *Hanguk Ilbo*, October 4, 1972.

51. D. Chung 1987: 435–436.

52. Hulbert 1911: 514.

53. *Kyong Hyang Sinmun* (November 8, 1973). Also, see K. J. Cho 1977; Kim and Kim 1967: 67–68; M. S. Kim et al. 1971: 61.

54. Huh 1989: 365–367.

55. Gragert1994.

56. K. J. Cho 1973: 445.

57. K. J. Cho 1973: 368, 409; Joseon Yonguwhae 1935: 299–300; Huh 1989: 362–365.

58. E. Choi 1992: 30; Tokanfu 1906: 54–55; K. J. Cho 1977: 47. Another report suggested that by 1910 there were as many as 2,250 such schools, of which as many as 823 had a religious affiliation. "Jonggyo Bagnyeon," the *Kyung-Hyang Shinmun*, August 30, 1974.

59. S. J. Ko 1988: 391; Bank of Korea 1948: I, 8.

60. Whereas the percentage of Japanese children attending school increased from 95.4 percent in 1911 to 99.9 percent in 1942, the number of Korean children attending school increased from less than 1 percent to only about 33 percent during the same period.

61. Grajdanzev 1944: 261–263, 266. Of the school age population of Korean children 55.2 percent attended primary school, while 2.8 percent attended schools other than primary schools, including secondary schools (S. B. McCune 1956: 53–54).

62. Sotokufu 1931: 257; J. C. Chung 1989: 451–453.

63. Grajdanzev 1944: 263; Bank of Korea 1948: I, 8.

64. These figures were reported in the *Korea Herald*, January 14, 1982: 5.

65. E. Choi 1992: 30; Tokanfu 1906: 54–55; K. J. Cho 1977: 47.

66. Takeo Suzuki 1941: 30–31; *Chosen Nenkan* 1941; Grajdanzev 1944: 265.

CHAPTER 5

1. Lewis 1955: 216, 239, 263–265.

2. K. Hosokawa 1941: 253.

3. An American traveler observed the following phenomena in 1920: "So perfect a road made the empty plateau look more desolate than ever. The dwellers in these squalid huts would never have built it; neither would the people of the valleys who used it only occasionally when they bartered with the people in the valleys beyond." According to the traveler, the new highways could have but one purpose: consolidating the conqueror's power (Alice Tisdale, "A Korean Highroad," quoted in H. Chung 1921: 109).

4. The Seoul-Inchon Line, which had been built by private railroad companies, and the Seoul-Busan Line were purchased by the Japanese government for a little over 20 million yen in June 1906, which were transferred to the charge of the Railway Bureau of the Residency General. By the close of the fiscal year ending March 31, 1907, the Japanese government had spent 33.2 million yen on the Seoul-Busan Line, 31.6 million on the Seoul-Wuiju Line, and 2.3 million on the Masanpo Line. Japanese expenditures for the construction and improvement of railroads in Korea reached 87.7 million yen by the end of 1909. It completed the Seoul-Wonsan Line in 1914 (Residency General of Korea 1909: 74–75;

Tokanfu 1909:197–98; Sotokufu 1937: 153–54, 156; Hosokawa 1941: 253; N. Hatobe 1931: 345).

5. Residency General of Korea 1907: 74; Sotokufu 1910: 585; ibid. 1914: 274; ibid.1931: 302; ibid. 1942: 177–178, 184, 189; ibid. 1939b: Appendix, 22; ibid. 1937: 578–579; Bank of Korea 1948: III, 57–158, 161; K Hosokawa 1941: 253.

6. N. Hatobe 1931: 53; Sotokufu 1942: 177, 183–188.

7. Sotokufu 1942: 177; Hatobe 1931: 53; Bank of Korea 1948: I, 157–159.

8. *Chosen Keizainenpo* 1940: 298; Grajdanzev 1944: 186, 215–216.

9. The number of such companies increased from 19 in 1911 to 532 in 1938 during 1923–1938, and the amount of paid-in capital increased from 0.8 million yen in 1911 to 32.5 million in 1923 and 98.3 million in 1938.

10. Sotokufu 1931: 341–342, 344–345; ibid. 1938: 220–221; ibid. 1942: 166–167.

11. This study adopts and uses the term *industry* in a manner that the Japanese government had used. Japanese statistics generally included in this category of industry most manufacturing and some public utilities, namely, gas and electricity, in the private sector. Japanese statistics did not include government or public enterprises in the category of industry.

12. Tokanfu 1907: 286–287; ibid. 1908: 325–330; ibid. 1910: 60.

13. Tokanfu 1910a: 60; Sotokufu 1937–1938: 143; Takeo Suzuki 1941: 240. The subscribed capital of industrial companies expanded to 194.1 million yen in 1921 and to 419.5 million yen in 1927. If electricity and gas production, transportation, and other industries (excluding mining) are included, then the paid-in capital of industrial companies was 642 million yen in 1938. Paid-in capital of commercial and industrial companies increased to 729 million yen in 1939.

14. There is no one consistent source for these data. They are found in Tokanfu 1907: 286–287; Sotokufu 1917: 222–225; ibid. 1927. Nihon Takumusho 1938; *Chosen Keizainenpo* 1940; Bank of Korea 1948: I, 100. The number of factories with more than five employees increased to 86 in 1911, 605 in 1917, and 2,424 in 1931.

15. Chosen Kogyo Kyokai 1931: 6; Chosen Ginko 1933: 35, 39; Shokusan Ginko 1940b: 35–37; Bank of Korea 1948: I, 318; Takeo Suzuki 1941: 240. Also, Nihon Takumusho 1938; *Chosen Keizainenpo* 1940.

16. Takeo Suzuki 1941: 223, 235; Bank of Korea 1948: I–318.

17. These were factories with more than five employees (Chosen Kogyo Kyokai 1933: 30; *Kokusei Gurafu* (State of Nation in Graph), January 1941; Takeo Suzuki 1941: 223, 235; Bank of Korea 1948: I, 100, 318; Himeno 1940: 330).

18. Bank of Korea 1948: I, 104; *Kokusei Gurafu* (State of Nation in Graph), January 1941; Takeo Suzuki 1941: 223, 235. The output in current prices between 1930 and 1943 increased by 22.3 times, showing an annual average increase of over 40 percent (Kawai and Yoon 1991: 34).

19. The number of metal and machinery factories increased from 182 in 1923 to 533 in 1938 and 1,354 in 1943 (Bank of Korea 1948: I–100–01, 318; *Kokusei Gurafu*, January 1941; Grajdanzev 1944: 157, 173, 176; Himeno 1940: 330).

20. In 1931 there were some 1,235 factories (51 percent of the total number of factories were in food-related industries) with more than five employees (Bank of Korea 1948: I, 100, 318; Himeno 1940: 330).

21. Bank of Korea 1948: I, 113, 318; Tokanfu 1907: 286–287; ibid. 1910: 330; Takeo Suzuki 1941: 212; Himeno 1940: 330; Kawai and Yoon 1991: 121.

22. By 1907 a total of 10 mechanized textile factories had been established. This number increased to 24 by 1910, 38 by 1913, 118 by 1921, and 264 by 1932 (Tokanfu 1907: 286–287; Sotokufu 1917; Bank of Korea 1948: I, 100, 318; Grajdanzev 1944: 173, 176; Himeno 1940: 330; S. J. Ko 1988: 301–303; C. H. Han 1971:160–164).

23. H. Shikata 1933: 202; B. M. Lee 1948: 294–295.

24. Sotokufu 1931: 236; ibid. 1938: 166; Grajdanzev 1944: 136.

25. Shokusan Ginko 1940b: 35–37; *Kokusai Gurafu*, April 1940; Bank of Korea 1948: I, 110.

26. Grajdanzev 1944: 136, 170, 176.

27. Bank of Korea 1948: I–85–87; Chosen Kogyo Kyokai 1931: 6; Chosen Ginko 1933: 35, 39; Shokusan Ginko 1940b: 35–37; Yamaguchi 1911: I, 922; K. Hosokawa 1941: 304–305; Government General of Chosen 1913–1914: 139; Takahashi 1935; *Kokusei Gurafu*, April 1940; S. J. Ko 1988: 385.

28. The number of mines increased from 40 in 1906 to 368 in 1909, 2,175 in 1927, 7,454 in 1937, and 10,534 in 1945. The number of applications for mining permits increased from 633 in 1912 to 10,000 in 1935 and 16,411 in 1939, and the number of mining companies increased from 35 in 1931 to 186 in 1939.

29. Paid-in capital in mining corporations increased from 9.6 million yen in 1914 to 105.7 million in 1931, 183.6 million in 1938, and 805.6 million in July 1945.

30. See Appendix 5.1.

31. A very influential Japanese financial newspaper editorialized that Korea's "contribution to the Empire's demand for rice . . . is very important" (Toyo Keizai Shinposha, *Shinbun*, October 20, 1940). See also, Porter 1936: 82.

32. Takahashi 1935: 79–80.

33. G. McCune 1950: 96.

34. Ban 1983: 18; Grajdanzev 1944: 102–103.

35. G. McCune 1950: 102–103; U.S. Department of Commerce 1940: 698; Takeo Suzuki 1941: 249.

36. Shirushi 1940: 28–29.

37. Gragert 1994: 210.

38. F. Fujita 1993: 412–413; T Suzuki 1941: 128; *Chosen Keizainenpo* 1939: Index, 7; G. McCune 1950: 100; Suh 1978: 77; Grajdanzev 1944: 100.

39. Unidentified government official quoted in Takeo Suzuki 1941: 112.

40. H. K. Lee 1936: 183.

41. Residency General of Korea 1907: 80–81.

42. *Chosen Keizainenpo* 1939: 177; G. McCune 1950: 126.

43. Sotokufu 1942: 4–5; Shokusan Ginko 1940b: 35–37; Chosen Ginko 1933: 39; Bank of Korea 1948: I, 74; Kin 1965: 161; Y. Lim 1968: 79; Grajdanzev 1944: 130, 175; H. Shikata 1933: 202.

44. Another source states that total (subscribed) capital invested in fishing was about 40 million yen in 1940.

45. Sotokufu 1910: 60. Takeo Suzuki (1941: 284) reported that the paid-in capital of commercial and industrial companies increased to 729 million yen in 1939.

46. Chosen Kogyo Kyokai 1931: 6; Chosen Ginko 1933: 35, 39; Shokusan Ginko 1940b: 35–37; Sotokufu 1932: 275–277; ibid. 1942: 125; Bank of Korea 1948: I, 277 and III, 73–77; Hosokawa 1941: 335–336.

47. Sotokufu 1932: 275–277; ibid. 1942: 125; Bank of Korea 1948: III, –73; Chosen Kogyo Kyokai 1931: 6; Chosen Ginko 1933: 35–39; Shokusan Ginko 1940b: 35–37.

48. K. J. Cho 1977: 477–482. The Industrial Bank was the arm of the Government-General (S. J. Ko 1988: 327–337); F. Fujita 1993: 2, 100–130, 209, 426; Mizuda and Tsuchiya 1962: 49.

49. Bank of Korea 1948: III, 76; Shokusan Ginko 1930; Hosokawa 1941: 327; F. Fujita 1993: 1, 217, 234–235; Joseon Yeonguwhae 1935: 308–309.

50. Sotokufu 1932: 294–295; ibid. 1942: 68, 130–131; Bank of Korea 1948: III, 76–79, 84–85.

51. Bank of Korea 1948: III, 78–79.

52. Tokanfu 1910b: 339, 342, 347; Bank of Korea 1948: III, 73, 80–81, 86–87; K. J. Cho 1973: 383–384; Huh 1989: 371; Mizuda and Tsuchiya 1962: 76–77; Takahashi 1935: 508; S. Suzuki 1939: 332; *Kokusei Gurafu*, April 1940.

53. Residency General of Korea 1908–1909: 19; Sotokufu 1916: 110–113; ibid. 1926: 108; ibid. 1935: 98; ibid. 1942: 68; K. J. Cho 1994: 429–434; F. Fujita 1993: 119, 202. This amount was a portion of 100,000 *jeong* of land confiscated by the Japanese government.

54. To raise the capital, various groups subscribed, purchasing a total of 288,300 shares: the Korean king (1,700 shares), the Japanese imperial household (5,000), other members of the royalty (1,000), and the general public in both countries (142,300). Three million yen were subscribed by the Korean government in the form of land (11,400 *jeong*), and 440,000 yen were invested by the imperial households of Japan and Korea. Most of the rest (about 7 million yen) came from the general public. More than two-thirds of the shares were bought by the Japanese, and the rest by Koreans.

55. F. Fujita 1993: 82–83; Sotokufu 1916: 110–113; ibid. 1926: 108; ibid. 1932: 294–295; ibid. 1935: 98; ibid. 1942: 68, 130–131; Bank of Korea 1948: III, 84–85.

56. Tokanfu 1910b: 339, 342, 347; Bank of Korea 1948: III, 73, 80–81, 86–87; Huh 1989: 371; Mizuda and Tsuchiya 1962: 76–77, 94–95; Takahashi 1935: 508; S. Suzuki 1939: 332; H. Shikata 1933: 202; B. M. Lee 1948: 294–295; *Kokusei Gurafu* April 1940; K. J. Cho 1973: 383–385.

57. Bank of Korea 1948: III, 80–81, 86–87; Takahashi 1935: 508; S. Suzuki 1939: 332; Grajdanzev 1944: 173.

58. Examples are numerous and include the so-called wildcat and other commercial banks that existed in the United States between the 1820s and the Civil War, as well as the commercial banks chartered by the government of Japan in the 1870s.

59. Shokusan Ginko 1940b: 35–37; *Kokusei Gurafu* April 1940.

60. H. Shikata 1933: 202; B. M. Lee 1948: 294–95.

61. Shokusan Ginko 1940b: 35–37; *Kokusei Gurafu* April 1940; Huh 1989: 378.

62. The number of factories in Japanese hands increased from 79 in 1908 to 183 in 1911, 738 in 1917, 1,276 in 1921, 2,279 in 1927, and 3,026 in 1938, while their investment in factories, which began modestly with 2.2 million yen in 1908, increased to about 250 million by 1938 (Tokanfu 1910a: 325–330; Sotokufu 1917: 222–225; Chosen Kogyo Kyokai 1933: 30; Government General of Chosen 1935–1936: 63; H. Shikata 1933: 202; ibid. 1976: 174–178; Grajdanzev 1944: 172; Ahn 1971: 79–102; B. M. Lee 1948: 292–293, 296–297, 352–53; K. J. Cho 1973: 413, 428–429; ibid. 1977: 346). These figures include mining, which was responsible for about one-third of the total (Himeno 1940: 330; Kawai and Yoon 1991: 130; Shokusan Ginko 1940b: 35–37; Nihon Noshomusho 1905: 111–112; *Kokusei Grafu* April 1940; Moon 1966: 103–104; K. Park 1973: 104).

63. Himeno calculates this as 12.5 times that of the Koreans (1940: 330).

64. There is no one consistent source of data. What does exist is found in Shokusan Ginko 1940b: 35–37; Bank of Korea 1948: I, 100; K. J. Cho 1973: 413, 419–429; Grajdanzev 1944: 172; H. J. Choi 1962: 406; B. M. Lee 1948: 352–353.

65. K. J. Cho 1977: 404–408; Himeno 1940: 330.

66. The number of factories with more than five employees mushroomed from only 6 in 1908 to 605 in 1917, 1,088 in 1921, and 2,457 in 1927. The number of factories under Korean ownership that had more than ten employees and motorized machinery increased from 86 in 1911 to 2,897 in 1930 and 4,332 in 1938. As a result, the number of factories owned and operated by Koreans increased from 7.6 percent of the Japanese owned in 1908 to 47 percent in 1911, 82 percent in 1917, and 123.7 percent in 1928.

67. Similarly, the reported amount of Korean investment in factories rose in 1908 from 2.7 percent compared with that of the Japanese to 5.6 percent in 1917 and 14 percent in 1939 (Shokusan Ginko 1940b: 35–37).

68. Huh 1989: 378; Grajdanzev 1944: 173. Himeno 1940: 330.

69. Joseon Yeonguwhae 1935: 293.

70. As noted in chapter 3, the first installation of electricity in Korea was by a company jointly established with Westerners in 1898, with capital of $1 million. It employed about 260 workers. Another company, which operated a power station with 500,000 yen in capital, employed about twenty workers. It was jointly owned with Americans (Tokanfu 1907: 286–287).

71. Sotokufu 1917: 222–225; Bank of Korea 1948: I, 318; Grajdanzev 1944: 172; Takahashi 1935: 348; H. Shikata 1933: 202; B. M. Lee 1948: 296–297; K. J. Cho 1973: 413; Himeno 1940: 330; Takeo Suzuki 1941: 240; Joseon Yeonguwhae 1935: 285–286.

72. Grajdanzev 1944: 173; Himeno 1940: 330. The Bank of Korea calculated the ratio between the Japanese- and Korean-owned companies at ninety-one to nine in 1941 (1948: I, 318).

73. The Government General spent 1.07 billion yen on government enterprises between 1910 and 1930 alone (Chosen Ginko 1933: 28–29; Government General 1925: 74–76; ibid. 1932: 65–67). No comparable data are available for the period between 1931 and 1945, but based on the analyses presented earlier, the Japanese government's investment may have been at least half as much as the sum spent in the previous two decades, or at least about 500 million yen, making the total public investment about 1.5 billion yen in 1938 prices.

74. In terms of the share of industrial production, government "plants" accounted for approximately 8 percent of industrial production in 1935, although this rapidly diminished to 1 or 2 percent (Kawai and Yoon 1991: 39).

75. Total mining production in 1932 was valued at 38.7 million yen, of which 80 percent was produced by the Japanese. Production by mines owned and operated by the Japanese in 1933 was 82 percent of the total output in mining (Sotokufu 1916: 174; ibid. 1928: 168; ibid. 1936: 142; Bank of Chosen 1920: 39, 135; Shokusan Ginko 1940b: 35–37; Bank of Korea 1948: I, 86–87; S. J. Ko 1959: 340–341; ibid. 1988: 384; B. M. Lee 1948: 353; Yamaguchi 1911: I, 922; *Kokusei Gurafu* April 1940).

76. The number of mines operated by the Japanese increased to 1,727 in 1927, 3,942 in 1937, and 7,250 in 1945.

77. Takeo Suzuki 1941: 187; Bank of Korea 1948: I, 86–87.

78. Bank of Chosen 1920: 135; Residency General of Korea 1909–1910: 125; Bank of Korea 1948: I, 86–87; Iwaya Hosai, cited in Brown 1921: 9; Yamaguchi 1911: I, 922. An English-owned mine in Suwon was bought out by the Japanese in 1937, and an American-owned mine in Wunsan was sold to the Japanese in 1939 (Hosokawa 1941: 304).

79. Sotokufu 1916: 174; S. J. Ko 1959: 168; ibid. 1936: 142; ibid. 1959: 340–341; ibid. 1988: 384.

80. Residency General of Korea 1907: 80; Bank of Chosen 1920: 135; Bank of Korea 1948: I, 86.

81. The number of mines operated by Koreans increased from 44 in 1908 to 161 in 1910, 461 in 1917, and 3,512 in1937, although the number declined slightly, to 3,284, in 1945.

82. Chosen Ginko 1933: 35; Shokusan Ginko 1940b: 35–37; Sotokufu 1916: 174; ibid. 1928: 168; ibid. 1936: 142; Bank of Korea 1948: I, 86–87; *Far Eastern Survey* 1939: 295; *Kokusei Gurafu* April 1940; S. J. Ko 1959: 340–341; ibid. 1988: 384.

83. This represented 3.8 million yen out of 38.7 million's worth of total mining production in 1932.

84. Grajdanzev 1944: 146.

85. Some authors have claimed that purchases of farmland, especially by the Japanese, constituted an investment in agriculture. However, the purchase of land itself did not

constitute real investment in land or agriculture. It represented individual financial, but not real, investment. These financial investments in land or agricultural companies merely constituted the transfer of ownership from sellers to buyers, and such transactions did not lead to a net addition to productive capital or an increase in productivity of land. The so-called investment by the buyers was canceled out by the disinvestment of the sellers. If the proceeds from the sale of land were invested in new businesses, there would have been real investment. It is possible and probable that some portion of such proceeds was invested in commerce, industry, or even agriculture. Some landlords and farmers sold land as a means of financing new businesses. In most instances, however, Koreans sold land to finance events such as marriages and funerals, to pay for emergencies, or to repay debts previously incurred, much of which were the customs continued from the traditional period.

86. In this regard, some scholars have argued that large landowners who acquired additional land for the sake of security or profit hindered Korean investment in industry, retarded the development of entrepreneurs, and transformed Koreans into the servants of Japan. Certainly, they supported Japan's cause by supplying it with much-needed grain (K. J. Cho 1977: 559).

87. Shokusan Ginko 1940b: 35–37, 39; Joseon Yonguwhae 1935: 293; J. B. Kim 1977: 209; *Kokusei Gurafu* April 1940. *Far Eastern Survey* 1939: 293.

88. The paid-in capital of Korean companies in the agriculture, fishing, and forestry sector increased from 3.6 million yen in 1923 to 14.4 million in 1939, a quadrupling in sixteen years (Grajdanzev 1944: 173).

89. Shokusan Ginko 1940b: 35–37. Chosen Ginko 1933: 39; Bank of Korea 1948: I, 74; H. Shikata 1933: 202; B. M. Lee 1948: 294–295.

90. J. B. Kim 1977: 209; Himeno 1940: 40; H. Shikata 1933: 202; B. M. Lee 1948: 294–295.

91. Shokusan Ginko 1940a: 26–28; Chosen Ginko 1933: 39; *Chosen Nenkan* 1942: 35; H. Shikata 1933: 202; B. M. Lee 1948: 294–95; Grajdanzev 1944: 175.

92. Chosen Ginko 1933: 39; J. B. Kim 1977: 209; Huh 1989: 378; H Shikata 1933: 202; B. M. Lee 1948: 294–295; *Kokusei Gurafu* April 1940.

93. Shokusan Ginko 1940b.

94. The main banks in Japan had paid-in capital of 4.15 million yen, which increased from 4.4 million yen in 1907 to 4.85 million in 1909 (Residency General of Korea 1909–1910: 75; Bank of Korea 1948: I, 278 and III, 80, 86–87; Mizuda and Tsuchiya 1962: 76–77; *Kokusei Gurafu* April 1940; K. J. Cho 1977: 540; Takahashi 1935: 508; S. Suzuki 1939: 332).

95. The commercial banks organized by Koreans were the Joseon, Hanheung, Jeguk, Cheonil, Hanseong, and Hanil. The first Korean bank, the Cheonil, was established in 1899 with capital of 50,000 yen and reorganized in 1906 with capital of 150,000 yen. The bank received a loan of 240,000 yen without interest during the 1905 financial crisis as a support fund (*seiri shikin*). After the Annexation, it was again reorganized as the Korea Commerce Bank, owned jointly with the Japanese. The second bank, the Hanseong, was launched in 1903 with capital of 10,000 yen. It was reorganized as a joint stock company in 1905, at the urging of a Japanese financial adviser, with capital of 150,000 yen. The bank received a loan of 100,000 yen without interest in 1905 as a support fund. It increased its paid-in capital to 300,000 yen in 1907. The paid-in capital of a third bank, the Hanil (Dongil), was 150,000 yen in 1906. Residency General of Korea 1907–1910, 54–56; ibid. 1909–1910: 75; Tokanfu 1910b: 168; K. J. Cho 1977: 320, 398–401, 540. Cho wrote that it had a capital of 30,000 yen and received a subsidy (*bojokum*) of 150,000 yen (1973: 364, 368–370, 381–382, 385); Grajdanzev 1944: 173; S. J. Ko 1988: 349–353; Bank of Korea 1948: I, 278, III, 73.

96. Shokusan Ginko 1940b: 35–37; Chosen Ginko 1933: 39; *Kokusei Gurafu* April 1940; Huh 1989: 378.

97. Shokusan Ginko 1940b: 35–37; Chosen Ginko 1933: 39; *Kokusei Gurafu* April 1940.

98. Tokanfu 1907: 286–287; ibid. 1908: 330; Shokusan Ginko 1940b: 35–37; Chosen Ginko 1933: 39. *Kokusei Gurafu* April 1940.

99. Bank of Korea 1948: I, 100, 318; Himeno 1940: 330; Grajdanzev 1944: 173, 176.

100. Tokanfu 1907: 286–287; Bank of Korea 1948: I, 100, 318; Kawai and Yoon 1991: 130; Grajdanzev 1944: 173, 176; Himeno 1940: 330.

101. Bank of Korea 1948: I, 100, 318; Himeno 1940: 330; Kawai and Yoon 1991: 130; *Kokusei Gurafu*, April 1940; Chosen Kogyo Kyokai 1931: 6; Chosen Ginko 1933: 35, 39; Shokusan Ginko 1940b: 35–37.

102. Bank of Korea 1948: I, 100, 318; Chosen Kogyo Kyokai 1931: 6; Chosen Ginko 1933: 35, 39; Shokusan Ginko 1940b: 35–37; *Kokusai Gurafu* April 1940.

103. Grajdanzev 1944: 176; Himeno 1940: 330. Similarly, the number of Korean chemical factories increased to about 23 percent of all manufacturing facilities and was more than 2.6 times that of the Japanese, while their paid-in capital increased from 5.3 million yen in 1923 to about 10 million in 1938. The share of Korean investment in chemical factories decreased from about 4 percent of paid-in capital in the industry in 1923 to less than 3 percent in 1938 and less than 2 percent relative to the Japanese in 1941 (Bank of Korea 1948: I, 318).

104. K. J. Cho 1977: 515–528, 526–527; S. J. Ko 1988: 307–308.

105. Notable among Korean rubber-shoe companies were four prominent producers: the Continental Rubber Company, established in 1922 with 500,000 yen in capital; the Peninsula Rubber Company, established in 1921 with 50,000 yen; the Joseon Rubber Company, established in 1922 with 50,000 yen in capital, which was increased to 120,000, and employing 150 workers in 1936; and the Seoul Rubber Company, established in 1924 with 80,000 yen, which was increased to 180,000 in 1930. Many of these companies were established by former high- and middle-level government officials, so-called giant merchants (*geosang*), landowners, merchants, and technicians. Many of the officers of the Continental Rubber Company were former Korean-government officials, and the other three companies were operated by former merchants and technicians (K. J. Cho 1977: 518–521, 526; S. J. Ko 1988: 302, 306–308).

106. Suh 1978: 107.

107. Bank of Korea 1948: I, 318.

108. These included the American-Korean Electric Company, established in 1898; the Electric Power Co., established in 1907; the Townsend Rice Cleaning Mill, established in 1892; and the Brick Manufacturing Co., which existed in 1906. Tokanfu 1907: 286–287.

109. Sotokufu 1921; ibid. 1927.

110. Before the Annexation, Koreans operated fourteen rice mills and four cigarette manufacturing firms that possessed four to ten motor-powered machines each and employed 100 to 300 workers. The number of Korean-owned factories increased to eighty-six in 1911 (twenty producing porcelain, fifteen milling rice, thirteen in metal wares, ten in weaving, nine in paper, and eight in cigarettes). Others produced flour, precious-metal crafts, leather goods, and printed materials (Bank of Korea 1948: I, 318; K. J. Cho 1977: 346).

111. Bank of Korea 1948: I, 318; Himeno 1940: 330; Kawai and Yoon 1991: 130; B. M. Lee 1948: 291.

112. Kawai and Yoon 1991: 121.

113. The Japanese invested heavily in the textile industry in Korea for several reasons. The first was to divert their facilities in Japan to war production. The second was the tax advantages in Korea. Taxation in Japan proper was increasing, while taxes on business in Korea were almost nonexistent. The third reason is that a number of industrial-control measures and legislation to protect workers enacted in Japan were completely absent in Korea.

114. Bank of Korea 1948: I, 100, 318; *Kokusei Gurafu* April 1940; Himeno 1940: 330.

115. Tokanfu 1908: 330; Bank of Korea 1948: I, 318; Grajdanzev 1944: 176.

116. K. J. Cho 1977: 501–515; Kawai and Yoon 1991: 121; Grajdanzev 1944: 155.

117. K. J. Cho 1977: 505–507; Kawai and Yoon 1991: 121.

118. Lewis 1955: 210.

119. Ibid.

120. The claim of benefit has often been made by former Japanese officials and sometimes by "official scholars," who were close allies of the government and who tended to justify all its policies.

121. Mizuda and Tsuchiya 1962: 29.

122. Lewis 1955: 250.

CHAPTER 6

1. To many Japanese, Koreans were "inferior in aptitude and knowledge" and in need of encouragement. In the early years, Japanese advisers believed that Koreans, especially the wealthy *yangban* leaders, lacked entrepreneurial expertise. Thus, economic development had to be mandated and monitored, and the highly centralized Japanese government in Korea ruled the colony with absolute power. These reform measures, which were forceful and heavy handed, were often enforced by the police. In the Japanese view, the "dictatorial encouragement" of the government was responsible for everything Korea achieved under its colonial rule (government official quoted in Takeo Suzuki 1941: 112). These prejudices contrast with the post–World War II economic success of the independent South Korea and led to many unsuccessful programs, such as rice-production plans, which are examined later in the chapter.

2. The proportion of the provincial governments' tax revenue decreased, for instance, from 29 percent in 1932 to 16 percent in 1939 (Nihon Takumusho 1938; Bank of Korea 1948: III, 113).

3. Himeno 1940: 99; F. Fujita 1993: 182; Ahn 1975: 10; Choo 1983: 95.

4. Bank of Korea 1948: III, 113.

5. Bank of Korea 1948: III, 113; Himeno 1940: 99. This was similar to the tax policy followed in the early years of the Meiji Restoration in Japan (Y-I. Chung 1965).

6. Himeno 1940: 99.

7. Measured in terms of the ratio of profits to expenditures, they ranged from about 40 to over 60 percent between 1929 and 1943, when such statistics were published. These calculations are based on data reported in Sotokufu 1932: 748–750; ibid. 1942: 350–351.

8. Government General of Chosen 1937–1938: 147. After a trip to Korea, Yashino, a professor at the Imperial University of Tokyo, described his impressions of road construction. His remarks were published in *Chuokoron* (cited in H. Chung 1921: 110–111).

9. Kim and Kim 1967: 162; H. Chung 1921: 110–111.

10. Government General of Chosen 1935–1936: 52; Grajdanzev 1944: 215; Bank of Korea 1948: III, 13.

11. In the case of Wunsan mine, the company annually paid 25,000 yen to the Korean government as a royalty (S. J. Ko 1959: 336–337; Residency General of Korea 1908–1909: 147; Hatada 1951: 214–215).

12. S. J. Ko 1988: 358.

13. Mizuda and Tsuchiya 1962: 141; Lockwood 1954: 221, 525.

14. Bank of Korea 1948: III, 13.

15. Grajdanzev 1944: 152.

16. Mizuda and Tsuchiya 1962: 20; Himeno 1940: 99; Grajdanzev 1944: 213–214.

17. K. J. Cho 1977: 555.

18. Government official quoted in Takeo Suzuki 1941: 112.

19. Resident General of Korea 1909–1910: 31, 121; Sotokufu 1926: 798; ibid. 1931: 762–763; ibid. 1938: 454–455; ibid. 1942: 376–379.

20. Takahashi 1935: 349–350.

21. Takeo Suzuki 1941: 184. Also see Resident General of Korea 1909–1910: 31, 121; Sotokufu 1926: 798; ibid. 1931: 762–763; ibid. 1932: 749, 841; ibid. 1938: 454–455; ibid. 1942: 376–379, 351–52; Hatada 1951: 216.

22. Resident General of Korea 1909–1910: 31, 121; ibid. 1926: 798; ibid. 1931: 762–763; ibid. 1932: 749, 841; ibid. 1938: 454–455; ibid. 1942: 376–379, 351–352.

23. Grajdenzev 1944: 222.

24. Sotokufu 1932: 294–295; ibid. 1942: 130–131. In 1937 the Japanese government developed a five-year plan to produce 135 tons of gold, of which Korea was responsible for 56 percent, or 75 tons, while Japan was responsible for less than half (F. Fujita 1993: 256; Takeo Suzuki 1941: 188–189; Grajdenzev 1944: 222; S. J. Ko 1988: 39).

25. Resident General of Korea 1908–1909: 18; Government General of Chosen 1937–1938: 160; *Chosen Keizainenpo* 1940: 201; Bank of Korea 1948: I, 159; Mizuda and Tsuchiya 1962: 94–95. Such financial aid often produced costly results, however. Malayan iron ores were better than Korean, and American mineral oil was many times less expensive than Korean oil, but generous subsidies were granted to support uneconomical Korean resources (Grajdanzev 1944: 140, 197, 221–235; Takeo Suzuki 1941: 188–189).

26. S. J. Ko 1988: 391.

27. Government General of Chosen 1937–1938: 160; Bank of Korea 1948: I, 159; Mizuda and Tsuchiya 1962: 51, 94–95.

28. Sotokufu 1932: 749, 841; ibid. 1942: 351–352; Mizuda and Tsuchiya 1962: 51; F. Fujita 1993: 403–404, 456; Takeo Suzuki 1941: 132.

29. Mizuda and Tsuchiya 1962: 90–91; F. Fujita 1993: 213; Resident General of Korea 1907: 57; 1908–1909: 18.

30. Sotokufu 1932: 280, 284.

31. Resident General of Korea 1907: 57; ibid.1908–1909: 18; Sotokufu 1932: 280, 284.

32. In the United States during the same period, the average charge per kilowatt hour was 4.3 cents for nonfarm commercial and industrial use, while the price charged to residential consumers was 2.52 times greater.

33. Bank of Korea 1938: 244–245; Government General of Chosen 1937–1938: 139; *Chosen Keizainenpo* 1940: 20.

34. *Chosen Keizainenpo* 1940: 201; Hatada 1951: 219; Grajdanzev 1944: 138, 142–143, 146, 235.

35. Hatada 1951: 219; Grajdanzev 1944: 138, 222; Joseon Yeonguwhae 1935: 276; S. J. Ko 1988: 270–273, 380; J. B. Kim 1977: 251; Inanuma 1982: 141.

36. An old German Foreign Office document was discovered and reported on by the *Kyong Hyang Shinmun*, March 13, 1979.

37. J. B. Kim 1977: 251.

38. Inanuma 1982: 141.

39. Examples include Tae-sik Min, Heung-sik Pak, and Yon-su Kim.

40. See Appendix 6.1.

41. Of all the loans made by financial institutions in 1938 and 1943, about 65.3 to 77.8 percent, respectively, were made by banks.

42. Most of the loans of the Oriental Development Company, for instance, were extended to the agricultural sector— during 1912 and 1927, respectively, between 67.2 and 83 percent of the total. Other loans were scattered among the transportation, gas, electricity, manufacturing, mining, and other sectors (Toyo Takushoku Kaisha 1928: 26–28).

43. These percentage shares are very different from Suh's findings (1978: 98). The institutional loans for industrial and "miscellaneous" uses increased rapidly, from about a tenth of the total in the 1910–1919 period to about 20 percent for the remaining period.

44. Toyo Keizai Shinposha *Toyo Keizai Shinbun* (Asian Economic Newspaper), October 20, 1940. See also Porter 1936: 82.

45. Zenkoku Keizai Chosakikan Rengyokai Chosenshibu 1940: 137–139; Bank of Korea 1948: I, 277.

46. Deposits in the bank were equal to approximately 12 to 14 percent of all deposits in banking and financial institutions during 1932 and 1934. The value of its notes increased from 13.4 million yen in 1909 to 148.2 million in 1933.

47. K. J. Cho 1977: 477–482.

48. Sotokufu 1931: 267; Hosokawa 1941: 335–336; Joseon Yeonguwhae 1935: 306–307; Lockwood 1954: 517.

49. F. Fujita 1993: 278; K. J. Cho 1977: 477; ibid. 1994: 580, 538; S. J. Ko 1988: 340, 396–397.

50. Although these were supposed to have been private banks financed by and established solely for Koreans, they functioned more like public banks.

51. Sotokufu 1942: 125–127; Shokusan Ginko 1938b:70–71; ibid. 1940b: 30–32; Bank of Korea 1948: I, 278 and III, 76–77, 82–87; Himeno 1940: 369–371, 374; S. Suzuki 1939: 321, 347; Takeo Suzuki 1941: 268–269; F. Fujita 1993: 126–127, 212; Takahashi 1935: 500–501.

52. F. Fujita 1993: 120–121, 213–215, 125–128, 257–258, 427, 451.

53. F. Fujita 1993: 288–289, 305–307, 427.

54. K. J. Cho 1977: 477–482; F. Fujita 1993: 1, 284, 288–289, 305–307, 427, 456–457, 500.

55. The Industrial Bank was the arm of the Government General (S. J. Ko, 1988: 327–337).

56. F. Fujita 1993: 2, 488–490, 500; S. J. Ko 1988: 384–385.

57. F. Fujita 1993: 209–210. The following distribution of Industrial Bank loans illustrates the purposes for which loans were made in three sample years. In 1928 25 percent of its loans were for irrigation projects; 8 percent for land-improvement projects, including land reclamation; 7 percent for land and house improvements; 28 percent for "farming"; and 11 percent for credit unions. Only 5 percent was allocated to commerce (Hosokawa 1941: 327). Similarly, in 1930 162 million (69 percent) out of 232 million yen in loans were made to increase rice production, which included irrigation projects (K. J. Cho 1977: 480). Loans for land improvement came in second, at 9.8 percent (J. B. Kim 1974: 172). The remaining loans supported sericulture, animal husbandry, and agriculture in general. In 1931 the bank allotted 42.8 percent of its loans to irrigation projects. The drainage project to convert so-called wasteland into cultivated land was carried out, with 40 percent of the costs paid with bank loans and owners' equity. Government subsidies covered the rest (F. Fujita 1993: 456).

58. Shokusan Ginko 1938b: 70–71; 1940: 30–31.

59. Shokusan Ginko 1938b: 70–71; ibid. 1940b: 30–32; F. Fujita 1993: 314; K. J. Cho 1977: 480.

60. K. J. Cho 1994: 584; Shokusan Ginko 1938b: 70–71; ibid. 1940b: 30–32; F. Fujita 1993: 264–265, 270, 317, 330.

61. Shokusan Ginko 1938b: 70–71; ibid. 1940b: 30–32; Mizuda and Tsuchiya 1962: 133.

62. F. Fujita 1993: 265, 325–327, 487; K. J. Cho 1977: 474, 482; S. J. Ko 1988: 235, 384.

63. F. Fujita 1993: 264, 268–282, 322, 323, 459–466; S. J. Ko 1988: 256, 395.

64. F. Fujita 1993: 268–269, 322–324.

65. Many of these were for irrigation projects on paddy rice land and for the development of military industries. F. Fujita 1993: 305–307, 488–490; K. J. Cho 1994: 538.

66. F. Fujita 1993: 380, 383, 386, 406.

67. These complaints were reported by the Dong-A Ilbosa1922–1932.

68. Choo 1983: 96–97.

69. F. Fujita 1993: 362, 398, 406, 417.

70. F. Fujita 1993: 408–410, 464.

71. Bank of Korea 1948: I, 278, III, 78–79, 82–83; Himeno 1940: 369, 371, 374.

72. Bank of Korea 1948: III, 80–83; Himeno 1940: 369–371, 374.

73. Bank of Korea 1948: I, 278; Himeno 1940: 369, 374.

74. Takahashi 1935: 521.

75. The value of its regular or long-term loans (excluding commercial paper discounts) increased from less than 400,000 yen in 1910 to 5.2 million in 1915, 27.8 million in 1920, 73.7 million in 1930, and 84 million in 1935. Toyo Takushoku Kaisha 1928: 26–28; Sotokufu 1925; ibid. 1942: 68; Himeno 1940: 369, 371, 374; Moskowitz 1974; H. J. Kim 1990: 360. About 9 percent of these loans were made by the Oriental Development Company and the Trust Company (Takahashi 1935: 500–501; Takeo Suzuki 1941: 268–269; Bank of Korea 1948: III–82–87; Hosokawa 1941: 329).

76. Toyo Takushoku Kaisha 1928: 26–28; F. Fujita 1993: 120; K. Hosokawa 1941: 329–331. It invested in mining (10.5 million yen), textiles (9 million yen), gas and electric (6.8 million yen), and other industries (172.5 million yen).

77. Takahashi 1935: 540; S. Suzuki 1938: 358; K. J. Cho 1977: 482–485.

78. K. J. Cho 1994: 538.

79. Grajdanzev 1944: 208.

80. Official indebtedness in the agricultural sector was 435.8 million yen in 1930. To finance this debt, the rural credit unions advanced loans to meet 23.2 percent of it, the banks 54.6 percent, and individuals 13.3 percent. The rest was supplied by PNBFIs and government agencies. According to Lee, however, this did not include the value of loans contracted between private individuals, a figure he estimated to have been 101.1 million in 1930 yen (H. K. Lee 1936: 233).

81. Bank of Korea 1948: I, 345.

82. Bank of Korea 1948: III, 86–87; *Kokusei Gurafu* April 1940.

83. H. Shikada 1933: 202; B. M. Lee 1948: 283, 286, 294–295; Grajdanzev 1944: 173, 208.

84. There were forty-three Japanese loan operators in Seoul, twelve in Inchon city, and fifty-nine (out of seventy-four Japanese households) in Gaeseong city.

85. S. J. Ko 1988: 257–258.

86. Sotokufu 1942: 125–127; Takahashi 1935: 500–501; Hosokawa 1941: 324–325.

87. These new intermediaries were similar to such government-sponsored financial institutions as the agricultural banks, development banks, or industrial-finance corporations, which borrowed in foreign capital markets, under government guarantee, and reinvested in small firms at home. The United Kingdom, for example, established the Colonial Development Corporation with government funds. It was intended primarily to invest directly, but it also lent money to private undertakings, public utilities, and public corporations (Lewis 1955: 262).

88. Credit unions charged, on average, a 9.1 percent annual interest rate, which was lower than the market rate. Interest rates of credit unions also varied depending on whether the borrower was a member. The rate charged to members without collateral was 11.3 percent in September 1939, while rates of 18 percent or more charged to nonmembers were not uncommon. The maximum amount of loans to individual members who could supply collateral was as high as 1,000 yen; for those without collateral, there was a limit of 200 yen.

89. *Chosen Nenkan* 1939: 244–245.

90. Grajdanzev 1944: 207–208; D. Chung 1987.

91. S. J. Ko, for instance, contends that loan policies of the financial institutions favored Japanese landlords and businesses without offering the same services to Koreans (1988: 270–273).

92. Mizuda and Tsuchiya 1962: 108.

93. F. Fujita 1993: 402–403; Ahn 1975: 14, 16–17; Sotokufu 1932: 122–123, 125–126, 151–152.

94. In contrast, nearly three-quarters of the irrigated land owned by the Koreans was held by small and medium-sized landowners (those with less than 50 *jeong*). There probably was irrigated land before Japanese takeover of the country or land located in the areas where irrigation projects were undertaken for large Japanese landholdings.

95. 0.35/0.15 = 2.3 and 5/0.24 = 2.1.

96. 0.50/0.76 = 0.67 and 0.65/0.85 = 0.76.

97. Loans totaled 371.4 million yen to Japanese, 301.5 million to Koreans, and 3.8 million to others (Bank of Korea 1948: I, 277).

98. The Koreans' share of loans increased from about 29 percent of total loans in 1910 to 39.8 percent in 1937 and 45 percent in 1939, while the Japanese share of loans conversely decreased from 71 percent to 55 percent during the same period (S. Suzuki 1939: 324–326; Himeno 1940: 379; Takahashi 1935: 515, 519; Bank of Korea 1948: I, 277).

99. These were businessmen who cultivated relationships with the state and the Japanese and who gained the trust (*sinyo*) and support of bank administrators and bureaucratic officials in the colonial government. Apparently, their close ties to leading local Japanese business figures reinforced their credibility with the Japanese administration, which opened further channels for investment during the late colonial period.

100. S. J. Ko 1988: 270–273; *Chosen Keizainenpo* 1939: Appendix, 36; K. J. Cho 1994: 538, 623; K. Hosokawa 1941: 335–336; Joseon Yonguwhae 1935: 306–307.

101. F. Fujita 1993: 217, 235.

102. F. Fujita 1993: 402–403; Sotokufu 1932: 122–123, 125–126, 151–152; Ahn 1975: 14, 16–17.

103. Japanese government and bank officials calculated that as long as an entrepreneur put up 10 percent of the cost of a land-improvement project, the rest could easily be financed with low-interest bank loans and government subsidies. Some Japanese alleged that even if an entrepreneur invested less than 10 percent, he could borrow money from the Industrial Bank, receive government subsidies, pay off the loan in ten years, and become a landowner. In the case of irrigation projects, the colonialist further argued that even if less than 8 percent was invested, he could still become a successful landlord, according to officials (F. Fujita 1993: 310, 346–347, 389, 381, 402).

104. F. Fujita 1993: 402; Sotokufu 1932: 2.

105. When a plan to increase rice production was developed, many Korean landowners complained that the charges (actually taxes) for water, construction costs, and interest rates were too high. They also alleged that Korean landowners had no control over the management of the associations, as the associations were in Japanese hands, and that members were responsible for the debts of the irrigation associations. Dong-A Ilbosa 1922–1932; Hamanuma 1982: 141; Grajdanzev 1944: 97, 99.

106. Sotokufu 1932: 122–123. 125–126, 151–152; F. Fujita: 1993: 402–403; Ahn 1975: 16–17; Choo 1983: 97; Hamanuma 1982: 141.

107. Hagen 1968: 293–294.

108. The combined total of owners' equity in paid-in capital and retained earnings of all financial institutions was about 230.4 million yen in 1938 and 362.7 million in 1943.

109. Deposits increased from 3 to 7 million yen in 1909 to 242 million in 1921, 652 million in 1935, 1.1 billion in 1938, 2.03 billion in 1940, 4.8 billion in 1943, and 6.46 billion in 1944 (Sotokufu 1932: 275–277; ibid. 1942: 125; Hosokawa 1941: 324–336; S. Suzuki, 1938: 315–318; Takahashi 1935: 532–533; Bank of Korea 1948: III, 74–105).

110. Bank deposits increased rapidly from a very small sum in 1905 to 193.1 million yen in 1926, 684 million in 1938, 2.6 billion in 1943, and 3.3 billion in 1944.

111. Banks held 63 percent of the total in 1938 and 58.1 percent in 1943 and about 35.3 percent and 27.2 percent of deposits in all financial institutions in 1938 and 1943, respectively. Bank of Korea 1948: III, 74–83; Himeno 1940: 374; Hosokawa 1941: 335–336.

112. Deposits in the Bank of Korea increased from 10 million yen in 1910 to 508 million in 1943, more than fivefold.

113. Its predecessors, the Agricultural and Industrial Banks, did not have many deposits; for example, the largest sum of 7.9 million yen in 1918, representing only a fifth of deposits in all banks in Korea, which was rather small until later years. The deposits of the Industrial Bank increased to 65.7 million yen in 1926, 191.1 million in 1938, and 809 million in 1943 (Bank of Korea 1948: III, 76–77; Hosokawa 1941: 335–336; F. Fujita 1993: 212).

114. K. J. Cho 1977: 474, 477–482. Their deposits in the Industrial Bank and other public banks increased from a small sum in 1910 to 38.5 million yen in 1929, 234.3 million in 1940, and 1.41 billion in 1944.

115. Deposits increased from 21.4 million yen in 1929 to 366.1 million in 1943. Sotokufu 1932: 294–295; Sotokufu 1942: 130–131; Bank of Korea 1948: I, 277–278; III, 78–79.

116. Sotokufu 1932: 294–295; ibid. 1942: 130–131. Bank of Korea 1948: III, 84–85; Mizuda and Tsuchiya 1962: 56, 133.

117. The deposits of the credit unions increased from 400,000 yen in 1918 to 76.9 million in 1929, 229 million in 1938, 432.1 million in 1940, and 1.1 billion in 1943.

118. Deposits in postal savings increased from 3.2 million yen in 1910 to 37.8 million in 1934, 223 million in 1942, and 688.3 million in 15 million accounts in June 1945. Deposits increased by seventy times between 1910 and 1942, averaging 74 yen apiece and 45.83 yen per account, respectively (Sotokufu 1932: 356; ibid. 1942: 171; Bank of Korea 1948: III, 104–105).

119. They increased from about 5 million yen in 1910 to 105.6 million in 1926, 228 million in 1938, 949 million in 1943, and 1.38 billion in 1944 (Bank of Korea 1948: III, 80–83, 87).

120. The estimated amount of currency in circulation in Korea increased from 23.7 million yen in 1906 to 30 million in 1910, 98.1 million in 1920, 322 million in 1938, 1.45 billion in 1943, and 3.14 billion in 1944 (Bank of Korea 1948: I, 264, 278, III, 65–67, 145).

121. The outstanding sum of bonds issued by financial institutions was 724.7 million yen in 1938, which was increased to 1.65 billion in 1940, the year before Japan entered the war against the Allies, and 1.2 billion in 1943. Mizuda remembers that practically the entire amount of capital came from the financial market in Japan (Mizuda and Tsuchiya 1962: 18, 56, 101).

122. Shokusan Ginko 1938b: 236–237; Toyo TakushokuKaisha 1928: 156; Sotokufu 1916: 110–13; ibid. 1926: 108; ibid. 1935: 98; ibid. 1942: 68.

123. The outstanding sums were valued at 147.2 million yen in 1929 and 150.6 million in 1930, which appears to have been related to the issuance of Bank of Korea notes (Joseon Yeonguwhae 1935: 306–307).

124. Its predecessors, the Agricultural and Industrial Banks, were more or less self-supporting banks with stock shares and deposits. They attempted to raise debenture capital to fill the banks' needs, but was not successful to raise sufficient funds to meet their financial needs at the time. They were able to raise only 60,000 yen, or one-sixth of the targeted sum, and their needs were partially met with 3 million yen of bank bonds issued directly to the Oriental Development Company and the Industrial Bank (Kogyo Ginko) of Japan (F. Fujita 1993: 108–109, 117–120, 212, 245, 250, 301, 333–341, 426; K. J. Cho 1977: 482).

125. It had 6 million yen in outstanding bonds in 1918, which was quickly increased to 17.5 million in 1919, 49.6 million in 1921, and 100 million in 1923.

126. The value of bonds issued increased to 173.4 million yen in 1927 (Shokusan Ginko 1938b: 236; Bank of Korea 1948: I, 277; F. Fujita 1993: 301–302, 304; K. J. Cho 1977: 482; Takeo Suzuki 1941: 270).

127. The value of bank bonds issued climbed to 242.2 million yen in 1930 and 389.6 million in 1938. During World War II, the bank issued 450 million yen's worth of bonds. By 1943 and 1945, outstanding bonds reached 832.8 million and 967.2 million yen, respectively, which represented approximately sixteen to eighteen times its paid-in capital. At the end of World War II, it had floated 399.15 million yen's worth of government-guaranteed bank bonds, 558.68 million in ordinary bank bonds, and 15 million in discount bank bonds, totaling 1.06 billion yen.

128. Shokusan Ginko 1938b: 236–237; F. Fujita 1993: 250, 262, 301–302, 305–307, 336–341; K. J. Cho 1994: 603, 607; S. J. Ko 1988: 327–337.

129. A sum of 895 million yen was raised through bank bond issues between 1921 and 1937.

130. Loans of 21.5 million yen from the Deposit Bureau of Japan and 233.1 million in bond issues represented 35.9 percent of the loanable funds of all banks in Korea, which totaled 710.2 million yen.

131. A total of 405 million yen in government-guaranteed Industrial Bank bonds were issued after 1938.

132. The Industrial Bank held 445.5 million yen in nongovernment guaranteed ordinary bonds.

133. F. Fujita 1993: 304, 337–338, 341.

134. Toyo Takushoku Kaisha 1928: 156; ibid. 1938; Sotokufu 1942: 68; Mizuda and Tsuchiya 1962: 51; F. Fujita 1993: 120; Takeo Suzuki 1941: 270.

135. The sum borrowed increased from 1.5 million yen in 1910 to 30 million in 1935 and 42.8 million in 1940. As a result, the outstanding bonds of the company, which were valued at 19.4 million yen in 1912, quickly increased to 41 million in 1918, 168.2 million in 1927, 375.9 million in 1939, and 422.2 million in 1940.

136. Sotokufu 1932: 294–295, 749; ibid. 1942: 130–131; Bank of Korea 1948: 84–85. The outstanding bonds were valued at 28.5 million and 31.8 million yen in 1939 and 1940, respectively (Takeo Suzuki 1941: 270). These amounts might have been mistaken for the bonds issued in those years. They were equal to about half of the credit unions' loans in the early years and a little more than one-fifth in later years. The borrowing of the credit unions increased from an outstanding balance of a few million yen prior to 1920 to 46.8 million in 1929, 82.1 million in 1935, and 123.1 million in 1940 (Takeo Suzuki 1941: 270; K. J. Cho 1977: 478).

137. The bonds were valued at 28.5 million yen and 31.8 million, respectively.

138. The Irrigation Association, which started out with 1 million yen in 1913, had issued 104 million yen's worth of bonds by 1932 (Sotokufu 1932: 749, 841).

139. The commercial banks borrowed funds in the amount of 16.7 million yen in 1926, 47.8 million 1937, and 19.2 million in 1942 (Bank of Korea 1948: III, 80–81).

140. The amount of financial resources raised through bond issues by the public banks and GNBFIs was large: 675.6 million yen in 1938 and 1.46 billion in 1943 (Sotokufu 1942: 125–127; Takeo Suzuki 1941: 270; Mizuda and Tsuchiya 1962: 101; Takahashi 1935: 500–501; Hosokawa 1941: 324–325).

141. In 1943 they held 86 percent of the total (the Bank of Korea, 29.6 percent; the Industrial Bank, 26.4 percent; the Savings Bank, 3.1 percent; the Oriental Development Company, 7.2 percent; the credit unions, 15.9 percent; the Postal Savings System, 4 percent; and the private commercial banks and PNBFIs, 13.8 percent.

142. K. J. Cho 1977: 477. Unfortunately, history repeated itself in South Korea after World War II, and similar practices resulted in the financial crisis of the mid-1990s.

143. The exception to these expansionary and risky loan practices was found, surprisingly, during World War II, when the amount of deposits in Korea exceeded that of loans (5.8 billion yen in deposits, compared with 4.5 billion in loans in 1944). Otherwise, the inflationary spiral during World War II would have been far greater. This probably occurred because saving was forced on people and opportunities for consumption and investment in consumer-goods-oriented industries were limited during the war.

CHAPTER 7

1. Bank of Korea 1948: III, 43.
2. Takahashi 1935: 383; Grajdanzev 1944: 236.
3. Mizuda and Tsuchiya 1962: 86. Grajdanzev 1944: 236.
4. Grajdanzev 1944: 237.
5. Mizuda and Tsuchiya 1962: 109. Bank of Korea 1948: III, 145.
6. Daiichi Ginko 1926: 72ff.; B. M. Lee 1948: 263; *Chosen Keizainenpo* 1940: 514; Grajdanzev 1944: 236.
7. Tokanfu 1908: 585–586, 603. K. J. Cho estimates (1977: 189–192, 247, 248–249) the amount of Korean government loans from Japan during the 1905–1910 period at 44.71 million yen. If Japanese-government expenditures for administration and the military are included, the total for the same period is 79.44 million yen.
8. Sotokufu 1932: 748–750; ibid. 1942: 350–351; Government General of Chosen 1910, 1938, 1942; Chosen Ginko 1933: 28–29; Himeno 1940: 102, 131; Takahashi 1935: 447–451; Mizuda and Tsuchiya 1962: 11.
9. Former Japanese officials claimed that these bonds were never used to cover the deficit in the budget. Chosen Ginko 1933: 28–29; Mizuda and Tsuchiya 1962: 14–15, 30–31.
10. This estimate is supported by both Takahashi (1935: 441) and Grajdanzev (1944: 221). According to Takahashi, the Japanese Treasury carried the great burden of Korea on three counts: expenditures on the army and navy, grants to the Korean government, and payments of interest on debts connected with Korea. He estimated that between 1907 and 1931 these represented 343.3 million, 159.5 million, and 148.6 million yen, respectively, totaling 651.4 million. Grajdenzev estimated that the total for 1907–1938 could be as high as 1.27 billion yen. According to Takahashi's calculation, the total Japanese government "subsidy" to Korea between 1907 and 1931 was approximately equal to its military expenditures in Korea, which was also estimated at 651.4 million yen (441).
11. Tokanfu 1910a: 585–586, 596, 603; Residency General of Korea 1910: 110–111; Sotokufu 1914: 20–21; ibid. 1932: 748–750; ibid.1942: 350–351; Himeno 1940: 102, 131; Mizuda and Tsuchiya 1962: 14–15, 30–31; Takahashi 1935: 447–451, 466; K. J. Cho 1994: 463; Hosokawa 1941: 333–334.
12. There was a 5.96 million yen loan in 1908, a 4.66 million yen loan in 1909, and bond issues valued at 3.9 million yen in 1908 and 6.44 million in 1909. The Korean government also raised 3.73 million yen in 1908 and 18.44 million in 1909 for investment (*giop jagum*). As noted above, most of these loans were forgiven when Japan annexed Korea in 1910.
13. Nihon Takumusho 1938; *Chosen Nenkan* 1941; Bank of Korea 1948: III, 145; K. J. Cho 1977: 249; S. J. Ko 1988: 327–37; Mizuda and Tsuchiya 1962: 14–15, 18, 30, 71.
14. A total of 405 million yen in government-guaranteed Industrial Bank bonds were issued after 1938.

15. Hosokawa 1941: 333–334; Mizuda and Tsuchiya 1962: 108.

16. Mizuda and Tsuchiya 1962: 30.

17. Nihon Takumusho 1938; *Chosen Nenkan* 1941.

18. Himeno 1940: 133.

19. Sotokufu 1916: 110–113; ibid. 1926: 108; ibid.1935: 98; ibid. 1942: 68; Shokusan Ginko 1938b: 236–37; Toyo Takushoku Kaisha 1928: 156.

20. Another estimate shows that more than 70 percent of the 733.7 million yen that financed Japanese companies headquartered in Korea as of 1943 was financed in Japan in the form of loans, which came either from bond issues or as direct loans from banks and other financial institutions in Japan. As of 1943, borrowing through corporate bond issues floated in Japan financed about 8.2 percent of the total capital of companies headquartered in Korea and represented about 4 percent of the capital of all companies in Korea in that year. The major portion (e.g., 61.9 percent of capital financed from Japan in companies headquartered in Korea as of 1943) was in the form of direct loans from banks and other financial institutions in Japan, which represented 32.8 percent of the total capital of all companies in Korea. According to a study covering the period between 1910 and 1932, direct investment made up 28.4 percent of the total, which comprised the capital of companies headquartered in Korea (11.8 percent) and of companies headquartered in Japan (16.6 percent) (Hosokawa 1941: 333–334; Mizuda and Tsuchiya 1962: 108).

21. Hosokawa 1941: 333–334; Mizuda and Tsuchiya 1962: 108.

22. It is difficult to calculate all foreign direct investment in Korea, but in the case of companies, nearly 30 percent of the 733.7 million yen that was estimated to have financed Japanese companies headquartered in Korea as of 1943 was in the form of direct investment. It represented about 14 percent of the 1.57 billion yen of aggregate capital in all types of Japanese companies headquartered in Korea in 1943. However, according to a foreign report in 1939, Japanese investment in Korea was small in comparison with that made in Manchuria (*Far Eastern Survey* 1939: 295).

23. The investment of 279.2 million yen in private railroads (noted in chapter 4) was financed 37.3 percent with paid-in capital, 61.5 percent in bonds and loans, and 1.2 percent from other sources, while 44 percent (58.4 million yen) of the investment of 132.6 million yen in private tracks was financed through paid-in capital, 29 percent by bonds and loans, and 27 percent from other sources (Tokanfu 1909: 585; Sotokufu 1914: 274; ibid. 1931: 302; ibid. 1932: 320, 338; ibid. 1942: 177–178, 184, 189; K. J. Cho 1973: 401).

24. Hosokawa 1941: 333–334.

25. Chosen Ginko 1933.

26. Shokusan Ginko 1940b: 13–43.

27. Toyo Keizai Shinposha 1942: 26–27.

28. Keizyo Shoko Kaigijo 1944: 39–42.

29. Mizuda and Tsuchiya 1962: 108; *Kokusei Gurafu* 1942: 26–27; Kawai and Yoon 1991: 134–135.

30. The computations are based on the following equations: 2.62 billion yen $= 5{,}600 \times 0.468$. The figure, 5.6 billion yen, represents the capital stock of all companies headquartered in Korea as of 1943, which was estimated in chapter 4, and the number 46.8 percent stands for capital stock invested in Japanese companies headquartered in Korea by residents of Japan: $0.54 = (2{,}620 + 900)/6{,}520)$; and $0.452 = (2{,}620 + 900)/7{,}780$.

31. According to Mizuda, a former high-ranking Government General official in charge of the Finance Department, “retained earnings proper” represented 9 percent of company financing in 1943, while the “capital depreciation allowances” constituted 8 percent (Mizuda and Tsuchiya 1962: 108).

32. Mizuda and Tsuchiya 1962: 108.

33. Suh1 978: 69. Mizuda and Tsuchiya1962: 108.

34. Sotokufu 1932: 356; ibid. 1933: 336; Nihon Takumusho 1938; *Chosen Keizai-nenpo*1940: 513, quoted in Grajdanzev 1944: 199.

35. Shokusan Gingko 1941b and 1943c; Grajdanzev 1944: 220; Mizuda and Tsuchiya 1962; Ahn 1971: 97; Bank of Korea 1948: I, 318.

36. The deposits of Japanese residents in banks in Korea increased about thirtyfold in twenty-eight years, from 12 million yen in 1910 to 360 million in 1938 (Grajdanzev 1944: 234). This represents a large portion of Japanese financing of its investment in Korea, probably as much as one-fifth of the total Japanese investment. Investment in Korea by special companies such as the Oriental Development Company and Industrial Bank affiliate companies represented 18 percent of total capital. The rest was contributed by other companies (*Kokusei Gurafu* 1942: 26–27; Kawai and Yoon 1991: 134–135).

37. Chosen Ginko 1933: 39; Mizuda and Tsuchiya 1962: 108.

38. 1,190 million = 2,380 million × 0.5.

39. 1,140 million = (2,380 million × 0.5 + 600 million × 0.3) × 0.83.

40. 2,330 million = 2,380 million × 0.5 + (2,380 million × 0.5 + 600 million × 0.3) × 0.83).

41. 0.9 = (2,330 + 2,620 + 900)/(5,600 + 900).

42. Sotokufu 1932: 356; ibid. 1937–38: 169; ibid. 1942: 171.*Chosen Keizainenkan* 1940: 513.

43. Grajdanzev 1944: 234.

44. Mizuda and Tsuchiya 1962: 34. In the traditional period, there was no appropriate institution for the safekeeping of savings, and people in general had no clear idea of a bank. The number of Korean depositors in 1908 was only about 4,200, and their savings amounted to no more than 30,000 yen (Government General of Chosen 1937–1938: 168).

45. Sotokufu 1932: 336; ibid. 1933: 336.

46. 420 million = 600 million × 0.7.

47. Chosen Ginko 1933: 39; Mizuda and Tsuchiya 1962: 108.

48. 230 million = (2,380 million × 0.5 + 600 million × 0.3) × 0.17.

49. 650 million = 420 million + 230 million.

50. 0.532 = 2.98/5.60 and 0.468 = 2.62/5.60

51. 0.602 = (2.62 + 900)/5.85 and 0.398 = 2.33/5.85.

52. 0.021 = 50/2,380.

53. Mizuda and Tsuchiya 1962: 14–15, 30–31; Himeno 1940: 133. As of 1933, 368.8 million yen was allocated for investment projects, 48.1 million for institutional reforms and new investment projects, and 15 million for other purposes (Takahashi 1935: 468).

54. Tokanfu 1909: 585; Sotokufu 1914: 274; ibid. 1930b: Appendix, 22; ibid. 1931: 302; 1937: 578–579; ibid. 1942: 178, 184, 189; Shokusan Ginko 1940b: 17–18; Mizuda and Tsuchiya 1962: 87.

55. 2,062 million yen = 1,953 + 109.

56. 0.55 = (1,952+ 2,620 + 900)/9,950.

57. 0.45 = (217 + 2330 + 650 + 560 + 720)/9,950.

58. Saving is a habit that can to some extent be created through incentives and propaganda, as well as by supplying safe institutions in which to keep savings (Lewis 1955: 229; F. Fujita 1993: 324). As examined in chapter 9, the majority of Koreans under Japanese rule continued to exhibit a high propensity to spend, making large outlays for funerals, weddings, and other social or religious obligations of a formal character, as was the case during the traditional period. Such expenditures were commonly a heavy drain on personal and village income and thus deterred saving (Mizuda and Tsuchiya 1962: 34). It is interesting to note that a similar policy was implemented under President Chung Hee Park's leadership after South Korea became independent.

59. F. Fujita 1993: 245; G. McCune 1950: 120; Kwon 1984: 404–407; Mizuda and Tsuchiya 1962: 18, 71; S. J. Ko 1988: 258.

60. Kwon 1984: 400–402.

61. Kwon 1984: 403–404.

62. Sotokufu 1940: 728–729.

63. Mizuda and Tsuchiya 1962: 111.

64. Mizuda and Tsuchiya 1962: 111; Bank of Korea 1948: I, 318; Grajdanzev 1944: 220; Ahn 1971: 97–99.

65. The calculation is based on Ahn 1971: 97.

66. Bank of Korea 1948: I, 318.

67. Grajdanzev 1944: 220.

CHAPTER 8

1. Tokanfu 1909: 53; Sotokufu 1942: 2–3; Bank of Korea 1948: III, 11. Suh estimates an average of 1.5 percent per annum (1978: 41, 43).

2. These totals represent the net value of commodity production at constant prices, based on statistics provided by Sotokufu (1942: 4–5) and in the statistical appendixes of the *Chosen Keizainenpo*. The gross value of commodity production, which was 3.18 billion yen in 1938, was about 13 percent that of Japan.

3. Because of the lack of an appropriate price index, the wholesale price index is used to correct inflationary biases.

4. The net value of Korea's total production, estimated according to the coefficients that the Government Bureau of Statistics in Japan used for the census of 1930, was only 1.7 to 1.8 billion yen in 1938.

5. The official estimate shows commodity production for the three-year period to have been worth 972.6 million yen. In fact, it would have been close to 1.26 billion, based on commodity production in the later years.

6. Bank of Korea 1948: I, 264.

7. Suh 1978: 38, 43, 170–171.

8. Grajdanzev 1944: 84, 236.

9. Suh 1978: 43. Per farm, the gross value of production in U.S. dollars in 1938 for Korea was $153, compared with $248 for Japan and $1,828 for the United States (Grajdanzev 1944: 84–86).

10. N. Shikata 1938: 13–14.

11. Yoon Keun Lee's research paper, "Estimate of Korean National Income and Its Make-up, 1926–36," was reported in *Joong Ahng Ilbo*, October 10, 1967.

12. Suh 1978: 43; Kahng 1984: 1602.

13. This result is consistent with recent, more reliable national income statistics and growth rates after the 1960s. According to another source, the gross value of production per capita in 1938 was 138 yen, or US$35. This amount seems to be in line with another estimate, related to farm production. The gross value of production per farm was $153 in 1938 U.S. prices. On the assumption that each farm had, on average, six members, the per capita income in the farming sector would be $25.50.

14. Kahng 1984: 1602; Y. K. Lee 1971: 380–381.

15. *Chosen Keizainenpo*, 1939; *Chosen Nenkan* 1941.

16. Inanuma 1982: 141; Takahashi 1935: 79–80.

17. Some have argued that the government's successes were not remarkable: while some afforestation was chiefly the result of private efforts and was achieved in the south and

center, deforestation proceeded rapidly in the northern provinces, the only places where good stands of forests were to be found.

18. Grajdanzev 1944: 51–52.

19. Takahashi 1935: 79–80.

20. Sotokufu 1937–1938: 143; Grajdanzev 1944: 85. There were 23,000 in 1920, over 200,000 in 1936, 270,439 in 1939, and 280,000 in 1943.

21. Industrial production increased from 9 million yen in 1910 to 27.9 million in 1913, 201 million in 1921, 1.14 billion in 1938, and over 2.05 billion in 1943 (Tokanfu 1907: 286–287; *Chosen Keizainenpo* 1939: Appendix, 2–16; 1940; Sotokufu 1942: 4–5; Bank of Korea 1948: I, 98–99; Kawai and Yoon 1991: 32; H Shikata 1976: 174–175; Takeo Suzuki 1941: 215). The factories produced 195,000 yen's worth of output in 1907 (Suh 1978: 38; B. M. Lee 1948: 352–353; Grajdanzev 1944: 172; Kin 1965: 161; Y. Lim 1968: 79).

22. Nihon Takumusho 1938; Shokusan Ginko 1939: 60; *Chosen Keizainenpo* 1939: Appendix, 2–16; Sotokufu 1942: 4–5; Bank of Korea 1948: I, 98–111; B. M. Lee 1948: 352–353; Grajdanzev 1944: 172; Kin 1965: 161; Suh 1978: 46–47, 170–171.

23. Suh 1978: 38, 52, 146; Bank of Korea 1948: I, 100–1, 106, 111. Viewing the economy in terms of primary, secondary, and tertiary sectors, Kajimura estimates that the primary sector declined from somewhat less than 60 percent of "national domestic product" around 1910 to about 48 percent in the late 1930s, while the share of the secondary sector increased from about 4 percent to about 18 percent during the same period. The tertiary sector increased only slightly, from about 25 to 30 percent. The remaining share is attributed to "statistical discrepancy" (1983: 250).

24. Kawai and Yoon 1991: 34.

25. Kawai and Yoon 1991: 34; Takeo Suzuki 1941: 223, 235; Bank of Korea 1948: I, 106–109; Grajdanzev 1944: 150.

26. The value of output (all in 1930 prices) increased from 82.2 million yen in 1930 to 189.6 million in 1936 and 190.7 million in 1939. The value of production decreased to 175.7 million yen in 1943.

27. Takeo Suzuki 1941: 223, 235; Bank of Korea 1948; Kawai and Yoon 1991: 34; Grajdanzev 1944: 150, 155. The value of output expanded from 45.7 million yen in 1930, which placed textiles second only to the food industry, to 94.4 million in 1936, 116.9 million in 1939, and 151.5 million in 1943 (all in 1930 prices).

28. Bank of Korea 1948: I, 109–110; Kawai and Yoon 1991: 34.

29. The value of production increased from 10.5 million yen in 1930 to 39.5 million in 1943.

30. Figures are calculated on the basis of data found in Gradanjev 1944: 301; Bank of Korea 1948: I, 106, 100–101, 111; Kawai and Yoon 1991: 34.

31. This represented about 62,000 workers.

32. Takeo Suzuki 1941: 223, 235; Bank of Korea 1948: I, 106–109; Kawai and Yoon 1991: 34. The value of its output rose from 42.1 million yen in 1930 to 185.4 million in 1936, 291.4 million in 1939, and 455.8 million in 1943 (all in 1930 prices).

33. Grajdanzev 1944: 160–161; Suh 1978: 107.

34. Sotokufu 1939, 1941, 1942; Kawai and Yoon 1991: 34; Grajdanzev 1944: 141.

35. Pig-iron production alone increased from 2,000 tons in 1917 to 800,000 in 1943. The production of pig iron and steel was particularly encouraged after 1941. As a result of such rapid expansion, the value of production increased from an insignificant amount in 1905 to 6 million yen in 1930, 32 million in 1936, 79 million in 1939, and 134.7 million in 1943 (all in 1930 prices).

36. *Chosen Nenkan* 1941; Bank of Korea 1948: I, 104; Kawai and Yoon 1991: 34; Grajdanzev 1944: 157; Takeo Suzuki 1941: 223, 235. The value of output in current prices between 1930 and 1943 increased 22.3 times, an annual average increase of over 40 percent.

37. The increase was from 3,400 workers in 1929 to 47,821 in 1943.

38. The value of output increased from an insignificant amount in 1905 to 10.1 million yen in 1930, 30.9 million in 1939, and 51 million in 1943 (all in 1930 prices).

39. Suh 1978: 66.

40. Production was 1,825 kilowatt hours in 1912, 8,000 in 1917, 225,100 in 1929, 668,206 in 1937, and 1.24 million in 1942 (Takeo Suzuki 1941: 223, 235; Bank of Korea 1948: I, 137–38).

41. Bank of Korea 1948: III, 19; Suh 1978: 52.

42. The value of mining output grew from a few million yen in 1905 to 6.1 million in 1910, 26.5 million in 1929, 110 million in 1936, and 445.5 million in 1942. Tokanfu 1909: 562; Sotokufu 1942: 4–5; Kawai and Yoon 1991: 34; Tokanfu 1909: 562; Bank of Korea 1948; *Chosen Keizainenpo* 1939: 195; Hosokawa 1941: 304–305; Y. Lim 1968: 79. According to Suh, the production in mining increased at annual average rate of 9.9 percent (1978: 46–47, 170–171).

43. The Wunsan mines fluctuated somewhat from year to year but produced more than 14,000 kilograms between 1910 and 1944. Gold production alone increased from 5,641 kilograms in 1927 to 11,507 in 1933 and 17,489 in 1936, while the value of output increased from 3.7 million yen in 1910 to 5.6 million in 1927, 9 million in 1931, 49.9 million in 1936, and an average of 325 million (a total of 1.3 billion) between 1941 and 1944 (Hosokawa 1941: 306; S. J. Ko 1988: 380, 390; Takeo Suzuki 1941: 184).

44. Iron-ore production increased forty five times, from 140,000 tons in 1910 to 522,000 in 1933 and 6.3 million in 1943 (*Chosen Keizainenpo* 1939; U.S. Department of State 1945: 96; S. J. Ko 1956: 120; Grajdanzev 1944: 140).

45. Output was estimated at 42 million tons in 1932, 1.34 billion in 1936, and 1.75 billion in 1939.

46. The output of coal increased from less than 78,000 tons in 1910 to 2.3 million in 1936 and 6.9 million in 1941. The extraction of anthracite alone increased from 289,000 tons in 1920 to 2.3 million in 1938.

47. There were 1,167 locomotives, 2,027 coaches, 15,352 boxcars, and a work force of over 10,000 workers (Tokanfu 1909: 585; Sotokufu 1914: 274; ibid. 1931: 302, 917; ibid. 1940: 224–226; ibid. 1942: 178, 184, 189; Bank of Korea 1948: III, 161; Grajdanzev 1944: 188).

48. Private spur lines expanded from 328 kilometers in 1910 to 1,632 kilometers in 1942; other private tracks totaled 94.3 kilometers in 1942. The total length of private tracks in 1942 was 1,726 kilometers.

49. Government General of Chosen 1937–1938: 161–162; Grajdanzev 1944: 193.

50. Sotokufu 1931: 344–345; ibid. 1938: 220–221; ibid. 1942: 166–167.

51. Tokanfu 1909: 63–79; Bank of Korea 1948: III, 18–19; Kawai and Yoon 1991: 95.

52. Sotokufu 1942: 4–5.

53. This amount is smaller than that computed by Ban (1983: 4), which was 2.13 percent during the period between 1911 and 1941. The main reason for the lower figure is that Ban computes the growth rate of agricultural production between 1911 and 1917 too high resulting in an upward bias (1983: 16, 21). See also Suh 1978F. Fujita 1993: 355.

54. Y. Lim 1968: 79.

55. Suh 1978: 11–13. The rate of agricultural production increase should have been 1.7 percent per annum on average. Suh calculates that the value of agricultural production (in 1936 prices) increased from some 553 million yen in 1910 to 903 million in 1940, a rise of 63.3 percent at an average annual increase of 2.1 percent.

56. Ban's calculation shows that the average annual rate of agricultural output during the years 1911–1917 was a whopping 6.27 percent, while the average annual rate of growth for the period 1911–1941 was 2.13 percent, about a third of the former (1983: 18, 21).

57. Tokanfu 1909: 307; Sotokufu 1942: 4–5.

58. Suh 1978: 146.

59. Sotokufu 1932: 98; ibid. 1942: 44–45; Bank of Korea 1948: III, 26–27; Chosun Yonguwhae 1935: 259; Hosokawa 1941: 345; Suh 1978: 73, 143. Rice productivity in Taiwan was 1.45 *seok* (equivalent to 7.42 bushels) in 1938.

60. U.S. Supreme Commander for the Allied Powers, GHQ 1947a: 13–18; ibid. GHQ 1947b; *Chosen Keizainenpo*: 1936; 1939: Index, 7; ibid. 1942; *Chosen Nenkan*, 1941; G. McCune 1950: 100; Takeo Suzuki 1941: 128; Takahashi 1935: 262.

61. *Chosen Keizainenpo* 1939: Appendix, 2–16; ibid. 1940; Sotokufu 1940: 4–5; Bank of Korea 1936, 1944, 1948; Suh 1978: 38. Some scholars placed the share of the agricultural sector at about 85 percent of Korea's GDP in 1910–12 (B. M. Lee 1948: 352–53; Grajdanzev 1944: 172).

62. Suh's calculations, based on current and 1936 prices, had a slightly different result (1978: 46–47, 170–171).

63. Sotokufu 1910: 28–35; ibid. 1931: 46–57; ibid. 1942: 26–35; Nihon Takumusho 1938; *Chosen Keizainenpo* 1940; Kin 1965: 161; Suh 1978: 52.

64. *Chosen Keizainenpo* [1940; Kin 1965:161; Grajdanzev 1944: 86.

65. Sotokufu 1942: 4–5.

66. B. M. Lee 1948: 352–353; Grajdanzev 1944: 172; *Chosen Keizainenpo* 1939: Appendix, 2–16; ibid. 1940; Bank of Korea 1948.

67. The value of fish production increased from 9.4 million yen in 1911 to 190 million in 1938 and 372.7 million in 1941, while the number of fishing households increased from 72,000 to 192,200 (*Chosen Keizainenpo* 1939: Appendix, 2–16; Sotokufu 1942: 4–5; Bank of Korea 1948: I, 74, 78 and III, 48; Kin 1965: 161; Y. Lim 1968: 79; B. M. Lee 1948: 352–353; Grajdanzev 1944: 172).

68. The proportion of exports as a share of domestic production increased from 27.7 percent in 1920–1921 to 63.2 percent in 1939–1941 (Bank of Korea 1948: III, 43).

69. Grajdanzev 1944: 121; Lockwood 1954: 367, 401.

70. The first group, for instance, is not composed exclusively of consumption goods. It contained such products as ginned cotton, fishnets, and gunny sacks, while the second group includes bicycles and enamelware (Grajdanzev 1944: 234–235).

71. K. D. Kim 1987.

72. Bank of Korea 1948: III, 44–45; *Toyo Keizai Shinposha*, October 20, 1940; Grajdanzev 1944: 117–119; Kawai and Yoon 1991: 148–151.

73. H. K. Lee 1936.

74. *Far Eastern Survey* 1939: 294; S. B. McCune 1956: 88–90; Lockwood 1954: 533; Kajimura 1989: 237; Grajdanzev 1944: 92–94, 105.

75. Sotokufu 1939: Index, 19; Bank of Korea 1948: I, 104, III, 44–45; Kawai and Yoon 1991: 148–151.

76. Grajdanzev 1944: 228.

77. These figures are computed from the Bank of Korea 1948: I, 117, III, 50–59.

78. Grajdanzev 1944: 235.

79. Bank of Korea 1948: I, 101, III, 48; Suh 1978: 64; Kawai and Yoon 1991: 158–165, 175.

80. Takeo Suzuki 1941: 291; Kawai and Yoon 1991: 175.

81. Chosen Boeki Kyokai 1943; Bank of Korea 1948: 112–113.

82. Nor did Japan depend solely on its colonies to meet its essential requirements. With the exception of foodstuffs, only 10 percent of Japan's industrial materials, both raw and semiprocessed, were supplied by its colonies and by countries within its sphere of influence, including Korea. Despite its best efforts, Japan was never able to satisfy its import requirements for fibers, metals, petroleum, or fertilizers strictly from within the empire. In

1936 all the dependent areas together furnished no more than 15 percent of Japan's total imports of industrial materials (Porter 1936: 82; Lockwood 1954: 536).

83. There were only ninety-two factories with motor power in 1908: seventy-nine Japanese owned, three American owned, five Chinese owned, and five Korean owned (Tokanfu 1908: 325–330; Grajdanzev 1944: 152).

84. Sotokufu 1910: 28–35; ibid. 1931: 46–57; ibid. 1942: 26–35; *Chosen Keizainenpo* 1940; Joseon Yeonguwhae 1935: 237.

85. K. J. Cho 1977; Kim and Kim 1967: 67–70.

86. Joseon Yeonguwhae 1935: 237; B. M. Lee 1948: 292–293; Moon 1966: 103–104; K. Park 1973: 104.

87. Takeo Suzuki 1941: 215; Joseon Yeonguwhae 1935: 237; Grajdanzev 1944: 151–152.

88. Bank of Korea 1948: I, 100; Government General of Chosen 1937–1938: 143; Kajimura 1989: 325; Himeno 1940: 286; Suh 1978: 338, 170–171.

89. Companies with more than a million yen of paid-in capital in the industrial sector had 69 percent of the country's total paid-in capital in 1932. As few as 24 percent of all companies (171 out of 714) possessed 66 percent of the total capital of 185 million yen in industry in 1934. The paid-in capital of large factories (with more than 1 million yen in capital) expanded to possess 102 million in 1940 (Government-General of Chosen 1910: 260; ibid. 1931: 190–193; ibid. 1942; Shokusan Ginko 1939: 60). Similarly, the average paid-in capital of industrial enterprises with more than five workers increased from 98,684 yen in 1910 to 160,000 in 1929, 276,000 in 1935, and 358,000 in 1938. Sotokufu 1931: 190–93; Bank of Korea 1948: I, 100; Joseon Yeonguwhae 1935: 249; K. J. Cho 1973: 413, 419–429; Grajdanzev 1944: 172; H. J. Choi 1962: 406; B. M. Lee 1948: 352–353; Kawai 1943: 252–253.

90. Miyake 1937: 75, 143–144; Grajdanzev 1944: 136.

91. Bank of Korea 1948: I, 100.

92. K. J. Cho 1977: 518; Y. M. Kim 1972.

93. See Appendix 8.1.

94. Sotokufu 1932: 195; *Chosen Keizainenpo* 1939: 38–39; Moon 1966: 144–146; K. J. Cho 1973: 99, 413; J. B. Kim 1970: 18; B. M. Lee 1948: 352–353.

95. These were the Japan Soy Sauce Manufacturing Co. (200,000 yen in capital), the Saito Rice Cleaning Mill (100,000 yen in capital), the Fuzan Electric Light Generating Co. (100,000 yen in capital), the Jinseng Electric Joint Stock Co. (125,000 yen in capital), and the Dairin Lumber Co. (110,000 yen in capital) (K. J. Cho 1973: 413).

96. See Appendix 8.2.

97. Hatada 1951: 219; S. J. Ko, 1988: 399.

98. Sotokufu 1917: 222–225; ibid. 1921; ibid. 1927; K. J. Cho 1973: 419–420. There were four joint Korean-Japanese enterprises with 410,000 yen in capital and thirteen foreign companies with 3.1 million yen in capital.

99. B. M. Lee 1948: 352–353; Sotokufu 1910: 260.

100. Sotokufu 1925; ibid. 1932: 195; Moon 1966: 144–146; J. B. Kim 1970: 18; K. J. Cho 1965: 99.

101. Sotokufu 1921; ibid. 1927; Grajdanzev 1944: 51–52; K. J. Cho 1977: 527; Himeno 1940: 330.

102. See Appendix 8.3.

103. According to one source, nearly three-quarters of Korea's industrial production in 1928 was produced in Japanese enterprises. However, this statistic is misleading in one respect: the number of enterprises includes only those that had five or more workers. If we exclude household industries, the Korean part would shrink by at least one-half and perhaps by three-quarters.

104. Sotokufu 1917: 222–225; ibid. 1921; ibid. 1927; Bank of Korea 1948: I, 318; K. J. Cho 1973: 413, 419–420; ibid. 1977: 518; ibid. 1994: 548; B. M. Lee 1948: 292–293; Moon 1966: 103–104; K. Park 1973: 104; *Kokusei Gurafu* April 1940.

105. The figures are those of Y. M. Kim, who presented at a colloquium, cited in the *Hanguk Ilbo*, October 4, 1972.

106. Hosokawa 1941.

107. Toyo Keizai Shinposha 1942: 26–27.

108. Toyo Keizai Shinposha 1942: 26–27; Kawai and Yoon 1991: 134–135; K. J. Cho 1977: 448.

109. Sotokufu 1916: 174; ibid. 1928: 168; ibid. 1936: 142; Bank of Korea 1948: I, 86; Grajdanzev 1944: 147; S. J. Ko 1988: 389–395; K. J. Cho 1994: 580; Katadoshi 1939: 33.

110. Lockwood 1954: 221.

111. Grajdanzev 1944: 169; Mizuda and Tsuchiya 1962: 74–75; K. J. Cho 1973: 383–384; Huh 1989: 371; Lockwood 1954: 221; Hatada 1951: 216.

112. Grajdanzev 1944: 164.

113. Grajdanzev 1944: 177; Lockwood 1954: 221.

114. Ahn 1971: 83, 92–93. This type of arrangement appears to have persisted in South Korea after the Korean War.

115. Mizuda and Tsuchiya 1962: 76–77; Grajdanzev 1944: 176–177; K. J. Cho 1973: 383–385; S. J. Ko, 1988: 338–340, 344–349.

116. See Appendix 8.4.

117. Sotokufu *Tokeinenkan;* J. B. Kim 1970: 46; 1974: 96–97; Chosen Nokai 1944; Grajdanzev (1944: 106–107, 284) calculated that the area of land classified as Japanese increased from 242,500 *jeong* in 1921, to 346,200 in 1927, or by 43 percent. See also H. K. Lee 1936: 146; *Far Eastern Survey* 1939: 293; Brunner 1928: 71–72, 126; S. J. Ko, 1988: 262.

118. Sotokufu 1912: 19; B. M. Lee 1948: 346–347; S. J. Ko 1959: 342; K. J. Cho 1994: 429–434; J. B. Kim 1970: 46; ibid. 1974: 96–97.

119. Brunner 1928: 126.

120. Kobayakawa 1944: 94; Van Buskirk 1931: 71–72; Grajdanzev 1944: 106–107, 284.

121. One Korean newspaper reported that 25 percent of arable land and 70 percent of urban land were in Japanese hands.

122. These percentages are based on the following computations: 4.7 million *jeong*/20.583 million *jeong*; 3.71 million/10.477 million; 3.71 million/15.804 million; and 1 million/4.419 million.

123. Hatobe 1931: 116.

124. Chosen Nokai 1944: 591; J. B. Kim 1970: 46; ibid. 1974: 96–97; ibid. 1977: 224; K. J. Cho 1977: 392. The figures in 1909 and 1915 may reflect understated landholdings by Koreans before the land survey.

125. The computation of Japanese landholding is based on a number of fragmentary and incomplete data related to landownership. In South Korea in 1943 the Japanese owned 446,729 *jeong* of farmland (18.1 percent of the total of 2,472,177 *jeong*). Since total farmland in Korea in 1943 was 4,419,334 *jeong*, the farmland in North Korea would be 1,947,157 *jeong* (4,419,334 − 2,472,177 = 1,947,157). Assuming that the Japanese held about 14 percent of total farmland in North Korea (because their share of landholding there was somewhat smaller than in South Korea), their farm holdings could be estimated at 272,602 *jeong*. The sum of Japanese landholdings in South and North Koreas would be 719,331 *jeong*, which is about 16.3 percent of the total farmland in Korea. Bank of Korea 1948: I, 29–36 and III, 17.

126. Based on fragmentary and incomplete data related to landownership, the share of the Japanese may be estimated at a minimum of about 15.8 percent of total land in Korea.

This was calculated based on the following four facts and assumptions. According to landownership figures by nationality in South Korea in 1943, (1) South Korean farmland represented 56 percent of the total farmland in Korea and (2) Japanese owned 18.1 percent of it. Since the Japanese share of landholding in North Korea was somewhat smaller than that in South Korea, (3) it is assumed that the Japanese landholding was about 14 percent of total farmland in North Korea, and (4) the shares of the ownership of the nonfarm land in South and North Korea were distributed in the same ratios as those of farmland ($0.181 \times 0.56 + 0.14 \times 0.44 = 0.16$. Assuming that Japanese holdings of all land, including farm and forest land, was the same (16 percent), the figure of 3,293,280 was derived from the following equation: 20,582,882 (total acreage in *jeong*) x 0.16. Bank of Korea 1948: I, 29–36, III, 17.

127. These calculations set Japanese ownership of cultivated land at about 400,000 *jeong* and 3.5 million *jeong* of forest land. These computations appear to be in agreement with Grajdanzev's estimate (1944: 106).

128. In 1940 the price was 93 yen per 344 *pyeong* of paddy field in Korea, compared with 167 yen in Japan (Grajdanzev 1944: 292). However, Edwin H. Gragert refutes the reports that Japanese corporations and entrepreneurs snapped up prime land at fire-sale prices. He argues that the notorious Oriental Development Company, at least initially, rarely displaced Korean landholders and that they tended instead to purchase inferior land from absentee landlords. He shows that these effects were most pronounced in villages closely integrated into the Japanese rice market (1994: 210). Also, see K. J. Cho 1994: 435; G. McCune 1950: 81; S. J. Ko 1988: 235; Grajdanzev 1944: 81; the Chosen Shokusan Ginko Survey (quoted in Takeo Suzuki 1941: 264).

129. B. M. Lee 1948: 360; Nasu 1941: 129–131; Kanbe 1931: 205–210; Nihon Tokeikyoku 1939: 4–5; Lockwood 1954: 240; S. Suzuki 1939: 456. Rates were computed from surveys by Shokusan Ginko (cited in T. Fujita 1940: 85). The return on dry land was higher than on paddy field during the 1931 to 1940 period (Takeo Suzuki 1941: 266).

130. B. K. Choo 1981; B. M. Lee 1948: 360.

131. Included was land that had been used as collateral and ended up in the possession of lenders (Mizuda and Tsuchiya 1962: 51).

132. Based on their customs, many Koreans treated collateral loans as sales of land and did not pay them off. People in general did not have a clear concept of landownership.

133. B. M. Lee 1948: 357; *Chosen Keizainenpo* 1939: 38–39; F. Fujita 1993: 108, 186; Hatobe 1931: 116; Mizuda and Tsuchiya 1963: 23–24, 51.

134. *Korea Repository* 1896: 317.

135. Residency General of Korea 1907–1910; 1908–1909: 20.

136. Gragert 1994; Kim and Kim 1967: 162.

137. M. K. Park 1978; 530, 548–554; K. J. Cho cites 20.4 million yen (1977: 350; 1994: 500, 504–505, 508); G. McCune reported that the cost of the survey was 30 million yen (1950: 54). See also F. Fujita 1993: 202, 283; Guksa Pyonjib Uiwonwhae 1994: 686–690; Hosokawa 1941: 250–251; Shin 1978: 487–591; Takeo Suzuki 1941: 72–73.

138. H. Chung 1921: 110–111.

139. K. J. Cho estimated that about 10 percent (357,000-plus *jeong*) of all farmland and 58 percent (9,240,000 *jeong*) of wooded land were transferred to the Government General (1979: 5).

140. Kim and Kim 1967: 162; K. J. Cho 1977: 364–367; F. Fujita 1993: 196–201.

141. K. J. Cho 1977: 365.

142. Government General of Chosen 1937–1938: 147.

143. Kwon 1984: 305–306. These calculations are based on Sotokufu 1935: 262–278; Kim and Kim 1967: 162.

144. Gragert 1994: 210.

145. Bank of Korea 1948: I, 28–29; M. K. Park 1978: 548–554; Takeo Suzuki 1941: 72–73.

146. Ahn 1975: 7–8.

147. Takeo Suzuki 1941: 262–263; H. K. Lee 1936: 146; S. J. Ko 1988: 244–245; J. B. Kim 1970: 46.

148. Bank of Chosen 1920: 132; Bank of Korea 1948: I, 30; Kobayakawa 1941: 94; J. B. Kim 1970: 51; ibid. 1977: 225. The Mitsubishi Company, for example, owned large plantations (H. J. Choi 1962: 345; H. K. Lee 1936: 145–146).

149. Sotokufu 1910: 182; S. J. Ko 1988: 237. Another report indicated that 692 large Japanese landlords had invested 7.9 million yen in agriculture as early as 1909.

150. See Appendix 8.5.

151. Sotokufu 1916: 110–113; ibid. 1917: 132; ibid. 1926: 108; ibid. 1935: 98; ibid. 1942: 68; K. J. Cho 1965; Hosokawa 1941: 341; Bank of Korea 1948: I, 29–30; Daehan Geumnyung Johap 1955; Huh 1989: 372.

152. See Appendix 8.6.

153. A similar situation developed in South Korea after the 1960s. Most large *zaibatsu*-owned and speculated in nonagricultural real estate, from which they were able to make huge profits.

154. Kobayakawa 1944: 94.

155. Joseon Yeonguwhae 1935: 293; H. J. Kim 1990: 360; K. J. Cho 1977: 450; S. B. McCune 1956: 53–54; Grajdanzev 1944: 114.

156. Bank of Korea 1948: I, 28–29, 338–339; M. K. Park 1978: 548–554; Takeo Suzuki 1941: 72–73, 246. According to government statistics, the share of farming by pure tenant farmers increased from 41 percent of all cultivators in 1914 to 53.8 percent in 1941, a 31.2 percent rise during the twenty-seven-year period.

157. *Chosen Nenkan* 1939; Bank of Korea 1948: I, 28–29, 338–343; M. K. Park 1978: 548–54; Takeo Suzuki 1941: 72–73, 246, 248; Hosokawa 1941: 250. According to Suzuki, of a farming population of 2.9 million households in 1938, about 80 percent (2.3 million families) were tenants or part-owner/cultivators who were mostly poor and farmed on a small scale (Sotokufu 1944: 534). Similarly, in 1943, of over 3 million farm households, about one-half rented all the land they farmed, one-third rented a substantial portion, and only about one-sixth owned all the land they farmed.

158. M. K. Park 1978: 544 548; Takeo Suzuki 1941: 47–48. Legally, landownership was in the hands of the king; strictly speaking, landlords did not have the right to sell and buy land (F. Fujita 1993: 183).

159. See Appendix 8.7.

160. Nihon Takumusho 1939: 184–185; *Chosen Keizainenpo* 1939: 100; G. McCune 1950: 115–116; H. K. Lee 1936; Hosokawa 1941: 250–251; S. J. Ko 1988: 279–287; Grajdanzev 1944: 116.

CHAPTER 9

1. Grajdenzev 1944: 293.

2. Tokanfu 1909: 585; Sotokufu 1914: 274; ibid. 1931: 302, 917; ibid. 1942: 178, 182–184, 189; Suh 1978: 147.

3. *Chosen Keizainenpo*, 1940; Bank of Korea 1949: IV, 35; H. J. Choi 1962: 396; J. B. Kim 1977: 383.

4. Grajdanzev 1944: 86.

5. Grajdanzev 1944: 114; Takeo Suzuki 1941: 87; Bank of Korea 1948: I, 343. It was estimated that aggregate rentals in rice farming were, on average, about 60 percent of the crop (Asano 1941; Takeo Suzuki 1941: 251–253; F. Fujita 1993: 398).

6. Grajdanzev 1944: 292; Asano 1941; Takeo Suzuki 1941: 251–253; Ahn 1975.

7. Rent in kind in Korea was five to ten times that in Western countries at the time. The Bank of Korea (1948: I, 343) lists the following survey: rents in Korea, 7.97–11.95 yen (1930); 2.5 yen in England (1910–1914); 2 yen in Scotland (1912–1920); 1.8 yen in Ireland (1881–1920); 1.92 yen in Germany (1913); 1.5 yen in Austria (1913); 1.2–1.6 yen in France (1913); and 1–1.5 yen in U.S. (1913).

8. The landlords, who constituted less than 2 percent of the farming class, acquired nearly 40 percent of the rice produced in 1932, about twenty times the national average. This constituted more than one-third of the total rice output for 1932. It was speculated that the ulterior motive of this plan was to export 8 million *seok* of rice (which was 87 percent of 9.2 million *seok*) to Japan (Grajdanzev 1944: 117).

9. The agricultural population was made up of about 56 percent tenants, 19 percent owner/cultivators, and 23 percent owner/tenants. The tenants' share of rice production in 1938 was 19.8 percent, and the shares of owner-cultivators and owner-tenants were 14.8 percent and 28.1 percent, respectively (Grajdanzev 1944: 117).

10. Government General of Chosen 1937–1938: 218; Grajdanzev 1944: 117; F. Fujita 1993: 398; Takeo Suzuki 1941: 251–253.

11. While the cultivated area per Japanese farm in Japan averaged about 2.7 acres, the average size of Korean farms reached 3.7 acres. The average Korean farm, however, had a lower unit yield than the average in Japan. The Korean peasant yielded about 58 percent of the Japanese (*Far Eastern Survey* 1939; Grajdanzev 1944: 292). This amount was slightly larger than the average in Japan (Bank of Korea 1948: I, 343; Ugaki 1935: 33).

12. Shirushi 1940: 14–15; Government-General 1937–38: 218.

13. Takeo Suzuki 1941: 249; Hatada 1951: 225; Grajdanzev 1944: 82.

14. Ugaki 1935: 82.

15. Choo 1981: 11–30.

16. Grajdanzev 1944: 156, 176–177, 205; *Toyo Keizai Shinposha,* October 11, 1941; Lockwood 1954: 287.

17. Harrington 1944: 166; Lockwood 1954: 287; F. Fujita 1993: 324, 341.

18. Takahashi 1935: 508.

19. *Toyo Keizai Shinposha,* October 11, 1941, cited in Grajdanzev 1944: 156.

20. Sotokufu 1914: 274; ibid. 1931: 302, 917; ibid. 1942: 178, 182–184, 189; Bank of Korea 1948: III, 145.

21. The inflation was caused by expansionary fiscal and monetary policies related to the Government General financing its deficit budget, especially during World War II. The money supply increased about 210 times between 1904 and 1945 at an annual rate of about 17 percent. The expansion of the money supply between 1937 and 1945, when Japan launched the military conquest in Asia, was especially rapid, averaging about 52 percent a year. At the end of World War II, the Bank of Korea issued a total of 4.3 billion yen in banknotes against 1 billion yen in loans and 1 billion yen in deposits. According to the official wholesale price index of Seoul (a national index did not exist), the price level rose about 415 percent between 1910 and 1944, the annual average rise being about 4.2 percent. The price rises during 1937 and 1944 were more explosive, officially estimated at about 30 percent per annum.

22. Westphal 1982: 35; Suh 1978: 149.

23. Mizuda and Tsuchiya 1962: 109.

24. Himeno 1940: 294; Grajdanzev 1944: 184. All hours given are exclusive of time for lunch and recesses.

25. Grajdanzev 1944: 152, 182–184.

26. According to Hosokawa (1941: 333), the tax burdens of national, provincial, and local governments per person in 1939 were 48.56 yen for Japanese city dwellers and 47.36 for Japanese rural dwellers, while those of the Koreans were 8.66 and 2.78 yen, respectively. The figures of 48.21 and 4.84 were derived through the following computations: $48.56 \times 0.71 + 47.36 \times 0.29$ and $8.66 \times 0.35 + 2.78$ x 0.65, respectively. The numbers 0.71 and 0.29 represent the urban and rural populations of Japanese in Korea, respectively, and 0.35 and 0.65 represent those of Koreans.

27. Takeo Suzuki, 1941: 262.

28. D. H. Yun 1999. Increases in the income and wealth of Korean landlords were not limited to increases in agricultural productivity and rent alone. Other factors enabled them to be well off. Some landowners became rich through mining ore on their land or constructing a port on a hitherto empty coast. A few former high-ranking Korean government officials, who were typically landlords, became wealthy when they received generous Japanese government rewards and pensions for their roles in the Annexation. According to one historian, Wan Yong Yi, who was the last prime minister of the Joseon dynasty and who signed the Annexation treaty with Japan, was reputed to have been the second wealthiest man in Seoul in the 1920s.

29. Mizuda and Tsuchiya 1962: 101; Grajdanzev 1944: 161, 176–177.

30. Grajdanzev 1944: 161, 177.

31. Koreans had to pay higher interest rates when borrowing money (D. Chung 1987).

32. Grajdanzev 1944: 176–177; a German Foreign Office document discovered and reported by the *Kyong Hyang Sinmun*, March 13, 1979: 3; Huh 1989: 362–367.

33. Tokanfu 1909: 307; Sotokufu 1942: 4–5; Tokunaga 1907: 904; Kanbe 1931: 5–6; H. Shikata 1933: 103; Grajdanzev 1944: 79.

34. S. S. Kim 1985: 95.

35. Sotokufu 1909: 307; ibid. 1916: 28–35; ibid. 1931: 46–57; ibid. 1942: 4–5, 26–35; Suh 1978: 117.

36. Reeve 1963: 7.

37. Sotokufu 1941, 1942, 1943; Bank of Korea 1948: I, 87, 100; K. S. Lee 1990: 321; Ahn 1989: 430–431.

38. Tokanfu 1909: 307; Sotokufu 1932: 50–9; ibid. 1942: 4–5, 28–35; Kawai and Yoon 1991: 95; Himeno 1940: 40.

39. Sotokufu 1941, 1942, 1943; Bank of Korea 1948: I, 87, 100; Ahn 1989: 430–431.

40. As a result, the departure of the Japanese after World War II left a management vacuum (Huh 1989: 374).

41. Senior government officials were appointed at different levels of ranking, similar to military ranking.

42. Ahn 1989: 417.

43. J. C. Chung 1989: 469.

44. S. S. Kim 1985: 95; Grajdanzev 1944: 182–183.

45. Of the Korean workers in the mining industry, 75.2 percent had no education, compared with only 4.7 percent of the Japanese. Nearly 99 percent of Korean but only 27.8 percent of Japanese workers in mining had an education at the elementary school level or less. About 72.2 percent of Japanese mine workers stopped short of a high school education, and 43.2 percent had a high school education (Ahn 1989: 417).

46. In the case of railroads, Koreans made up about 40 percent of all employees until the 1930s, but only 11 to 24 percent of them had received any formal education (Bank of Korea 1948: I, 8).

47. Grajdanzev 1944: 199, 267. The hiring of Japanese workers by Japanese enterprises was obviously based more on nationality rather than on economic considerations. Hatobe, the first editor of the Japanese newspaper in Korea, *Keijo Nippo,* urged the Japanese government and businesses to provide opportunities for Korean workers (1931: 202–217).

48. The least discriminatory employer under Japanese rule was reputed to have been the Industrial Bank, which set a quota of 30 percent Korean workers (F. Fujita 1993: 242; Moskowitz 1979).

49. Kawai and Yoon 1991: 19.

50. Sotokufu 1942: 400–405; F. Fujita 1993: 244, 259; Grajdanzev 1944: 178; Reeve 1963: 7; K. Hosokawa 1941: 364.

51. Surveys and reports on wage levels in manufacturing, construction, and services indicate that Korean workers typically received about 50 percent of Japanese workers' salaries and wages in the same positions. In 1919 the daily wages of Japanese workers in industry were higher than those of their Korean counterparts—between 33 and 400 percent more. According to most reports, the pay ratio between Japanese and Korean factory workers, for both males and females, was at least two to one even as late as the early 1930s. According to a survey conducted in 1932, Korean laborers' daily wage was 0.9 yen, as compared with 1.90 yen for Japanese workers. A similar investigation of enterprises with fifty or more workers conducted by the Government General in 1933 found that the daily pay of an average blue-collar Japanese worker was 1.93 yen a day, while that of a Korean was 0.92. Official statistics on large-scale businesses in 1939 gave a pay rate of 2.32 yen a day for a Japanese worker and 1.10 for a Korean.

52. S. Suzuki (1939: 300–301) cited surveys conducted by Sotokufu in Korea and the Tokyo Chamber of Commerce in Tokyo.

53. F. Fujita 1993: 242; Moskowitz 1979.

54. In 196 factories with more than fifty employees engaged in thirty-seven varieties of businesses during 1929 and 1931, the average daily wage of Korean male adult workers in 1930 was 0.94 yen, as compared with 1.96 for Japanese adult male workers. The average Korean female worker's wage was 0.61 yen, which was lower than a Japanese female worker's wage of 1.02 yen. If comparisons are made among firms that employed fewer than fifty workers, the wage differentials were even greater. While the Japanese women were paid 1 yen a day in 1933, a Korean woman received half that (50 *sen*) (Himeno 1940: 302; Hosokawa 1941: 351–352; S. Suzuki, 1939: 298–305; Sotokufu 1910: 270; ibid. 1942: 150–157; Kawai and Yoon 1991: 101; S. S. Kim 1985: 255).

55. Hosokawa 1941: 333.

56. Sotokufu 1920; ibid. 1933: 148; Joseon Yeonguwhae 1935: 267–269; S. S. Kim 1985: 95–96; Reeve 1963: 7, 64; Takahashi 1935: 430; Himeno 1940: 301; S. Suzuki 1939: 289 (based on a Sotokufu survey); Mizuda and Tsuchiya 1962: 13, 152.

57. Mizuda and Tsuchiya 1962: 152.

58. It was alleged that the Koreans were lazy and indifferent to technical improvements, had no desire to advance or use their intellect in work, had a very weak sense of responsibility, lacked inventiveness, and disliked discipline and rules. (Takahashi 1935: 402; Ito 1942: 214; Bank of Chosen 1920: 11. Yet there were many accolades accorded to them. Korean workers were thought to be healthy; to possess "sufficient strength" to withstand long hours of monotonous work; and to have the ability to perform the required work. Those who had obtained an education were considered efficient (Grajdanzev 1944: 152, 179).

59. Kawai and Yoon 1991: 107; Grajdanzev 1944: 179.

60. S-W. Park 1999.

61. Takeo Suzuki 1941: 249; Hatada 1951: 225; Grajdanzev 1944: 82.

62. Hosokawa 1941: 333.

63. Bank of Korea 1948: III, 14; H. K. Lee 1936: 18. Some of the land that was distributed/leased to Japanese immigrants included that acquired through either confiscation (Shin 1978: 545) or purchase by Japanese private and public entities, such as land-development companies (Hosokawa 1941: 250–251; K. J. Cho 1977: 360, 368). When the Oriental Development Company awarded these lands to Japanese immigrants, the Korean farmers lost their land, and some moved to Manchuria (F. Fujita 1993: 202).

64. Sotokufu 1930: 113, 115; ibid. 1942: 68; H. K. Lee 1936: 284. The company sought 13,095 Japanese farmers between 1910 and 1926, for which 21,832 applied and 9,096 were granted permission to immigrate (Toyo Takushoku Kaisha 1938: 171; K. J. Cho 1994: 621).

65. B. M. Lee 1948: 349.

66. Governor General of Chosen 1914; Nihon *Takumutokei* 1938; Bank of Korea 1948; Grajdanzev 1944: 79–80, 105, 291.

67. Sotokufu 1910: 182; Bank of Chosen 1920: 132; *Far Eastern Survey* 1939: 293.

68. Grajdanzev 1944: 130.

69. Bank of Korea 1948: I, 318.

70. Suh 1978: 65; Kajimura 1989: 343; Sotokufu 1932: 24–25, 206; ibid. 1942: 16, 193.

71. S. B. McCune 1956: 53–54; Hosokawa 1941: 350–351; Kimura 1993: 629–652.

72. *Chosen Keizainenpo* 1939: 17–18; Gajdanzev 1944: 192.

73. H. Shikata 1929: 437–441; Kimura 1993: 629–652; Grajdanzev 1944: 234.

74. Sotokufu 1932: 248–250; S. Suzuki 1939: 272–273; Grajdanzev 1944: 139; *Chosen Keizainenpo* 1939; Bank of Korea 1948: I, 146.

75. Sotokufu 1932: 360–361, 363–364; ibid. 1942, 168; *Chosen Keizainenpo* 1940: 514; Grajdanzev 1944: 200.

76. Sotokufu 1932: 408–409; Nihon Takumusho 1938; Grajdanzev 1944: 260, 269; Hosokawa 1941: 350–351.

77. Bank of Korea 1948: III, 18, 28; J. H. Cho 1970: 92; Grajdanzev 1944: 118; Kajimura 1989: 237; Chosen Boeki Kyokai 1943; S. B. McCune 1956: 9.

78. Sotokufu 1934; H-J. Choi 1962: 399; Nihon Noshomusho 1941: 270; H. Shikata 1929: 437–441; Grajdanzev 1944: 294.

79. Bank of Korea 1948: III, 28; Suh1978: 86–87; *Far Eastern Survey* 1939; Grajdanzev: 119, 294.

80. Kimura 1993: 629–652.

81. A number of government investigations in Korea revealed that the proportion of marginal income spent on rice was quite high. For example, in the provinces of Chung Cheong Namdo, Joella Bukdo, and Joella Namdo, which produced most of the rice in South Korea, the marginal propensity to consume rice at the lowest income levels was 0.93 or above. For higher income levels in the same provinces the marginal propensity ranged from 0.7 to 0.85. In the major rice-producing province of Joella Namdo, when after-rent rice income increased by 65.5 percent or 3.8 *seok* (from 5.8 to 9.6 *seok*), the entire increase was consumed. Only when the farmers' income was above 9.6 *seok* did they not consume all of their additional harvest of rice. As the after-rent income rose by 5.3 *seok*, in going from 9.6 to 14.8 *seok*, they consumed 4.4 *seok*, setting the marginal propensity to consume between these higher income levels at 0.85. Only at the highest income levels (from 14.8 *seok* to 23.7 *seok*) was the marginal propensity to consume less than half, or 0.48.

82. F. Fujita 1993: 108, 137, 142.

83. Higuma 1943: 425–26; Takeo Suzuki 1941: 250.

84. K. Takahashi 1935: 201; Grajdanzev 1944: 119; K. J. Cho 1977: 389; J. B. Kim 1977: 354.

85. Shirushi 1940.

86. Ugaki 1935: 33; Bank of Korea 1948: I, 344; Foreign Affairs Association of Japan 1939–1940: 918; Grajdanzev 1944: 209.

87. Takeo Suzuki 1941: 251–253; Grajdanzev 1944: 119, 208; Ugaki 1935: 82; Hatada 1951: 225; *Far Eastern Survey* 1939.

88. Grajdanzev 1944: 180–182.

89. Kimura 1993: 629–652.

90. Drake 1930: 196.

91. It is certain that the Japanese deprivation of Korean national sovereignty through colonization and the strict Japan-first colonial policy depressed most Koreans. As a result, Korean mental health also seems to have suffered (Grajdanzev 1944: 80, 117).

92. J. B. Kim 1974: 148.

93. In 1932 the average rice income per member of the landlord families was 11.43 *seok*. Taking 1.5 *seok* as the maximum per capita rice consumption for the year, the total quantity that could be consumed by the landlord class was estimated at about 850,000 *seok*. The remainder, over 5.6 million *seok*, was "landlords' surplus." This constituted more than one-third of the total rice output for 1932. It was speculated that the ulterior motive of this plan was to export 8 million *seok* of rice (which was 87 percent of 9.2 million *seok*) to Japan. This constituted more than one-third of the total rice output for 1932.

94. F. Fujita 1993: 137, 186; Takahashi 1935: 220, 223–224, 529; K. J. Cho 1977; D. Chung 1987: 165.

95. In 1931 there were 8,664 Korean, 3,387 Japanese, and 37 foreigner lenders.

96. According to one report, of the total indebtedness of farm families in 1932, 25.6 percent was owed to individuals or to mutual-aid societies. The rest came from credit unions (17.4 percent in 1932 and 56.9 percent in 1936), *gae* (mutual-aid associations, 9 percent), and banks (10 percent). According to a 1936 Korean Farm Association survey, cited in D. Chung (1987: 165) the average owner/tenant contracted 43.1 percent of his loans with private individuals. Also, several investigations conducted in 1933 indicated that loans from individuals (mostly well-to-do landlords) made up more than 60 percent of the total debt of farmers in 1932.

97. Takahashi 1935: 221–222. By province, the percentage of farm households carrying debt ranged from 55 to 85 percent in 1930 (Bank of Korea 1948: I, 344; K. J. Cho 1977: 389; S. J. Ko 1988: 258). The governor of a southern province (Jeonbuk) reported in 1932 that 92.6 percent of sampled households in the province carried debt (Kwon 1984: 400; Grajdanzev 1944: 208).

98. Government General of Chosen 1937–1938: 220; Higuma 1943: 425. Takeo Suzuki 1941: 249; S. J. Ko 1988: 258.

99. Lee estimates the average figures at 251 yen and nearly 300 yen in the same year (H. K. Lee 1936: 233). According to a survey of farm families in Hamgyeong-bukdo Province, individual lenders financed as much as 55 percent of total loans of 225,914 yen. This sum included the mutual-aid societies. See also Bank of Korea 1948: I, 344; K. Takahashi 1935: 220–223; Grajdanzev 1944: 208.

100. Porter 1936: 87.

101. Bank of Korea 1948: I, 344.

102. This estimate appears to have been too low, since the amount borrowed by the farmers from private persons was apparently underestimated. In 1932 it was given as 128 million yen, or 26 percent of the total indebtedness. Several investigations conducted among the farmers in 1933, however, showed that loans from individuals made up more than 60 percent of the total (Grajdanzev 1944: 208).

103. The total indebtedness of the agricultural sector in 1930 was 435.8 million yen. But according to Lee's estimate, this amount did not include the unascertainable data of amounts

of loans between individuals and loans advanced by banks without collateral. The "legal value" of all arable land in Korea in 1930 was estimated to have been 846 million yen. The sales value of the land was supposed to have been, on the average, about three times the legal value. Accordingly, the total sales value of arable land would have been 2,538 million yen. Thus, in 1930 no less than 60 percent of the total land area of Korea was mortgaged (H. K. Lee 1936: 233).

104. The interest rates charged for loans supplied by private persons (mostly usurers) ranged as high as 30 to 48 percent per annum (Grajdanzev 1944: 208). See also Takahashi 1935: 224.

105. Takahashi 1935: 223–224, 228–229; J. B. Kim 1977: 352–353; S. Suzuki 1939: 468, 470; Himeno 1940: 176–177; Foreign Affairs Association of Japan 1939–1940: 918; Grajdanzev 1944: 208. Though somewhat moderated, Koreans' propensity to adhere to "proper" Confucian ethics (*leigi*) prevailed after the Annexation. Huge expenditures were made on ceremonies such as funerals, weddings, and anniversaries (F. Fujita 1993: 108, 142).

106. Lewis 1955: 229.

107. Based on these statistics, Suh (1978: 149) also concluded that all productivity increases were rewarded to entrepreneurs.

CHAPTER 10

1. Moulton aptly declared, "From a fiscal point of view, the colonies as a whole have . . . clearly been a liability rather than asset" (1944: 234). Grajdanzev (1944: 441) calculated that the Japanese Treasury carried a financial burden of 1.272 billion yen during the 1907–1938 period. This included expenditures on the army and navy (52.7 percent of the total), grants to the Korean government (24.5 percent), and payments of interest on national debts connected with Korea (22.8 percent). See also Takahashi 1935: 441.

2. Lockwood 1954: 577.

3. Sotokufu 1940.

BIBLIOGRAPHY

Ahn, Byong-jik. 1969. "Sikminjiha Joseon ui Gukje Suji wa Jabon Suchilip, 1910–1945" (The Balance of Payment and Capital Export and Import under Colonial Rule). *Gyeongje Nonjip* (The Korean Economic Journal), IV. Seoul, Korea: Seoul National University Press.

———. 1971. "1930-nyon ifu Joseon ue Chimip han Ilbon Dokjeom Jabon ui Jeongtae" (Nature of Japanese Monopoly Capital in Korea after 1930). *Gyeongje Nonjip* (The Korean Economic Journal), X-4, December. Seoul: Seoul National University Press.

———. 1975. "Sikminjiha Joseonin Daejiju ui Yeongu 1920 yondae eul Jungsimuro" (Large Korean Landowners during the Colonial Period in the 1920s)." *Gyeongje Nonjip* (The Korean Economic Journal), XIV, 3, September. Seoul, Korea: Seoul National University Press.

———. 1981. *Hanguk Geundae Gyeongjesa* (Recent Economic History of Korea). Seoul: Bibongsa.

———. 1989. "Sikminji Joseon ui Goyong Guzo uc Gwanhan Yeongu" (Study of Employment Structure in Colonial Korea). In Byong-jik Ahn et al. eds., *Geundae Joseon ui Gyeongje Gujo* (Economic Structure of Recent Korea). Seoul, Korea: Bibong Publishing.

Ahn, Byong-jik, et al., eds. 1989. *Geundae Joseon ui Gyeongje Gujo* (Economic Structure of Recent Korea). Seoul: Bibong Publishing.

Akihishi, Sawano, ed. 1942. *Tairiku Kaisha Benran, 1942* (Handbook of Companies on the Continent, 1942). Tokyo: Toyo Keizai Shinposha.

Allen, Horace N. 1908. *Things Korean.* New York: Fleming H. Revell.

Altman, Albert A. 1984. "Korea's First Newspaper: The Japanese Chosen Shinpo," *Journal of Asian Studies,* XLIII, 4, August.

Asada, Kyoji. 1968. *Nihon Teikokushugi to Kyushokuminchi Jinushi sei* (Japanese Imperialism and Patterns of Landownership in Colonial Territories). Tokyo: Ochanomizu.

Asano, Shuji. 1941. "Chosen ni okeru Nokakeizai no Hensen" (Changes in Farm Economics in Korea). *Shokusan Geppo* (Industry Monthly), XXXIII. Keizyo: Chosen Shokusang Ginko.

Ban, Sung Hwan. 1983. "Growth of Korean Agriculture under Japanese Colonialism." *Seoul National University Economic Review,* XVII, December. Seoul: Seoul National University Press.

Bank of Chosen. 1920. *Economic History of Chosen.* Keizyo: Bank of Korea.

Bank of Korea. Annual. *Economic Statistics Yearbook.* Seoul: Bank of Korea.

Barro, Robert J. 1991. "Economic Growth in a Cross Section of Countries." *Quarterly Journal of Economics,* CVI, May.

Bishop, Isabella Bird. 1897. *Korea.* New York: Fleming H. Revell.

———. 1898. *Korea and Her Neighbors.* London: J. Murray.

Borton, Hugh. 1944. "Korea." *U.S. Department of State Bulletin,* XXII, November. Washington, D.C.: U.S. Government.

Brandt, Vincent S. R. 1972. *A Korean Village: Between Farm and Sea.* Cambridge, Mass.: Harvard University Press.

Brown, Arthur Judson. 1921. *The Mastery of the Far East.* New York: Charles Scribner and Sons.

Brudony, David. 1970. "Japan's Experiment in Korea." *Monumenta Nipponica,* XXV. Tokyo: Sophia University Press.

Brunner, Edmund deS. 1928. *Rural Korea.* New York: International Missionary Council.

Buruma, Ian. 2003. *Inventing Japan 1853–1964.* New York: The Modern Library.

Carles, W. R. 1888. *Life in Korea.* London, New York: Macmillan.

Cha, Byung-kwon. 1980. "Iljeha ui Gyeongjejok Uisan gwa Migunjongki ui Chogijokun ae daehan Gochal" (Economic Legacy under Japanese Rule and Early U.S. Military Governance). *Gyeongje Nonjip* (The Korean Economic Journal), XIX, 2. Seoul: Seoul National University Press.

Cha, Ki-byok, ed. 1985. *Ilje ui Hanguk Sikmin Tongchi* (Colonial Administration in Korea under Japanese Imperial Rule). Seoul: Chongumsa.

Cho, Jae H. 1970. "Modernization Effect upon Exports of Agricultural Produce: South Korea." *American Journal of Agricultural Economics,* LII, 1, February.

Cho, Ki Joon. 1965. "Hanguk eh Yuip dwaen Il-in Jabonaek Chujoeng mit keu Seong-kyeok Bunseok" (Estimation of Japanese Capital Inflow into Korea and Analysis of Its Character). In the *Social Science Edition of Nonmun-jip: Sahwae Gwahak-pyon.* Seoul: Koryo University Press.

———. 1973. *Hanguk Gyongjesa* (Economic History of Korea). Rev. ed. Seoul: Ilshin Sa.

———. 1977. *Hanguk Jabonjui Songnipsaron* (History of Capitalism in Korea). Seoul: Taewangsa.

———. 1983. *Hanguk Giepkasa* (A History of Korean Entrepreneurs). Seoul: Pagyongsa.

———. 1991. *Hanguk Jabonjui Baljunsa* (Development History of Korean Capitalism). Seoul: Taiwangsa.

———. 1994. *Hanguk Gyeongje Singang* (New Lectures on Korean Economic History). Seoul: Ilshinsa.

Cho, Ki Joon, et al. 1988. *Hanguk Jabonjui Seongkyok Ronjang* (Debate on Characteristics of Korean Capitalism). Seoul: Daiwangsa.

Choi, Eun-hee. 1992. *Hanguk Gaewha Yosong Yeoljon* (Biographies of Enlightened Korean Women). Reported in *Newsreview,* March 7. Seoul: The Korea Foundation.

Choi, Ho-jin. 1957. "Yijomalki ue issosoui Golidae Jabon Gejeong (Usury Loan Creditor Class during the Late Yi Period)." *Gyeongjehak Yeongu* (Economic Review), V, December. Seoul.

———. 1962. *Hanguk Gyeongje Kairon* (Outline of Korean Economic History). Seoul: Bomoonsa.

———. 1982. *Geundae Hanguk Gyeongjesa Yeongu* (Recent Korean Economic History). Seoul: Bakyongsa.

Choo, Bong Kyu. 1977. "Iljeha Saum ae kwanhan Yeongu" (Agent of Landlord under Japanese Rule) in *Gyeongje Nonjip* (The Korean Economic Journal), XVI, 3, September. Seoul: Seoul National University.

———. 1979. "Iljeha Nongchon Jinheung Wundong ae kwanhan Yeongu" (Farming Community Rejuvenation Movement under Japanese Domination) in *Gyeongje Nonjip* (The Korean Economic Journal), XVIII, 4, December. Seoul: Seoul National University.

———. 1981. "Iljeha Nongjilyeong ui Seongkyeok ae kwanhan Yeongu" (Characteristics of Farmland under Japanese Rule) in *Gyeongje Nonjip* (The Korean Economic Journal), XX, 1, March. Seoul: Seoul National University.

———. 1983. "Iljeha Surijohap Seolchi ui kwanhan Yeongu" (Establishment of Farmland Irrigation Association under Japanese Rule) in *Gyeongje Nonjip* (The Korean Economic Journal), XXII, 1, March. Seoul: Seoul National University.

Chosen Boeki Kyokai. 1892, 1942, 1943, and 1945. *Chosen Boekishi* (Trade History of Korea). Keizyo: Taikaido.

Chosen Ginko. 1933. "Chosen ni okeru Naichi Shihon Ryushutsunyu ni tsuite" (Japanese Capital Export to Korea). *Chosa Nenpo*. Keizyo: Chosen Ginko.

———. Annual. *Chosa Nenpo*, Keizyo: Chosen Ginko.

Chosen Keizai Kenkyusho. 1931. *Chosen Tokei Soran* (Korean Statistics). Keizyo: Chosen Keizai Kenkyusho.

Chosen Keizainenpo (Economic Annual of Korea). Annual. Tokyo: Kaizosha.

Chosen Kinyu Kumiai Kyokai. 1929, 1935. *Chosen Kinyu Kumiaishi* (History of Korea Credit Union). Keizyo: Chosen Kinyu Kumiai Kyokai.

———. Annual. *Kinyu Kumiai Nenkan* (Annal of Korea Credit Association). Keizyo: Chosen Kinyu Kumiai Kyokai.

Chosen Kogyo Kyokai. 1931, 1932, 1933, 1936, and 1940. *Chosen Kojo Meiran* (Factory Directory in Korea). Keizyo: Chosen Kogyo Kyokai.

———. 1937. *Chosen no Kogyo to sono Shigen* (Industry and Industrial Resources in Korea). Keizyo: Chosen Kogyo Kyokai.

Chosen Kyokai. 1892. "Kankoku Kahei Mondai Chosa Shiryo" (Source Materials for Korean Money) in Kaiho (Association Journal), I. Tokyo: Chosen Kyokai.

———. Annual. *Kaiho* (Association Journal). Tokyo: Chosen Kyokai.

Chosen Nenkan (Korea Annual). 1937, 1939, 1941, and 1942. Keizyo: Keizyo Nipponsha.

Chosen Nokai. 1944. *Chosen Nogyo Hattatsushi, Hattatsuhen* (Agricultural Development of Korea, Development). Keizyo. Chosen Nokai.

Chun, Hae-Jong. 1976. "Korean Attitude toward Foreigners in Earlier Times." Paper presented at the 4th Annual International Symposium on History and Culture of East Asia, sponsored by the Korean National Academy of Sciences, Seoul, Korea, October 26.

Chung, Dukhi. 1972. "Joseon Wangjomalki Kolidae Jabon ui Seongkyeok (Characterter of Usury Capital in the Late Yi Dynasty)." Paper presented at the 15th Korean Historial Association Meeting, Sookmyong Women's University, Seoul, Korea, May 26.

———. 1987. *Hanguk Sawhae Gyeongjesa Yeongu* (Socioeconomic History of Korea). Seoul: Yongsul Publishing.

Chung, Henry. 1921. *The Case of Korea*. New York: Fleming H. Revell.

Chung, Jai Chong. 1989. "Joseon Chongdokbu Choldoguk ui Koyong Kujo" (Employment Structure of the Korean Government: General's Railroad Bureau). In Byong-jik Ahn et al., eds., *Geundae Joseon ui Gyeongje Gujo* (Economic Structure of Recent Korea). Seoul, Korea: Bibong Publishing.

Chung, Young-Iob. 1965. "The Role of Government in Savings in Japan during 1868–1898." Ph.D. diss., Columbia University, New York.

———. 1973. "Japanese Investment in Korea, 1904–1945." In Andrew C. Nahm, ed., *Korea under Japanese Colonial Rule*. Kalamazazoo, Michigan: Western Michigan University.

———. 1974. "*Gae*, a Traditional Economic Institution in Korea." In Andrew C. Nahm, ed., *Traditional Korea: Theory and Practice*. Kalamazoo, Michigan: Western Michigan University Center for Korean Studies.

———. 1977. "Korean Investment under Japanese Rule," In C. I. Eugene Kim and Doretha E. Mortimore, eds., *Korea's Response to Japan: The Colonial Period 1910–1945*, Kalamazazoo, Michigan: Western Michigan University Center for Korean Studies.

———. 1984. "The Traditional Economy of Korea." *The Journal of Modern Korean Studies*, I, April. Fredericksburg, Va.: Mary Washington College.

———. 1989. "The Impact of Chinese Culture on Korea's Economic Development." In Hung-chao Tai, ed., *Confucianism and Economic Development, an Oriental Alternative*. Washington, D.C.: The Washington Institute Press.

———. 2000. "Financing Investment in Korea under Japanese Rule." *The Journal of Modern Korean Studies*, VII, April. Fredericksburg, Va.: Mary Washington College.

Conroy, Hilary. 1960. *The Japanese Seizure of Korea: 1868–1910*. Philadelphia: University of Pennsylvania Press.

Cumings, Bruce. 1984. "The Legacy of Japanese Colonialism in Korea." In Ramon H. Myers and Mark R. Peattie, eds., *The Japanese Colonial Empire, 1895–1945*. Princeton, N.J.: Princeton University Press.

———. 1997. *Korea's Place in the Sun*. New York and London: Norton.

Curzon, George M. 1896. *Problems of the Far East: Japan, Korea, China*. London: Constable.

Daehan Gumnyung Johap (Korea Credit Cooperative Federation). 1955. *Hanguk Nongeop Yeongan* (Korean Agricultural Annual). Seoul: Daihan Kumnyung Chohap.

Daiichi Ginko. 1908. *Kankoku Kakushiten Shutsuchojo Kaigyo Irai Eigyo Jokyo* (Conditions of Business at Branches in Korea since Opening). Tokyo: Daiichi Ginko.

———. 1926. *Daiichi Ginko 50nen Shoshi* (A 50-Year Short History of the First Bank). Tokyo: Daiichi Ginko.

Dallet, Charles. [1874] 1954. *Traditional Korea*. Behavior Science Translations. New Haven: Human Relations Area Files.

De Bary, William Theodore. 1970. "Conversations and Concerns: China in Perspective." *Columbia Forum*, XIII, 1, Spring. New York: Columbia University.

De Long, J. Gradford, and Lawrence H. Summers. 1991. "Equipment Investment and Economic Growth." *Quarterly Journal of Economics,* CVI, May.

Deuchler, Martina. 1977. *Confucian Gentlemen and Barbarian Envoy: The Opening of Korea, 1875–1885*. Seatle: University of Washington Press.

———. 1993. *The Confucian Transformation of Korea: A Study of Society and Ideology*. Cambridge, Mass., and London: Council of East Asian Studies, Harvard University Press.

Dong-A Ilbosha. *Dong-A Ilbo*. 1922--1932. Seoul: Dong-A Ilbosha.

Dower, John W. 1999. *Embracing Defeat: Japan in the Wake of World War II*. New York: Norton and The New Press.

Drake, H. B. 1930. *Korea of the Japanese*. London: John Lane.

Duus, Peter. 1984. "Economic Dimensions of Meiji Imperialism." In Ramon H. Myers and Mark R. Peattie, eds., *The Japanese Colonial Empire, 1895–1945*. Princeton, N.J.: Princeton University Press.

———. 1995. *The Abacus and the Sword: The Japanese Penetration of Korea, 1895–1910*. Berkeley: University of California Press.

Eckert, Carter J. 1991. *Offspring of Empire: The Koch'ang Kims and the Kyongsong Spinning and Weaving Company, 1876–1945*. Seattle: University of Washington Press.

Eckert, Carter J., Ki-baik Lee, Young Ick Lew, Michael Robinson, and Edward W. Wagner. 1990. *Korea Old and New: A History*. Seoul, Korea: Ilchokak Publishers for the Korea Institute, Harvard University.

Edwards, Corwin D., et al. 1946. *Report of Mission on Japanese Combines.* General Headquarters, Supreme Commander for the Allied powers. March. RG 407, National Archives.

Far Eastern Survey. 1939. December 20.

Farnsworth, Helen. 1958. "The Role of Wheat in Improving Nutritional Status and Labor Productivity in Lesser Developed Countries." *International Wheat Surplus Utilization Conference Proceedings*. Brookings, South Dakota.

Fogel, Robert W. 1994. "Economic Growth, Population Theory, and Physiology: Bearing of Long-Term Processes on the Making of Economic Policy," The Nobel Prize Lecture, *The American Economic Review*, LXXXIIII, 3, June.

Foreign Affairs Association of Japan. 1939–1940. *The Japan Year Book*. Tokyo: Japan Times Press.

Fujita, Fumiyoshi. 1993. *Chosen Sangyo Keizai no Kindaika to Chosen Shokusan Ginko* (Modernization of Industrial Economy of Korea and Korea Industrial Bank). Tokyo: Nishita Shoten.

Fujita, Tsuyoshi. 1940. "Chosen ni okeru Nochi Kakaku no Henseini tsuite (Changes in Land Price in Korea), Shokusan Ginko survey reported in *Shokusan Ginko Chosa Geppo* (Research Monthly of Industrial Bank), September. Keizyo: Shokusan Ginko.

Fukuda, Tokuzo. 1921. "Kankoku no Keizaisoshiki to Keizaitani" (Economic Organization of Korea and its Economic Unit) in *Kokumin Keizai Kowa*. Tokyo: Keizaikaku Kenkyukai.

Gale, James S. 1893. *Korean Sketches*. Boston: F. H. Revell.

———. 1909. *Korea in Transition*. Cincinnati: Jennings & Graham, New York: Easton and Mains.

———. 1972. *History of the Korean People*. Seoul: Royal Asiatic Society.

Gerschenkron, Alexander. 1962. *Economic Backwardness in a Historical Perspective*. Cambridge, Mass.: Harvard University Press.

Gifford, Daniel L. 1898. *Everyday Life in Korea: A Collection of Studies and Stories*. Chicago and New York: Fleming H. Revell.

Gould, David M., and Roy J. Ruffin. 1993a. "Human Capital Externalities, Trade, and Economic Growth," Federal Reserve Bank of Dallas Research Paper no. 9301, January.

———. 1993b. "What Determines Economic Growth?" Federal Reserve Bank of Dallas, *Economic Review*, second quarter.

Government General of Chosen. 1910–1911. *Annual Report on Reforms and Progress, 1910–1911*. Keizyo: Government General of Chosen.

———. 1912—1938 (annual). *Annual Reports of Administration of Chosen*. Keizyo: Government General of Chosen.

———. 1914. *Results of Three Years Administration of Chosen Since Annexation*. Keizyo: Government General of Chosen.

Gragert, Edwin Harold. 1994. *Landownership under Colonial Rule: Korea's Japanese Experience, 1900–1935*. Honolulu: University of Hawaii Press.

Grajdanzev, Andrew J. 1944. *Modern Korea*. New York: Institute of Pacific Relations and John Day.

Graves, Louis. 1922. *Willard Straight in the Orient*. New York: Asia Publishing.

Griffis, William E. [1889] 1907. *Corea: The Hermit Nation*. New York: Charles Scribner's Sons.

Guksa Pyeonjib Uiwonwhae. 1994. *Ilje Chimryakwa Hanguk 36-nyonsa* (A Thirty-Six-Year History of Korea under Japan). Vol. IV. Seoul: Minjok Munwhasa.

Hagen, Everett E. 1968. *The Economics of Development*, Homewood, Ill.: Richard D. Irwin.

Hamanuma, Jiro. 1982. "Niteika ni okeru Nogyo Kakumei" (Agricultural Revolution under Japanese Administration) in *Chosenshiso* (Korean History), V and VI. Tokyo: Chosenshisokai.

Hamilton, Angus. [1904] 1910. *Korea*. London: Heiniman, Boston: J. B. Millet.

Han, Chang Ho. 1971. "Iljeha ui Hanguk Kwangkongeop ui kwanhan Yeongu" (Mining and Industry Under Japanese Rule). In Moon Shik Kim et al., eds., *Ilche ui Gyeongje Chimtalsa* (History of Economic Exploitation of Japanese Imperialism) Seoul: Minjung Sokwan.

Han, Woo-Keun. 1971. *The History of Korea*. Translated by Kyong-shik Lee and Grafton K. Mintz. Honolulu: East-West Center Press.

———. 1974. *Hanguk Gaehanggi ui Sangeop Yeongu* (Studies of Commerce During Korea's Opening). Seoul: Ilchogak.

Hanguk Eunhaeng. 1952. *Hanguk Nongeup ui Jeonge Kwajeong* (Development Processes of Korean Agriculture). Saneop Josa no. 8. Seoul: Hanguk Eunhaeng.

Harrington, Fred Harvey. 1944. *God, Mammon, and the Japanese: Dr. Horace N. Allen and Korean-American Relations, 1884–1905*. Madison: University of Wisconsin Press.

Hatada, Takashi. 1951. *Chosenshi* (Korean History). Tokyo: Iwanami Shoten.

Hatobe, Noboru. 1931. *Chosen oyobi Chosenjin no Keizaiseikatsu* (Korea and Economic Life of Koreans). Keizyo: Teikoku Chiho Gyosei Kakukai Chosen Hombu.

Henderson, Gregory. 1968. *Korea: The Politics of Vortex*. Cambridge: Harvard University Press.

Higuma, Kenichi. 1935. *Chosen Nogyo no Kindaiteki Yoso* (Modern Features of Korean Agriculture). Tokyo: Nishihara Kankokai.

———. 1937. "Chosen ni okeru Kosaku Mondai no Hattensei-tokuni Jinushi to Nomin no Saikaku o Chusin to shite (Development of the Tenant Problem in Korea: Essence of the Relationship Between Landowners and Peasants)." *Nogyo to Keizai*, IV, 6, June.

———. 1943. *Chosen Nosei no Kadai Yoso* (Critical Problems of Korean Agricultural Policy). Tokyo: Meguro Shoten.

Himeno, Minoru. 1940. *Chosen Keizai Tohyo* (Economic Graph of Korea). Keizyo: Chosen Tokeikyokai.

Ho, Samuel Pao-San. 1984. "Colonialism and Development: Korea, Taiwan, and Kwantung." In Ramon H. Myers and Mark R. Peattie, eds., *The Japanese Colonial Empire, 1895–1945*. Princeton, N.J.: Princeton University Press.

Hosokawa, Karoku. 1941. *Chosen no Shokumin Shi* (History of Colony), a series in Gendai Nihon Bunmeishi (History of Modern Japanese Civilization). Volume X. Tokyo: Toyo Keizai Shimposha.

Huang, Sung-mo. 1967. "Protestant Churches in Korea: Their Impact on Cultural Change," *Korean Quarterly*, VIII, 4, and IX, 1, Winter 1966–Spring 1967.

Huh, Suyul. 1989. "Ilbon Jegukjuiha Joseonin Gongjang ui Dongte" (The State of Korean Factories under Japanese Imperialism) in Byong-jik Ahn et al., eds., *Geundae Joseon ui Gyeongje Gujo* (Economic Structure of Recent Korea). Seoul: Bibong Publishing.

Hulbert, Homer B. 1905. *History of Korea*. Seoul: Methodist Publishing House.

———. [1906] 1911. *The Passing of Korea*. New York: Doubleday, Page.

Hunter, Janet. 1977. "Japanese Government Policy, Business Opinion, and the Seoul-Pusan Railway, 1894–1906." *Modern Asian Studies,* XI.

Im, Pyong-yun. 1971. *Shokuminchi ni okeru Shogyoteki Nogyo no Hatten* (The Development of Commercial Agriculture in Colonial Lands). Tokyo: Tokyo Daigakku Shuppankai.

In, Chung Shik. 1949. *Chosen Nogyo Keizai Ron* (Korean Agriculture), Tokyo: Hakubun Shuppansha.

Inanuma, Nichiro. 1982. "Nichiteika ni Okeru Nogyo Kakumei" (Agricultural Revolution under the Japanese Imperial Rule). *Chosen Shiso,* V and VI, January.

Ito, Seikaku. 1937. *Chosen ni okeru Katei Kogyo Chosa* (Investigation of Korean Household Industry). Keizyo: Keizyo Shokokai.

Ito, Seikaku, ed. 1942. *Keizyo Shoko Kaigijo Nijugonenshi* (A Twenty-Five-Year History of the Keizyo Chamber of Commerce and Industry). Keizyo: Keizyo Shoko Kaigijo.

Jindan Hakhwae, comp. 1961a. *Hanguksa* (History of Korea). Vol. IV, Late Pre-Modern Age, edited by Sang-baek Lee. Seoul: Eulyu Publishing.

———. 1961b. *Hanguksa* (History of Korea). Vol. V, Early Modern Period, edited by Sungun Lee. Seoul: Eulyu Publishing.

Jo, Yung-Hwan, ed. 1971. *Korea's Response to the West.* Kalamazoo: The Korea Research and Publications.

Joseon Yeonguwhae. 1935. *Joseon Gongeop kwa Geumnyungjabon Yeongu* (Korean Industry and Financial Capital). Seoul: Joseon Yeonguwhai.

Kahng, Sun-Myong. 1984. "Korean Development in Historical Perspective." *Proceedings of International Convention of Korean Economists: Papers.* Vol. IV, August 20–21, 1984. Seoul: The Korean Economic Association.

Kajimura, Hideki. 1977. *Chosen ni okeru Shihon-shugi no Keisei to Tenkai* (The Structure and Development of Capitalism in Korea). Tokyo: Ryukei Shosha.

———. 1983. "Minjok Jabon gwa Yesok Jabon" (National Capital and Dependent Capital) in Kajimura, Hideki et al., eds. *Hanguk Geundae Gyeongjesa Yeongu* (Modern Korean History). Seoul: Sagyechol.

———. 1989. "1910-nyon dae ui Gyeongje Sunwhan kwa Sonong Gyeongyeong" (Economic Activities of Korea and Small-Farm Management in the 1910s). In Byung-jik Ahn et al., eds., *Geundae Joseon ui Gyeongje Guzo* (Economic Structure of Recent Korea). Seoul: Bibong Publishing.

Kanbe, Masao. 1931. *Chosen Nogyo Imin Ron* (Agricultural Immigration). Tokyo: Yuhikaku.

Kang, Dong-jin. 1980. *Ilche ui Hanguk Chinmyaek Jeongchaeksa: 1920 nyondae rul chungsim uro* (Imperialist Policy to Conquer Korea: Focusing on the 1920s). Seoul: Hangilsa.

Kang, Man Gil. 1966. "Joseonfugi Sugongeopja wa Sangin kwa ui Kwange" (The Relationship between Handicraft Industry Workers and Merchants during the Late Joseon Period) *Asia Yeongu,* no. 23, September.

———. 1970. "Yijofugi Sangeop Jabon ui Seongjang (Growth of Business Capital in the Late Yi Period)." Paper presented at a seminar sponsored by the Asian Research Institute, Seoul.

———. 1973. *Joseon Fugi SangupJabon ui Baldal* (Development of Commercial Capital during the Late Joseon Period). Seoul: Korea University Press.

———. 1963. "Reflections on the Centenary of the Opening of Korea." *Korea Journal* XVI, 2, February: 10–18.

———. 1963. "The Modernization of Korea from the Historical Point of View." *Asiatic Research Bulletin* VI, 1, March: 1–6.

Kang, Shin-pyo. 1982. Paper presented at the Conference on U.S.-Korean Relations held at the University of Hawaii, jointly sponsored by the American Studies Institute of Seoul National University and the Center for Korean Studies of the University of Hawaii, May 21–27.

Katadoshi, Ryukichi. 1939. *Hanto no Jigyojin Noguchi* (Penninsula's Entrepreneur Noguchi). Keizyo.

Kawai, Akitake. 1943. *Chosen Kogyo no Gendankai* (Current Stage of Korean Industry), Keizyo: Toyo Keizai Shinposha Keizyo Shikyoku.

Kawai, Kazuo, and Myong Ho Yoon. 1991. *Shokumin Chiki no Chosen Kogyo* (Korean Industry during the Colonial Period). Tokyo: Miraisha.

Keizyo Shoko Kaigisho. 1933–1938. *Keizai Geppo* (Economic Monthly). Keizyo: Keizyo Shoko Kaigijo.

———. 1944. "Chosen ni okeru Naichi Shihon no Toka Genkyu" (Japanese Capital Investment in Korea." *Keizai Geppo* (Economic Monthly), September. Keizyo: Keizyo Shoko Kaigijo.

———. Annual. *Tokei Nenpo* (Statistical Annual). Keojo: Keizyo Shoko Kaigijo.

Kennan, George. 1905a. "The Japanese in Korea," *Outlook*, XXXI. New York.

———. 1905b. "Korea: A Degenerated State," *Outlook*, XXXI. New York.

Kim, Byong Yoon. 1983. *Guhanmal ui Sawhae wa Gyeongje* (Social and Economic Conditions in the Late Han Period). Translated from a Russian Ministry of Treasury report prepared in 1900. Seoul: Yupoongsa.

Kim, Han Joo. 1990. "Nongjeongsa" (History of Agricultural Policy). In Suk Dam Chun and Ko Chai Park et al., eds., *Joseon Gyeongje Kyongjesa Tamgu* (Economic History of Korea). Seoul: Bomwoosa.

Kim, Hyun-kil. 1971. "Land Use Policy in Korea with Special References to the Oriental Development Company." Ph.D. diss., University of Washington.

Kim, Joon Bo. 1970 (I), 1974 (II), and 1977 (III). *Hanguk Jabonjuisa Yeongu* (History of Korean Capitalism). Seoul: Ilchosa.

Kim, Kyong-tae. 1982. "Historical Features of the Soldiers Revolt in 1882." Reported in the *Korea Herald*, June 25, 1982.

Kim, Kyung-dong. 1987. *Dependency Issues in Korean Development*. Seoul: Seoul National University Press.

Kim, Moon Shik, et al. 1971. *Ilje ui Gyeongje Chimtalsa* (Economic Exploitation History of Japanese Imperialism). Seoul: Minjung Sokwan.

Kim, Sung Su. 1985. *Hanguk Gyeongjesaron* (Economic History of Korea). Seoul: Kyongjinsa.

Kim, Tu-Yong. 1947. *Chosen Kindai Keizaishiwa* (Recent Economic History of Korea). Tokyo: Kyodo Shobo.

Kim, Yong Ho. 1972 "Jinbopa Jean han Waeguk Chagwan ui Toron" (Debates on Foreign Loan Proposed by the Progressives). Reported in the *Hanguk Sinmun*, May 30.

Kim, Yong Mo. 1972. "Hanmal Yuhaksaeng ui Siltae" (Situation of Korean Students at the End of Yi Dynasty). Paper presented at the Korea Sociology Meeting at Seoul National University, March 4.

Kim, Yong-sop. 1978. "Hanmal Iljeha ui Jijusei. Sayesam: Kobu Kimsiga ui Jiju Kyeongyeong gwa Jabon Jonhwan (System of Landownership in the LateYi Dynasty Under Japanese Rule. The Fourth Case: Land Administration and Capital Movement in the Kim Family of Kobu)." *Hanguksa Yeongu* (Study of Korean History), XIX.

Kim, Han-Kyo, and C. I. Eugene Kim. 1967. *Korea and the Politics of Imperialism, 1876–1910*. Berkeley: University of California Press.

Kim, C. I. Eugene, and Doretha E. Mortimore, eds. 1977. *Korea's Response to Japan: The Colonial Period, 1910–1945*. Kalamazazoo, Michigan: Western Michigan University Center for Korean Studies.

Kimura, Mitsuhiko. 1993. "Standards of Living in Colonial Korea: Did the Masses Become Worse Off or Better Off under Japanese Rule?" *The Journal of Economic History*, LIII, 3, September.

Kin, Tetsu. 1965. *Kankoku no Jinko to Keizai* (Population and Economy of Korea). Tokyo: Iwanami Shoten.

Kitakawa, Osamu. 1932. "Nisshin Sensozen no Nissin Boeki" (Japan-China Trade Before Sino-Japanese War) in *Rekishi Gakaku Ronshu* (Science of History). First issue. Tokyo: Tokyo University.

Ko, Byong Woon. 1995. *Ryakutatsu sareta Sokoku* (Stolen Mother Country). Tokyo: Yusankaku Publishing.

Ko, Sung Je. 1959. *Geunse Hanguk Saneopsa Yeongu* (Modern Korean Industrial History). Seoul: Taedong Munwhasa.

———. 1975. *Hanguk Gyeongyeongsa Yeongu* (History of Korean Entrepreneurship). Seoul: Hankook Nungyul Hyopwhai (Korea Productivity/Efficiency Association).

———. 1988. *Hanguk Sawhae Gyongjesaron* (Socioeconomic History of Korea). Seoul: Ilchisa.

Kobayakawa, Kuro. 1944. *Chosen Nogyo Hattatsushishi* (Korean Agricultural Development History). Keizyo: Chosen Nokai.

Kobayashi, Hideo. 1968. "1930 nendai Chosen Kogyoka Seisaku no Tenkai Katei" (Development of Korean Industrialization Policy in the 1930s). *Chosenshi Kenkyukai Ronbunshu* 3. Tokyo: Kyokuto Shoten.

———. 1973. "1930 nendai Nippon Chisso Hiryo Kabushiki Kaisha no Chosen e no Shishutsu ni tsuite" (The Advance of Japanese Nitrogenous Fertilizers into Korea in the 1930s). In Yamada Hideo ed., *Shokuminchi Keizaishi no Shomondai* (Issues in Colonial Economic History). Tokyo: Institute of Developing Economies.

Kokusei Gurafu (State of Nation in Graph). April 1940, July 1940, and January 1941. Tokyo: Kaizosha.

Koo, Young-nok. 1982. Paper presented at the Conference on U.S.-Korean Relations held at the University of Hawaii, jointly sponsored by the American Studies Institute of Seoul National University and the Center for Korean Studies of the University of Hawaii, May 21–27.

Korea Repository. Ohlinger, F., H. G. Appenzeller, and George Heber Jones, eds. 1892 (I), 1895 (II), 1896 (III), 1897 (IV), and 1898 (V). Seoul: Trilingual Press.

Kwon, Byong Tack. 1984. *Hanguk Gyeongjesa* (Economic History of Korea). Seoul: Bakyongsa.

Lee, Buk Man. 1948. *Yijo Sawhae Gyeongjesa Yeongu* (A Study of Socioeconomic History during the Yi Dynasty). Seoul: Daisung Publishing.

Lee, Byong Do. 1979–1981. "Wuri nun Nuguinga, (Who Are We?)." Series of twelve articles reported in the magazine *Sam-Toh.*

Lee, Changsoo, ed. 1981. *Modernization of Korea and the Impact of the West.* Los Angeles: University of Sothern California.

Lee, Hoon Koo. 1936. *Land Utilization and Rural Economy in Korea.* New York: Greenwood.

Lee, Hyo-chae. 1978. A series of articles on "The Status of Korean Women," in the *Korea Herald* between January 18 and February 9.

Lee, Ki Soo. 1990. "Gyeongjesa" (Economic History). In Suk Dan Chin and Kuje Park et al., eds., *Joseon Kyongjesa Tamku* (Economic History of Korea). Seoul: Bomwoosa.

Lee, Nang Nyung. 1963. "The Korean's Way of Thinking," *Koreana Quarterly,* V, 3. Seoul: The International Research Center.

Lee, Won-ho. 1991. "Modern System Came Hard Way to Korea," *Koreana,* V, 3.

Lee, Yun Keun. 1971. "Hanguk Gukminsodeok Chuge wa Naeyong" (Estimate of Korea's National Income and Its Structure). In Ki Joon Cho et al., eds., *Ilcheha ui Minjok Sangwhalsa* (Korean Living Standard under Japanese Imperialism) Vol. V. in the series Study of Korea under Japanese Imperialism. Seoul: Minjung Sokwan.

Lee, Yur-bok. 1988. *West Goes East: Paul Georg von Mollendorff and Great Power Imperialism in Late Yi Korea.* Honolulu: University of Hawaii Press.

Levine, Ross, and David Renelt. 1992. "A Sensitivity Analysis of Cross-Country Growth Regression," *American Economic Review* LXXXII, September.

Lew, Young-ick. 1972. "The Kap-O Reform Movement: Korean and Japanese Reform Efforts in Korea, 1894." Ph.D. diss., Harvard University.

Lewis, W. Arthur. 1955. *The Theory of Economic Growth.* Homewood, Ill.: Richard D. Irwin.

Lim, Jong-Chul. 1969. "Iljemal Hanguk ui Gongepwha ae kwanhan Ilgochal" (An Examination of Korean Industrialization in Later Japanese Rule). *Gyeongje Nonjip* (The Korean Economic Journal), VIII, 3, September. Seoul: Seoul National University.

Lim, Youngil. 1968. "Foreign Influence on the Economic Change in Korea, a Survey," *The Journal of Asian Studies,* November.

Lockwood, William W. 1954. *The Economic Development of Japan.* Princeton, N.J.: Princeton University.

Longford, Joseph H. 1911. *The Story of Korea.* London: T. Fisher Unwin.

Lowell, Percival. 1888. *Chosen: The Land of the Morning Calm.* Boston: Ticknar.

Maeil Sinbosa. 1910–1944. *Maeil Sinbo.* Keizyo: Maeil Sinbosa.

Mankew, N. Gregory, David Romer, and David N. Weil. 1992. "A Contribution to the Empirics of Economic Growth," *Quarterly Journal of Economics* CVII, May.

McCune, George M. 1950. *Korea Today.* Cambridge, Mass.: Harvard University Press.

McCune, George M., and John A. Harrison, eds. 1951. *Korean-American Relations: Documents Pertaining to the Far Eastern Diplomacy of the United States.* Berkeley and Los Angeles: University of California Press.

McCune, Shannon Boyd. 1956. *Korea's Heritage: A Regional and Social Geography.* Tokyo-Rutland, Vt.: Tuttle.

McGinn, Noel E., Donald R. Snodgrass, Yung Bong Kim, Shin-Bok Kim, and Quee-Young Kim. 1980. *Education and Development in Korea.* Cambridge, Mass: Harvard University Press.

McKenzie, F. A. 1908. *The Tragedy of Korea.* New York: Dutton.

McNamara, Dennis. 1989. "The Keisho and the Korean Business Elite." *The Journal of Asian Studies* XLVIII, 2, May.

McNamara, Dennis. 1990. *The Colonial Origin of Korean Enterprises, 1919–1945.* New York: Cambridge University Press.

Miyajima, Hiroshi. 1982. "Shokuminchika Chosenjin Daijinushi no Sonzai Keitai ni kansuru Shiron (A Study of Patterns of Existence Among Korean Large Landowners during the Colonial Period.)" *Shokuminchi Chosen no Shakai to Teiko* (Society and Resistance in Colonial Korea). Tokyo: Miraisha.

Miyake, Seiki. 1937. *Shinko Kontsuerun Tokuhon* (New Monopoly Reader). Tokyo: Shunjusha.

Miyamoto, Mataji. 1944. "Taisen Boeki no Shocho to Nisshin Senso" (Development of Japan-Korea Trade and Sino-Japan War), *Keizaishi Kenkyu* (Study of Economic History), XXXI, 7–8. Kyoto: Keizaishi Kenkyukai.

Mizoguchi, Toshiyuki, and Yuzo Yamamoto. 1984. "Capital Formation in Taiwan and Korea," In Ramon H. Myers and Mark R. Peattie, eds., *The Japanese Colonial Empire, 1895–1945*. Princeton, N.J.: Princeton University Press.

Mizuda, Naomasa, and Takao Tsuchiya. 1962. *Zaisei Kinyu Seisaku kara mita Chosen Tochi to sono Shukyoku* (The Governance of Korea and Its End), Chosen Kindai Shiryo Chosen Sotokufu Kaankei Juyo Bunsho Senshu, III. Tokyo: Chosen Shiryo Hensankai, Korean Yuho Kyokai.

Molony, Barbara. 1984. "Japan's Strategic Investment in High Technology in Korea, 1925–1945." Paper presented at the Association for Asian Studies, March.

Moon, Chung Chan. 1966. *Gunkuk Ilbon Joseon Gangjum 36-nyeonsa* (History of Japan's Military Occupation of Korea for 36 Years), Middle Volume. Seoul: Bakmun Dang.

Moose, J. Robert. 1911. *Village Life in Korea*. Nashville, Tenn.: Publishing House of the M. E. Church, South.

Moskowitz, Karl. 1974. "The Creation of the Oriental Development Company: Japanese Illusion Meets Korean Reality." In *Occasional Papers on Korea,* ed. James B. Palais, no. 1. Seattle: Joint Committee on Korean Studies of the American Council of Learned Societies and the Social Science Research Council.

———. 1979. "Current Assets: The Employees of Japanese Banks in Colonial Korea." Ph.D. diss., Harvard University.

Moulton, Harold G. 1944. *An Economic Appraisal and Financial Appraisal*. Washington D.C.: The Brookings Institution.

Myers, Ramon H., and Mark R. Peattie, eds. 1984. *The Japanese Colonial Empire,1895–1945*. Princeton, N.J.: Princeton University Press.

Na, Ik-chin. 1984. *Hanguk ui Sanggongeop Baeknyon* (One Hundred Years of Korean Commerce and Industry). Seoul: Korean Chamber of Commerce and Industry.

Nahm, Andrew C. 1988. Korea, *Tradition and Transformation*. Elizabeth, New Jersey: Hollym International.

Nahm, Andrew C., ed. 1973. *Korea under Japanese Colonial Rule*. Kalamazoo, Michigan: Western Michigan University Center for Korean Studies.

———. 1974. *Traditional Korea: Theory and Practice*. Kalamazee, Michigan: Western Michigan University Center for Korean Studies.

Nakamura, Kichiji. 1941. *Nihon Keizaishi Gairon* (General History of Japan). Tokyo: Nihon Hyoronsha.

Nakatsuka, Akira. 1968. *Kindai Nihon to Chosen* (Recent Japan and Korea). Tokyo: Sanseido.

Nasu, Shiroshi. 1941. *Aspects of Japanese Agriculture; A Preliminary Survey*. New York: Institute of Pacific Relations.

Nelson, M. Frederick. 1945. *Korea and the Old Orders in Eastern Asia*. Baton Rouge, La.: Lousiana State University Press.

Nihon Noshomusho. 1905. *Rokoku Okurasho Kankokushi* (Russian Korean History). Russian Treasury Department's report in 1900. Japanese Ministry of Agriculture and Commerce translated. Tokyo: Nihon Noshomusho.

———. 1901–1907 (annual). *Kankoku Boeki Nenpo* (Korean Foreign Trade Yearbook). Tokyo: Nihon Noshomusho.

———. 1932. *Nihon Nogyo Nenpo* II. Tokyo: Nihon Noshomusho.

———. 1941. *Nihon Nogyo Nenkan*. Tokyo: Nihon Noshomusho.

Nihon Okurasho. 1910. *Gaikoku Boeki Gairon* (General Survey of Foreign Trade, 1891–1910). Tokyo: Nihon Okurasho.

Nihon Takumusho. 1938–1940 (annual). *Takumu Yoran* (A Survey of Colonies). Tokyo: Nihon Takumusho.

———. Annual. *Takumutokei*. Tokyo: Nihon Takumusho.

Nihon Tokeikyoku. Annual. *Nippon Teikoku Tokei Nenkan* (Statistical Annual of Japan). Vol. LVIII. Tokyo: Nihon Tokeikyoku.

Nurkse, Ragner. 1953. *Problems of Capital Formation in Underdeveloped Countries*. Oxford: Blackwell.

Oh, Sung. 1989. *Joseon Fugi Sangin Yeongu* (Merchants in the Lste Joseon Period). Seoul: Ilchogak.

Oppert, Earnest Jakob. 1880. *A Forbidden Land: Voyages to Corea*. New York: Putnam.

Osgood, Cornelious. 1951. *The Koreans and Their Culture*. New York: The Ronald Press.

Paik, George N. 1929. *The History of Protestant Missions in Korea, 1832–1910*. Pyong-Yang, Korea: Union Christian College Press.

Palais, James B. 1975. *Politics and Policies in Traditional Korea*. Cambridge: Harvard University Press.

———. 1996. *Confucian Statecraft and Korean Institutions, Yu Hyungwon and the Late Chosen Dynasty*. Seattle: University of Washington Press.

Palmer, Spencer J., ed. 1963. *Korean-American Relations, 1887–1895*. Berkeley: University of California Press.

Park, Chong Wha. 1970. "Records of Twentieth Century." Reported in Hanguk Ilbo, July 19, 1970.

Park, Ki Hyok. 1965. "Hanguk Sijok Burak ui Sawhae Gyeongje Yeongu Silche Josa: 1961–1962" (Socioeconomic Study of Korean Kinship Village, Field Survey: 1961–1962). In *Yonse Daehakkyo Palsip-Junyeon Ginyeomji* (Yonsei University 80th Anniversary Essay Collection). Seoul: Yonsei University.

Park, Ki Hyuk, et al. 1966. *A Study of the Land Tenure System in Korea*. Seoul: Korea Land Economics Research Center.

Park, Kyungshick. 1973. *Nihon Teikoku Shugi no Chosen Shihai* (Imperial Japan's Domination of Korea). 2 vol. Tokyo: Aoki Shoten.

Park, Moon Kyu. 1933 (1978). "Tochi Chosa Jigyo ni tsuite" (Land Survey Project) in *Chosen Shakai Keizaishi Kenkyu*. Keizyo: Keizyo Imperial University.

Park, Soon-Woon. 1999. *Colonial Industrialization and Labor in Korea*. Cambridge, Mass.: Harvard University Asia Center.

Park, Sun-young. 1991. "Confucianism Molds Core of the System," *Koreana*, III. Seoul: International Research Center.

Porter, Catherine. 1936. *Far Eastern Survey*, April.

Reeve, W. D. 1963. *The Republic of Korea: A Political and Economic Study*. London and New York: Oxford University Press.

Reischauer, Edwin O., and John Fairbanks. 1960. *East Asia: The Great Tradition*. Boston: Houghton Mifflin.

Repetto, Robert, Tai Hwan Kwon, Son-Ung Kim, Dae Young Kim, John E. Sloboda, and Peter Donaldson. 1981. *Economic Development, Population Policy, and Demographic Transition in the Republic of Korea*. Cambridge, Mass.: Harvard University Press.

Republic of Korea. 1955. *Handbook of Korea*. Seoul: Office of Public Information.

Residency General of Korea. 1906–1910 (annual). *Annual Reports on Reforms and Progress in Korea*. Seoul: Tokanfu.

———. 1910. *The Material Progress of Korea for the Last Five Years, 1905–1910*. Seoul: Residency General of Korea.

Richthofen, F. F. von. 1943. *Sina Ryoko Nikki* (Diary of China Trip). Translated by Masao Uminohara. Tokyo: Hakubunsha.

Rockhill, William Woodville. 1905. *China's Intercourse with Korea from the 15th Century to 1895*. London: Luzac.

Sachs, Jeffrey, and Andrew Warner. 1999. "Economic Convergence and Economic Policies," NBER Working Paper no. 5039.

Sands, William F. 1930. *Undiplomatic Memories*. New York: McGraw-Hill.

Savage-Landor, A. Henry. 1885. *Corea or Cho-sen, A Travellogue of 1890–1891*. New York: Macmillan.

Shibuya, Reiji. 1936. *Chosen ni okeru Kogyo Kinyu Jijo* (The Financial Situation of Industry in Korea) in Chosen Kogyo Kyokai 1937. Part II. Keizyo: Chosen Kogyo Kyokai.

Shikata, Hiroshi. 1929. "Shijo ou tsujite mitaru Chosen no Keijai" (Korean Economy Viewing through Market). In Keizyo Teitai Hobunkaku Daiichibu Ronshu, eds., *Chosen Keijai no Kenkyu* (Study of Korean Economy). Vol. II. Keijyo: Keizyo Taikaku.

———. 1933. *Chosen ni okeru Kindai Shihon Shugi no Seiritsu Katei* (Development Stages of Recent Capitalism in Korea). A series in the study of socioeconomic history of Korea (Chosen Shakai Keizaishi Kenkyu) sponsored by Keizyo Teikoku Taikaku Habunkakukai (Law and Literature Association of Seoul Imperial University). Tokyo: Tokoshoin.

———. 1976. *Chosen Shakai Keizaishi Kenkyu* (Socioeconomic History of Korea). 3 vols. Tokyo: Tosho Kankosha.

Shikata, Nariyoshi. 1938. "Saikin Akoku Kokumin Shotoku" (Our Recent National Income). *Rekishikaku Ronshu*, VIII, 7, July. Tokyo: Tokyo University.

Shin, Yong Ha. 1967. "Yijomalgi ui 'Sejikwon kwa Iljeha ui 'Yongsojak' ui Gwange" (The Relationship between 'The Cultivating Right' during the Late Yi Dynasty and 'Permanent Tenancy' under Japanese Rule), *Gyeongje Nonjip* (The Korean Economic Journal), VI, 1, March. Seoul: Seoul National University.

———. 1978. "Ilje ui 'Chosen Toji Chosa Saup' ue isoso ui 'Gugyuji' Changchul kwa 'Yokdonji' Chosa," (Identification of "National Land" and "Station Land" in Korean Land Survey Project under Japanese Rule). *Gyeongje Nonjip* (The Korean Economic Journal), XVII, 4, December. Seoul: Seoul National University.

———. 1982. *Joseon Tojijosaeop Yeongu* (Study of Land Survey of Korea). Seoul: Chishik Sanupsa.

Shinobu, Jumpei. 1901. *Kan Hanto* (Korean Peninsula). Tokyo: Tokyodo Shoten.

Shiokawa, Ichitaro. 1895. *Chosen Tsusho Jijo* (The Condition of Korean Trade). Tokyo: Yao Shoten.

Shirushi, Sadanao. 1940. *Chosen no Nogyo Chitai* (Korea's Agricultural Region). Tokyo: Seikatsusha.

Shokusan Ginko. 1928. *Chosen Shokusan Ginko Junenshi* (A Ten-Year History of the Chosen Industrial Bank). Keizyo: Chosen Shokusan Ginko.

———. 1930. *Chosen Kinyujijo Kaikan* (Overview of Korean Finance). Keizyo: Chosen Shokusan Ginko.

———. 1935. *Chosen ni okeru Kogyo Kaisha no Shihon Kosei Chosa* (A Study of Capital Formation in Korean Industrial Companies). Keizyo: Chosen Shokusan Ginko.

———. 1938a. "Chosen ni okeru Dochaku Shihon no Kenkyu" (A Study of Indigenous Capital in Korea). *Shokugin Chosa Geppo,* April. Keijyo: Chosen Shokusan Ginko.

———. 1938b. *Chosen Shokusan Ginko Nijunenshi* (A Twenty Year History of the Chosen Industrial Bank). Keizyo: Chosen Shokusan Ginko.

———. 1939. "Chosen no Kogyo to Kojo" (Industrial Factories in Korea). *Shokugin Chosa Geppo,* XXXIII, December. Keizyo: Chosen Shokusan Ginko.

———. 1940a. "Chosen ni okeru Hantojin Shihaika no Shakai Josei (The Social Conditions of the Indigenous Population in Korea under Japanese Rule)." *Shokugin Chosa Geppo,* January. Keizyo: Chosen Shokusan Ginko.

———. 1940b. "Chosen Toka Naichi Shihon go kore ni yoru Jigyo (The Enterprises of Japanese Capital Invested in Korea)." *Shokugin Chosa Geppo,* LXV, June. Keizyo: Chosen Shokusan Ginko.

———. 1941a. "Chosen Shikin Mondai no Shindankai" (A New Phase in the Problem of Capital in Korea), part 2. *Shokugin Chosa Geppo,* LXXVI, May; 77, June. Keizyo: Chosen Shokusan Ginko.

———. 1941b. "Chosen ni okeru Kokumin Chojiku ni tsuite" (National Savings in Korea). *Shokugin Chosa Geppo,* XXXVI, May. Keizyo: Chosen Shokusan Ginko.

———. 1943a. "Chosen ni okeru Dochaku Shihon no Kenkyu" (A Study of Indigenous Capital in Korea). *Shokugin Chosa Geppo*. Keijyo: Chosen Shokusan Ginko.

———. 1943b. *Zensen Tanden Baibai Kakaku oyobi Shuekicho* [A Study of Prices and Profits in the Sale of Land in Korea]. Keizyo: Chosen Shokusan Ginko.

———. 1943c. "Ginko Yokin ou Chusin to shite mitaru Sennai Chojiku no Jitsseki" (Record of Savings in Korea viewed from Bank Deposits). *Shokugin Chosa Geppo* (Research Monthly of Industrial Bank) LVIII, March. Keizyo: Chosen Shokusan Ginko.

Sotokufu. 1910–1942 (annual). *Tokeinempo* (Statistical Annual). Keizyo: Chosen Sotokufu.

———. 1915. *Chosen Tesudoshi* (History of Korean Railroads). Keizyo: Chosen Sotokufu.

———. 1928. *Chosen no Tochi Kairyo Jigyo* (Land Improvement Projects). Keizyo: Chosen Sotokufu.

———. 1930. *Shisei Nijunenshi* (Twenty-Year History of Administration). Keizyo: Chosen Sotokufu.

———. 1934. *Chosen Beikoku Yoran* (Overview of Korean Rice). Keizyo: Chosen Sotokufu.

———. 1935. *Shisei 25-nenshi (*Twenty-Five-Year History of Governance). Keizyo: Chosen Sotokufu.

———. 1937. *Chosen Tetsudoshi* (Railroad History of Korea). I. Keizyo: Chosen Sotokufu.

———. 1939a. *Chosen Kinyu Jijo Sankosho* (Reference Sources of Financial Conditions of Korea). Keizyo: Chosen Sotokufu.

———. 1939b. *Chosen Tetsudo Yonjunenshi* (Forty-Year History of Korean Railroad). Keizyo: Chosen Sotokufu.

———. 1940a. "Chosen ni okeru Katei Kogyo Chosa" (Survey of Household Industry in Korea) *Chosen Keizai Nenpo*. Keizyo: Chosen Sotokufu.

———. 1940b. *Shisei Sanjunenshi* (A Thirty-Year History of Administration). Appendix: "Nempyo" Keizyo: Chosen Insatsu.

———. 1941, 1942, and 1943. *Chosen Rodo Gijutsu Tokei Chosa Kekka Hokoku* (Report of Statistical Survey of Korean Workers and Skilled Workers in Korea). Keijyo: Chosen Sotokufu.

———. Annual. *Chosen Boeki Nenpo* (Korean Trade Annual) Keizyo: Chosen Sotokufu

Suenaga, Joonichiro. 1895. *Chosen Shooho* (Reports from Korea). Toho Sosho by Toho Kyokai. Tokyo: Toho Shoten.

Suh, Sang-Chul. 1978. *Growth and Structural Change in the Korean Economy, 1910–1940.* Cambridge, Mass.: Harvard University Press.

Suzuki, Seibun. 1939. *Chosen Keizai no Kentankai* (Current Stage of Korean Economy). Keizyo: Teikoku Chiho Kyosei Kakukai.

Suzuki, Takeo. 1941. *Chosen no Keizai* (Korean Economy). Tokyo: Nihon Hyoronsha.

Suzuki, Takesizu. 1942. *Chosen Toji no Seikaku to Jitsuseki* (Character and Records of Governmance of Korea). Tokyo: Toyo Seijai Shimposha.

Takahashi, Kamekichi. 1935. *Gendai Chosen Keizairon* (Current Economy of Korea). Tokyo: Chigura.

Takasugi, Togo. 1940. *Chosen Kinyu Kikan Hattatsushi* (A History of the Development of Financial Institutions in Korea). Keizyo: Jitsugyo Taimususha.

Teikoku Nokai. 1931. *Nogyo Nenkan* (Agriculture). Tokyo: Teikoku Nokai.

Tokanfu. 1906–1910 (annual). *Tokanfu Tokei Nenpo* (First Resident-General Statistical Annual). Seoul: Chosen Tokanfu.

———. 1910b. *Kankoku Zaisei Shisetsu Koyo* (Korean Financial Structure). Seoul: Chosen Tokanfu.

Tokunaga, Isamu. 1907. *Kankoku Soran* (Overview of Korea). Tokyo: Hakunsha.

Toyo Keizai Shinposha. 1935. *Nihon Boeki Seiron* (Survey of Japan's Trade), Tokyo: Toyo Keizai Shimposha.

———. 1936–1941. *Keizai Nenkan* (Economic Yearbook), Tokyo: Toyo Keizai Shimposha.

———. 1942. *Chosen Nenkan*, (Korea Annual). Tokyo: Toyo Keizai Shinposha.

———. Daily. *Toyo Keizai Shinbun*. Tokyo: Toyo Keizai Shinposha.

Toyo Takushoku Kaisha. 1918. *Totaku Junenshi* (Ten-Year History of Oriental Development Comapny). Tokyo: Toyo Takushoku Kaisha.

———. 1928. *Toyo Takushiki Kaisha Nizyunenshi* (Twenty Year History of Oriental Development Company). Tokyo: Toyo Takushoku Kaisha.

———. 1938. *Toyo Takushoku Kaisha Sanjunenshi* (Thirty Year History of Oriental Development Company). Tokyo: Toyo Takushoku Kaisha.

Tsuchiya, Takao, and Saburo Okazaki. 1937. *Nihon Shihonshugi Hatasushi Kaisetsu* (Outline of Development History of Japanese Capitalism). Tokyo: Yuhigaku.

Ugaki, Kazunari. 1935. *Chosen o Kataru* (Story of Korea). Tokyo: Jitsugyono Nihonsha.

Underwood, Horace G. 1992. "Missionaries Bring Modern Learning: Americans Aid Korean Education," in *The Korea Herald*, January 1.

U.S. Department of Commerce. 1940. *Statistical Abstract of the United States*. U.S. Government Printing Office, Washington, D.C.

U.S. Department of State. 1945. *Japanese Economic Penetration into Korea as of 1940 as Shown by an Analysis of Corporations Operating in Korea*. October 23. U.S. Department of State, RG 407, box 2052, National Archives.

———. 1962. *A Historical Summary of U.S.-Korea Relations*. Washington, D.C.

U.S. Foreign Economic Administration, Enemy Branch, Japanese Special Services Staff. 1945. *Summary Industrial Survey of Korea*. April 17. RG 407, National Archives.

U.S. Supreme Commander for Allied Forces in the Pacific General Headquarters, *Civil Property Custodian, External Assets Division. 1948. Japanese External Assets as of August 1945: Korea*, I. Washington, D.C.: National Archives.

———. 1947a. Natural Resources Section Report 86, *Field Experiments with Fertilizers in Japan*. Tokyo.

———. 1947b. Natural Resources Section Report No. 93, *Fertilizer Practices in Japan*. Tokyo.

———. 1948. *Japanese External Assets as of August 1945*. Part I, "Korea," and Part II, "Manchuria." September 30. RG 59, National Archives.

Van Bushirk, James Dale. 1931. *Korea, Land of Dawn*. New York: Missionary in Education Movement of the United States and Canada.

Wagner, Edward W. 1975. "Report on a Conference: Traditional Korean Society," *Items*, Social Science Research Council, XXIX, 4, December.

Weber, Max. 1951. *The Religion of China*. Translated by Hans H. Gerth. Glencoe, Ill.: The Free Press.

Westphal, Larry E. 1982. "The Private Sector as 'Principal Engine of Development: Korea,' " *Finance and Development*, June. Washington, D.C.: International Monetary Fund.

Whigham, H. J. 1904. *Manchuria and Korea*. London: Isbister.

Williamson, Jeffrey G. 1979. "Why Do Koreans Save So Little?" *Journal of Development Economics*, V.

Yamada, Yuzo. 1937. *Nihon Kokumin Shotoku Suikei Shiryo* (Data for Estimating National Income of Japan). Tokyo: Toyo Keizai Simposha.

Yamaguchi, Toyomasa. 1911. *Chosen no Kenkyu* (Study of Korea). Tokyo: Ganshodo Shoten.

Yim, Seong Hi. 1963. "The Problem of Human Metabolism in Korea," *Koreana Quarterly,* V, 2.

Yoo, Bong Chul. 1971. "Iljeha ui Gukmin Saegwhal Sujyun" (Standard of Living under Japanese Rule) in Ki Joon Cho et al. *Iljeha wi Minjok Sangwhalsa* (Korean Living Standard under Japanese Imperialism), V, theseries of Study of Korea under Japanese Imperialism. Seoul: Minjoong Sokwan.

Yoo, Won Dong. 1968. *Yicho Fugi Sangkongeopsa Yeongu* (Commercial and Industrial History of Late Yi Period). Seoul: Hanguk Yeonguwon.

———. 1977. *Hanguk Gundae Gyeongjesa Yeongu* (Recent Economic History of Korea). Seoul: Ilchosa.

Yun, Dok-han. 1999. *The Critical Biography of Yi Wan-yong*. Reported in *Korea Newsreview,* XXVIII, 49, December 4.

Yun, Tae-sop. 1949. *Daehan Sanggong Hoeuiso Samnyonsa* (A Three-Year History of the Korean Chamber of Commerce and Industry). Seoul: Namyangsa.

Zenkoku Keizai Chosakikan Rengyokai Chosenshibu. Annual. *Chosen Keizai Nenpo* (Economic Annal of Korea). Tokyo: Yamamoto Sansei.

Zimmerman, L. J. 1965. *Poor Lands, Rich Lands: The Widening Gap*. New York: Random House.

Zinsenfu. 1933. *Zinsenfusi* (History of Zinsen City). Keizyo: Kanezawa Shoten.

INDEX

Page numbers in italics indicate tables or charts.